Cold Canning

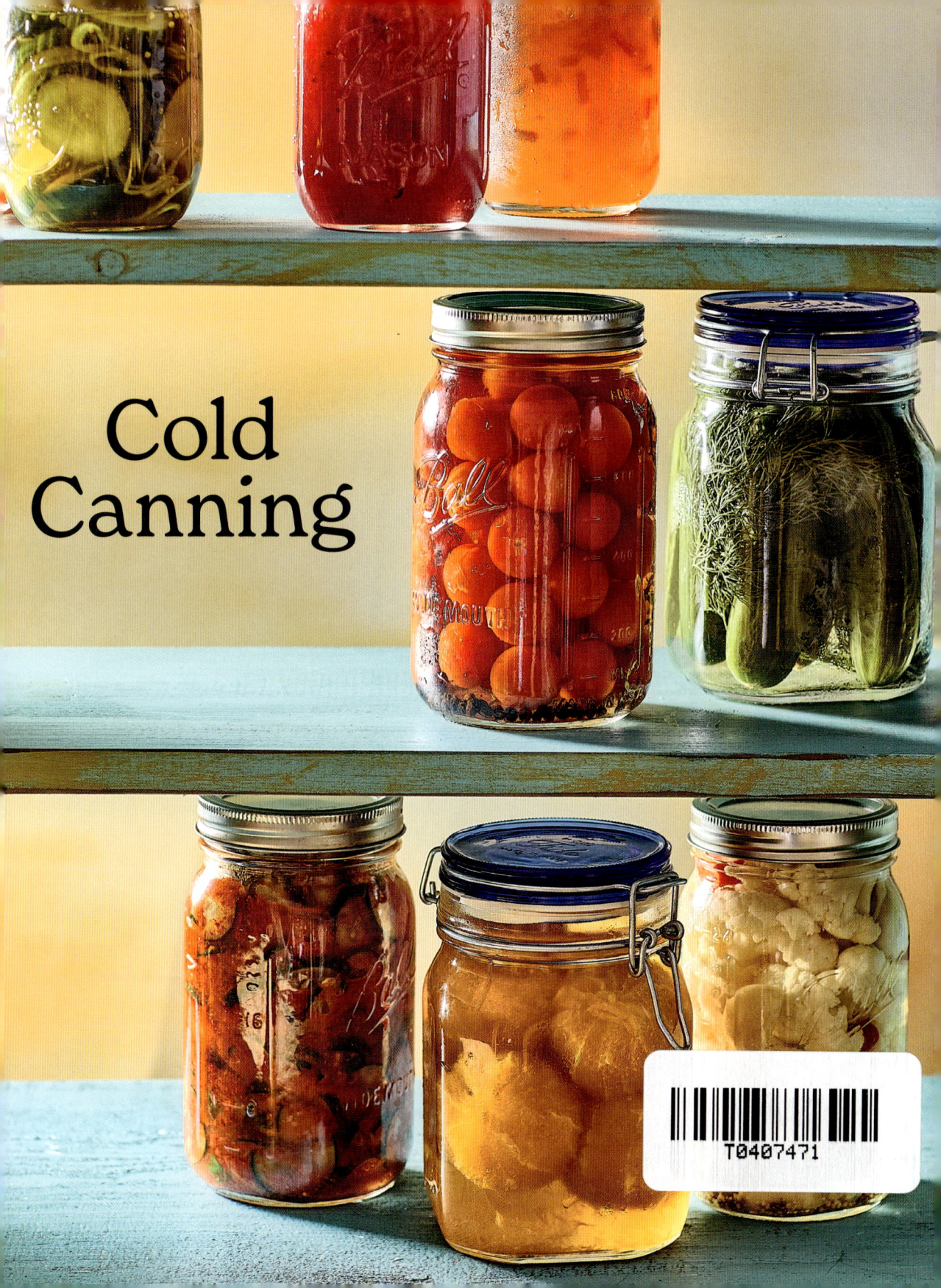

Also by Bruce Weinstein & Mark Scarbrough

Pressure Cooker and Instant Pot Cookbooks

The Instant Pot Bible

Instant Pot Bible: The Next Generation

Instant Pot Bible: Copycat Recipes

From Freezer to Instant Pot: The Cookbook

The Great Big Pressure Cooker Book

Air Fryer Cookbooks

The Essential Air Fryer Cookbook

The Look and Cook Air Fryer Bible

The Instant Air Fryer Bible

The Ultimate Series

The Ultimate Cook Book

The Ultimate Ice Cream Book

The Ultimate Party Drink Book

The Ultimate Candy Book

The Ultimate Shrimp Book

The Ultimate Brownie Book

The Ultimate Potato Book

The Ultimate Muffin Book

The Ultimate Chocolate Cookie Book

The Ultimate Frozen Dessert Book

The Ultimate Peanut Butter Book

Other Cookbooks

The Kitchen Shortcut Bible

Great Grilling

Cooking for Two

Pizza: Grill It! Bake It! Love It!

Cooking Know-How

Ham: An Obsession with the Hindquarter

Real Food Has Curves

Goat: Meat, Milk, Cheese

Lobsters Scream When You Boil Them

The Complete Quick Cook

Grain Mains

The Great American Slow Cooker Book

Vegetarian Dinner Parties

The Boozy Blender

À La Mode

The Turbo Blender Dessert Revolution

All-Time Favorite Sheet Cakes and Slab Pies

Cold Canning

The Easy Way to Preserve the Seasons
Without Hot Water Processing

425 Small-Batch Jams, Jellies, Chutneys, Chili Crisps,
Pickles, Sauerkrauts, Kimchis & More

Bruce Weinstein &
Mark Scarbrough

PHOTOGRAPHS BY ERIC MEDSKER

VORACIOUS
Little, Brown and Company
NEW YORK   BOSTON   LONDON

Voracious / Little, Brown and Company
Hachette Book Group
1290 Avenue of the Americas, New York, NY 10104
voraciousbooks.com

First Edition: July 2025

Voracious is an imprint of Little, Brown and Company, a division of Hachette Book
Group, Inc. The Voracious name and logo are trademarks of Hachette Book Group, Inc.

The publisher is not responsible for websites (or their content)
that are not owned by the publisher.

The Hachette Speakers Bureau provides a wide range of authors for
speaking events. To find out more, go to hachettespeakersbureau.com or email
hachettespeakers@hbgusa.com.

Little, Brown and Company books may be purchased in bulk for business, educational,
or promotional use. For information, please contact your local bookseller or the
Hachette Book Group Special Markets Department at special.markets@hbgusa.com.

ISBN 9780316577977
LCCN 2024948857

10 9 8 7 6 5 4 3 2 1

APS

Printed in China

Contents

Don't Skip This! (An Introduction) 13

CHAPTER 1

Jams, Jellies, Preserves, and Marmalades

Strawberry Preserves 32
Strawberry Jam 34
Strawberry Jewels 34
Sugar-Free Strawberry Preserves................... 35
Strawberry-Rhubarb Jam 36
Strawberry-Jalapeño Jam............................... 37
Concord Grape Jelly.. 37
Concord Grape Jam 38
Green Grape Jam 40
Red Grape Jam 40
Grape-Ginger Jelly 41
Spiced Grape Jelly 42
The Best Blueberry Preserves 42
Sugar-Free Blueberry Jam 44
Blueberry-Orange Jam 44
Blueberry–Chia Seed Jam.............................. 45
Blackberry Preserves 47
Sugar-Free Blackberry Jam............................ 47
Blackberry-Balsamic Jam............................... 48
Blackberry-Lavender Jam............................... 49
Blackberry–Chia Seed Jam............................ 49
Raspberry Preserves 50
Raspberry Jam 50
Raspberry Jelly... 52
Sugar-Free Raspberry Jam 53
Raspberry-Chipotle Jam................................. 53
Raspberry–Chia Seed Jam............................. 54
Boysenberry Jam 54
Elderberry Jam... 56

Three-Berry Jam... 57
Four-Berry Holiday Jam 57
Peach Preserves... 59
Sugar-Free Peach Jam...................................60
Peach Melba Jam 60
Peach Margarita Jam...................................... 61
Peach-Ginger Jam.. 61
Peach-Mango Jam 62
Apricot Preserves 64
Apricot-Gochujang Jam.................................. 64
Plum Preserves.. 65
Sour Cherry Preserves................................... 66
Sweet Cherry Preserves 66
Sugar-Free Sweet Cherry Jam 67
Cherry Pie Jam 67
Spiced Black Cherry Jelly 69
Rhubarb Jam 70
Rhubarb-Ginger Jam...................................... 70
Apple Jelly.. 71
Candy Apple Jelly... 71
Apple-Amaretto Jelly 72
Sugar-Free Apple Jam....................................74
Apple-Cardamom Jam....................................74
Apple-Caramel Jam 75
Spiced Apple Preserves 76
Brandied Apple Preserves 77
Easy Apple Butter 77
Oven-Roasted Apple Butter 78
Pear Preserves...80
Brown Sugar–Pear Preserves 80
Pear Butter 81
Pumpkin Butter.. 81
Fig Jam.. 83
Fig-Ginger Jam... 84
Dried Fig–Lemon Jam.................................... 84
Chestnut Jam... 86
Black Currant Jelly 87

Black Currant–Port Jam..................................89
Red Currant Jelly 89
White Currant–Lemon Jelly............................90
Pineapple Jelly 91
Pineapple Jam 91
Pineapple-Coconut Jelly 93
Pomegranate Jelly..94
Kiwi Jam...94
Quince Jelly..96
Mango Jam 97
Persimmon Jam 97
Lychee Jelly..98
Guava Jam 99
Lime-Ginger Jelly...99
Rose Jelly 100
Hibiscus Jelly 102
Spiced Hibiscus Jelly 102
Coffee Jelly 103
Chai Jelly.. 104
Sweet Orange Marmalade 105
Sour Orange Marmalade............................... 105
Sugar-Free Orange Marmalade......................107
Blood Orange Marmalade 108
Clementine-Ginger Marmalade 109
Grapefruit Marmalade 110
Lemon Marmalade 110
Three-Citrus Marmalade 111
Carrot Marmalade..112

Carrot Jam..122
Spicy Carrot Jam...122
Red Pepper Jam..124
Pineapple-Horseradish Jam 125
Celery Root–Cardamom Jam.........................125
Tomato-Ancho Jam 127
Tomato-Basil Jam..128
Tamarind-Chili Jam.......................................128
Kimchi Jam..129
Blackberry Conserve.....................................129
Peach–Sour Cherry Conserve....................... 130
Apple Pie Conserve.......................................132
Spicy Pineapple-Coconut Conserve 132
Sweet-and-Sour Pear Conserve 133
Maple-Rhubarb Conserve 134
Spicy Tomato Conserve 134
Spicy Cranberry Conserve 135
Ginger Jam 137
White Wine Jelly 137
Red Wine Jelly 138
Rosemary–Red Wine Jelly 138
Jalapeño Jam 139
Mint Jelly..141
Tarragon Jelly..142
Smooth Cranberry Sauce 142
Chunky Cranberry Sauce 144
Sugar-Free Cranberry Sauce 144
Spiced Cranberry Sauce 145
Cranberry Walnut Sauce................................146
Classic Mango Chutney 146
Major Grey's Chutney 147
Sugar-Free Mango Chutney 147
Easy Onion Chutney......................................149
Red Onion–Molasses Chutney....................... 150
Apple Chutney.. 150
Apple Pie Chutney...151
Nearly Sugar-Free Apple Chutney 153
Spiced Plum Chutney....................................153
Rhubarb-Raisin Chutney 154
Rhubarb-Chipotle Chutney 154
Hot Tomato Chutney 155
Green Tomato Chutney...................................156

CHAPTER 2

Savory Jams, Conserves, Chutneys, Relishes, and Tapenades

Bacon Jam 118
Onion-Bourbon Jam.. 118
Blueberry-Onion Jam......................................120
Shallot Jam 120
Shallot-Bacon Jam 121

Fig-Tamarind Chutney 156

Cranberry-Cardamom Chutney 158

Apricot–Garam Masala Chutney........159

Pineapple-Chili Chutney 159

Mint Chutney.. 160

Parsley–Pumpkin Seed Chutney 160

Spicy Coconut-Cashew Chutney 161

Shallot-Dal Chutney 163

Sweet Pickle Relish 163

Dill Pickle Relish 164

Sweet Corn Relish................................166

Spicy Corn Relish.................................166

Jalapeño Relish....................................167

Carrot-Ginger Relish 168

Sweet-and-Sour Zucchini Relish.................... 168

Lemon–Summer Squash Relish 169

Fennel Relish.......................................171

Beet Relish 172

Shredded Mango Relish 172

English Piccalilli 173

Southern Piccalilli.............................. 174

Sticky Brown Cauliflower Pickle 174

Sweet Chow Chow 175

Chili Chow Chow 177

Watermelon Rind Chow Chow 177

Caponata 178

Super Sour Iranian-Style Pickle...................179

Black Olive Tapenade 181

Anchovy-Free Tapenade 181

Green Olive Tapenade..........................182

Fig-Olive Tapenade 182

Caper Tapenade...................................183

Beet Tapenade.....................................184

Puttanesca Tapenade...........................184

Garlicky Sun-Dried Tomato Tapenade 186

Spiced Tapenade 186

Artichoke-Lemon Tapenade.................187

CHAPTER 3

Salsas, Chili Crisps, Chili Sauces, and Chili Pastes

Salsa Fresca...193

Charred Salsa.......................................194

Simmered Salsa....................................194

Salsa Verde 196

Smooth Green Salsa.............................196

Green Tequila Salsa 197

Jalapeño Salsa 198

Pineapple-Cumin Salsa 200

Corn–Black Bean Salsa 200

Peach-Mango Salsa.............................. 201

Go-to Salsa Macha...............................202

Pineapple–Pine Nut Salsa Macha....................202

Smoky Pecan–Cacao Nib Salsa Macha...........204

Cherry-Pistachio Salsa Macha....................205

Cranberry-Walnut Salsa Macha 205

Maple-Sesame Salsa Macha 206

Coconut-Pecan Salsa Macha 208

Almost Everything Chili Crisp....................209

Star Anise–Smoked Paprika Chili Crisp.......... 210

Five-Spice Chili Crisp 210

Garlic-Scallion Chili Crisp................... 212

Gochugaru Chili Crisp.........................213

Sumac-Cinnamon Chili Crisp 213

Shiitake–Szechuan Peppercorn Chili Crisp 214

Curried Chili Crisp..............................215

Wasabi-Nori Chili Crisp 215

Fiery Red Sambal 217

Tomato-Lemongrass Sambal.....................217

Green Sambal 218

Peanut-Tamarind Sambal........................220

Sour-Funky Sambal 221

Lemon-Ginger Mazavaroo 221

Peri Peri Sauce 223

Fermented Chili Sauce.........................223

Easy Red Chili Paste 224

Calabrian Chili Paste 225

Garlicky Chili Paste.............................225

Aji Amarillo Paste 226

Aji Panca Paste 229

Smoky Macadamia Nut Chili Paste.................. 229

Red Curry Paste..230

Yellow Curry Paste..231

Green Curry Paste 232

Black Mole...232

Shortcut Black Mole 233

Red Mole 235

Shortcut Red Mole 236

Green Mole 236

Go-to Harissa.. 237

Rose Harissa... 238

Smoky-Sweet Harissa......................................240

Shortcut Gochujang 240

CHAPTER 4

Pickles, Preserved Vegetables, and Syrupy Fruits

Classic Dill Pickles... 247

Half Sour Pickles.. 247

Garlic Sour Pickles 248

Fiery Pickles..248

Green Tea Pickles 250

Horseradish Pickles 251

Mustard Pickles 251

Zucchini Pickles 252

Bread and Butter Pickles.................................. 252

Sweet Gherkins 254

Cornichons 255

Pickled Jalapeño Rings..................................... 255

Cowboy Candy 256

Pickled Cubanelles... 256

Pickled Red Onions 258

Cocktail Onions.. 258

Pickled Ginger.. 259

Pickled Turmeric... 261

Pickled Green Tomatoes................................... 261

Giardiniera.. 262

Dilly Beans.. 262

Vinegary Cherry Tomatoes 263

Pickled Asparagus.. 264

Pickled Celery 264

Pickled Red Cabbage 266

Pickled Radishes 266

Gingery Pickled Broccoli 267

Fiery Sugar Snaps... 267

Hot and Sour Pickled Okra 268

Spicy-Garlicky Cauliflower Pickles 269

Pickled Tarragon Carrots..................................269

Pickled Eggplant 271

Sweet-and-Sour Butternut Squash 271

Pickled Jicama 272

Lime-Sesame Pickled Daikon.......................... 273

Pickled Daikon and Carrots.............................. 273

Sweet-and-Sour Pickled Beets 274

Horseradish-Pickled Beets 275

Pickled Roasted Beets 275

Harvard Beets... 276

Preserved Lemons 276

Gingered Watermelon Rinds............................. 278

Sweet-and-Sour Cherries 279

Spiced Pickled Cherries 280

Pickled Spiced Pears 280

Pickled Spiced Plums....................................... 282

Pickled Grapes... 282

Pickled Kumquats... 283

Garlic Confit.. 285

Roasted Tomatoes in Oil 285

Seared Mushrooms in Oil 286

Roasted Bell Peppers in Oil..............................288

Marinated Artichokes 288

Marinated Roasted Vegetables........................ 289

Spiced Peach Quarters 290

Prunes in Armagnac..290

Apples in Syrup... 291

Cherries in Almond Syrup 293

Pear Quarters in Spiced Syrup......................... 293

Dried Pears in Fennel-Orange Syrup 294

Figs in Honey Syrup 296

Pineapple in Black Pepper Syrup 296

Oranges in Brandy Syrup 297

Kumquats in Cognac Syrup 299

CHAPTER 5

Kimchis and Sauerkrauts

Go-to Kimchi 306

Summer Kimchi 308

Napa Cabbage Kimchi 308

White Kimchi 310

Radish Kimchi 311

Savoy Cabbage Kimchi 311

Baby Bok Choy Kimchi 313

Cucumber Kimchi 314

Carrot Kimchi 315

Go-to Sauerkraut............................... 317

Shortcut Vinegary Red Sauerkraut..............318

Red Cabbage Sauerkraut 318

Caraway-Cranberry Sauerkraut 319

Apple Sauerkraut 320

Pineapple Sauerkraut........................ 321

Celery Root Sauerkraut..................... 323

Beet Sauerkraut 324

Fennel Sauerkraut 325

Jalapeño Sauerkraut......................... 326

Turmeric-Onion Sauerkraut 327

Gin Sauerkraut 328

Pistachio-Duqqa Sauerkraut 329

Carrot Sauerkraut..............................330

Rutabaga Sauerkraut 332

Turnip Sauerkraut 333

Curtido... 335

CHAPTER 6

Savory Sauces, Spreads, and Dips

Tomato Ketchup.................................340

Curried Ketchup 340

Five-Spice Ketchup............................ 342

Plum Ketchup..................................... 343

Blueberry-Jalapeño Ketchup............ 343

Banana Ketchup 344

Mushroom Ketchup...........................346

Kecap Manis 346

Steak Sauce 347

Hoisin Sauce 348

Thick Red Chili Sauce....................... 349

Sweet Red Chili Sauce 349

Classic Barbecue Sauce 351

Vinegary Barbecue Sauce 351

Brown Sugar Barbecue Sauce........ 352

Five-Alarm Barbecue Sauce............ 353

Raspberry-Chipotle Barbecue Sauce 355

Peanut Butter–Ginger Barbecue Sauce......... 355

Peachy Barbecue Sauce...................356

Roasted Garlic–Maple Barbecue Sauce.......... 357

Pineapple-Sesame Barbecue Sauce............. 357

Gold Barbecue Sauce 358

Alabama White Sauce 360

Char Siu Sauce................................... 360

Prepared Yellow Mustard 361

Dijon Mustard 361

Coarse-Grained Mustard.................. 363

Honey Mustard 364

Brown Mustard 364

Wheat Beer Mustard 365

Fiery Brown Mustard 365

Maple Mustard 366

Molasses Mustard 366

Garlic Mustard................................... 367

Super Hot Yellow Mustard............... 369

Szechuan-Inspired Red Mustard 369

Spicy Peanut Sauce 370

Duck Sauce 370

Worcestershire Sauce 372

CHAPTER 7

Sweet Sauces and Dips

Applesauce 378

Cranberry Applesauce 378

Sugar-Free Applesauce 380

Pear Sauce 380

Pear-Ginger Sauce 381

Chocolate Sauce 382

Hot Fudge Sauce 382

White Chocolate Sauce 384

Butterscotch Sauce 385

Toffee Sauce 385

Salted Caramel Sauce 386

Coconut Caramel Sauce..................................388

Praline Sauce..388

Peanut Butter Sauce......................................389

Marshmallow Sauce.......................................389

Strawberry Sauce 390

Pineapple Sauce 392

Lemon Sauce 392

Blackberry Sauce 393

Raspberry-Orange Sauce 393

Apple Dessert Sauce 395

Coffee Sauce..396

Wet Walnuts...396

Dulce de Leche...398

Easy Dulce de Leche 398

Cajeta...399

CHAPTER 8

Infused Oils, Vinegars, Syrups, and Liqueurs

Basil Oil..404

Chive Oil 404

Rosemary-Garlic Oil 406

Citrus Oil 406

Eighteen-Spice Chili Oil..................................407

Eighteen-Spice Curry Oil 408

Raspberry Vinegar 408

Plum Vinegar 410

Cranberry Vinegar 411

Sour Cherry Vinegar 411

Fig Vinegar... 413

Lemon-Sage Vinegar...................................... 413

Lavender-Thyme Vinegar................................ 414

Tarragon Vinegar 414

Fresh Chili Vinegar..416

Dried Chili Vinegar..416

Grenadine 417

Tonic Syrup 417

Demerara Syrup..418

Coconut Syrup...418

Lemon Syrup...420

Almond Syrup...420

Coffee Syrup... 421

Chai Syrup... 421

Lavender Syrup 422

Rose Syrup 422

Elderberry Syrup 423

Strawberry Syrup.. 423

Chocolate Syrup 425

Caramel Syrup.. 426

Root Beer Syrup.. 426

Cranberry Liqueur... 427

Raspberry Liqueur... 428

Strawberry Liqueur.. 428

Blueberry Liqueur..430

Black Currant Liqueur 430

Cacao Liqueur.. 431

Coffee Liqueur.. 433

Hazelnut Liqueur 433

Triple Sec 434

Appendix: How to Can Some of These Recipes the Traditional Way 436

Acknowledgments 438

Index 439

Don't Skip This!
(An Introduction)

Cold canning is the modern way to save the best of the seasons without the work, cost, risks, heat, steam, or hair nets of traditional preserving techniques.

Skip the hot water bath or pressure canner. From now on, use your refrigerator or freezer to store (and sometimes craft) *small batches* of your favorite jam, condiment, spread, oil, or sauce. Leave two or three jars safe in the chill for weeks, months, or even up to a year.

Nix your worries about rehashing the twelve labors of Hercules in your kitchen. And brush away any niggles about pests or pathogens in shelf-stable condiments. Instead, revel in homemade jams, jellies, chutneys, pickles, relishes, kimchis, ketchups, and liqueurs without any hot water processing *and* without any chemical additives. What's more satisfying than knowing you made the best for yourself?

Well, lots more. Here's why we love cold canning:

- It's **easier**. There's no need for the unwieldy, specialized, sterilized equipment that's required to can the old-fashioned way with boiling water, pressure, or steam.

- It's **smaller**. You craft just a few jars of your favorite jelly, condiment, or sauce—enough to give away while saving back some for yourself.

- It **preserves fresher flavors**. There's no double-cooking as in the old-school technique (once on the stove, again in the canner).

- It **saves money**. You won't have to break the bank on a bushel of fruit. Instead, pick up a couple of containers of berries anywhere and turn them into a few jars of sugar-free jam or spicy chutney.

- It **saves time**. The prep and cooking are quicker. Waiting 30 minutes for a kettle of old-fashioned jam to come to a boil or a few months for a big box of cucumbers to pickle has always been a pain in disparate parts of the body.

- It's often **healthier**, because refrigerator or freezer canning requires less sugar and sometimes less salt than shelf-stable items that need more of either (or both!) to give them extra oomph to ward off bad bugs.

- It can be **more gut-friendly**, because you can keep more of the probiotics intact in pickled and fermented items by nixing the heat of the canner.

- It **eliminates the backache** of traditional canning. You don't need to lift a huge pot or haul yourself to the hardware store to buy a truckload of jars, sealing rings, and lids. Many neighborhood grocery stores sell canning jars in four-packs.

- Plus, it's just **more fun**. So you'll want to do it more often!

We'll show how to make luscious conserves and spicy chili crisps, complex chili sauces and syrup-soaked fruits, English pickles and deli half sours, infused oils and rich tapenades, savory sauces and vinegary relishes, dessert toppings and liqueurs...*without* a container ship of produce, *without* barrels of booze, *without* a Rube Goldberg–style canner setup, *without* overloading your pantry shelves, *without* putting up enough stuff to survive the apocalypse, and *without* worrying about safety.

Cold canning is DIY for today. It condenses a weekend project into something doable anytime—like a half hour after waffles on Sunday morning or 45 minutes before you order DoorDash on Tuesday evening.

For example, take that all-time favorite, Concord Grape Jelly (page 37). Our technique is super fast and absurdly easy. Buy a bottle of Concord grape juice, some sugar, and a box of pectin. Bring it all to a boil. Pour it into a few jars, seal with lids, and stash in the fridge or freezer. Done. Almost no work. Certainly no fuss. And a treat all year long.

Just imagine opening your own jar of applesauce one morning. Or chili crisp one evening. Or half-sour pickles mid-afternoon. Your meals just got better. Your life, too.

How Does Cold Canning Work?

These recipes for preserves, pickles, condiments, sauces, syrups, and sauerkrauts start at the stove, on a cutting board, or in a mixing bowl. After that, they skip the canner, get bottled or jarred without a lot of fuss, and stored in the fridge or freezer. Hence, the name: cold canning. (We sometimes even ferment in the fridge!)

Just to be super clear, *none* of these products is shelf-stable. But who needs to do that much work these days? It's easier to store a few small jars on a refrigerator shelf or in the freezer door than it is to put in all the work to store them on a pantry shelf until time has no meaning. And let's face it: If you aren't going to eat that peach jam in 6 months, will you ever? These condiments last as long as you're likely to want them. (For more information, see "How Long Will Something Last?" on page 25.)

Cold canning is totally safe, so long as you don't leave things out on the counter too long or go beyond the storage times we recommend. Here's the deal: Bad bugs thrive above 40°F or 4°C. Set your fridge for that temperature (or a bit lower) and what you've made is out of the danger zone. Plus, your freezer is already set well below that temperature. (FYI, we recommend 0°F or −18°C.)

Beyond temperatures, we've also set strict guidelines throughout this book to ensure our methods produce safe and stable results. Our research includes consulting with both the USDA and the National Center For Home Food Preservation, as well as cross-referencing with agriculture schools at Purdue University, North Dakota State University, Texas A&M, and the NC State University Extension Food Safety program.

But sure, there may be times when you may want to make these preserves and store them at room temperature. Perhaps you want to take a few jars home for the holidays. We've still got you covered! If the recipe includes enough sugar, acid (vinegar or lemon juice), and/or salt to remain

▲ The range of what you can make with our cold canning method is way beyond what you'll find in a standard canning book.

safe at room temperature *and isn't harmed by going into a hot-water-bath canner*, we mark it as being suitable for traditional canning. Check out our primer on that technique in the appendix on page 436.

Tools

You don't need much equipment to get started. Only a handful of recipes call for specialized tools like a food mill or a jelly bag. But we want to offer a few guidelines for these and other gadgets in a bid to ensure your efforts are successful.

Wooden spoons

These are the gold standard of home cooking. Although no wooden spoon can blaze a clear-cut trail through a boiling cauldron as well as a silicone spatula, we *strongly* recommend wooden spoons because they have large surface areas that can push and drag around a great deal of not only what's *on* the bottom of the pot but also what's *in* it. Simply put, stirring is more efficient.

However, wooden spoons are not as durable as you might think.

- They shouldn't be put in a dishwasher because the drying cycle can crack them over time.

- They should be deeply cleaned on occasion, by immersing them overnight in a one-to-one solution *by volume* of distilled white vinegar and water or by scrubbing them with a paste of baking soda and water.

- And they should be replaced whenever they split or splinter.

Serrated vegetable peeler

Although there are old-fashioned, boiling-water methods for skinning tomatoes, peaches, and other ripe, fleshy fruits and vegetables, this new-fangled tool is a true time-saver and much easier to use. A serrated peeler takes the skin right off the most delicate pear or luscious apricot. Just don't *squeeze* the ripe produce as you work with the peeler!

▲ A serrated vegetable peeler makes short work of peeling tomatoes, peaches, and more!

Saucepans

Saucepans should be heavy and level with a tight-fitting lid. All standard advice, to be sure. But when we call for a specific size of saucepan in this book, it's important. A pan's volume determines the rate of evaporation, the primary way you'll get the right consistency in jams, chutneys, pastes, and sauces. Don't swap one pan size for another.

- A small saucepan = 1 quart or 1 liter
- A medium saucepan = 2 quarts or 2 liters
- A large saucepan = 3 quarts or 3 liters
- A very large saucepan = 4 quarts or 4 liters

Food mill

A food mill is the best way to make sure you get a plush texture in jams and pastes. Admittedly, it's pretty old-school: a wide-mouthed basin, usually metal but now sometimes plastic, often with footed grips to hold on to the rim of a bowl or a pot set below. A food mill almost always has a hand-turned crank that spins something like fan blades over a wire mesh to remove *and* contain skins, seeds, and pulpy solids, while liquids or a thin puree drips into the bowl or pot below.

As an alternative, use a *fine-mesh* strainer. The webbing should be tight. Set the strainer over a large bowl and dump what you've made into the strainer without filling it more than halfway (most likely, that is, using a smaller amount than you've made). Let the contents drip into the bowl, stirring *very gently and only occasionally* to keep the pulpy or translucent drips coming without also pushing through bits of the spices, seeds, or stems. Dump out the solids and pour in another portion. FYI, this alternative process with a fine-mesh strainer can take 30 minutes or more. A more traditional food mill takes perhaps 5 minutes and does a better job. Enough said.

Jelly bag

A jelly bag is the only way you can strain a pulpy mixture to produce *perfectly* clear jellies and liqueurs. Set up a jelly bag over a pot or a bowl to let the juice drip for several hours or sometimes overnight. Work *in* the sink to save on cleanup down the line.

In the old days, home canners made a muslin bag and tied it around a rolling pin perched over a pot. Some people still use homemade bags tied and hung from faucets (yikes: the fit of the plumbing washers!) or cabinet door handles.

These days, modern jelly bags are made from fine-grained cloth (cotton, nylon, or a plastic mesh) with an elastic opening. Most are washable and reusable. Follow the manufacturer's instructions.

▲ Your great-grandmother was right: A food mill makes you a canning pro!

▲ A jelly bag turns a cooked puree into clear juice with no more effort than your patience.

As an alternative, you can use a fine-mesh sieve—preferably, a conical sieve with a metal mesh *much* finer than even a fine-mesh strainer. To use a conical sieve as a substitute, set the sieve over a large bowl or a deep pot and pour what you've made into the sieve. The process is tricky because the sieve rarely stands up straight. You must hold it in place as you pour. You may even have to hold it for a while as you await the majority of the drips. They can take a long time! You can speed the process (slightly) by *gently* rearranging the solids to let more juice flow and by occasionally wiping down the *outside* of the mesh with a rubber spatula.

Another alternative to a jelly bag is to puree what you've made in a food processor or a high-powered blender and then transfer the thick mess to a cheesecloth-lined colander. This alternative is time-consuming, for sure. But the real problem is that you'll inevitably grind things like bitter seeds into the juices and end up with a cloudy or bitter product.

Or you can try a cheesecloth-lined potato ricer, but you'll have to work in about a zillion micro batches and the cheesecloth rarely stays put—which means you'll inevitably have to sieve the results again to extract unwanted bits. Best to just buy a jelly bag and be done with it.

Colanders and strainers

A colander has large, circular holes; a strainer has a mesh, about like the screens on your windows. We call for both. If you only have a strainer, you *can* use it in place of a colander but the dripping will take longer. If you only have a colander, you need to buy a fine-mesh strainer (sorry!) because there's no great substitute.

Can you line a colander with cheesecloth and call it a strainer? Yes, but we dare you to keep that cheesecloth in place as you pour a hot brine through it. And we dare you to balance a cheesecloth-lined colander over a small canning jar as you pour molten jam into it. What's more,

- The most common are stretched over a ring on metal or plastic legs to stand in or around a pot or a bowl set below. (If the legs are to be set *into* something, a pot is a better choice because the bottom is flat; the legs won't tip as easily.)

- Some jelly bags—also called *wine* or *brew bags*—can be pulled over the opening of a pot or bowl to stretch into a sack for holding what you've made. (Don't pull it too tight and make a trampoline—there's got to be some bowl-shaped give to hold what's coming.)

- A few jelly bags stretch over a ring with a long handle. You must hold it over a pot or a bowl. Frankly, we find this type of jelly bag awkward since we're never adept at balancing the grip in one hand and pouring something scalding from a saucepan with the other.

▲ A fine-mesh strainer catches all the tiny bits of the spices to clarify this chai syrup.

by the time you purchase more cheesecloth for your colander, you could have bought a strainer.

In our kitchen, we often use a mid-size fine-mesh strainer over a wide funnel set in the mouth of a canning jar to make pouring as easy as possible.

And one final note: We do not put our strainers in the dishwasher since the mesh can degrade and weaken with watery abuse. Plus, we can never get all the dishwasher soap out of the mesh. To put it bluntly, ick.

Culinary thermometer

Some recipes call for a thermometer, sometimes in a bid for safety (have you cooked something long enough to kill any pathogens?), but more often to get the right consistency. In other words, have you cooked the sugar long enough for the mixture to gel?

We prefer a candy-making thermometer. It can be clipped to the inside of the pan so you don't have to hold it as the mixture roils underneath. For the best results, stir as required so that the boiling mixture is moving around the saucepan and you're not just getting a reading off one small spot in the batch.

You can also use an instant-read meat thermometer, although you'll have to have a bit more dexterity than we do to steady the thermometer in the mixture as you stir and stir. Also, make sure the thermometer has been cleaned thoroughly since your last pork roast.

We don't recommend a laser thermometer. Although it's a cool kitchen tool, it accurately measures only the surface temperature of whatever is in the pan.

One more thing: If you substitute an instant-read meat thermometer for a candy thermometer, make sure the probe is long enough to keep your hand away from any spatters. Some old-school meat thermometers have short probes. Our grandmothers were tough. Most of us, not so much.

Culinary kitchen gloves

These are disposable latex gloves, sort of like thin surgical gloves. You've probably seen television chefs and barbecue pit masters wear them. We prefer the black ones because it's easier to see bits of this and that adhering to them. We refer to them as *culinary kitchen gloves* to distinguish them from so-called *rubber gloves*, used for cleaning.

When you're canning, even with our simplified technique, you want to keep out as many contaminants as possible. You can repeatedly clean and dry your hands as you work, but snapping on a new pair of culinary kitchen gloves ensures that you're preserving the seasons as safely as possible.

Never reuse these gloves, even within the steps of a recipe.

For the quickest cleanup, strip them off over a trash can.

Jars and storage containers

Our recipes have been written with traditional canning jars, lids, and sealing rings in mind. Throughout, we call for ½ pint (1 cup or 236 ml) jars, 1 pint (2 cup or 472 ml) jars, 1 quart (4 cup or about 1 liter) jars, and (rarely) 2 quart (8 cup or a little less than 2 liter) jars.

Can you mix and match? Of course, so long as the total volume of all the containers adds up to the volume the recipe produces.

Can you use other containers? Probably, as long as their lids afford a tight seal, particularly when brining and pickling. But always take note of the amount of headspace left after filling one. You'll see the requirements in the individual recipes, almost always about ½ inch or 1 centimeter. If there's more headspace than that, the contents can oxidize, mold, or rot, even in the fridge.

If you're *not* using canning jars, your containers should be heat-safe and made of glass to avoid reactive substances or glazes, particularly when it comes to relishes, sauces, and liqueurs. And while we're at it, they should be made of *tempered* glass to hold super hot jams, chutneys, and chili sauces straight from the pan. (Tempered glass has been made sturdier than standard glass through either chemical or thermal processes— it's what standard canning jars are made of.) We find the best alternative to canning jars are square or rectangular tempered glass containers with sturdy, plastic, lock-tight lids.

We have also stored jams and the like in resealable, dishwasher-safe, *silicone* bags. But getting the spreads out of these containers is messy (at best). There's inevitably some waste in the corners. What's more, ones filled with brine always seem to gap open and spill in the fridge. Finally, these silicone bags are *not* suitable for pickling or fermentation.

Zip-closed plastic bags (like sandwich or freezer storage bags) are *not* suitable for any of our recipes. The seals are too fiddly. Plus, the plastic may not be rated for high-heat or acidic ingredients.

This discussion of storage jars and containers invariably brings us to the one about *cleaning* them. No, we don't have to be as persnickety for most of what goes in a fridge or a freezer as we'd need to be if we were making shelf-stable condiments. But even brand-new jars or containers should be scrupulously cleaned, if not sterilized (particularly for pickling and fermenting), to inhibit the growth of nasty bacteria and keep you safe. Once cleaned, use them within a few hours. To get the jars or containers ready, you can:

- boil any jars, containers, canning lids, and sealing bands in a very large saucepan or a pot of water over high heat for a couple of minutes—this is our preferred method;

- or run all the storage paraphernalia through the hot wash and heated dry cycle of an empty dishwasher without any detergent.

▲ Although you can sterilize jars and lids in a dishwasher, we prefer the old-school method of boiling them.

Common Ingredients

Throughout these recipes, we've kept the North American and European supermarket in mind. To that end, we've adapted some condiments to use ingredients that are more easily within reach—like our version of zobo (Spiced Hibiscus Jelly, page 102) and kuchela (Shredded Mango Relish, page 172). A few times, we offer you all-out DIY options, like making your own garam masala (page 153). But there are a few common ingredients that need a little explanation from the get-go.

Salt

Kosher salt. Period. Its mineral flavor works best with sweet, sour, and bitter condiments. It's highly standardized: The kosher salt you buy from one manufacturer is almost always chemically identical to the kosher salt you buy from another. Despite internet myths, it doesn't come from religiously sanctioned salt mines (it's mostly refined from sea salt). But it has been used for eons to draw out the blood in the koshering of meat.

Although all kosher salt is kosher salt, not all kosher salt is ground the same. In our kitchen, 1 tablespoon from a common manufacturer weighed as much as 15 grams; 1 tablespoon from another, 10 grams. Our standard throughout this book is: 1 *tablespoon* kosher salt = 12 grams; 1 *teaspoon* = 4 grams.

Can you use standard table salt? No, it has a murkier flavor and contains additives. (There's more about this in the introduction to Chapter 4 on page 243.)

Can you use less refined sea salt, like sel gris? Yes, but you must grind down large crystals so they'll dissolve easily. And you must measure this salt solely by weight.

Can you use pink Himalayan salt? Maybe, but why would you waste it on something cooked or even boiled, destroying those prized, sweet-salty flavors? Stick with kosher salt and you'll end up with the right flavor every time.

Sugar

With few exceptions, we call for granulated white sugar. Do not use brown sugar, turbinado sugar, muscovado sugar, or other less refined sugars *unless* they are specifically called for. And don't ever substitute confectioners' or icing sugar.

Sounds SOP, right? But there's an international problem. (There's *always* an international problem.) What we in the US call *granulated white sugar* actually falls in its coarseness somewhere between what's called *granulated sugar* (or *table sugar*) and what's called *caster sugar* in the UK and elsewhere. If you live outside the US, you can use either granulated or caster sugar in our recipes. But always measure it *by weight*, not by volume.

Sugar substitutes

For sugar-free recipes, we tried a range of white sugar replacements: Stevia, sucralose (with maltodextrin for bulk), and erythritol sweeteners. Also, we tried several varieties of brown-sugar substitute, with its more caramelized flavor. (Both white and brown sugar baking substitutes can be found in the baking aisle at the supermarket.)

All that we tried worked in our sugar-free recipes with minor variations in texture and aftertaste. Some people don't even notice a slightly bitter tang from some of the brands; others can't stand it. Pick whichever substitute you prefer so long as it can be measured *one-to-one by volume* with granulated white sugar or brown sugar (depending on which is called for in the recipe). *Do not* measure the substitute by weight. And do not use more concentrated versions like packets of fake sugar from a coffee shop or liquid artificial sweeteners served up in drops.

The sugar substitutes you should use are the ones sold exclusively for baking recipes. Most are labeled either *1:1* or *= sugar* on the packaging.

Finally, these sugar substitutes *only* work in recipes designated sugar-free. Do not attempt to make sugar substitutions in other recipes.

Distilled white vinegar

Or *white distilled vinegar*? Because there's recently been a change. Just a few years ago, distilled white vinegar was 5 percent acidic brand over brand. However, 4 percent is the minimum acidity required by many governmental agencies worldwide. So several US, UK, and EU producers have started selling a 4 percent distilled vinegar in a bid to cut costs. To make a distinction, some reverse the word order and (confusingly!) label it *white distilled vinegar.*

For eons, distilled white vinegar was the canning standard. Its clean, straightforward taste doesn't get in the way of other flavors. And its 5 percent acidity ensured that preserved foods stayed safe. Four percent vinegar cannot hold foods safely *in traditional canning.*

But we're all about *cold* canning. So the variation between 4 and 5 percent doesn't hold as much weight for us, since we're not leaving things on a room-temperature shelf for months. However, 4 percent distilled white vinegar will result in murkier brines over time (things degrade more quickly) and will test the limits of our refrigerator storage guidelines (sometimes shaving off as much as a week). It will have no effect on our freezer guidelines. Still, best to read the labels and buy 5 percent distilled white vinegar.

Molasses and black treacle

We call for both, always interchangeably. But although they're related, they're not the same. Yes, both are a step out of the sugar-making process: Cane or beet juice is boiled for a while, the sucrose crystals removed, and the resulting liquid bottled or further reduced.

Molasses is reduced further than treacle and has more tannic or bitter undertones. To put it another way, black treacle is milder. But oddly, black treacle is also not as *pourable* as molasses. To get either one out of measuring cups or spoons, you'll need a thin, small, silicone spatula for scraping.

We prefer treacle for all the recipes in this book, although it can be hard to track down in North America. (We order it online.) Just FYI, there are grades of treacle, from light (or golden) to dark (or black), depending on the reduction (and caramelization). We call for only *black* treacle.

Pectin

It's a dissolvable polysaccharide found in or around the seeds or skins of many fruits. It's extracted, dried, and ground to a powder that can set preserves, jams, and jellies to a viscous consistency or a glassier, less spreadable firmness.

We call for only *granulated less-sugar pectin* (sometimes labeled *low-sugar pectin* or even *low- or no-sugar pectin*). You can find it at most large supermarkets, hardware stores, and health-food stores. However, we almost always order the stuff online. It's simpler than chancing availabilities at the store.

Why have we continually made this pectin choice over decades of preserving? We prefer to cut down on the added sugar, so we have to use a gelling agent specifically designed to work with less.

And why are we so keen on reducing the amount of sugar? Not for health reasons. Instead, for flavor. We're always let down by how many preserves, jams, and jellies taste like little more than colored sugar.

There are a few solely-no-sugar pectins on the market, often available at health-food stores. We *do not* recommend this specialty pectin for our recipes. Ours do not need such a powerful push to get them to set because we do add some sugar (which has its own gelling properties after cooking).

And we *do not* recommend pectins specifically designed for freezer or refrigerator jams. For one thing, these pectins prove hard to find. For another thing, we found that freezer pectin often required us to dramatically up the amount of sugar to get the proper set, (again) a move we want to avoid. Worse yet, these solely-no-sugar pectins give jams and jellies a consistency like Jell-O. Blech.

We also *do not* recommend liquid pectin. Yes, it was our grandmothers' preferred pectin. It's added to cooked fruits *after* they've reached a temperature-marked point...which means it requires a canning thermometer. It's also finicky. A degree or two off and the set is a no-go. For our purposes, granulated pectin is *much* more forgiving and a better match for refrigerator and freezer recipes that are by nature quicker and easier.

One final note: There are a few brands of less- or no-sugar pectins made *entirely* from citrus peels. These specialty pectins require you to stir in monocalcium phosphate to activate the gelling properties. We find the set from this sort of pectin too firm for our liking. That said, you can use this pectin variety in our recipes, but you must follow the instructions on the package. You may find you have to alter our directions, based on the manufacturer's requirements. And there's no standardization for what those alterations are, so you'll be doing a little recipe-testing on your own.

Olive oil

There's a persistent myth that if you put olive oil in the fridge and it remains a liquid, it isn't olive oil at all but some other refined oil masquerading as the prized commodity. Not true. What refrigerating *may* indicate is how refined the olive oil is. If still a liquid after a while, the oil may have been refined more than its *extra virgin* label indicates. If you live in the US and are concerned about the issue of quality on any front, buy only olive oils with the North American Olive Oil Association (NAOOA) seal of approval.

When it's all said and done, olive oil solidifies based on its triglyceride count. And triglycerides can be resistant to solidifying because of the oil's surrounding fat molecules. Still, over time, even the most high-quality olive oil may well solidify in a fridge set at 40°F or 4°C.

One more thing: A condiment with a thin, preserving layer of olive oil on top or some olive oil mixed into it will probably solidify in the chill. Do not microwave or heat these condiments to get them ready to serve. Doing so can change the set and degrade the flavors. Leave them sealed at room temperature for several hours so that the oil can reliquefy as its temperature increases.

Dried herbs and spices

They go bad. Or if not outright bad, then tasteless. Paprika becomes a coloring agent, familiar from your great-aunt's deviled eggs. Ground allspice tastes like bark. Dried thyme, like lawn clippings.

If a bottle has been around for 2 years, even in a cool, dark pantry, get a new one. If there are ground chilis in the mix or if it's a ground, dried spice, consider 1 year your toss-out point.

Yes, spices are expensive. Just ask the Middle Ages. But there's no point in holding on to something that's lost its savor. (Consider this relationship advice, too.)

Technical Questions

You'll see a fair amount of repetition in our recipes. The techniques are pretty standardized across, say, the chutney recipes. What's significant (and the result of years of testing) are the *ratios* among the ingredients and the specifics about timings, including some admittedly small variations—for example, *boil undisturbed for 1 minute* v. *boil undisturbed for 2 minutes.*

You still might have some questions. We can't anticipate all of them. Contact us under our own names on social media, check out the Facebook group *Cooking with Bruce and Mark*, or send us an email through our website, cookingwithbruceandmark.com. But here are some pertinent questions that our testers brought up or that we've imagined as we wrote this book.

What's with the volumes and metric equivalents in the ingredient lists?

If we had our way, we'd write a cookbook using *only* weights for all ingredients, even the liquids. But since current cookbook practice calls for volumes in some countries and weights in others, yet *liquid* amounts in volumes in almost all countries (whether in cups or milliliters), we offer both volumes and weights where we can.

But there's a minor wait-a-minute lurking behind our compromise: We've often rounded our numbers for the sake of simplicity. For example, 2¼ pounds is not exactly 1 kilogram, but it's close enough for almost every recipe. And 1 tablespoon of maple syrup isn't exactly 20 grams. But again, almost always close enough. The one glaring exception happens with the sauerkraut and kimchi recipes. These require a much more finessed precision. But we'll get to that problem down the road.

In the lists of ingredients, you'll also notice an inconsistent variation between *market amounts*, like 4 medium jalapeño chilis, and *by-weight amounts*, like 8 ounces (225 grams) apricots. We give market amounts when small variations won't matter to the outcome.

But small variations often *do* matter. These are, after all, preserving recipes. If the amount required *must* be specific, we list the ingredient by weight, often with an approximate market amount in parentheses to help you at the store — like this: 8 ounces (225 grams) plum tomatoes (about 3 medium). In cases like this, consider the weight the rule and the market amount a mere suggestion.

What's a boil you can't stir down?

In essence, stirring is a cooling process, lifting some of a mixture off the pan's bottom and exposing some or even all of that mixture to the (relatively) cooler air above. You also stir to keep ingredients from glomming onto the pan's super hot surface near the burner.

That said, after many ingredients have dissolved in a mixture (that is, are in suspension if not altogether bonded to the surrounding liquid), there's often less urgency for stirring. Now the liquid can come to a boil, although a good stir can bring them back to a very low simmer, even to outright stillness.

However, we often want a mixture to go *beyond* this boiling point. We're looking for a farrago, above some of the boiling points of the components — in other words, a boil you can't stir down. Give the mixture a couple of full stirs with a wooden spoon and see if the boil remains constant or at least *immediately* comes back to its former bubble when the spoon stops. If so, the mixture has now hit the right temperature to continue with the recipe.

▲ Even as it's stirred, the boiling doesn't stop (Raspberry–Chia Seed Jam, page 54).

Why do we skip the plate test?

Longtime canners work to caramelize sugars until the attendant liquids set in distinct ways: quite loose, sticky, a bit firmer, etc. These canners will test for the desired results by dripping a little jam on a chilled, heat-safe plate to immediately see the final consistency.

We forgo this time-tested technique for a few reasons:

- We call for granulated less-sugar pectin in many recipes—even with pectin-rich blackberries and apples—thereby assuring the final set.

- These smaller batches are easier to see in the saucepan (rather than in a pot or a Dutch oven), so they more readily reveal their final consistency for visual cues: perhaps *thickened like pancake batter* or *jammy*.

- And we often ask you to run a wooden spoon through the mixture at the bottom of the pan to create a line that holds its edges for a second. When you're working with 2 gallons of, say, blueberry jam, it's almost impossible to make that kind of a line. But in a medium saucepan, it's no sweat. (There's more on this specific, line-making technique on page 117 in the introduction to Chapter 2.)

How much does a recipe make?

We weighed our ingredients and tried to accommodate the variables. But there's no way we can tell if your blueberries hold more or less water than ours, if you start counting a boil the same second we do, or if you push every drop through a sieve or leave behind a little for the sake of speed.

So your batch may make slightly less or more than ours. Less is a bit of a problem, since we must worry about oxidation in the jars, even in cold canning. If one jar is not quite as full as we suggest, *either* put it in the fridge and use it quickly *or* let it cool and pop it in the freezer to kill the chances of its discoloring. Once frozen, it can last as long as our guidelines state.

A yield greater than ours is really no problem. If you find some left in the pot after bottling, scrape the remainder into a heat-safe, glass storage vessel, like a Pyrex custard cup. Cover and refrigerate for a day or two. Who doesn't want a sneak peek at the final results?

Can I double a recipe?

Unfortunately, *no.*

Pectin and sugar work in an algorithmic ratio, not an arithmetic nor even a geometric one. There's no way to look at most of these recipes and simply multiply by two (or more). Everything, even the rise of the pH from added lemon juice, has to be rejiggered for a proper gel or consistency.

If you want to double or even triple a recipe, make two or three batches. Given that most of these recipes can be completed in under 30 minutes, doing so is no big deal.

What does *cover or seal* mean?

Time and again, we tell you to fill the jars or containers, often with a still-hot sweet or savory condiment, then *cover or seal* them. If you're using mason-style jars, lay a flat lid on each jar with the silicone gasket down, then screw on the sealing band (or ring). If you're using a one-piece, lid-ring combination (sometimes called a *cap*), screw one on each jar. If you're using canning jars that don't have a screw-on lid design, that have, say, flat glass lids with silicon rings on the bottom side and metal clips to hold the lids tight, follow the manufacturer's instructions for sealing these. And if you're using some other storage con-tainer—in other words, *not* a canning jar of some sort—snap or clip on its lid.

Why? It's a bid to keep contaminants out of what you've made and to keep you and yours safe. However, you should let sealed, hot things cool down on the counter a bit before chilling—sometimes, no more than 30 minutes—to avoid straining your refrigerator or even thawing nearby items in your freezer.

All in all, traditional canning jars remain your best option. Otherwise, be forewarned on three counts:

- Do not cover hot contents with plastic wrap, even if the wrap never touches the product. The plastic wrap can warp from the heat and melt onto the jar.

- Flimsy plastic lids on glass containers will warp over time and lose their seal, particularly as they get locked over very warm condiments and as they are run through your dishwasher.

- Check to make sure the alternative containers you're using are freezer-safe. Many cheap knock-offs will shatter in the freezer, sometimes within minutes, sometimes during long storage. And many cheap glass containers will crack when still-warm condiments are put in them.

How long will something last?

This answer varies dramatically, mostly based on the condiment's sugar and/or salt content, both of which can be preservatives. And don't forget: There's naturally occurring sugar and salt in many vegetables and fruits, as well as salt added to some purchased ingredients like tamarind paste.

In general, jellies, syrups, and liqueurs have the highest amount of sugar and last the longest in the fridge, anywhere from 1 month to up to 6 months in some cases. Some low-salt, low-sugar, or sugar-free condiments stay fresh only a week or so in the fridge. And some uncooked, raw things like tapenades have a very short shelf life, sometimes only a few days, tops.

As to freezer condiments, the vast majority in this book can stay in the deep chill for up to a year. A few fresher things, particularly with uncooked ingredients, can't stay more than 6 months in the freezer. And several snacks or condiments, like pickles and sauerkraut, should never be frozen.

▲ You don't need fancy labels. Mark the lids of your jars!

Why would we skip the freezer? Take pickled okra, for example. The spears expand while freezing, then collapse while thawing, resulting in something that resembles squishy chunks of slimy relish, none too appealing. That's why some recipes are designed *only* for the fridge. Check the storage guidelines to be sure.

For safety's sake, err on the conservative side with our guidelines, even if you think the jam or sauerkraut is still…um, good. Toss out anything molded, funky, darkly discolored, or acrid.

We always mark the lids of our jars with a date in indelible ink, so we know exactly when we made it (and thus, when we should throw it out).

Can I heat-process my results?

For the vast majority of these recipes, no. Certainly not the ferments, the relishes, the low-sugar conserves, the sugar-free and chia-seed jams, the salsas, most of the sauces, all of the chili crisps, and any of the recipes with tomatoes. Most of these recipes were not crafted with a pH that permits them to become shelf-stable. However, there are some recipes that can indeed produce pantry products, particularly those in the first two chapters.

You'll find them marked with a call-out indicating you can process these old-school. To find out more, see the appendix on page 436. Just to be abundantly clear, do not process the results of any recipe without this call-out, even sweet jams and chutneys. Either the sugar content is too low or the pectin ratio is too delicate to withstand time in a traditional canner.

Will freezing compromise what I made?

It's really about thawing, not freezing. So the short answer goes like this: mostly, *no*; sometimes, *a little*; rarely, *yes*. Follow the guidelines on each recipe for the best results.

For jellies, jams, liqueurs, most chutneys, most sauces, and almost all syrups, there's no problem. For somewhat drier *or* chunkier condiments like preserves, chili crisps, and chili pastes, thawing can cause a mildly compromised, mushier texture, although it's often detectable only by sensitive palates. For coarser, wetter, vegetable-forward things like relishes and chow chows, the change in texture is more noticeable, although the condiment is perfectly edible,

just squishier. And for some things like pickles, sauerkrauts, and kimchis, there's a huge problem, since the vegetable mixture can not only turn spongy, but also start to rot as it thaws. These recipes do not list a freezer storage option.

Another thawing problem is oxidation. Some condiments turn a bit brown as the thawed ingredients are exposed again to room-temperature air. Scrape off those bits and there's no problem… unless you notice very dark or blackish patches in or even (gads!) below the oxidation. In these cases, throw out the entire condiment. The jar may not have been perfectly clean at bottling; an unseen, dirty residue may have been left on the vegetable; or the condiment wasn't quite cooked enough, leaving too much residual moisture in the mix, which then leads to rot.

Finally, if you open a condiment, thawed or just refrigerated, and notice a tidal pond aroma, a rotten smell, or a corroded battery odor, throw the thing out. It's not worth a day in the bathroom for a spoonful of corn relish.

Can I refreeze something that's previously been frozen? Or freeze an opened jar of something from the fridge?

Again, the short answers: *sort of* and *no*.

First, a freezer condiment that has been thawed in a 40°F or 4°C refrigerator and left *unopened* for under 3 days can indeed be refrozen (for example, so you can go on an unexpected trip). But here's the *sort of* part of that short answer: The texture will be greatly compromised. Chutneys and preserves can become like baby food; chili crisps and harissas, like purees.

And no, you cannot freeze an opened, half-eaten jar of strawberry preserves or coarse-grained mustard. There are too many possible pathogens introduced by both contact with the air and contact with spoons stuck in the jar. Don't morph your penurious habits into a dangerous gambit.

▲ Good-quality jars will get frosty but won't crack in the freezer.

Ready, set…

You're ready to enter a world of better meals! Or maybe better takeout as you top tacos with homemade salsa macha, fried rice with your own chili crisp, or bagels with your own blackberry conserve. Just wait until you break out your own pickled asparagus spears with a turkey sandwich, your own apples in syrup with some Greek yogurt for breakfast, or your own Harvard beets with a rotisserie chicken quarter for an easy dinner. And think how pleased you'll be when you crack open a jar of fiery red sambal, a container of nose-spanking mustard, or a bottle of smooth, homemade triple sec for your next patio party.

We can't wait for you to join us on this adventure. We've been at it for years. We want to share it with you. Don't skip the chapter introductions. But do have great fun with the recipes. We always do.

1

Jams, Jellies, Preserves, and Marmalades

There are good reasons why fruit concoctions take the first spot for most of us canners. Homemade jams, preserves, and marmalades are less sweet than the mass-processed stuff. They sparkle more brilliantly in the light. And they taste more like the fruit or berry that was their inception.

Back when we got serious about canning, back when Bruce was an advertising copywriter and Mark was in grad school—and long before we were together—we both started with jams and preserves...but strictly old-school: with a water-bath canner, a pot rack, a jar grip, the whole rigamarole.

But after years of traditional canning, we came to see that we could retain even fresher flavors if we put up fruits and berries with cold canning. Less processing = less effort = more flavor—a win-win-win. Plus, we were left with smaller batches in a tiny Manhattan apartment!

Now that we've decamped to more spacious digs in rural New England, do we still drag out our time-tested equipment? Of course! Like when the bushes in our backyard produce 5 gallons of blueberries. But not when we find 2 quarts of sun-fresh strawberries at a local farmers' market. Or when we drive an hour and a half to a big box store and find a bag of frozen blackberries at an unbeatable price.

Cold canning is just easier. We sometimes even use bottled fruit juices for small batches of jelly. (Admittedly, there are a *few* times when it's worthwhile to pull out a jelly bag.) We can also create a jammy pulp right in the saucepan without a rigorous prep and cooking process (mostly by just mashing the fruit against the inside of the pan). And since none of these recipes involves a second heating in a canner—which can dull the flavor—they produce spreads that taste more like blackberries, blueberries, mangoes, or what have you.

Before we bounce to our first cold canning adventures, let's talk through some key points.

Nailing down some definitions

As writers, we love definitions. So here goes:

- **preserves** and **marmalades** are made from whole fruit;

- **jams**, from fruit pulp;

- and **jellies**, from fruit juice.

Or to put it another way, preserves and marmalades are thick and chunky; jams, smoother if pulpy, yet also velvety; and jellies, translucent and more subtly flavored. (Conserves, a less-sweet and separate category altogether, are found in the next chapter.)

▲ Clockwise from top in ramekins: Red Currant Jelly (page 89), Clementine-Ginger Marmalade (page 109), Plum Preserves (page 65), and Kiwi Jam (page 94)

Using fresh v. frozen ingredients

Whenever we're putting up a small batch and want to get the best flavor out of the fruit or berries, we most often opt for fresh. But when we're cooking a fruit or berry mixture a bit longer, particularly to get a pulpy jam, we often use *either* fresh or frozen, depending on what our wallets allow.

In fact, frozen fruits and berries are often picked closer to ripeness than the fresh ones in our supermarkets. Those in the produce section ripen (or, um, change color) during transit. But those in the freezer case don't have the luxury of time on the open road. They're often flash-frozen right in the fields or within a few hours of harvest.

If you use frozen fruit or berries, consider thawing them right in their bag or container, rather than in a colander set in the sink. If you've got the right *weight* when you buy the frozen stuff, you want to preserve any liquid that's released during thawing and add it along with the fruit or berries to the saucepan.

Truth be told, the fruits and vegetables at a farmers' market may be the best choice all around if you're putting yourself through even the small trouble of cold canning. Local producers have to present their goods at their peak. Even so, don't discount supermarket sales, particularly on berries. There's no call for lofty idealism when raspberries are marked *buy two, get one free*.

Crushing berries and fruit

To cut down on the prep and cleanup, we often advocate for crushing berries and fruits right in the saucepan (rather than dirtying another bowl). You can get the job done in one of three ways:

- Use a potato masher (our preferred method)—it will let you mush up whatever you have in the pan without a lot of effort;

- Use the back of a wooden spoon, which is a bit more labor intensive and certainly not as effective;

- Or if the recipe says you should put the fruit pieces or berries in a bowl or even in a saucepan to crush them before you heat them, put on culinary kitchen gloves (see page 18) to do the job by hand. However, we *don't* advocate for a hand-crushing technique if we want more of the pulp or even bits of fruit left in the mix. Your hands are just too forceful!

Mixing the sugar and pectin

Throughout these recipes, we include a seemingly fussy step of mixing some of the sugar and the low-sugar pectin in a separate bowl. Why not just add them together to the cauldron at the appointed time in the cooking? We tried it. We ended up with little clumps of pectin throughout the boiling mixture. These lumps proved hard to

▲ Keep spills to a minimum: Work with a ladle spoon and a canning funnel.

dissolve. We even resorted to a potato masher to get rid of them, thereby also destroying some of the fruit or berries. So this preliminary step isn't busywork. It's necessary for success.

▲ Press lightly with a vegetable peeler to take only the zest off citrus.

▲ Removing the peel reveals the individual segments in an orange or other citrus.

Taking caution!

Keep in mind that you're often working with extremely hot sugar syrups, far beyond the boiling point of water. Don't handle jars or pans with wet hot pads. If your kitchen has laminate countertops, consider filling the jars in the sink to prevent scorch marks. And don't attempt to bottle preserves and their like with children or pets in the kitchen.

To fill the jars (or other containers), the best tools are a relatively shallow, tapered ladle (often called a *ladle spoon*) and a canning funnel. Can you pour from the saucepan directly into a jar? Yes, but you'll end up with scalding drips on the counter. Clean these as they cool.

Special matters for marmalades

At the end of this chapter, you'll also find small-batch marmalades. These recipes require two considerations.

First, you must often use the brightly colored citrus *zest* but not the white *pith* underneath (unless called for, of course). The best tool to extract a strip of zest is a vegetable peeler. Don't press into the fruit. Instead, use the peeler to take off a colored strip from just the outer layer of the pith. The strip needn't be translucent. It can even have specks of white pith attached to it, so long as it's mostly the same color on both sides.

Second, marmalades sometimes require you to extract the pulpy fruit from the citrus. To do so, first remove the zest as directed. Then slice a little circle from the top (that is, the blossom end) and the bottom (the stem end). Now the fruit can sit flat on your cutting board with chambers of those inner, pulpy bits revealed at the top and bottom. Run a sharp knife down the exterior curve of the fruit, slicing off a strip of the white pith and revealing some of the chambers with bright fruit inside. Work all the way around the fruit to remove as much of the pith as you can and reveal all the bright fruit, then pare off any bits of pith that remain here and there. The inner segments (also called *supremes*) are now visible, although there's still a white membrane between each segment. For our recipes, you can usually chop or tear up the fruit at this point. For these recipes, there's no call to remove those inner membranes. Yes, they're bitter. But we find they can complement the zest and pulp, particularly with all the sugar in the mix.

Ready, set…

At this point, you're ready to turn fruits and berries into the best things that toast, crackers, bagels, and English muffins have ever seen. Or the best condiments for cheese and charcuterie boards. Or for an afternoon treat with a scone. *And* you'll have a couple of extra jars in the freezer for friends and family (or to resupply your fridge stash when you're ready).

Strawberry Preserves

MAKES: about 3 cups (720 ml)
FRIDGE: up to 3 weeks
FREEZER: up to 1 year
May be traditionally canned (see page 436)

Is there anything better than popping open a jar of homemade strawberry preserves? You breathe in that sweet perfume from summer's height, even in the winter. You see the dark chunks of fruit—and among them, the lighter specks of gelled juice, as brilliant as rubies between the berries. You spoon up a little and know the jar was worth the effort. To achieve this gold standard of preserves, we've nixed cooking the strawberries. Instead, we crush them a bit, keeping them as whole as the best preserves warrant (that is, in chunks and pieces). Then we make a thick pectin mixture, which the strawberries touch for only a minute before bottling.

> 1¼ pounds (565 g) fresh strawberries, rinsed and hulled (about 4 cups)
> 2 teaspoons (10 ml) lemon juice
> 1½ cups (300 g) granulated white sugar
> ½ cup (120 ml) water
> 2 tablespoons (24 g) *granulated less-sugar* pectin

1. Use a potato masher or your clean hands to partially crush the strawberries in a medium bowl, leaving the strawberries in chunks and pieces. Do *not* create a puree. Stir in the lemon juice.

2. Combine the sugar, water, and pectin in a medium saucepan. Set the pan over medium-high heat and whisk until the sugar dissolves. Raise the heat to medium-high and bring to a boil you cannot stir down, whisking occasionally. Boil undisturbed for 1 minute, as the liquid turns clear.

3. Turn off the heat and remove the saucepan from the burner. Add the strawberry mixture (be careful of scalding plops). *Gently* stir for 1 minute.

Front to back: Strawberry Preserves (page 32) and Strawberry Jam (page 34)

4. Transfer to three *clean* ½ pint (236 ml) jars or other containers, leaving about ½ inch (1 cm) headspace in each. Cover or seal. Cool at room temperature for no more than 1 hour, then refrigerate or freeze. In the fridge, the preserves may not gel until cold.

Tip

Can you use frozen strawberries? Yes, but why? For the best results, use ripe strawberries. The fresher, the better. You'll know by their characteristic aroma and perky stems.

Strawberry Jam

MAKES: about 4 cups (960 ml)
FRIDGE: up to 3 weeks
FREEZER: up to 1 year
May be traditionally canned (see page 436)

This pulpy jam may well represent the whole jam category! It's a sumptuous spread that remains our preferred *J* in a PB&J. When making Strawberry Preserves (page 32), you crush the fruit for lots of chunks and pieces. Here, you smash the fruit into a viscous puree. It needn't be smooth, certainly not like strawberry sauce, but more like canned, crushed tomatoes.

> 2 cups (400 g) granulated white sugar
>
> 2 tablespoons (24 g) *granulated less-sugar* pectin
>
> 1 pound 14 ounces (840 g) fresh strawberries, rinsed and hulled; or thawed frozen strawberries, hulled (about 6 cups for either)
>
> 1 tablespoon (15 ml) lemon juice

1. Mix ¼ cup (50 g) sugar and the pectin in a small bowl until uniform.

2. Crush the strawberries in a medium saucepan with a potato masher or the back of a wooden spoon until a pulpy puree. Stir in the lemon juice.

3. Set the pan over medium-high heat and add the pectin mixture. Stir constantly to dissolve the granulated ingredients. Bring the mixture to a boil you can't stir down, stirring often.

4. Add the remaining 1¾ cups (350 g) sugar and stir constantly to dissolve the sugar. Bring back to a full boil, stirring occasionally. Boil undisturbed for 1 minute.

5. Turn off the heat and remove the saucepan from the burner. Let stand for 1–2 minutes, then skim any foamy impurities with a tablespoon.

6. Transfer to four *clean* ½ pint (236 ml) jars or other containers, leaving about ½ inch (1 cm) headspace in each. Cover or seal. Cool at room temperature for no more than 1 hour, then refrigerate or freeze.

More

For a more sophisticated take, add up to 1 teaspoon ground black pepper with the remaining sugar in step 4. Or 2 teaspoons stemmed fresh thyme leaves. Or ½ teaspoon red pepper flakes.

Strawberry Jewels

MAKES: about 4 cups (960 ml)
FRIDGE: up to 1 month
FREEZER: up to 1 year

When we stroll through a farmers' market at the start *or* at the end of New England's growing season, we often spot small, super sweet strawberries that beg us to go all out. We oblige with this old-school, French technique. It renders *small* strawberries into something like luscious, edible cabochon rubies suspended in a thick yet pectin-free syrup. Admittedly, this recipe is a multi-day affair. But you'll end up with something like candied strawberries that are a step up from the most prized preserves and an unrivaled treat.

> 3 pounds (1.4 kg) *small* fresh strawberries (about 12 cups), rinsed and hulled
>
> 3 cups (600 g) granulated white sugar
>
> 2½ tablespoons (35 ml) lemon juice

1. Place one-third of the berries in a large bowl; sprinkle evenly with ½ cup (100 g) sugar. Repeat this process twice, eventually using all the berries and a total of 1½ cups (300 g) sugar. Cover the bowl and set in the coolest part of the kitchen for 24 hours.

2. Pour the strawberry mixture into a large colander set over a very large saucepan to drain for about 1 hour. Remove the colander with the berries. Stir the remaining 1½ cups (300 g) sugar into the drained syrup.

3. Set the pan over medium-high heat and bring the syrup to a full boil, stirring often. Stir in the strawberries and lemon juice. Bring back to a boil, stirring occasionally *but gently*. Boil undisturbed for 5 minutes.

4. Use a slotted spoon to transfer the strawberries to a clean bowl. Continue boiling the syrup, stirring occasionally, until reduced by half of its volume when the strawberries were removed, about 8 minutes.

5. Return the strawberries to the pan and bring back to a boil, stirring *gently* and occasionally. Reduce the heat to low and simmer, *gently* stirring a few times, until the syrup has thickened quite a bit, not to a glaze, but to a corn syrup–like texture, about 5 minutes.

6. Turn off the heat, remove the pan from the burner, and transfer the strawberries and syrup to four *clean* ½ pint (236 ml) jars or other containers, dividing the strawberries evenly among them and leaving about ½ inch (1 cm) headspace in each. There may be a little syrup left over. Save it, covered, in the fridge for pancakes. Cover or seal the jars or containers. Cool at room temperature for no more than 30 minutes, then refrigerate or freeze. These jewels will never set as firmly as traditional preserves.

Next
Spoon the strawberry jewels onto a slice of vanilla cream pie instead of (or with!) whipped cream.

Sugar-Free Strawberry Preserves

MAKES: about 3 cups (720 ml)
FRIDGE: up to 2 weeks
FREEZER: up to 6 months

Maybe you're helping someone cut down on sugar. Maybe *you* want to cut down. Or maybe, midyear you'd like to put back a nice gift in the freezer for a new year's resolution yet to come. In any case, you don't need sugar to make chunky, strawberry-rich preserves. Use any artificial sweetener you like, so long as it works *in a 1:1 ratio* (*by volume*) *in baking recipes*. (For more information, see page 20 in the introduction.)

> 1¼ pounds (565 g) fresh strawberries, rinsed and hulled; or thawed frozen strawberries, hulled (about 4 cups for either)
> 2 teaspoons (10 ml) lemon juice
> 1 cup *1-to-1 (by volume)* granulated white-sugar substitute
> ½ cup (120 ml) water
> 2 tablespoons (24 g) *granulated less-sugar* pectin

1. Use a potato masher or the back of a wooden spoon to partially crush the strawberries in a medium bowl, leaving many pieces and small chunks. Do not make a puree. Stir in the lemon juice.

2. Put the sugar substitute, water, and pectin in a medium saucepan. Set over medium-high heat and stir until the granulated ingredients dissolve. Raise the heat to medium-high and bring to a boil that you can't stir down, stirring often. Boil undisturbed for 1 minute, as the liquid turns clear.

3. Turn off the heat and remove the pan from the burner. Slowly add the strawberry mixture. (Watch out for the scalding plops!) *Gently* stir for 1 minute.

4. Transfer the strawberry mixture to three *clean* ½ pint (236 ml) jars or other containers, leaving about ½ inch (1 cm) headspace in each. Cover or seal. Cool at room temperature for no more than 1 hour, then refrigerate or freeze.

Next

For a sugar-free breakfast, stir these preserves into warm oatmeal and top with a dollop of fat-free plain Greek yogurt.

Strawberry-Rhubarb Jam

MAKES: about 4 cups (960 ml)
FRIDGE: up to 3 weeks
FREEZER: up to 1 year
May be traditionally canned (see page 436)

Ever snuggle farther down into a comfy bed on a winter morning? We have! Inevitably, one of us will realize the day *must* go on and climb out into the New England cold. Why? Usually, it's the call of a toasted bagel with a jam like this one, with a bright pop to remind us of early summer mornings. Rhubarb pairs best with the texture of pulpy *jam*, given the way rhubarb itself cooks down to a mash. And a tiny bit of vanilla mutes some of the sweetness for a smoother finish. If you make this jam when rhubarb is fresh, you, too, will be braced for those winter mornings when a hot cup of coffee and your own jam are the best reasons to face the chill.

> 1¼ pounds (565 g) fresh strawberries, rinsed and hulled; or thawed frozen strawberries, hulled (about 4 cups for either)
>
> 1 teaspoon (5 ml) vanilla extract
>
> 2½ cups (500 g) granulated white sugar
>
> 2 tablespoons (24 g) *granulated less-sugar* pectin
>
> Two 12 inch (30 cm) thin rhubarb stalks, cut into ½ inch (1.25 cm) half-moon slices
>
> ¼ cup (60 ml) water

1. Use a potato masher or the back of a wooden spoon to crush the strawberries in a medium bowl until they're the consistency of canned crushed tomatoes. Do not make a puree. Stir in the vanilla.

2. Mix ¼ cup (50 g) sugar and the pectin in a large bowl until uniform. Stir into the strawberries until well combined.

3. Bring the rhubarb and water to a boil in a large saucepan set over medium-high heat, stirring occasionally. Reduce the heat to medium-low, cover, and cook, stirring once, for 3 minutes.

4. Uncover and stir in the strawberry mixture. Raise the heat to medium-high. Do not cover. Bring the mixture to a boil you can't stir down, stirring often.

5. Add the remaining 2¼ cups (450 g) sugar and stir constantly to dissolve the sugar. Bring back to a full boil, stirring often. Boil undisturbed for 1 minute.

6. Turn off the heat and remove the pan from the burner. Let stand for 1–2 minutes, then skim any foamy impurities with a tablespoon.

7. Transfer to four *clean* ½ pint (236 ml) jars or other containers, leaving about ½ inch (1 cm) headspace in each. Cover or seal. Cool at room temperature for no more than 1 hour, then refrigerate or freeze. In the fridge, the jam may not set for 24 hours.

Tip

Because of the relatively short cooking time, the tough "threads" on the curved, exterior side of large rhubarb stalks won't get tender. If you're working with very thin stalks, it's really not much of a problem. But with stalks wider than about 1 inch (2.5 cm), nick up those threads at the smaller end and zip them off before chopping the rhubarb.

Strawberry-Jalapeño Jam

MAKES: about 4 cups (960 ml)
FRIDGE: up to 3 weeks
FREEZER: up to 1 year
May be traditionally canned (see page 436)

Although we're unabashed fans of fresh berry flavors like those in Strawberry Preserves (page 32), cooking strawberries for jam gives them a more intense savor with distinctly caramel undertones. All the better then to pair with bright, spicy jalapeños, which arrive late to the cooking process so they retain a bit of their crunch (and their burn). The heady blend is balanced with a splash of balsamic vinegar to bring in a few sour notes. All in all, this jam is a sophisticated treat, terrific on a cream cheese–smeared bagel.

> 2¼ cups (450 g) granulated white sugar
>
> 2 tablespoons (24 g) *granulated less-sugar* pectin
>
> 1 pound 14 ounces (840 g) fresh strawberries, rinsed and hulled; or thawed frozen strawberries, hulled (about 6 cups for either)
>
> Up to 4 medium fresh jalapeño chilis, stemmed, halved lengthwise, and *very* thinly sliced
>
> 1 tablespoon (15 ml) balsamic vinegar

1. Mix ¼ cup (50 g) sugar and the pectin in a small bowl until uniform.

2. Use a potato masher or the back of a wooden spoon to crush the strawberries in a large saucepan, until they're the consistency of canned crushed tomatoes. Do not make a puree.

3. Set the pan over medium-high heat and add the pectin mixture. Stir constantly until the granulated ingredients dissolve. Bring to a boil you can't stir down, stirring often.

4. Add the remaining 2 cups (400 g) sugar, the jalapeños, and vinegar. Stir constantly to dissolve the sugar. Raise the heat to medium-high and bring back to a full boil, stirring often. Boil undisturbed for 1 minute.

5. Turn off the heat and remove the pan from the burner. Let stand for 1–2 minutes, then skim any foamy impurities with a tablespoon.

6. Transfer to four *clean* ½ pint (236 ml) jars or other containers, leaving about ½ inch (1 cm) headspace in each. Cover or seal. Cool at room temperature for no more than 30 minutes, then refrigerate or freeze. In the fridge, the jam may not set for 24 hours.

Tip
Make a less spicy jam by seeding the chilis after stemming and halving them.

Concord Grape Jelly

MAKES: about 4 cups (960 ml)
FRIDGE: up to 1 month
FREEZER: up to 1 year
May be traditionally canned (see page 436)

We're old enough to cherish memories of bygone Concord grape jelly, an amethyst-purple, translucent spread that had to be paired with (chunky!) peanut butter (or snuck out of the jar by the spoonful). Over the years, mass-produced Concord grape jelly has gotten sweeter and lost the tart-lush contrast we once craved. But *bottled* Concord grape juice still has the flavor we love. So this easy, small-batch jelly is as tasty as the stuff from back in the day.

> 2 cups (400 g) granulated white sugar
>
> 2½ tablespoons (30 g) *granulated less-sugar* pectin
>
> 3½ cups (840 ml) *unsweetened pure* Concord grape juice
>
> ⅛ teaspoon kosher salt, optional

1. Mix ¼ cup (50 g) sugar and the pectin in a small bowl until uniform.

2. Pour the juice into a medium saucepan, set over medium-high heat, and add the pectin mixture. Stir constantly to dissolve the granulated ingredients. Bring the mixture to a boil you can't stir down, stirring often.

3. Stir in the remaining 1¾ cups (350 g) sugar and the salt, if using. Stir constantly to dissolve the sugar. Bring back to a full boil, stirring often. Boil undisturbed for 1 minute.

4. Turn off the heat and remove the pan from the burner. Let stand for 1–2 minutes, then skim any foamy impurities with a tablespoon.

5. Transfer to four *clean* ½ pint (236 ml) jars or other containers, leaving about ½ inch (1 cm) headspace in each. Cover or seal. Cool at room temperature for no more than 1 hour, then refrigerate or freeze.

Tip
Use *unsweetened* Concord grape juice. And read the label to make sure the juice is from only Concord grapes, not cut with less-expensive juices.

Concord Grape Jam

MAKES: about 5 cups (1200 ml)
FRIDGE: up to 3 weeks
FREEZER: up to 1 year
May be traditionally canned (see page 436)

Bottled grape juice is all well and good for an easy jelly, but the pulpier texture of jam requires the grapes themselves, as well as (unfortunately) a bit more work. We scour our New England farmers' markets in the early autumn for Concord grapes. These days, the grapes are expensive, so a small batch better fits our budget. We end up with that prized, luxurious jam texture: looser and more velvety than jelly.

    4 cups (750 g) stemmed fresh Concord grapes (do
        not seed them)
    ½ cup (120 ml) water
    1 tablespoon (15 ml) lemon juice
    2½ cups (500 g) granulated white sugar
    2 tablespoons (24 g) *granulated less-sugar* pectin

1. Mix the grapes, water, and lemon juice in a large saucepan. Set it over medium-high heat and stir almost constantly as the grapes begin to break down, about 2 minutes. Cover and bring to a simmer, stirring frequently.

2. Reduce the heat to low, keep covered, and cook, stirring occasionally, for 10 minutes. Turn off the heat, uncover, and cool for 15 minutes. (The grapes should be crushable with a wooden spoon.)

3. Working in batches, crank the grape mixture through a food mill and into a large bowl underneath, thereby removing the seeds and skins. (For an alternative to a food mill, see page 16.)

4. Mix ½ cup (100 g) sugar and the pectin in a small bowl until uniform.

5. Wipe out the saucepan, return the milled grape mixture to it, and set it over medium-high heat. Add the pectin mixture. Stir constantly to dissolve the granulated ingredients. Bring the mixture to a boil you can't stir down, stirring often.

6. Add the remaining 2 cups (400 g) sugar and stir constantly to dissolve the sugar. Bring back to a full boil, stirring often. Boil undisturbed for 1 minute.

7. Turn off the heat and remove the saucepan from the burner. Let stand for 1–2 minutes, then skim any foamy impurities with a tablespoon.

8. Transfer to five *clean* ½ pint (236 ml) jars or other containers, leaving about ½ inch (1 cm) headspace in each. Cover or seal. Cool at room temperature for no more than 1 hour, then refrigerate or freeze.

Next
Concord Grape Jam and Cowboy Candy (page 256) are a perfect combo with a smear of chopped liver on a cracker!

Bottom to top, on toast with peanut butter: Red Grape Jam (page 40) and Concord Grape Jam (page 38)

Green Grape Jam

MAKES: about 3 cups (720 ml)
FRIDGE: up to 3 weeks
FREEZER: up to 1 year
May be traditionally canned (see page 436)

Fresh, green grapes are a strange lot. They're sweet, no doubt. But the ones from the supermarket can taste like colored sugar water— that is, until they're simmered. Then they take on a white-wine flavor: a little tart, a little floral, quite rounded. We feel the pulpy thickness of jam is a better complement to that flavor than a jelly would be. But since we want to keep the work for a small batch to a minimum, we opt for seedless green grapes (and are then able to swear off a food mill).

> 2½ cups (500 g) granulated white sugar
> 2 tablespoons (24 g) *granulated less-sugar* pectin
> 5 cups (750 g) stemmed *seedless* green grapes

1. Mix ¼ cup (50 g) sugar and the pectin in a small bowl until uniform.

2. Dump the grapes into a large saucepan. Use the back of a wooden spoon or a potato masher to crush the grapes against the side of the pan, leaving lots of pulp and smaller bits without making a puree.

3. Set the pan over medium-high heat and bring the grape mash to a simmer, stirring frequently. Reduce the heat to low and cook, stirring often, until the mash is reduced to about two-thirds of its original volume, about 10 minutes.

4. Add the pectin mixture and raise the heat to medium-high. Stirring constantly to dissolve the granulated ingredients, then less frequently but still fairly often, bring the mixture to a boil you can't stir down.

5. Add the remaining 2¼ cups (450 g) sugar and stir constantly to dissolve the sugar. Bring back to a full boil, stirring occasionally. Boil undisturbed for 1 minute.

6. Turn off the heat and remove the saucepan from the burner. Let stand for 1–2 minutes, then skim any foamy impurities with a tablespoon.

7. Transfer to three *clean* ½ pint (236 ml) jars or other containers, leaving about ½ inch (1 cm) headspace in each. Cover or seal. Cool at room temperature for no more than 1 hour, then refrigerate or freeze.

More

Add up to ½ teaspoon ginger juice, ½ teaspoon vanilla extract, *or* ¼ teaspoon brandy extract with the pectin mixture.

Red Grape Jam

MAKES: about 4 cups (960 ml)
FRIDGE: up to 3 weeks
FREEZER: up to 1 year
May be traditionally canned (see page 436)

The difference between this jam and Concord Grape Jam (page 38) is a bit like the difference between red wine and grape juice. Red grape jam has a lighter but somehow more sophisticated, mildly tannic flavor. It also holds a brighter, jewel-tone color. (Check out the photo on page 39.)

> 2¼ cups (450 g) granulated white sugar
> 2 tablespoons (24 g) *granulated less-sugar* pectin
> 1 pound 9 ounces (720 g) stemmed *seedless* red grapes (about 5 cups)
> ½ cup (120 ml) *unsweetened* red grape juice concentrate (thawed if frozen)
> 2 tablespoons (30 ml) lemon juice

1. Mix ¼ cup (50 g) sugar and the pectin in a small bowl until uniform.

2. Place the grapes in a food processor (work in batches as necessary), cover, and pulse to chop them without turning them into a puree. Pour them into a large saucepan. Stir in the juice concentrate and lemon juice.

3. Set the pan over medium-high heat and add the pectin mixture. Stirring constantly at first to dissolve the granulated ingredients, then less frequently but still fairly often, bring the mixture to a boil you can't stir down.

4. Add the remaining 2 cups (400 g) sugar and stir constantly to dissolve the sugar. Bring back to a full boil, stirring occasionally. Boil undisturbed for 1 minute.

5. Turn off the heat and remove the saucepan from the burner. Let stand for 1–2 minutes, then skim any foamy impurities with a tablespoon.

6. Transfer to four *clean* ½ pint (236 ml) jars or other containers, leaving about ½ inch (1 cm) headspace in each. Cover or seal. Cool at room temperature for no more than 1 hour, then refrigerate or freeze. In the fridge, the jam may not set until cold.

Next
Try the jam on crackers with a bit of runny, room-temperature Camembert. Or stir a little bit into a beef or root vegetable stew at the end of cooking to mellow and balance the flavors.

Grape-Ginger Jelly

MAKES: about 4 cups (960 ml)
FRIDGE: up to 1 month
FREEZER: up to 1 year
May be traditionally canned (see page 436)

Texture v. flavor: This changing dynamic is a focus for all canners. Take this simple recipe as an example. We combine bottled white grape juice with more assertive ginger juice for a morning wake-up poke or a great addition to a charcuterie board. But because of that ginger kick, and even though this recipe makes a translucent jelly, we still wanted its texture to be a bit more luxurious than that of standard jelly, so we adjusted the sugar-pectin ratio for a slightly softer, swankier set to contrast the spikier flavors.

2 cups (400 g) granulated white sugar
2 tablespoons (24 g) *granulated less-sugar* pectin
3 cups (720 ml) *unsweetened pure* white grape juice
2 tablespoons (30 ml) ginger juice (see TIP)

1. Stir ¼ cup (50 g) sugar with the pectin in a small bowl until uniform.

2. Pour the grape juice and ginger juice into a medium saucepan. Set it over medium-high heat and add the pectin mixture. Stirring constantly at first to dissolve the granulated ingredients, then less frequently but still fairly often, bring this mixture to a boil you can't stir down.

3. Add the remaining 1¾ cups (350 g) sugar and stir constantly to dissolve the sugar. Bring back to a full boil, stirring occasionally. Boil undisturbed for 1 minute.

4. Turn off the heat and remove the saucepan from the burner. Let stand for 1–2 minutes, then skim any foamy impurities with a tablespoon.

5. Transfer to four *clean* ½ pint (236 ml) jars or other containers, leaving about ½ inch (1 cm) headspace in each. Cover or seal. Cool at room temperature for no more than 1 hour, then refrigerate or freeze. In the fridge, the jelly may not fully set for 24 hours.

Tip
Press fresh minced ginger through a garlic press to make ginger juice. You'll need up to 5 inches (13 cm) fresh ginger to get the 2 tablespoons for this recipe. Or use bottled ginger juice.

Spiced Grape Jelly

MAKES: about 4 cups (960 ml)
FRIDGE: up to 1 month
FREEZER: up to 1 year
May be traditionally canned (see page 436)

Winter holidays are all about warming spices like cinnamon, cloves, and allspice. Maybe the connection is primal: to hunker down near a fire, to feel some comfort in our bellies. Or maybe it's a centuries-long tradition of using those spices during the chilly months, a link now bred in our bones. No matter: Make this clear, firm jelly for all winter celebrations, along with a few extra jars for your loved ones who'll stick with you close by the fire.

- 4 cups (960 ml) *unsweetened pure* white grape juice
- 1 teaspoon (5 ml) white wine vinegar
- One 2 x 2 inch (5 x 5 cm) strip of orange zest
- One 3 inch (7.5 cm) cinnamon stick
- 5 whole allspice berries
- 5 whole cloves
- 2 cups (400 g) granulated white sugar
- 3 tablespoons (36 g) *granulated less-sugar* pectin

1. Pour the grape juice into a large saucepan set over medium-high heat. Stir in the vinegar, orange zest strip, cinnamon stick, allspice berries, and cloves. Bring to a simmer, stirring once in a while. Turn off the heat, remove the pan from the burner, cover, and cool at room temperature for at least 2 hours or up to 4 hours.

2. Strain the cooled liquid through a colander into a bowl and discard the solids. Pour the juice back into the saucepan and set the pan over medium-high heat.

3. Mix ¼ cup (50 g) sugar and the pectin in a small bowl until uniform. Add this mixture to the juice. Stirring constantly at first to dissolve the granulated ingredients, then less frequently but still fairly often, bring the mixture to a boil you can't stir down.

4. Add the remaining 1¾ cups (350 g) sugar and stir constantly to dissolve the sugar. Bring back to a full boil, stirring occasionally. Boil undisturbed for 1 minute.

5. Turn off the heat and remove the saucepan from the burner. Let stand for 1–2 minutes, then skim any foamy impurities with a tablespoon.

6. Transfer to four *clean* ½ pint (236 ml) jars or other containers, leaving about ½ inch (1 cm) headspace in each. Cover or seal. Cool at room temperature for no more than 1 hour, then refrigerate or freeze.

More

For a more aromatic jelly, add 2 *green* cardamom pods and 1 star anise pod with the spices.

The Best Blueberry Preserves

MAKES: about 4 cups (960 ml)
FRIDGE: up to 3 weeks
FREEZER: up to 1 year
May be traditionally canned (see page 436)

Low-bush blueberries from Maine or the Canadian Maritimes make the best blueberry preserves—and without a ton of sugar, to boot! Although blueberries hold lots of natural pectin, you still need to cook the berries a long time to activate it and get the preserves to set. We prefer a fresher flavor, so we use granulated pectin for the faster set, the better to preserve the intense flavors of the tiny berries and keep them relatively whole. For the best results, *weigh* frozen blueberries whole, then thaw them and use the berries plus any released juice.

- 2¼ cups (450 g) granulated white sugar
- 2 tablespoons (24 g) *granulated less-sugar* pectin
- 1¾ pounds (790 g) fresh, tiny low-bush blueberries or thawed frozen wild blueberries, such as Wyman's (about 5 cups)
- 1 tablespoon (15 ml) lemon juice

The Best Blueberry
Preserves (page 42)

1. Mix ¼ cup (50 g) sugar and the pectin in a small bowl until uniform.

2. Put the blueberries and lemon juice in a large saucepan. Set it over medium-high heat and add the pectin mixture. Stir constantly to dissolve the granulated ingredients and smash some of the berries to release some of their juice. Bring the mixture to a boil you can't stir down, stirring often.

3. Add the remaining 2 cups (400 g) sugar and stir constantly to dissolve the sugar. Bring back to a full boil, stirring often. Boil undisturbed for 1 minute.

4. Turn off the heat and remove the saucepan from the burner. Let stand for 1–2 minutes, then skim any foam with a tablespoon.

5. Transfer to four *clean* ½ pint (236 ml) jars or other containers, leaving about ½ inch (1 cm) headspace in each. Cover or seal. Cool at room temperature for no more than 1 hour, then refrigerate or freeze.

Tip

Unless you live in Maine or Canada's Maritimes, you'll most likely find tiny blueberries in your supermarket's freezer section.

Sugar-Free Blueberry Jam

MAKES: about 2 cups (480 ml)
FRIDGE: up to 2 weeks
FREEZER: up to 6 months

The two of us double up on New Year's resolutions. If one of us decides to have a dry January, the other goes along. The same goes for cutting calories. We do it together. But we do have our limits. We won't compromise on homemade jam. This sugar-free blueberry jam is cooked a long time so it'll set without pectin, which means it also has a deep, rich, almost caramelized flavor, even without granulated sugar—the best answer to anyone's resolution.

1 pound 6 ounces (640 g) fresh blueberries (about 4 cups)

1 cup *1-to-1 (by volume)* granulated white-sugar substitute

¼ cup (60 ml) *unsweetened* apple juice

1 tablespoon (15 ml) lemon juice

1. Stir everything in a large saucepan and set it over medium-high heat. Stir constantly to dissolve the sugar substitute. Bring the mixture to a boil you can't stir down, stirring often.

2. Use the back of a wooden spoon to mash about half of the blueberries into the simmering liquid. Reduce the heat to low and cook, stirring often, until thickened, 20–25 minutes.

3. Turn off the heat and remove the pan from the burner. Let stand for 1–2 minutes, then skim any foamy impurities with a tablespoon.

4. Transfer to two *clean* ½ pint (236 ml) jars or other containers, leaving about ½ inch (1 cm) of headspace in each. Cover or seal. Cool at room temperature for no more than 1 hour, then refrigerate or freeze. In the fridge, the jam may not set for 24 hours.

More

For a more sophisticated flavor, substitute white wine for the apple juice. Or stir ¼ teaspoon ground cinnamon into the finished jam for a subtle contrast to the blueberries.

Blueberry-Orange Jam

MAKES: about 3 cups (720 ml)
FRIDGE: up to 3 weeks
FREEZER: up to 1 year
May be traditionally canned (see page 436)

Years ago, we started adding orange zest to blueberry pies to give them a citrus pop. Thinking of that more complex flavor combo, we also wanted the long-cooked taste of a great pie filling in a jam. That meant that we don't need added pectin, given the natural amount in blueberries. We ended up with a sweet but caramelized blueberry concoction that holds a splash of orange-vanilla overtones.

> **1¾ pounds (790 g) fresh blueberries or thawed frozen blueberries (about 5 cups for either)**
>
> **2 cups (400 g) granulated white sugar**
>
> **The finely minced zest (*no white pith!*) and seeded juice of 1 medium orange**
>
> **1 tablespoon (15 ml) lemon juice**
>
> **⅛ teaspoon ground cinnamon, optional**

1. Mix all the ingredients in a very large saucepan. Set it over low heat and stir until the sugar dissolves, using the back of a wooden spoon to smash about a quarter of the berries against the inside of the pan to release their juice.

2. Raise the heat to medium-high and bring the mixture to a simmer, stirring frequently. Use the back of a wooden spoon to smash even more of the blueberries, about half in total, against the inside of the saucepan. Reduce the heat to low and simmer slowly, stirring often, until thickened, 20–25 minutes.

3. Turn off the heat and remove the pan from the burner. Let stand for 1–2 minutes, then skim any foamy impurities with a tablespoon.

4. Transfer to three *clean* ½ pint (236 ml) jars or other containers, leaving about ½ inch (1 cm) headspace in each. Cover or seal. Cool at room temperature for no more than 1 hour, then refrigerate or freeze. In the fridge, the preserves will not reach their best flavor for 24 hours.

Next
Use this jam as a glaze on roast ham, smearing a little on the meat for the last 5–10 minutes of roasting.

Blueberry–Chia Seed Jam

MAKES: about 3 cups (720 ml)
FRIDGE: up to 2 weeks
FREEZER: up to 6 months

One of the things culinary influencers have taught us old cookbook dogs is the wonder of chia seeds. They thicken jam without added pectin…*and* without long cooking. Plus, they're a terrific source of natural sugar. (Not to mention fiber.) Yes, the texture is not quite as smooth as standard jam. But life's all about trade-offs, no? And new tricks.

> **1¾ pounds (790 g) fresh blueberries or thawed frozen blueberries (about 5 cups for either)**
>
> **½ cup (100 g) granulated white sugar**
>
> **3 tablespoons (36 g) chia seeds**

1. Mix the blueberries and sugar in a medium saucepan. Set it over medium-low heat. Use the back of a wooden spoon to mash about half the blueberries against the inside of the pan to release their juice. Cook, stirring almost constantly, until the sugar dissolves.

2. Raise the heat to medium-high and bring the mixture to a boil you can't stir down, stirring often. Boil undisturbed for 1 minute.

3. Turn off the heat and remove the pan from the burner. Let stand for 1–2 minutes, then skim any foamy impurities with a tablespoon. Stir in the chia seeds until uniform, then cool uncovered at room temperature for 1 hour.

4. Transfer the jam to three *clean* ½ pint (236 ml) jars or other containers, leaving about ½ inch (1 cm) headspace in each. Cover or seal. Cool at room temperature for no more than 1 hour, then refrigerate or freeze.

Next
Stir a little of this jam into overnight muesli or refrigerator oatmeal for a healthy kick! (Reduce or omit the honey or other sweetener you might use.)

Blackberry Preserves
(page 47) in thumbprint
cookies

Blackberry Preserves

MAKES: about 3 cups (720 ml)
FRIDGE: up to 3 weeks
FREEZER: up to 1 year
May be traditionally canned (see page 436)

Blackberries were once an expensive treat. These days, you can find sales! When you do, stock up and make a small batch of blackberry preserves. We roughly chop the blackberries because they have a relatively large white core that won't cook properly in the short time over the heat. The chopped berries give the jam a better texture while reducing the cooking time to preserve that quintessential berry flavor: tart but sweet, mellow but still bright—an affordable luxury for the months ahead.

> 1½ cups (300 g) granulated white sugar
>
> 2 tablespoons (24 g) *granulated less-sugar* pectin
>
> 1⅓ pounds (605 g) fresh blackberries (about 4 cups), roughly chopped
>
> 1 tablespoon (15 ml) lemon juice

1. Stir ½ cup (100 g) sugar and the pectin in a small bowl until uniform.

2. Stir the blackberries and lemon juice in a large saucepan. Set it over medium-high heat and add the pectin mixture. Stir constantly to dissolve the granulated ingredients. Bring the mixture to a boil you can't stir down, stirring often. Boil undisturbed for 1 minute.

3. Add the remaining 1 cup (200 g) sugar and stir constantly to dissolve the sugar. Bring back to a full boil, stirring often. Boil undisturbed for 1 minute.

4. Turn off the heat, remove the pan from the burner, and set aside for 1–2 minutes. Skim any foamy impurities with a tablespoon.

5. Transfer to three *clean* ½ pint (236 ml) jars or other containers, leaving about ½ inch (1 cm) headspace in each. Cover or seal. Cool at room temperature for no more than 1 hour, then refrigerate or freeze.

More

Use this technique to make MARIONBERRY or OLALLIEBERRY PRESERVES by substituting 1⅓ pounds (605 g) of those berries for the blackberries. (Go strictly *by weight*, not volume).

Sugar-Free Blackberry Jam

MAKES: about 2 cups (480 ml)
FRIDGE: up to 2 weeks
FREEZER: up to 6 months

The tradition of preserving and canning is about saving summer: making the most flavorful fruits and vegetables last into the chill. Since that's the case, you usually want to start with the freshest fruit you can find when making *sugar-free* preserves. Not always, of course. Sometimes, you want to cook down the fruit for a deeper flavor. But there's no doubt about it: Granulated white sugar offers a texture that's hard to beat. So when it comes to blackberry jam, you can get close to that texture in a sugar-free alternative if the berries are fresh, not frozen.

> 1⅓ pounds (605 g) fresh blackberries (about 4 cups), roughly chopped
>
> 2 cups *1-to-1 (by volume)* granulated white-sugar substitute
>
> ¼ cup (60 ml) *unsweetened* red grape juice
>
> 2 tablespoons (24 g) *granulated less-sugar* pectin
>
> 1 tablespoon (15 ml) lemon juice

1. Combine all the ingredients in a medium saucepan set over medium-high heat. Stir well to dissolve the sugar substitute while also crushing about half of the blackberries against the sides of the pan with a wooden spoon to release their juice.

2. Bring the mixture to a boil you can't stir down, stirring often. Boil undisturbed for 1 minute.

3. Turn off the heat, remove the pan from the burner, and set aside for 1–2 minutes. Skim any foamy impurities with a tablespoon.

4. Transfer to two *clean* ½ pint (236 ml) jars or other containers, leaving about ½ inch (1 cm) headspace in each. Cover or seal. Cool at room temperature for no more than 1 hour, then refrigerate or freeze. In the fridge, the preserves may not reach their best flavor for 48 hours.

Next
Beat a little of this jam into whipped cream to make a refined sugar-free topping for any dessert.

Blackberry-Balsamic Jam

MAKES: about 4 cups (960 ml)
FRIDGE: up to 3 weeks
FREEZER: up to 1 year
May be traditionally canned (see page 436)

Whenever the house is quiet (we *do* have excitable collies), we so enjoy time in the kitchen. But even on these special days, we like to save time. That's why we've developed most of our blackberry jam recipes to cut down on the cooking and provide plenty of time to take our collies on a walk down a New England country road. This pulpy jam has a slightly bitter edge, thanks to the quicker cooking of the chopped blackberries and the added balsamic vinegar. It's a treat spread over fresh goat cheese on toast.

> 2⅓ cups (467 g) granulated white sugar
> 2 tablespoons (25 g) *granulated less-sugar* pectin
> 2 pounds (900 g) fresh blackberries (about 6 cups)
> 1 tablespoon (15 ml) balsamic vinegar

1. Stir ⅓ cup (67 g) sugar and the pectin in a small bowl until uniform.

2. Chop each blackberry widthwise into thirds or quarters (depending on their size) to release as much pulp and juice as possible. Scrape all the blackberries, any pulp, and juice into a large saucepan. Stir in the vinegar.

3. Set the pan over medium-high heat and add the pectin mixture. Stir constantly to dissolve the granulated ingredients. Bring the mixture to a boil you can't stir down, stirring often.

4. Add the remaining 2 cups (400 g) sugar and stir constantly to dissolve the sugar. Bring the mixture back to a full boil, stirring often. Boil undisturbed for 1 minute.

5. Turn off the heat, remove the pan from the burner, and set aside for 1–2 minutes. Skim any foamy impurities with a tablespoon.

6. Transfer to four *clean* ½ pint (236 ml) jars or other containers, leaving about ½ inch (1 cm) headspace in each. Cover or seal. Cool at room temperature for no more than 1 hour, then refrigerate or freeze. In the fridge, the preserves may not reach their best flavor for 48 hours.

More
Make the jam slightly more savory by adding ½ teaspoon ground black pepper and ¼ teaspoon kosher salt with the balsamic vinegar.

Blackberry-Lavender Jam

MAKES: about 3 cups (720 ml)
FRIDGE: up to 3 weeks
FREEZER: up to 1 year
May be traditionally canned (see page 436)

Although we've sung the praises of cooking blackberries more quickly to retain their freshest flavor, big pairings (like this one, with lavender) need a more *cooked* flavor—that is, the slightly bitter notes from caramelized sugars. Long cooking has other perks, too. Here, we can forgo chopping the blackberries because they cook so long that the white centers soften. And we can skip the added pectin because of the abundance of natural pectin in blackberries.

- 2 tablespoons (4 g) *dried* culinary lavender buds
- ½ cup (120 ml) *boiling* water
- 1⅔ pounds (750 g) fresh blackberries or thawed frozen blackberries (about 5 cups for either)
- 2 cups (400 g) granulated white sugar
- 1 tablespoon (15 ml) lemon juice

1. Put the lavender buds in a small heat-safe bowl or mug and pour the boiling water over them. Steep at room temperature for 30 minutes.

2. Strain the lavender tea into a large saucepan. Discard the solids. Stir the blackberries, sugar, and lemon juice into the lavender tea.

3. Set the pan over medium-high heat and stir constantly to dissolve the sugar. Bring the mixture to a boil you can't stir down, stirring often.

4. Use the back of a wooden spoon to crush about half of the blackberries against the side of the pan. Reduce the heat to medium and simmer, stirring often, until thickened and jam-like, 15–20 minutes.

5. Turn off the heat, remove the pan from the burner, and set aside for 1–2 minutes. Skim any foamy impurities with a tablespoon.

6. Transfer to three *clean* ½ pint (236 ml) jars or other containers, leaving about ½ inch (1 cm) headspace in each. Cover or seal. Cool at room temperature for no more than 1 hour, then refrigerate or freeze. In the fridge, the jam may not set for 24 hours.

Tip
Use only culinary-grade lavender, available at large supermarkets in the spice aisle or from online spice suppliers. Do not use decorative lavender or lavender intended for potpourri bags.

Blackberry–Chia Seed Jam

MAKES: about 3 cups (720 ml)
FRIDGE: up to 2 weeks
FREEZER: up to 6 months

Not only do chia seeds give jams a soft, velvety gel, they also add texture, like the little pop of berry seeds. Since they're a great source of sugar (and fiber!), we can cut down on the added sugar and feel a little less guilt with each spoonful. Chia seeds do have a slightly bitter edge, so they often work best with added flavor notes, like vanilla.

- 1⅓ pounds (605 g) fresh blackberries or thawed frozen blackberries, roughly chopped (about 4 cups)
- 1 cup (200 g) granulated white sugar
- 1 tablespoon (15 ml) lemon juice
- ⅛ teaspoon vanilla extract
- ¼ cup (48 g) chia seeds

1. Combine the blackberries, sugar, lemon juice, and vanilla extract in a medium saucepan set over medium-high heat. Stir well with a wooden spoon to crush most of the blackberries against the inside of the pan as the mixture comes to a simmer. Do not boil.

2. Turn off the heat and remove the pan from the burner. Stir in the chia seeds and cool uncovered at room temperature for 1 hour.

3. Transfer to three *clean* ½ pint (236 ml) jars or other containers, leaving about ½ inch (1 cm) headspace in each. Cover or seal. Cool at room temperature for no more than 1 hour, then refrigerate or freeze. In the fridge, the jam may not set for 24 hours.

More
Make a spiced jam by stirring ½ teaspoon ground cinnamon, ¼ teaspoon ground ginger, ¼ teaspoon ground allspice, ¼ teaspoon grated nutmeg, and ¼ teaspoon kosher salt into the cooked blackberry mixture with the chia seeds.

Raspberry Preserves

MAKES: about 3 cups (720 ml)
FRIDGE: up to 3 weeks
FREEZER: up to 1 year
May be traditionally canned (see page 436)

We eagerly wait to pick raspberries on a summer afternoon. A local spot near us has dozens of bushes, although the Puritan farmer stands at the barn with a pair of binoculars to catch you when you try to make a meal out of the berries. He has good reason to be careful. Fresh raspberries are tart and bright, gorgeous and soft, like the best summer day encased in red bijoux. To save that goodness, we've crafted these preserves to put the berries over the heat as little as possible for a loose set and a velvety finish, with bits of whole berries throughout.

> 1 pound (450 g) fresh raspberries (about 4 cups)
> 1¾ cups (350 g) granulated white sugar
> ½ cup (120 ml) *unsweetened* apple juice
> 3 tablespoons (36 g) *granulated less-sugar* pectin

1. Put the raspberries and sugar in a *heat-safe* medium bowl. Gently crush the raspberries against the inside of the bowl with a potato masher or the back of a wooden spoon, leaving some in chunks, even whole. Do not make a puree.

2. Mix the juice and pectin in a small saucepan set over medium-high heat and stir constantly to dissolve the granulated ingredients. Bring the mixture to a boil you can't stir down, stirring often. Boil undisturbed for 1 minute.

3. Pour the boiling mixture into the berry mixture. Stir well to dissolve the sugar.

4. Transfer to three *clean* ½ pint (236 ml) jars or other containers, leaving about ½ inch (1 cm) headspace in each. Cover or seal. Cool at room temperature for no more than 1 hour, then refrigerate or freeze. In the fridge, the preserves may not set for 24 hours.

More
For RASPBERRY ALMOND PRESERVES, add ¼ teaspoon almond extract to the raspberry puree before you add the hot pectin mixture.

Raspberry Jam

MAKES: about 4 cups (960 ml)
FRIDGE: up to 3 weeks
FREEZER: up to 1 year
May be traditionally canned (see page 436)

Over the years, we've come to believe that a proper raspberry jam should be a little herbaceous and only moderately sweet. Although we love the intense flavor of Raspberry Preserves (above), we also know the pleasures a little more cooking can bring to the berries: mellowing them and adding a few elegant, slightly tannic notes to their natural pop.

> 2¼ cups (450 g) granulated white sugar
> 2 tablespoons (24 g) *granulated less-sugar* pectin
> 1¼ pounds (565 g) fresh raspberries or thawed frozen raspberries (about 5 cups for either)

Front to back: Raspberry
Preserves (page 50) and
Raspberry Jelly (page 52)

1. Mix ¼ cup (50 g) sugar and the pectin in a small bowl until uniform.

2. Pour the raspberries into a very large saucepan. Set it over medium-high heat and add the pectin mixture. Stir constantly to dissolve the granulated ingredients and squash most of the raspberries against the inside of the pan. Bring the mixture to a boil you can't stir down, stirring often.

3. Add the remaining 2 cups (400 g) sugar and stir constantly to dissolve the sugar. Bring back to a full boil, stirring often. Boil undisturbed for 1 minute.

4. Turn off the heat, remove the pan from the burner, and set aside for 1–2 minutes. Skim any foamy impurities with a tablespoon.

5. Transfer to four *clean* ½ pint (236 ml) jars or other containers, leaving about ½ inch (1 cm) headspace in each. Cover or seal. Cool at room temperature for no more than 1 hour, then refrigerate or freeze.

More

Stir up to 1 teaspoon (2 g) finely minced lemon zest and/or ½ teaspoon vanilla extract into the raspberries before you add the pectin mixture.

Raspberry Jelly

MAKES: about 3 cups (720 ml)
FRIDGE: up to 1 month
FREEZER: up to 1 year
May be traditionally canned (see page 436)

Holding a jar of homemade, shimmering, ruby-red raspberry jelly up to a sunny window is an experience like few others: to watch the sunlight swirl in the color and know that you've created something that captures not only summer's height but the light itself…at any time of the year, even in the middle of winter if you catch frozen raspberries on sale. This jelly seems too good to spread on toast. Seems.

1½ pounds (680 g) fresh raspberries or thawed frozen raspberries (about 6 cups for either)
¼ cup (60 ml) *unsweetened* apple juice
1 tablespoon (15 ml) lemon juice
1½ cups (300 g) granulated white sugar
2 tablespoons (24 g) *granulated less-sugar* pectin

1. Use your clean (or better, gloved!) hands or a potato masher to *thoroughly* crush the berries in a large saucepan until fully juiced. Stir in the apple juice and lemon juice. Set the pan over medium-high heat and bring to a boil, stirring often. Reduce the heat to low and simmer, stirring occasionally, for 2 minutes.

2. Set up a jelly bag over a clean large bowl (for alternatives to a jelly bag, see page 17). Pour the hot raspberry mixture into the bag. Drain for at least 4 hours or up to 24 hours to end up with 2½ cups (600 ml) liquid.

3. Mix ¼ cup (50 g) sugar and the pectin in a small bowl until uniform.

4. Pour the drained raspberry liquid into a medium saucepan. Set it over medium-high heat and add the pectin mixture. Stir constantly to dissolve the granulated ingredients. Bring the mixture to a boil you can't stir down, stirring often.

5. Add the remaining 1¼ cups (250 g) sugar and stir constantly to dissolve the sugar. Bring back to a full boil, stirring often. Boil undisturbed for 1 minute.

6. Turn off the heat, remove the pan from the burner, and set aside for 1–2 minutes. Skim any foamy impurities with a tablespoon.

7. Transfer to three *clean* ½ pint (236 ml) jars or other containers, leaving about ½ inch (1 cm) headspace in each. Cover or seal. Cool at room temperature for no more than 1 hour, then refrigerate or freeze.

Next

Soften a little of this jelly in a small glass jar in the microwave, then brush it over tarts or pastries for a shiny glaze.

Sugar-Free Raspberry Jam

MAKES: about 2 cups (480 ml)
FRIDGE: up to 2 weeks
FREEZER: up to 6 months

Consider for a moment the difference in taste between a regular raspberry hard candy and a sugar-free one. Now you'll understand the problem with sugar-free jams. They almost always need a little help because granulated white sugar heightens tasty flavor notes and diminishes bitter ones in ways that sugar substitutes cannot. Over the years, we've developed tricks to craft sugar-free jams with the flavor highs and lows beloved in more traditional jams. Here, the secret is a little super-tart cranberry juice for the brightest pops.

- 1¼ pounds (565 g) fresh raspberries or thawed frozen raspberries (about 5 cups for either)
- 1 cup *1-to-1 (by volume)* granulated white-sugar substitute
- ¼ cup (60 ml) *unsweetened* cranberry juice (see TIP)
- 2 tablespoons (24 g) *granulated less-sugar* pectin
- 1 tablespoon (15 ml) lemon juice

1. Combine all the ingredients in a medium saucepan. Use a potato masher or the back of a wooden spoon to crush about two-thirds of the raspberries against the inside of the pan.

2. Set the pan over medium-high heat and stir constantly to dissolve the granulated ingredients. Bring the mixture to a boil you can't stir down, stirring often. Boil undisturbed for 1 minute.

3. Turn off the heat, remove the pan from the burner, and set aside for 1–2 minutes. Skim any foamy impurities with a tablespoon.

4. Transfer to two *clean* ½ pint (236 ml) jars or other containers, leaving about ½ inch (1 cm) headspace in each. Cover or seal. Cool at room temperature for no more than 1 hour, then refrigerate or freeze. In the fridge, the jam may not set for 24 hours.

Tip

Use *unsweetened* cranberry juice, not *sugar-free* cranberry juice (usually sweetened by a sugar substitute). You can find this more esoteric sort of cranberry juice in your grocery store's health-food aisle and most health-food stores.

Raspberry-Chipotle Jam

MAKES: about 3 cups (720 ml)
FRIDGE: up to 3 weeks
FREEZER: up to 1 year
May be traditionally canned (see page 436)

Canned chipotle chilis in adobo sauce have a sour, vinegary edge and a muskier taste than plain dried chipotles. These complexly flavored chilis are a good match for raspberries, but with one caveat: The raspberries need to be cooked a little longer to give them a caramelized flavor that balances those aggressive flavors in the chilis. But as a bonus, there's no need for added pectin, given the quantity of it that naturally occurs in the berries.

- 1½ pounds (680 g) fresh raspberries or thawed frozen raspberries (about 6 cups for either)
- 2½ cups (500 g) granulated white sugar
- 2 canned chipotle chilis in adobo sauce, stemmed, seeded (if desired), and finely chopped
- 1 tablespoon (15 ml) adobo sauce from the can
- 1 tablespoon (15 ml) lemon juice

1. Combine all the ingredients in a very large saucepan set over medium-high heat. Stir constantly to dissolve the sugar and crush most of the raspberries against the inside of the pan. Bring the mixture to a full boil, stirring often.

2. Reduce the heat to medium-low and simmer, still stirring often, until thickened and jam-like, about 10 minutes.

➡️

3. Turn off the heat, remove the pan from the burner, and set aside for 1–2 minutes. Skim any foamy impurities with a tablespoon.

4. Transfer to three *clean* ½ pint (236 ml) jars or other containers, leaving about ½ inch (1 cm) headspace in each. Cover or seal. Cool at room temperature for no more than 1 hour, then refrigerate or freeze.

Next

Soften this jam slightly in a glass jar in the microwave, then put little dollops of it across a spicy bean dip or even a spicy bean chili.

Raspberry–Chia Seed Jam

MAKES: about 3 cups (720 ml)
FRIDGE: up to 2 weeks
FREEZER: up to 6 months

Here's a great (but quick) house gift to whip up for a dinner party or overnight visit. Easier still, you can buy frozen raspberries when they're on sale, then prepare this simple jam with little fuss (and not much sugar) after you get the invite. The jam needs to sit in the fridge overnight to set up.

> 1⅓ pounds (605 g) fresh raspberries or thawed frozen raspberries (about 5½ cups for either)
> ¾ cup (150 g) granulated white sugar
> 1 tablespoon (15 ml) lemon juice
> 3 tablespoons (36 g) chia seeds

1. Put the raspberries in a medium saucepan. Use a clean (or better, gloved!) hand or a potato masher to mash them against the inside of the pan, releasing their juice. Do not make a puree but make sure the raspberry juice is more pronounced than raspberry pulp. Stir in the sugar and lemon juice.

2. Set the pan over medium-high heat and stir constantly to dissolve the sugar. Bring to a boil you can't stir down, stirring often. Boil undisturbed for 1 minute.

3. Turn off the heat and remove the pan from the burner. Stir in the chia seeds and cool uncovered at room temperature for 1 hour.

4. Transfer the preserves to three *clean* ½ pint (236 ml) jars or other containers, leaving ½ inch (1 cm) headspace in each. Cover or seal, then refrigerate or freeze. In the fridge, the preserves will not set for 24 hours.

Tip

Chia seeds quickly go rancid at room temperature. Store any unused seeds in the freezer for up to 6 months. Bring them to room temperature before using them in any preserving recipe since a deep chill can affect the set.

Boysenberry Jam

MAKES: about 3 cups (720 ml)
FRIDGE: up to 3 weeks
FREEZER: up to 1 year
May be traditionally canned (see page 436)

Back in the day, Mark begged his grandparents to take him to O'Mealey's Cafeteria in Oklahoma City to brave the ladies in hairnets behind the counter and snag a slice of boysenberry pie. All these years later, he still hankers for boysenberries, maybe because they're a berry lover's dream: a hybrid of European raspberries, European blackberries, North American dewberries, and loganberries. Fresh ones can be hard to find, but you can spot frozen boysenberries in large supermarkets, sometimes even on sale. (Do not substitute canned boysenberries.) Boysenberries have a mild, vanilla-scented flavor that makes a pitch-perfect, silky jam.

> 1¼ pounds (565 g) fresh boysenberries or thawed frozen boysenberries (about 4 cups for either)
> 2 tablespoons (30 ml) lemon juice
> 3 cups (600 g) granulated white sugar

1. Use a potato masher or the back of a wooden spoon to crush the boysenberries in a large

Raspberry–Chia Seed Jam (page 54) on a buttered split scone

saucepan. Make sure the berries have released their juice but do not create a juiced puree. Stir in the lemon juice.

2. Set the pan over medium-high heat and bring the mixture to a simmer, stirring occasionally.

3. Add the sugar and stir constantly to dissolve. Bring the mixture to a boil, stirring often. Reduce the heat to low and simmer, stirring occasionally, until thickened and jam-like, about 10 minutes.

4. Turn off the heat, remove the pan from the burner, and set aside for 1–2 minutes. Skim any foamy impurities with a tablespoon.

5. Transfer to three *clean* ½ pint (236 ml) jars or other containers, leaving about ½ inch (1 cm) headspace in each. Cover or seal. Cool at room temperature for no more than 1 hour, then refrigerate or freeze.

More
For a more herbal jam, add up to 1 tablespoon (3 g) minced fresh rosemary leaves with the berries as you crush them.

Elderberry Jam

MAKES: about 3 cups (720 ml)
FRIDGE: up to 3 weeks
FREEZER: up to 1 year
May be traditionally canned (see page 436)

When we moved to rural New England from Manhattan, the first thing we planted were elderberry bushes because of the promise of jam and liqueur. The first thing we ripped out were elderberry bushes because we ended up with moose in the yard, mowing down the plants. Now we settle for elderberries from our local farmers' market. But this delicate, luxurious jam keeps those surprising undertones that elderberries carry: smooth brandy, tart blackberries, and vanilla.

1½ pounds (680 g) stemmed elderberries (about 5 cups)
1 cup (240 ml) water
2½ cups (500 g) granulated white sugar
2 tablespoons (24 g) *granulated less-sugar* pectin
¼ cup (60 ml) lemon juice

1. Stir the elderberries and water in a large saucepan set over medium-high heat. Bring the mixture to a simmer, stirring occasionally. Reduce the heat to low and simmer for 20 minutes, still stirring occasionally. Turn off the heat, remove the pan from the burner, cover, and cool at room temperature for 20–30 minutes.

2. Mix ½ cup (100 g) sugar and the pectin in a small bowl until uniform.

3. Run the elderberry mixture through a food mill in batches and into a medium bowl set below to extract as much juice and pulp as possible. (For an alternative to a food mill, see page 16.)

4. Clean that large saucepan and pour the strained juice and pulp into it. Stir in the lemon juice and set the pan over medium-high heat. Add the pectin mixture and stir constantly to dissolve the granulated ingredients. Bring to a boil you can't stir down, stirring often.

5. Add the remaining 2 cups (400 g) sugar and stir constantly to dissolve the sugar. Bring back to a full boil, stirring often. Boil undisturbed for 1 minute.

6. Turn off the heat, remove the pan from the burner, and set aside for 1–2 minutes. Skim any foamy impurities with a tablespoon.

7. Transfer to three *clean* ½ pint (236 ml) jars or other containers, leaving about ½ inch (1 cm) headspace in each. Cover or seal. Cool at room temperature for no more than 1 hour, then refrigerate or freeze.

More
Stir up to ½ teaspoon ground cinnamon, ½ teaspoon ground allspice, and/or ½ teaspoon vanilla extract into the elderberry mixture with the pectin mixture.

Three-Berry Jam

MAKES: about 5 cups (1200 ml)
FRIDGE: up to 3 weeks
FREEZER: up to 1 year
May be traditionally canned (see page 436)

There's something wonderful about mixing different kinds of berries: the various levels of sweet and sour; the interplay of the herbal notes; and the lovely range of textures, from pulpy blueberries to jammy blackberries. This three-berry mix is a flavorful, rich jam that's like the best berry pie filling you've ever had.

- 2½ cups (500 g) granulated white sugar
- 2 tablespoons (24 g) *granulated less-sugar* pectin
- 12 ounces (345 g) fresh blueberries or thawed frozen blueberries (about 2½ cups for either)
- 7½ ounces (215 g) fresh blackberries or thawed frozen blackberries (about 1½ cups for either)
- 7½ ounces (215 g) fresh raspberries or thawed frozen raspberries (about 1½ cups for either)

1. Mix ¼ cup (50 g) sugar and the pectin in a small bowl.

2. Use a potato masher or the back of a wooden spoon to crush all the berries against the inside of a large saucepan. Release the juice but do not make a puree.

3. Set the pan over medium-high heat and add the pectin mixture. Stir constantly to dissolve the granulated ingredients. Bring to a boil you can't stir down, stirring often.

4. Add the remaining 2¼ cups (450 g) sugar and stir constantly to dissolve the sugar. Bring back to a full boil, stirring often. Boil undisturbed for 1 minute.

5. Turn off the heat, remove the pan from the burner, and set aside for 1–2 minutes. Skim any foamy impurities with a tablespoon.

6. Transfer to five *clean* ½ pint (236 ml) jars or other containers, leaving about ½ inch (1 cm) headspace in each. Cover or seal. Cool at room temperature for no more than 1 hour, then refrigerate or freeze. In the fridge, the jam will not reach its best flavor for 24 hours.

More
For a slightly more mellow flavor, add ½ teaspoon vanilla extract with the remaining sugar in step 4.

Four-Berry Holiday Jam

MAKES: about 3 cups (720 ml)
FRIDGE: up to 3 weeks
FREEZER: up to 1 year
May be traditionally canned (see page 436)

Here's our version of *Christmas jam*, a North American tradition, usually made with strawberries and cranberries (and maybe orange zest or juice). We love to pack even more berries into the mix and leave the jam a bit longer over the heat for the deeper blend of berry flavors and warming spices. We always make this jam as a special treat for a holiday breakfast. Then we have a jar or two left over for our favorite people to take home after the feast.

- 5 ounces (140 g) fresh cranberries or thawed frozen cranberries (about 1 cup for either)
- 4½ ounces (130 g) fresh strawberries, hulled; or thawed frozen strawberries, hulled (about 1 cup for either)
- 7½ ounces (215 g) fresh raspberries or thawed frozen raspberries (about 1½ cups for either)
- 2 cups (400 g) granulated white sugar
- 7½ ounces (215 g) fresh blueberries or thawed frozen blueberries (about 1½ cups for either)
- 1 tablespoon (15 ml) lemon juice
- 1 teaspoon (2 g) finely grated orange zest
- ⅛ teaspoon ground cinnamon
- ⅛ teaspoon ground cloves

Four-Berry Holiday Jam
(page 57) on a waffle with
whipped cream

1. Chop the cranberries and strawberries into small bits, then add them to a large saucepan. Add the raspberries and crush them against the side of the pan with a potato masher or the back of a wooden spoon. Do not make a smooth puree.

2. Set the pan over medium-high heat and stir in the sugar, blueberries, lemon juice, orange zest, cinnamon, and cloves. Stir constantly to dissolve the sugar. Bring the mixture to a boil, stirring often.

3. Reduce the heat to low and simmer, stirring occasionally, until thickened and jam-like, about 12 minutes.

4. Turn off the heat, remove the pan from the burner, and set aside for 1–2 minutes. Skim any foamy impurities with a tablespoon.

5. Transfer to three *clean* ½ pint (236 ml) jars or other containers, leaving about ½ inch (1 cm) headspace in each. Cover or seal. Cool at room temperature for no more than 1 hour, then refrigerate or freeze. In the fridge, the jam will not reach its best flavor for 24 hours.

Next
This jam is particularly tasty on gingerbread or a warm slice of spiced holiday quick bread.

Peach Preserves

MAKES: about 3 cups (720 ml)
FRIDGE: up to 3 weeks
FREEZER: up to 1 year
May be traditionally canned (see page 436)

A ripe peach is a thing of beauty…but not forever. (Sorry, Keats.) A fresh peach is hard and tasteless one afternoon, perfect the next morning, and mushy by midnight. You need perfect timing for the best peach preserves. Watch your market carefully. Remember the selection criteria: 1) that peachy aroma, 2) heavy to the hand, and 3) slightly soft with no mushy bits.

2¼ cups (450 g) granulated white sugar
3 tablespoons (36 g) *granulated less-sugar* pectin
1⅓ pounds (605 g) fresh peaches (3–4 large), pitted, peeled, and chopped (about 3½ cups)
1½ tablespoons (22 ml) lemon juice

1. Mix ¼ cup (50 g) sugar and the pectin in a small bowl until uniform.

2. Mix the peaches and lemon juice in a large saucepan. Use the back of a wooden spoon (but *not* a potato masher because it's too forceful) to smoosh about half of the peaches against the side of the pan. Release the juice but leave plenty of chunky pulp.

3. Set the pan over medium-high heat and add the pectin mixture. Stir constantly to dissolve the granulated ingredients. Bring to a boil you can't stir down, stirring often.

4. Add the remaining 2 cups (400 g) sugar and stir constantly to dissolve the sugar. Bring back to a full boil, stirring often. Boil undisturbed for 1 minute.

5. Turn off the heat, remove the pan from the burner, and set aside for 1–2 minutes. Skim any foamy impurities with a tablespoon.

6. Transfer to three *clean* ½ pint (236 ml) jars or other containers, leaving about ½ inch (1 cm) headspace in each. Cover or seal. Cool at room temperature for no more than 1 hour, then refrigerate or freeze. In the fridge, the preserves may not gel for 24 hours.

More
For PEACH-THYME JAM, add 1 teaspoon stemmed fresh thyme leaves with the sugar in step 4.

Sugar-Free Peach Jam

MAKES: about 3 cups (720 ml)
FRIDGE: up to 2 weeks
FREEZER: up to 6 months

If there's ever a moment when fresh (not frozen) fruit is called for, it's with this recipe. Frozen peaches, while flavorful, often lose some of their moisture during the freezing process. Without all the natural juice, frozen slices just can't make up for the lack of sugar. Buy fresh peaches at the peak of their flavor and ripeness.

> 1⅓ pounds (605 g) fresh peaches (3–4 large), pitted, peeled, and chopped (about 3½ cups)
>
> 1 cup *1-to-1 (by volume)* granulated white-sugar substitute
>
> 3 tablespoons (36 g) *granulated less-sugar* pectin
>
> ¼ cup (60 ml) orange juice
>
> 2 tablespoons (30 ml) lemon juice

1. Mix all the ingredients in a medium saucepan until well combined. Use the back of a wooden spoon to crush a little more than half of the peaches against the inside of the pan.

2. Set the pan over medium-high heat and stir constantly to dissolve the granulated ingredients. Bring to a boil you can't stir down, stirring often. Boil undisturbed for 2 minutes.

3. Turn off the heat, remove the pan from the burner, and set aside for 1–2 minutes. Skim any foamy impurities with a tablespoon.

4. Transfer to three *clean* ½ pint (236 ml) jars or other containers, leaving about ½ inch (1 cm) headspace in each. Cover or seal. Cool at room temperature for no more than 1 hour, then refrigerate or freeze. In the fridge, the jam will not reach its best flavor for 48 hours.

More

For SUGAR-FREE SPICED PEACH JAM, stir in ½ teaspoon apple pie spice mix with the sugar substitute and pectin.

Peach Melba Jam

MAKES: about 3 cups (720 ml)
FRIDGE: up to 3 weeks
FREEZER: up to 1 year
May be traditionally canned (see page 436)

We've long loved making peach melba jam, not only because of that sweet-tart, peach-raspberry meld but also because of the long tradition of this combo, a favorite of the groovy 1960s. Sure, peach melba is retro, but it's nice to recall such time-tested duos. For the best texture, make sure you *dice* the peaches. Cut them into ½-inch-thick (1-cm-thick) slices at the widest part, then slice these into ½ inch (1 cm) sections.

> 1½ cups (300 g) granulated white sugar
>
> 2 tablespoons (24 g) *granulated less-sugar* pectin
>
> 10 ounces (285 g) fresh raspberries or thawed frozen raspberries (about 2 cups for either)
>
> 12 ounces (340 g) fresh peaches (about 2 medium), peeled, pitted, and *diced* (about 1½ cups)
>
> 2 teaspoons (10 ml) lemon juice

1. Mix ¼ cup (50 g) sugar and the pectin in a small bowl until uniform.

2. Pour the raspberries into a medium saucepan. Use a potato masher or the back of a wooden spoon to crush the berries into pulp but not a puree.

3. Set the pan over medium-high heat, stir in the peaches and lemon juice, then add the pectin mixture. Stir constantly to dissolve the granulated ingredients. Bring the mixture to a thick, burbling bubble you can't stir down, stirring often. (There's not enough liquid for a proper boil.)

4. Add the remaining 1¼ cups (250 g) sugar and stir constantly to dissolve the sugar. Bring back to a full boil, stirring often. Boil undisturbed for 1 minute.

5. Turn off the heat, remove the pan from the burner, and set aside for 1–2 minutes. Skim any foamy impurities with a tablespoon.

6. Transfer to three *clean* ½ pint (236 ml) jars or other containers, leaving about ½ inch (1 cm) headspace in each. Cover or seal. Cool at room temperature for no more than 1 hour, then refrigerate or freeze.

Next
This jam is terrific in jam oat bars. For a video on how to make them, look for Blackberry Bar Cookies on our YouTube channel, Cooking With Bruce & Mark. (Substitute this jam for the blackberry jam.)

Peach Margarita Jam

MAKES: about 4 cups (960 ml)
FRIDGE: up to 3 weeks
FREEZER: up to 1 year
May be traditionally canned (see page 436)

Once in a while, you gotta have a maraschino cherry with your oh-so-flashy frozen peach margarita, if only to honor your time in college dive bars. (We may have gone to a different sort of dive bar than you did….) In that spirit, we've gone all out with this booze-free, slightly silly confection that tastes deliciously like that cocktail from long ago (without any regrets the next morning).

- 2½ cups (500 g) granulated white sugar
- 3 tablespoons (36 g) *granulated less-sugar* pectin
- 1½ pounds (680 g) fresh peaches (about 5 large), peeled, pitted, and roughly chopped (about 4 cups)
- ¼ cup (40 g) drained pitted maraschino cherries, cut into quarters
- ¼ cup (60 ml) fresh orange juice (*not* from concentrate)
- 2 tablespoons (30 ml) lime juice
- 2 teaspoons (4 g) finely grated orange zest
- 2 teaspoons (4 g) finely grated lime zest

1. Mix ¼ cup (50 g) sugar and the pectin in a small bowl until uniform.

2. Mix the peaches, maraschino cherries, orange juice, lime juice, orange zest, and lime zest in a large saucepan. Set it over medium-high heat and add the pectin mixture. Stir constantly to dissolve the granulated ingredients. Bring to a boil you can't stir down, stirring often.

3. Add the remaining 2¼ cups (450 g) sugar and stir constantly to dissolve the sugar. Bring back to a full boil, stirring often. Boil undisturbed for 1 minute.

4. Turn off the heat, remove the pan from the burner, and set aside for 1–2 minutes. Skim any foamy impurities with a tablespoon.

5. Transfer to four *clean* ½ pint (236 ml) jars or other containers, leaving about ½ inch (1 cm) headspace in each. Cover or seal. Cool at room temperature for no more than 1 hour, then refrigerate or freeze.

Next
Save this jam to brighten up a bran muffin or a slice of pound cake.

Peach-Ginger Jam

MAKES: about 4 cups (960 ml)
FRIDGE: up to 3 weeks
FREEZER: up to 1 year
May be traditionally canned (see page 436)

Why are peaches so versatile? Perhaps it's the subtle vanilla undertone. Or the rounded sweetness. Or the velvety texture. Whatever it is, peaches adapt to so many flavors, even the sharp spiciness of ginger. That said, we've found that fresh ginger is too big a flavor to balance with the subtler notes in peaches. So we opt for crystallized ginger and the earthy notes of ground ginger.

- 2½ cups (500 g) granulated white sugar
- 3 tablespoons (36 g) *granulated less-sugar* pectin
- 1½ pounds (680 g) fresh peaches (about 5 large), peeled, pitted, and roughly chopped (about 4 cups)
- ¼ cup (55 g) *minced* crystallized ginger
- 3 tablespoons (45 ml) lemon juice
- ½ teaspoon ground ginger

1. Stir ¼ cup (50 g) sugar and the pectin in a small bowl until uniform.

2. Put the chopped peaches, crystallized ginger, lemon juice, and ground ginger in a large saucepan. Set the pan over medium-high heat and add the pectin mixture. Stir constantly to dissolve the granulated ingredients. Bring to a boil you can't stir down, stirring often.

3. Add the remaining 2¼ cups (450 g) sugar and stir constantly to dissolve the sugar. Bring back to a full boil, stirring occasionally. Boil undisturbed for 1 minute.

4. Turn off the heat, remove the pan from the burner, and set aside for 1–2 minutes. Skim any foamy impurities with a tablespoon.

5. Transfer to four *clean* ½ pint (236 ml) jars or other containers, leaving about ½ inch (1 cm) headspace in each. Cover or seal. Cool at room temperature for no more than 1 hour, then refrigerate or freeze. In the fridge, the jam may not set for 24 hours.

Next
Mix this jam with chili crisp in a 1-part-jam-to-2-parts-chili-crisp ratio for a great dip for egg rolls or steamed pork dumplings. (Our recipes for chili crisps start on page 209.)

Peach-Mango Jam

MAKES: about 4 cups (960 ml)
FRIDGE: up to 3 weeks
FREEZER: up to 1 year
May be traditionally canned (see page 436)

Double the tantalizing perfume in jam by combining fresh peaches and mangoes for a morning treat that's silky and aromatic. We'll admit to dragging a peanut butter–laden spoon through this one in the middle of the night. Beware: If you're sharing a fridge, it may be best to have your own jar. Some people get upset when they find bits of peanut butter in their jam. No names, of course.

- 2½ cups (500 g) granulated white sugar
- 2 tablespoons (24 g) *granulated less-sugar* pectin
- 1 pound 2 ounces (500 g) ripe mango (about 1 very large), pitted, peeled, and *diced* (about 1½ cups)
- 1 pound (450 g) fresh peaches (about 3 medium), peeled, pitted, and *diced* (about 2 cups)
- 1½ tablespoons (22 ml) lemon juice

1. Mix ½ cup (100 g) sugar and the pectin in a small bowl until uniform.

2. Put the mango, peaches, and lemon juice in a medium saucepan. Set the pan over medium-high heat and add the pectin mixture. Stir constantly to dissolve the granulated ingredients and smash up about half the fruit against the inside of the pan. Bring the mixture to a thick, burbling bubble you can't stir down, stirring often. (There's not enough liquid for a proper boil.)

3. Add the remaining 2 cups (400 g) sugar and stir constantly to dissolve the sugar. Bring back to a full boil, stirring occasionally. Boil undisturbed for 1 minute.

4. Turn off the heat, remove the pan from the burner, and set aside for 1–2 minutes. Skim any foamy impurities with a tablespoon.

5. Transfer to four *clean* ½ pint (236 ml) jars or other containers, leaving about ½ inch (1 cm)

Clockwise from bottom:
Peach-Mango Jam (page 62),
Apricot Preserves (page 64),
and Plum Preserves (page 65)

headspace in each. Cover or seal. Cool at room temperature for no more than 1 hour, then refrigerate or freeze. In the fridge, the jam will not reach its best flavor for 48 hours.

Tip

You *can* use frozen fruit here, but the fruit doesn't have as much juice as its fresh kin. To make sure it all breaks down into a luxurious jam, the thawed peach and mango slices must be exactingly *diced*. Also, use all the juice in their bags once thawed.

Apricot Preserves

MAKES: about 3 cups (720 ml)
FRIDGE: up to 3 weeks
FREEZER: up to 1 year
May be traditionally canned (see page 436)

By now, you know the preserving drill: mostly fresh, ripe, perfume-rich fruit…*except* when it comes to apricots. Somehow, even hard, late winter, globally shipped apricots turn into perfect preserves. That's great news on two fronts: You can make these preserves any time you see apricots on sale. And you can save the ripest, summery apricots for an afternoon snack.

> 2¼ cups (450 g) granulated white sugar
> 2 tablespoons (24 g) *granulated less-sugar* pectin
> 1⅔ pounds (750 g) fresh apricots (about 16 medium), pitted (do not peel) and roughly chopped (about 3 cups)
> 1 tablespoon (15 ml) lime juice

1. Mix ¾ cup (150 g) sugar and the pectin in a small bowl until uniform.

2. Stir the apricots and lime juice in a large saucepan. Set the pan over medium heat and add the pectin mixture. Stir constantly to dissolve the granulated ingredients and squash about half of the apricot pieces against the inside of the pan. Continue cooking, stirring often, until the remaining apricot pieces soften and give off some of their juice, about 3 minutes.

3. Raise the heat to medium-high and cook, stirring often, until the mixture comes to a boil you can't stir down.

4. Add the remaining 1½ cups (300 g) sugar and stir constantly to dissolve the sugar. Bring back to a full boil, stirring occasionally. Boil undistributed for 1 minute.

5. Turn off the heat, remove the pan from the burner, and set aside for 1–2 minutes. Skim any foamy impurities with a tablespoon.

6. Transfer to three *clean* ½ pint (236 ml) jars or other containers, leaving about ½ inch (1 cm) headspace in each. Cover or seal. Cool at room temperature for no more than 1 hour, then refrigerate or freeze. In the fridge, the preserves may not gel for 24 hours.

Tip

Although you needn't peel the apricots (the skin almost disappears in the jam), do cut off any blemishes or dark blotches. Those bits can affect the final, jewel-tone color of the jam.

Apricot-Gochujang Jam

MAKES: about 3 cups (720 ml)
FRIDGE: up to 3 weeks
FREEZER: up to 1 year
May be traditionally canned (see page 436)

Apricots take to spicy heat like almost no other fruit. Their aromatic sweetness perfectly matches the fermented, fiery notes in gochujang, the Korean spice paste made from glutinous rice, soybeans, and dried chilis and other aromatics. Because of the gelling agents in commercial packagings of the spice paste, we can't double up with additional pectin and still get the luxurious texture of apricot jam. So in this case, we nix the pectin and use a candy thermometer to get the right set.

1⅔ pounds (750 g) fresh apricots (about 16 medium), pitted (do not peel) and roughly chopped (about 3 cups)

2½ cups (500 g) granulated white sugar

¼ cup (60 ml) lemon juice

¼ cup (60 ml) water

2 tablespoons (45 g) gochujang (or use your own homemade, page 240)

1. Stir the apricots and sugar in a large saucepan until the apricot pieces are thoroughly and evenly coated in the sugar. Set aside at room temperature for 30 minutes.

2. Stir in the lemon juice, water, and gochujang until uniform. Set the pan over medium heat and bring the mixture to a simmer, stirring often.

3. Attach a candy-making thermometer to the inside of the pan and continue cooking, stirring quite often, until the mixture reaches 220°F (105°C), about 10 minutes.

4. Turn off the heat, remove the pan from the burner, and set aside for 1–2 minutes. Skim any foamy impurities with a tablespoon.

5. Transfer to three *clean* ½ pint (236 ml) jars or other containers, leaving about ½ inch (1 cm) headspace in each. Cover or seal. Cool at room temperature for no more than 1 hour, then refrigerate or freeze. In the fridge, the jam may not set for 48 hours.

Next

Mix this jam in a 1:1 proportion *by volume* with *unseasoned* rice vinegar for a barbecue glaze.

Plum Preserves

MAKES: about 4 cups (960 ml)
FRIDGE: up to 3 weeks
FREEZER: up to 1 year
May be traditionally canned (see page 436)

Every summer, we anxiously wait for a postal box of Santa Rosa plums from Bruce's family in California's Silicon Valley. When we've got the fruit in hand, we lurch into preserving mode (after gorging on the ripest ones). But you needn't have the same family connections or even use the same varietal. Purple, red, yellow, or green plums will work in this tasty jam, so long as the plums are sweet, heavy to the hand, and slightly soft to the touch. One caveat: Prune plums of any varietal don't have enough juice for this recipe.

3 cups (600 g) granulated white sugar

2 tablespoons (24 g) *granulated less-sugar* pectin

2 pounds (900 g) ripe plums, quartered and pitted (do not peel)

¼ cup (60 ml) water

2 tablespoons (30 ml) lemon juice

1. Mix ¼ cup (50 g) sugar and the pectin in a small bowl until uniform.

2. Stir the plums, water, and lemon juice in a large saucepan. Set the pan over medium-high heat and add the pectin mixture. Stir constantly to dissolve the granulated ingredients. Bring to a boil you can't stir down, stirring often.

3. Add the remaining 2¾ cups (550 g) sugar and stir constantly to dissolve the sugar. Bring back to a full boil, stirring often. Boil undisturbed for 1 minute.

4. Turn off the heat, remove the pan from the burner, and set aside for 1–2 minutes. Skim any foamy impurities with a tablespoon.

5. Transfer to four *clean* ½ pint (236 ml) jars or other containers, leaving about ½ inch (1 cm) headspace in each. Cover or seal. Cool at room temperature for no more than 1 hour, then refrigerate or freeze.

More

For plum preserves that are definitely extra, substitute dry red wine or even port for the water.

Sour Cherry Preserves

MAKES: about 4 cups (960 ml)
FRIDGE: up to 3 weeks
FREEZER: up to 1 year
May be traditionally canned (see page 436)

In our part of New England, sour cherries are a prize. No, they're actually a required reservation. We call a farm and place an order long before the harvest begins. But the effort is worth it for these tart, ruby-red preserves that we dole out to only our closest friends. You can also find frozen sour cherries at large supermarkets and from online suppliers. However, we must admit that the freezing process degrades that puckering pop. If you see fresh sour cherries at the store or a farmers' market, grab them!

> 2½ cups (500 g) granulated white sugar
> 2 tablespoons (24 g) *granulated less-sugar* pectin
> 1¾ pounds (790 g) small sour cherries, stemmed, pitted, and roughly chopped (about 4 cups)
> 2 tablespoons (30 ml) lemon juice

1. Mix ¼ cup (50 g) sugar and the pectin in a small bowl until uniform.

2. Put the cherries and lemon juice in a large saucepan. Set the pan over medium-high heat and add the pectin mixture. Stir constantly to dissolve the granulated ingredients. Bring to a boil you can't stir down, stirring often.

3. Add the remaining 2¼ cups (450 g) sugar and stir constantly to dissolve the sugar. Bring back to a full boil, stirring often. Boil undisturbed for 1 minute.

4. Turn off the heat, remove the pan from the burner, and set aside for 1–2 minutes. Skim any foamy impurities with a tablespoon.

5. Transfer to four *clean* ½ pint (236 ml) jars or other containers, leaving about ½ inch (1 cm) headspace in each. Cover or seal. Cool at room temperature for no more than 1 hour, then refrigerate or freeze. In the fridge, the preserves may not gel for 24 hours.

Tip

Buy a cherry pitter! Even so, make sure you *and* any surfaces are protected from the staining splatters.

Sweet Cherry Preserves

MAKES: about 3 cups (720 ml)
FRIDGE: up to 3 weeks
FREEZER: up to 1 year
May be traditionally canned (see page 436)

Sweet cherries, available almost all year round, are much easier to find than sour cherries. And here's a bonus: Sweet cherries (like bing cherries) are larger than sour cherries, so there are fewer to pit. Even though sweet cherries have a subtle flavor, we find we need to up the lemon juice quite a bit to keep the jam from becoming cloyingly sweet.

> 2¼ cups (450 g) granulated white sugar
> 2 tablespoons (24 g) *granulated less-sugar* pectin
> 1½ pounds (680 g) sweet cherries, stemmed, pitted, and halved (about 3 cups)
> ¼ cup (60 ml) lemon juice

1. Mix ¼ cup (50 g) sugar and the pectin in a small bowl until uniform.

2. Put the cherries and the lemon juice in a large saucepan. Set the pan over medium-high heat and add the pectin mixture. Stir constantly to dissolve the granulated ingredients. Bring the mixture to a boil you can't stir down, stirring often.

3. Add the remaining 2 cups (400 g) sugar and stir constantly to dissolve the sugar and smash about half of the cherries against the inside of the pan to release their juice and pulp. Bring back to a full boil, stirring often. Boil undisturbed for 1 minute.

4. Turn off the heat, remove the pan from the burner, and set aside for 1–2 minutes. Skim any foamy impurities with a tablespoon.

5. Transfer to three *clean* ½ pint (236 ml) jars or other containers, leaving about ½ inch (1 cm) headspace in each. Cover or seal. Cool at room temperature for no more than 1 hour, then refrigerate or freeze.

More
Add up to 1 teaspoon vanilla extract and/or up to ¼ teaspoon orange extract with the lemon juice.

Sugar-Free Sweet Cherry Jam

MAKES: about 3 cups (720 ml)
FRIDGE: up to 2 weeks
FREEZER: up to 6 months

Feel free to use frozen pitted cherries for this recipe, especially since you're going to cook the cherries a bit longer to make a thick, rich jam—in other words, deepening the flavors of the natural sugars to make up for the lack of granulated sugar. Most people have a preferred sugar substitute based on subtle differences in flavor. For our part, we've long thought that stevia baking substitutes have the most neutral flavor. They work particularly well in this subtle jam.

> 1½ pounds (680 g) sweet cherries, stemmed, pitted, and *finely* chopped (about 3 cups)
> 1 cup *1-to-1 (by volume)* granulated white-sugar substitute
> ¼ cup (60 ml) lemon juice
> 2 tablespoons (24 g) *granulated less-sugar* pectin
> ½ teaspoon vanilla extract

1. Mix all the ingredients in a medium saucepan until well combined. Set the pan over medium-high heat and stir constantly to dissolve the granulated ingredients. Bring to a boil you can't stir down, stirring often. Boil undisturbed for 2 minutes.

2. Turn off the heat, remove the pan from the burner, and set aside for 1–2 minutes. Skim any foamy impurities with a tablespoon.

3. Transfer to three *clean* ½ pint (236 ml) jars or other containers, leaving about ½ inch (1 cm) headspace in each. Cover or seal. Cool at room temperature for no more than 1 hour, then refrigerate or freeze. In the fridge, the preserves may not set for 24 hours.

Next
This jam is great in a smoothie, particularly one with almond butter, banana, and wheat bran.

Cherry Pie Jam

MAKES: about 2 cups (480 ml)
FRIDGE: up to 3 weeks
FREEZER: up to 1 year
May be traditionally canned (see page 436)

The best cherry pie includes a little almond extract. Problem is, we've found that almond extract is too powerful in preserves and overwhelms the cherries. So we substitute either almond syrup or almond liqueur for a softer, more mellow flavor with the sweet cherries.

> 1½ cups (300 g) granulated white sugar
> 2 tablespoons (24 g) *granulated less-sugar* pectin
> 1 pound (450 g) sweet cherries, stemmed and pitted (about 2 cups)
> ¼ cup (60 ml) almond syrup, orgeat, Amaretto, or other almond-flavored liqueur (or use your own homemade, page 420)
> 1 tablespoon (15 ml) lemon juice

1. Mix ¼ cup (50 g) sugar and the pectin in a small bowl until uniform.

Top to bottom, with graham crackers: Cherry Pie Jam (page 67) and Peach Melba Jam (page 60)

2. Put about half of the pitted cherries in a food processor. Cover and pulse until finely chopped. Pour them into a medium saucepan and stir in the remaining cherries, almond syrup or its substitute, and lemon juice.

3. Set the pan over medium-high heat and add the pectin mixture. Stir constantly to dissolve the granulated ingredients. Bring to a boil you can't stir down, stirring often.

4. Add the remaining 1¼ cups (250 g) sugar and stir constantly to dissolve the sugar. Bring back to a full boil, stirring often. Boil undisturbed for 1 minute.

5. Turn off the heat, remove the pan from the burner, and set aside for 1–2 minutes. Skim any foamy impurities with a tablespoon.

6. Transfer to two *clean* ½ pint (236 ml) jars or other containers, leaving about ½ inch (1 cm) headspace in each. Cover or seal. Cool at room temperature for no more than 1 hour, then refrigerate or freeze. In the fridge, the jam may not gel for 24 hours.

Next
This jam makes an easy dessert with purchased individual graham-cracker pie crusts. Line the shells or crusts with the jam, then top with sweetened whipped cream. Shave bittersweet chocolate on top.

Spiced Black Cherry Jelly

MAKES: about 3 cups (720 ml)
FRIDGE: up to 1 month
FREEZER: up to 1 year
May be traditionally canned (see page 436)

Want to make a super easy, smooth, translucent jelly without a jelly bag? Try this spiced cherry jelly, made with bottled black cherry juice. The only trick is that the juice *must* be unsweetened. Some juice is sweetened with corn syrup or even cane syrup, which makes the gelling trickier. Find unsweetened black cherry juice in bottles near the organic juices at the supermarket, in health-food stores, or from online suppliers.

> 3 cups (720 ml) *unsweetened* black cherry juice
> One 2 inch (5 cm) cinnamon stick
> 1 teaspoon whole allspice berries
> 6 whole cloves
> 2¼ cups (450 g) granulated white sugar
> 2 tablespoons (24 g) *granulated less-sugar* pectin

1. Put the black cherry juice, cinnamon stick, allspice berries, and cloves in a large saucepan. Set the pan over medium-low heat and bring to a gentle simmer, stirring occasionally. Turn off the heat and remove the pan from the burner. Cover the pan and steep at room temperature for 30 minutes.

2. Meanwhile, mix ¼ cup (50 g) sugar and the pectin in a small bowl until uniform.

3. Fish out and discard the whole spices from the juice. Set the pan over medium-high heat and add the pectin mixture. Stir constantly to dissolve the granulated ingredients. Bring to a boil you can't stir down, stirring often.

4. Add the remaining 2 cups (400 g) sugar and stir constantly to dissolve the sugar. Bring back to a full boil, stirring occasionally. Boil undisturbed for 1 minute.

5. Turn off the heat, remove the pan from the burner, and set aside for 1–2 minutes. Skim any foamy impurities with a tablespoon.

6. Transfer to three *clean* ½ pint (236 ml) jars or other containers, leaving about ½ inch (1 cm) headspace in each. Cover or seal. Cool at room temperature for no more than 1 hour, then refrigerate or freeze.

Next
This jelly is spectacular in an old-school jelly roll (or Swiss roll) with sweetened whipped cream.

Rhubarb Jam

MAKES: about 4 cups (960 ml)
FRIDGE: up to 3 weeks
FREEZER: up to 1 year
May be traditionally canned (see page 436)

There's nothing like the sour pop of rhubarb, the spring delight that tells us in New England that winter is over. Rhubarb grows like a weed up here. Some people refuse to plant it because it's almost invasive. But there's always a neighbor willing to share. The best thank-you in return is a jar of this thick pulpy jam. (For the problem with thick, tough rhubarb stems, see the TIP for Strawberry-Rhubarb Jam on page 36.)

- 1 pound 10 ounces (740 g) sliced, trimmed rhubarb (about 5 cups)
- 3 cups (600 g) granulated white sugar
- 2 tablespoons (24 g) *granulated less-sugar* pectin

1. Mix the rhubarb and 2¾ cups (550 g) sugar in a large saucepan until the slices are evenly coated in the sugar. Set aside at room temperature to macerate for at least 12 hours or up to 24 hours, stirring every once in a while.

2. Mix the remaining ¼ cup (50 g) sugar and the pectin in a small bowl until uniform.

3. Set the saucepan with the rhubarb mixture over medium heat. Bring the mixture to a simmer, stirring constantly to extract even more juice and dissolve the sugar. Reduce the heat to low and simmer, stirring often, for 5 minutes.

4. Add the pectin mixture. Stir constantly to dissolve the granulated ingredients. Bring to a full boil, stirring often. Boil undisturbed for 1 minute.

5. Turn off the heat, remove the pan from the burner, and set aside for 1–2 minutes. Skim any foamy impurities with a tablespoon.

6. Transfer to four *clean* ½ pint (236 ml) jars or other containers, leaving about ½ inch (1 cm) headspace in each. Cover or seal. Cool at room temperature for no more than 1 hour, then refrigerate or freeze. In the fridge, the jam may not set for 24 hours.

More

Add up to 1 teaspoon (5 ml) vanilla extract or ¼ teaspoon rum extract with the pectin mixture.

Rhubarb-Ginger Jam

MAKES: about 4 cups (960 ml)
FRIDGE: up to 3 weeks
FREEZER: up to 1 year
May be traditionally canned (see page 436)

Ginger has a delightful, spiky kick that pairs beautifully with sour-savory rhubarb in this rich jam, cooked until the rhubarb becomes luxuriously soft. That said, we've found that fresh ginger morphs the jam into something like a savory condiment for roast beef. So we use crystallized ginger for a more subtle finish, suitable for scones.

- 1 pound 10 ounces (740 g) sliced, trimmed rhubarb (about 5 cups)
- 3 cups (600 g) granulated white sugar
- 1½ tablespoons (23 ml) ginger juice
- 2 tablespoons (24 g) *granulated less-sugar* pectin
- 3 tablespoons (42 g) *minced* crystallized ginger
- ¼ teaspoon vanilla extract

1. Mix the rhubarb, 2¾ cups (550 g) sugar, and the ginger juice in a large saucepan until the slices are evenly and thoroughly coated. Set aside to macerate at room temperature for at least 12 hours or up to 24 hours, stirring every once in a while.

2. Mix the remaining ¼ cup (50 g) sugar and the pectin in a small bowl until uniform.

3. Set the saucepan with the rhubarb mixture over medium heat and stir in the crystallized ginger. Stir constantly to dissolve the sugar. Cook, stirring often, until the mixture comes to a simmer. Reduce the heat to low and simmer, stirring often, for 5 minutes.

4. Add the pectin mixture and the vanilla. Stir constantly to dissolve the granulated ingredients. Bring the mixture to a full boil, stirring often. Boil undisturbed for 1 minute.

5. Turn off the heat, remove the pan from the burner, and set aside for 1–2 minutes. Skim any foamy impurities with a tablespoon.

6. Transfer to four *clean* ½ pint (236 ml) jars or other containers, leaving about ½ inch (1 cm) headspace in each. Cover or seal. Cool at room temperature for no more than 1 hour, then refrigerate or freeze. In the fridge, the jam may not gel for 24 hours.

Next
Swirl a tablespoon or two of this jam into slightly softened vanilla or strawberry ice cream.

Apple Jelly

MAKES: about 4 cups (960 ml)
FRIDGE: up to 1 month
FREEZER: up to 1 year
May be traditionally canned (see page 436)

We swore off making apple jelly for a while because it was too difficult: cooking the apples, straining them, getting rid of the pulp, clarifying the juice, gelling it…and all *that* for not much apple flavor. Then we discovered an easier solution: frozen unsweetened apple juice concentrate. Its subtle flavors survive vigorous boiling. And we don't need to clarify the jelly because it's already been done for us as the concentrate is processed. Voilà: more apple flavor than the stuff you get at diners and breakfast spots.

2 cups (400 g) granulated white sugar
3 tablespoons (36 g) *granulated less-sugar* pectin
2½ cups (600 ml) water
One 12 ounce (355 ml) can of frozen *unsweetened* apple juice concentrate, thawed
1 tablespoon (15 ml) lemon juice

1. Mix ¼ cup (50 g) sugar and the pectin in a small bowl until uniform.

2. Stir the water, apple juice concentrate, and lemon juice in a large saucepan. Set the pan over medium-high heat and add the pectin mixture. Stir constantly to dissolve the granulated ingredients. Bring to a boil you can't stir down, stirring often.

3. Add the remaining 1¾ cups (350 g) sugar and stir constantly to dissolve the sugar. Bring back to a full boil, stirring occasionally. Boil undisturbed for 1 minute.

4. Turn off the heat, remove the pan from the burner, and set aside for 1–2 minutes. Skim any foamy impurities with a tablespoon.

5. Transfer to four *clean* ½ pint (236 ml) jars or other containers, leaving about ½ inch (1 cm) headspace in each. Cover or seal. Cool at room temperature for no more than 1 hour, then refrigerate or freeze.

Next
We love this jelly on French toast with lots of butter!

Candy Apple Jelly

MAKES: about 4 cups (960 ml)
FRIDGE: up to 1 month
FREEZER: up to 1 year
May be traditionally canned (see page 436)

Here's a clear jelly with the flavor of candied apples—and even the red color. As the cinnamon candies melt, their flavor softens to create a cinnamon-laced apple jelly that's a great afternoon treat on a graham cracker. Red food coloring is optional, but be careful: Too much can turn the jelly lurid. And food colorings vary dramatically in strength. Start with a single drop and see how it goes.

- 3½ cups (840 ml) pure *unsweetened* apple juice (do not use apple cider)
- 5½ ounces (155 g) pill-sized red cinnamon candies, such as Red Hots or Cinnamon Imperials
- 2 cups (400 g) granulated white sugar
- 3 tablespoons (36 g) *granulated less-sugar* pectin
- 1–3 drops of red food coloring, optional

1. Mix the juice and candies in a large saucepan set over medium heat. Cook until the candies melt and dissolve, stirring almost constantly. Turn off the heat, remove the pan from the burner, and cool at room temperature for 15 minutes.

2. Mix ½ cup (100 g) sugar and the pectin in a small bowl until uniform.

3. Set the juice mixture back over medium-high heat and add the pectin mixture. Stir constantly to dissolve the granulated ingredients. Bring to a boil you can't stir down, stirring often.

4. Add the remaining 1½ cups (300 g) sugar and the food coloring (if using). Stir constantly to dissolve the sugar. Bring back to a full boil, stirring often. Boil undisturbed for 1 minute.

5. Turn off the heat, remove the pan from the burner, and set aside for 1–2 minutes. Skim any foamy impurities with a tablespoon.

6. Transfer to four *clean* ½ pint (236 ml) jars or other containers, leaving about ½ inch (1 cm) headspace in each. Cover or seal. Cool at room temperature for no more than 1 hour, then refrigerate or freeze.

Tip

Some bottlings of apple juice are cut with white grape juice or even a blend of juices. For the best flavor, read the label and make sure you're using pure unsweetened apple juice.

Apple-Amaretto Jelly

MAKES: about 4 cups (960 ml)
FRIDGE: up to 1 month
FREEZER: up to 1 year
May be traditionally canned (see page 436)

Here's an up-market apple jelly, best spread on a buttered cracker alongside a steaming cup of milky black tea on a winter afternoon. The cinnamon notes are actually pretty moderate, what with all the cooking and added almond flavor.

- 4 cups (960 ml) pure *unsweetened* apple juice (do not use apple cider)
- One 3 inch (7.5 cm) cinnamon stick
- 2½ cups (500 g) granulated white sugar
- 3 tablespoons (36 g) *granulated less-sugar* pectin
- 2 tablespoons (30 ml) amaretto or other almond-flavored liqueur

1. Pour the juice into a large saucepan, add the cinnamon stick, and set the pan over high heat. Bring the juice to a simmer, then turn off the heat, cover the pan, and remove it from the burner. Cool to room temperature, about 2 hours.

2. Mix ½ cup (100 g) sugar and the pectin in a small bowl until uniform.

3. Fish out and discard the cinnamon stick from the pan. Set it over medium-high heat and add the pectin mixture. Stir constantly to dissolve the granulated ingredients. Bring to a boil you can't stir down, stirring often.

4. Add the remaining 2 cups (400 g) sugar and stir constantly to dissolve the sugar. Bring back to a full boil, stirring occasionally. Boil undisturbed for 1 minute.

5. Turn off the heat, remove the pan from the burner, and set aside for 1–2 minutes. Skim any foamy impurities with a tablespoon. Stir in the amaretto.

Front to back: Apple-Amaretto Jelly (page 72) and Apple-Caramel Jam (page 75)

6. Transfer to four *clean* ½ pint (236 ml) jars or other containers, leaving about ½ inch (1 cm) headspace in each. Cover or seal. Cool at room temperature for no more than 2 hours, then refrigerate or freeze.

More

If you'd rather not include any amaretto or don't want the residual taste of alcohol, substitute an equal amount of almond syrup or use your own homemade syrup (page 420). Unfortunately, the jelly may have less sparkle and a murkier color.

Sugar-Free Apple Jam

MAKES: about 3 cups (720 ml)
FRIDGE: up to 2 weeks
FREEZER: up to 6 months

If you prefer pulpier jams over smooth jellies, you may have found your grail. Although *sugar-free* often means a texture problem in jellies and jams, the solutions are simple with apples. For one thing, we can use sweeter apples so there are complex, natural sugars in tow, adding a breadth of flavor without refined sugar. Second, we can use softer apples so they'll cook into a thick jam with a velvety texture that makes up for the lack of granulated sugar. And we can add a few spices to give the jam deeper, warmer notes.

- 1 cup *1-to-1 (by volume)* granulated white-sugar substitute
- 2 tablespoons (24 g) *granulated less-sugar* pectin
- ½ teaspoon ground cinnamon
- ⅛ teaspoon grated nutmeg
- 1½ pounds (680 g) *sweet* apples, such as Gala or Braeburn (about 3 large), peeled, cored, and chopped
- ½ cup (120 ml) *unsweetened* apple juice
- 2 tablespoons (30 ml) lemon juice

1. Mix the sugar substitute, pectin, cinnamon, and nutmeg in a medium bowl until uniform.

2. Place the apple pieces, apple juice, and lemon juice in a large saucepan. Set it over medium heat and bring to a simmer, stirring often.

3. Reduce the heat to low, cover, and simmer, stirring often, until the apples are tender, about 10 minutes.

4. Raise the heat to medium and add the pectin mixture. Stir constantly to dissolve the granulated ingredients. Bring to a boil you can't stir down, stirring often. Boil undisturbed for 1 minute.

5. Turn off the heat, remove the pan from the burner, and set aside for 1–2 minutes. Skim any foamy impurities with a tablespoon.

6. Transfer to three *clean* ½ pint (236 ml) jars or other containers, leaving about ½ inch (1 cm) headspace in each. Cover or seal. Cool at room temperature for no more than 1 hour, then refrigerate or freeze.

Next

Controlled studies show that freezing bread, then toasting it, results in a change to the starches that reduces its glycemic load. With sugar-free jam, breakfast can truly be a tasty win-win.

Apple-Cardamom Jam

MAKES: about 4 cups (960 ml)
FRIDGE: up to 3 weeks
FREEZER: up to 1 year
May be traditionally canned (see page 436)

The old-school French jam combo of apples and cardamom is a great way to keep those autumnal flavors in your pantry for the colder days ahead. Sour, hard apples are the key to making this jam. If the apples are the slightest bit soft, they will become no better than applesauce and you'll lose the thick, pulpy texture of true *jam*. (This advice may seem to contradict what we wrote about Sugar-Free Apple Jam, at left, but there, we want a softer apple to make up for the loss of refined sugar.)

- 2½ cups (500 g) granulated white sugar
- 2 tablespoons (24 g) *granulated less-sugar* pectin
- 1¾ pounds (790 g) hard sour apples, preferably Granny Smith (about 5 large), peeled, cored, and *diced*
- ½ cup (120 ml) *unsweetened* apple juice (do not use apple cider)
- 2 tablespoons (30 ml) lemon juice
- 2–3 *green* cardamom pods, crushed

1. Mix ½ cup (100 g) sugar and the pectin in a large bowl until uniform.

2. Stir the apples, apple juice, lemon juice, and cardamom pods (and seeds) in a large saucepan. Set it over medium-high heat. Bring the mixture to a simmer, stirring often. Reduce the heat to low and simmer, stirring occasionally, until the apples soften, about 10 minutes.

3. Raise the heat to medium-high and add the pectin mixture. Stir constantly to dissolve the granulated ingredients. Bring to a boil you can't stir down, stirring often.

4. Add the remaining 2 cups (400 g) sugar and stir constantly to dissolve the sugar. Bring back to a full boil, stirring occasionally. Boil undisturbed for 1 minute.

5. Turn off the heat, remove the pan from the burner, and set aside for 1–2 minutes. Skim any foamy impurities with a tablespoon. Fish out and discard any bits of cardamom hull, leaving the seeds behind.

6. Transfer to four *clean* ½ pint (236 ml) jars or other containers, leaving about ½ inch (1 cm) headspace in each. Cover or seal. Cool at room temperature for no more than 1 hour, then refrigerate or freeze. In the fridge, the jam will not reach its best flavor for 48 hours.

Next
Add a little of this jam to your next chicken salad. Or spread it on a chicken sandwich with lots of deli mustard.

Apple-Caramel Jam

MAKES: about 3 cups (720 ml)
FRIDGE: about 1 month
FREEZER: about 1 year
May be traditionally canned (see page 436)

We've long been fans of so-called *burned sugar*, ever since Mark's grandmother, a professional baker, started making what she called *burned sugar pie*. Essentially, she melted and mildly caramelized sugar (she called that "burning" it), then added it to the custard in a cream pie. We've taken her method as the inspiration for this jam. We *burn* (ahem) the sugar, then add apples for a sophisticated set of flavors with sweet-bitter notes throughout the dark, brown jam—like crustless tarte tatin in a jar. Be careful: The darker the melted sugar's color, the more bitter its flavors. And remember that sugar continues to caramelize off the heat. Look for a mellow, golden amber that will darken a bit as it cools, rather than a deep brown.

- 2 pounds (900 g) hard, sour apples, preferably Granny Smith (about 6–8 large), peeled, cored, and *diced*
- 2 tablespoons (30 ml) lemon juice
- 2 cups (400 g) granulated white sugar

1. Toss the apples and lemon juice in a large bowl to thoroughly coat the apple pieces and keep them from browning.

2. Pour the sugar into a very large saucepan and set it over medium-high heat. Stir occasionally until the sugar melts and turns golden amber, even very pale brown.

3. Turn off the heat and remove the pan from the burner. Add the apple mixture, taking care since everything may roil. The sugar will also harden.

4. Set the pan over low heat and cook, stirring gently but often, until the sugar melts again. Continue cooking, stirring occasionally, until the mixture returns to a boil.

5. Reduce the heat and continue cooking, stirring occasionally, until the apples soften and the mixture thickens enough that you can run a wooden spoon across the bottom of the pan and create a line that holds its edges for a second, about 15 minutes.

6. Turn off the heat, remove the pan from the burner, and set aside for 1–2 minutes. Skim foamy impurities with a tablespoon.

7. Transfer to three *clean* ½ pint (236 ml) jars or other containers, leaving about ½ inch (1 cm) headspace in each. Cover or seal. Cool at room temperature for no more than 1 hour, then refrigerate or freeze. In the fridge, the jam may not reach its best flavor for 48 hours.

Next
Since this jam has a bitter edge, it's best on toast spread with soft goat cheese or even sour cream.

Spiced Apple Preserves

MAKES: about 3 cups (720 ml)
FRIDGE: up to 3 weeks
FREEZER: up to 1 year
May be traditionally canned (see page 436)

We've long experimented with apple *preserves*. The problem we've been trying to solve? How to prevent the apples from breaking down into sauce or apple butter. It's hard to keep that whole-fruit texture found in the best preserves. So we've settled on this technique of grating the apples and squeezing the juice, then setting aside those apple shreds to be added later in the process. The exact amount of warming spices here is a matter of personal preference. If you're not sure, err on the light side the first time you make these preserves.

2 pounds (900 g) hard, sour apples (6–8 large), such as Granny Smith or McIntosh
1 tablespoon (15 ml) lemon juice
1 cup (200 g) granulated white sugar
½ teaspoon ground cinnamon
Up to ¼ teaspoon ground cloves
Up to ¼ teaspoon grated nutmeg

1. Set up a jelly bag over a large saucepan. (For alternatives to a jelly bag, see page 17.) Grate the apples (peels too, but not the cores) through the large holes of a box grater into the bag. For the safest results, use a hand guard to grip each apple, then grate one side of the fruit down to the core, turn the apple a bit, grate another side, and so on, until you have only a core left on the guard.

2. Gather the jelly bag into a bundle. Remove the stand. Squeeze the apple shreds gently to get as much juice as possible into the saucepan, working the bag from several different angles.

3. Pour the squeezed apple shreds into a large bowl and stir in the lemon juice to keep them from browning.

4. Set the saucepan with the juice over medium heat and add the sugar. Stir constantly to dissolve the sugar. Bring to a full boil, stirring often. Boil, stirring frequently, until reduced to a syrup, about 3 minutes.

5. Stir in the apple shreds (and any juice in their bowl), the cinnamon, cloves, and nutmeg. Bring the mixture back to a boil, stirring often. Reduce the heat to low and cook, stirring frequently, until the apple shreds absorb most of the syrup and the mixture thickens considerably.

6. Turn off the heat, remove the pan from the burner, and set aside for 1–2 minutes. Transfer to three *clean* ½ pint (236 ml) jars or other containers, leaving about ½ inch (1 cm) headspace in each. Cover or seal. Cool at room temperature for no more than 1 hour, then refrigerate or freeze.

More
Skip the three individual spices and use up to 1 teaspoon dried apple-pie spice mix instead.

Brandied Apple Preserves

MAKES: about 3 cups (720 ml)
FRIDGE: up to 3 weeks
FREEZER: up to 1 year
May be traditionally canned (see page 436)

Rather than the more complex technique of grating the apples that we used for Spiced Apple Preserves (page 76), the method here results in a thick, syrupy set, something like a cross between apple preserves and apple butter. It's not as much work as the grating technique, but the final results are thick and pulpy, not perfectly the texture of preserves, but close enough to be quite satisfying. The brandy (or Calvados) offers a sweet, woody flavor and deep, caramelized notes for a particularly sophisticated finish.

- 1¼ cups (250 g) granulated white sugar
- 2 tablespoons (24 g) *granulated less-sugar* pectin
- 2 pounds (900 g) hard sour apples, such as Granny Smith or McIntosh (about 6–8 large), peeled, cored, and *roughly chopped*
- ¾ cup (180 ml) apple brandy or Calvados (do not use apple schnapps)
- 2 tablespoons (30 ml) lemon juice
- ¾ cup (160 g) packed light brown sugar
- ¼ teaspoon ground cinnamon, optional

1. Mix ¼ cup (50 g) white sugar and the pectin in a small bowl until uniform.

2. Mix the apples, brandy, and lemon juice in a large saucepan. Set it over medium heat, add the pectin mixture, and stir constantly to dissolve the granulated ingredients. Bring the mixture to a simmer, stirring often.

3. Reduce the heat to low and simmer steadily but slowly, stirring often, until the apples begin to break down, up to 15 minutes.

4. Add the remaining 1 cup (200 g) white sugar, the brown sugar, and cinnamon (if using). Stir well to dissolve the sugar, crushing about half of the apple bits against the inside of the pan. Bring the mixture back to a simmer, stirring often. Boil undisturbed for 1 minute.

5. Turn off the heat, remove the pan from the burner, and set aside for 1–2 minutes. Skim any foamy impurities with a tablespoon.

6. Transfer to three *clean* ½ pint (236 ml) jars or other containers, leaving about ½ inch (1 cm) headspace in each. Cover or seal. Cool at room temperature for no more than 2 hours, then refrigerate or freeze. In the fridge, the preserves will not reach their best flavor for 48 hours.

More
For a cleaner flavor, use plain brandy.

Easy Apple Butter

MAKES: about 3 cups (720 ml)
FRIDGE: up to 3 weeks
FREEZER: up to 1 year

We've got a more labor-intensive roasted apple butter coming up on page 78. Still, this one gives you almost as much of that prized, creamy, smooth texture for a lot less work. True, the flavors are not as intense, but the trade-off for less work may sometimes be worth it if you want to make a housewarming present or a small sick-day gift for someone you care about—as well as keeping a jar or two for yourself.

- One 48 ounce (1.36 kg) jar of *unsweetened* applesauce
- ¼ cup (85 g) honey
- 1 cup (215 g) packed light brown sugar
- ½ teaspoon ground cinnamon
- ¼ teaspoon ground cloves
- ¼ teaspoon grated nutmeg

1. Stir together all of the ingredients in a very large saucepan until uniform. Set the pan over medium heat and bring to a simmer, stirring quite often so the honey and sugar don't burn.

2. Reduce the heat to low and simmer gently, stirring often, until the mixture is dark golden brown and (most importantly) thick enough that you can run a wooden spoon across the bottom of the pan and create a line that holds its edges for a second, about 40 minutes.

3. Turn off the heat, remove the pan from the burner, and set aside for 1–2 minutes.

4. Transfer to three *clean* ½ pint (236 ml) jars or other containers, leaving about ½ inch (1 cm) headspace in each. Cover or seal. Cool at room temperature for no more than 1 hour, then refrigerate or freeze. In the fridge, the apple butter may not reach its best flavor for 48 hours.

Next
This apple butter is a great spread for a dessert pizza, used as you would tomato sauce on a savory pizza. Top with chocolate chunks and caramel sauce.

Oven-Roasted Apple Butter

MAKES: about 2 cups (480 ml)
FRIDGE: up to 3 weeks
FREEZER: up to 6 months

Now we're not taking any shortcuts. We're making the best apple butter you can imagine: chopped apples, roasted in brown sugar until caramelized, then morphed into perfection for toast. Yes, you *must* peel the apples for the smoothest, creamiest texture. And watch the roasting, particularly in the last 15 minutes, because the apple pieces are prone to burning. So be sure to stir often. But the effort pays off in an apple butter that's bliss: a velvety set, caramelized sweet-bitter tones, and hints of cinnamon throughout.

4 pounds (1.8 kg) tart juicy apples, preferably McIntosh (about 12 medium), peeled, cored, and *roughly chopped*

1 cup (240 ml) water

¾ cup (160 g) packed light brown sugar

¼ teaspoon ground cinnamon

1. Set the rack in the center of the oven and heat the oven to 400°F (200°C), no fan or convection.

2. Stir the apple chunks, water, brown sugar, and cinnamon in a large roasting pan until uniform.

3. Roast until the apples are very soft and dark brown and the mixture is thick and caramelized, stirring about every 10 minutes at first, then more frequently until about every 3 minutes when things are really browning, about 1 hour in total. As you stir the ingredients, particularly during the last 30 minutes, the apples will have become softer and start to smoosh in the pan. No worries: Just stir more often without fully breaking them up.

4. Transfer the baking dish to a wire rack. Cool for a few minutes, then stir into a smooth mush.

5. Transfer to two *clean* ½ pint (236 ml) jars or other containers, leaving about ½ inch (1 cm) headspace in each. Cover or seal. Cool at room temperature for no more than 1 hour, then refrigerate or freeze.

Tip
Don't have brown sugar on hand? Substitute granulated white sugar and add ¼ teaspoon (6 g) of molasses for every ¼ cup (50 g) granulated sugar as a stand-in for light brown sugar. For dark brown sugar, use ½ teaspoon (12 g) molasses for every ¼ cup (50 g) granulated white sugar.

Pear Preserves
(page 80)

Pear Preserves

MAKES: about 5 cups (1200 ml)
FRIDGE: up to 3 weeks
FREEZER: up to 1 year
May be traditionally canned (see page 436)

For these simple preserves, you'll need to start with semi-soft, juicy pears, like ripe Comice or Bartlett pears, *not* firmer Bosc, Seckel, or Forelle pears. The softer pears break down more readily to create a thick syrup that suspends larger chunks of pear in the jars. The final consistency is a matter of taste. We like bigger pear chunks, but you might like smaller ones for an overall smoother texture. Just remember that these are *preserves*: They should still retain the feel of *whole* fruit.

> 2¼ cups (450 g) granulated white sugar
>
> 3 tablespoons (36 g) *granulated less-sugar* pectin
>
> 1 pound 14 ounces (850 g) semi-soft ripe pears (about 5 large), peeled, cored, and chopped (4 cups)
>
> 1 tablespoon (15 ml) lemon juice

1. Mix ¼ cup (50 g) sugar and the pectin in a small bowl until uniform.

2. Stir the pear pieces and lemon juice in a large saucepan. Set it over medium-high heat and add the pectin mixture. Stir constantly to dissolve the granulated ingredients. Bring to a boil you can't stir down, stirring often.

3. Add the remaining 2 cups (400 g) sugar and stir constantly to dissolve the sugar. Bring back to a full boil, stirring occasionally. Boil undisturbed for 1 minute.

4. Turn off the heat, remove the pan from the burner, and set aside for 1–2 minutes. Skim any foamy impurities with a tablespoon.

5. Transfer to five *clean* ½ pint (236 ml) jars or other containers, leaving about ½ inch (1 cm) headspace in each. Cover or seal. Cool at room temperature for no more than 1 hour, then refrigerate or freeze.

More

Spice these pear preserves with up to ½ teaspoon ground cinnamon, ¼ teaspoon ground ginger, and/or ¼ teaspoon ground mace. Stir any or all into the pan when you take it off the heat in step 4.

Brown Sugar–Pear Preserves

MAKES: about 5 cups (1200 ml)
FRIDGE: up to 3 weeks
FREEZER: up to 1 year
May be traditionally canned (see page 436)

These pear preserves are a complex luxury: slightly tannic notes from the molasses (in the brown sugar) underneath sweet, aromatic chunks of pears in a thick syrup. Because of the longer cooking time needed to create those deeper flavors, you'll want to use fairly firm pears, not the soft, ripe, luscious ones you might prefer for a snack or dessert. And to achieve a luxurious texture that better suits the flavors, cut the pears into large chunks, maybe even 2 inch (5 cm) pieces, so that there are big pieces suspended in the thick syrup.

> 1½ cups (300 g) granulated white sugar
>
> 3 tablespoons (36 g) *granulated less-sugar* pectin
>
> 1 pound 14 ounces (850 g) *firm* ripe pears, preferably Bosc or Seckel (about 5), peeled, cored, and cut into big chunks
>
> ½ cup (120 ml) *unsweetened* apple juice
>
> ¾ cup (160 g) packed light brown sugar

1. Mix the granulated white sugar and pectin in a medium bowl until uniform.

2. Stir the pear chunks and apple juice in a large saucepan. Set it over medium-high heat and add the pectin mixture. Stir constantly to dissolve the granulated ingredients. Bring to a full boil, stirring often. Reduce the heat to medium-low and simmer, stirring frequently, for 2 minutes.

3. Add the brown sugar and stir constantly until it dissolves. Bring back to a full boil, stirring often. Boil undisturbed for 2 minutes.

4. Turn off the heat, remove the pan from the burner, and set aside for 1–2 minutes. Skim any foamy impurities with a tablespoon.

5. Transfer to five *clean* ½ pint (236 ml) jars or other containers, leaving about ½ inch (1 cm) headspace in each. Cover or seal. Cool at room temperature for no more than 1 hour, then refrigerate or freeze. In the fridge, the preserves may not gel for 24 hours.

Next
These are the perfect preserves to accompany pungent soft goat cheeses like Cypress Grove's Humboldt Fog.

Pear Butter

MAKES: about 3 cups (720 ml)
FRIDGE: up to 3 weeks
FREEZER: up to 6 months

The difference between a fruit butter and jam is all about texture. Butters are smoother and creamier—not pulpy at all. Given that difference, it makes sense to use canned pears in juice (not heavy syrup) for a rich pear butter. We puree the pears, then reduce them until the final texture offers a velvety elegance. As a bonus, the canning process has already softened the pears, making our cooking time (relatively) shorter.

> One 28 ounce (794 g) can of sliced pears *in juice*
> 1 cup (200 g) granulated white sugar
> ¼ teaspoon almond extract
> ⅛ teaspoon kosher salt

1. Put all the ingredients (including any juice from the can) in a blender. Cover and blend until smooth, scraping down the inside of the canister as necessary.

2. Pour the pear mixture into a medium saucepan and set over medium heat. Bring to a simmer, stirring often. Reduce the heat to low, partially cover the pan, and simmer for 15 minutes, stirring often as the mixture spits and sputters.

3. Reduce the heat even more if possible. Uncover the pan and continue simmering *slowly*, stirring quite often, until thickened and amber colored, about 30 more minutes.

4. Turn off the heat and remove the pan from the burner. Cool for 5 minutes.

5. Transfer to three *clean* ½ pint (236 ml) jars or other containers, leaving about ½ inch (1 cm) headspace in each. Cover or seal. Cool at room temperature for no more than 1 hour, then refrigerate or freeze.

More
For a more complex flavor, stir in up to 1 tablespoon (15 ml) cognac, Calvados, or pear brandy with the other ingredients.

Pumpkin Butter

MAKES: about 3 cups (720 ml)
FRIDGE: up to 3 weeks
FREEZER: up to 6 months

Canned solid-pack pumpkin gives you a head start when making creamy pumpkin butter. There's no need to peel, seed, and chop that big squash! Plus, the results with this canned cheat are irresistible: The more complex, vegetal sugars (as opposed to the sweeter ones in, say, apples or pears) and the less watery pumpkin from the solid-pack can produce a butter that's so thick it'll stand up on a spoon, not to mention an English muffin.

> Two 15 ounce (425 g) cans of solid-pack pumpkin puree (do not use pumpkin pie filling)
> 1 cup (240 ml) *unsweetened* apple juice
> ½ cup (100 g) granulated white sugar
> ¼ cup (78 g) maple syrup
> 1 tablespoon (15 ml) lemon juice

Pumpkin Butter (page 81)
on cornbread

½ teaspoon ground cinnamon
½ teaspoon ground ginger
¼ teaspoon grated nutmeg
¼ teaspoon ground cloves
⅛ teaspoon kosher salt

1. Stir everything together in a very large saucepan. Set the pan over low heat and bring to a simmer, stirring quite often.

2. Simmer, stirring once every 5 minutes at first but *more and more frequently* after about 25 minutes, until dark orange and thick, about 1 hour in total. Here's the whole process: 1) the mixture begins to bubble and splatter because it's wet, like the mud paint pots at Yellowstone National Park; 2) the splattering slows and the holes created by the steam stay open as steam jets escape; 3) the mixture begins to momentarily hold its shape as you run a wooden spoon across the bottom of the pan; 4) the moisture has reduced enough that the mixture starts to darken and caramelize.

3. Transfer to three *clean* ½ pint (236 ml) jars or other containers, leaving about ½ inch (1 cm) headspace in each. Cover or seal. Cool at room temperature for no more than 1 hour, then refrigerate or freeze.

More
Although maple syrup gives pumpkin butter an autumnal flavor, you can substitute agave syrup for a cleaner finish, honey for a more aromatic flavor, or birch syrup for a slightly bitter sweetness.

Fig Jam

MAKES: about 3 cups (720 ml)
FRIDGE: up to 3 weeks
FREEZER: up to 1 year
May be traditionally canned (see page 436)

A ripe fig is a sensuous experience: the soft texture under the slight give of the skin, the subdued flavors, not to mention its gorgeous appearance. It's almost too much in jam. *Almost.* In fact, when we concentrate the flavors and allow the figs to turn into a sticky jam, the results rival the exquisite taste and texture of the figs themselves. Because figs have a lot of natural pectin, this recipe allows you to customize the jam's set. Cook it for a shorter time for a more velvety texture; cook it longer for a chewy set, like the filling of a Fig Newton cookie.

2¼ pounds (1 kg) fresh green or black figs, stemmed and chopped (about 4 cups)
2½ cups (500 g) granulated white sugar
½ cup (120 ml) water
¼ cup (60 ml) lemon juice
1 teaspoon molasses or black treacle

1. Stir the figs and sugar in a large saucepan until the fruit is evenly and thoroughly coated. Set aside *at room temperature* for 30 minutes.

2. Stir in the water, lemon juice, and molasses until uniform. Set the pan over medium-high heat and bring the mixture to a simmer, stirring quite often.

3. Reduce the heat to low and continue simmering, stirring often, until just thickened, about 12 minutes, or until quite thickened and even a little pasty, about 16 minutes.

4. Turn off the heat, remove the pan from the burner, and set aside for 1–2 minutes. Transfer to three *clean* ½ pint (236 ml) jars or other containers, leaving about ½ inch (1 cm) headspace in each. Cover or seal. Cool at room temperature for no more than 1 hour, then refrigerate or freeze.

More
Double the molasses for more pronounced bitterness under the sweetness. And/or add up to 1 tablespoon brandy or cognac with the molasses for mellow, vanilla notes.

Fig-Ginger Jam

MAKES: about 3 cups (720 ml)
FRIDGE: up to 3 weeks
FREEZER: up to 1 year
May be traditionally canned (see page 436)

Black Mission figs are a better match in this jam than Calimyrna or Adriatic figs because ginger has an assertive flavor. Plus, Black Mission figs are sweeter and a little pulpier, creating a denser texture against the ginger. We use fresh ginger in addition to crystallized ginger because we cook the jam a bit longer to help it break down over the heat. Just make sure that the fresh ginger is truly fresh—that is, markedly juicy under a thin skin.

- 2¼ pounds (1 kg) fresh Black Mission figs, stemmed and chopped (about 4 cups)
- 2¼ cups (450 g) granulated white sugar
- ¼ cup (55 g) *minced* crystallized ginger
- 2 tablespoons (30 g) minced peeled fresh ginger
- ½ cup (120 ml) water
- 2 teaspoons (10 ml) white wine vinegar
- ½ teaspoon (3 ml) vanilla extract

1. Stir the figs, sugar, crystallized ginger, and fresh ginger in a large saucepan until the fruit is evenly and thoroughly coated. Set aside *at room temperature* for 30 minutes.

2. Stir in the water, vinegar, and vanilla. Set the pan over medium-high heat and bring the mixture to a simmer, stirring often.

3. Reduce the heat to low and continue simmering, stirring often, until the fruit is pulpy-soft and the liquid has a thick, viscous texture, 15–18 minutes.

4. Turn off the heat, remove the pan from the burner, and set aside for 1–2 minutes.

5. Transfer to three *clean* ½ pint (236 ml) jars or other containers, leaving about ½ inch (1 cm) headspace in each. Cover or seal. Cool at room temperature for no more than 1 hour, then refrigerate or freeze.

More

Add one 2 inch (5 cm) cinnamon stick with the water. Remove and discard the cinnamon stick when the pan comes off the heat.

Dried Fig-Lemon Jam

MAKES: about 3 cups (720 ml)
FRIDGE: up to 3 weeks
FREEZER: up to 1 year
May be traditionally canned (see page 436)

Dried figs produce a super thick jam, almost like a fruit paste. It's a fine spread on toast but also a great condiment to go on a cheese board or even *in* a grilled cheese sandwich. For the best color, use dried Calimyrna or Adriatic (aka Turkish) figs. Their skin is soft and pale, as opposed to dried Black Mission figs, which have a leathery skin and make an inky jam.

- 1 pound (450 g) dried Calimyrna or Adriatic figs, stemmed and chopped
- 1¾ cups (420 ml) water
- 1½ cups (300 g) granulated white sugar
- ½ cup (120 ml) lemon juice
- 1 tablespoon (6 g) finely grated lemon zest
- ½ teaspoon (3 ml) vanilla extract

1. Stir the figs and water in a large saucepan. Set the pan over medium-high heat and bring to a boil, stirring occasionally. Turn off the burner, remove the pan from the heat, and set aside at room temperature for 30 minutes to let the dried figs rehydrate.

2. Set a colander over a bowl. Pour the contents of the saucepan through the colander, catching the liquid in the bowl. Pour that liquid back into the saucepan.

3. Set the pan back over medium-high heat. Add the sugar, lemon juice, zest, and vanilla. Stir constantly to dissolve the sugar. Bring to a full boil, stirring often.

Dried Fig–Lemon Jam (page 84) in cookie sandwiches

4. Reduce the heat to low and simmer, stirring occasionally, until slightly thickened, about 5 minutes. Add the rehydrated figs, raise the heat to medium-high, and bring the mixture back to a full boil, stirring often.

5. Reduce the heat again to low and continue to simmer slowly, stirring more and more often to prevent scorching, until the mixture has thickened enough that you can run a wooden spoon across the bottom of the pan and create a line that holds its edges for a second, about 10 minutes.

6. Turn off the heat, remove the pan from the burner, and set aside for 1–2 minutes. Transfer to three *clean* ½ pint (236 ml) jars or other containers, leaving about ½ inch (1 cm) headspace in each. Cover or seal. Cool at room temperature for no more than 1 hour, then refrigerate or freeze.

Next
For easy sandwich cookies, buy small sugar cookies or even digestive biscuits. Spread the flat side of a cookie or biscuit with this jam, then top with a second cookie, flat side down. Press gently to seal.

Chestnut Jam

MAKES: about 2 cups (480 ml)
FRIDGE: up to 3 weeks
FREEZER: up to 1 year

Not really a jam, more like a sticky spread, chestnut jam is an old-school treat that used to be a labor of love, mostly because picking, roasting, and shelling those chestnuts added up to such a pain. These days, you can buy jars of cooked, peeled chestnuts. Admittedly, they can be pricey. But you also can find smaller, cooked, peeled chestnuts in pouches in Asian grocery stores and from online suppliers. Those chestnuts make this treat super easy *and* affordable.

1¼ pounds (565 g) jarred or packaged cooked peeled chestnuts (about 4 cups)

As much water as necessary for processing the chestnuts into a paste

1¾ cups (350 g) granulated white sugar

½ cup (120 ml) water

1 teaspoon (15 ml) vanilla extract

1. Put the chestnuts in a food processor. Cover and process, dribbling in water through the center hole as the processor runs, until you've created a thick paste, not watery or loose in any way. Depending on the moisture content of the chestnuts, you'll end up using between ¼ cup (60 ml) and perhaps ¾ cup (180 ml) water. Uncover the processor; scrape down and remove the blade.

2. Combine the sugar, the ½ cup (120 ml) water, and the vanilla in a medium saucepan. Set the pan over medium heat and stir constantly to dissolve the sugar. Bring to a full boil, stirring often. Boil for 2 minutes, still stirring often.

3. Add every speck of the chestnut paste from the food processor, then *whisk* constantly and bring the mixture to a low simmer. Reduce the heat to very low and cook, whisking more and more often to prevent scorching, until thickened enough that you can run the whisk along the bottom of the pan and create a line that holds its edges for a second, about 5 minutes.

4. Turn off the heat, remove the pan from the burner, and set aside for 1–2 minutes.

5. Transfer to two *clean* ½ pint (236 ml) jars or other containers, leaving about ½ inch (1 cm) headspace in each. Cover or seal. Cool at room temperature for no more than 1 hour, then refrigerate or freeze.

Next
For an easy dessert, spread the chestnut jam into the bottom of a baked (or purchased) tart shell, then top with lots of sweetened whipped cream.

Black Currant Jelly

MAKES: about 3 cups (720 ml)
FRIDGE: up to 1 month
FREEZER: up to 1 year
May be traditionally canned (see page 436)

We suspect that if you go to the trouble of tracking down black currants, you'll also be willing to go to jelly-bag and candy-thermometer extents for this dark purple jelly with a characteristic yet more subtle taste of cassis, the liqueur made from black currants. At our house, the bushes make dozens of quarts of black currants at summer's height. But there are always stragglers on the branches that take longer to ripen. We developed this small-batch recipe for that last gasp of summer fruit, long after most of the black currants have been harvested. It's a bow toward the autumn orange glow already starting to glimmer on the swamp maples down the road.

> 1⅔ pounds (750 g) stemmed and trimmed fresh black currants (about 5 cups)
>
> 1¼ cups (300 ml) water
>
> 2½ cups (500 g) granulated white sugar
>
> Additional water to even up the volume (optional)

1. Put the black currants (stems and all) and water in a medium saucepan. Set it over medium-high heat and bring to a boil, stirring occasionally. Reduce the heat to low, cover, and cook, stirring often, until the currants are very soft and have started to break down into a pulp, about 20 minutes.

2. Turn off the heat and remove the pan from the burner. Use a potato masher or the back of a wooden spoon to mash the cooked currants against the inside of the pan. Cool for 5 minutes. Meanwhile, set up a jelly bag on a stand over a large bowl or pot. (For alternatives to a jelly bag, see page 17.)

3. Pour the black currant mixture into the jelly bag. Let the mixture drip until the pulp in the bag is dry, up to 8 hours. (You can even leave this dripping for 12 hours or overnight.)

4. Measure the juice. You should have 2½ cups (600 ml). If not, gently press the pulp in the bag with a wooden spoon to extract more juice, although the jelly will then be cloudier. If aesthetics are important, you can instead make up the difference in volume with water.

5. Clean the medium saucepan and pour the juice into it. Set the pan over medium-high heat and add the sugar. Stir constantly to dissolve the sugar. Bring to a full boil, stirring often.

6. Attach a candy thermometer to the inside of the pan. Continue boiling, stirring often, until the mixture reaches 220°F (104°C), about 15 minutes.

7. Turn off the heat, remove the pan from the burner, and set aside for 1–2 minutes. Skim any foamy impurities with a tablespoon.

8. Transfer to three *clean* ½ pint (236 ml) jars or other containers, leaving about ½ inch (1 cm) headspace in each. Cover or seal. Cool at room temperature for no more than 1 hour, then refrigerate or freeze.

More
Use this same technique to make GOOSEBERRY JELLY. Substitute 1⅔ pounds (750 g) *red* gooseberries for the black currants.

Clockwise from bottom:
Red Currant Jelly (page 89),
White Currant–Lemon Jelly
(page 90), and Black Current
Jelly (page 87)

Black Currant–Port Jam

MAKES: about 3 cups (720 ml)
FRIDGE: up to 3 weeks
FREEZER: up to 1 year
May be traditionally canned (see page 436)

In terms of effort, black currant jam is certainly easier to make than Black Currant Jelly (page 87)! You don't need a jelly bag to strain the juice. Even better, there's no call for an expensive vintage port in this jam. A ruby port is a great choice because of its dark red color and berry-like flavor. One note: Because this jam is not strained, you'll still have the pop of tiny black currant seeds throughout.

> 1½ pounds (680 g) stemmed and trimmed fresh black currants (about 4½ cups)
> 2 cups (400 g) granulated white sugar
> ½ cup (120 ml) ruby port

1. Stir everything together in a large saucepan. Set it over medium heat and stir constantly until the sugar dissolves. Cook until the black currants begin to break down and release their juice, stirring often.

2. Raise the heat to medium-high and bring the mixture to a boil, stirring often. Continue cooking, stirring more and more often to prevent scorching and smashing about half of the currants against the inside of the pan, until the mixture thickens but isn't paste-like, 6–7 minutes.

3. Turn off the heat, remove the pan from the burner, and set aside for 1–2 minutes. Skim any foamy impurities with a tablespoon.

4. Transfer to three *clean* ½ pint (236 ml) jars or other containers, leaving about ½ inch (1 cm) headspace in each. Cover or seal. Cool at room temperature for no more than 1 hour, then refrigerate or freeze.

More

For a pure black currant *jam* (that is, without the port), substitute 6 tablespoons (90 ml) water plus 2 tablespoons (30 ml) cassis for the port.

Red Currant Jelly

MAKES: about 3 cups (720 ml)
FRIDGE: up to 1 month
FREEZER: up to 1 year
May be traditionally canned (see page 436)

Every July, we go into battle mode: the two of us v. a billion chipmunks. The fought-for prize is a batch of red currants off our bushes. We never win. So we get to make (at most!) a small batch of this precious jelly. Or we resort to buying red currants at a local farmers' market. They're expensive, but we can't live without that sweet-sour, delicate, floral flavor.

> 4 cups (900 g) fresh red currants (do not stem)
> 1 cup (240 ml) water
> Additional water to even up the volume (optional)
> 2½ cups (500 g) granulated white sugar

1. Place the red currants (stems and all) and the water in a medium saucepan. Set it over medium heat. Bring to a boil, stirring occasionally. Cover, reduce the heat to low, and cook, stirring occasionally, until the currants are very soft and pulpy, about 20 minutes.

2. Turn off the heat and remove the pan from the burner. Use a potato masher or the back of a wooden spoon to mash the cooked currants against the inside of the pan. Cool for 5 minutes. Meanwhile, set up a jelly bag on a stand over a large bowl or pot. (For alternatives to a jelly bag, see page 17.)

3. Pour the red currant mixture into the jelly bag. Let the mixture drip until the pulp in the bag is dry, up to 8 hours. (You can even leave this dripping for 12 hours or overnight.)

4. Measure the juice. You should have 2½ cups (600 ml). If not, gently press the pulp in the bag with a wooden spoon to extract more juice, although the jelly will be cloudier. If aesthetics are important, you can instead make up the difference in volume with water.

5. Clean the saucepan and pour the juice into it. Add the sugar and set the pan over medium-high heat. Stir constantly to dissolve the sugar. Bring to a boil, stirring often.

6. Attach a candy thermometer to the inside of the pan. Continue boiling, stirring often, until the temperature reaches 220°F (104°C), about 15 minutes.

7. Turn off the heat, remove the pan from the burner, and set aside for 1–2 minutes. Skim any foamy impurities with a tablespoon.

8. Transfer to three *clean* ½ pint (236 ml) jars or other containers, leaving about ½ inch (1 cm) headspace in each. Cover or seal. Cool at room temperature for no more than 1 hour, then refrigerate or freeze.

Next
Red currant jelly is the perfect final touch for beef stews and soups. Only a teaspoon or two, stirred in during the final moments of cooking, will brighten all the flavors considerably.

White Currant–Lemon Jelly

MAKES: about 2 cups (480 ml)
FRIDGE: up to 1 month
FREEZER: up to 1 year
May be traditionally canned (see page 436)

White currants are rare! They're sometimes called *champagne currants*, despite an arc of pale pink blush along one section of each currant. They're larger than red currants and not quite as tart, more floral, although still with a bright, sunny pop.

They're best in jelly because the flavors are so subtle—a pulpy texture somehow interferes. Because white currants can be hard to find, a mini batch of this special jelly fits the bill. The jelly is a bit floral, almost like one made from elderberries, but paler, vaguely golden, and with a tart flavor that's still somehow ephemeral.

> **2 large lemons**
> **1 pound (450 g) fresh white currants (do not stem)**
> **1 cup (240 ml) water**
> **1½ cups (300 g) granulated white sugar**
> **Additional water to even up the volume (optional)**

1. Remove the zest from the lemons, preferably with a vegetable peeler, taking it off in wide strips. Put the zest in a medium saucepan. (Reserve the zested lemons for later in the recipe.) Add the white currants (stems and all) and the water. Set the pan over medium-high heat. Bring to a boil, stirring often.

2. Cover, reduce the heat to low, and simmer *slowly*, stirring occasionally, until the currants are soft and pulpy, about 20 minutes.

3. Turn off the heat and remove the pan from the burner. Use a potato masher or the back of a wooden spoon to mash the cooked currants against the inside of the pan. Cool for 5 minutes. Meanwhile, set up a jelly bag over a large bowl or pot. (For alternatives to a jelly bag, see page 17.)

4. Pour the white currant mixture into the jelly bag. Let the mixture drip until the pulp in the bag is dry, up to 8 hours. (You can even leave this dripping for 12 hours or overnight.)

5. Measure the currant juice. Juice the zested lemons and add the seeded juice to the currant juice. You should have 1½ cups (360 ml). If not, gently press the pulp in the bag with a wooden spoon to extract more juice, although the jelly will be cloudier. If aesthetics are important, you can instead make up the difference in volume with water.

6. Clean the saucepan and pour the juice into it. Add the sugar and set the pan over medium-high heat. Stir constantly to dissolve the sugar. Bring to a boil, stirring often.

7. Attach a candy thermometer to the inside of the pan. Continue boiling, stirring often, until the temperature reaches 220°F (104°C), about 10 minutes.

8. Turn off the heat, remove the pan from the burner, and set aside for 1–2 minutes. Skim any foamy impurities with a tablespoon.

9. Transfer to two *clean* ½ pint (236 ml) jars or other containers, leaving about ½ inch (1 cm) headspace in each. Cover or seal. Cool at room temperature for no more than 1 hour, then refrigerate or freeze.

Next
This jelly is great as a last-minute addition to vegetable or fish curries, particularly Thai red and green curries. Add no more than 2 teaspoons in the final moments of cooking.

Pineapple Jelly

MAKES: about 4 cups (960 ml)
FRIDGE: up to 1 month
FREEZER: up to 1 year
May be traditionally canned (see page 436)

Because fresh pineapple has protein-dissolving enzymes, it's tough to make clear pineapple jelly from scratch…unless you start with bottled pineapple juice! It's already been processed, so the enzymes have been neutralized and can't affect the final set. Even better, pineapple juice makes this jelly an easy weekend project without the need of a jelly bag or a food mill.

> 2 cups (400 g) granulated white sugar
> 3 tablespoons (36 g) *granulated less-sugar* pectin
> 3 cups (720 ml) *unsweetened* pineapple juice

1. Mix ¼ cup (50 g) sugar and the pectin in a small bowl until uniform.

2. Pour the pineapple juice into a large saucepan. Set it over medium-high heat and add the pectin mixture. Stir constantly to dissolve the granulated ingredients *and* keep the mixture from boiling over. Bring the mixture to a boil you can't stir down, stirring quite often. (See the TIP for more information.)

3. Add the remaining 1¾ cups (350 g) sugar and stir constantly to dissolve the sugar. Bring back to a full boil, stirring often. Boil undisturbed for 1 minute.

4. Turn off the heat, remove the pan from the burner, and set aside for 1–2 minutes. Skim any foamy impurities with a tablespoon.

5. Transfer to four *clean* ½ pint (236 ml) jars or other containers, leaving about ½ inch (1 cm) headspace in each. Cover or seal. Cool at room temperature for no more than 1 hour, then refrigerate or freeze.

Tip
Pineapple juice foams and roils as it comes to a boil. Stir carefully to avoid burns (a long-handled wooden spoon works best). Don't step away from the pan. If you can't control the roiling, reduce the heat a bit while maintaining the necessary boil.

Pineapple Jam

MAKES: about 4 cups (960 ml)
FRIDGE: up to 3 weeks
FREEZER: up to 1 year
May be traditionally canned (see page 436)

Because a jam usually has a looser set than a jelly, we can use fresh pineapple to create a velvety jam—no natural, protein-dissolving enzymes to worry about, since the ways they compromise the pectin are exactly what we want for that softer set. As a bonus, peeled and cored fresh pineapple chunks are available in the produce section of most supermarkets (as well as the peeled and cored whole pineapple that you must then cut into chunks). This jam has the satiny texture of fresh

Front to back: Pineapple
Jelly (page 91) and
Pineapple Jam (page 91)

pineapple as well as its soft perfume. But because of those enzymes, the jam may become looser as it rests in the fridge, so the freezer is the best option for long storage.

- 1¾ cups (375 g) granulated white sugar
- 2 tablespoons (24 g) *granulated less-sugar* pectin
- 1 pound 2 ounces (510 g) peeled, cored, and chopped fresh pineapple (about 3 cups)
- 1 tablespoon (15 ml) lime juice
- ⅛ teaspoon vanilla extract

1. Mix ¼ cup (50 g) sugar and the pectin in a small bowl until uniform.

2. Place the pineapple chunks, lime juice, and vanilla in a large saucepan. Use a potato masher or the back of a wooden spoon to mash the pineapple into a pulpy mess. Do not make a puree.

3. Set the pan over medium-high heat and add the pectin mixture. Stir constantly to dissolve the granulated ingredients. Bring to a boil you can't stir down, stirring often.

4. Add the remaining 1½ cups (350 g) sugar and stir constantly to dissolve the sugar. Bring back to a full boil, stirring often. Boil undisturbed for 1 minute.

5. Turn off the heat, remove the pan from the burner, and set aside for at least 3 minutes to let all the bubbling stop. Skim any foamy impurities with a tablespoon.

6. Transfer to four *clean* ½ pint (236 ml) jars or other containers, leaving about ½ inch (1 cm) headspace in each. Cover or seal. Cool at room temperature for no more than 1 hour, then refrigerate or freeze.

More

For PINEAPPLE-RUM JAM, substitute rum extract for the vanilla extract.

Pineapple-Coconut Jelly

MAKES: about 4 cups (960 ml)
FRIDGE: up to 1 month
FREEZER: up to 1 year
May be traditionally canned (see page 436)

Our most tropical jelly, this one is fairly simple to make, with pineapple juice concentrate and coconut water as its base. The jelly is almost transparent, since you use coconut water without any pulp. All in all, this jelly is great stirred into hot oatmeal on a winter morning. It's certainly cheaper than a trip to the Caribbean!

- 2 cups (400 g) granulated white sugar
- 2 tablespoons (24 g) *granulated less-sugar* pectin
- 3 cups (720 ml) *unsweetened* plain coconut water without pulp
- ¾ cup (180 ml) thawed frozen unsweetened pineapple juice concentrate

1. Mix ¼ cup (50 g) sugar and the pectin in a small bowl until uniform.

2. Stir the coconut water and pineapple juice concentrate in a large saucepan. Set it over medium-high heat and add the pectin mixture. Stir constantly to dissolve the granulated ingredients. Bring to a boil you can't stir down, stirring often.

3. Add the remaining 1¾ cups (350 g) sugar and stir constantly to dissolve the sugar. Bring back to a full boil, stirring occasionally. Boil undisturbed for 2 minutes.

4. Turn off the heat, remove the pan from the burner, and set aside for 1–2 minutes to let all the bubbling stop. Skim any foamy impurities with a tablespoon.

5. Transfer to four *clean* ½ pint (236 ml) jars or other containers, leaving about ½ inch (1 cm) headspace in each. Cover or seal. Cool at room temperature for no more than 1 hour, then refrigerate or freeze.

More

Beat about 1 tablespoon (12 g) of this jelly into whipping cream, instead of sugar, for a tasty topping for tropical desserts or sundaes.

Pomegranate Jelly

MAKES: about 4 cups (960 ml)
FRIDGE: up to 1 month
FREEZER: up to 1 year
May be traditionally canned (see page 436)

Too many versions of pomegranate jelly are so sweet that the natural, sour-bitter notes from pomegranates are lost. The whole thing tastes like red sugar water. We cut down on the sugar in our batches so that the clear, beautiful jelly retains those prized flavors. And we add pomegranate molasses, a thick, reduced pomegranate condiment that gives us an even bigger flavor punch, for an even more urbane treat.

> 2¼ cups (450 g) granulated white sugar
> 3 tablespoons (36 g) *granulated less-sugar* pectin
> 4 cups (960 ml) *unsweetened pure* pomegranate juice
> 1 tablespoon (16 g) pomegranate molasses
> 1 tablespoon (15 ml) lemon juice

1. Mix ¼ cup (50 g) sugar and the pectin in a small bowl until uniform.

2. Put the pomegranate juice, pomegranate molasses, and lemon juice in a large saucepan. Set it over medium-high heat and add the pectin mixture. Stir constantly to dissolve the granulated ingredients. Bring to a boil you can't stir down, stirring often.

3. Add the remaining 2 cups (400 g) sugar and stir constantly to dissolve the sugar. Bring back to a full boil, stirring occasionally. Boil undisturbed for 1 minute.

4. Turn off the heat, remove the pan from the burner, and set aside for 1–2 minutes to let all the bubbling stop. Skim any foamy impurities with a tablespoon.

5. Transfer to four *clean* ½ pint (236 ml) jars or other containers, leaving about ½ inch (1 cm) headspace in each. Cover or seal. Cool at room temperature for no more than 1 hour, then refrigerate or freeze.

More

Spice the jelly by adding one 2 inch (5 cm) cinnamon stick, 3–5 allspice berries, and/or 1 star anise pod with the pectin mixture. Fish out and discard the spices before jarring.

Kiwi Jam

MAKES: 4 cups (960 ml)
FRIDGE: up to 3 weeks
FREEZER: up to 1 year

Kiwi jam is a rare delicacy: emerald green, thick yet refreshing, a little slushy but also light on the palate. The subtle flavors need time to ripen in the fridge or freezer before they're at their peak. Although kiwi jam is great on toast and other breakfast goodies, it's also a nice treat painted across white chocolate bark.

> 1½ cups (300 g) granulated white sugar
> 3 tablespoons (36 g) *granulated less-sugar* pectin
> 1 pound 14 ounces (850 g) kiwi fruit (about 6 large)
> 1 tablespoon (15 ml) lime juice

1. Mix ¼ cup (50 g) sugar and the pectin in a small bowl until uniform.

2. Halve each kiwi through its equator (that is, the horizontal center line if you were to stand the fruit on its stem or blossom end). Skin the fruits (see the TIP on page 96), then cut out the white inner middles. Chop the remaining fruit into ½ inch (1 cm) pieces.

Clockwise from bottom: Kiwi Jam (page 94), Pomegranate Jelly (page 94), and Mango Jam (page 97)

3. Put the kiwi into a large saucepan and stir in the lime juice. Set the pan over medium-high heat and add the pectin mixture. Stir constantly to dissolve the granulated ingredients. Bring to a boil you can't stir down, stirring often.

4. Add the remaining 1¼ cups (250 g) sugar. Stir constantly to dissolve the sugar and mash some of the fruit against the inside of the pan. Bring back to a full boil, stirring often. Boil undisturbed for 1 minute.

5. Turn off the heat, remove the pan from the burner, and set aside for 1–2 minutes to let all the bubbling stop. Skim any foamy impurities with a tablespoon.

6. Transfer to four *clean* ½ pint (236 ml) jars or other containers, leaving about ½ inch (1 cm) headspace in each. Cover or seal. Cool at room temperature for no more than 1 hour, then refrigerate or freeze. In the fridge, the jam may not gel for 24 hours.

Tip
The best way to peel a kiwi is use a flatware spoon to run it around the *inside* of the peel of the halved fruit, thereby skinning (or shelling) the green fruit from its fuzzy exterior.

Quince Jelly

MAKES: about 3 cups (720 ml)
FRIDGE: up to 1 month
FREEZER: up to 1 year
May be traditionally canned (see page 436)

Time was, people harvested quinces to wrap in tissue paper and stash in drawers for the pleasant scent. The fruit would last rock-hard for quite a while, even beyond late autumn. But we can't imagine wasting quinces on a sachet! They make a gorgeous, delicately pink jelly with a flavor so subtle that it can actually be overpowered by butter. Best then to enjoy the jelly on a slice of warm quick bread.

2 pounds (900 g) ripe but hard quinces (about 4 large)
Water as necessary to cook the quinces
3 tablespoons (45 ml) lemon juice
About 3 cups (600 g) granulated sugar, or as necessary for the proper *volume* amount

1. Roughly chop the quinces: stems, seeds, skin, and all. Scrape the pieces, pulpy bits, and any juice on the cutting board into a large saucepan. Fill the pan with water until the quince bits are covered.

2. Set the pan over medium heat and bring to a simmer, stirring occasionally. Reduce the heat to medium-low and cover the pan. Cook, stirring once in a while, until the quince bits are quite tender when prodded with a fork, about 20 minutes.

3. Set up a jelly bag on a stand over a large bowl or a pot. (For alternatives to a jelly bag, see page 17.) Ladle and pour the contents of the pan into the bag. Set aside to drip for at least 12 hours or overnight.

4. Add the lemon juice to the liquid. Measure the volume of the amount of liquid in the bowl. You should have 3 cups (720 ml). If you have less, you must use as much sugar *by volume* in the next step as you have juice.

5. Clean that saucepan, pour the liquid into it, and set it over medium-high heat. Add the sugar (that is, the equivalent amount *by volume* to the liquid you have). Stir constantly to dissolve the sugar. Bring to a full boil, stirring often.

6. Attach a candy thermometer to the inside of the pan. Reduce the heat to medium and continue boiling, stirring occasionally, until the temperature reaches 220°F (104°C), about 12 minutes.

7. Turn off the heat, remove the pan from the burner, and set aside for 1–2 minutes. Skim any foamy impurities with a tablespoon.

8. Transfer to three *clean* ½ pint (236 ml) jars or other containers, leaving about ½ inch (1 cm) headspace in each. Cover or seal. Cool at room temperature for no more than 1 hour, then refrigerate or freeze. In the fridge, the jelly may not set for up to 48 hours.

More

For QUINCE-WINE JELLY, pour 1½ cups (180 ml) dry white wine into the saucepan with the quince bits. Then add more water to reach the required depth in the pan before cooking.

Mango Jam

MAKES: about 3 cups (720 ml)
FRIDGE: up to 3 weeks
FREEZER: up to 1 year
May be traditionally canned (see page 436)

Although many jams need pectin to reach a pulpy texture, mango jam is an exception because of the cooking process. For the best flavor, the mango puree must be cooked quite a while, allowing the fruit to give up its perfumy essence and concentrate as it bubbles. The results are quite amazing: a clean taste of fresh mangoes rendered into a smooth but opaque jam that cries out for buttered toast.

> 4¼ pounds (2 kg) mangoes (about 4 large), pitted, peeled, and roughly chopped
> 3 cups (600 g) granulated white sugar
> ½ cup (120 ml) lime juice

1. Scrape the chopped mango, any pulp, and all the juice into a food processor. Cover and pulse until the mixture looks like chunky applesauce.

2. Scrape every drop of that mixture into a large saucepan and set it over medium-high heat. Add the sugar and lime juice. Stir constantly to dissolve the sugar. Bring to a steady simmer *but not a full boil*, stirring often.

3. Reduce the heat to low and continue simmering *slowly*, stirring more and more often to prevent scorching, until the mixture has turned a light

honey color and thickened quite a bit, about 15 minutes.

4. Turn off the heat, remove the pan from the burner, and set aside for 1–2 minutes. Skim any foamy impurities with a tablespoon.

5. Transfer to three *clean* ½ pint (236 ml) jars or other containers, leaving about ½ inch (1 cm) headspace in each. Cover or seal. Cool at room temperature for no more than 1 hour, then refrigerate or freeze. In the fridge, the jam may not gel for 24 hours.

Next

Spread a little mango jam on a turkey sandwich with deli mustard, lettuce, and sliced tomatoes.

Persimmon Jam

MAKES: about 2 cups (480 ml)
FRIDGE: up to 3 weeks
FREEZER: up to 1 year

For the best persimmon jam, with a refined perfume and elegant sweetness, use only squatter Fuyu persimmons, the sort that can be sliced like tomatoes for winter salads. Hachiya persimmons are too soft to make a decent jam (and unfortunately too astringent before they're too soft). To pick the perfect Fuyus, look for a deep orange color and a firm texture but with some give in the skin. They should feel heavy to the hand and have a *very* delicate fragrance. Beware of dark spots, which can mold almost before you get the fruit home.

> 1¾ pounds (790 g) ripe, vaguely soft Fuyu persimmons (about 6)
> ¼ cup (60 ml) lime juice
> ¼ cup (60 ml) water
> 1¼ cups (250 g) granulated white sugar

1. Cut off the tops (or the brown, leafy bits and stems) of the persimmons. Chop them into ½ inch (1 cm) pieces.

2. Scrape all of the persimmon pieces, any pulp, and juice on the cutting board into a medium saucepan. Set it over medium heat and add the lime juice and water. Cook, stirring often, until the mixture comes to a medium simmer.

3. Cover the pan, reduce the heat to low, and simmer slowly, stirring quite often, until the persimmon pieces are very soft, about 10 minutes.

4. Uncover the pan, add the sugar, and increase the heat to medium-high. Stir constantly to dissolve the sugar. Bring to a full boil, stirring often.

5. Again, reduce the heat to low. Simmer *slowly*, stirring more and more often to prevent scorching, until the mixture is thick enough that you can run a wooden spoon through it at the bottom of the pan to create a line that holds its edges for a second, about 10 minutes.

6. Turn off the heat, remove the pan from the burner, and set aside for 1–2 minutes. Skim any foamy impurities with a tablespoon.

7. Transfer to two *clean* ½ pint (236 ml) jars or other containers, leaving about ½ inch (1 cm) headspace in each. Cover or seal. Cool at room temperature for no more than 1 hour, then refrigerate or freeze.

More

Spice this jam by adding up to 2 crushed *green* cardamom pods with the sugar. Remove the hulls (but not the seeds) before bottling.

Lychee Jelly

MAKES: about 3 cups (720 ml)
FRIDGE: up to 1 month
FREEZER: up to 1 year
May be traditionally canned (see page 436)

Bottled lychee juice is the answer to capturing the fruit's superlative, delicate perfume in this easy jelly. (The fruit itself can be difficult to work with, given its large pits and pulpy texture.) Admittedly, the juice has been processed, but that means the flavors are concentrated enough that it can become an almost translucent jelly in no time.

> 2 cups (400 g) granulated white sugar
> 2 tablespoons (24 g) *granulated less-sugar* pectin
> 3 cups (720 ml) *unsweetened* lychee juice

1. Mix ¼ cup (50 g) sugar and the pectin in a small bowl until uniform.

2. Pour the juice into a large saucepan. Set it over medium-high heat and add the pectin mixture. Stir constantly to dissolve the granulated ingredients. Bring to a boil you can't stir down, stirring often.

3. Add the remaining 1¾ cups (350 g) sugar and stir constantly to dissolve the sugar. Bring back to a full boil, stirring often. Boil undisturbed for 1 minute.

4. Turn off the heat, remove the pan from the burner, and set aside for 1–2 minutes. Skim any foamy impurities with a tablespoon.

5. Transfer to three *clean* ½ pint (236 ml) jars or other containers, leaving about ½ inch (1 cm) headspace in each. Cover or seal. Cool at room temperature for no more than 1 hour, then refrigerate or freeze. In the fridge, the jelly may not set for up to 48 hours.

More

Balance that characteristic lychee perfume with a kick of heat: Add 2–3 stemmed, dried chilis de árbol with the sugar. Fish out and discard the chilis before bottling.

Guava Jam

MAKES: about 2 cups (480 ml)
FRIDGE: up to 3 weeks
FREEZER: up to 1 year

Here's a tropical wonder, an almost juicy, red jam that's got guava's sour pop as well as that irresistible fragrance. We like to make *jam* with fresh guavas (rather than a jelly from guava juice) because the pulpy fruit allows for a luxurious, silken texture. Choose yellow guavas with a hint of pink blush but no brown spots. The fruit should give just a little when gently squeezed and should have its distinct if subtle perfume.

> 1 pound (450 g) ripe guavas (about 12 medium)
> 3 cups (720 ml) water
> 1 cup (200 g) granulated white sugar
> 2 tablespoons (30 ml) lime juice

1. Trim and discard the ends from the guavas, then cut each into quarters. Set them in a medium saucepan and add the water. Set the pan over medium-high heat and bring the mixture to a boil, stirring occasionally.

2. Reduce the heat to low and simmer, stirring more and more often to prevent scorching, until the fruit is very soft and mushy, about 15 minutes.

3. Turn off the heat and remove the pan from the burner. Cool for 5 minutes. Run the contents of the pan through a food mill into a medium bowl set below, thereby removing the seeds. (For an alternative to a food mill, see page 16.)

4. Clean the pan and return the guava puree to it. Set over medium-high heat and add the sugar and lime juice. Stir constantly to dissolve the sugar. Bring to a steady simmer *but not a full boil*, stirring often.

5. Reduce the heat to low and simmer slowly, stirring quite often, until thickened enough that you can run a wooden spoon through the mixture at the bottom of the pan to make a line that holds its edges for a second, about 10 minutes.

6. Turn off the heat, remove the pan from the burner, and set aside for 1–2 minutes. Skim any foamy impurities with a tablespoon.

7. Transfer to two *clean* ½ pint (236 ml) jars or other containers, leaving about ½ inch (1 cm) headspace in each. Cover or seal. Cool at room temperature for no more than 1 hour, then refrigerate or freeze. In the fridge, the jam may not gel for 24 hours.

Next
Guava jam is a treat with sorbet, particularly pineapple or lemon sorbet. Spoon just a little on top, then sprinkle on some chopped salted nuts, particularly shelled pistachios.

Lime-Ginger Jelly

MAKES: about 2 cups (480 ml)
FRIDGE: up to 1 month
FREEZER: up to 1 year
May be traditionally canned (see page 436)

This sour confection is a great antidote to winter. Since it's made with several juices, all of which you can buy, it's not a lot of effort for a bit of sunshine during gray days. Lime is the predominant flavor, so it's best to use fresh juice, rather than one from concentrate, for a bold pop. If you're going to the trouble to squeeze fresh lime juice, remember that limes can dry out as they sit in storage. Look for large limes that are heavy to the hand without thick, leathery skins. You'll need 6 to 8 for this recipe.

> 1½ cups (300 g) granulated white sugar
> 2 tablespoons (24 g) *granulated less-sugar* pectin
> 1¼ cups (300 ml) lime juice
> ¾ cup (180 ml) *unsweetened* pineapple juice
> 2 tablespoons (30 ml) ginger juice
> ⅛ teaspoon vanilla extract

1. Mix ¼ cup (50 g) sugar and the pectin in a small bowl until uniform.

2. Combine the lime juice, pineapple juice, ginger juice, and vanilla in a medium saucepan. Set it over medium-high heat and add the pectin mixture. Stir constantly to dissolve the granulated ingredients. Bring to a boil you can't stir down, stirring often.

3. Add the remaining 1¼ cups (250 g) sugar and stir constantly to dissolve the sugar. Bring back to a full boil, stirring often. Boil undisturbed for 1 minute.

4. Turn off the heat, remove the pan from the burner, and set aside for 1–2 minutes. Skim any foamy impurities with a tablespoon.

5. Transfer to two *clean* ½ pint (236 ml) jars or other containers, leaving about ½ inch (1 cm) headspace in each. Cover or seal. Cool at room temperature for no more than 1 hour, then refrigerate or freeze.

Next

For COCONUT-LIME-GINGER JELLY substitute unsweetened, pulp-free coconut water for the pineapple juice.

Rose Jelly

MAKES: about 2 cups (480 ml)
FRIDGE: up to 1 month
FREEZER: up to 1 year
May be traditionally canned (see page 436)

Back in the day, rose jelly was made with roses from the garden, a perfumy treat that added a pale pink, glossy glow when spread on tarts. Unfortunately, most roses these days have chemical spray or fertilizer residue. Our best bet for rose jelly—and a far simpler solution than raising your own roses—is to use culinary-grade dried rosebuds, available in almost all Middle Eastern markets and from online suppliers. The resulting jelly is a floral wonder, best in small doses with a flaky pastry.

1 cup (20 g) dried culinary rosebuds
2 cups (480 ml) *boiling* water
2 cups (400 g) granulated white sugar
3 tablespoons (36 g) *granulated less-sugar* pectin
2 tablespoons (30 ml) *fresh* lemon juice (see the TIP)

1. Pinch off the stem end of each rosebud. Crumble the buds into a medium, heat-safe bowl or (better yet) a large, heat-safe glass measuring vessel. Add the boiling water, stir gently, and steep at room temperature for 1 hour.

2. Meanwhile, mix 2 tablespoons (25 g) sugar and the pectin in a small bowl until uniform.

3. Pour the rose water through a fine-mesh sieve or a cheesecloth-lined colander into a medium saucepan. Gently press against the rosebuds with the back of a wooden spoon to extract as much liquid as you can. The rose water will be an unpleasant gray-brown. No worries. Stir in the lemon juice.

4. Set the pan over medium-high heat and bring the mixture to a boil. (Notice it's turned pale pink.) Add the pectin mixture and stir constantly to dissolve the granulated ingredients. Bring to a boil you can't stir down, stirring often.

5. Add the remaining 1¾ cups plus 2 tablespoons (375 g) sugar and stir constantly to dissolve the sugar. Bring back to a full boil, stirring occasionally. Boil undisturbed for 1 minute.

6. Turn off the heat, remove the pan from the burner, and set aside for 1–2 minutes. Skim any foamy impurities with a tablespoon.

7. Transfer to two *clean* ½ pint (236 ml) jars or other containers, leaving about ½ inch (1 cm) headspace in each. Cover or seal. Cool at room temperature for no more than 1 hour, then refrigerate or freeze.

Tip

Lemon juice will change the pH enough that the gray-brown rose water will turn pink. However, some bottlings of lemon juice are ultra-processed and can have a lower pH. Use fresh lemon juice for the perfect color.

Front to back:
Rose Jelly (page 100)
and Hibiscus Jelly
(page 102)

Hibiscus Jelly

MAKES: about 4 cups (960 ml)
FRIDGE: up to 1 month
FREEZER: up to 1 year
May be traditionally canned (see page 436)

The intense floral flavor of perfumy, sour hibiscus jelly is a terrific addition to a deeply flavored beef stew; just stir in a little at the last moment of cooking. Look for dried hibiscus flowers in health-food stores and many large supermarkets among the teas and infusions. Hibiscus jelly is such a treat that we always make a slightly larger batch, since a jar is a great house gift.

> 5 cups (1200 ml) water
> 1½ cups (60 g) dried hibiscus flowers
> 1½ cups (300 g) granulated white sugar
> 3 tablespoons (36 g) *granulated less-sugar* pectin
> 2 tablespoons (30 ml) lemon juice

1. Bring the water to a boil in a medium saucepan set over high heat. Add the hibiscus flowers and turn off the heat. Remove the pan from the burner, cover, and steep for 1 hour.

2. Meanwhile, mix ½ cup (100 g) sugar and the pectin in a small bowl until uniform.

3. Strain the hibiscus water through a fine-mesh sieve or a cheesecloth-lined colander into a medium bowl. Do not press or squeeze the flowers in any way. (See the TIP.) Wipe out the saucepan and return the strained liquid to it. Stir in the lemon juice

4. Set the pan over medium-high heat and add the pectin mixture. Stir constantly to dissolve the granulated ingredients. Bring to a boil you can't stir down, stirring often.

5. Add the remaining 1 cup (200 g) sugar and stir constantly to dissolve the sugar. Bring back to a full boil, stirring often. Boil undisturbed for 1 minute.

6. Turn off the heat, remove the pan from the burner, and set aside for 1–2 minutes. Skim any foamy impurities with a tablespoon.

7. Transfer to four *clean* ½ pint (236 ml) jars or other containers, leaving about ½ inch (1 cm) headspace in each. Cover or seal. Cool at room temperature for no more than 1 hour, then refrigerate or freeze. The jelly may not reach its best flavor for 48 hours.

Tip
Dried hibiscus flowers can be dirty—not just sandy, but muddy. You *must* strain the tea through a fine-mesh sieve or cheesecloth to remove the grit. Do not press the flowers against the sieve or cloth, lest they release that muck into the jelly.

Spiced Hibiscus Jelly

MAKES: about 4 cups (960 ml)
FRIDGE: up to 1 month
FREEZER: up to 1 year
May be traditionally canned (see page 436)

Or maybe we should call it *spicy hibiscus jelly*? We modeled this recipe on a traditional jelly from Nigeria: zobo jelly, a blend of hibiscus flowers, spices, and fiery chilis. This one's probably not right for morning toast, but it's definitely right for charcuterie, hummus, and cheese boards. It'd also be great as a finish to coconut-based curries: Stir in 1 or 2 teaspoons at the end of the cooking process.

> 5 cups (1200 ml) water
> 1¾ cups (70 g) dried hibiscus flowers
> 1 fresh red thin chili, such as a bird's eye, stemmed and thinly sliced
> One 1 inch (2.5 cm) piece of peeled fresh ginger, thinly sliced
> One 1 inch (2.5 cm) cinnamon stick
> 1½ cups (300 g) granulated white sugar
> 3 tablespoons (36 g) *granulated less-sugar* pectin
> 2 tablespoons (30 ml) lemon juice

1. Bring the water to a boil in a large saucepan set over medium heat. Stir in the hibiscus flowers, chili, ginger, and cinnamon stick. Turn off the heat, take the pan off the burner, cover, and steep for 1 hour.

2. Meanwhile, mix ½ cup (100 g) sugar and the pectin in a small bowl until uniform.

3. Strain the hibiscus and spice tea through a fine-mesh sieve or a cheesecloth-lined colander into a bowl. Do not press against the flowers to drain them. (See the TIP for Hibiscus Jelly on page 102.) Wipe out the pan and return the strained tea to it. Stir in the lemon juice.

4. Set the pan over medium-high heat and add the pectin mixture. Stir constantly to dissolve the granulated ingredients. Bring to a boil you can't stir down, stirring often.

5. Add the remaining 1 cup (200 g) sugar and stir constantly to dissolve the sugar. Bring back to a full boil, stirring often. Boil undisturbed for 1 minute.

6. Turn off the heat, remove the pan from the burner, and set aside for 1–2 minutes. Skim any foamy impurities with a tablespoon.

7. Transfer to four *clean* ½ pint (236 ml) jars or other containers, leaving about ½ inch (1 cm) headspace in each. Cover or seal. Cool at room temperature for no more than 1 hour, then refrigerate or freeze. The jelly may not reach its best flavor for 48 hours.

More
Add up to 5 whole cloves, 5 allspice berries, and/or 10 black peppercorns with the other spices and aromatics.

Coffee Jelly

MAKES: about 2 cups (480 ml)
FRIDGE: up to 1 month
FREEZER: up to 1 year
May be traditionally canned (see page 436)

In essence, pectin works as a gelling agent when (and if) the pH of a mixture changes to become more acidic. That's why there's lemon or lime juice added to almost every preserve, jam, or jelly in this chapter. (Unless, of course, we reduce the liquid until the pH becomes more acidic naturally or we skip the pectin entirely for another technique, essentially candy-making by morphing sugar into a soft set.) The whole point of mentioning this is that the requisite amount of lemon or lime juice doesn't work well with the flavors of coffee. So we've added a little balsamic vinegar to this smooth, mellow jelly. Watch out: The coffee-pectin combo has a tendency to roil as it boils.

> 2 cups (400 g) granulated white sugar
> 3 tablespoons (36 g) *granulated less-sugar* pectin
> 2 cups (480 ml) water
> 2 tablespoons (30 ml) balsamic vinegar
> 2 tablespoons (12 g) instant espresso powder

1. Mix ¼ cup (50 g) sugar and the pectin in a small bowl until uniform.

2. Stir the water, vinegar, and espresso powder in a very large saucepan until the espresso powder dissolves. Set the pan over medium-high heat and add the pectin mixture. Stir constantly until the granulated ingredients dissolve. Bring to a boil you can't stir down, stirring often.

3. Add the remaining 1¾ cups (350 g) sugar and stir constantly to dissolve the sugar. Bring back to a full boil, stirring often. Boil undisturbed for 1 minute. If at any point the mixture roils up in a foamy mess, remove the pan from the burner, reduce the heat to low, and carry on.

4. Turn off the heat, remove the pan from the burner, and set aside for 1–2 minutes. Skim any foamy impurities with a tablespoon.

5. Transfer to two *clean* ½ pint (236 ml) jars or other containers, leaving about ½ inch (1 cm) headspace in each. Cover or seal. Cool at room temperature for no more than 1 hour, then refrigerate or freeze. The jelly may not reach its best flavor for 24 hours.

Next
Spread a little of this jelly (plus butter, of course!) on a slice of pound cake or even a plain cake donut.

Chai Jelly

MAKES: about 3 cups (720 ml)
FRIDGE: up to 1 month
FREEZER: up to 1 year
May be traditionally canned (see page 436)

Long ago, on a photo shoot for one of our previous cookbooks, the photographer's assistant made her a cup of chai every afternoon. It filled our kitchen with such spicy, warming notes that we both fell in love with that blend of flavors, particularly on busy days, as if a cup of chai could open a peaceful spot in a hectic schedule. It wasn't too long before we wanted to try making chai jelly. Although we can't add milk to a refrigerator jam, we can create the essential flavors of chai in this brown, translucent jelly.

> 5 tea bags of plain black tea, preferably English breakfast tea
> One 2 inch (5 cm) cinnamon stick
> One 1 inch (2.5 cm) piece of fresh ginger, peeled and cut into 3 pieces
> 2 *green* cardamom pods
> 1 teaspoon whole cloves
> 1 teaspoon coriander seeds
> 2 cups (480 ml) *boiling* water
> 2 cups (400 g) granulated white sugar
> 3 tablespoons (36 g) *granulated less-sugar* pectin
> 1 tablespoon (30 ml) lemon juice

1. Put the tea bags, cinnamon stick, ginger, cardamom pods, cloves, and coriander seeds in a medium heat-safe bowl or a large heat-safe glass measuring vessel. Pour in the boiling water. Steep at room temperature for 1 hour.

2. Meanwhile, mix ¼ cup (50 g) sugar and the pectin in a small bowl until uniform.

3. Strain the spiced tea through a fine-mesh strainer or a cheesecloth-lined colander into a small saucepan below. Squeeze the tea bags to extract as much tea as you can.

4. Set the pan over medium-high heat and add the pectin mixture and lemon juice. Stir constantly to dissolve the granulated ingredients. Bring to a boil you can't stir down, stirring often.

5. Add the remaining 1¾ cups (350 g) sugar and stir constantly to dissolve the sugar. Bring back to a full boil, stirring often. Boil undisturbed for 1 minute.

6. Turn off the heat, remove the pan from the burner, and set aside for 1–2 minutes. Skim any foamy impurities with a tablespoon.

7. Transfer to three *clean* ½ pint (236 ml) jars or other containers, leaving about ½ inch (1 cm) headspace in each. Cover or seal. Cool at room temperature for no more than 1 hour, then refrigerate or freeze. The jelly may not reach its best flavor for 24 hours.

More
Add even more spices with the other spices: up to 10 black peppercorns, 5 allspice berries, 1 bay leaf, and/or 1 makrut lime leaf.

Sweet Orange Marmalade

MAKES: about 4 cups (960 ml)
FRIDGE: up to 3 weeks
FREEZER: up to 1 year
May be traditionally canned (see page 436)

If you're not a fan of marmalades (that is, preserves made from citrus pulp and zest or sometimes even peel), you might want to start expanding your palate with this recipe. This is not the go-to standard orange marmalade—that's made with bitter Seville oranges, which are hard to find in North America. So we start our parade of marmalades with one made from sweeter navel oranges for a more delicate, less assertive flavor.

> 1 pound 10 ounces (750 g) navel oranges (about 5 medium)
> 1½ cups (360 ml) water
> 1 medium lemon
> 2 cups (400 g) granulated white sugar
> 3 tablespoons (36 g) *granulated less-sugar* pectin

1. Use a vegetable peeler to remove only the orange zest in strips from the oranges (for more information, see "Special matters for marmalades" on page 31). Get as much of the zest as you can, including smaller bits from either end of the oranges. Thinly shred the wider swaths crosswise into matchsticks.

2. Put the zest in a large saucepan. Add ¾ cup (180 ml) water and bring to a boil over medium-high heat. *Cover*, reduce the heat to very low, and simmer slowly for 10 minutes.

3. Meanwhile, slice off and discard the white pith from each of the oranges (as above, see page 31). Slice off and discard both the zest *and* pith from the lemon, too. Halve the oranges and lemon. Cut out the white core from all the citrus. Also, remove any seeds from the lemon.

4. Tear the oranges and lemons into chunks. Put them (and any juice) in a food processor. Add

¼ cup (50 g) sugar and the pectin. Cover and pulse the food processor repeatedly to create a chunky puree and dissolve the granulated ingredients.

5. Uncover and remove the processor's blade. Pour and scrape the contents into the pan with the simmering zest. Also add the remaining ¾ cup (180 ml) water. Raise the heat to medium and bring the mixture to a boil you can't stir down, stirring quite often.

6. Add the remaining 1¾ cups (350 g) sugar; stir constantly to dissolve the sugar. Bring back to a full boil, stirring often. Boil undisturbed for 1 minute.

7. Turn off the heat, remove the pan from the burner, and set aside for 1–2 minutes. Skim any foamy impurities with a tablespoon.

8. Transfer to four *clean* ½ pint (236 ml) jars or other containers, leaving about ½ inch (1 cm) headspace in each. Cover or seal. Cool at room temperature for no more than 1 hour, then refrigerate or freeze.

Next
Marmalade of any sort makes an excellent glaze on a pork loin or leg of lamb. Microwave a tablespoon or two with a little water, just until softened. Stir it into a glaze and paint on the roast for the final 15 minutes in the oven.

Sour Orange Marmalade

MAKES: about 4 cups (960 ml)
FRIDGE: up to 3 weeks
FREEZER: up to 1 year
May be traditionally canned (see page 436)

Nothing beats a jar of homemade marmalade: The glistening jelly holds the strips of zest and bits of pulpy fruit in the perfect way to catch the light. The grail of all marmalades is one made with bitter

Clockwise from bottom: Grapefruit Marmalade (page 110),
Sour Orange Marmalade (page 105), Sugar-Free Orange
Marmalade (page 107), Blood Orange Marmalade (page 108),
and Lemon Marmalade (page 110)

or sour oranges. Unfortunately, these are hard to find in North America. But we can get very close to the traditional flavor with sour or bitter orange *juice*, available at Hispanic supermarkets and from online suppliers. Make sure the juice is unsweetened—that is, pure and sour.

> 10½ ounces (300 g) navel oranges (about 2 medium)
> ½ cup (120 ml) water, plus more as necessary
> 2½ cups (500 g), granulated white sugar
> 2 tablespoons (24 g) *granulated less-sugar* pectin
> 2½ cups (600 ml) *unsweetened* bottled sour orange juice

1. Use a vegetable peeler to remove only the orange zest in strips from the oranges (for more information, see "Special matters for marmalades" on page 31). Get as much of the zest as you can, including smaller bits from either end of the oranges. Thinly shred the wider swaths into matchsticks.

2. Put all the zest in a large saucepan. Add the water and bring to a boil over medium-high heat. *Cover*, reduce the heat to very low, and simmer slowly for 10 minutes, making sure the pan doesn't dry out. (If it does, add a little more water and continue simmering.)

3. Meanwhile, mix ½ cup (100 g) sugar and the pectin in a small bowl until uniform.

4. Slice off and discard the white pith from each of the oranges (as above, see page 31). Cut the oranges in half and cut out the white cores. Tear the oranges into chunks, put them (and any juice) in a food processor, cover, and pulse until a chunky puree.

5. Uncover the processor and remove the blade. Pour and scrape the contents into the saucepan with the simmering zest. Stir in the juice and the pectin mixture. Raise the heat to medium and bring the mixture to a boil you can't stir down, stirring often.

6. Add the remaining 2 cups (400 g) sugar and stir constantly to dissolve the sugar. Bring back to a full boil, stirring often. Boil undisturbed for 1 minute.

7. Turn off the heat, remove the pan from the burner, and set aside for 1–2 minutes. Skim any foamy impurities with a tablespoon.

8. Transfer to four *clean* ½ pint (236 ml) jars or other containers, leaving about ½ inch (1 cm) headspace in each. Cover or seal. Cool at room temperature for no more than 1 hour, then refrigerate or freeze.

Tip

Citrus fruits are often sheathed in a thin, clear, food-grade wax for transport and storage. For the best results, use a clean sponge (and no soap) to gently wash the fruit, thereby removing the wax.

Sugar-Free Orange Marmalade

MAKES: about 3 cups (720 ml)
FRIDGE: up to 2 weeks
FREEZER: up to 6 months

Here's a guilt-free way to bring sunshine into a winter day…or to guarantee the hope for better weather ahead in the middle of winter when citrus floods our supermarkets and you want to be reminded that summer's on the way. A little *brown-sugar* substitute adds a depth of flavor to this sweet marmalade.

> 1 pound 10 ounces (750 g) navel oranges (about 5 medium)
> 1 cup (240 ml) water
> 1 medium lemon
> 3 tablespoons (36 g) *granulated less-sugar* pectin
> 1 cup *1-to-1 (by volume)* granulated white-sugar substitute
> ¼ cup *1-to-1 (by volume)* granulated brown-sugar substitute

1. Use a vegetable peeler to remove only the orange zest in strips from the oranges (see page 31). Get as much of the zest as you can, including smaller bits from either end of the oranges. Thinly shred the wider swaths into matchsticks.

2. Put the zest in a large saucepan. Add the water and bring to a boil over medium-high heat. *Cover*, reduce the heat to very low, and simmer slowly for 15 minutes.

3. Meanwhile, slice off and discard the white pith from each of the oranges (for more information, see "Special matters for marmalades" on page 31). Slice off and discard both the zest *and* pith from the lemon, too. Halve the oranges and lemon. Cut out the white core from the citrus. Also, remove any seeds from the lemon.

4. Tear the oranges and lemons into chunks. Put them (and any juice) in a food processor. Add the pectin. Cover and pulse the food processor repeatedly to create a chunky puree and dissolve the pectin.

5. Uncover and remove the processor's blade. Pour and scrape its contents into the pan with the simmering zest. Raise the heat to medium and bring the mixture to a boil you can't stir down, stirring often.

6. Add *both* sugar substitutes and cook, stirring constantly until dissolved. Bring back to a full boil, stirring often. Boil undisturbed for 1 minute.

7. Turn off the heat, remove the pan from the burner, and set aside for 1–2 minutes. Skim any foamy impurities with a tablespoon.

8. Transfer to three *clean* ½ pint (236 ml) jars or other containers, leaving about ½ inch (1 cm) headspace in each. Cover or seal. Cool at room temperature for no more than 1 hour, then refrigerate or freeze.

Next
Stir this marmalade until soft in a small bowl, then use it as a guilt-free topping for a cheesecake or between the layers of a layer cake.

Blood Orange Marmalade

MAKES: about 3 cups (720 ml)
FRIDGE: up to 3 weeks
FREEZER: up to 1 year
May be traditionally canned (see page 436)

We eagerly await the return of blood oranges to our supermarkets each winter. The fruit is less sweet than traditional oranges, often ruby in color, and a vitamin-rich treat on a cold day. Naturally, blood oranges make a gorgeous marmalade: the strips of zest and the fruit's pulp suspended in a translucent, red jelly, sometimes deeply carnelian, sometimes almost purple, and sometimes a pale red, almost pink, depending on the varietal. Less bitter than traditional orange marmalade, this one's a great addition to a cheese board, as well as a spread for toast.

> 2¼ pounds (1 kg) blood oranges (about 7 medium)
> 1¾ cups (420 ml) water
> 3 *small* lemons
> 2 tablespoons (24 g) *granulated less-sugar* pectin
> 2½ cups (500 g) granulated white sugar

1. Use a vegetable peeler to remove only the orange zest in strips from *three* of the oranges (see page 31). Get as much of the zest as you can, including smaller bits from either end of the oranges. Thinly shred the wider swaths crosswise into matchsticks.

2. Put the zest in a large saucepan. Add 1 cup (240 ml) water and bring to a boil over medium-high heat. *Cover*, reduce the heat to very low, and simmer slowly for 5 minutes.

3. Meanwhile, slice off and discard the white pith from each of the zested oranges (for more information, see "Special matters for marmalades" on page 31). Slice off and discard both the zest *and* pith from the remaining oranges and the lemons. Halve all of the oranges and lemon. Cut out the white cores from the citrus. Also, remove any seeds.

4. Tear the oranges and lemons into chunks. Put them (and any juice) in a food processor. Add the pectin. Cover and pulse the food processor repeatedly to create a chunky puree and dissolve the pectin.

5. Uncover and remove the processor's blade. Pour and scrape its contents into the pan with the simmering zest. Add the remaining ¾ cup (180 ml) water. Raise the heat to medium and bring the mixture to a boil you can't stir down, stirring often.

6. Add the sugar and stir constantly until dissolved. Bring back to a full boil, stirring often. Reduce the heat to low and simmer, stirring quite often, until the liquid is reduced to about half of its original volume and the mixture is darker and thick, about 15 minutes.

7. Turn off the heat, remove the pan from the burner, and set aside for 1–2 minutes. Skim any foamy impurities with a tablespoon.

8. Transfer to three *clean* ½ pint (236 ml) jars or other containers, leaving about ½ inch (1 cm) headspace in each. Cover or seal. Cool at room temperature for no more than 1 hour, then refrigerate or freeze.

More
For a little heat, add up to 1 teaspoon red pepper flakes with the sugar.

Clementine-Ginger Marmalade

MAKES: about 3 cups (720 ml)
FRIDGE: up to 3 weeks
FREEZER: up to 1 year
May be traditionally canned (see page 436)

Clementines are a sweet treat! They come into our markets in little boxes or bags, ready for noshing.

Save that flavor (and even enhance it with the spike of ginger) by turning them into a dark, full-bodied marmalade. By cooking whole slices of the clementines, rather than working with the zest and pulp separately, we can bring out the vanilla, herbaceous, and even sour notes of the fruit, a refined finish to this citrus preserve.

> 1 pound (450 g) *seedless* clementines (about 5 medium)
> 2 cups (480 ml) water
> 2½ cups (500 g) granulated white sugar
> 1 tablespoon (12 g) *granulated less-sugar* pectin
> ¼ cup (45 g) chopped crystallized ginger
> 2 tablespoons (30 ml) lemon juice

1. Slice each clementine in half through its equator (that is, the middle line between its blossom and stem ends). Slice the clementine halves as thinly as you can, removing and discarding all the seeds.

2. Place the clementine slices and water in a large saucepan. Set it over medium heat and bring to a simmer, stirring often. *Cover*, reduce the heat to very low, and simmer slowly until the fruit is quite soft, stirring occasionally, about 45 minutes.

3. Mix the sugar and pectin in a medium bowl until uniform. Pour it into the pan with the simmering clementines. Add the ginger and lemon juice. Raise the heat to medium and bring to a full simmer, uncovered, stirring often.

4. Reduce the heat to low and continue simmering, stirring occasionally, until the liquid in the pan is reduced to half of its original volume and the mixture is thick and jam-like, about 20 minutes.

5. Turn off the heat, remove the pan from the burner, and set aside for 1–2 minutes. Skim any foamy impurities with a tablespoon.

6. Transfer to three *clean* ½ pint (236 ml) jars or other containers, leaving about ½ inch (1 cm) headspace in each. Cover or seal. Cool at room temperature for no more than 1 hour, then refrigerate or freeze.

More

For SPICED CLEMENTINE MARMALADE, add 1 star anise pod and/or one 1 inch (2.5 cm) cinnamon stick to the clementines and water in step 2. Remove and discard them before continuing to step 3.

Grapefruit Marmalade

MAKES: about 4 cups (960 ml)
FRIDGE: up to 3 weeks
FREEZER: up to 1 year
May be traditionally canned (see page 436)

This marmalade is decidedly less assertive than most orange marmalades. It's more aromatic but less sour, particularly if you use pink or ruby-red grapefruits that have only the slightest bitter edge. Those grapefruits will make a gorgeous, thick marmalade, lots of fruit per spoonful. Make sure you save and use every bit of zest and pulp for the best texture.

- 2¼ pounds (1 kg) pink or ruby-red grapefruits (about 3 large), washed
- 1¼ cups (300 ml) water
- ⅛ teaspoon baking soda (to tone down the too-acidic notes)
- 3 cups (600 g) granulated white sugar
- 3 tablespoons (36 g) *granulated less-sugar* pectin

1. Remove only the zest in strips from *two* of the grapefruits with a vegetable peeler (for more information, see "Special matters for marmalades" on page 31). Get as much of the zest as you can, including smaller bits from either end. Thinly shred the wider strips lengthwise into matchsticks.

2. Put the zest in a large saucepan; add the water and baking soda. Bring to a boil over medium-high heat. *Cover*, reduce the heat to very low, and simmer slowly for 15 minutes.

3. Meanwhile, slice off and discard the white pith from the zested grapefruits (see page 31). Slice off and discard both the zest *and* the pith from the

remaining grapefruits. Halve all the grapefruits. Cut out the white cores.

4. Tear the grapefruits into chunks and remove any seeds. Put the chunks (and any juice) in a food processor. Add ¼ cup (50 g) sugar and the pectin. Cover and pulse the food processor repeatedly to create a chunky puree and dissolve the granulated ingredients.

5. Uncover and remove the processor's blade. Pour and scrape the contents into the pan with the simmering zest. Raise the heat to medium and bring the mixture to a boil you can't stir down, stirring often.

6. Reduce the heat to low and simmer for 2 minutes, stirring occasionally.

7. Raise the heat to medium and add the remaining 2¾ cups (550 g) sugar. Stir constantly until dissolved. Bring back to a full boil, stirring often. Boil undisturbed for 1 minute.

8. Turn off the heat, remove the pan from the burner, and set aside for 1–2 minutes. Skim any foamy impurities with a tablespoon.

9. Transfer to four *clean* ½ pint (236 ml) jars or other containers, leaving about ½ inch (1 cm) headspace in each. Cover or seal. Cool at room temperature for no more than 1 hour, then refrigerate or freeze.

More

For a more sophisticated marmalade, use 1 cup (240 ml) water plus ¼ cup (60 ml) Campari.

Lemon Marmalade

MAKES: about 3 cups (720 ml)
FRIDGE: up to 3 weeks
FREEZER: up to 1 year
May be traditionally canned (see page 436)

There's a choice when it comes to making a small batch of this bright, sour marmalade. You can use regular lemons for a bigger pucker in every spoonful. Or you can use Meyer lemons for a more delicate, aromatic flavor with natural notes of vanilla and almonds. Either way, you'll end up with a gorgeous spread.

> 1 pound (450 g) lemons (about 6 large)
> 1½ cups (360 ml) water
> 2 tablespoons (24 g) *granulated less-sugar* pectin
> 2½ cups (500 g) granulated white sugar

1. Remove only the zest in strips from the lemons with a vegetable peeler (for more information, see "Special matters for marmalades" on page 31). Get as much of the zest as you can, including smaller bits from either end. Thinly shred the wider strips lengthwise into matchsticks.

2. Put the zest in a large saucepan and add 1 cup (240 ml) water. Bring to a boil over medium-high heat, stirring occasionally. *Cover*, reduce the heat to very low, and simmer slowly for 5 minutes, stirring frequently.

3. Meanwhile, slice off and discard the white pith from the lemons (as above, see page 31). Halve the lemons and cut out their white cores.

4. Tear the lemons into chunks and remove any seeds. Put the chunks (and any juice) in a food processor. Add the pectin, cover, and pulse the food processor repeatedly to create a chunky puree and dissolve the pectin.

5. Uncover and remove the processor's blade. Pour and scrape the contents into the pan with the simmering zest. Add the remaining ½ cup (120 ml) water. Raise the heat to medium and bring the mixture to a boil you can't stir down, stirring often.

6. Raise the heat to medium, add the sugar, and stir constantly until dissolved. Bring back to a full boil, stirring often. Boil undisturbed for 1 minute.

7. Turn off the heat, remove the pan from the burner, and set aside for 1–2 minutes. Skim any foamy impurities with a tablespoon.

8. Transfer to three *clean* ½ pint (236 ml) jars or other containers, leaving about ½ inch (1 cm) headspace in each. Cover or seal. Cool at room temperature for no more than 1 hour, then refrigerate or freeze.

More
Lemon marmalade goes well with fresh herbs: Add up to 1 tablespoon (2 g) minced rosemary, thyme, mint, or tarragon leaves with the sugar.

Three-Citrus Marmalade

MAKES: about 4 cups (960 ml)
FRIDGE: up to 3 weeks
FREEZER: up to 1 year
May be traditionally canned (see page 436)

Although pink or ruby-red grapefruits make the best small-batch fridge or freezer grapefruit marmalade (page 110), more standard (and more sour) white grapefruit works best in this mélange of citrus fruits because of their more pronounced acidic notes and more assertive bitterness—all of which balances the sweet, vanilla-scented flavor of the tangerines.

> 1 large white grapefruit
> 2 *small* lemons
> 1⅓ pounds (605 g) thin-skinned tangerines (about 4 medium)
> 2½ cups (500 g) granulated white sugar
> 2 tablespoons (24 g) *granulated less-sugar* pectin
> ½ cup (120 ml) water
> Orange juice, as necessary to make up additional volume

1. Remove only the zest in strips from the grapefruit and lemons with a vegetable peeler (see page 31). Get as much of the zest as you can, including smaller bits from either end. Thinly shred the wider strips lengthwise into matchsticks.

2. Wash and peel 1 tangerine. Slice the peel into matchsticks. Peel all the remaining tangerines and discard these peels.

3. Mix ¼ cup (50 g) sugar and the pectin in a small bowl until uniform.

4. Put the grapefruit and lemon zest and the tangerine peel in a large saucepan. Add the water and bring to a boil over medium-high heat, stirring occasionally. *Cover*, reduce the heat to very low, and simmer slowly for 10 minutes, stirring frequently.

5. Meanwhile, slice off and discard the white pith from the grapefruit and lemons (for more information, see "Special matters for marmalades" on page 31). Halve all the citrus, including the tangerines. Cut out any white cores.

6. Tear the fruit into chunks and remove any seeds. Put the chunks (and any juice) in a food processor. Cover and pulse the food processor repeatedly to create a chunky puree. You should end up with 3 cups (720 ml) puree. If not, add orange juice as necessary to make up the *volume* amount.

7. Pour and scrape the puree into the pan with the simmering zest. Add the pectin mixture. Raise the heat to medium and bring the mixture to a boil you can't stir down, stirring often.

8. Add the remaining 2¼ cups (450 g) sugar; stir constantly to dissolve the sugar. Bring back to a full boil, stirring often. Boil undisturbed for 1 minute.

9. Turn off the heat, remove the pan from the burner, and set aside for 1–2 minutes. Skim any foamy impurities with a tablespoon.

10. Transfer to four *clean* ½ pint (236 ml) jars or other containers, leaving about ½ inch (1 cm) headspace in each. Cover or seal. Cool at room temperature for no more than 1 hour, then refrigerate or freeze.

More

For a much more sour marmalade, substitute limes for the lemons.

Carrot Marmalade

MAKES: about 3 cups (720 ml)
FRIDGE: up to 3 weeks
FREEZER: up to 1 year

Our last marmalade verges into territory covered in the next chapter: savory jams and conserves. We didn't put this recipe there because it is still a sweet treat without any dried spices, chopped nuts, or vinegar. It's definitely a preserve, but it's also the leading edge of what's to come: a less-sweet, slightly vegetal, elegant spread that has no pectin because it needs a long time over the heat to caramelize the sugars for a deeper, more layered finish.

> 3 medium lemons
> 1 pound 2 ounces (510 g) carrots (about 5 large), peeled
> 2 cups (480 ml) water
> 2½ cups (500 g) granulated white sugar
> 1 tablespoon (15 g) grated peeled fresh ginger

1. Grate the zest from the lemons with the large holes of a box grater. Make sure you leave as much of the white pith behind as you can.

2. Slice off and discard the remaining pith from each lemon, then *finely* chop the fruit and remove any seeds. Scrape the zest, fruit, and any juice on the cutting board into a large saucepan.

3. Grate the carrots into that saucepan through the large holes of a box grater. Pour in the water, then stir in the sugar and ginger.

4. Set the pan over medium-high heat. Attach a candy thermometer to the inside of the pan. Cook, stirring more and more often to prevent scorching, until the mixture reaches 220°F (104°C), about 15 minutes.

5. Turn off the heat, remove the pan from the burner, and set aside for 1–2 minutes.

6. Transfer to three *clean* ½ pint (236 ml) jars or other containers, leaving about ½ inch (1 cm) headspace in each. Cover or seal. Cool at room temperature for no more than 1 hour, then refrigerate or freeze.

More

Use this marmalade instead of sweet pickle relish on a hamburger or hot dog.

2

Savory Jams, Conserves, Chutneys, Relishes, and Tapenades

If you thought we went crazy with refrigerator and freezer jams, hold our beers. Or our baked potatoes. Or our grilled cheese sandwiches. Because this chapter has the condiments we pass around *after* breakfast to bump up the flavors for better meals. Sure, we often have a few opened jars of jelly in the fridge, but we always have a whole door shelf allocated to these spreads, dips, and toppers!

These are the first savory condiments in this book, the vast majority not right for toast, but each more assertively flavored than almost any of those in the first chapter. What's more, the sugar load drops in this chapter when compared to the first chapter. It also drops (generally, if not consistently) over the *course* of this chapter, from savory jams and conserves to relishes and tapenades.

Among the ingredients, we've got lots more nuts, chilis, vinegars, aromatics, and spices here than appeared in Chapter 1. In some ways, we've stepped into more polished territory—not that preserves are somehow unrefined, but that these recipes use a broader palette of flavors, most probably geared to adult palates. Before we get to them, let's talk through some overall points to make sure of your success.

More definitions

Since we writers love definitions, let's have a few more!

- A **savory jam** is, frankly, an oxymoron. It's sweet, yes; but it can include onions, shallots, or even bacon that tip the jam away from toast and toward a topper for proteins off the grill or root vegetables out of the oven. Over the years, we've pushed the notion of a savory jam to include carrots, cardamom, and kimchi for the sheer joy of wild and wooly flavors.

- By contrast, a **conserve** is admittedly closer to a traditional jam than a so-called savory jam. The major differences are 1) it's less sweet and 2) it often has other aromatics, tomatoes, and/ or nuts in tow, thus making it great with the likes of roasted root vegetables (although we do love a smear of Blackberry Conserve on toast—see page 129).

- A **chutney** is a vinegary-sweet condiment, traditionally served with curries or alongside flatbreads like naan. The two of us also use chutneys liberally on burgers, hot dogs, and grilled sausages. We'll even stir a dollop of chutney into chicken, tuna, or pasta salad. Most of our chutneys are in the English style— in other words, they sieve Indian flavors through Western European cooking techniques and so are sort of like vinegary jams, although we also include a few relatively dry or fresh chutneys.

- A **relish** may be the quintessential condiment: a vinegary, vegetable-based concoction, terrific as a topper for just about anything off the grill, as a spread in a packed sandwich, or as a dab on a cracker to curb the appetite before dinner.

- Finally, a **tapenade** is usually a minced olive-caper spread. (The name comes from the Provençal word for capers: *tapenas*.) A tapenade often includes minced anchovies (although not always). It may also include garlic, lemon juice, or herbs. There are probably as many so-called *authentic* tapenade recipes as there are cooks along the Mediterranean. Given those variations, we've felt free to blow up the concept to encompass sun-dried tomatoes and even jarred artichoke hearts, all in the spirit of creating a great spread for a cheese board or on plain crackers.

Equipment notes

You'll notice that many items in this chapter are cooked in a saucepan, when you might otherwise expect a skillet (for example, for frying bacon or caramelizing onions). Compared to a skillet, a saucepan offers a more concentrated heat source (because of the smaller bottom) and permits a more measured reduction (because of its depth, which exposes less of what's inside to the air above).

Some of these recipes, particularly for relishes, use a food processor (or less frequently, a blender). In no instance have we used a turbo blender, like a Vitamix. The final consistency of, say, a pickle relish out of that powerhouse is just too mushy.

Some of these recipes, especially tapenades, would traditionally be made in a mortar with a pestle. We've opted for more modern appliances but keep in mind this caveat: Watch a food processor or blender carefully so you don't inadvertently make baby food. Pulse the machine until you get the hang of turning it off at exactly the right moment.

▲ We find a food processor is a great, less-fussy tool for relishes and pickles.

▲ Take your time and work in batches. (Culinary kitchen gloves are the best!)

Squeezing by the handful

In many of these recipes, you must salt or brine a vegetable before proceeding, so you can extract some of the excess moisture. Afterwards, you pick up handfuls of the vegetable and squeeze the shreds dry.

Here are a few points for finessing this technique. First, start the process in a large bowl, even for relatively small amounts, because nothing is quite so irritating as sloshing salty liquid out of a small bowl and onto your counter. Second, clean and dry your hands or put on culinary kitchen gloves. Third, to extract more moisture, pick up small batches that easily fit in one hand, not giant wads that require a two-fisted effort. But once you have a single handful, give it a two-handed embrace (as in the photo above). Finally, squeeze the vegetable over the sink or a second bowl so you can easily get rid of the excess liquid.

The wooden spoon test

Longtime canners use a candy thermometer to determine the exact set in sugar-rich recipes like savory jams and chutneys. More professional canners may even use a litmus test to determine the pH. Unfortunately, since we're working with small batches, we often don't have a lot of liquid left in the pan for an accurate temperature measurement. And we're not aiming for shelf-stability, so we're less interested in the pH.

Our test is more visual. For many recipes, it means running a wooden spoon through the mixture to determine the amount of liquid left and its chance of gelling. To do so, scrape a wooden spoon through whatever you're making to reveal the bottom of the saucepan. You may have to dig down in chunkier chutneys. The line you make should hold its edges for a second or two before closing up. More importantly, there should still be enough (even solid-rich) liquid left so it *can* flow back in place. The liquid should also have a glossy if perhaps translucent look. Get the pan off the heat the moment you reach this point to avoid drying out the chutney or relish.

Yields

Many of these recipes make less than the ones in the first chapter. Some here are special-occasion condiments; others require more expensive ingredients. We tried to calibrate the yields based on about how quickly we use something at our house: more Red Pepper Jam (page 124), less Spiced Tapenade (page 186).

Mustard seeds

Since we use them a fair amount in this chapter, we should add a few words about this specialty spice. Essentially, mustard seeds come in three colors: yellow, brown, and black (although each color represents manifold varietals). As a rule, brown and black mustard seeds are spicier than yellow ones, which have a more rounded flavor with a hint of sweetness in the overtones. In light of our supermarkets and for the purposes of our recipes, brown and black mustard seeds are interchangeable, although black are often smaller than brown, which means you'll end up with more of them in a tablespoon and sometimes a more pungent flavor all around. If you don't like a bop in the nose, consider halving the amount of black mustard seeds when used for brown in this chapter's recipes (but *not* for recipes in other chapters).

All mustard seeds can go rancid, although they'll usually last a year or more in a cool dark pantry. If rancid, they give off a musty, funky smell. If you're not sure how often you'll use them, store them in a sealed jar or bag in the freezer, where they'll last indefinitely.

Ready, set...

Most of these condiments are terrific house gifts for weekend stays or even dinner parties. Our advice? If you've stored something in the freezer, tie a ribbon around it and bring it frozen. That way, your host can decide when to open it: tomorrow or several months from now.

▲ For a proper set, make a line that holds its shape for a second or two before it closes up. (Notice that you can *see* the bottom of the saucepan.)

Bacon Jam

MAKES: about 2 cups (480 ml)
FRIDGE: up to 2 weeks
FREEZER: up to 6 months

Is there anything better than this salty-sweet-porky miracle on a buttery baked potato? Or a charred steak? Or a cracker with ripe, runny cheese? Bacon jam is a true treat: aromatic and smoky, perhaps the best reason to start making savory jams. Although the quality of the bacon dramatically affects the jam here, you needn't spend a fortune. A solid, well-smoked, not-too-fatty store brand will do fine.

> 1 pound (450 g) thinly sliced US-style bacon (or streaky bacon), chopped
> 1 small yellow or white onion, peeled and chopped
> ¼ cup (60 ml) water
> ½ cup (108 g) packed light brown sugar
> 3 tablespoons (45 ml) red wine vinegar
> 4 teaspoons (20 ml) balsamic vinegar
> 2 medium garlic cloves, peeled and minced
> ½ teaspoon dried thyme
> ½ teaspoon ground black pepper

1. Cook the bacon in a medium saucepan set over medium heat until quite brown and distinctly crisp, stirring often, about 5 minutes.

2. Spoon out and discard all but about 1 tablespoon (15 ml) rendered fat (but *not* the bacon). Add the onion and cook, stirring often, until quite soft, 4–5 minutes.

3. Pour in the water and *quickly* scrape up the browned bits in the pan. Stir in the brown sugar, both types of vinegar, the garlic, thyme, and pepper. Continue cooking, stirring frequently, until most of the liquid has evaporated and the mixture is quite thick, about 5 minutes.

4. Turn off the heat and remove the pan from the burner. Transfer to two *clean* ½ pint (236 ml) jars or other containers, leaving about ½ inch (1 cm) headspace in each. Cover or seal. Cool at room temperature for no more than 1 hour, then refrigerate or freeze.

More
For over-the-top flavor, use pepper bacon for a hotter jam or maple bacon for a sweeter jam.

Onion-Bourbon Jam

MAKES: about 2 cups (480 ml)
FRIDGE: up to 3 weeks
FREEZER: up to 1 year

By softening the onions, rather than deeply caramelizing them, you can craft an onion jam that's mellow and aromatic, less markedly bittersweet, and thus better balanced by oaky bourbon. Although you won't spend an hour at the stove with the onions, you still must watch them carefully. Reduce the heat if you notice they're browning—or remove the pan from the burner for a minute or two before soldiering on. The point of all this fuss is to reach the middle ground between a sweet and savory jam.

> ¼ cup (60 ml) olive oil
> 2 pounds (900 g) yellow or white onions, peeled, halved, and sliced into paper-thin half-moons
> ½ cup (100 g) granulated white sugar
> 2 tablespoons (30 ml) bourbon
> 1 tablespoon (15 ml) apple cider vinegar
> 1 tablespoon (15 ml) soy sauce
> ½ teaspoon mild smoked paprika
> ½ teaspoon kosher salt
> ½ teaspoon ground black pepper

1. Set a large saucepan over low heat for a minute or two. Pour in the oil, then add the onions. Stir well. Reduce the heat further if possible, cover, and cook, stirring often, until the onions are limp and translucent if still fairly white, about 20 minutes.

2. Uncover the pan and continue cooking, stirring very often, until the onions are quite soft and golden but not yet browned, about 10 minutes.

Top to bottom: Blueberry-Onion Jam (page 120), Onion-Bourbon Jam (page 118), and Bacon Jam (page 118)

3. Stir in the sugar, bourbon, vinegar, soy sauce, smoked paprika, salt, and pepper. Raise the heat to medium and bring the mixture to a simmer, stirring constantly to dissolve the sugar. Cook, stirring often, until most of the liquid has evaporated and the mixture is quite thick, about 5 minutes.

4. Turn off the heat and remove the pan from the burner. Transfer to two *clean* ½ pint (236 ml) jars or other containers, leaving about ½ inch (1 cm) headspace in each. Cover or seal. Cool at room temperature for no more than 1 hour, then refrigerate or freeze.

Next
This is the best savory jam for burgers of any sort: beef, bison, turkey, or veggie.

Blueberry-Onion Jam

MAKES: about 2 cups (480 ml)
FRIDGE: up to 3 weeks
FREEZER: up to 1 year

This chunky savory jam tips a little more toward the sweet than the sour, thanks to the blueberries as well as a small amount of vinegar. The trick is all in the reduction: getting the jam to the state where it looks indeed like jam with very little liquid in the saucepan. Don't dry it out. But make sure it's got a *mounding consistency* when you bottle it.

- 1 tablespoon (15 ml) olive oil
- 1 large red onion, peeled, halved, and sliced into paper-thin half-moons
- 10 ounces (280 g) fresh blueberries (about 2 cups)
- ½ cup (108 g) packed light brown sugar
- ¼ cup (60 ml) red wine vinegar
- ½ teaspoon kosher salt
- ½ teaspoon ground black pepper
- ¼ teaspoon ground allspice

1. Set a large saucepan over low heat for a minute or two. Pour in the oil, then add the onion. Stir well. Reduce the heat further if possible and cook, stirring often, until the onion is quite soft and *a little* browned, about 20 minutes.

2. Stir in the blueberries, brown sugar, vinegar, salt, pepper, and allspice. Bring the mixture back to a simmer, stirring almost constantly to dissolve the brown sugar. Simmer slowly, crushing the berries against the pot with the back of a wooden spoon and stirring often, until thickened and jam-like, about 5 minutes.

3. Turn off the heat and remove the pan from the burner. Transfer to two *clean* ½ pint (236 ml) jars or other containers, leaving about ½ inch (1 cm) headspace in each. Cover or seal. Cool at room temperature for no more than 1 hour, then refrigerate or freeze.

Next
This jam is terrific with sausages off the grill, particularly if you've got sauerkraut and buttery boiled potatoes on the side.

Shallot Jam

MAKES: about 2 cups (480 ml)
FRIDGE: up to 3 weeks
FREEZER: up to 1 year

Look no further for a savory jam that takes full advantage of the bittersweet notes from very caramelized alliums—in this case, shallots with their slightly garlicky spark that pairs so well with red pepper flakes. This recipe calls for a bit of patience: stirring the mixture until it gets jam-like, until almost all (but not quite all) of the liquid has evaporated or been absorbed.

- 2 tablespoons (30 g) butter
- 1 tablespoon (15 ml) neutral-flavored oil, such as canola or vegetable oil
- 2 pounds (900 g) shallots (about 20 medium), peeled and chopped

½ cup (100 g) granulated white sugar

1 teaspoon ground black pepper

½ teaspoon dried thyme

½ teaspoon red pepper flakes

½ teaspoon kosher salt

6 tablespoons (90 ml) malt vinegar

1. Melt the butter in the oil in a large saucepan set over low heat. Add the shallots and stir well. Reduce the heat even further if possible, cover, and cook, stirring often, until the shallots are quite soft, translucent, but still mostly white, about 10 minutes.

2. Uncover and raise the heat to medium. Continue cooking, stirring more and more frequently, until the shallots begin to brown at their edges, about 10 minutes.

3. Add the sugar, black pepper, thyme, red pepper flakes, and salt. Stir constantly to dissolve the sugar. Reduce the heat to low and continue cooking, stirring often, until the mixture is golden brown, about 15 minutes.

4. Stir in the vinegar and continue cooking, stirring almost constantly, until the liquid in the pan has reduced to a thick glaze, about 5 minutes.

5. Turn off the heat and remove the pan from the burner. Transfer to two *clean* ½ pint (236 ml) jars or other containers, leaving about ½ inch (1 cm) headspace in each. Cover or seal. Cool at room temperature for no more than 1 hour, then refrigerate or freeze.

Next

We love to spread this jam on a crisp cracker, then top with an oil-cured white anchovy.

Shallot-Bacon Jam

MAKES: about 3 cups (720 ml)
FRIDGE: up to 2 weeks
FREEZER: up to 1 year

We've given this savory jam to countless people as a house gift and *we've* almost always gotten a thank-you phone call the next day. This one is more about the shallots than the bacon, which does give it a smoky, salty, porky flavor, but pales in comparison to the sweet flavors of the alliums, which have not darkened but just softened until they're garlicky-rich.

¼ pound (115 g) thinly sliced US-style bacon (or streaky bacon), chopped

2½ pounds (1.1 kg) shallots (about 25 medium), peeled and thinly sliced

4 fresh thyme sprigs

½ cup (120 ml) *sweet* vermouth

6 tablespoons (75 g) granulated white sugar

¼ cup (80 g) maple syrup

2 tablespoons (30 ml) red wine vinegar

½ teaspoon kosher salt

½ teaspoon ground black pepper

1. Set a medium saucepan over medium heat. Add the bacon and cook, stirring often, until quite browned and crisp (the pieces would shatter if cooled), about 5 minutes.

2. Use a slotted spoon to transfer the bacon bits to a small bowl (leaving the rendered bacon fat behind). Add the shallots to the pan as well as the thyme sprigs. Reduce the heat to low and stir until the shallots are well coated in the grease.

3. Stir in the vermouth and scrape up any browned bits in the pan. Cover and cook, stirring often, until the shallots are quite soft but still white, not yet brown, about 10 minutes.

4. Uncover, raise the heat to medium, and stir in the cooked bacon, sugar, maple syrup, vinegar, salt, and pepper. Continue cooking uncovered, stirring often, until the mixture is jam-like, about 10 minutes.

5. Turn off the heat and remove the pan from the burner. Remove and discard the thyme sprigs. Cool for about 10 minutes.

6. Transfer the jam to three *clean* ½ pint (236 ml) jars or other containers, leaving about ½ inch (1 cm) headspace in each. Cover or seal. Cool at room temperature for no more than 1 hour, then refrigerate or freeze.

Next
This savory jam is terrific inside omelets or set atop scrambled eggs.

Carrot Jam

MAKES: about 4 cups (960 ml)
FRIDGE: up to 3 weeks
FREEZER: up to 1 year
May be traditionally canned (see page 436)

Here's one of our personal favorites among the savory jams (although we'll admit it's more sweet than savory). It wouldn't be welcome on toast but can certainly make its way to roast pork or even a holiday turkey. The flavors are delicate at first blush but finish with the stronger flavor of carrots. Since a slightly crunchy texture is part of the joy of this jam and we don't want to turn the carrots into a puree, we use pectin to help the jam set.

- 2 cups (400 g) granulated white sugar
- 2½ tablespoons (30 g) *granulated less-sugar* pectin
- 1 pound (450 g) carrots, peeled and shredded through the large holes of a box grater (about 3 packed cups)
- 1 cup (240 ml) *pure unsweetened* bottled carrot juice
- 2 tablespoons (30 ml) lemon juice
- 2 tablespoons (30 ml) apple cider vinegar
- ½ teaspoon ground ginger

1. Mix ¼ cup (50 g) sugar and the pectin in a small bowl until uniform.

2. Mix the carrots, carrot juice, lemon juice, vinegar, and ground ginger in a large saucepan. Set it over medium-high heat and add the pectin

mixture. Stir constantly to dissolve the granulated ingredients. Bring to a boil you can't stir down, stirring often.

3. Add the remaining 1¾ cups (350 g) sugar and stir constantly to dissolve the sugar. Bring back to a full boil, stirring often. Boil undisturbed for 1 minute.

4. Turn off the heat, remove the pan from the burner, and set aside for 1–2 minutes. Skim any foamy impurities with a tablespoon.

5. Transfer to four *clean* ½ pint (236 ml) jars or other containers, leaving about ½ inch (1 cm) headspace in each. Cover or seal. Cool at room temperature for no more than 1 hour, then refrigerate or freeze.

More
Add up to ½ teaspoon ground cinnamon with the ground ginger.

Spicy Carrot Jam

MAKES: about 3 cups (720 ml)
FRIDGE: up to 3 weeks
FREEZER: up to 1 year
May be traditionally canned (see page 436)

Consider this concoction a halfway point between a savory jam and a chutney. To balance the fiery heat from the chilis and the warming spices, we cook this carrot jam longer than our more standard one (above) to caramelize the sugars and bring out a few sophisticated, bitter notes. We don't need to add pectin because the sugar cooks long enough to offer a soft set.

- 1½ pounds (680 g) carrots, peeled and shredded (about 4½ packed cups)
- 2¼ cups (450 g) granulated white sugar
- ¼ cup (60 ml) lemon juice
- 2 fresh green serrano chilis, stemmed, halved lengthwise, seeded (if desired), and *very thinly* sliced
- One 3 inch (7.5 cm) cinnamon stick
- ¼ teaspoon grated nutmeg
- ¼ teaspoon kosher salt

Front to back: Red Pepper Jam
(page 124) and Carrot Jam (page 122)

1. Combine all the ingredients in a large saucepan. Set it over medium-high heat and stir constantly to dissolve the sugar and bring out some of the liquid from the carrots. Then bring to a boil, stirring often.

2. Reduce the heat to low and simmer slowly but steadily, stirring quite often, until most of the liquid has been absorbed and the texture is jam-like, about 40 minutes.

3. Turn off the heat, remove the pan from the burner, and set aside for 1–2 minutes. Fish out and discard the cinnamon stick.

4. Transfer the jam to three *clean* ½ pint (236 ml) jars or other containers, leaving about ½ inch (1 cm) headspace in each. Cover or seal. Cool at room temperature for no more than 1 hour, then refrigerate or freeze.

Next

This jam is terrific on baked potatoes with butter and sour cream. It also makes a great dip for fries in a 50/50 mix with either ketchup or mayonnaise.

Red Pepper Jam

MAKES: about 4 cups (960 ml)
FRIDGE: up to 3 weeks
FREEZER: up to 1 year
May be traditionally canned (see page 436)

Although red bell peppers are sweet, even sweeter than green bell peppers, we add fresh chilis and a smattering of red pepper flakes to our pepper jam to give it a kick, if only because it seems (by name and appearance) as if it *should* have a kick. The jam is tangy and chunky, not smooth or pulpy. It's a terrific condiment alongside almost anything off the grill, on sandwiches (particularly those made with toasted rye bread), or stirred into sour cream for a dip with bagel chips.

1¾ cups (350 g) granulated white sugar

3 tablespoons (36 g) *granulated less-sugar* pectin

1⅓ pounds (605 g) red bell peppers (about 3 large), stemmed, cored, seeded, and roughly chopped

3 ounces (80 g) red hot chilis, preferably Fresno chilis (about 3 small), stemmed, seeded, and roughly chopped

⅔ cup (160 ml) white vinegar

2 tablespoons (30 ml) water

1 teaspoon red pepper flakes

½ teaspoon kosher salt

1. Mix ¼ cup (50 g) sugar and the pectin in a small bowl until uniform.

2. Put the red bell peppers and chilis in a food processor. Cover and pulse until the consistency of a relish. Scrape every drop of this relish into a medium saucepan.

3. Set the pan over medium-high heat and add the pectin mixture. Stir constantly to dissolve the granulated ingredients. Add the vinegar, water, red pepper flakes, and salt. Cook, stirring often, until the mixture comes to a boil you can't stir down. Reduce the heat to medium and boil, stirring quite often, until slightly thickened, about 4 minutes.

4. Add the remaining 1½ cups (300 g) sugar and stir constantly to dissolve the sugar. Bring back to a full boil, stirring often. Boil undisturbed for 1 minute.

5. Turn off the heat, remove the pan from the burner, and set aside for 1–2 minutes. Skim any foamy impurities with a tablespoon.

6. Transfer to four *clean* ½ pint (236 ml) jars or other containers, leaving about ½ inch (1 cm) headspace in each. Cover or seal. Cool at room temperature for no more than 1 hour, then refrigerate or freeze.

More

For a more elegant finish with slightly bitter notes, substitute Campari or Aperol for the water.

Pineapple-Horseradish Jam

MAKES: about 3 cups (720 ml)
FRIDGE: up to 3 weeks
FREEZER: up to 1 year

We modeled this sweet-savory jam on jezebel sauce, a US Gulf Coast classic, usually made by stirring together pineapple jam, apple juice, horseradish, and prepared mustard. We've morphed it into a bit of a DIY project, more jam than sauce. The flavor is piquant, right up in the nose. The traditional sauce is used with grilled meats or as a spread with mayonnaise on sandwiches. Do the same with this jam.

- 2 cups (400 g) granulated white sugar
- 2 tablespoons (24 g) *granulated less-sugar* pectin
- 1 cup (280 g) canned crushed pineapple packed in juice (do not drain)
- 1 cup (240 ml) *unsweetened* apple juice
- 2½ tablespoons (15 g) ground dried mustard
- 1 teaspoon ground black pepper
- 1 teaspoon red pepper flakes
- ½ cup (120 g) jarred prepared white horseradish

1. Mix ¼ cup (50 g) sugar and the pectin in a small bowl until uniform.

2. Combine the pineapple, apple juice, dried mustard, black pepper, and red pepper flakes in a medium saucepan. Set it over medium-high heat and add the pectin mixture. Stir constantly to dissolve the granulated ingredients. Bring the mixture to a boil you can't stir down, stirring often.

3. Add the remaining 1¾ cups (350 g) sugar and the horseradish. Stir constantly to dissolve the sugar. Bring back to a full boil, stirring often. Boil undisturbed for 1 minute.

4. Turn off the heat, remove the pan from the burner, and set aside for 1–2 minutes. Skim any foamy impurities with a tablespoon.

5. Transfer to three *clean* ½ pint (236 ml) jars or other containers, leaving about ½ inch (1 cm) headspace in each. Cover or seal. Cool at room temperature for no more than 1 hour, then refrigerate or freeze. In the fridge, the preserves may not reach their best flavor for 48 hours.

More

For a new take on tartar sauce, use this sauce in place of some or all of the pickle relish. (Omit any added horseradish you might put in tartar sauce.)

Celery Root-Cardamom Jam

MAKES: about 4 cups (960 ml)
FRIDGE: up to 3 weeks
FREEZER: up to 1 year

This one's a favorite: savory, aromatic, a little sweet, and even a little crunchy from the celery root (aka celeriac). We use this jam on sandwiches of all sorts, alongside steaks or chops, and even with fish fillets off the grill. It's a big batch of flavors that mellow during cooking, producing a celery-laced, perfume-rich mix with a consistency somewhere between a jam and a relish.

- 2¼ cups (450 g) granulated white sugar
- 3 tablespoons (36 g) *granulated less-sugar* pectin
- 1⅓ pounds (605 g) celery root (aka celeriac—about 1 large), trimmed, peeled, and shredded through the large holes of a box grater (about 3 cups)
- 1 cup (240 ml) *unsweetened* apple juice
- 1½ teaspoons decorticated (husked and removed from the pod) cardamom seeds

1. Mix ¼ cup (50 g) sugar and the pectin in a small bowl until uniform.

2. Combine the celery root, apple juice, and cardamom seeds in a medium saucepan. Set it over medium-high heat and add the pectin mixture. Stir constantly to dissolve the granulated ingredients. Bring to a boil you can't stir down, stirring often.

➡

Clockwise from left:
Pineapple-Horseradish
Jam (page 125), Tomato-
Ancho Jam (page 127),
Celery Root–Cardamom
Jam (page 125), and
Kimchi Jam (page 129)

3. Add the remaining 2 cups (400 g) sugar and stir constantly to dissolve the sugar. Bring back to a full boil, stirring often. Boil undisturbed for 1 minute.

4. Turn off the heat, remove the pan from the burner, and set aside for 1–2 minutes. Skim any foamy impurities with a tablespoon.

5. Transfer to four *clean* ½ pint (236 ml) jars or other containers, leaving about ½ inch (1 cm) headspace in each. Cover or seal. Cool at room temperature for no more than 1 hour, then refrigerate or freeze. In the fridge, the preserves may not reach their best flavor for 48 hours.

More

Introduce some heat by adding up to 1 teaspoon red pepper flakes or even just ground black pepper with the cardamom.

Tomato-Ancho Jam

MAKES: about 2 cups (480 ml)
FRIDGE: up to 3 weeks
FREEZER: up to 1 year

Ancho chilis (aka dried poblano chilis) have an earthy, bittersweet flavor without a great deal of heat, particularly if you remove the desiccated seeds. Anchos pair well with tomatoes to make this condiment a gorgeous spread for cheese platters, a mid-afternoon snack with crackers, or even a topper for hot dogs (skip the ketchup!). We use large, beefsteak tomatoes here because they're a little less sweet than cherry tomatoes, a better contrast to the anchos.

2 dried ancho chilis (about ¾ ounce or 20 g total weight), stemmed

Boiling water as necessary to soak the chilis

1⅔ pounds (750 g) beefsteak tomatoes (about 4 large), cored and chopped

1¼ cups (250 g) granulated white sugar

2 tablespoons (30 ml) lemon juice

1 tablespoon (15 g) grated peeled fresh ginger

1 teaspoon kosher salt

½ teaspoon ground cumin

¼ teaspoon ground cinnamon

¼ teaspoon ground cloves

1. Tear the dried chilis into chunks, removing the seeds for less heat if desired. Set the chili pieces in a small, heat-safe bowl and add enough boiling water to submerge them. Set a small heat-safe plate on the chilis to hold them down and soak at room temperature for 20 minutes.

2. Uncover and drain the chilis in a colander set in the sink. Put them in a food processor and add about one quarter of the chopped tomatoes. Cover and process to create a fairly smooth puree.

3. Pour and scrape this mixture into a medium saucepan. Add the remaining chopped tomatoes, the sugar, lemon juice, ginger, salt, cumin, cinnamon, and cloves. Set the pan over medium-high heat and bring to a boil, stirring often.

4. Reduce the heat to low and simmer, *stirring often*, until thick enough that you can run a wooden spoon across the bottom of the pan to make a line that holds its edges for a second, about 1 hour.

5. Turn off the heat and remove the pan from the burner. Transfer to two *clean* ½ pint (236 ml) jars or other containers, leaving about ½ inch (1 cm) headspace in each. Cover or seal. Cool at room temperature for no more than 1 hour, then refrigerate or freeze. In the fridge, the jam will not reach its best flavor for 24 hours.

More

Substitute other dried chilis (*by weight*) for the anchos: chipotles for a darker, smokier spice; guajillos for a tangy heat; or pasilla negro chilis for a sweeter, velvety heat.

Tomato-Basil Jam

MAKES: about 4 cups (960 ml)
FRIDGE: up to 3 weeks
FREEZER: up to 1 year

Since decent cherry tomatoes are available year-round, you don't have to wait until summer to make this fresh, sweet-and-a-little-sour jam. The only trick is the patience it requires to get the tomatoes to break down into a luscious, pulpy jam. Don't give up and you'll have a terrific condiment for burgers, sandwiches, hummus, cheese boards, and charcuterie platters.

- 3 pounds (1.4 kg) cherry tomatoes, halved
- 1 small yellow or white onion, peeled and finely chopped
- 1 cup (200 g) granulated white sugar
- 1 cup (35 g) packed fresh basil leaves, finely chopped
- 3 tablespoons (45 ml) balsamic vinegar
- 2 tablespoons (30 ml) lemon juice
- 1 teaspoon kosher salt
- ½ teaspoon ground black pepper

1. Combine all the ingredients in a medium saucepan and set over medium-high heat. Bring the mixture to a boil, stirring occasionally.

2. Reduce the heat to low and simmer slowly, stirring occasionally, until the liquid has been reduced to a third of its original volume and the mixture is getting jam-like, about 1 hour.

3. Turn off the heat and remove the pan from the burner. Transfer to four *clean* ½ pint (236 ml) jars or other containers, leaving about ½ inch (1 cm) headspace in each. Cover or seal. Cool at room temperature for no more than 1 hour, then refrigerate or freeze. In the fridge, the jam will not reach its best flavor for 24 hours.

More
For SPICED TOMATO-BASIL JAM, add ½ teaspoon ground coriander and/or ¼ teaspoon ground allspice.

Tamarind-Chili Jam

MAKES: about 4 cups (960 ml)
FRIDGE: up to 3 weeks
FREEZER: up to 1 year

Tamarind paste provides this savory jam with a pronounced, sour edge. The commercially processed paste is the sparky reduction of the pulp around the legumes from mature seed pods off a tamarind tree. For a jam like this, the additional flavors need to be more assertive for the right balance among them, all so that sour tamarind kick doesn't overshadow this rounded condiment when dolloped onto a bowl of beef stew, some grilled fish, or a slice of smoked salmon.

- 1½ cups (300 g) granulated white sugar
- 3 tablespoons (36 g) *granulated less-sugar* pectin
- 10½ ounces (300 g) beefsteak tomatoes (about 2 large), halved, cored, and cut into chunks
- 8 fresh red jalapeño chilis (more heat) or red Fresnos (less heat), stemmed, halved lengthwise, seeded, and roughly chopped
- 1 large red bell pepper, stemmed, cored, and cut into chunks
- 4 medium garlic cloves, peeled and chopped
- 2 tablespoons (30 g) grated peeled fresh ginger
- 3 tablespoons (45 ml) lime juice
- 2 tablespoons (30 g) tamarind paste
- 1 tablespoon (15 ml) fish sauce
- ½ teaspoon five-spice powder (or use your own homemade, see the MORE section of the Five-Spice Ketchup recipe on page 342)

1. Mix ¼ cup (50 g) sugar and the pectin in a small bowl until uniform.

2. Combine the tomatoes, chilis, bell pepper, garlic, and ginger in a food processor. Cover and process until just a little beyond the texture of a relish—that is, fairly slushy, not a chunky puree.

3. Pour and scrape the mixture into a medium saucepan and set over medium-high heat. Add the pectin mixture and stir constantly to dissolve the granulated ingredients. Stir in the lime juice, tamarind paste, fish sauce, and five-spice powder. Bring to a full boil, stirring often. Boil for 3 minutes, stirring occasionally.

4. Add the remaining 1¼ cups (250 g) sugar and stir constantly to dissolve the sugar. Bring back to a full boil, stirring often. Boil undisturbed for 1 minute.

5. Turn off the heat, remove the pan from the burner, and set aside for 1–2 minutes. Skim any foamy impurities with a tablespoon.

6. Transfer to four *clean* ½ pint (236 ml) jars or other containers, leaving about ½ inch (1 cm) headspace in each. Cover or seal. Cool at room temperature for no more than 1 hour, then refrigerate or freeze.

Tip
Make this vegan by substituting 1 tablespoon (15 ml) liquid coconut aminos for the fish sauce.

Kimchi Jam

MAKES: about 4 cups (960 ml)
FRIDGE: up to 3 weeks
FREEZER: up to 1 year

One of our biggest revelations as jam makers came with kimchi jam. We've long loved kimchi on red-rare hamburgers. But we had no idea that sour-spicy kick would translate so well to a savory jam. We add a little cinnamon to mellow the spike for a flavor more in keeping with our jam expectations. But we also increase the heat (!) with gochujang, a Korean spice paste, because we want to make sure we retain that characteristic fermented funk along with the high heat notes. (For more information about gochujang, see the headnote to Apricot-Gochujang Jam on page 64).

1⅔ pounds (750 g) kimchi (about 3 packed cups—do not drain)
1 cup (200 g) granulated white sugar
½ cup (108 g) packed light brown sugar

¼ cup (60 ml) mirin
1 tablespoon (25 g) gochujang (or use your own homemade, page 240)
½ teaspoon ground cinnamon

1. Put the kimchi in a food processor, cover, and process until the consistency of a relish.

2. Dump and scrape the kimchi into a medium saucepan. Add the white sugar, brown sugar, mirin, gochujang, and cinnamon. Set the pan over medium-high heat and stir constantly to dissolve the sugar. Bring the mixture to a boil, stirring often.

3. Reduce the heat to low and simmer, stirring often, until thickened and jam-like, about 12 minutes.

4. Turn off the heat and remove the pan from the burner. Transfer to four *clean* ½ pint (236 ml) jars or other containers, leaving about ½ inch (1 cm) headspace in each. Cool at room temperature for no more than 1 hour, then refrigerate or freeze. In the fridge, the jam will not reach its best flavor for 24 hours.

Next
Beyond burgers, use this savory jam in a dipping sauce for dumplings or spring rolls: Stir a little into equal parts soy sauce and rice wine vinegar.

Blackberry Conserve

MAKES: about 4 cups (960 ml)
FRIDGE: up to 3 weeks
FREEZER: up to 1 year
May be traditionally canned (see page 436)

A great conserve involves a layering of flavors: caramelized sugar (yet not as much as in most jams), earthy notes from nuts, and bright pops from whatever fruit is at the base, plus a few aromatics to round things out. This particular conserve may well be our favorite, the one we make time and again, especially when we find blackberries on sale. Although it's terrific with cream cheese or Brie, and great on charcuterie boards, we even like it on buttered toast, a less-sweet treat with our morning coffee.

> 1⅓ pounds (605 g) fresh blackberries or thawed frozen blackberries (about 4 cups for either)
>
> 2½ cups (500 g) granulated white sugar
>
> 3 tablespoons (36 g) chopped crystallized ginger
>
> 2 tablespoons (30 ml) lemon juice
>
> ¼ cup (30 g) chopped walnuts
>
> ⅛ teaspoon grated nutmeg

1. Put the blackberries in a medium saucepan. Use a potato masher or the back of a wooden spoon to *lightly* crush them against the inside and bottom of the pan. There should be some pieces visible. Don't make a puree.

2. Set the pan over medium-high heat and add the remaining ingredients. Stir constantly to dissolve the sugar. Bring to a boil, stirring often.

3. Reduce the heat to low and simmer, stirring more and more often to avoid scorching, until thickened and jam-like, about 12 minutes.

4. Turn off the heat, remove the pan from the burner, and set aside for 1–2 minutes. Skim any foamy impurities with a tablespoon.

5. Transfer to four *clean* ½ pint (236 ml) jars or other containers, leaving about ½ inch (1 cm) headspace in each. Cover or seal. Cool at room temperature for no more than 1 hour, then refrigerate or freeze.

More
For the walnuts, you can substitute an equivalent amount by weight of any chopped, shelled nut: skinned hazelnuts, pecans, pine nuts, or pistachios. (Do not use salted nuts.)

Peach–Sour Cherry Conserve

MAKES: about 4 cups (960 ml)
FRIDGE: up to 3 weeks
FREEZER: up to 1 year
May be traditionally canned (see page 436)

Although we love to nab fresh sour cherries for this sweet, almost sticky conserve, we have used pitted sour cherries from a can to fine success. The flavors are so layered that the sunny, upper notes from the sour cherries are actually muted, no matter which sort you use. And we add back a few sour notes with the sweet-sour dried goji berries, an Asian red fruit (not technically a berry) that's found in most supermarkets (among either the dried fruits or the herbal remedies) as well as in almost all health-food stores.

> 1¾ cups (350 g) granulated white sugar
>
> 2½ tablespoons (30 g) *granulated less-sugar* pectin
>
> 1 pound (450 g) fresh peaches (about 2 large), peeled, pitted, and chopped
>
> 10 ounces (285 g) stemmed and pitted sour cherries (about 2 cups)
>
> 2 tablespoons (30 ml) lemon juice
>
> ¼ cup (30 g) pecan pieces, toasted and chopped (see TIP)
>
> 2 tablespoons (11 g) dried *unsweetened* goji berries

1. Mix ¼ cup (50 g) sugar and the pectin in a small bowl until uniform.

2. Put the peaches (plus any pulp and juice from the cutting board), sour cherries, and lemon juice in a medium saucepan and set it over medium-high heat. Add the pectin mixture and stir constantly to dissolve the granulated ingredients. Bring to a boil you can't stir down, stirring often.

3. Add the remaining 1½ cups (300 g) sugar, the pecans, and goji berries. Stir constantly to dissolve the sugar. Bring back to a full boil, stirring occasionally. Boil undisturbed for 1 minute.

Front to back:
Blackberry Conserve
(page 129), Peach–Sour
Cherry Conserve (page
130), and Apple Pie
Conserve (page 132)

4. Turn off the heat, remove the pan from the burner, and set aside for 1–2 minutes. Skim any foamy impurities with a tablespoon.

5. Transfer to four *clean* ½ pint (236 ml) jars or other containers, leaving about ½ inch (1 cm) headspace in each. Cover or seal. Cool at room temperature for no more than 1 hour, then refrigerate or freeze. In the fridge, the conserve may not gel for 24 hours.

Tip

To toast pecans, it's easier to work with larger pieces, not chopped bits. Toast the pieces in a dry skillet set over low heat, stirring often, until darker brown in places and quite aromatic. Pour into a bowl and cool for 10 minutes before chopping.

Apple Pie Conserve

MAKES: about 4 cups (960 ml)
FRIDGE: up to 3 weeks
FREEZER: up to 1 year
May be traditionally canned (see page 436)

Given the name of this chunky conserve, you'd expect it to be fairly sweet. Indeed, it is, although it's not as sweet as Spiced Apple Preserves (page 76) or even Apple Butter (page 78). We've added lots of dates, warming spices, and even some celery to give it a more complex, even savory flavor, fit for a cheese or charcuterie spread.

- ¾ cup (180 ml) *unsweetened* apple juice
- 1 tablespoon (12 g) *granulated less-sugar* pectin
- 1½ pounds (680 g) tart firm apples (about 5 medium), such as Granny Smith, peeled, cored, and chopped
- 1 cup (200 g) granulated white sugar
- 2 medium celery stalks, halved lengthwise and thinly sliced
- 8 plump, pitted Medjool dates, chopped
- ½ cup (60 g) chopped walnut pieces
- 1 teaspoon ground cinnamon
- ½ teaspoon ground cloves
- ¼ teaspoon grated nutmeg

1. Whisk the apple juice and pectin in a small bowl until the pectin dissolves.

2. Stir the apples, sugar, celery, dates, walnuts, cinnamon, cloves, and nutmeg in a large saucepan until well combined. Set the pan over medium-high heat and stir in the pectin mixture. Stir constantly to dissolve the sugar. Bring to a full boil, stirring often.

3. Reduce the heat to low and simmer, stirring more and more often to prevent scorching, until thickened and medium brown (not golden, but also not dark brown), 15–20 minutes.

4. Turn off the heat, remove the pan from the burner, and set aside for 1–2 minutes. Skim any foamy impurities with a tablespoon.

5. Transfer to four *clean* ½ pint (236 ml) jars or other containers, leaving about ½ inch (1 cm) headspace in each. Cover or seal. Cool at room temperature for no more than 1 hour, then refrigerate or freeze. In the fridge, the conserve may not gel for 24 hours.

More

Substitute brandy, even apple brandy, for the apple juice for a more elegant if also slightly bitter flavor.

Spicy Pineapple-Coconut Conserve

MAKES: about 5 cups (1200 ml)
FRIDGE: up to 3 weeks
FREEZER: up to 1 year
May be traditionally canned (see page 436)

Fresh pineapple is naturally sweet. To make a spicy, tropical-influenced conserve, you need to cook it quite a while to get those sugars to break down into more complex flavors. Sounds good, except doing so involves a lot of stirring at the stove. But give this conserve the effort it deserves. You'll end up with an almost astonishing blend of bright flavors laced with fiery chilis, a great condiment to enhance most any simple skillet sauté or even take-out fried rice. Note that we call for large coconut flakes, not just shredded coconut. These flakes offer a better texture because they don't dissolve as readily. Look for them in Asian supermarkets and health-food stores.

- 2¼ pounds (1 kg) peeled, cored, and chopped fresh pineapple (about 6 cups)
- 2 cups (400 g) granulated white sugar
- 1 cup (60 g) *large unsweetened* dried coconut flakes
- 1 cup (240 ml) *unsweetened* coconut water without pulp
- ½ cup (170 g) honey
- 2–3 green or red fresh bird's eye chilis, stemmed and thinly sliced
- 2 tablespoons (30 ml) lime juice

1. Mix all the ingredients in a large saucepan. Set it over medium-high heat and stir constantly to dissolve the sugar. Bring to a full boil, stirring often.

2. Reduce the heat to low and simmer, stirring more and more often until almost constantly, until the pineapple has turned translucent (about like glacéed fruit) and the liquid is a thick syrup, about 20 minutes.

3. Turn off the heat, remove the pan from the burner, and set aside for 1–2 minutes. Transfer to five *clean* ½ pint (236 ml) jars or other containers, leaving about ½ inch (1 cm) headspace in each. Cover or seal. Cool at room temperature for no more than 1 hour, then refrigerate or freeze. In the fridge, the conserve may not gel for 24 hours.

More
Make this conserve a little more savory (and a little more like a chutney) by substituting apple cider vinegar for the lime juice.

Sweet-and-Sour Pear Conserve

MAKES: about 3 cups (720 ml)
FRIDGE: up to 3 weeks
FREEZER: up to 1 year
May be traditionally canned (see page 436)

To keep ultra sweet ripe pears from becoming a jam or preserve, we add a little vinegar and even some onions to this conserve, morphing it into a condiment that's halfway between a traditional conserve and a chutney. It's astounding with almost anything off the grill, even a platter of grilled vegetables, along with deli mustard to really give each bite some spike.

- 2 pounds (900 g) very ripe, soft pears (about 4 large), preferably Comice or Anjou, stemmed, peeled, halved, cored, and chopped (about 4 cups)
- ½ cup (100 g) granulated white sugar
- ½ cup (75 g) golden raisins
- ⅓ cup (80 ml) apple cider vinegar
- 1 small yellow bell pepper, stemmed, cored, and *finely* chopped
- ¼ cup (35 g) chopped peeled yellow or white onion
- 3 tablespoons (45 g) grated peeled fresh ginger
- ½ teaspoon yellow mustard seeds
- ½ cup (57 g) slivered almonds

1. Combine the pears, sugar, raisins, vinegar, bell pepper, onion, ginger, and mustard seeds in a large saucepan set over medium heat. Cook, stirring often, until the mixture comes to a simmer.

2. Reduce the heat to low and simmer *slowly*, stirring more and more often to avoid scorching, until somewhat thickened, about 30 minutes.

3. Stir in the almonds. Continue simmering *slowly*, stirring almost constantly, until so thick that you can run a wooden spoon across the pan's bottom to create a line that holds its edges for a second, about 10 more minutes.

4. Turn off the heat, remove the pan from the burner, and set aside for 1–2 minutes. Transfer to three *clean* ½ pint (236 ml) jars or other containers, leaving about ½ inch (1 cm) headspace in each. Cover or seal. Cool at room temperature for no more than 1 hour, then refrigerate or freeze.

Next

Try this conserve as a condiment with Indian fare: chicken tikka masala, vindaloo of any sort, or aloo gobi.

Maple-Rhubarb Conserve

MAKES: about 2 cups (480 ml)
FRIDGE: up to 3 weeks
FREEZER: up to 1 year
May be traditionally canned (see page 436)

This conserve is fairly sweet, although the sour notes from the rhubarb definitely spark its overall finish. The sugars are also deepened by long cooking, which creates a few bitter notes. Stirring is key to the conserve's success: Stick with it, especially as it begins to become jam-like. The results are a unique gift for friends and family: warming, sweet-bitter, earthy, and complex, a great condiment on a baked potato with butter and sour cream.

- 1 pound (450 g) thin rhubarb stalks (about 3), thinly sliced (about 4 cups)
- 1 cup (320 g) maple syrup, preferably a dark amber or even dark maple syrup
- 1 tablespoon (6 g) finely grated orange zest
- ½ cup (120 ml) orange juice, preferably freshly squeezed
- ½ cup (75 g) golden raisins
- ⅛ teaspoon ground cinnamon
- ⅛ teaspoon kosher salt
- ½ cup (70 g) walnut pieces, toasted and chopped (for toasting nuts, see the TIP with Peach–Sour Cherry Conserve recipe on page 132)

1. Stir the rhubarb, maple syrup, orange zest, orange juice, raisins, cinnamon, and salt in a medium saucepan until well combined. Set the pan over medium-high heat and stir constantly to dissolve the sugar. Bring to a full boil, stirring often.

2. Reduce the heat to low and simmer *slowly*, stirring quite often, for 5 minutes. Stir in the nuts.

3. Keep cooking at a low simmer, stirring more and more frequently until almost constantly, until the mixture is so thick that you can run a wooden spoon across the bottom of the pan and create a line that holds its edges for a second or two before flowing back into place, about 30 minutes.

4. Turn off the heat, remove the pan from the burner, and set aside for 1–2 minutes. Transfer to two *clean* ½ pint (236 ml) jars or other containers, leaving about ½ inch (1 cm) headspace in each. Cover or seal. Cool at room temperature for no more than 1 hour, then refrigerate or freeze.

More

For a more sophisticated if slightly sweeter flavor, substitute triple sec for the orange juice (or use your homemade triple sec—see page 434).

Spicy Tomato Conserve

MAKES: about 3 cups (720 ml)
FRIDGE: up to 3 weeks
FREEZER: up to 1 year

Long ago, in New York City, we were at the Union Square Greenmarket, talking to a jam maker about her process. She told us the secret to her jams' velvety texture was tomato juice, which cooks down and loses its vegetal flavor but offers a luxurious finish. We're still not sold on the flavors of tomato juice in most jams, but we do know she was right when it comes to recipes like this one for tomato conserve, a decidedly wonderful treat later in winter when summery tomatoes are nowhere to be found.

- 1 pound (450 g) beefsteak tomatoes (about 2 large), halved, cored, and chopped
- 1 large tart green apple, such as Granny Smith, stemmed, cored, and chopped (do not peel)
- 1 medium yellow or white onion, peeled and finely chopped
- 2 fresh green serrano chilis, stemmed and very thinly sliced
- 2 medium garlic cloves, peeled and minced
- 1½ cups (360 ml) tomato juice
- 1 cup (200 g) granulated white sugar
- ½ cup (120 ml) apple cider vinegar
- 1 teaspoon brown mustard seeds
- ½ teaspoon ground allspice
- ½ teaspoon kosher salt
- ½ cup (70 g) chopped walnut pieces

1. Stir the tomatoes, apple, onion, chilis, garlic, tomato juice, sugar, vinegar, mustard seeds, allspice, and salt in a large saucepan until well combined. Set the pan over medium-high heat and stir constantly to dissolve the sugar. Bring to a full boil, stirring often. Reduce the heat to medium and simmer, stirring quite often, for 20 minutes.

2. Stir in the walnuts. Reduce the heat to low and simmer *slowly*, stirring more and more until almost constantly, until you can run a wooden spoon across the bottom of the pan and create a line that holds its edges for a second, about 40 minutes.

3. Turn off the heat, remove the pan from the burner, and set aside for 1–2 minutes. Transfer to three *clean* ½ pint (236 ml) jars or other containers, leaving about ½ inch (1 cm) headspace in each. Cover or seal. Cool at room temperature for no more than 1 hour, then refrigerate or freeze.

More
For a slightly sweeter conserve, substitute a firm but ripe pear, stemmed, seeded, and chopped (but not peeled) for the apple.

Spicy Cranberry Conserve

MAKES: about 4 cups (960 ml)
FRIDGE: up to 3 weeks
FREEZER: up to 1 year
May be traditionally canned (see page 436)

This cranberry concoction might replace the more traditional Smooth Cranberry Sauce (page 142) at your holiday table. It's got a deep if still sweet flavor. It's also got walnuts for a bit of crunch. But don't wait for a holiday. Serve this one with any chicken or turkey off the grill in the middle of summer.

- 12 ounces (340 g) fresh cranberries or thawed frozen whole cranberries (about 3 cups for either)
- 1 cup (240 ml) orange juice, preferably freshly squeezed
- ½ cup (100 g) granulated white sugar
- ½ cup (107 g) packed light brown sugar
- 6 tablespoons (45 g) walnut pieces, toasted and chopped (for toasting nuts, see the TIP with Peach–Sour Cherry Conserve recipe on page 132)
- 4 plump dried Calimyrna or Adriatic (aka Turkish) figs, stemmed and finely chopped
- 3 fresh green or red serrano chilis, stemmed, halved lengthwise, and thinly sliced
- ⅛ teaspoon ground cloves
- ⅛ teaspoon kosher salt

1. Stir together all the ingredients in a large saucepan until well combined. Set the pan over medium-high heat and stir constantly to dissolve the sugar. Bring to a full boil, stirring often.

2. Reduce the heat to low and simmer, stirring often so you can crush about three-quarters of the cranberries against the inside of the pan, until thick and jam-like, about 7 minutes.

3. Turn off the heat, remove the pan from the burner, and set aside for 1–2 minutes. Transfer to four *clean* ½ pint (236 ml) jars or other containers, leaving about ½ inch (1 cm) headspace in each. Cover or seal. Cool at room temperature for no more than 1 hour, then refrigerate or freeze.

Spicy Tomato Conserve (page 134)
with a grilled cheese sandwich

More

For more warming spice flavor, add up to ¼ teaspoon ground cinnamon, ¼ teaspoon ground allspice, and ⅛ teaspoon grated nutmeg.

Ginger Jam

MAKES: about 2 cups (480 ml)
FRIDGE: up to 3 weeks
FREEZER: up to 1 year
May be traditionally canned (see page 436)

This one is a spicy-sweet English tradition, often served with toast or scones and definitely a strong flavor in the morning (*and* far better with tea than coffee). The fresher the ginger, the better. Tough ginger will produce a fibrous jam. The ginger should be still moist with a thin, almost translucent skin you can nick with your fingernail. For the best specimens, head to an Asian supermarket.

> 1 cup (200 g) granulated white sugar
>
> 2 tablespoons (24 g) *granulated less-sugar* pectin
>
> 8 ounces (240 g) fresh ginger, peeled and grated through the large holes of a box grater (about 1 cup)
>
> 1 cup (240 ml) water
>
> 2 tablespoons (30 ml) lemon juice
>
> 1 tablespoon (6 g) finely grated lemon zest

1. Mix ¼ cup (50 g) sugar and the pectin in a small bowl until uniform.

2. Combine the ginger, water, lemon juice, and zest in a medium saucepan. Set it over medium-high heat and add the pectin mixture. Stir constantly to dissolve the granulated ingredients. Bring to a boil you can't stir down, stirring often.

3. Add the remaining ¾ cup (150 g) sugar and stir constantly to dissolve the sugar. Bring back to a full boil, stirring occasionally. Boil undisturbed for 1 minute.

4. Turn off the heat, remove the pan from the burner, and set aside for 1–2 minutes. Skim any foamy impurities with a tablespoon.

5. Transfer to two *clean* ½ pint (236 ml) jars or other containers, leaving about ½ inch (1 cm) headspace in each. Cover or seal. Cool at room temperature for no more than 1 hour, then refrigerate or freeze.

Tip

To peel ginger with the least loss, scrape the thin skin from the ginger with the edge of a flatware spoon. Although a box grater may be the easiest way to grate the ginger, if you want to get fancy, use the julienne blade of a mandoline.

White Wine Jelly

MAKES: about 3 cups (720 ml)
FRIDGE: up to 1 month
FREEZER: up to 1 year
May be traditionally canned (see page 436)

Why would anyone go to the trouble to make wine jelly? Easy! To stir into beef, pork, chicken, or vegetable stew during the last minutes to brighten the flavors. To soften a spoonful in a microwave for a glaze to brush on a tart or other baked good. To use as a glaze on a pork roast (particularly ham) during the last 15 minutes of cooking. To add jazz to a cheese board. Or finally, to enjoy as a topper for tapenade or caponata on a cracker.

> 1½ cups (300 g) granulated white sugar
>
> ¼ cup (48 g) *granulated less-sugar* pectin
>
> One 750 ml bottle of sweet white wine, such as a sweet Riesling (but not a dessert wine)

1. Mix ¼ cup (50 g) sugar and the pectin in a small bowl until uniform.

2. Pour the wine into a medium saucepan and set it over medium-high heat. Add the pectin mixture and stir constantly to dissolve the granulated ingredients. Bring to a boil you can't stir down, stirring often.

➡

3. Add the remaining 1¼ cups (250 g) sugar and stir constantly to dissolve the sugar. Bring back to a full boil, stirring occasionally. Boil undisturbed for 1 minute.

4. Turn off the heat, remove the pan from the burner, and set aside for 1–2 minutes. Skim any foamy impurities with a tablespoon.

5. Transfer to three *clean* ½ pint (236 ml) jars or other containers, leaving about ½ inch (1 cm) headspace in each. Cover or seal. Cool at room temperature for no more than 1 hour, then refrigerate or freeze. In the fridge, the jelly will not reach its best flavor for 48 hours.

More

Add herbs, spices, or aromatics: a small rosemary stalk, a couple of thyme sprigs, a tarragon sprig, a few allspice berries, a *green* cardamom pod or two, a halved and seeded fresh bird's eye chili, or a small, peeled piece of fresh ginger. Fish out and discard any of these before bottling.

Red Wine Jelly

MAKES: about 3 cups (720 ml)
FRIDGE: up to 1 month
FREEZER: up to 1 year
May be traditionally canned (see page 436)

Red wine jelly is a bit trickier than white wine jelly, mostly because it's oddly easier to mask the flavors of red wine with too much sugar. Since we need to cut down on the sugar to bring out those mellow, tannic notes, we must then compensate by adding cardamom pods for a gentle herbal flavor, almost a background note that helps bring the wine flavors forward again.

1 cup (200 g) granulated white sugar
¼ cup (48 g) *granulated less-sugar* pectin
One 750 ml bottle of a full-bodied red wine, such as Cabernet, Merlot, Rioja, or Chianti
Up to 4 *green* cardamom pods, crushed

1. Mix ¼ cup (50 g) sugar and the pectin in a small bowl until uniform.

2. Pour the wine into a medium saucepan and set it over medium-high heat. Add the cardamom pods and the pectin mixture. Stir constantly to dissolve the granulated ingredients. Bring to a boil you can't stir down, stirring often.

3. Add the remaining ¾ cup (150 g) sugar and stir constantly to dissolve the sugar. Bring back to a full boil, stirring occasionally. Boil undisturbed for 1 minute.

4. Turn off the heat, remove the pan from the burner, and set aside for 1–2 minutes. Skim any foamy impurities with a tablespoon. Fish out and discard any bits of cardamom hull. (You'll never get all the seeds).

5. Transfer to three *clean* ½ pint (236 ml) jars or other containers, leaving about ½ inch (1 cm) headspace in each. Cover or seal. Cool at room temperature for no more than 1 hour, then refrigerate or freeze. In the fridge, the jelly will not reach its best flavor for 48 hours.

Tip

Although we call for ¼ cup (48 g) pectin, feel free to use the whole box if it's the standard 1¾ ounces (50 g).

Rosemary–Red Wine Jelly

MAKES: about 3 cups (720 ml)
FRIDGE: up to 1 month
FREEZER: up to 1 year
May be traditionally canned (see page 436)

Because there's rosemary in this jelly, we've cut down the sugar compared to our Red Wine Jelly (above), so this concoction tastes less like a sweet confection and more like a sophisticated, herbal cocktail. You can tame the rosemary notes by steeping the sprigs in the wine for only 10 minutes, rather than our suggested 20 minutes. Use this jelly as a finish for ragus of all sorts, mushroom or root vegetable stews, and even as a topper (with butter) for roasted carrots.

> One 750 ml bottle of dark, bold red wine, preferably Merlot
> Two 4 inch (10 cm) fresh rosemary sprigs
> ¾ cup (150 g) granulated white sugar
> ¼ cup (48 g) *granulated less-sugar* pectin

1. Pour the wine into a medium saucepan. Set it over medium-high heat and add the rosemary. Warm until steam rises from the wine but it doesn't begin to simmer. Turn off the heat, cover the pan, and steep at room temperature for 20 minutes.

2. Meanwhile, mix ¼ cup (50 g) sugar and the pectin in a small bowl until uniform.

3. Fish out and discard the rosemary sprigs. Set the pan back over medium-high heat and add the pectin mixture. Stir constantly to dissolve the granulated ingredients. Bring to a boil you can't stir down, stirring often.

4. Add the remaining ½ cup (100 g) sugar and stir constantly to dissolve the sugar. Bring back to a full boil, stirring occasionally. Boil undisturbed for 1 minute.

5. Turn off the heat, remove the pan from the burner, and set aside for 1–2 minutes. Skim any foamy impurities with a tablespoon.

6. Transfer to three *clean* ½ pint (236 ml) jars or other containers, leaving about ½ inch (1 cm) headspace in each. Cover or seal. Cool at room temperature for no more than 1 hour, then refrigerate or freeze. In the fridge, the jelly will not reach its best flavor for 48 hours.

More
Add up to 1 teaspoon black peppercorns and/or one dried red chili with the rosemary. Get rid of these when you discard the rosemary.

Jalapeño Jam

MAKES: about 3 cups (720 ml)
FRIDGE: up to 3 weeks
FREEZER: up to 1 year
May be traditionally canned (see page 436)

Here's a spicy kick, great in dollops on tacos, burritos, and nachos, or spread with mayonnaise on toasted-bread sandwiches. We don't strain the mixture so it stays pulpy, a better contrast to the burn. The fresh chilis will leave an invisible residue of the fiery chemical capsaicin on your fingers: Wear culinary kitchen gloves (see page 18) when prepping them, then strip the gloves off, so you don't have to worry about your eyes or other sensitive parts. If you don't have culinary kitchen gloves, rub your hands with vegetable or canola oil *after* handling the chilis, then wash thoroughly with soap and water.

> 2 cups (400 g) granulated white sugar
> 2 tablespoons (24 g) *granulated less-sugar* pectin
> 5 large fresh green jalapeño chilis
> 1 large red or yellow bell pepper
> ½ cup (120 ml) apple cider vinegar

1. Mix ¼ cup (50 g) sugar and the pectin in a small bowl until uniform.

2. Cut the stem end off each chili, stand it up on its cut side on a cutting board, and slice down to remove the flesh in strips, leaving the core and seeds behind. Do the same operation with the bell pepper.

3. Roughly chop the chili strips and pieces of bell pepper. Put them and the vinegar in a food processor. Cover and pulse several times until the mixture looks like a slushy relish, not a puree.

4. Pour and scrape the contents of the food processor into a medium saucepan. Set it over medium-high heat and add the pectin mixture. Stir constantly to dissolve the granulated ingredients. Bring to a boil you can't stir down, stirring often.

Jalapeño Jam
(page 139)

5. Add the remaining 1¾ cups (350 g) sugar and stir constantly to dissolve the sugar. Bring back to a full boil, stirring occasionally. Boil undisturbed for 1 minute.

6. Turn off the heat, remove the pan from the burner, and set aside for 1–2 minutes. Skim any foamy impurities with a tablespoon.

7. Transfer to three *clean* ½ pint (236 ml) jars or other containers, leaving about ½ inch (1 cm) headspace in each. Cover or seal. Cool at room temperature for no more than 1 hour, then refrigerate or freeze.

Next
Mix a little of this jelly into softened cream cheese and use in flour tortilla roll-ups with sprouts, shredded carrots, and/or shredded zucchini.

Mint Jelly

MAKES: about 3 cups (720 ml)
FRIDGE: up to 1 month
FREEZER: up to 1 year
May be traditionally canned (see page 436)

This clear, brilliant jelly has a more subtle flavor than the lurid green stuff often sold with lamb chops. We've long experimented with mint in preserves. Frankly, the herb needs taming! To that end, we've gotten more sophisticated results by adding apples to the mix—which means, yes, we have to use a jelly bag and (ultimately) a candy thermometer for the right consistency. But the results speak for themselves: soft, aromatic, and smooth as glass.

> 2 pounds (900 g) hard sour apples, such as Granny Smith or McIntosh
> 4 cups (960 ml) water
> 2 cups (170 g) packed fresh mint leaves
> Additional water as necessary to make up the volume
> 1 cup (200 g) granulated white sugar
> 2 tablespoons (24 g) *granulated less-sugar* pectin
> 2 tablespoons (30 ml) lemon juice
> 1 drop of green food coloring

1. Roughly chop the apples: peels, cores, stems, and all. Put them in a large saucepan and stir in 3½ cups (840 ml) water. Set the pan over medium-high heat and bring the mixture to a simmer, stirring occasionally. Reduce the heat to low, cover the pan, and simmer, stirring occasionally, until the apples are so soft they can be mashed with the back of a wooden spoon, about 15 minutes. Turn off the burner and remove the pan from the heat.

2. Put the mint and the remaining ½ cup (120 ml) water in a food processor. Cover and pulse until the mint is finely chopped into a thick tapenade-like mixture. Stir this mixture into the apples in the pan, cover, and set aside at room temperature for 30 minutes.

3. Set up a jelly bag on a stand over a clean, large saucepan. (For alternatives to a jelly bag, see page 17.) Pour the apple-mint mixture into the bag and drain for at least 8 hours or overnight. You should end up with 3 cups of liquid. If the amount is shy, add a little water to make up the deficit.

4. Mix the sugar and pectin in a small bowl until uniform. Set the saucepan with the strained liquid over medium-high heat and add the pectin mixture. Stir constantly to dissolve the granulated ingredients. Stir in the lemon juice and food coloring.

5. Clip a candy thermometer to the inside of the pan. Bring the mixture to a full boil, stirring often. Continue cooking until the temperature reaches 220°F (104°C), about 7 minutes.

6. Turn off the heat, remove the pan from the burner, and set aside for 1–2 minutes. Skim any foamy impurities with a tablespoon.

7. Transfer to three *clean* ½ pint (236 ml) jars or other containers, leaving about ½ inch (1 cm) headspace in each. Cover or seal. Cool at room temperature for no more than 1 hour, then refrigerate or freeze.

More
To spice it up, add up to 1 teaspoon red pepper flakes with the mint in the food processor.

Tarragon Jelly

MAKES: about 3 cups (720 ml)
FRIDGE: up to 1 month
FREEZER: up to 1 year
May be traditionally canned (see page 436)

Just as we did with Mint Jelly (page 141), we use apples to soften this herb jelly. It's delicately aromatic, a great addition to a cheese board or even to a grilled cheese sandwich before you toast it. We're also fond of the jelly with deli mustard on turkey or roast beef sandwiches. Or with mayonnaise on classic tomato sandwiches.

> 2 pounds (900 g) hard sour apples, such as Granny Smith or McIntosh
> 4 cups (960 ml) water
> 4 large tarragon sprigs
> Additional water as necessary to make up the volume
> 1 cup (200 g) granulated white sugar
> 2 tablespoons (24 g) *granulated less-sugar* pectin
> 1 tablespoon (30 ml) white wine vinegar

1. Roughly chop the apples: peels, cores, stems, and all. Put them in a large saucepan and stir in the water. Set the pan over medium-high heat and bring the mixture to a simmer, stirring occasionally. Reduce the heat to low, cover the pan, and simmer, stirring occasionally, until the apples are so soft they can be mashed with the back of a wooden spoon, about 15 minutes. Turn off the burner and remove the pan from the heat.

2. Stir in the tarragon sprigs, cover the pan, and steep at room temperature for at least 30 minutes or up to 1 hour.

3. Set up a jelly bag on a stand over a clean, large saucepan. (For alternatives to a jelly bag, see page 17.) Pour the apple-tarragon mixture into the bag and drain for at least 8 hours or overnight. You should end up with 3 cups of liquid. If the amount is shy, add a little water to make up the deficit.

4. Mix the sugar and pectin in a small bowl until uniform. Set the saucepan with the strained liquid

over medium-high heat and add the pectin mixture. Stir constantly to dissolve the granulated ingredients. Stir in the vinegar.

5. Clip a candy thermometer to the inside of the pan. Bring the mixture to a full boil, stirring often. Continue cooking until the temperature reaches 220°F (104°C), about 7 minutes.

6. Turn off the heat, remove the pan from the burner, and set aside for 1–2 minutes. Skim any foamy impurities with a tablespoon.

7. Transfer to three *clean* ½ pint (236 ml) jars or other containers, leaving about ½ inch (1 cm) headspace in each. Cover or seal. Cool at room temperature for no more than 1 hour, then refrigerate or freeze.

More
Make other herb jellies with this technique: substitute 6 large thyme sprigs, 4 large oregano sprigs, or two 4 inch (10 cm) rosemary sprigs for the tarragon.

Smooth Cranberry Sauce

MAKES: about 5 cups (1200 ml)
FRIDGE: up to 1 month
FREEZER: up to 1 year
May be traditionally canned (see page 436)

This is a firm, almost transparent cranberry jelly, known to *The Simpsons* fans as Cranberry Sauce à la Bart…or perhaps known to most of us as the stuff that plops out of the can as a jellied log. Ours is far less sweet, more fruit-tart, certainly less rigid, and so more in keeping with the natural flavors of cranberries. We think it's a better condiment with the holiday bird or any roasted poultry.

> 1¼ cups (250 g) granulated white sugar
> ¼ cup (48 g) *granulated less-sugar* pectin
> 4 cups (960 ml) *unsweetened* cranberry juice

1. Mix ¼ cup (50 g) sugar and the pectin in a small bowl until uniform.

Front to back: Smooth Cranberry Sauce (page 142) and Cranberry Walnut Sauce (page 146)

2. Pour the juice in a medium saucepan. Set it over medium-high heat and add the pectin mixture. Stir constantly to dissolve the granulated ingredients. Bring to a boil you can't stir down, stirring often.

3. Add the remaining 1 cup (200 g) sugar and stir constantly to dissolve the sugar. Bring back to a full boil, stirring often. Boil undisturbed for 1 minute.

4. Turn off the heat, remove the pan from the burner, and set aside for 1–2 minutes. Skim any foamy impurities with a tablespoon.

5. Transfer to five *clean* ½ pint (236 ml) jars or other containers, leaving about ½ inch (1 cm) headspace in each. Cover or seal. Cool at room temperature for no more than 1 hour, then refrigerate or freeze.

More
Layer more flavor with ¼ teaspoon orange extract or ¼ teaspoon rum extract with the sugar in step 3.

Chunky Cranberry Sauce

MAKES: about 3 cups (720 ml)
FRIDGE: up to 3 weeks
FREEZER: up to 1 year

As we did with Smooth Cranberry Sauce (page 142), we intentionally reduced the sugar in this chunky sauce so we could highlight the sour pop of cranberries. This recipe is easy to accomplish as long as you're patient, stirring the mixture until it becomes jam-like. Lots of stirring also wards off scorching, which introduces unwanted bitter notes among the sweet-sour flavors.

> 12 ounces (340 g) fresh whole cranberries or thawed frozen cranberries
> ¾ cup (180 ml) water
> ¼ cup (60 ml) orange juice, preferably freshly squeezed
> ¾ cup (160 g) packed light brown sugar
> ½ teaspoon vanilla extract
> ⅛ teaspoon kosher salt

1. Combine all the ingredients in a medium saucepan. Set it over medium-high heat and cook, stirring often, until the mixture comes to a boil, about 5 minutes.

2. Reduce the heat to low and simmer *slowly*, stirring more and more often, until the cranberries burst and the mixture thickens to a jam-like consistency, about 10 minutes.

3. Turn off the heat, remove the pan from the burner, and set aside for 1–2 minutes. Transfer to three *clean* ½ pint (236 ml) jars or other containers, leaving about ½ inch (1 cm) headspace in each. Cover or seal. Cool at room temperature for no more than 1 hour, then refrigerate or freeze. In the fridge, the sauce will not come to its best flavor for 48 hours.

More
For a more complex flavor, use ½ cup (120 ml) water and ¼ cup (60 ml) plain brandy, bourbon, or Cointreau.

Sugar-Free Cranberry Sauce

MAKES: about 3 cups (720 ml)
FRIDGE: up to 2 weeks
FREEZER: up to 6 months

This sauce is smooth but not clear, since we call for some *brown*-sugar substitute as well as the more familiar white-sugar substitute. The deeper flavors in the brown-sugar substitute make up some of the layers of flavoring that granulated sugar brings out in many preserved foods. Also, we use cranberries, rather than cranberry juice, because they have slightly earthy undertones that add more body to the sauce.

> 12 ounces (340 g) fresh whole cranberries or thawed frozen cranberries
> 1 cup (240 ml) water

½ cup *1-to-1 (by volume)* granulated *brown*-sugar substitute

¼ cup *1-to-1 (by volume)* granulated *white*-sugar substitute

1. Combine all the ingredients in a medium saucepan. Set it over medium-high heat. Cook, stirring quite often, until the mixture comes to a simmer, about 5 minutes.

2. Reduce the heat to low and simmer *slowly*, stirring more and more often, until the cranberries burst and the mixture thickens to a jam-like consistency, about 10 minutes.

3. Turn off the heat, remove the pan from the burner, and set aside for 1–2 minutes. Skim any foamy impurities with a tablespoon.

4. Transfer to three *clean* ½ pint (236 ml) jars or other containers, leaving about ½ inch (1 cm) headspace in each. Cover or seal. Cool at room temperature for no more than 1 hour, then refrigerate or freeze.

More

Add up to ½ teaspoon vanilla extract and/or ¼ teaspoon almond extract.

Spiced Cranberry Sauce

MAKES: about 3 cups (720 ml)
FRIDGE: up to 3 weeks
FREEZER: up to 1 year
May be traditionally canned (see page 436)

It's hard to describe this sophisticated cranberry sauce: not a chutney (because there's no vinegar), but still somewhat chunky, more like a highly spiced, pulpy sauce that's sweeter than most conserves but not quite as sweet as a jam. We've been making this sauce for years—but just a single batch at a time for a holiday table or a rib-roast celebration. Then we decided we should make more to squirrel away in the fridge or freezer so we'd always have a jar at the ready.

12 ounces (340 g) fresh whole cranberries or thawed frozen cranberries

1 cup (240 ml) water

1 cup (200 g) granulated white sugar

½ teaspoon ground cinnamon

½ teaspoon ground ginger

¼ teaspoon ground allspice

¼ teaspoon ground cloves

⅛ teaspoon kosher salt

1. Combine all the ingredients in a medium saucepan. Set it over medium-high heat and cook, stirring often, until the mixture comes to a boil, about 5 minutes.

2. Reduce the heat to low and simmer *slowly*, stirring more and more frequently, until the cranberries burst and the mixture thickens to a jam-like consistency, about 10 minutes.

3. Turn off the heat, remove the pan from the burner, and set aside for 1–2 minutes. Transfer to three *clean* ½ pint (236 ml) jars or other containers, leaving about ½ inch (1 cm) headspace in each. Cover or seal. Cool at room temperature for no more than 1 hour, then refrigerate or freeze. In the fridge, the sauce will not come to its best flavor for 48 hours.

Next

Mix the sauce with equal parts *by volume* chili crisp and softened cream cheese and use as a spread on veggie sandwiches, particularly with a layer of hummus and lots of sprouts.

Cranberry Walnut Sauce

MAKES: about 3 cups (720 ml)
FRIDGE: up to 3 weeks
FREEZER: up to 1 year
May be traditionally canned (see page 436)

To give this chunky sauce a bit more depth and a slightly more mellow flavor, we use unsweetened *cherry* juice, rather than cranberry juice. The cherry juice seems to smooth the pop of the cranberries, making a nice contrast to the earthy-sweet walnuts. If you want even more flavor, toast the shelled walnut pieces before you chop them.

> 12 ounces (340 g) fresh whole cranberries or thawed frozen cranberries
>
> 1 cup (240 ml) *unsweetened* cherry juice
>
> ¾ cup (160 g) packed light brown sugar
>
> ¼ cup (50 g) granulated white sugar
>
> ½ cup (56 g) walnut pieces, chopped
>
> ½ teaspoon ground ginger
>
> ½ teaspoon ground cinnamon

1. Combine all the ingredients in a medium saucepan. Set it over medium-high heat and cook, stirring often, until the mixture comes to a boil, about 5 minutes.

2. Reduce the heat to low and simmer *slowly*, stirring more and more often, until the cranberries burst and the mixture thickens to a jam-like consistency, about 10 minutes.

3. Turn off the heat, remove the pan from the burner, and set aside for 1–2 minutes. Transfer to three *clean* ½ pint (236 ml) jars or other containers, leaving about ½ inch (1 cm) headspace in each. Cover or seal. Cool at room temperature for no more than 1 hour, then refrigerate or freeze. In the fridge, the sauce will not come to its best flavor for 48 hours.

More
For an even more savory sauce, reduce the cherry juice to ½ cup (120 ml) and add ½ cup (120 ml) dry red wine.

Classic Mango Chutney

MAKES: about 5 cups (1200 ml)
FRIDGE: up to 3 weeks
FREEZER: up to 1 year
May be traditionally canned (see page 436)

We start our chutneys with one that may be unfamiliar to some: *not* the slightly musky Major Grey's (that's up next), but one with a bright orange color and a fresh flavor, still redolent of the mangoes' perfume. Ours is not spicy; it's more spiky, thanks to the crystallized ginger. Although it would be welcome with raita and/or dal along with almost any curry, it's also great mixed into egg or chicken salad.

> 4¼ pounds (2 kg) ripe mangoes (about 4 large), pitted, peeled, and chopped (about 6 cups)
>
> 2 cups (400 g) granulated white sugar
>
> 6 tablespoons (90 ml) lime juice
>
> 6 tablespoons (90 ml) distilled white vinegar
>
> ¼ cup (45 g) chopped crystallized ginger
>
> One 3 inch (7.5 cm) cinnamon stick
>
> 2 teaspoons fenugreek seeds
>
> 1 teaspoon yellow mustard seeds
>
> ½ teaspoon kosher salt
>
> ¼ teaspoon ground dried turmeric

1. Combine all the ingredients in a large saucepan. (Make sure you also scrape any juice or pulp from the mangoes on the cutting board into the pan.) Set the pan over medium-high heat and cook, stirring often, until the mixture comes to a boil, about 5 minutes.

2. Reduce the heat to low and simmer, stirring more and more often to prevent scorching, until so thick that you can run a wooden spoon across the bottom of the pan and create a line that holds its edges for a second, 45–50 minutes.

3. Turn off the heat, remove the pan from the burner, and set aside for 1–2 minutes. Skim any foamy impurities with a tablespoon. Fish out and discard the cinnamon stick.

4. Transfer to five *clean* ½ pint (236 ml) jars or other containers, leaving about ½ inch (1 cm) headspace in each. Cover or seal. Cool at room temperature for no more than 1 hour, then refrigerate or freeze.

More

For a more aromatic but less sour chutney, use just ¼ cup (60 ml) distilled white vinegar and add 2 tablespoons (30 ml) ginger juice.

Major Grey's Chutney

MAKES: about 5 cups (1200 ml)
FRIDGE: up to 3 weeks
FREEZER: up to 1 year
May be traditionally canned (see page 436)

This old-school chutney has a powerful flavor thanks to the brown sugar, the molasses (or treacle), and the aromatics. The condiment holds up well to freezing (and thawing), the flavors still broad and rich. Although truly ripe mangoes make a better chutney, you can still use those with only a bit of a red hue but without any distinct perfume. The many aromatics will bring out the missing flavor notes.

- 4¼ pounds (2 kg) ripe mangoes (about 4 large), pitted, peeled, and chopped (about 6 cups)
- 1 cup (240 ml) apple cider vinegar
- 1¼ cups (270 g) packed dark brown sugar
- ¾ cup (150 g) granulated white sugar
- ½ cup (170 g) molasses or black treacle
- 1 medium red onion, peeled and *finely* chopped
- 1 medium lime, peeled, cored, seeded, and the pulp chopped
- 1 cup (150 g) golden raisins
- One 2 inch (5 cm) piece of fresh ginger, peeled and *minced*
- 1 teaspoon red pepper flakes
- 1 teaspoon yellow or brown mustard seeds
- 1 teaspoon coriander seeds
- ½ teaspoon decorticated (husked and removed from the pods) cardamom seeds
- ½ teaspoon kosher salt
- ½ teaspoon ground black pepper

1. Combine all the ingredients in a large saucepan. (Scrape any juice or pulp from the mangoes on the cutting board into the pan.) Set the pan over medium-high heat and cook, stirring often, until the mixture comes to a boil, about 5 minutes.

2. Reduce the heat to low and simmer *slowly*, stirring more and more often to prevent scorching, until dark and so thick that you can run a wooden spoon across the bottom of the pan and create a line that holds its edges for a second, 45–50 minutes.

3. Turn off the heat, remove the pan from the burner, and set aside for 1–2 minutes. Transfer to five *clean* ½ pint (236 ml) jars or other containers, leaving about ½ inch (1 cm) headspace in each. Cover or seal. Cool at room temperature for no more than 1 hour, then refrigerate or freeze.

Next

Beyond curries, we love this chutney with sour cream on a baked potato.

Sugar-Free Mango Chutney

MAKES: about 4 cups (960 ml)
FRIDGE: up to 2 weeks
FREEZER: up to 6 months

We add lots of dried fruit to this guilt-free chutney to give it heft and layered flavors. The result is fairly chunky, although certainly not like preserves, more like a rich, less-sweet conserve. Use thick, plump Medjool dates, not chopped baking dates.

Front to back:
Classic Mango Chutney
(page 146) and Major
Grey's Chutney (page 147),
served with samosas

3⅓ pounds (1.5 kg) ripe mangoes (about 3 large), pitted, peeled, and chopped (about 4½ cups)

½ cup (120 ml) orange juice, preferably freshly squeezed

¼ cup (60 ml) white wine vinegar

¼ cup *1-to-1 (by volume)* granulated *brown*-sugar substitute

¼ cup (38 g) golden raisins

8 large, plump Medjool dates, pitted and chopped

1 large shallot (about 1¾ ounces or 50 g), peeled and *minced*

1 medium garlic clove, peeled and minced

One 1 inch (2.5 cm) piece of fresh ginger, peeled and *minced*

1 tablespoon (6 g) minced orange zest

1 teaspoon yellow or brown mustard seeds

⅛ teaspoon ground cloves

⅛ teaspoon kosher salt

1. Combine all the ingredients in a large saucepan. (Scrape any juice or pulp from the mangoes on the cutting board into the pan.) Set the pan over medium-high heat and cook, stirring often, until the mixture comes to a boil, about 5 minutes.

2. Reduce the heat to low and simmer *slowly*, stirring more and more often to prevent scorching, until dark and so thick that you can run a wooden spoon across the bottom of the pan and create a line that holds its edges for a second, about 40 minutes.

3. Turn off the heat, remove the pan from the burner, and set aside for 1–2 minutes. Transfer to four *clean* ½ pint (236 ml) jars or other containers, leaving about ½ inch (1 cm) headspace in each. Cover or seal. Cool at room temperature for no more than 1 hour, then refrigerate or freeze.

More
Double or even triple the garlic for lots of aromatic bounce in this chutney.

Easy Onion Chutney

MAKES: about 3 cups (720 ml)
FRIDGE: up to 3 weeks
FREEZER: up to 1 year

Onions are naturally sweet…and even more so after long cooking. However, they also become quite soft during a prolonged stint over the heat, which means that onion chutney can often become something like a spiced onion spread. Our version keeps the onions more intact so they offer more texture. That said, they must soften. So do watch them over the heat, stirring fairly often to keep them from turning dark brown. And FYI, the total weight of the onions is more important to the success of this chutney than any certain number of onions.

3 tablespoons (45 ml) olive oil

2 pounds (900 g) yellow or white onions, peeled, halved, and sliced into paper-thin half-moons

¼ cup (80 g) maple syrup

¼ cup (50 g) granulated white sugar

¼ cup (60 ml) white wine vinegar

One 1 inch (2.5 cm) piece of fresh ginger, peeled and *minced*

3 medium garlic cloves, peeled and minced

1 teaspoon coriander seeds

½ teaspoon red pepper flakes

½ teaspoon mild smoked paprika

¼ teaspoon ground cinnamon

¼ teaspoon kosher salt

1. Set a very large saucepan over low heat for a minute or two. Add the oil, then the onions and stir well to coat. Continue cooking, stirring often, until the onions are softened and golden, about 20 minutes.

2. Add the maple syrup, sugar, vinegar, ginger, garlic, coriander seeds, red pepper flakes, smoked paprika, cinnamon, and salt. Raise the heat to medium and stir constantly to dissolve the sugar. Bring back to a simmer, stirring often.

3. Reduce the heat to low and continue cooking, stirring more and more often to prevent scorching, until so thick that you can run a wooden spoon across the bottom of the pan and create a line that holds its edges for a second, about 10 minutes.

4. Turn off the heat, remove the pan from the burner, and set aside for 1–2 minutes. Transfer to three *clean* ½ pint (236 ml) jars or other containers, leaving about ½ inch (1 cm) headspace in each. Cover or seal. Cool at room temperature for no more than 1 hour, then refrigerate or freeze.

Next
Stir a little of this chutney into tuna or chicken salad (even purchased tuna or chicken salad!) for a terrific flavor burst.

Red Onion–Molasses Chutney

MAKES: about 3 cups (720 ml)
FRIDGE: up to 3 weeks
FREEZER: up to 1 year

Here, we let the onions cook a little longer than in our Easy Onion Chutney (page 149). The onions will then turn darker, get extremely sweet, and (as a bonus) pick up a few, subtle bitter notes for a more complex flavor—which is then darkened further with molasses or black treacle. The flavors are very assertive, a great combo on rice and dal with just about any curry.

- 3 tablespoons (45 ml) olive oil
- 2 pounds (900 g) red onions, peeled, halved, and sliced into paper-thin half-moons
- 1 cup (200 g) granulated white sugar
- ½ cup (120 ml) red wine vinegar
- 3 tablespoons (65 g) molasses or black treacle
- 3 medium garlic cloves, peeled and minced
- 1 tablespoon (16 g) coarse-grained mustard (or use your own homemade, page 63)
- ½ teaspoon ground dried ginger
- ½ teaspoon red pepper flakes
- ¼ teaspoon kosher salt

1. Set a very large saucepan over low heat for a minute or two. Add the oil, then the onions and stir well to coat. Reduce the heat to low and cook *slowly*, stirring more and more often, until the onions soften and begin to darken at their edges, about 30 minutes.

2. Raise the heat to medium and add the sugar, vinegar, molasses or treacle, garlic, mustard, ground ginger, red pepper flakes, and salt. Stir constantly to dissolve the sugar. Bring to a simmer, stirring occasionally.

3. Reduce the heat to low and simmer at a slow, steady bubble, stirring more and more often to prevent scorching, until so thick that you can run a wooden spoon across the bottom of the pan and create a line that holds its edges for a second, about 15 minutes.

4. Turn off the heat, remove the pan from the burner, and set aside for 1–2 minutes. Transfer to three *clean* ½ pint (236 ml) jars or other containers, leaving about ½ inch (1 cm) headspace in each. Cover or seal. Cool at room temperature for no more than 1 hour, then refrigerate or freeze.

Tip
The thinner the onion slices, the better. Use a large, heavy chef knife and sharpen it first. Or at least run it along a steel. But for the best results, use the slicing blade of a mandoline.

Apple Chutney

MAKES: about 3 cups (720 ml)
FRIDGE: up to 3 weeks
FREEZER: up to 1 year

Here's a sweeter chutney than most, thanks to the apples…and a chunkier chutney, too, thanks to the way tart apples can hold their shape over the heat. The flavors are brighter, even a little more intense, than some of the other chutneys, for a balanced sweet-sour mix that is a great introduction to making chutneys at home.

- 1½ pounds (680 g) hard tart apples, such as Granny Smith or McIntosh, stemmed, peeled, cored, and chopped
- 1 large white sweet onion, such as Vidalia, peeled and chopped
- ½ cup (75 g) golden raisins
- ½ cup (107 g) packed light brown sugar
- ¼ cup (60 ml) apple cider vinegar
- 2 tablespoons (24 g) chopped crystallized ginger
- 1 tablespoon (6 g) mustard seeds
- 1 teaspoon decorticated (husked and removed from the pods) cardamom seeds
- ½ teaspoon celery seeds
- ½ teaspoon kosher salt

1. Mix all the ingredients in a medium saucepan. Set it over medium-high heat and stir constantly to dissolve the brown sugar. Bring to a steady simmer (if not a boil), stirring often.

2. Reduce the heat to low and simmer *slowly*, stirring more and more often to prevent scorching, until so thick that you can run a wooden spoon across the bottom of the pan and create a line that holds its edges for a second, about 40 minutes.

3. Turn off the heat, remove the pan from the burner, and set aside for 1–2 minutes. Transfer to three *clean* ½ pint (236 ml) jars or other containers, leaving about ½ inch (1 cm) headspace in each. Cover or seal. Cool at room temperature for no more than 1 hour, then refrigerate or freeze.

Next
Apple chutney + coarse-grained mustard + a grilled brat + a whole-grain bun = bliss.

Apple Pie Chutney

MAKES: about 3 cups (720 ml)
FRIDGE: up to 3 weeks
FREEZER: up to 1 year
May be traditionally canned (see page 436)

We've upped the sugar, cut out the onion, and swapped out a more assertive vinegar for smoother malt vinegar to give this chutney a sweet flavor but a mellow finish. Because the chutney is sweeter, it's terrific with bold, spicy flavors, like those in a vindaloo. But don't stop there. Match it with mayo and sliced fresh jalapeño chilis on a burger…or combine it with Jalapeño Relish (page 167) on pork or lamb chops off the grill.

- 2¼ pounds (1 kg) moderately sweet baking apples, such as Braeburn or Honeycrisp, stemmed, peeled, cored, and chopped
- 1⅔ cups (334 g) granulated white sugar
- ¾ cup (180 ml) malt vinegar
- ⅓ cup (50 g) raisins
- ½ cup (120 ml) *unsweetened* apple juice
- One 1 inch (2.5 cm) piece of fresh ginger, peeled and *minced*
- 1 teaspoon ground cinnamon
- ½ teaspoon ground dried ginger
- ½ teaspoon kosher salt
- ¼ teaspoon grated nutmeg
- ¼ teaspoon ground cloves

1. Mix all the ingredients in a medium saucepan. Set it over medium-high heat and stir constantly to dissolve the sugar. Bring to a steady simmer (if not a boil), stirring often.

2. Reduce the heat to low and simmer *slowly*, stirring more and more often to prevent scorching, until so thick that you can run a wooden spoon across the bottom of the pan and create a line that holds its edges for a second, about 30 minutes.

3. Turn off the heat, remove the pan from the burner, and set aside for 1–2 minutes. Transfer to three *clean* ½ pint (236 ml) jars or other containers, leaving about ½ inch (1 cm) headspace in each. Cover or seal. Cool at room temperature for no more than 1 hour, then refrigerate or freeze.

More
For deeper flavors, substitute apple brandy for the apple juice.

In jars from top to bottom: Apple Chutney (page 150) and Spiced Plum Chutney (page 153)

Nearly Sugar-Free Apple Chutney

MAKES: about 2 cups (480 ml)
FRIDGE: up to 2 weeks
FREEZER: up to 6 months

In order to get the thick consistency of traditional chutney without any granulated sugar, we add sticky raisins, then we cook the mixture a fairly long time to let those natural sugars in the apples and raisins caramelize. Control the final consistency by how finely you chop the ingredients. We like a chunky chutney; but that also means we use more in a serving because we have to get larger bits out of the jar. This chutney is not sugar-free since crystallized ginger does indeed include some sugar.

- 1⅓ pounds (605 g) moderately sweet baking apples, such as Braeburn or Honeycrisp, stemmed, peeled, cored, and chopped
- 1 medium yellow or white onion, peeled and chopped
- ½ cup *1-to-1 (by volume)* granulated *brown*-sugar substitute
- ½ cup (120 ml) apple cider vinegar
- ½ cup (120 ml) *unsweetened* apple juice
- ¼ cup (45 g) chopped crystallized ginger
- ¼ cup (38 g) golden raisins
- ½ teaspoon coriander seeds
- ½ teaspoon yellow mustard seeds
- ¼ teaspoon garam masala

1. Combine all the ingredients in a medium saucepan. Set it over medium-high heat and stir constantly to dissolve the sugar substitute. Bring to a steady simmer (if not a boil), stirring often.

2. Reduce the heat to low and simmer *slowly*, stirring more and more often to prevent scorching, until so thick that you can run a wooden spoon across the bottom of the pan and create a line that holds its edges for a second, about 20 minutes.

3. Turn off the heat, remove the pan from the burner, and set aside for 1–2 minutes. Transfer to two *clean* ½ pint (236 ml) jars or other containers, leaving about ½ inch (1 cm) headspace in each. Cover or seal. Cool at room temperature for no more than 1 hour, then refrigerate or freeze.

More
Garam masala is a blend of warming spices. To make your own, grind 2 teaspoons fennel seeds in a spice grinder until powdery, then pour this powder into a small bowl and stir in 1 tablespoon ground coriander, 2 teaspoons ground cumin, 2 teaspoons mild paprika, 1 teaspoon ground cinnamon, 1 teaspoon ground allspice, and ¼ teaspoon grated nutmeg. Store in a sealed, small glass jar for up to 1 year.

Spiced Plum Chutney

MAKES: about 4 cups (960 ml)
FRIDGE: up to 3 weeks
FREEZER: up to 1 year
May be traditionally canned (see page 436)

Although we occasionally cheat with conserves and add pectin to help them gel like preserves, the best route to the more complex flavors of chutneys is *long* cooking. By stirring quite a bit, we can create a depth of flavor unmatched in purchased bottlings. Given the work involved, we go all out with this plum concoction. Almost all kinds of plums—yellow, red, green, purple, or a mix—will work, so long as they're juicy and aromatic. Only prune plums won't work.

- 2 pounds (900 g) ripe plums, quartered and pitted
- ¾ cup (150 g) granulated white sugar
- ¼ cup (54 g) packed light brown sugar
- ⅓ cup (80 ml) apple cider vinegar
- ¼ cup (36 g) minced peeled yellow or white onion
- 3 tablespoons (45 g) minced peeled fresh ginger
- 2 tablespoons (28 g) *minced* crystallized ginger
- 2 tablespoons (20 g) raisins, chopped
- 1 medium garlic clove, peeled and minced
- 1 teaspoon yellow or brown mustard seeds
- Up to 1 teaspoon red pepper flakes
- ¼ teaspoon kosher salt

1. Combine all the ingredients in a medium saucepan. Set it over medium-high heat and stir constantly to dissolve the sugar. Bring to a gurgling simmer (but not a boil), stirring often.

2. Reduce the heat to low and simmer *slowly*, stirring more and more often to prevent scorching, until so thick that you can run a wooden spoon across the bottom of the pan and create a line that holds its edges for a second, about 40 minutes.

3. Turn off the heat, remove the pan from the burner, and set aside for 1–2 minutes. Transfer to four *clean* ½ pint (236 ml) jars or other containers, leaving about ½ inch (1 cm) headspace in each. Cover or seal. Cool at room temperature for no more than 1 hour, then refrigerate or freeze.

Next
Make an easy spread for crackers by mixing a little of this chutney, a splash of rice vinegar, and a tiny bit of Plum Preserves (see page 65) into softened cream cheese.

Rhubarb-Raisin Chutney

MAKES: about 3 cups (720 ml)
FRIDGE: up to 3 weeks
FREEZER: up to 1 year
May be traditionally canned (see page 436)

Rhubarb has a tart, vegetal flavor that seems made for the richer, more vinegary flavors of chutney. In fact, those flavors, although seemingly perfect for chutney, can actually be a bit overpowering in the blend of spices. So we've worked to balance rhubarb's natural flavors with apples and raisins, as well as tamarind paste, the sweet-sour reduction of a tropical fruit. They all bring forward the high, bright flavors of the rhubarb after cooking.

1¼ pounds (565 g) fresh rhubarb (about 4 large stalks), trimmed and sliced into 1 inch (2.5 cm) pieces (about 5 cups)

1 large hard sour apple, such as Granny Smith, stemmed, peeled, cored, and *diced*

1 medium yellow or white onion, peeled, halved, and sliced into paper-thin half-moons

1 cup (215 g) packed light brown sugar

¾ cup (180 ml) apple cider vinegar

½ cup (75 g) raisins

¼ cup (85 g) honey

2 tablespoons (30 g) chopped fresh peeled ginger

2 teaspoons (10 g) tamarind paste

2 teaspoons yellow or brown mustard seeds

½ teaspoon ground fenugreek

½ teaspoon kosher salt

1. Combine all the ingredients in a large saucepan. Set it over medium-high heat and stir constantly to dissolve the sugar. Bring to a gurgling simmer (but not a boil), stirring often.

2. Reduce the heat to low and simmer *slowly*, stirring more and more often to prevent scorching, until so thick that you can run a wooden spoon across the bottom of the pan and create a line that holds its edges for a second, about 40 minutes.

3. Turn off the heat, remove the pan from the burner, and set aside for 1–2 minutes. Transfer to three *clean* ½ pint (236 ml) jars or other containers, leaving about ½ inch (1 cm) headspace in each. Cover or seal. Cool at room temperature for no more than 1 hour, then refrigerate or freeze.

Next
This is the perfect chutney for a turkey sandwich with crisp lettuce, thinly sliced red onion, and mayonnaise.

Rhubarb-Chipotle Chutney

MAKES: about 3 cups (720 ml)
FRIDGE: up to 3 weeks
FREEZER: up to 1 year
May be traditionally canned (see page 436)

Here's a fiery rhubarb chutney with the smoky flavor of chipotles (aka smoked jalapeños), all tied together by the sweet perfume of ripe pear. Make sure the pear actually has a distinct aroma so it will indeed do its best among its competitors. Canned chipotles in adobo are a terrific shortcut in a recipe like this one, but you almost never use the whole can. Stem and very finely chop what remains, then spread it in small plastic bags and freeze flat so you can chip off 1 or 2 tablespoons as required by a recipe.

- 1¼ pounds (565 g) fresh rhubarb (about 4 large stalks), trimmed and sliced into 1 inch (2.5 cm) pieces (about 5 cups)
- 2½ ounces (75 g) ripe firm pear (about 1 medium), preferably Comice or Bartlett, stemmed, peeled, cored, and chopped
- 1 large (1¾ ounce or 50 g) shallot, peeled and minced
- ¾ cup (150 g) granulated white sugar
- ½ cup (120 ml) apple cider vinegar
- 3 canned chipotles in adobo sauce, stemmed and chopped (seeded, if you want less heat)
- 1 tablespoon (15 g) adobo sauce from the can
- 2 tablespoons (42 g) honey
- 1 medium garlic clove, peeled and minced
- ½ teaspoon dried ground ginger
- ½ teaspoon ground cinnamon
- ½ teaspoon kosher salt
- ¼ teaspoon ground cloves
- ⅛ teaspoon ground dried turmeric

1. Combine all the ingredients in a medium saucepan. Set it over medium-high heat and stir constantly to dissolve the sugar. Bring to a gurgling simmer (but not a boil), stirring often.

2. Reduce the heat to low and simmer *slowly*, stirring more and more often to prevent scorching, until so thick that you can run a wooden spoon across the bottom of the pan and create a line that holds its edges for a second, about 40 minutes.

3. Turn off the heat, remove the pan from the burner, and set aside for 1–2 minutes. Transfer to three *clean* ½ pint (236 ml) jars or other containers, leaving about ½ inch (1 cm) headspace in each. Cover or seal. Cool at room temperature for no more than 1 hour, then refrigerate or freeze.

More

For a super garlicky version of this chutney, omit the shallot and use 6 to 8 medium garlic cloves, peeled and slivered.

Hot Tomato Chutney

MAKES: about 4 cups (960 ml)
FRIDGE: up to 3 weeks
FREEZER: up to 1 year

Tomato chutney can be cloyingly sweet, so we opt for a spicy blend of ginger-laced flavors in our recipe, complete with both bell peppers and chilis. Since tomatoes break down as they cook over a long time, this chutney has a smoother consistency than some others in this chapter. You might be surprised that we keep the skins on the tomatoes. We feel they add a little more texture to the sauce-like consistency the tomatoes eventually develop over the heat.

- 2 pounds (900 g) globe tomatoes (about 5 medium), chopped (about 4 cups)
- 1 small red bell pepper, stemmed, cored, and *diced*
- 1–2 fresh red chilis, preferably serrano or jalapeño, stemmed, cored, and *minced*
- ½ cup (100 g) granulated white sugar
- ½ cup (120 ml) distilled white vinegar
- 1 large (1¾ ounce or 50 g) shallot, peeled and minced
- 2 tablespoons (20 g) raisins
- One 2 inch (5 cm) piece of fresh ginger, peeled and minced
- 1 medium garlic clove, peeled and minced
- ½ teaspoon red pepper flakes
- ¼ teaspoon dried ground mustard
- ¼ teaspoon ground cloves
- ¼ teaspoon kosher salt

1. Combine all the ingredients in a large saucepan. Set it over medium-high heat and stir constantly to dissolve the sugar. Bring to a gurgling simmer (but not a boil), stirring often.

2. Reduce the heat to low and simmer *slowly*, stirring more and more often to prevent scorching, until so thick that you can run a wooden spoon across the bottom of the pan and create a line that holds its edges for a second or two before flowing back into place, about 45 minutes.

3. Turn off the heat, remove the pan from the burner, and set aside for 1–2 minutes. Transfer to four *clean* ½ pint (236 ml) jars or other containers, leaving about ½ inch (1 cm) headspace in each. Cover or seal. Cool at room temperature for no more than 1 hour, then refrigerate or freeze.

Next

This chutney is exceptional with melted butter on steamed or roasted green beans, asparagus, broccoli, or cauliflower.

Green Tomato Chutney

MAKES: about 3 cups (720 ml)
FRIDGE: up to 3 weeks
FREEZER: up to 1 year

By *green tomatoes*, we mean *unripe* ones. In our part of New England, they're a prized commodity at the end of the season, usually around the first of October, just before the first hard freeze stabs the plants. Unripe tomatoes are sour, with astringent notes that must be balanced by lots of aromatics and big flavors, even (as here) with a whole lime. Any sort of tomatoes will do in this recipe, from large to small, so long as they're unripe and the total *weight* is 2 pounds.

- 2 pounds (900 g) green (unripe) tomatoes, quartered
- 1 cup (215 g) packed light brown sugar
- ⅓ cup (80 ml) apple cider vinegar
- ¼ cup (38 g) raisins
- 1 small yellow or white onion, peeled and chopped
- 1 small lime, thinly sliced, *seeded*, and finely chopped (rind and all)
- 1 medium garlic clove, peeled and minced

- 2 tablespoons (30 g) minced peeled fresh ginger
- 1 teaspoon brown mustard seeds
- 1 teaspoon (5 g) tamarind paste
- 1 teaspoon (5 ml) sambal oelek
- ¼ teaspoon ground allspice
- ¼ teaspoon kosher salt

1. Put the green tomato quarters in a food processor, cover, and pulse until finely chopped, almost like a relish.

2. Pour and scape every speck of the tomato relish into a medium saucepan. Add the remaining ingredients. Set the pan over medium-high heat and stir constantly to dissolve the sugar. Bring to a gurgling, steady simmer (but not a boil), stirring often.

3. Reduce the heat to low and simmer *slowly*, stirring more and more often to prevent scorching, until so thick that you can run a wooden spoon across the bottom of the pan and create a line that holds its edges for a second, about 45 minutes.

4. Turn off the heat, remove the pan from the burner, and set aside for 1–2 minutes. Transfer to three *clean* ½ pint (236 ml) jars or other containers, leaving about ½ inch (1 cm) headspace in each. Cover or seal. Cool at room temperature for no more than 1 hour, then refrigerate or freeze.

Next

Stir a little of this chutney with oil and vinegar to drizzle over chopped vegetable salads for a burst of flavor.

Fig-Tamarind Chutney

MAKES: about 4 cups (960 ml)
FRIDGE: up to 3 weeks
FREEZER: up to 1 year
May be traditionally canned (see page 436)

This chutney probably has the deepest flavor of any in this book: a rich mix of sour notes from

Bottom to top: Fig-Tamarind Chutney (page 156) on Brie and Cranberry-Cardamom Chutney (page 158) on cream cheese

vinegar and tamarind paste, sweetened by both oranges and dried figs. There's also an earthy flavor at the base because of the caramelization, the better to stand up to sweeter curries and stews. This chutney also has a sticky yet smooth consistency, not chunky at all, like a conserve.

- 8½ ounces (240 g) dried Calimyrna or Adriatic (aka Turkish) figs, stemmed and *finely* chopped
- 1¾ cups (420 ml) *unsweetened* apple juice
- ½ cup (120 ml) apple cider vinegar
- ½ cup (72 g) golden raisins
- 6 ounces (172 g) mandarin oranges (about 2 medium), peeled, seeded, and chopped
- 1 very large shallot (about 3 ounces or 82 g), peeled and minced
- 2 tablespoons (30 g) chopped peeled fresh ginger
- 2 tablespoons (30 g) tamarind paste
- ½ teaspoon ground cinnamon
- ½ teaspoon kosher salt
- ½ teaspoon ground black pepper

1. Combine all the ingredients in a large saucepan. Set it over medium-high heat and stir constantly to dissolve the sugar. Bring to a gurgling, steady simmer (but not a boil), stirring often.

2. Reduce the heat to low and simmer *slowly*, stirring more and more often to prevent scorching, until so thick that you can run a wooden spoon across the bottom of the pan and create a line that holds its edges for a second, about 25 minutes.

3. Turn off the heat, remove the pan from the burner, and set aside for 1–2 minutes. Transfer to four *clean* ½ pint (236 ml) jars or other containers, leaving about ½ inch (1 cm) headspace in each. Cover or seal. Cool at room temperature for no more than 1 hour, then refrigerate or freeze.

More

For a bit of heat, add up to 2 teaspoons red pepper flakes with all the ingredients.

Cranberry-Cardamom Chutney

MAKES: about 3 cups (720 ml)
FRIDGE: up to 3 weeks
FREEZER: up to 1 year
May be traditionally canned (see page 436)

This chutney has a looser set and *fewer* caramelized flavors than some others. It's brighter in both color and flavor. Cardamom is the main player, but it can be quite assertive. For a milder chutney, consider halving the amount (or halve it the first time you make the chutney to be sure you like the sweet musky flavor).

- 12 ounces (340 g) fresh cranberries or thawed frozen cranberries
- 1 cup (200 g) granulated white sugar
- 1 cup (240 ml) orange juice, preferably freshly squeezed
- 6 tablespoons (125 g) honey
- 1 tablespoon (30 ml) red wine vinegar
- 1 tablespoon (15 g) minced peeled fresh ginger
- 1 teaspoon decorticated (husked and removed from the pods) cardamom seeds
- ½ teaspoon kosher salt

1. Combine all the ingredients in a medium saucepan. Set it over medium-high heat and stir constantly to dissolve the sugar. Bring to a gurgling simmer (but not a boil), stirring often.

2. Reduce the heat to low and simmer *slowly*, stirring more and more often to prevent scorching, until thick and jam-like without being caramelized, about 10 minutes.

3. Turn off the heat, remove the pan from the burner, and set aside for 1–2 minutes. Transfer to three *clean* ½ pint (236 ml) jars or other containers, leaving about ½ inch (1 cm) headspace in each. Cover or seal. Cool at room temperature for no more than 1 hour, then refrigerate or freeze.

More

For deeper flavor, stir 2 teaspoons (15 g) molasses or black treacle into the mix with the other ingredients.

Apricot–Garam Masala Chutney

MAKES: about 3 cups (720 ml)
FRIDGE: up to 3 weeks
FREEZER: up to 1 year

We love this fresh, chunky combo of apricots and nuts so much that we often buy apricots in the summer, quarter them, and freeze them to make a batch of this chutney in the winter months when we've got lots of stews and curries on the menu. The nuts are added at the end so they don't become too toasty and overwhelm the delicate apricots.

- 1 pound 2½ ounces (525 g) fresh apricots (about 15 medium), stemmed, halved, pitted, and *finely* chopped
- ½ cup (108 g) packed light brown sugar
- ⅓ cup (80 ml) white wine vinegar
- 1 small shallot (about ¾ ounce or 22 g), peeled and *minced*
- 2 tablespoons (20 g) *dried* cranberries, chopped
- 1 tablespoon (15 g) grated peeled fresh ginger
- 1½ teaspoons garam masala (or use your own homemade; see MORE on page 153)
- ¼ cup (35 g) chopped walnut pieces

1. Combine the apricots, brown sugar, vinegar, shallot, dried cranberries, ginger, and garam masala in a medium saucepan. Set it over medium-high heat and stir constantly to dissolve the sugar. Bring to a gurgling, steady simmer (but not a boil), stirring often.

2. Reduce the heat to low and simmer *slowly*, stirring more and more often to prevent scorching, until so thick that you can run a wooden spoon across the bottom of the pan and create a line that holds its edges for a second, about 25 minutes.

3. Turn off the heat and remove the pan from the burner. Stir in the walnuts. Set the pan aside for a few minutes.

4. Transfer to three *clean* ½ pint (236 ml) jars or other containers, leaving about ½ inch (1 cm) headspace in each. Cover or seal. Cool at room temperature for no more than 1 hour, then refrigerate or freeze.

More

Boost the heat with up to 2 dried long red chilis (such as árbol chilis), stemmed, added with the apricots. Remove the chilis before stirring in the nuts.

Pineapple-Chili Chutney

MAKES: about 3 cups (720 ml)
FRIDGE: up to 3 weeks
FREEZER: up to 1 year

This chutney is super spicy with sweet-sour notes and a decidedly tropical flair. It should be cooked until the pineapple is quite soft so that the consistency is right about in the middle ground between preserves and jam. The results are terrific on a buffalo burger, with grilled game meat (elk! venison!), or with roasted, sweet-but-earthy root vegetables like carrots and parsnips.

- 2⅔ pounds (1.2 kg) fresh pineapple (about 1 medium), trimmed, peeled, cored, and *finely* chopped (about 4 cups)
- 5¼ ounces (150 g) hot chilis, preferably aji cristal, red hot cherry, or red jalapeño, stemmed, cored, and chopped
- ⅓ cup (72 g) packed dark brown sugar
- ¼ cup (60 ml) apple cider vinegar
- 2 tablespoons (30 g) minced peeled fresh ginger
- 1 star anise pod
- 8 whole cloves
- ½ teaspoon fenugreek seeds
- ½ teaspoon kosher salt

1. Mix all the ingredients in a medium saucepan. Set it over medium heat and stir constantly to dissolve the brown sugar. Bring to a simmer with intermittent bubbles, stirring occasionally.

2. Reduce the heat to medium-low and simmer steadily, stirring more and more often to prevent scorching, until the mixture has thickened and the pineapple is translucent, about 20 minutes.

3. Turn off the heat, remove the pan from the burner, and set aside for 1–2 minutes. Fish out and discard the star anise pod.

4. Transfer to three *clean* ½ pint (236 ml) jars or other containers, leaving about ½ inch (1 cm) headspace in each. Cover or seal. Cool at room temperature for no more than 1 hour, then refrigerate or freeze.

More

For fewer bitter notes, grate jaggery (a South Asian cane sugar sold in clumps or blocks) to substitute the required *weight* of the brown sugar.

Mint Chutney

MAKES: about 2 cups (480 ml)
FRIDGE: up to 10 days
FREEZER: up to 6 months

This chutney is not cooked…and thus not jammy. It's a grainy, somewhat thick concoction, not an herbal sauce, but a topper for cooked lentils and rice of all sorts. It's also terrific as a dip for rice crackers with ice-cold cocktails before dinner. For the best consistency, discard all of the mint stems and the larger, fibrous cilantro stems.

- 3 ounces (85 g) fresh cilantro *leaves* (about 2 packed cups)
- 1½ ounces (43 g) fresh mint *leaves* (about 1 packed cup)
- 1 small shallot (about ¾ ounce or 22 g), peeled and *minced*
- 2 medium green serrano chilis, stemmed, cored, and chopped
- 2 tablespoons (10 g) shredded unsweetened coconut
- 2 medium garlic cloves, peeled and minced
- 2 teaspoons (10 g) minced peeled fresh ginger
- 2 tablespoons (30 ml) lime juice
- 1 teaspoon kosher salt
- Water as necessary to make a puree
- A neutral-flavored oil, such as vegetable or canola oil, as necessary to cover the chutney

1. Combine all the ingredients *except the water and oil* in a blender or food processor. Cover and blend or process, adding water in 1 tablespoon (15 ml) increments to get the blades spinning and grinding. The final chutney's consistency should be a thick if still grainy puree.

2. Transfer to two *clean* ½ pint (236 ml) jars or other containers, leaving about ½ inch (1 cm) headspace in each. Pour the slightest amount of oil over the top of the raw chutney, just to seal it from the air so that the chutney doesn't oxidize. Cover or seal, then refrigerate or freeze.

Tip

Fresh cilantro and mint can be sandy. Wash the leaves or sprigs, then put them through a salad spinner. Or float the leaves in a large bowl of water, agitating several times over about 20 minutes, to let the grit fall to the bottom of the bowl. Scoop out the leaves from the surface and dry between sheets of paper towel.

Parsley–Pumpkin Seed Chutney

MAKES: about 2 cups (480 ml)
FRIDGE: up to 10 days
FREEZER: up to 6 months

We modeled this fresh, no-cook, herb chutney on Afghani green chutney, a condiment served across west-central Asia with rice and dal. Pumpkin seeds are not traditional, but we add them because they give the chutney a mild flavor and a slightly coarse texture, less like a sauce, and more in keeping with our notions of the more traditional chutneys that don't involve a pseudo-jam-making technique.

> 3 ounces (85 g) fresh cilantro *leaves* (about 2 packed cups)
>
> 1½ ounces (43 g) fresh parsley *leaves* (about 1 packed cup)
>
> ¼ cup (60 ml) white wine vinegar
>
> 2 tablespoons (16 g) pepitas (small shelled pumpkin seeds)
>
> 1 large green jalapeño chili, stemmed, cored, and chopped
>
> 2 medium garlic cloves, peeled and minced
>
> 2 teaspoons (8 g) granulated white sugar
>
> ¼ teaspoon kosher salt
>
> Water as necessary to make a puree

1. Combine all the ingredients *except the water* in a blender or a food processor. Cover and blend or process, adding water in 1 tablespoon (15 ml) increments to get the blades spinning and grinding. The final chutney's consistency should be a thick but slightly grainy puree.

2. Transfer to two *clean* ½ pint (236 ml) jars or other containers, leaving about ½ inch (1 cm) headspace in each container. Cover or seal, then refrigerate or freeze.

Next
Afghani chutney is often mixed into plain yogurt for a creamy sauce, particularly great on grilled vegetables, cooked grains, or even brown rice. It's also great stirred into sour cream or even room-temperature cream cheese for an aromatic dip.

Spicy Coconut-Cashew Chutney

MAKES: about 2 cups (480 ml)
FRIDGE: up to 2 weeks
FREEZER: up to 6 months

Talk about addictive! This chili-laced, dry (even powdery) chutney (that is, *not* a sauce or even a jam) is a staple in our fridge. We love it spooned on baked potatoes, dolloped onto cooked dal or lentils, and even scooped up with thick-cut potato chips. Even better, mix it into crème fraîche for a dip, or use it with sour cream as an add-in to mashed potatoes.

> 1¼ cups (106 g) shredded unsweetened coconut
>
> ½ cup (57 g) *unsalted* roasted cashews
>
> 2 medium green serrano chilis, stemmed, cored, seeded if desired, and chopped
>
> One 1 inch (2.5 cm) piece of fresh ginger, peeled and chopped
>
> 1 medium garlic clove, peeled and chopped
>
> 1 teaspoon kosher salt
>
> 1 tablespoon (15 ml) neutral-flavored oil, such as corn, vegetable, or canola oil
>
> 1 teaspoon cumin seeds
>
> 1 teaspoon yellow mustard seeds
>
> 1 cup (240 ml) water
>
> ¼ cup (60 ml) lemon juice

1. Put the coconut, cashews, chilis, ginger, garlic, and salt in a blender or food processor.

2. Set a small skillet over low heat for a minute or two. Add the oil, then the cumin and mustard seeds. Stir until the seeds pop, probably less than 1 minute. Turn off the heat and set the skillet off the burner for a few minutes.

3. Scrape the contents of the skillet into the blender or food processor. Add the water and lemon juice. Cover and blend or process until almost smooth, just a tad coarse.

4. Transfer to two *clean* ½ pint (236 ml) jars or other containers, leaving about ½ inch (1 cm) headspace in each. Cover or seal. Cool at room temperature for no more than 30 minutes, then refrigerate or freeze.

More
For more intense flavors, add up to 1 teaspoon coriander seeds and/or 2 *green* cardamom pods with the other seeds.

Left to right: Mint Chutney (page 160)
and Spicy Coconut-Cashew Chutney (page 161)

Shallot-Dal Chutney

MAKES: about 2 cups (480 ml)
FRIDGE: up to 2 weeks
FREEZER: up to 6 months

This spicy, tomato-laced chutney is modeled on kara chutney, which is common in Tamil Nadu cuisine. Our version won't win authenticity awards, but it gets close to the flavors of the original with ingredients found in most large supermarkets near us. Although the chutney is often a dipping sauce for dosas or a spread for flatbreads, we love it with a plate of cut-up vegetables like cucumbers and carrots for an easy summer supper…or as a spread for thick whole-grain crackers before the meal.

- 4 tablespoons (60 ml) olive oil
- 2 tablespoons (24 g) raw chana dal (or yellow split peas)
- 1 very large shallot (about 3 ounces or 82 g), peeled and thinly sliced
- 6 dried long thin red chilis, preferably Kashmiri or árbol chilis, stemmed and seeded (if desired)
- 6 medium garlic cloves, peeled and thinly sliced
- 1¼ pounds (565 g) globe tomatoes (about 3 medium), chopped
- 1½ teaspoons (7 g) tamarind paste
- 1 teaspoon kosher salt
- 2 teaspoons brown mustard seeds
- 4 dried or fresh curry leaves
- ½ cup (120 ml) water, plus more as necessary to make a smooth sauce

1. Set a medium skillet over medium heat for a minute or two. Add 3 tablespoons (45 ml) oil, then the chana dal. Toast, stirring often, until golden brown, about 3 minutes.

2. Add the shallot and cook, stirring often, until brown at the edges, about 3 minutes. Add the chilis and garlic; cook, stirring constantly, until fragrant, about 30 seconds.

3. Add the tomatoes and cook, stirring occasionally, until the chunks have softened and even begun to break down, about 10 minutes. Stir in the tamarind paste and salt. Turn off the heat, set the skillet off the burner, and cool for 1–2 minutes. Scrape and pour the contents of the skillet into a blender.

4. Wipe out the still-warm skillet and set it over medium heat for a minute or two. Add the remaining 1 tablespoon (15 ml) oil. Stir in the mustard seeds and curry leaves. Cook, stirring quite often, until the seeds pop, less than 1 minute. Scrape the contents of the skillet into the blender.

5. Add ½ cup (120 ml) water. Cover and blend, adding more water in 1 tablespoon (15 ml) increments, until a smooth, thick, but spreadable sauce forms.

6. Transfer to two *clean* ½ pint (236 ml) jars or other containers, leaving about ½ inch (1 cm) headspace in each. Cover or seal, then refrigerate or freeze.

More
For a bigger punch of flavor, substitute sesame oil for the olive oil.

Sweet Pickle Relish

MAKES: about 3 cups (720 ml)
FRIDGE: up to 3 weeks
FREEZER: up to 1 year

Why buy mushy sweet pickle relish when you can make your own? Its texture is coarser, more in the spirit of a traditional relish. And its flavors are fresher yet more layered, without a heavy dose of corn syrup masking the mustard seeds. For the best texture, the cucumbers should be finely chopped, a daunting task. To be honest, we usually let the food processor do the job for us, cutting the cucumbers into 3 inch (7.5cm) chunks and pulsing the machine to produce a finely chopped mix.

1¾ pounds (790 g) pickling cucumbers (about 8), preferably Kirby, finely chopped (no more than ¼ inch or 1 cm pieces, with many smaller)

1½ tablespoons (18 g) kosher salt

Distilled water as necessary to submerge the cucumbers

1 small yellow or white onion, peeled and finely chopped

1 cup (240 ml) apple cider vinegar

1 cup (200 g) granulated white sugar

1 teaspoon celery seeds

1 teaspoon yellow mustard seeds

1. Mix the cucumbers with the salt in a large bowl until evenly salted. Add enough *distilled* water to reach the top of the cucumbers. Set aside at room temperature for 2 hours.

2. Clean and dry your hands or put on culinary kitchen gloves. Pick up the cucumbers by the handful and squeeze them as dry as you can, before putting each handful into a medium saucepan.

3. Add the onion, vinegar, sugar, celery seeds, and mustard seeds to the pan. Set it over medium-high heat and stir constantly to dissolve the sugar. Bring to a *boil* (not a simmer), stirring often.

4. Reduce the heat to low and simmer *slowly*, stirring more and more often to prevent scorching, until the liquid has reduced enough that you can run a wooden spoon across the bottom of the pan and create a line that holds its edges for a second, about 12 minutes.

5. Turn off the heat, remove the pan from the burner, and set aside for 1–2 minutes. Transfer to three *clean* ½ pint (236 ml) jars or other containers, leaving about ½ inch (1 cm) headspace in each. Cover or seal. Cool at room temperature for no more than 1 hour, then refrigerate or freeze.

Next
We think that one of the best burger toppers is a mix of equal parts *by volume* of this relish with Jalapeño Relish (page 167) and mayonnaise.

Dill Pickle Relish

MAKES: about 3 cups (720 ml)
FRIDGE: up to 3 weeks
FREEZER: up to 1 year

Although we often eschew corn syrup, we feel it's needed here because it offers a slightly smoother texture to this classic relish…and thus a better contrast to its sour, spiky flavors. Since we can use less of it than granulated sugar, it also doesn't mute the dill. We opt for fresh dill because it has a gorgeous color in the relish and offers a summery flavor.

1¾ pounds (790 g) pickling cucumbers (about 8), preferably Kirby, finely chopped (no more than ¼ inch or 1 cm pieces, with many smaller)

1½ tablespoons (18 g) kosher salt

Distilled water as necessary to submerge the cucumbers

1 small yellow or white onion, peeled and finely chopped

¼ cup (10 g) *packed* minced fresh dill

1 cup (240 ml) distilled white vinegar

2 tablespoons (25 g) granulated white sugar

1 tablespoon (20 g) light corn syrup

1 teaspoon yellow mustard seeds

1. Toss the cucumbers with the salt in a large bowl until evenly salted. Add enough *distilled* water just to reach the top of the cucumbers. Set aside at room temperature for 2 hours.

2. Clean and dry your hands or put on culinary kitchen gloves. Pick up the cucumbers by the handful and squeeze them as dry as you can, before putting each handful into a medium saucepan.

3. Add the onion, dill, vinegar, sugar, corn syrup, and mustard seeds. Set the pan over medium-high heat and stir constantly to dissolve the sugar. Bring to a *boil* (not a simmer), stirring often.

4. Reduce the heat to low and simmer *slowly*, stirring more and more often, until the liquid has reduced enough that you can run a wooden

Clockwise from left:
Sweet Pickle Relish
(page 163), Carrot-Ginger
Relish (page 168), Spicy
Corn Relish (page 166), and
Dill Pickle Relish (page 164)

spoon across the bottom of the pan and create a line that holds its edges for a second, about 12 minutes.

5. Turn off the heat, remove the pan from the burner, and set aside for 1–2 minutes. Transfer to three *clean* ½ pint (236 ml) jars or other containers, leaving about ½ inch (1 cm) headspace in each. Cover or seal. Cool at room temperature for no more than 1 hour, then refrigerate or freeze.

More
For a fiery dill pickle relish, add up to 2 medium jalapeño chilis, stemmed, cored, and finely chopped, with the onion and other ingredients in step 3.

Sweet Corn Relish

MAKES: about 3 cups (720 ml)
FRIDGE: up to 2 weeks
FREEZER: up to 1 year

You probably have to be from the US South to understand the glories of this relish. Yes, corn is sweet by nature. And yes, corn relish is sweeter still. But we add lots of vinegar and aromatics to round out the flavors. Longtime canners may be surprised by the little bit of ground cloves and grated nutmeg. Sure, you can omit them for a more traditional flavor, but we love the depth they add, making a good match for burgers, hot dogs, or brats.

> 2½ cups (450 g) fresh corn kernels or thawed frozen corn kernels
>
> 1 cup (100 g) *packed* shredded cored green cabbage
>
> 1 small yellow or white onion, peeled and *minced*
>
> 1 small yellow bell pepper, stemmed, cored, and diced
>
> ½ cup (100 g) granulated white sugar
>
> ½ cup (120 ml) apple cider vinegar
>
> ½ teaspoon celery seeds
>
> ½ teaspoon yellow mustard seeds
>
> ¼ teaspoon ground cloves
>
> ¼ teaspoon grated nutmeg
>
> ¼ teaspoon kosher salt

1. Combine all the ingredients in a medium saucepan. Set it over medium heat and stir constantly until the sugar dissolves. Continue cooking, stirring often, until the mixture comes to a *boil* (not just a simmer).

2. Reduce the heat to low and simmer *slowly*, stirring more and more often to prevent scorching, until most of the liquid has evaporated and the remainder has reduced to a syrup so thick that you can run a wooden spoon across the bottom of the pan and create a line that holds its edges for a second, about 20 minutes.

3. Turn off the heat, remove the pan from the burner, and set aside for 1–2 minutes. Transfer to three *clean* ½ pint (236 ml) jars or other containers, leaving about ½ inch (1 cm) headspace in each. Cover or seal. Cool at room temperature for no more than 1 hour, then refrigerate or freeze.

Next
Use this relish as part of the dressing for a chopped vegetable salad. Combine a dollop with a hearty glug of olive oil, and perhaps a splash of white wine vinegar to round out the flavors.

Spicy Corn Relish

MAKES: about 3 cups (720 ml)
FRIDGE: up to 2 weeks
FREEZER: up to 1 year

Sweet corn relish is all well and good, but the spicy stuff has our hearts. Although this recipe says you can use *up to four* chilis, we use them all. The seeds, too! This relish is a complex amalgam, including lots of dried spices. It offers a tongue-popping bit of flavor that's the best companion for smoked turkey or brisket.

> 2½ cups (450 g) fresh corn kernels or thawed frozen corn kernels
>
> 1 medium yellow or white onion, peeled and chopped
>
> Up to 4 medium red chilis, preferably Fresno or red jalapeño, stemmed, seeded (if desired), and chopped

2 celery stalks, halved lengthwise and very thinly sliced

¾ cup (180 ml) distilled white vinegar

½ cup (100 g) granulated white sugar

½ teaspoon yellow mustard seeds

½ teaspoon celery seeds

½ teaspoon kosher salt

⅛ teaspoon ground dried turmeric

1. Combine all the ingredients in a medium saucepan. Set it over medium heat and stir constantly until the sugar dissolves. Continue cooking, stirring often, until the mixture comes to a *boil* (not just a simmer).

2. Reduce the heat to low and simmer *slowly*, stirring more and more often to prevent scorching, until most of the liquid has evaporated and the remainder has reduced to a syrup so thick that you can run a wooden spoon across the bottom of the pan and create a line that holds its edges for a second, about 20 minutes.

3. Turn off the heat, remove the pan from the burner, and set aside for 1–2 minutes. Transfer to three *clean* ½ pint (236 ml) jars or other containers, leaving about ½ inch (1 cm) headspace in each. Cover or seal. Cool at room temperature for no more than 1 hour, then refrigerate or freeze.

More

For a sweeter relish to balance the spicy chilis, substitute a sweet white onion, such as a Vidalia, for the more standard yellow or white onion.

Jalapeño Relish

MAKES: about 3 cups (720 ml)
FRIDGE: up to 3 weeks
FREEZER: up to 1 year

We clearly love spicy condiments! And with this relish, we mean it! Although we surely have tongues made out of some noncorrosive material, we *still* seed about half of the chilis. And the chilis also calm down in storage, particularly if you freeze the relish. Still, it's rambunctious at the best of times, a spike of heat that'll pop chicken salad over the roof.

14 large fresh jalapeño chilis, preferably half red and half green, stemmed and halved (seeded, if desired)

3 celery stalks, halved lengthwise and very thinly sliced

1 very large shallot (about 3 ounces or 82 g), peeled and minced

1½ cups (300 g) granulated white sugar

1 cup (240 ml) distilled white vinegar

½ teaspoon kosher salt

1. Put the jalapeños in a food processor. Cover and pulse until finely chopped, like a slushy relish (do not process into a mush).

2. Pour and scrape the jalapeños into a medium saucepan. Add the celery, shallot, sugar, vinegar, and salt. Set the pan over medium heat and stir constantly until the sugar dissolves. Continue cooking, stirring often, until the mixture comes to a *boil* (not just a simmer).

3. Reduce the heat to low and simmer *slowly*, stirring more and more often to prevent scorching, until most of the liquid has evaporated and the remainder has reduced to a syrup so thick that you can run a wooden spoon across the bottom of the pan and create a line that holds its edges for a second, about 25 minutes.

4. Turn off the heat, remove the pan from the burner, and set aside for 1–2 minutes. Transfer to three *clean* ½ pint (236 ml) jars or other containers, leaving about ½ inch (1 cm) headspace in each. Cover or seal. Cool at room temperature for no more than 1 hour, then refrigerate or freeze.

More

For added depths of flavor, add a star anise pod to the saucepan as it goes over the heat. Fish out and discard that pod before bottling.

Carrot-Ginger Relish

MAKES: about 2 cups (480 ml)
FRIDGE: up to 3 weeks
FREEZER: up to 1 year

Let's step away from the über spicy and toward a gentler relish, a great condiment for roasted or grilled vegetables (with some butter, of course), a nice addition to a cheese board (particularly with blue cheeses), and a terrific topper for purchased hummus (especially artichoke hummus). We want to keep this relish's texture a little crunchy, a more traditional take on carrots, so we add them after we've created a sugar cauldron over the heat.

- 1 cup (200 g) granulated white sugar
- ½ cup (120 ml) water
- ¼ cup (60 ml) apple cider vinegar
- ¼ cup (60 g) minced peeled fresh ginger
- 1 teaspoon cumin seeds
- 1 teaspoon brown mustard seeds
- ½ teaspoon kosher salt
- 4 cups (575 g) shredded carrots (5–6 medium carrots)

1. Combine the sugar, water, vinegar, ginger, cumin seeds, mustard seeds, and salt in a medium saucepan. Set it over medium heat and stir until the sugar dissolves. Continue cooking, stirring often, until the mixture comes to a *boil* (not just a simmer). Boil undisturbed for 1 minute.

2. Add the shredded carrots. Bring back to a boil, stirring constantly. Reduce the heat to low and simmer *slowly*, stirring more and more often to prevent scorching, until most of the liquid has evaporated and the remainder has reduced to a syrup so thick that you can run a wooden spoon across the bottom of the pan and create a line that holds its edges for a second, about 12 minutes.

3. Turn off the heat, remove the pan from the burner, and set aside for 1–2 minutes. Transfer to two *clean* ½ pint (236 ml) jars or other containers, leaving about ½ inch (1 cm) headspace in each. Cover or seal. Cool at room temperature for no more than 1 hour, then refrigerate or freeze.

More

For a spikier flavor, reduce the water to 6 tablespoons (90 ml) and add 2 tablespoons (30 ml) ginger juice.

Sweet-and-Sour Zucchini Relish

MAKES: about 3 cups (720 ml)
FRIDGE: up to 3 weeks
FREEZER: up to 1 year

If you're looking for a relish that's full-flavored but a nice change from pickle or corn relish, look no further! Zucchini relish is sweet and aromatic, a fusion of gentle if still present herbal and vegetal flavors. The only problem is that zucchini hold lots of natural moisture. For the best-tasting relish, you must salt, squeeze, and drain the shredded vegetable to get a proper reduction of the liquid in the pan.

- 1¾ pounds (790 g) zucchini (about 4 medium)
- 1 teaspoon kosher salt
- 1 medium yellow or white onion, peeled and *minced*
- 1 cup (200 g) granulated white sugar
- 1 cup (240 ml) distilled white vinegar
- ½ teaspoon celery seeds
- ½ teaspoon yellow mustard seeds
- ½ teaspoon ground dried turmeric
- ½ teaspoon ground black pepper

1. Shred the zucchini through the large holes of a box grater or with the shredding blade of a food processor. Put the shreds in a large bowl. Sprinkle on the salt and toss well to distribute evenly. Set aside for 20 minutes to leach excess water from the vegetable.

2. Clean and dry your hands or put on culinary kitchen gloves. Pick up the zucchini by handfuls and squeeze it dry over the sink before putting the handfuls in a medium saucepan. Stir the onion, sugar, vinegar, celery seeds, mustard seeds, turmeric, and pepper into the pan.

3. Set the pan over medium heat and stir constantly to dissolve the sugar. Continue cooking, stirring quite often, until the mixture comes to a *boil* (not just a simmer).

4. Reduce the heat to low and simmer *slowly*, stirring more and more often to prevent scorching, until most of the liquid has evaporated and the remainder has reduced to a syrup so thick that you can run a wooden spoon across the bottom of the pan and create a line that holds its edges for a second, about 25 minutes.

5. Turn off the heat, remove the pan from the burner, and set aside for 1–2 minutes. Transfer to three *clean* ½ pint (236 ml) jars or other containers, leaving about ½ inch (1 cm) headspace in each. Cover or seal. Cool at room temperature for no more than 1 hour, then refrigerate or freeze.

Next
Zucchini relish is excellent on grilled or pan-seared fish fillets.

Lemon–Summer Squash Relish

MAKES: about 3 cups (720 ml)
FRIDGE: up to 3 weeks
FREEZER: up to 1 year

This unusual concoction is reminiscent of Middle Eastern condiments made with preserved lemons. In this case, we boil a lemon to soften its peel and tame the bitter notes. You can shred the yellow summer squash with either the large holes of a box grater or the shredding blade of a food processor, although the box grater will inevitably juice the vegetable a bit because you're working more slowly

(and usually with duller blades). FYI, the total weight of the squash is the most important factor in the success of this recipe.

> 1¾ pounds (790 g) yellow crook-neck summer squash, shredded
>
> 1 teaspoon kosher salt
>
> 1 large lemon, well washed
>
> Water as necessary to boil the lemon
>
> 1 large yellow or white onion, peeled and *finely* chopped
>
> ¾ cup (180 ml) dry white wine or *unsweetened* apple juice
>
> ½ cup (72 g) golden raisins, chopped
>
> ½ cup (170 g) honey
>
> 6 tablespoons (90 ml) lemon juice

1. Put the squash shreds in a large bowl. Sprinkle on the salt and toss well to distribute evenly. Set aside for 30 minutes to leach *lots* of excess water from the vegetable.

2. Meanwhile, set the lemon in a small saucepan and add enough water to cover. Set the pan over high heat and bring the water to a boil. Cover, reduce the heat to low, and simmer until the lemon is quite tender, about 15 minutes. Drain and cool the lemon at room temperature for 10 minutes.

3. Slice the lemon in half. Scoop out and discard the flesh and seeds. Cut the rind into a few chunks and slice these as thinly as possible, even thinner than matchsticks if you can. Put these in a medium saucepan.

4. Clean and dry your hands or put on culinary kitchen gloves. Pick up the summer squash by handfuls and squeeze it dry over the sink before putting the handfuls in a medium saucepan. Stir in the onion, wine, raisins, honey, and lemon juice. Set the pan over medium-high heat and stir until the sugar has dissolved. Continue cooking, stirring quite often, until the mixture comes to a *boil* (not just a simmer).

5. Reduce the heat to low and simmer *slowly*, stirring more and more often to prevent scorching, until most of the liquid has evaporated and the remainder has reduced to a syrup so thick that you

Clockwise from right:
Zucchini Relish (page 168),
Fennel Relish (page 171), and
Shredded Mango Relish
(page 172)

can run a wooden spoon across the bottom of the pan and create a line that holds its edges for a second, about 15 minutes.

6. Turn off the heat, remove the pan from the burner, and set aside for 1–2 minutes. Transfer to three *clean* ½ pint (236 ml) jars or other containers, leaving about ½ inch (1 cm) headspace in each. Cover or seal. Cool at room temperature for no more than 1 hour, then refrigerate or freeze.

More
For a slightly more mellow relish, omit the raisins and use an equivalent *weight* of chopped, pitted dates.

Fennel Relish

MAKES: about 4 cups (960 ml)
FRIDGE: up to 3 weeks
FREEZER: up to 1 year

This relish stands in the gap between a savory jam and a more standard relish. Yes, it's sweet, even sticky; but the fennel (and vinegar) tip it toward a classic sandwich relish with a licorice-tinged flavor and plenty of lemon juice to brighten it up. Here's a trick: If you don't cut off the woody, thick bottoms of the fennel bulbs, they'll hold together as you grate them on a box cutter.

> 2¼ pounds (1 kg) fennel bulbs (about 2 large)
> 1 cup (240 ml) distilled white vinegar
> ½ cup (108 g) packed light brown sugar
> ½ cup (120 ml) water
> ¼ cup (50 g) granulated white sugar
> 3 tablespoons (45 ml) lemon juice
> 2 teaspoons fennel seeds
> 2 teaspoons yellow mustard seeds
> 1 teaspoon kosher salt
> ½ teaspoon red pepper flakes

1. Trim the fennel bulbs of their stalks, fronds, and any brown spots. (You can freeze the stalks and fronds for soups and stews another time.) Holding the woody bottoms of the bulbs, shred the fennel through the large holes of a box grater; or shred with the shredding blade of a food processor. If you use a box grater, invest in a pair of washable, cut-safe kitchen gloves to protect your knuckles. Discard the tough, woody bottoms of the bulbs.

2. Dump the shredded fennel and all the remaining ingredients into a large saucepan. Set it over medium-high heat and stir constantly to dissolve the sugar.

3. Reduce the heat to low and simmer *slowly*, stirring more and more often to prevent scorching, until light golden and you can run a wooden spoon across the bottom of the pan and create a line that holds its edges for a second, about 25 minutes.

4. Turn off the heat, remove the pan from the burner, and set aside for 1–2 minutes. Transfer to four *clean* ½ pint (236 ml) jars or other containers, leaving about ½ inch (1 cm) headspace in each. Cover or seal. Cool at room temperature for no more than 1 hour, then refrigerate or freeze.

More
For a sweeter relish, substitute dry white wine for the water.

Beet Relish

MAKES: about 4 cups (960 ml)
FRIDGE: up to 3 weeks
FREEZER: up to 1 year

If you're a fan of sweeter, velvety relishes, this one is for you! Beets are loaded with natural sugars and get even sweeter as they cook and tenderize. Watch carefully for scorching, even when the covered pan is at a simmer. If you notice any sticking, take the pan off the heat, reduce the heat further, then soldier on with a more watchful eye and more stirring.

> 10½ ounces (300 g) red beets, peeled and shredded (about 3 packed cups)
>
> 1 small yellow or white onion, peeled and *finely* chopped
>
> 1 medium hard sour green apple, such as a Granny Smith, stemmed, cored, and *finely* chopped
>
> ½ cup (120 ml) apple cider vinegar
>
> ½ cup (120 ml) water
>
> ¼ cup (50 g) granulated white sugar
>
> 3 tablespoons (65 g) honey
>
> 2 tablespoons (30 g) minced peeled fresh ginger
>
> 1 teaspoon kosher salt

1. Combine all the ingredients in a large saucepan. Set it over medium-high heat and stir to dissolve the sugar. Bring the mixture to a *boil* (not just a simmer), stirring often.

2. Reduce the heat to very low. Cover and simmer *very slowly but steadily*, stirring occasionally, for 20 minutes.

3. Uncover and raise the heat to medium-low. Continue simmering *slowly*, stirring more and more often to prevent scorching, until you can run a wooden spoon across the bottom of the pan and create a line that holds its edges for a second, about 10 minutes.

4. Turn off the heat, remove the pan from the burner, and set aside for 1–2 minutes. Transfer to four *clean* ½ pint (236 ml) jars or other containers, leaving about ½ inch (1 cm) headspace in each.

Cover or seal. Cool at room temperature for no more than 1 hour, then refrigerate or freeze.

Next
Serve this relish at Passover with gefilte fish. Or mix with canned tuna for a non-creamy but brightly flavored tuna salad.

Shredded Mango Relish

MAKES: about 3 cups (720 ml)
FRIDGE: up to 3 weeks
FREEZER: up to 1 year

This is our take on a Trinidadian relish: kuchela. The original uses hard green mangoes, perhaps familiar from Thai green mango salads but not readily available in North America. We've adapted the standard recipe to use hard, sort-of-ripe mangoes, the kind that feel like lead and have absolutely no aroma but still appear in most supermarkets. Use the greenest you can find, with no red spots and few yellow areas. The original is also made with amchar masala, fried in lots of oil. It gives the relish an almost black color and a more bitter flavor. We've substituted dried spices so that we can keep the relish brighter and offer a slightly more varied palette of flavors.

> 3 pounds (1.4 kg) hard unripe mangoes
>
> ½ cup (100 g) granulated white sugar
>
> ¼ cup (54 g) packed light brown sugar
>
> 3 tablespoons (45 ml) lime juice
>
> 1 teaspoon coriander seeds
>
> 1 teaspoon cumin seeds
>
> 1 teaspoon fennel seeds
>
> 1 teaspoon fenugreek seeds
>
> 1 teaspoon brown mustard seeds
>
> 1 teaspoon red pepper flakes
>
> 1 teaspoon ground black pepper
>
> ½ teaspoon garlic powder
>
> ½ teaspoon kosher salt

1. Peel the unripe mangoes (a paring knife works best!), then grate them through the holes of a box grater into a medium saucepan, turning the fruit this way and that to get down to the pit in each.

2. Add all the remaining ingredients. Set the pan over medium heat and stir to dissolve the sugar. Bring to a simmer, stirring often.

3. Reduce the heat to low and simmer *slowly*, stirring more and more often to prevent scorching, until most of the liquid has evaporated and the remainder has reduced to a syrup so thick that you can run a wooden spoon across the bottom of the pan and create a line that holds its edges for a second, about 12 minutes.

4. Turn off the heat, remove the pan from the burner, and set aside for 1–2 minutes. Transfer to three *clean* ½ pint (236 ml) jars or other containers, leaving about ½ inch (1 cm) headspace in each. Cover or seal. Cool at room temperature for no more than 1 hour, then refrigerate or freeze.

Next
Serve this relish with sandwiches of all sorts, even grilled cheese, for a spicy, aromatic kick.

English Piccalilli

MAKES: about 2 cups (480 ml)
FRIDGE: up to 3 weeks
FREEZER: up to 1 year

Piccalilli is a cauliflower-based condiment, an English version of a Southeast Asian pickle. It's often bright yellow, thanks to turmeric (which also gives it an earthy muskiness). We use mellow malt vinegar, not exactly traditional, but a bow perhaps to its English roots. We find that riced cauliflower gives this relish a luxurious texture with our fridge or freezer method since we don't need to cook the relish a second time by pressure- or steam-canning to further cook larger pieces of cauliflower.

¾ pound (340 g) riced cauliflower (about 3 cups)

1 medium yellow or white onion, peeled and *minced*

¾ cup (180 ml) malt vinegar

¾ cup (150 g) granulated white sugar

2 tablespoons (30 ml) water

2 teaspoons (5 g) jarred, drained capers, *minced*

1 teaspoon ground dried mustard

½ teaspoon ground dried turmeric

½ teaspoon celery seeds

½ teaspoon kosher salt

1 tablespoon (15 ml) white balsamic vinegar

½ teaspoon cornstarch

1. Combine the cauliflower, onion, malt vinegar, sugar, water, capers, ground mustard, turmeric, celery seeds, and salt in a medium saucepan. Set it over medium heat and stir until the sugar dissolves. Cook, stirring frequently, until the mixture comes to a *boil* (not a simmer).

2. Reduce the heat to low and simmer *slowly*, stirring more and more often to prevent scorching, until the vegetables are soft and most of the liquid has reduced to a syrup so thick that you can run a wooden spoon across the bottom of the pan and create a line that holds its edges for a second, about 15 minutes.

3. Whisk the white balsamic vinegar and cornstarch in a small bowl until uniform, then stir into the mixture. Cook, stirring constantly, until thickened, less than 1 minute.

4. Turn off the heat, remove the pan from the burner, and set aside for 1–2 minutes. Transfer to two *clean* ½ pint (236 ml) jars or other containers, leaving about ½ inch (1 cm) headspace in each. Cover or seal. Cool at room temperature for no more than 1 hour, then refrigerate or freeze.

Next
Follow the English example and enjoy this pickle with fried eggs, sausages, and potatoes!

Southern Piccalilli

MAKES: about 2 cups (480 ml)
FRIDGE: up to 3 weeks
FREEZER: up to 1 year

Here's a complicated origin story: A Southeast Asian pickle, translated through English cuisine, is dropped into United States preserving methods from the South. To say the least, this green tomato relish now bears little resemblance to its origins! Look for green tomatoes at the end of the growing season, when the frosts are just in the offing. They'll give this relish a slightly bitter, decidedly sour edge.

- 1 pound (450 g) green unripe tomatoes, quartered
- 1 medium yellow or white onion, peeled and quartered
- 1 medium green bell pepper, stemmed, cored, and cut into small chunks
- ½ cup (100 g) granulated white sugar
- ¼ cup (60 ml) apple cider vinegar
- ½ teaspoon celery seeds
- ½ teaspoon yellow mustard seeds
- ¼ teaspoon kosher salt

1. Put the tomatoes, onion, and bell pepper in a food processor. Cover and pulse until the mixture is the texture of coarse relish. You will probably need to uncover the machine a couple of times to rearrange larger pieces.

2. Uncover the machine; scrape down and remove the blade. Clean and dry your hands or put on culinary kitchen gloves. Pick up the processed vegetables by the handful and squeeze dry before putting in a small saucepan.

3. Add the sugar, vinegar, celery seeds, mustard seeds, and salt. Set the pan over medium heat and stir to dissolve the sugar. Bring to a simmer, stirring often.

4. Reduce the heat to low and simmer *slowly*, stirring more and more often to prevent scorching, until the vegetables are soft and the remaining liquid has reduced to a syrup so thick that you can run a wooden spoon across the bottom of the pan and create a line that holds its edges for a second, about 15 minutes.

5. Turn off the heat, remove the pan from the burner, and set aside for 1–2 minutes. Transfer to two *clean* ½ pint (236 ml) jars or other containers, leaving about ½ inch (1 cm) headspace in each. Cover or seal. Cool at room temperature for no more than 1 hour, then refrigerate or freeze.

More
For heat, add up to 1 teaspoon red pepper flakes with the seeds.

Sticky Brown Cauliflower Pickle

MAKES: about 3 cups (720 ml)
FRIDGE: up to 3 weeks
FREEZER: up to 1 year

Here's our version of an English staple: Branston pickle. Although the standard bottling includes rutabagas, we use only cauliflower to offer a slightly easier prep and a gentler flavor. This pickle is terrific with aged, hard cheese, even a dry Asiago or an aged Gouda. Or go with the classic: buttered bread slices sandwiching slices of strong English cheddar and the pickle.

- ¾ pound (350 g) cauliflower florets; or a very small cauliflower head, trimmed, cored, and cut into florets
- 1 medium yellow or white onion, peeled and finely chopped
- 1 small zucchini, diced
- 1 large carrot, peeled and finely chopped
- 1 medium hard sour green apple, stemmed, cored, and finely chopped
- 6 plump pitted Medjool dates, finely chopped
- 1 cup (215 g) packed dark brown sugar
- 1 cup (240 ml) malt vinegar
- ½ cup (120 ml) water
- 2 tablespoons (30 ml) lemon juice
- 1 tablespoon (21 g) molasses or black treacle

- 1 tablespoon (15 ml) Worcestershire sauce (or use your own, page 372)
- 1 teaspoon brown mustard seeds
- 1 teaspoon ground allspice
- 1 teaspoon kosher salt
- ½ teaspoon red pepper flakes

1. Put the cauliflower florets in a food processor, cover, and pulse until they're ground to coarse bits, about like raisins, not like fine, riced cauliflower. Work in batches as necessary.

2. Pour the cauliflower bits into a large saucepan and add all the remaining ingredients. Set the pan over medium-high heat and stir constantly to dissolve the brown sugar. Bring to a simmer, stirring often.

3. Reduce the heat to low and simmer *slowly*, stirring more and more often to prevent scorching, until darkly colored and the liquid has reduced to a syrup so thick that you can run a wooden spoon across the bottom of the pan and create a line that holds its edges for a second, about 35 minutes.

4. Turn off the heat, remove the pan from the burner, and set aside for 1–2 minutes. Transfer to three *clean* ½ pint (236 ml) jars or other containers, leaving about ½ inch (1 cm) headspace in each. Cover or seal. Cool at room temperature for no more than 1 hour, then refrigerate or freeze.

More

Although not traditional by any means, we often add up to ¼ teaspoon grated nutmeg with the other spices.

Sweet Chow Chow

MAKES: about 3 cups (720 ml)
FRIDGE: up to 3 weeks
FREEZER: up to 1 year

Chow chow is something of a staple in the US South. Originally a Cantonese import but morphed into a Western-style condiment with turmeric and mustard, it's designed to preserve vegetables from the height of summer, like cabbage and bell peppers. There are probably as many versions of chow chow below the Mason-Dixon Line as there are grandmothers. We lean into the cabbage in our sweet version because it develops an earthy funkiness as it cooks, giving the condiment a more sophisticated blush, not just a sweet pop.

- 3 cups (270 g) chopped cored green cabbage
- 1 medium yellow bell pepper, stemmed, cored, and chopped
- 1 medium red bell pepper, stemmed, cored, and chopped
- 1 cup (240 ml) distilled white vinegar
- 1 cup (200 g) granulated white sugar
- 2 teaspoons (10 g) prepared yellow mustard (not Dijon or coarse-grained mustard)
- ½ teaspoon ground dried turmeric
- ½ teaspoon celery seeds
- ½ teaspoon kosher salt

1. Combine all the ingredients in a medium saucepan. Set it over medium heat and stir to dissolve the sugar. Bring to a simmer, stirring often.

2. Reduce the heat to low and simmer *slowly*, stirring more and more often to prevent scorching, until the vegetables are soft and most of the liquid has reduced to a syrup so thick that you can run a wooden spoon across the bottom of the pan and create a line that holds its edges for a second, about 15 minutes.

3. Turn off the heat, remove the pan from the burner, and set aside for 1–2 minutes. Transfer to three *clean* ½ pint (236 ml) jars or other containers, leaving about ½ inch (1 cm) headspace in each. Cover or seal. Cool at room temperature for no more than 1 hour, then refrigerate or freeze.

Next

This chow chow is delicious on a baked potato with lots of sour cream and a little butter.

On cocktail toasts with ham, from light to dark: English Piccalilli (page 173) and Sticky Brown Cauliflower Pickle (page 174)

Chili Chow Chow

MAKES: about 4 cups (960 ml)
FRIDGE: up to 3 weeks
FREEZER: up to 1 year

This cabbage-based condiment is given a kick in the (leafy?) pants with fresh chilis for a big spoonful of flavor to serve alongside grilled meats, vegetables, even buttered corn on the cob. Remember: The heat from chilis is tamed by fat, not water. Have some of this chow chow with full-fat mayonnaise or even crème fraîche to calm it down and create an unbeatable spread for sandwiches.

> 5 cups (450 g) chopped cored green cabbage
>
> 1 medium *sweet* onion, such as Vidalia, peeled and finely chopped
>
> 1 medium red bell pepper, stemmed, cored, and finely chopped
>
> 4 medium fresh green chilis, such as jalapeño or serrano, stemmed and thinly sliced
>
> 2 teaspoons kosher salt
>
> 1½ cups (360 ml) distilled white vinegar
>
> 1½ cups (300 g) granulated white sugar
>
> 2 medium garlic cloves, peeled and minced
>
> 1½ teaspoons brown mustard seeds
>
> 1 teaspoon celery seeds
>
> 1 teaspoon red pepper flakes
>
> ½ teaspoon ground cumin
>
> ½ teaspoon ground dried turmeric
>
> ½ teaspoon ground dried ginger

1. Mix the cabbage, onion, bell pepper, and chilis in a large bowl. Sprinkle on the salt and toss well to combine evenly. Cover and refrigerate for at least 8 hours or overnight.

2. Uncover the bowl and hold the vegetables in place with the back of a wooden spoon. Tip the bowl to drain as much of the water as you can into the sink. Clean and dry your hands or put on culinary kitchen gloves. Pick up the vegetables by the handful and squeeze them dry before putting them in a second bowl.

3. Mix the vinegar, sugar, garlic, mustard seeds, celery seeds, red pepper flakes, cumin, ground turmeric, and ground ginger in a large saucepan. Set it over medium-high heat and stir to dissolve the sugar. Continue cooking, stirring occasionally, until the mixture comes to a boil. Reduce the heat to very low and simmer *slowly but steadily* for 10 minutes, stirring occasionally.

4. Add the vegetable mixture and raise the heat back to medium-high. Stirring almost constantly, bring the liquid to a boil. Reduce the heat to low and again simmer *slowly*, stirring more and more often to prevent scorching, until the vegetables are soft and the remaining liquid has reduced to a syrup so thick that you can run a wooden spoon across the bottom of the pan and create a line that holds its edges for a second, about 15 minutes.

5. Turn off the heat, remove the pan from the burner, and set aside for 1–2 minutes. Transfer to four *clean* ½ pint (236 ml) jars or other containers, leaving about ½ inch (1 cm) headspace in each. Cover or seal. Cool at room temperature for no more than 1 hour, then refrigerate or freeze.

Next
This chow chow is great in egg salad or simply dolloped on fried eggs. Or use it as you would sauerkraut.

Watermelon Rind Chow Chow

MAKES: about 4 cups (960 ml)
FRIDGE: up to 3 weeks
FREEZER: up to 1 year

Watermelon rind is something of a preserving wonder in the US South. It's often pickled for a condiment in the colder (or slightly less hot) months. Here, we take our cue from those pickles to create a chow chow with the rind. We've loved this condiment ever since we first crafted a version for *Cooking Light* magazine, where it proved to be one of their most popular recipes.

> One 5 pound (2.25 kg) watermelon
> Water as necessary to boil the watermelon rind
> 1 cup (200 g) granulated white sugar
> 1 cup (240 ml) distilled white vinegar
> 1 tablespoon (15 g) minced peeled fresh ginger
> 1 tablespoon ground dried mustard powder
> 2 teaspoons ground dried turmeric
> ½ teaspoon kosher salt

1. Halve the watermelon; scoop out its insides and save for eating later. Use a sharp knife to slice off and discard the green outer layer of the rind, leaving only the white part behind. Cut the rind into manageable chunks (based on what you're about to do next). Either grate the chunks through the large holes of a box grater, or feed the chunks through the tube of a food processor and onto the running shredding blades. You should end up with about 6 packed cups of shreds (discard any remainder or use for composting).

2. Fill a very large saucepan about three-quarters full with water. Set the pan over high heat and bring the water to a boil. Add the watermelon rind shreds. Cook, stirring once or twice, for 3 minutes (from the time the shreds hit the water, not from the time it comes back to a boil). Drain the shreds in a colander set in the sink.

3. Combine the sugar, vinegar, ginger, ground mustard, turmeric, and salt in that same very large saucepan. Set it over medium-high heat and stir until the sugar dissolves. Bring the mixture to a boil, stirring occasionally. Reduce the heat to low and simmer *slowly* for 2 minutes, stirring occasionally.

4. Add the watermelon shreds and raise the heat back to medium-high. Stirring almost constantly, bring the liquid to a boil. Reduce the heat to low and again simmer *slowly*, stirring more and more often to prevent scorching, until the rind shreds are soft and the remaining liquid has reduced to a syrup so thick that you can run a wooden spoon

across the bottom of the pan and create a line that holds its edges for a second, about 12 minutes.

5. Turn off the heat, remove the pan from the burner, and set aside for 1–2 minutes. Transfer to four *clean* ½ pint (236 ml) jars or other containers, leaving about ½ inch (1 cm) headspace in each. Cover or seal. Cool at room temperature for no more than 1 hour, then refrigerate or freeze.

More
Substitute light brown sugar for the granulated sugar and apple cider vinegar for the distilled white vinegar for a more chutney-style chow chow.

Caponata

MAKES: about 3 cups (720 ml)
FRIDGE: up to 1 week
FREEZER: up to 1 year

Caponata was (perhaps originally?) a Sicilian eggplant mélange of eggplant, tomatoes, capers, and olives in a sweet-sour sauce. It now encompasses hundreds of variations that reach far beyond that Mediterranean island. Our version sticks close to something like what the original may have been, although we've used more common vegetables available at most supermarkets rather than Sicilian varietals. We also add raisins to offer a slightly more cooked (or caramelized) flavor without a prolonged stir at the stove.

> 14 ounces (400 g) eggplant (about 2 medium), stemmed, peeled, and *diced*
> 6 tablespoons (90 ml) olive oil
> ½ teaspoon kosher salt
> 1 small yellow or white onion, peeled and chopped
> 1 medium red bell pepper, stemmed, cored, and chopped
> 2 small celery ribs, chopped
> 7 ounces (200 g) small cherry tomatoes, halved (about 1½ cups)
> ¼ cup (38 g) raisins, chopped
> ¼ cup (32 g) pitted green olives, chopped
> 2 tablespoons (15 g) drained capers, chopped

1 tablespoon (21 g) honey

¼ cup (60 ml) dry white wine

¼ cup (60 ml) red wine vinegar

½ teaspoon red pepper flakes

1. Position the rack in the oven's middle and heat the oven to 375°F (190°C), no fan or convection.

2. Toss the eggplant, 3 tablespoons (45 ml) oil, and the salt in a bowl until the eggplant is well coated. Scrape and spread the eggplant pieces on a large, lipped baking sheet. Roast, stirring once, until golden and somewhat softened, about 25 minutes. Set aside to cool as you continue the recipe.

3. Set a very large saucepan over medium heat for a minute or two. Add the remaining 3 tablespoons (45 ml) oil, then stir in the onion, bell pepper, and celery. Cook, stirring occasionally, until softened, about 5 minutes.

4. Stir in the tomatoes, raisins, olives, capers, honey, wine, vinegar, and red pepper flakes. Cook, stirring often, until bubbling. Reduce the heat to low and continue cooking, stirring occasionally, until the vegetables break down to become almost a sauce, about 10 minutes.

5. Stir in the roasted eggplant pieces and simmer *slowly*, stirring more and more often to prevent scorching, until quite thick, almost pasty (if not quite), about 3 minutes.

6. Turn off the heat, remove the pan from the burner, and set aside for 1–2 minutes. Transfer to three *clean* ½ pint (236 ml) jars or other containers, leaving about ½ inch (1 cm) headspace in each. Cover or seal. Cool at room temperature for no more than 30 minutes, then refrigerate or freeze.

Next

Stirring caponata into plain Greek yogurt makes a gorgeous dip for chips or crackers.

Super Sour Iranian-Style Pickle

MAKES: about 4 cups (960 ml)
FRIDGE: up to 3 weeks
FREEZER: up to 1 year

In Iranian culture, there's a long tradition of pickling vegetables or fruits with vinegar, salt, and spices—*and not much sugar at all*. In fact, the Farsi name for this condiment (*torshi*) is derived from a word meaning *sour*. Torshi is often made in the autumn months as a preparation for cooler weather ahead. Trust us: This pickle will yank your palate out of any winter doldrums.

1 pound (450 g) cauliflower (about half a large head), trimmed of its thick stem and cut into chunks

12 ounces (340 g) eggplant (about 1 medium), stemmed, peeled, and cut into chunks

7 ounces (200 g) carrot (about 1 large), peeled and cut into chunks

5 ounces (140 g) cucumber (about 1 medium), cut into chunks

2 cups (480 ml) apple cider vinegar

1 large shallot (about 1¾ ounces or 50 g), peeled

Up to 2 fresh green serrano chilis, stemmed, seeded (if desired), and *finely* chopped

2 medium garlic cloves, peeled and minced

1 teaspoon decorticated (husked and removed from the pods) cardamom seeds

1 teaspoon coriander seeds

1 teaspoon kosher salt

½ teaspoon ground dried turmeric

¼ cup (60 g) tomato paste

2 tablespoons (32 g) pomegranate molasses

1. Working in batches, put the cauliflower, eggplant, carrot, and cucumber in a food processor, cover, and pulse until very finely chopped, not pureed or juiced, but in tiny bits. Uncover the processor as necessary and rearrange the chunks with a rubber spatula. As you work, pour the finely chopped bits into a medium bowl and continue processing the remainder.

Front to back: Caponata (page 178)
and Black Olive Tapenade (page 181)

2. Pour the vinegar into a very large saucepan. Stir in the finely chopped vegetables as well as the shallot, chilis, garlic, cardamom, coriander, salt, and turmeric. Set the pan over medium-high heat and bring to a boil, stirring often.

3. Reduce the heat to medium-low and simmer steadily, stirring quite often, until the liquid has reduced quite a bit and the vegetables are tender, about 15 minutes.

4. Stir in the tomato paste and pomegranate molasses. Reduce the heat to low and simmer *slowly*, stirring almost constantly, until the mixture is quite thick, like a chunky relish, and the liquid has almost all evaporated, about 5 more minutes.

5. Turn off the heat, remove the pan from the burner, and set aside for 1–2 minutes. Transfer to four *clean* ½ pint (236 ml) jars or other containers, leaving about ½ inch (1 cm) headspace in each. Cover or seal. Cool at room temperature for no more than 1 hour, then refrigerate or freeze.

More

Since there's no added sugar to this mix, it may be too sour for many North American tastes. For a sweeter finish, add 2 tablespoons (25 g) sugar with the tomato paste.

Black Olive Tapenade

MAKES: about 2 cups (480 ml)
FRIDGE: up to 2 weeks
FREEZER: up to 1 year

A jar of classic tapenade is an extraordinary gift for friends and family. For the best results, look for *plump* pitted brine-cured black Kalamata olives. Combine them with *plump* tinned anchovy fillets, which add a briny depth of flavor. The better the anchovies, the better the tapenade. Look for tinned or jarred anchovies from Spain or Portugal. They're fat, rich, and bursting with flavor.

2¼ cups (320 g) pitted black Kalamata olives
½ cup (120 ml) olive oil, preferably extra virgin
¼ cup (30 g) drained capers
4 tinned anchovy fillets
2 tablespoons (30 ml) lemon juice
2 tablespoons (30 ml) red wine vinegar
3 medium garlic cloves, peeled and halved lengthwise
1 tablespoon (2 g) fresh thyme leaves
1 teaspoon kosher salt
½ teaspoon ground black pepper

1. Put all the ingredients in a food processor. Cover and pulse repeatedly, uncovering and rearranging ingredients with a rubber spatula as necessary, until the mixture has the consistency of a coarse, slushy relish.

2. Transfer to two *clean* ½ pint (236 ml) jars or other containers, leaving about ½ inch (1 cm) headspace in each. Cover or seal, then refrigerate or freeze.

Tip

All our tapenades make a small amount because a little tapenade goes a long way. Freeze them in even smaller containers than our suggestion and pull them out whenever you've got friends over.

Anchovy-Free Tapenade

MAKES: about 2 cups (480 ml)
FRIDGE: up to 2 weeks
FREEZER: up to 1 year

Although tinned anchovies are customary in black olive tapenade, they're not required. However, once we leave them out, we have to compensate for the loss to make a successful condiment. We do so by using a *mix* of olives, both brine- and dry-cured (or sometimes called *salt-cured*). And we swap out the thyme for more assertive oregano in a bid to layer the flavors dramatically.

- ¾ cup (112 g) pitted dry-cured black olives
- ¾ cup (105 g) pitted Niçoise olives
- ¾ cup (105 g) pitted black Kalamata olives
- 6 tablespoons (90 ml) olive oil, preferably extra virgin
- 3 tablespoons (23 g) drained capers
- 2 medium garlic cloves, peeled and halved lengthwise
- 1 tablespoon (2 g) packed fresh oregano leaves, *minced*
- 2 teaspoons (4 g) finely grated lemon zest
- ½ teaspoon ground black pepper

1. Put all the ingredients in a food processor. Cover and pulse repeatedly, uncovering and rearranging ingredients with a rubber spatula as necessary, until the mixture has the consistency of a coarse, slushy relish.

2. Transfer to two *clean* ½ pint (236 ml) jars or other containers, leaving about ½ inch (1 cm) headspace in each. Cover or seal, then refrigerate or freeze.

Tip
If you're buying olives *with* their pits, you'll need to buy about 25 percent more *by weight* than our stated amount before you pit them at home.

Green Olive Tapenade

MAKES: about 2 cups (480 ml)
FRIDGE: up to 2 weeks
FREEZER: up to 1 year

We got our inspiration for this tapenade from a version we enjoyed in a Madrid restaurant. Since green olives are not the standard for tapenade, the chef felt free to go crazy and added Marcona almonds. These almonds are prized for their buttery flavor and creamy texture. They're sometimes sold salted—and if indeed yours are, you might want to cut down or omit the added salt. This tapenade is best with a cold cocktail or mocktail in the heat of summer.

- 2 cups (250 g) pitted plump green olives
- ½ cup (120 ml) olive oil, preferably extra virgin
- ¼ cup (35 g) Marcona almonds
- 3 tablespoons (23 g) drained capers
- 2 tablespoons (30 ml) lemon juice
- 1 tablespoon (15 ml) white wine vinegar
- 3 medium garlic cloves, peeled and halved lengthwise
- 1 teaspoon kosher salt

1. Put all the ingredients in a food processor. Cover and pulse repeatedly, uncovering and rearranging ingredients with a rubber spatula as necessary, until the mixture has the consistency of a coarse, slushy relish.

2. Transfer to two *clean* ½ pint (236 ml) jars or other containers, leaving about ½ inch (1 cm) headspace in each. Cover or seal, then refrigerate or freeze.

Next
Use this tapenade on fish fillets off the grill or on top of hummus with crunchy rye crackers for an easy lunch.

Fig-Olive Tapenade

MAKES: about 2 cups (480 ml)
FRIDGE: up to 2 weeks
FREEZER: up to 1 year

Now we're pushing the limits of what a tapenade can be! And we might as well, given the many variations even among so-called *authentic* versions. This one with dried figs has more sweetness, is a bit richer, and is perhaps better before a winter holiday dinner (with a second jar saved to the side for someone special to take home).

- 6 dried Calimyrna or Adriatic (aka Turkish) figs, stemmed and quartered
- 1 tablespoon (15 ml) balsamic vinegar
- 1 small fresh rosemary sprig
- 1 fresh thyme sprig
- Water as necessary to simmer the figs
- 1 cup (128 g) pitted green olives

½ cup (56 g) walnut pieces

1 teaspoon kosher salt

½ teaspoon ground black pepper

Olive oil, as necessary to process effectively

1. Combine the figs, vinegar, rosemary, and thyme in a small saucepan. Add just enough water to cover the ingredients. Set the pan over medium-high heat and bring to a simmer. Reduce the heat to low and simmer *slowly but steadily*, stirring occasionally, until the figs are soft and the liquid in the pan has reduced to a thick glaze, about 12 minutes. Turn off the heat and remove the pan from the burner. Cool to room temperature, about 1 hour.

2. Remove and discard the rosemary and thyme sprigs. Pour and scrape the figs and any liquid into a food processor. Add the olives, nuts, salt, and pepper. Cover and pulse repeatedly, uncovering and rearranging ingredients as necessary and adding olive oil in 1 tablespoon (15 ml) increments to get the mixture to process effectively, until it has the consistency of a coarse, slushy relish.

3. Transfer to two *clean* ½ pint (236 ml) jars or other containers, leaving about ½ inch (1 cm) headspace in each. Cover or seal, then refrigerate or freeze.

More

Add ½ teaspoon finely grated lemon zest to the food processor.

Caper Tapenade

MAKES: about 2 cups (480 ml)
FRIDGE: up to 2 weeks
FREEZER: up to 1 year

Since the origins of tapenade may actually be tied more to capers than olives, we've crafted a version that uses tons of capers, the better to foreground their briny, herbaceous flavors. Because capers are more assertive than olives, we've balanced them with some mustard and honey, all in a bid to give this tapenade a smoother finish—less jagged in its flavors, but still quite salty.

¼ cup (60 ml) olive oil

½ cup (60 g) drained capers

¼ cup (28 g) pecan pieces or halves

1 small (¾ ounce or 22 g) shallot, peeled and *minced*

2 medium garlic cloves, peeled and thinly sliced

1 tablespoon (2 g) packed fresh rosemary leaves, finely chopped

1½ cups (213 g) pitted black Kalamata olives

1 tablespoon (30 ml) lemon juice

1 teaspoon (7 g) honey

1 teaspoon (5 g) Dijon mustard

1. Set a small skillet over medium heat for a minute or two. Swirl in the oil, then add the capers, pecans, shallot, garlic, and rosemary. Cook, stirring almost constantly, until sizzling and quite fragrant (do not let the pecans burn), about 2 minutes. Turn off the heat and remove the skillet from the burner. Cool to room temperature, about 30 minutes.

2. Pour and scrape the contents of the skillet into a food processor. Add the olives, lemon juice, honey, and mustard. Cover and pulse repeatedly, uncovering and rearranging ingredients as necessary, until it has the consistency of a coarse, slushy relish.

3. Transfer to two *clean* ½ pint (236 ml) jars or other containers, leaving about ½ inch (1 cm) headspace in each. Cover or seal, then refrigerate or freeze.

Next

This tapenade is particularly great as a brunch condiment with stuffed, cheesy omelets.

Beet Tapenade

MAKES: about 2 cups (480 ml)
FRIDGE: up to 2 weeks
FREEZER: up to 1 year

Beet tapenade is a culinary revelation: sweet, earthy, and salty…even quite flavorful in this version, thanks to the orange zest and red pepper flakes. We love the way this tapenade brightens plates. But do remember that beets stain everything. Have lots of (paper?) napkins on hand.

- ¾ pound (350 g) beet (about 1 large), peeled and cut into 2 inch (5 cm) chunks
- 1 cup (142 g) pitted black Kalamata olives
- ¼ cup (60 ml) olive oil, preferably extra virgin
- 1 tablespoon (6 g) finely grated orange zest
- 2 tablespoons (30 ml) lemon juice
- 2 tablespoons (15 g) drained capers
- ½ teaspoon red pepper flakes
- ½ teaspoon kosher salt

1. Position the rack in the oven's center and heat the oven to 375°F (190°C), no fan or convection.

2. Tightly seal the beet chunks in an aluminum foil packet. Roast until tender when pierced with a knife, about 45 minutes. Open the packet and cool the beets to room temperature, about 1 hour.

3. Place the beets in a food processor. Add the olives, olive oil, orange zest, lemon juice, capers, red pepper flakes, and salt. Cover and pulse repeatedly, uncovering and rearranging ingredients with a rubber spatula as necessary, until the mixture has the consistency of a coarse, slushy relish.

4. Transfer to two *clean* ½ pint (236 ml) jars or other containers, leaving about ½ inch (1 cm) headspace in each. Cover or seal, then refrigerate or freeze.

Tip

Look for packages of roasted peeled beets in your supermarket's produce section. Substitute the same amount *by weight*.

Puttanesca Tapenade

MAKES: about 2 cups (480 ml)
FRIDGE: up to 2 weeks
FREEZER: up to 1 year

Although we used dry-packed sun-dried tomatoes in our Garlicky Sun-Dried Tomato Tapenade (page 186) for both their texture and earthy flavor, here we use oil-packed sun-dried tomatoes, which are often sweeter and offer a more velvety finish when blended. Dry vermouth also adds herbaceous notes. Remember that there's a wide disparity among vermouths, from basically flavored water to rich, herbal concoctions. As a general rule, you get what you pay for.

- 2 cups (300 g) pitted dry-packed oil-cured black olives
- 6 tablespoons (90 ml) olive oil, preferably extra virgin
- 8 sun-dried tomato halves packed in oil
- ¼ cup (30 g) drained capers
- 2 tablespoons (24 g) jarred minced pimentos
- 2 tablespoons (30 ml) dry (or white) vermouth
- 8 fresh basil leaves
- 3 medium garlic cloves, peeled and halved lengthwise
- 2 tinned anchovy fillets
- ½ teaspoon ground black pepper

1. Put all the ingredients in a food processor. Cover and pulse repeatedly, uncovering and rearranging ingredients with a rubber spatula as necessary, until the mixture has the consistency of a coarse, slushy relish.

2. Transfer to two *clean* ½ pint (236 ml) jars or other containers, leaving about ½ inch (1 cm) headspace in each. Cover or seal, then refrigerate or freeze.

Next

For an easy dinner, cook and drain some pasta of any sort, then toss with some of this tapenade, a little of the cooking water to make a sauce, and lots of ground black pepper.

With tinned anchovies, from left: Beet Tapenade (page 184) and Spiced Tapenade (page 186)

Garlicky Sun-Dried Tomato Tapenade

MAKES: about 2 cups (480 ml)
FRIDGE: up to 2 weeks
FREEZER: up to 1 year

Less sweet than Beet Tapenade (page 184), this olive spread is quite aromatic, thanks to the copious amounts of garlic. Don't use sun-dried tomatoes packed in oil. They're too unctuous with a more complicated blend of flavors (and so perfect for our Puttanesca Tapenade on page 184). Look for the dry-packed sun-dried tomatoes in the produce section of most supermarkets. If they're loose, pick through the bin to choose plump, soft ones, not ones that are desiccated or hard.

- ½ cup (120 ml) olive oil
- 8 medium garlic cloves, peeled and thinly sliced
- 2 tablespoons (15 g) drained capers
- ½ cup (85 g) dry-packed sun-dried tomatoes, thinly sliced
- 1½ cups (213 g) pitted black Kalamata olives
- ¼ cup (60 ml) red wine vinegar
- 1 teaspoon dried oregano
- 1 teaspoon kosher salt

1. Set a small skillet over medium heat for a minute or two. Swirl in the oil, then add the garlic and capers. Cook, stirring often, until the garlic has begun to brown at the edges, about 2 minutes.

2. Turn off the heat and remove the skillet from the burner. Stir in the sun-dried tomatoes until well combined. Cool to room temperature, about 30 minutes.

3. Pour and scrape the contents of the skillet into a food processor. Add the olives, vinegar, oregano, and salt. Cover and pulse repeatedly, uncovering and rearranging ingredients with a rubber spatula as necessary, until the mixture has the consistency of a coarse, slushy relish.

4. Transfer to two *clean* ½ pint (236 ml) jars or other containers, leaving about ½ inch (1 cm) headspace in each. Cover or seal, then refrigerate or freeze.

More

For heat, add up to two stemmed long thin dried chilis to the skillet with the capers. Remove them before pouring the contents of the skillet into the food processor.

Spiced Tapenade

MAKES: about 2 cups (480 ml)
FRIDGE: up to 2 weeks
FREEZER: up to 1 year

We modeled this tapenade from the flavors more common along the North African shores of the western Mediterranean: something like a Moroccan spice blend or perhaps even a taste of a Tunisian tagine. It's a bit of whimsy on our part, but one that has paid off well with rounds of cocktails on summer evenings. Frying the spices in the oil enhances their flavors and makes your kitchen smell amazing!

- ½ cup (120 ml) olive oil
- 1 teaspoon ground coriander
- 1 teaspoon ground cumin
- 1 teaspoon ground dried ginger
- ½ teaspoon ground black pepper
- ¼ teaspoon ground cinnamon
- ⅛ teaspoon ground dried turmeric
- 2 cups (256 g) pitted green olives
- 4 medium garlic cloves, peeled and halved lengthwise
- 2 tablespoons (30 g) seeded and chopped jarred preserved lemon (or use your own homemade, page 276)
- 2 tablespoons (32 g) pomegranate molasses
- 1 teaspoon kosher salt

1. Set a small skillet over medium heat for a minute or two. Swirl in the oil, then add the coriander, cumin, ground ginger, black pepper, cinnamon, and turmeric. Stir until the spices sizzle and smell fragrant, probably less than 1 minute. Turn off the heat, remove the skillet from the burner, and cool to room temperature, about 20 minutes.

2. Pour and scrape every drop in the skillet into a food processor. Add the olives, garlic, preserved lemon, pomegranate molasses, and salt. Cover and pulse repeatedly, uncovering and rearranging ingredients with a rubber spatula as necessary, until the mixture has the consistency of a coarse, slushy relish.

3. Transfer to two *clean* ½ pint (236 ml) jars or other containers, leaving about ½ inch (1 cm) headspace in each. Cover or seal, then refrigerate or freeze.

Next
Stir a little of this tapenade into warm cooked lentils, beans, or brown rice for a tasty side dish.

Artichoke-Lemon Tapenade

MAKES: about 2 cups (480 ml)
FRIDGE: up to 2 weeks
FREEZER: up to 1 year

We always have a jar or two of marinated artichoke hearts in the pantry for pizzas, omelets, and nibbles…and to make this tapenade! The overall blend is fairly simple, so nothing impedes those bright notes from the lemon juice and zest along with that wonderful flavor from the artichokes.

> 1½ cups (192 g) pitted green olives
>
> One 12 ounce (340 g) jar of marinated artichoke hearts (or make your own—see page 288), drained
>
> Finely grated zest and seeded juice of 1 large lemon
>
> 3 tablespoons (45 ml) olive oil, preferably extra virgin
>
> 2 medium garlic cloves, peeled and halved lengthwise

1. Put all the ingredients in a food processor. Cover and pulse repeatedly, uncovering and rearranging ingredients with a rubber spatula as necessary, until the mixture has the consistency of a coarse, slushy relish.

2. Transfer to two *clean* ½ pint (236 ml) jars or other containers, leaving about ½ inch (1 cm) headspace in each. Cover or seal, then refrigerate or freeze.

More
For a layered and sophisticated heat, add 1 stemmed pickled Calabrian chili.

3

Salsas, Chili Crisps, Chili Sauces, and Chili Pastes

Bring on the heat! This chapter is about chilis (threaded with aromatics, of course). Some of these condiments and sauces can be stirred into soups, stews, and braises for a flavor bump. (More later in this introduction about a specific problem with dairy and some of these condiments.) Many are terrific on deviled eggs, deli meats, hummus, noodles of all sorts, and takeout. And a few can be thinned out with broth, wine, and/or beer to become the base for a simmering sauce or a pan sauté.

Before we get started, let's talk about the source of a chili's heat. The incendiary chemical is an organic compound, a member of the lipid group capsaicin ($C_{18}H_{27}NO_3$). In practice, it's the chili's defense mechanism. We (and many other mammals) experience it as a burning or tingling sensation because our molars grind the fruit's precious seeds. But it has no effect on birds. They gulp parts of the fruit, can't digest its seeds, and so, um, spread them far and wide.

Capsaicin is also *not* water soluble. Neither iced tea nor a daiquiri can serve as a fire extinguisher. But the chemical is *fat* soluble. A buttered tortilla, a spoonful of full-fat sour cream, or a drizzle of olive oil will help stop the burn…not immediately, but quickly.

The burn is worth it for the metabolic functions capsaicin gooses and for the endorphins it stimulates. That's why most of us come back for more the moment the burn dies down.

Before we get to the recipes, let's be more precise about the condiments you can find in this chapter, then dig a little deeper into chilis as an ingredient and turn to a few technique notes.

More definitions

Here are the categories of condiments in this chapter:

- A **salsa**, by both nature and etymology, is a sauce. It can be fresh or cooked, chopped or pureed. It often includes either tomatoes or tomatillos. It is frequently made with some sort of allium, whether an onion, a shallot or two, or some garlic cloves.

- **Salsa macha** is an oily, thick chili sauce, originally from Veracruz, Mexico. It often includes nuts and a wider range of aromatics than salsas. Given its bigger concept, we've always felt free to push the notion of a salsa macha until we now include maple syrup or cranberries in some recipes. The point is a rich, chunky sauce that can be spooned on roasted vegetables, added to tacos, dolloped onto nachos, or used to garnish bowls of chili.

- A **chili crisp** was once a chunky *ingredient* in Szechuan cooking. Now an international phenomenon, it has morphed into a *condiment* for fried rice, stir-fries, roasted vegetables, or hummus. Many of us are familiar with the almost ever-present bottles of Lao Gan Ma Spicy Chili Crisp. But as you'll see, chili crisp variations can be mind-boggling, given the simplicity of the technique: Sizzling oil is poured over spices and aromatics to create a thick sauce that verges on a paste.

- A **chili sauce** is sometimes cooked, sometimes not, but is definitely more assertive (aka hotter) than a salsa. Some of ours are versions of **sambal** (again, *sauce*), a condiment found across Indonesia. All can be used to garnish cooked noodles or vegetables, offered as a condiment for braises and stir-fries, or added to many stews for a fiery finish.

- Finally, a **chili paste** is almost always an *ingredient*, not a condiment. It's the beginning of a stir-fry (as in **curry pastes**) or a braise (as in **moles**). Some can indeed be thinned to become dips and drizzles, but many can only be used as the base of more involved recipes.

Dried chilis

You'll find lots of dried chilis in this chapter: chipotles to árbol chilis, guajillos to pasillas, anchos to moritas. Larger supermarkets should have a decent supply, although dried chilis may not move quickly and can then degrade (that is, mold or mutate into something with no more than a dry, dusty flavor, about as appetizing as sand). Unless you live near a Latin American supermarket, consider buying dried chilis online from reputable purveyors.

A dried chili should be plump, still tender (or at least bendable), *maybe* breakable into two or three discrete sections, but *not* into a zillion shards. The stem should be attached; it should be pale but not desiccated. Store dried chilis in a plastic bag, squirreled away in a cool dark pantry for up to 6 months if you live in a humid climate, or up to 1 year in a dry climate.

Measuring dried chilis: When it comes to chili amounts in these recipes, you'll notice some variations as to how we measure them—that is, from market quantities (like "5 fresh red jalapeño chilis") to exact weight amounts (like "3 ounces or 85 grams fresh red bird's eye chilis"). In general, market quantities indicate a more forgiving recipe; weight amounts, a more exacting recipe. True, some of these weight amounts get a bit persnickety (like ⅔ ounce or 18.7 grams). Whenever we're this precise, we believe that more chilis will up the heat quotient enough to mute the subtler flavors of the herbs, spices, aromatics, and/or vegetables in the mix.

For example, take the first recipe, for Salsa Fresca (page 193). We call for 2 pounds (900 grams) cherry tomatoes, but also for *up to 4 fresh serrano chilis* (with no weight given). This tells you that we think the amount of tomatoes is important to the recipe's success but the amount of chilis is a matter of personal taste: How hot do you want this fresh salsa? However, in the recipe for Jalapeño Salsa (page 198), we call for *4 ounces or 125 grams fresh green jalapeños*. Here, we think

the amount of jalapeños has to be more precise to balance the other aromatics.

To be clear, whenever we work with ingredient *weights*, we always work in grams in our kitchen. As we developed these recipes, we naturally found that in many cases, a specific weight of an ingredient, particularly a chili, works best for the right flavor. Given our preference for working in grams, that desired weight might then come out to, say, 20 grams of dried chilis. But here's the rub: That gram amount has led us to some strange imperial amounts (0.7 ounce, in this case).

Since we work mostly in grams, we encourage you to set your kitchen scale to grams and follow us down the road to greater recipe success. That said, we almost always give you a market equivalent for any stated weights (about 30 dried chilis, for instance), mostly so you know about how many chilis you should purchase at the market. (But always err on the side of buying a few more than our recommendation.) Even so, when you're standing at the counter in *your own* kitchen and making the recipe, we urge you to get as fussy as we have been in these cases.

Prepping dried chilis: The easiest way to stem and seed a dried chili is with kitchen shears. Snip off the stem, preferably over a bowl or even a trash can, since seeds may spill out. Then cut along the chili's skin to reveal more seeds and their membranes.

Discarding the seeds is a matter of preference: more seeds = more heat. But we suggest removing the desiccated, off-white membranes since these can add unwanted bitter notes (unless we specifically call for them in a recipe as a balance against other flavors). In our recipe shorthand, whenever we ask you to *seed* a chili, we mean that you should remove *both* its seeds and membranes.

Red Szechuan chili powder

Some recipes in this chapter (and elsewhere in the book) call for *coarsely ground* red Szechuan

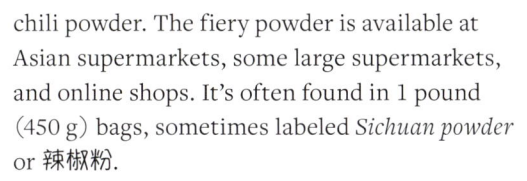

▲ Kitchen shears are the best tools for seeding chilis.

▲ Our preferred grind for red Szechuan chili powder.

chili powder. The fiery powder is available at Asian supermarkets, some large supermarkets, and online shops. It's often found in 1 pound (450 g) bags, sometimes labeled *Sichuan powder* or 辣椒粉.

Sounds simple, right? But there are two problems: first the chilis, then the grind. When it comes to the chilis, look for ground, dried *er jing tiao* chilis, prized for their sour bite, (somewhat) moderate heat, and fruit-like finish. That said, less expensive packagings may well include other ground chilis. If there's dried cayenne chili in the blend, the powder will be less complex and *super* hot. As a general rule, a blend of dried chilis won't ruin any of these recipes. And unfortunately, many brands do not label the types of ground chilis used, so you must rely on…

The grind. There's a huge difference among packagings: from a few that are almost powdery, to many more that are about as coarse as red pepper flakes and several that look more like slim shards of red chilis. We prefer a coarse blend, a little finer than red pepper flakes, but still grainy, certainly not like red talcum powder. In a pinch, we have used the sort in shards. But we wouldn't

recommend the powdery packagings for any recipe in this chapter. In short, the finer the grind, the *less* successful the chili crisp (because the texture gets pastier).

If you want to go all out, stem then grind *dried* er jing tiao chilis in a spice grinder or a mini food processor to create a coarsely ground chili powder. Store dried er jing tiao chilis as you would any dried chili: in a sealed plastic bag tucked into a cool, dark pantry for several months.

The types and temperatures of oils

Throughout this chapter, we're heating oil for frying, sizzling, browning, or singeing pastes, aromatics, and alliums. Always use an oil with a high smoke point (that is, the temperature beyond which it can ignite). Oils with high smoke points include almost any refined oil: vegetable, corn, canola, safflower, and the like. Grape seed and avocado oils are terrific but absurdly expensive. Refined peanut oil or even standard olive oil will work, although the latter will have a distinct and probably unwanted flavor in a chili crisp. Both these latter two may solidify in the fridge, resulting in a too-thick salsa macha or a salsa with a pale, firm film around its edges. You'll need to bring condiments or pastes made with these up to room temperature and then stir them to again be at their best.

Although we've written these recipes so that the oil is good to go near 300°F (150°C), here are some finessed guidelines:

- If the oil's temperature is between 275°F (135°C) and 290°F (143°C), the color of the final condiment will be more glorious but the flavors will be less pronounced;

- If the oil's temperature is at least 300°F (150°C) but no more than 330°F (165°C), the resulting condiment will have duller colors but more brilliant flavors;

- And if the oil's temperature is above 330°F (165°C) and on up to about 360°F (182°C), the condiment will look dark brown and take on toasty, even bitter notes, preferred by some (but not by us).

The chopstick test for hot oil: Although a candy-making or deep-frying thermometer gives the most accurate temperature for heated oil, we often work with amounts too small to give the necessary depth for a solid reading. While a laser thermometer can tell the temperature of the oil's surface and is a fine gauge for the small amounts we're using (particularly if you gently swirl the small amount of oil in the pan or skillet), you can go low-tech with the chopstick test.

Pour the oil into the skillet or saucepan and set it over the heat. After 20 seconds or so, stick an unglazed, unpainted, wooden chopstick *thick side down* in the oil and against the bottom surface. When the oil begins to bubble under the chopstick, it's hot enough for our purposes.

▲ The oil is hot enough when bubbles appear under an unglazed wooden chopstick.

The dairy problem

Many of these condiments include acids of some sort, sometimes just plain vinegar but also sometimes the acidic components found naturally in ingredients like chilis. As such, these condiments will by and large curdle most dairy products, including many faux dairy products like oat milk. They can also cause sour cream or yogurt to break if they are simmered or boiled with these last two ingredients, rather than just spooned on top of them as a garnish.

What all that means is that you can't use them as add-ins for simmering soups, stews, or braises that include milk, cream, sour cream, or yogurt. You can, of course, enjoy them on a tortilla or a chip alongside, say, a cream-rich tomato soup. You can even put some salsa on the sour cream atop a baked potato. But if you're set on making a creamy, rich soup and including one of these condiments in the cooking process, consider coconut milk your best alternative.

More about storage and safety

The recipes here are a little more, well, dangerous than those in previous chapters, not because these are going to singe your tongue (most will!), but because many involve tomatoes or chilis, both of which can be prone to bad bugs during preserving. What's more, some of these recipes include fresh aromatics that are not cooked to safety standards (or even cooked at all).

Make sure your jars, containers, and lids are *clean*, preferably boiled in water. And don't push the storage life with these condiments: If a brand-new jar has been stored unopened in the fridge a few days and you see that you won't eat it in the next few, freeze it (if the recipe says you can).

Also, make sure you're preparing the recipe in nonreactive, heat-safe vessels, such as tempered-glass measuring cups or stainless-steel bowls. Don't work in receptacles with glazes; don't work with unlined copper or tin-lined pans. The high acidity of some of the salsas and sambals can react with glazes or metals and lead to bad consequences for your health.

And one more note: Fresh *salsas* (that is, those not cooked) can indeed be frozen but the texture suffers in the thaw. Nevertheless, the flavor remains solid. Here's why: Billions of ice crystals form *inside* the fruit and vegetable bits during the freeze. These crystals then thaw and the microscopic amount of water in each pours out. The now-empty hole collapses, so you're left with a watery, mushy texture. You can drain off the excess liquid (there's lots of flavor in it!) or just make do with a more squishy but flavorful condiment after freezing.

Ready, set...

You'll need lots of napkins for your friends who sneeze when they eat spicy foods! But you'll soon have a stock of chili-infused condiments to blow away any winter doldrums or brighten any deck party this summer.

Salsa Fresca

MAKES: about 4 cups (960 ml)
FRIDGE: up to 1 week
FREEZER: up to 6 months

Fresh, straightforward, and not cooked, this salsa is our go-to for tacos, burritos, nachos, tortilla chips, hamburgers, or grilled chops. Or try it on a baked potato with lots of sour cream. One warning: If you freeze the salsa, it'll get watery when thawed. Drain off that liquid for Bloody Marys. Or be content with a looser, watery sauce that's then better garnished *on* things, rather than spooned *inside* the likes of burritos.

- 2 pounds (900 g) grape or small cherry tomatoes
- 1 small yellow or white onion, peeled and finely chopped
- Up to 4 medium fresh green serrano chilis, stemmed, seeded, and minced
- ¼ cup (8 g) *packed* fresh cilantro leaves, finely chopped
- 3 tablespoons (30 ml) lime juice, preferably freshly squeezed
- 1 teaspoon kosher salt

1. For the best texture, don't chop the tomatoes. Instead, halve each, then cut each half into four pieces. This is a laborious process but it does give the best texture to the salsa and doesn't mash (or juice) the tomatoes before they're mixed with the other ingredients. A sharp knife is a must!

2. Stir the chopped tomatoes (plus any juice and seeds on the cutting board), onion, chilis, cilantro, lime juice, and salt in a bowl until well combined.

3. Transfer to four *clean* ½ pint (236 ml) jars or other containers, leaving about ½ inch (1 cm) headspace in each. Cover or seal, then refrigerate or freeze.

More

Add up to 2 peeled and minced garlic cloves, 1 tablespoon (15 ml) white or silver tequila, and/or 1 teaspoon (2 g) finely minced lime zest with the other ingredients.

Charred Salsa

MAKES: about 4 cups (960 ml)
FRIDGE: up to 1 week
FREEZER: up to 6 months

Well, maybe not exactly *charred*. But we broil the tomatoes and garlic to blacken their edges and give this salsa a fire-roasted flavor. We essentially do the same with the onion, cooking it over *high* heat, all in a bid to give this moderately chunky salsa more complex notes, a great pairing with salty chips.

- 2 pounds (900 g) plum tomatoes (about 8 medium), halved lengthwise
- 4 medium garlic cloves, peeled and halved lengthwise
- 4 tablespoons (60 ml) olive oil
- 1 medium yellow or white onion, peeled, halved, and sliced into paper-thin half-moons
- 3 canned chipotles in adobo sauce, stemmed (for sure) and seeded (if desired)
- ½ cup (15 g) fresh cilantro leaves
- ¼ cup (60 ml) red wine vinegar
- 1½ teaspoons kosher salt
- 1 teaspoon (4 g) granulated white sugar

1. Toss the tomatoes and garlic with 3 tablespoons (45 ml) oil in a large bowl until well coated.

2. Position an oven rack about 6 inches (15 cm) from the broiler; heat the broiler. Pour the tomatoes and garlic onto a large, lipped baking sheet. Scrape every drop of oil from the bowl on top. Broil until the tomatoes and garlic are wilted and blackened in spots, about 6 minutes. Transfer to a rack to cool at room temperature for 10 minutes.

3. Meanwhile, set a small skillet over high heat. Add the remaining 1 tablespoon (15 ml) oil and heat until waggly and even smoking. Add the onion and cook, stirring constantly, until wilted and even blackened in a few spots, about 4 minutes. Turn off the heat and set the skillet off the burner for a couple of minutes to cool slightly, stirring often.

4. Pour and scrape the contents of the baking pan *and* the skillet into a food processor. Add the canned chipotles, cilantro, vinegar, salt, and sugar. Cover and pulse until coarsely chopped.

5. Transfer to four *clean* ½ pint (236 ml) jars or other containers, leaving about ½ inch (1 cm) headspace in each. Cover or seal. Cool at room temperature for no more than 30 minutes, then refrigerate or freeze.

More
To add the flavor of a raw allium to this salsa, add 1 small (¾ ounce or 22 g) shallot, peeled and quartered, to the food processor with the other ingredients in step 4.

Simmered Salsa

MAKES: about 4 cups (960 ml)
FRIDGE: up to 2 weeks
FREEZER: up to 1 year

Although you can keep this cooked, relatively smooth salsa in the fridge, it's actually *better* after freezing. It gets a wetter texture after thawing, more in keeping with a lot of bottled salsa brands. Yes, the refrigerated salsa has brighter flavors. But if you're looking for the classic jarred texture, avail yourself of the freezer, even if only for a day or two with each jar.

- 2 pounds (900 g) plum tomatoes (about 8 medium), quartered
- 1 medium red onion, peeled and cut into about 6 chunks
- 1 medium green bell pepper, stemmed, cored, and cut into 2 inch (5 cm) chunks
- 2 fresh green jalapeño chilis, stemmed, seeded (if desired), and quartered
- ¼ cup (60 g) tomato paste
- ¼ cup (60 ml) lime juice
- 3 medium garlic cloves, peeled and minced
- 1½ teaspoons kosher salt
- ½ teaspoon ground black pepper
- ¼ cup (8 g) *packed* fresh cilantro leaves, minced

Clockwise from bottom: Salsa Fresca (page 193), Charred Salsa (page 194), and Salsa Verde (page 196)

1. Put the tomato quarters in a food processor, cover, and pulse repeatedly until finely chopped but not pureed. Uncover the machine, remove the blade, and dump the tomatoes into a large saucepan.

2. Return the canister and blade to the food processor. Add the onion, bell pepper, and jalapeños. Cover and again pulse repeatedly until finely chopped but not pureed. Uncover the machine, remove the blade, and dump the bits into the saucepan.

3. Set the pan over medium-high heat. Stir in the tomato paste, lime juice, garlic, salt, and pepper. Bring to a *boil* (not just a simmer), stirring quite often. Reduce the heat to low and simmer slowly but steadily, stirring more and more frequently, until the sauce is slightly thickened and the onion has lost its raw flavor, about 10 minutes. Turn off the heat and remove the pan from the burner. Stir in the cilantro.

4. Transfer to four *clean* ½ pint (236 ml) jars or other containers, leaving about ½ inch (1 cm) headspace in each. Cover or seal. Cool at room temperature for no more than 30 minutes, then refrigerate or freeze.

More
If you want a much more classic texture, you'll need to peel the tomatoes. Either dip them whole into boiling water for 1 minute, then immerse them in an ice bath before pulling off the skins; or invest in a serrated vegetable peeler (see page 15).

Salsa Verde

MAKES: about 2 cups (480 ml)
FRIDGE: up to 1 week
FREEZER: up to 6 months

We can tell Mexican and Central American cuisine has gone global, if only because our local supermarket in rural New England routinely stocks fresh tomatillos. It's a cinch these days to sub them for tomatoes in this classic, chunky, green salsa. This is a fresh (or uncooked) salsa, so the flavors remain bright, even acidic. After freezing, the texture does soften and the flavors get muted. But a squeeze of lime juice and a little salt will help to brighten them up.

> 1 pound (450 g) small fresh tomatillos (about 15), husked (if necessary), rinsed to remove sticky residue, halved, cored, and roughly chopped
>
> 1 cup (25 g) *packed* fresh cilantro leaves
>
> Up to 3 green serrano chilis, stemmed, seeded (if desired), and roughly chopped
>
> 2 tablespoons (30 ml) lime juice
>
> 1½ teaspoons (6 g) granulated white sugar
>
> 1 teaspoon kosher salt

1. Place all the ingredients in a food processor, making sure the tomatillos and cilantro are at the bottom near the blade. Cover and process until fairly smooth, stopping the machine at least once to rearrange everything and to scrape down the inside of the canister.

2. Transfer to two *clean* ½ pint (236 ml) jars or other containers, leaving about ½ inch (1 cm) headspace in each. Cover or seal, then refrigerate or freeze.

Next
Although it's great in tacos or burritos, we also love salsa verde as a dip for cooked shrimp or spooned onto fried eggs.

Smooth Green Salsa

MAKES: about 4 cups (960 ml)
FRIDGE: up to 1 week
FREEZER: up to 6 months

There's no char in this ultra luxurious if slightly sour salsa. We boil the vegetables so they get velvety soft, then puree them with oil for a creamy finish. This salsa is exceptionally delicious in tacos of any sort…or better yet, spooned over enchiladas. As you can tell from the way the ingredients are noted, we find that the ratio between the tomatillos (given as a weight) and the poblanos (also given as a weight) is a crucial balance for success. But as to the serranos? They're less important to the flavor profile and more important to the overall heat of the salsa.

- 3½ ounces (100 g) fresh tomatillos (about 2 large), husked (if necessary), rinsed to remove sticky residue, peeled, and quartered
- 2 ounces (57 g) fresh poblano chilis (about 2 large), stemmed, seeded, and roughly chopped
- 2 medium green serrano chilis, stemmed, seeded (if desired), and cut into quarters lengthwise
- 1 small shallot (about ¾ ounce or 22 g), peeled and quartered
- Water as necessary to simmer the ingredients
- 12 fresh cilantro sprigs
- 2 medium garlic cloves, peeled and halved lengthwise
- 1 cup (240 ml) olive oil
- 2 tablespoons (30 ml) lime juice, preferably freshly squeezed
- 1 teaspoon kosher salt

1. Put the tomatillos, poblanos, serranos, and shallot in a medium saucepan. Add enough water to cover these ingredients. Set the pan over medium-high heat and bring to a boil. Cover, reduce the heat to medium, and simmer for 10 minutes.

2. Uncover the pan and turn the heat back to medium-high. Boil, stirring more and more frequently to prevent scorching, until the liquid has reduced to about half its original volume, 7–10 minutes. Turn off the heat, remove the pan from the burner, and cool to room temperature, about 1 hour.

3. Pour the contents of the pan into a large blender; add the cilantro and garlic. Cover and process, drizzling in the oil through the hole in the blender's lid, until smooth and luscious. Add the lime juice and salt. Blend well.

4. Transfer to four *clean* ½ pint (236 ml) jars or other containers, leaving about ½ inch (1 cm) headspace in each. Cover or seal, then refrigerate or freeze.

More

For a creamier salsa, add half a ripe pitted and peeled avocado to the blender before adding the oil. This avocado version will *not* freeze well.

Green Tequila Salsa

MAKES: about 4 cups (960 ml)
FRIDGE: up to 1 week
FREEZER: up to 1 year

More than three decades ago, the Silver Palate, an iconic New York City food store, broke new ground with a boozy salsa that won tons of awards when it was launched. Theirs was admittedly a red salsa, but we frankly prefer to spike a cooked, green salsa with tequila because the brighter flavors from tomatillos and green jalapeños pair so well with the liquor and lime juice. Just a heads-up: The tequila is not cooked long enough for the alcohol to burn off in this salsa.

- 12 ounces (340 g) tomatillos (about 12 small), husked (if necessary), peeled, and halved
- 8 medium scallions, trimmed and cut into 2 inch (5 cm) sections
- 4 tablespoons (60 ml) olive oil
- 2 ounces (57 g) fresh poblano chilis (about 2 large)
- ½ cup (15 g) *packed* fresh cilantro leaves
- ¼ cup (60 ml) white or silver tequila
- 2 tablespoons (30 ml) lime juice
- 2 medium green jalapeño chilis, stemmed, seeded (if desired), and quartered lengthwise
- 2 medium garlic cloves, peeled and halved lengthwise
- 1 teaspoon kosher salt

1. Position an oven rack 4 inches (10 cm) from the broiler; heat the broiler. Put the tomatillo halves cut side up and the scallion bits on a large lipped baking sheet. Drizzle the chilis and scallions with 2 tablespoons (30 ml) oil. Broil undisturbed until charred in spots, about 2 minutes.

2. Scrape the contents of the baking sheet into a food processor. Put the poblanos on that sheet and broil, turning once or twice, until blackened evenly on all sides, about 4 minutes. Set the baking sheet on a rack and cool at room temperature for 10–15 minutes.

3. Peel the blackened skin off the poblanos. Stem them and cut them open. Scrape out and discard the seeds, then put the poblanos in the food processor. Add the cilantro, tequila, lime juice, jalapeños, garlic, and salt. Cover and process until a somewhat chunky sauce forms, not pureed but also not coarse. Stop the machine and rearrange the pieces with a rubber spatula as necessary.

4. Set a medium skillet over medium heat for a minute or two. Swirl in the remaining 2 tablespoons (30 ml) oil. Scrape in every drop of the sauce from the food processor. Fry, stirring almost constantly, until reduced slightly if a little runny (but not watery), about 2 minutes. Turn off the heat and set the skillet off the burner. Cool for 1–2 minutes.

5. Transfer to four *clean* ½ pint (236 ml) jars or other containers, leaving about ½ inch (1 cm) headspace in each. Cover or seal. Cool at room temperature for no more than 30 minutes, then refrigerate or freeze.

More
For a smokier salsa, substitute mescal for the tequila.

Jalapeño Salsa

MAKES: about 2 cups (480 ml)
FRIDGE: up to 1 week
FREEZER: up to 6 months

Brace yourself: Things are about to get fiery with this cooked, moderately smooth, green salsa made from jalapeños, rather than tomatillos or tomatoes. We got this idea years ago, not from a restaurant in Texas or New Mexico, but from a tiny, long-gone joint in New York City's Greenwich Village (Mexicana Mama, if anyone remembers!). Their salsa about took the skin off our tongues, yet we kept going back for more. Of any salsa in this chapter, this one needs *salty* tortilla chips, or even Fritos…and maybe some full-fat sour cream on the side to tame the heat.

> 1¼ cups (300 ml) olive oil
> 4 ounces (125 g) fresh green jalapeño chilis (about 5 large), stemmed and halved lengthwise
> 6 medium garlic cloves, peeled
> ½ cup (15 g) packed fresh cilantro leaves
> 2 tablespoons (30 ml) lime juice
> 1 teaspoon kosher salt

1. Set a large skillet, preferably nonstick or seasoned cast-iron, over medium-high heat for a minute or two. Add 2 tablespoons (30 ml) oil, then add the jalapeños and garlic. Turn the stove vent on high if your eyes are sensitive. Cook, stirring often and turning things on all sides, until well browned, about 5 minutes. Turn off the heat and set the skillet off the burner. Cool to room temperature, about 1 hour.

2. Scrape the contents of the skillet into a blender and add the cilantro. Cover and blend, drizzling in the remaining 1 cup plus 2 tablespoons (270 ml) oil through the hole in the blender's lid, until smooth and almost creamy. Add the lime juice and salt. Scrape down the inside of the canister, cover, and blend until well combined.

3. Transfer to two *clean* ½ pint (236 ml) jars or other containers, leaving about ½ inch (1 cm) headspace in each. Cover or seal, then refrigerate or freeze.

More
Decrease the burn by substituting 1 or 2 green Hatch chilis for a couple of the jalapeños (just make sure the total *weight* matches our recipe). Or increase the heat by substituting 1 or 2 green habaneros for 1 of the jalapeños (again, the total *weight* must remain the same).

Clockwise from center: Jalapeño Salsa (page 198), Corn–Black Bean Salsa (page 200), Peach-Mango Salsa (page 201), and Pineapple-Cumin Salsa (page 200)

Pineapple-Cumin Salsa

MAKES: about 4 cups (960 ml)
FRIDGE: up to 1 week
FREEZER: up to 6 months

Caramelizing pineapple pieces brings a greater flavor depth to (and because of) their natural sugars. It also reduces their characteristic perfume to make a more balanced, chunky salsa. We increase the smoky notes even more with canned chipotles in adobo sauce. FYI, there's a wide disparity among the canned chipotles that you can find in large supermarkets. Read the ingredients to make sure yours is not a corn syrup–doped, culinary nightmare.

- 1 teaspoon cumin seeds
- At least 2 tablespoons (30 ml) neutral-flavor oil, such as canola or vegetable oil
- One 2½ pound (1.1 kg) fresh pineapple, topped, peeled, cored, and cut into 1-inch-thick (2.5-cm-thick) chunks (about 6 cups)
- One 4 ounce (113 g) jar of diced pimentos, drained
- ¼ cup (8 g) *packed* fresh cilantro leaves, minced
- 2 canned chipotle chilis in adobo sauce, stemmed, seeded (if desired), and minced
- 1 tablespoon (15 ml) adobo sauce from the can
- 1 teaspoon (4 g) light brown sugar
- 1 teaspoon kosher salt

1. Set a large heavy skillet over medium-high heat. Add the cumin seeds and toss until fragrant, about 30 seconds. Pour the seeds into a large bowl.

2. Return the skillet to the heat. Add 1 tablespoon (15 ml) oil, then about half of the pineapple chunks. Don't crowd them—they must lie in one layer. Sear on one side until golden brown, about 3 minutes. Transfer the chunks to a cutting board. Add the remaining 1 tablespoon (15 ml) oil and the remaining pineapple chunks to the pan…and repeat the process. (If you have to work in more than two batches, add 1 tablespoon or 15 ml oil for each batch.)

3. Cool the pineapple chunks for a few minutes, then chop into fine pieces, about as you'd find in a chunky salsa.

4. Scrape the pineapple pieces into the bowl with the cumin seeds. Add the pimentos, cilantro, chipotles, adobo sauce, brown sugar, and salt. Stir until well combined.

5. Transfer to four *clean* ½ pint (236 ml) jars or other containers, leaving about ½ inch (1 cm) headspace in each. Cover or seal, then refrigerate or freeze.

More
Add up to 1 teaspoon (2 g) minced grated lime zest for a brighter flavor. Add up to 1 stemmed, seeded, and minced small green serrano chili for a bigger kick.

Corn-Black Bean Salsa

MAKES: about 4 cups (960 ml)
FRIDGE: up to 1 week
FREEZER: up to 6 months

Call us purists. We don't think a chunky corn salsa like this one should include tomatoes because we want more corn in every spoonful! Although we give instructions for broiling the corn to deepen its flavors, feel free to grill the husked ears for an even better result. Set the ears over medium heat and grill, turning a few times, for about 3 minutes. If the grill grate is not in perfect condition, first spritz the ears with nonstick spray to keep them from sticking.

- 1½ pounds (680 g) ears of corn (about 3 medium), husked and any silks removed
- One 15 ounce (439 g) can of black beans, drained and rinsed
- One 4 ounce (113 g) can of mild chopped green chilis
- ¼ cup (30 g) pickled jalapeño chili rings, chopped
- 2 tablespoons (30 ml) lime juice
- 2 teaspoons (9 g) granulated white sugar

1 teaspoon dried oregano

½ teaspoon ground cumin

½ teaspoon kosher salt

¼ teaspoon ground cinnamon

1. Set an oven rack 4 inches (10 cm) from the broiler; heat the broiler. Set the ears of corn on a lipped baking sheet. Broil, turning often, until well browned on all sides, about 4 minutes. Transfer the ears to a wire rack and cool at room temperature for 20 minutes.

2. Cut the kernels off the ears. The easiest way to do this job is to cut the thicker end off the ear so it will stand up flat on this end on a cutting board. Run a knife down the ear, removing the kernels, then working around the ear to get them all. (Watch out for your fingers!)

3. Scrape the kernels into a large bowl. Stir in the beans, green chilis, jalapeños, lime juice, sugar, oregano, cumin, salt, and cinnamon until uniform.

4. Transfer to four *clean* ½ pint (236 ml) jars or other containers, leaving about ½ inch (1 cm) headspace in each. Cover or seal, then refrigerate or freeze.

Next

This salsa is particularly good in cheesy quesadillas. For the best results, drain off the liquid and spread only a little of the vegetable mixture in each quesadilla.

Peach-Mango Salsa

MAKES: about 4 cups (960 ml)

FRIDGE: up to 2 weeks

FREEZER: up to 1 year

This smooth, rich salsa is cooked…in fact, reduced, sort of like a chutney or a jam but without the sugar that would make a glossy sauce around the vegetables. The final texture is largely a matter of preference: We like a looser salsa than some because we like a lot of moisture around the vegetables for messy dipping. If you like a drier salsa, reduce the salsa even further over the heat. As the salsa begins to thicken, you'll need to stir almost constantly to avoid scorching.

1¼ pounds (565 g) fresh peaches (about 3 large), peeled, pitted, and finely chopped

1 pound (450 g) fresh ripe mango (about 1 large), pitted, peeled, and finely chopped

6 ounces (170 g) plum tomatoes (about 6 medium), halved lengthwise, cored, and finely chopped

1 medium shallot (about 1 ounce or 30 g), peeled and minced

1 medium red bell pepper, stemmed, cored, and finely chopped

2 medium jalapeño chilis, stemmed, seeded (if desired), and minced

2 medium garlic cloves, peeled and minced

¼ cup (8 g) *packed* fresh cilantro leaves, minced

2 tablespoons (30 ml) distilled white vinegar

1 tablespoon (21 g) honey

1 teaspoon ground cumin

1 teaspoon kosher salt

½ teaspoon ground dried cayenne

1. Put all the ingredients in a large saucepan. Set over medium heat and bring to a simmer, stirring quite a bit.

2. Reduce the heat to low and simmer at a steady gurgle, stirring more and more often to prevent scorching, until the liquid in the pan has been reduced to about a third of its original volume, about 15 minutes.

3. Turn off the heat and remove the pan from the burner. Cool at room temperature for 1–2 minutes.

4. Transfer to four *clean* ½ pint (236 ml) jars or other containers, leaving about ½ inch (1 cm) headspace in each. Cover or seal. Cool at room temperature for no more than 30 minutes, then refrigerate or freeze.

More

For a brighter heat, leave one of the minced jalapeños out of the saucepan and stir it in after cooking and before bottling.

Go-to Salsa Macha

MAKES: about 2 cups (480 ml)
FRIDGE: up to 1 month
FREEZER: up to 1 year

Here's the salsa macha you'll want to return to again and again: a deeply flavored, chunky mix of two kinds of chilis (rich pasilla negro and spiky-hot árbol chilis), two kinds of seeds (pumpkin and sunflower), and a few aromatics (including orange zest for vanilla-toned brightness among the flavors). We'd be hard-pressed to tell you how quickly we go through this stuff!

- 1 cup (240 ml) neutral-flavored oil, such as canola or vegetable oil
- 1 ounce (30 g) dried pasilla chilis (about 4), stemmed, seeded, and cut into 3 inch (7.5 cm) pieces
- 1 ounce (28 g) dried small árbol chilis (about 65), stemmed and halved lengthwise (seeds and membranes retained as much as possible)
- ¾ cup (113 g) raw pepitas (small shelled pumpkin seeds)
- ¼ cup (30 g) raw shelled sunflower seeds
- 1 tablespoon (15 ml) apple cider vinegar
- 1 teaspoon (4 g) granulated white sugar
- 1 teaspoon (2 g) finely grated orange zest
- 1 teaspoon dried oregano
- 1 teaspoon kosher salt

1. Set a large skillet over medium-high heat and pour in the oil. Heat until shimmering and waggly. If you've got a laser thermometer, it should register about 300°F or 150°C. Or use the chopstick test (see page 192). Add all the dried chilis and stir gently to toast for 1 minute. Use a slotted spoon to transfer them to a heat-safe, nonreactive bowl.

2. Add the pepitas and sunflower seeds to the skillet and stir gently to toast lightly, about 30 seconds. Pour and scrape the contents of the skillet into the bowl. Add the vinegar, sugar, zest, oregano, and salt to the bowl; stir until well combined. Cool at room temperature for 30 minutes.

3. Pour and scrape the contents of the bowl into a food processor. Cover and process until a coarse paste forms, not a smooth puree. There should be bits of seed and chili throughout.

4. Transfer to two *clean* ½ pint (236 ml) jars or other containers, leaving about ½ inch (1 cm) headspace in each. Cover or seal, then refrigerate or freeze.

Next
We love this salsa macha on roast pork of any sort, on roasted root vegetables (particularly carrots, parsnips, and potatoes), and dolloped freely on cheese nachos.

Pineapple–Pine Nut Salsa Macha

MAKES: about 3 cups (720 ml)
FRIDGE: up to 1 month
FREEZER: up to 1 year

Here's a gentler salsa macha, particularly if you seed the chilis. (We never do. But you certainly can if you or yours don't like sauces quite so fiery.) This utterly nontraditional salsa macha is otherwise fairly straightforward, with a hint of sweetness from dried pineapple (fresh pineapple won't keep as long in the fridge) and a bump of cozy warmth from ground cloves.

- 1 cup (240 ml) neutral-flavored oil, such as canola or vegetable oil
- 2 ounces (54 g) dried small árbol chilis (about 150 or 2 heaping cups), stemmed and halved lengthwise (seeds and membranes retained, if desired)
- ¾ cup (100 g) pine nuts
- 2 tablespoons (10 g) dehydrated onion flakes
- 1 teaspoon (5 ml) white wine vinegar
- 1 teaspoon kosher salt
- ¼ teaspoon ground cloves
- 3 tablespoons (30 g) chopped *dried* pineapple

Go-to Salsa Macha (page 202)
on cheese nachos

1. Set a large skillet over medium-high heat and pour in the oil. Heat until shimmering and waggly. If you've got a laser thermometer, it should register about 300°F or 150°C. Or use the chopstick test (see page 192). Add the chilis and stir gently to toast for 1 minute. Use a slotted spoon to transfer them to a heat-safe bowl.

2. Add the pine nuts and onion flakes to the skillet. Stir gently to toast lightly, about 30 seconds. Pour and scrape the contents of the skillet into the bowl. Stir in the vinegar, salt, and cloves until well combined. Cool at room temperature for 30 minutes.

3. Pour and scrape the contents of the bowl into a food processor. Add the dried pineapple. Cover and process just until a coarse paste forms, not a smooth puree, stopping the machine at least once to scrape down the inside of the canister. In the end, there should be bits of seed and chili visible throughout.

4. Transfer to three *clean* ½ pint (236 ml) jars or other containers, leaving about ½ inch (1 cm) headspace in each. Cover or seal, then refrigerate or freeze.

Tip
This salsa macha is only as good as the dried pineapple. The pieces should be plump and glistening, not hard or desiccated.

Smoky Pecan–Cacao Nib Salsa Macha

MAKES: about 2 cups (480 ml)
FRIDGE: up to 1 month
FREEZER: up to 1 year

Dried chipotles (that is, smoked jalapeños) can be hard to seed since they're so shriveled, almost desiccated. Although it may be worth it to seed a lot of them for a bigger batch of salsa macha, we cut down on the prep time here by using canned chipotles in adobo sauce, lending this small-batch sauce a smoky edge that pairs wonderfully with the slightly bitter, chocolaty flavor of cacao nibs as well as the (perhaps surprising) dried figs.

> 1 cup (240 ml) neutral-flavored oil, such as canola or vegetable oil
>
> 1 large garlic clove, peeled and thinly sliced
>
> 2¾ ounces (78 g) dried New Mexican red chilis (about 13), stemmed, seeded, and cut into 3 inch (7.5 cm) pieces
>
> ½ cup (56 g) pecan pieces, coarsely chopped
>
> 3 canned chipotles in adobo sauce, stemmed and halved
>
> 1 teaspoon kosher salt
>
> ½ teaspoon ground cinnamon
>
> ½ teaspoon ground cumin
>
> 4 dried figs, preferably Calimyrna or Adriatic (aka Turkish) figs, stemmed and chopped
>
> 2 tablespoons (15 g) cacao nibs

1. Set a large skillet over medium-high heat and pour in the oil. Heat until shimmering and waggly. If you've got a laser thermometer, it should register about 300°F or 150°C. Or use the chopstick test (see page 192). Add the sliced garlic and stir until lightly browned, less than 1 minute. Use a slotted spoon to transfer the garlic to a heat-safe bowl.

2. Add the chilis and pecans to the skillet. Stir gently until toasty, about 1 minute. Do not let the pecans blacken! Pour the chilis, pecans, and oil into the bowl. Stir in the canned chipotles, salt, cinnamon, and cumin until well combined. Cool at room temperature for 30 minutes.

3. Pour and scrape the contents of the bowl into a food processor. Add the dried figs and cacao nibs. Cover and process just until a coarse paste forms, not a smooth puree, stopping the machine at least once to scrape down the inside of the canister. At the end, there should be bits of nuts, nibs, and figs visible throughout.

4. Transfer to two *clean* ½ pint (236 ml) jars or other containers, leaving about ½ inch (1 cm) headspace in each. Cover or seal, then refrigerate or freeze.

Next

This salsa macha is particularly good in chicken or turkey tacos, or with enchiladas, either as a garnish or stirred into the cooked meat mixture before serving.

Cherry-Pistachio Salsa Macha

MAKES: about 2 cups (480 ml)
FRIDGE: up to 1 month
FREEZER: up to 1 year

This salsa macha has never made an appearance in Veracruz! But we felt free to flex our culinary know-how to create a pleasing, complex amalgam that is in keeping with a more traditional salsa macha in its texture and a few of its flavor notes, but otherwise much more of a walk on the culinary wild side. There's a blend of two distinct and perhaps unusual dried chilis in this sauce: 1) moritas, or dried red jalapeños, which are smoky with an almost citrus finish; and 2) mulatos, dried green poblanos that are milder, brighter, and even acidic. These chilis combine with dried cherries and pistachios to make a sweet, light salsa macha.

- 1 cup (240 ml) neutral-flavored oil, such as canola or vegetable oil
- 2½ ounces (70 g) dried morita chilis (about 14), stemmed, seeded, and cut into 2 inch (5 cm) pieces
- 2 ounces (58 g) dried mulato chilis (about 4), stemmed, seeded, and cut into 2 inch (5 cm) pieces
- ½ cup (56 g) raw unsalted shelled pistachios
- ¼ cup (40 g) raw pepitas (small shelled pumpkin seeds)
- 3 tablespoons (30 g) *unsweetened* dried cherries, chopped
- 2 teaspoons (10 ml) red wine vinegar
- 1 medium garlic clove, peeled and minced
- 1 teaspoon ground cumin
- 1 teaspoon kosher salt

1. Set a large skillet over medium-high heat and pour in the oil. Heat until shimmering and waggly. If you've got a laser thermometer, it should register about 300°F or 150°C. Or use the chopstick test (see page 192). Add both kinds of chilis and stir gently to toast for 1 minute. Use a slotted spoon to transfer them to a heat-safe bowl.

2. Add the pistachios and pepitas to the skillet. Stir gently to toast *lightly*, about 30 seconds. Pour and scrape the contents of the skillet into the bowl. Stir in the cherries, vinegar, garlic, cumin, and salt until well combined. Cool at room temperature for 30 minutes.

3. Pour and scrape the contents of the bowl into a food processor. Cover and process just until a coarse paste forms, not a smooth puree, stopping the machine at least once to scrape down the inside of the canister. In the end, there should be bits of seed and chili visible throughout.

4. Transfer to two *clean* ½ pint (236 ml) jars or other containers, leaving about ½ inch (1 cm) headspace in each. Cover or seal, then refrigerate or freeze.

Next

You *need* this salsa macha on fried eggs…plus a little Chive Oil (page 404).

Cranberry-Walnut Salsa Macha

MAKES: about 2 cups (480 ml)
FRIDGE: up to 1 month
FREEZER: up to 1 year

Skip the cranberry sauce this holiday and serve this spiky-sweet salsa macha with the turkey and mashed potatoes. This salsa macha has bold, burly flavors, thanks especially to the reddish-brown, moderately hot guajillo chilis. Although we often tell you to seed the chilis or not based on your heat tolerance, we *strongly* suggest here that you remove the seeds and membranes from the guajillos since the bits can introduce unwanted bitter notes that then mute the cranberries.

- 1 cup (240 ml) neutral-flavored oil, such as canola or vegetable oil
- 6 medium garlic cloves, peeled and very thinly sliced lengthwise
- 2½ ounces (72 g) dried guajillo chilis (about 12), stemmed, seeded, and cut into 3 inch (7.5 cm) pieces
- ½ cup (58 g) walnut pieces
- 2 tablespoons (18 g) white sesame seeds
- ½ cup (80 g) unsweetened dried cranberries
- 1 teaspoon (5 ml) red wine vinegar
- 1 teaspoon dried oregano
- 1 teaspoon kosher salt

1. Set a large skillet over medium-high heat and pour in the oil. Heat until shimmering and waggly. If you've got a laser thermometer, it should register about 300°F or 150°C. Or use the chopstick test (see page 192). Add the garlic and stir gently to toast until crispy and golden brown, less than 1 minute. Use a slotted spoon to transfer the garlic slices to a heat-safe bowl.

2. Add the chilis to the skillet and stir gently to toast lightly, about 30 seconds. Again, use a slotted spoon to get them into that bowl.

3. Finally, add the walnuts and sesame seeds to the skillet. Stir just until browned. Do not blacken! Pour and scrape the contents of the skillet into the bowl. Stir in the cranberries, vinegar, oregano, and salt until well combined. Cool at room temperature for 30 minutes.

4. Pour and scrape the contents of the bowl into a food processor. Cover and process just until a coarse paste forms, not a smooth puree, stopping the machine at least once to scrape down the inside of the canister. In the end, there should be bits of sesame seeds, nuts, and chili visible throughout.

5. Transfer to two *clean* ½ pint (236 ml) jars or other containers, leaving about ½ inch (1 cm) headspace in each. Cover or seal, then refrigerate or freeze.

More

Add a little smoky flavor by substituting 1 stemmed and halved canned chipotle in adobo sauce for 2 of the guajillo chilis. Do not fry the canned chipotle. Rather, stir it into the bowl with the cranberries and spices.

Maple-Sesame Salsa Macha

MAKES: about 2 cups (480 ml)
FRIDGE: up to 1 month
FREEZER: up to 1 year

As you can probably tell, we love to get creative with salsa macha. This one is admittedly a flight of culinary fancy: maple syrup + sesame seeds + cinnamon + cloves. Given that rowdy mix, we use a fairly standard chili here: anchos (that is, dried poblanos). We like their milder flavor and slightly bitter heat to pair with this otherwise untraditional mix.

- 1 cup (240 ml) neutral-flavored oil, such as canola or vegetable oil
- 4 medium garlic cloves, peeled and thinly sliced
- 5¼ ounces (150 g) medium dried ancho chilis (about 10), stemmed, seeded, and cut into 3 inch (7.5 cm) pieces
- ½ cup (72 g) white sesame seeds
- ¼ cup (28 g) slivered almonds
- 2 tablespoons (40 g) maple syrup (the darker, the better)
- 1 teaspoon kosher salt
- ¼ teaspoon ground cinnamon
- ¼ teaspoon ground cloves

1. Set a large skillet over medium-high heat and pour in the oil. Heat until shimmering and waggly. If you've got a laser thermometer, it should register about 300°F or 150°C. Or use the chopstick test (see page 192). Add the garlic and stir gently until golden and crispy, less than 1 minute. Use a slotted spoon to transfer the garlic slices to a heat-safe bowl.

Cranberry-Walnut Salsa Macha
(page 205) in chicken tacos

2. Add the chilis to the skillet. Stir gently to toast and render quite fragrant, about 1 minute. Again, use that slotted spoon to get the chili pieces into the bowl.

3. Add the sesame seeds and almonds to the skillet. Toast, stirring constantly, until golden but not darkened, about 30 seconds. Pour and scrape the contents of the skillet into the bowl. Stir in the maple syrup, salt, cinnamon, and cloves until well combined. Cool at room temperature for 30 minutes.

4. Pour and scrape the contents of the bowl into a food processor. Cover and process just until a coarse paste forms, not a smooth puree, stopping the machine at least once to scrape down the inside of the canister. In the end, there should be bits of seed and chili visible throughout.

5. Transfer to two *clean* ½ pint (236 ml) jars or other containers, leaving about ½ inch (1 cm) headspace in each. Cover or seal, then refrigerate or freeze.

More
To up the heat considerably, substitute half or even all of the anchos with dried New Mexican red chilis, stemmed, seeded, and cut into 2 inch (5 cm) pieces.

Coconut-Pecan Salsa Macha

MAKES: about 2 cups (480 ml)
FRIDGE: up to 1 month
FREEZER: up to 1 year

Here, we bend salsa macha a little toward the Caribbean with coconut and brown sugar, offering sweet and savory notes under the heat. The flavors are a bit subtle, not quite the punch of some of our other versions of salsa macha…and so perhaps better with more delicately flavored things like avocado toast or even as a crazy garnish for a chocolate brownie. Keep in mind that nuts go

rancid over time. Bad pecans make bad salsa macha. Store shelled nuts in the freezer for up to 1 year. For recipes like this one (and almost all non-baking recipes), you can use them right out of the freezer.

> 1 cup (240 ml) neutral-flavored oil, such as canola or vegetable oil
> 2 medium garlic cloves, peeled and thinly sliced
> 1.4 ounces (40 g) dried guajillo chilis (about 8), stemmed, seeded, and cut into 3 inch (7.5 cm) pieces
> ¾ cup (75 g) pecan pieces
> 3 tablespoons (15 g) shredded unsweetened coconut
> 1 tablespoon (5 g) dehydrated onion flakes
> 1 tablespoon (15 ml) apple cider vinegar
> 1 tablespoon (13 g) dark brown sugar
> 1 teaspoon kosher salt

1. Set a large skillet over medium-high heat and pour in the oil. Heat until shimmering and waggly. If you've got a laser thermometer, it should register about 300°F or 150°C. Or use the chopstick test (see page 192). Add the garlic and stir gently until golden and crispy, less than 1 minute. Use a slotted spoon to transfer the garlic to a heat-safe bowl.

2. Add the chilis to the skillet. Stir gently to toast and render quite fragrant, about 1 minute. Again, use that slotted spoon to get the chili pieces into the bowl.

3. Add the pecans, coconut flakes, and onion flakes to the skillet. Toast, stirring constantly, until golden but not darkened, about 30 seconds. Pour and scrape the contents of the skillet into the bowl. Stir in the vinegar, brown sugar, and salt until well combined. Cool at room temperature for 30 minutes.

4. Pour and scrape the contents of the bowl into a food processor. Cover and process just until a coarse paste forms, not a smooth puree, stopping the machine at least once to scrape down the inside of the canister. In the end, there should be bits of coconut and chilis visible throughout.

5. Transfer to two *clean* ½ pint (236 ml) jars or other containers, leaving about ½ inch (1 cm) headspace in each container. Cover or seal, then refrigerate or freeze.

More
For a brighter flavor, add up to 1 tablespoon minced *dried* orange peel with the vinegar, brown sugar, and salt.

Almost Everything Chili Crisp

MAKES: about 2 cups (480 ml)
FRIDGE: up to 1 month
FREEZER: up to 1 year

Decades ago, Huabi Tao sold her version of chili crisp at a small market in Guizhou, China. Culinary mavens and even government bureaucrats began traveling miles to pick up her shortcut sauce to add spicy goodness to stir-fries, braises, and dumpling dips. Soon, the Lao Gan Ma brand was born and quickly became a global industry. Here's our version of *kitchen sink* chili crisp, a wild concoction that gets close to her original while adding depth beyond crispy garlic and shallots with cardamom and cumin.

- ¾ cup (75 g) coarsely ground red Szechuan chili powder (see page 190)
- One 2 inch (5 cm) piece of fresh ginger, peeled and minced
- 2 tablespoons (30 g) packaged Chinese fermented black beans, chopped
- 2 tablespoons (20 g) black Szechuan peppercorns, crushed under a saucepan or a rolling pin
- 2 tablespoons (10 g) dried shiitake mushroom powder
- 1½ tablespoons (18 g) granulated white sugar
- 1½ tablespoons (15 g) roasted unsalted peanuts, *chopped*
- 2 teaspoons kosher salt

- 1½ teaspoons decorticated (husked and removed from the pods) cardamom seeds, lightly crushed under a saucepan or a rolling pin
- 1½ teaspoons ground cumin
- ½ teaspoon star anise powder
- ½ teaspoon finely ground black pepper
- ½ teaspoon MSG, optional
- 1¼ cups (300 ml) neutral-flavored oil, such as canola or vegetable oil
- 1 medium shallot (about 1 ounce or 30 g), peeled and *minced*
- 8 medium garlic cloves, peeled and *minced*

1. Stir the chili powder, ginger, fermented beans, Szechuan peppercorns, mushroom powder, sugar, peanuts, salt, cardamom seeds, cumin, star anise powder, black pepper, and MSG (if using) in a large heat-safe bowl until uniform.

2. Set a large skillet over medium-high heat and pour in the oil. Heat until quite hot but not yet smoking. If you've got a laser thermometer, it should register between 275°F (135°C) and 325°F (163°C). Or use the chopstick test (see page 192). Add the shallot and garlic. Cook, stirring often, until well browned, even crispy, up to 2 minutes (depending on the oil's temperature).

3. Turn off the heat and pour the sizzling hot oil and aromatics over the ingredients in the bowl. When the sizzling stops, stir until uniform, avoiding splashes and burns. Cool at room temperature for no more than 1 hour.

4. Transfer to two *clean* ½ pint (236 ml) jars or other containers, leaving about ½ inch (1 cm) headspace in each. Cover or seal, then refrigerate or freeze.

Tip
Dried shiitake mushroom powder can be hard to find except online. As an alternative, grind 4 small dried shiitake mushroom caps (about 0.35 ounce or 10 g) one at a time in a spice grinder until powdery.

Star Anise–Smoked Paprika Chili Crisp

MAKES: about 2 cups (480 ml)
FRIDGE: up to 1 month
FREEZER: up to 1 year

This chili crisp is certainly simpler to make than our Almost Everything Chili Crisp (page 209), probably within the reach of a weekend evening. There's no frying, no belabored chopping, and few obscure ingredients. (We even omitted the more traditional Szechuan red chili powder.) That said, the one harder-to-find but necessary ingredient is ground Aleppo pepper. It adds a spicy bitterness, an attempt to bring this simpler chili crisp to more sophisticated standards.

- 9 medium garlic cloves, peeled and minced
- ½ cup (80 g) dehydrated onion flakes
- ¼ cup (20 g) red pepper flakes
- ¼ cup (20 g) ground Aleppo pepper
- 3 tablespoons mild smoked paprika
- 1 teaspoon ground star anise
- 1 teaspoon kosher salt
- 1¼ cups (300 ml) neutral-flavored oil, such as canola or vegetable oil

1. Mix the garlic, dehydrated onion, red pepper flakes, Aleppo pepper, smoked paprika, star anise, and salt in a heat-safe bowl.

2. Pour the oil into a small skillet set over medium-high heat. Heat until quite hot but not yet smoking. If you've got a laser thermometer, it should register between 275°F (135°C) and 325°F (163°C). Or use the chopstick test (see page 192).

3. Pour this hot oil over the ingredients in the bowl. When the sizzling stops, stir until uniform, avoiding splashes and burns. Set aside at room temperature until the side of the bowl is cool to the touch, about 2 hours.

4. Transfer to two *clean* ½ pint (236 ml) jars or other containers, leaving about ½ inch (1 cm) headspace in each. Cover or seal, then refrigerate or freeze.

More

Add up to 1 teaspoon grated nutmeg and/or 1 teaspoon ground cinnamon with the other spices in the bowl.

Five-Spice Chili Crisp

MAKES: about 2 cups (480 ml)
FRIDGE: up to 1 month
FREEZER: up to 1 year

This is our version of a Taiwanese chili crisp, which often calls for dried "facing heaven" chilis (so named because they curve up and face the sky as they grow). The flavor relies on those fruit-forward, wine-scented, spiky-bright chilis, although they can be hard to track down, except from online suppliers. You can substitute other, easier-to-find dried chilis: either dried cascabel chilis, a Southwestern variety; or a 50/50 combo of dried árbol chilis and dried guajillo chilis. Both of these subs will result in a less aromatic chili crisp; but it's worth the effort in a pinch to create a chili crisp laced with warming spices like cinnamon and fennel seeds (found in the five-spice powder).

- 5¼ ounces (150 g) dried facing heaven chilis, stemmed, seeded, and ground to a coarse, even flaky powder
- 2 medium garlic cloves, peeled and minced
- 2 tablespoons (20 g) dehydrated onion flakes
- 1½ teaspoons five-spice powder (or to use your own homemade, see the MORE section at the Five-Spice Ketchup recipe on page 342)
- 1½ teaspoons kosher salt
- 1¼ cups (300 ml) neutral-flavored oil, such as canola or vegetable oil

Front to back: Star Anise–Smoked Paprika Chili Crisp (page 210) and Shiitake–Szechuan Peppercorn Chili Crisp (page 214) on bowls of rice

1. Mix the ground chilis, garlic, dehydrated onion flakes, five-spice powder, and salt in a heat-safe bowl.

2. Pour the oil into a small skillet set over medium-high heat. Heat until quite hot but not yet smoking. If you've got a laser thermometer, it should register between 275°F (135°C) and 325°F (163°C). Or use the chopstick test (see page 192).

3. Pour the hot oil over the ingredients in the bowl. When the sizzling stops, stir until uniform, avoiding splashes and burns. Cool at room temperature for no more than 1 hour.

4. Transfer to two *clean* ½ pint (236 ml) jars or other containers, leaving about ½ inch (1 cm) headspace in each. Cover or seal, then refrigerate or freeze.

Tip

To grind dried facing heaven chilis, you'll need a spice grinder and the patience to work in many batches. Or you can use a mini food processor, although you'll never get them ground quite fine enough. Stem the chilis before using with either appliance.

Garlic-Scallion Chili Crisp

MAKES: about 2 cups (480 ml)
FRIDGE: up to 3 weeks
FREEZER: up to 1 year

The hotter the red pepper flakes, the better this moderately fiery, quite chunky, garlicky chili crisp. Unfortunately, red pepper flakes have become increasingly wan and flavorless over the last few decades, at least in North America. Search out hotter (and better!) red pepper flakes from spice sellers or online stores. They'll give a big spike to this aromatic condiment, a great mix with Eighteen-Spice Chili Oil (page 407) and as a dip for just about anything fried: egg rolls to chicken wings.

3 tablespoons (15 g) red pepper flakes

1½ tablespoons (14 g) white sesame seeds

1½ teaspoons (7 g) granulated white sugar

1½ teaspoons kosher salt

1⅔ ounces (48 g) dried New Mexican red chilis (about 8)

1 cup plus 2 tablespoons (270 ml) neutral-flavored oil, such as canola or vegetable oil

18 medium garlic cloves, peeled and minced

3 medium scallions, trimmed and thinly sliced

1. Mix the red pepper flakes, sesame seeds, sugar, and salt in a heat-safe bowl until uniform.

2. Stem and seed the chilis, removing even the dried membranes that used to hold the seeds. Tear the chilis into small bits. Grind these in batches in a spice grinder or a mini food processor until the consistency of red pepper flakes. Stir into the mixture in the bowl.

3. Pour the oil into a large skillet set over medium-high heat. Heat until quite hot but not yet smoking. If you've got a laser thermometer, it should register between 275°F (135°C) and 325°F (163°C). Or use the chopstick test (see page 192).

4. Add the garlic and scallions to the skillet. Fry until golden and crisp, stirring occasionally, up to 2 minutes (depending on the oil's temperature).

5. Pour and scrape the contents of the skillet into the bowl. When the sizzling stops, stir until uniform, avoiding splashes and burns. Set aside at room temperature to cool for no more than 1 hour.

6. Transfer to two *clean* ½ pint (236 ml) jars or other containers, leaving about ½ inch (1 cm) headspace in each. Cover or seal, then refrigerate or freeze.

Next

Use this chili crisp as a topper to French onion dip or serve with thick-cut potato chips.

Gochugaru Chili Crisp

MAKES: about 3 cups (720 ml)
FRIDGE: up to 3 weeks
FREEZER: up to 1 year

Gochugaru is ground red Korean chili flakes (it's also sometimes sold as a powder, although we *only* call for the flakes). It's often used in braises like kimchi-jjigae (one of our go-to comfort foods, a stew of onions, kimchi, tofu, and pork). We nix any dried chilis and use spiky gochugaru as the basis for this chili crisp. It's got the sweet-spiky flavors of scallions, garlic, and ginger, which are fried in the oil, then discarded to give the chili crisp a smoother, more luxurious texture.

- ½ cup (136 g) gochugaru flakes
- ½ cup (40 g) red pepper flakes
- 2 tablespoons (18 g) white sesame seeds
- 2 tablespoons (25 g) granulated white sugar
- 2 teaspoons kosher salt
- 2 cups (480 ml) neutral-flavored oil, such as canola or vegetable oil
- 24 medium scallions, trimmed and cut in half widthwise
- 12 medium garlic cloves, peeled
- Two 2 inch (5 cm) pieces of fresh ginger, peeled and sliced into thin coins

1. Stir the gochugaru, red pepper flakes, sesame seeds, sugar, and salt in a heat-safe bowl until uniform.

2. Combine the oil, scallions, garlic, and ginger in a large saucepan. Set over medium-high heat and cook, stirring occasionally, until the aromatics are sizzling and browned, about 6 minutes.

3. Use a slotted spoon to remove *and discard* the aromatics, retaining as much of the oil as possible. Pour the hot oil over the gochugaru mixture. When the sizzling stops, stir until uniform, avoiding splashes and burns. Set aside at room temperature until the side of the bowl is cool to the touch, about 2 hours.

4. Transfer to three *clean* ½ pint (236 ml) jars or other containers, leaving about ½ inch (1 cm) headspace in each. Cover or seal, then refrigerate or freeze.

Next
This chili crisp is exceptionally good on cooked white rice, dished up with almost any stir-fry you can name.

Sumac-Cinnamon Chili Crisp

MAKES: about 2 cups (480 ml)
FRIDGE: up to 1 month
FREEZER: up to 1 year

In this whimsical version of chili crisp, we've bent the flavors toward the Middle East with sour ground sumac, lots of ground Aleppo pepper, and even lemon zest. The chili crisp has a dark, rich color that makes it quite appealing as a gift…and certainly far beyond anyone's idea of the norm. It's terrific mixed with honey as a spread for thick, crunchy rye crackers.

- ½ cup (60 g) ground Aleppo pepper
- 2 tablespoons (30 g) ground sumac
- Two 2 inch (5 cm) cinnamon sticks, broken into two pieces each
- 1½ cups (360 ml) neutral-flavored oil, such as canola or vegetable oil
- 2 large shallots (about 1¾ ounces or 50 g *each*), peeled and finely chopped
- 4 medium garlic cloves, peeled and finely chopped
- 1 teaspoon kosher salt
- 1 teaspoon (2 g) finely grated lemon zest

1. Mix the Aleppo pepper, sumac, and cinnamon sticks in a heat-safe bowl.

2. Pour the oil into a medium saucepan and set it over medium-high heat. Heat until quite hot but not yet smoking. If you've got a laser thermometer, it should register between 275°F (135°C) and 325°F (163°C). Or use the chopstick test (see page 192).

3. Add the shallots to the skillet and fry, stirring occasionally, until golden and crisp *but not burned*, about 4 minutes. Add the garlic and fry for 30 seconds, just until golden.

4. Pour and scrape the contents of the saucepan over the pepper mixture in the bowl. When the sizzling stops, add the salt and lemon zest. Stir until uniform, avoiding splashes and burns. Cool at room temperature for no more than 1 hour.

5. Fish out and discard the cinnamon sticks. Transfer to two *clean* ½ pint (236 ml) jars or other containers, leaving about ½ inch (1 cm) headspace in each. Cover or seal, then refrigerate or freeze.

Tip

Ground Aleppo pepper is often coarse, somewhere in texture between red pepper flakes and ground black pepper. There are now a few finely ground varietals on the market. *Only* the more coarsely ground type works well in all our recipes.

Shiitake–Szechuan Peppercorn Chili Crisp

MAKES: about 2 cups (480 ml)
FRIDGE: up to 1 month
FREEZER: up to 1 year

The manufacturer of the world-famous Lao Gan Ma Spicy Chili Crisp makes a version of this earthy, numbing chili crisp as an alternative to their popular, go-to bottling. Although the chili crisp is imported into North America, it's hard to find, even in large Asian supermarkets. That's too bad, because the condiment has a markedly savory flavor, even a little funky from the fermented black beans and miso paste. We've created our own version, close to the original with an even more pronounced mushroom flavor.

¾ cup (75 g) coarsely ground red Szechuan chili powder (see page 190)

3 tablespoons (60 g) doubanjiang (a Chinese paste of fermented broad beans, chilis, and aromatics, not to be confused with Korean doenjang or gochujang)

¼ cup (60 g) packaged Chinese fermented black beans, chopped

3 tablespoons (27 g) unsalted shelled peanuts, chopped

1 tablespoon (15 g) white miso paste

1½ teaspoons ground Szechuan peppercorn powder

1 teaspoon (4 g) granulated white sugar

1¼ cups (300 ml) neutral-flavored oil, such as canola or vegetable oil

5 ounces (140 g) large *fresh* shiitake mushroom caps (about 6), *diced*

2 medium scallions, trimmed and very thinly sliced

3 medium garlic cloves, peeled and minced

1 tablespoon (15 g) peeled minced fresh ginger

1. Mix the Szechuan chili powder, doubanjiang, fermented black beans, peanuts, miso paste, peppercorn powder, and sugar in a heat-safe bowl.

2. Pour the oil into a large skillet set over medium-high heat. Heat until quite hot but not yet smoking. If you've got a laser thermometer, it should register between 275°F (135°C) and 325°F (163°C). Or use the chopstick test (see page 192).

3. Add the mushrooms and fry, stirring often, until brown and even crisp *but not burned*, about 10 minutes. Add the scallions, garlic, and ginger. Continue frying, stirring often, just until fragrant, about 10 seconds.

4. Pour and scrape the contents of the skillet over the ingredients in the bowl. When the sizzling stops, stir until uniform, avoiding splashes and burns. Cool at room temperature for no more than 1 hour.

5. Transfer to two *clean* ½ pint (236 ml) jars or other containers, leaving about ½ inch (1 cm) headspace in each. Cover or seal, then refrigerate or freeze.

Next

Although already flavorful with mushrooms, make it more so by adding up to 1 tablespoon ground shiitake mushroom powder (see page 209) to the bowl in step 1.

Curried Chili Crisp

MAKES: about 2 cups (480 ml)
FRIDGE: up to 1 month
FREEZER: up to 1 year

Another flight of chili crisp fancy, this recipe makes a gorgeously complex condiment that's great with curries of all sorts, even dolloped right on top of the raita or rice. This chili crisp is hot, to be sure, but also has a sparky flavor from lemongrass and some earthy notes from turmeric. While we prefer Madras curry powder for its spicier kick in this chunky sauce, feel free to substitute much milder, more standard yellow curry powder for a tamer flavor.

- ⅔ ounce (19 g) dried árbol chilis (about 51 or ¾ cup), stemmed, seeded, and ground in batches to a coarse texture like red pepper flakes
- 6 tablespoons (90 g) minced peeled fresh ginger
- 6 tablespoons (36 g) minced trimmed fresh lemongrass (preferably only the tender inner parts)
- 1½ tablespoons (12 g) curry powder, preferably Madras curry powder
- 1½ tablespoons (19 g) granulated white sugar
- 1½ teaspoons kosher salt
- 1 teaspoon ground cumin
- 1 teaspoon ground dried turmeric
- 1 cup plus 2 tablespoons (270 ml) neutral-flavored oil, such as canola or vegetable oil
- 8 medium garlic cloves, peeled and minced

1. Mix the ground chilis, ginger, lemongrass, curry powder, sugar, salt, cumin, and turmeric in a heat-safe bowl.

2. Pour the oil into a large skillet set over medium-high heat. Heat until quite hot but not yet smoking. If you've got a laser thermometer, it should register between 275°F (135°C) and 325°F (163°C). Or use the chopstick test (see page 192).

3. Add the garlic and fry, stirring often, until golden brown, about 2 minutes (depending on the oil's temperature).

4. Pour and scrape the contents of the skillet over the ingredients in the bowl. When the sizzling stops, stir until uniform, avoiding splashes and burns. Cool at room temperature for no more than 1 hour.

5. Transfer to two *clean* ½ pint (236 ml) jars or other containers, leaving about ½ inch (1 cm) headspace in each. Cover or seal, then refrigerate or freeze.

Tip

Curry powder isn't one blend. It's a category of spice blends. Search spice stores and online shops for more aromatic, sweeter, milder, or hotter blends to suit your palate.

Wasabi-Nori Chili Crisp

MAKES: about 2 cups (480 ml)
FRIDGE: up to 1 month
FREEZER: up to 1 year

One last chili crisp…and perhaps our favorite, especially with fried shrimp or crab cakes. We give this condiment a decided briny flavor with dried seaweed (the nori sheets). We also spike it with the wasabi powder, found as a coating on purchased wasabi peas, available just about everywhere. In fact, we grind those whole peas to give this chili crisp even more body. The results are unlike any other chili crisp we know: salty, nose-spanking, briny, and fiery.

- Five 7 inch x 8 inch (17 cm x 20 cm) sheets of nori, torn to small pieces
- ¾ cup (90 g) crunchy wasabi peas
- ½ cup (40 g) red pepper flakes
- 3 medium scallions, trimmed and very thinly sliced
- 1 tablespoon (15 g) minced peeled fresh ginger
- 1 cup plus 2 tablespoons (270 ml) neutral-flavored oil, such as canola or vegetable oil
- 1 tablespoon (15 ml) toasted sesame oil

Front to back: Curried Chili Crisp (page 215)
and Wasabi-Nori Chili Crisp (page 215)

1. Place the bits of nori and the wasabi peas in a food processor. Cover and process until coarsely ground, not a powder.

2. Uncover, remove the blade, and scrape the contents of the canister into a heat-safe bowl. Add the red pepper flakes, scallions, and ginger. Stir well to combine.

3. Pour the oil into a small saucepan and set it over medium-high heat. Heat until quite hot but not yet smoking. If you've got a laser thermometer, it should register between 275°F (135°C) and 325°F (163°C). Or use the chopstick test (see page 192).

4. Pour the hot oil over the ingredients in the bowl. When the sizzling stops, add the sesame oil and stir until uniform, avoiding splashes and burns. Cool at room temperature for no more than 1 hour.

5. Transfer to two *clean* ½ pint (236 ml) jars or other containers, leaving about ½ inch (1 cm) headspace in each. Cover or seal, then refrigerate or freeze.

Next
We love this chili crisp tossed with cooked gnocchi, a little of the cooking water, some drained capers, and lots of grated Parmigiano-Reggiano.

Fiery Red Sambal

MAKES: about 2 cups (480 ml)
FRIDGE: up to 3 weeks
FREEZER: up to 1 year

Here's our version of sambal oelek, the well-known Indonesian chili sauce. Why buy a monochromatic bottling when you can make a more flavorful version with a blend of fresh chilis? And it's easy! It's not even cooked. Mix and match red chilis to get the desired spike you prefer. Use all red jalapeños, and the sambal will be searing. Mix red serranos and red jalapeños, and the sambal will be a little brighter but still hot. Mix in a few fresh

cayennes or even their Turkish counterparts, aci sivri, and the sambal will be fit for only the bravest. Or if you want sour notes in the heat, mix in a few red Fresno chilis.

> 1 pound (450 g) *fresh* red chilis, such as red jalapeño, red serrano, red Fresno, bird's eye chili, or cayenne, or a mix of any of these (or more), stemmed, seeded (if desired), and roughly chopped
>
> 2 medium garlic cloves, peeled and halved lengthwise
>
> 2 tablespoons (30 ml) lime juice
>
> 2 tablespoons (30 ml) *unseasoned* rice vinegar
>
> 1 tablespoon (12 g) kosher salt

1. Place all the ingredients in a food processor. Cover and pulse until a coarse paste forms, not a puree.

2. Uncover the machine and remove the blade. Transfer to two *clean* ½ pint (236 ml) jars or other containers, leaving about ½ inch (1 cm) headspace in each. Cover or seal, then refrigerate or freeze.

More
The traditional way to make this sambal is in a mortar with a pestle. You'll need a large one. You'll also need patience because you'll probably have to work in batches. And you might want to wear culinary kitchen gloves.

Tomato-Lemongrass Sambal

MAKES: about 2 cups (480 ml)
FRIDGE: up to 3 weeks
FREEZER: up to 1 year

We modeled this chili sauce on an Indonesian favorite, sambal bajak. This one's less of a sledgehammer than our Fiery Red Sambal (above). It's sweeter and a bit more sophisticated, partly because there are tomatoes in the mix, partly because the chilis are first blanched to tame them, and partly because some of the aromatics are fried until fragrant. What's more, this sauce is a bit funky, given the shrimp paste. Search out a bottling of *oily* shrimp paste for the best results.

> Water as necessary to simmer the chilis, tomatoes, and garlic
>
> 5¼ ounces (150 g) *fresh* red chilis, preferably a mix of red jalapeño and red serrano, stemmed
>
> 3½ ounces (100 g) globe tomato (about 1 medium), halved through the stem end
>
> 3 medium garlic cloves, peeled
>
> ¼ cup (60 ml) neutral-flavored oil, such as canola or vegetable oil
>
> 3 small shallots (about ¾ ounce or 22 g *each*), peeled and minced
>
> 1 medium lemongrass stalk, trimmed of woody or frayed ends and peeled of woody leaves, the tender center minced
>
> One 2 inch (5 cm) piece of fresh ginger, peeled and minced
>
> 1 tablespoon (16 g) jarred shrimp paste
>
> 1 tablespoon (15 g) tamarind paste
>
> 1 teaspoon kosher salt

1. Bring a large saucepan of water to a boil over high heat. Add the chilis, tomato, and garlic. Boil just until the chilis are tender, about 3 minutes. Drain in a colander set in the sink. Cool for 10 minutes.

2. Pour the contents of the colander into a food processor. Cover and process until a *smooth* puree forms, stopping the machine at least once to scrape down the inside of the canister.

3. Set a large skillet over medium-high heat for a minute or two. Add the oil, then the shallots and lemongrass. Fry, stirring often, until everything's a bit crisp around the edges, about 2 minutes.

4. Pour and scrape the chili-tomato puree into the skillet. Add the ginger, shrimp paste, tamarind paste, and salt. Reduce the heat to low. Cook, stirring more and more often to prevent scorching, until thickened and somewhat paste-like, 10–15 minutes.

5. Turn off the heat and take the skillet off the burner. Transfer to two *clean* ½ pint (236 ml) jars or other containers, leaving about ½ inch (1 cm) headspace in each. Cover or seal. Cool at room temperature for no more than 30 minutes, then refrigerate or freeze.

Next

Because of the tomatoes, this sambal is a terrific condiment with fish of almost any sort, grilled, baked, or broiled.

Green Sambal

MAKES: about 5 cups (1200 ml)
FRIDGE: up to 3 weeks
FREEZER: up to 1 year

This is our version of sambal ijo (literally, *green sambal*). It's quite luxurious, even comforting, given the bright notes from the tomatillos and the way those notes are then mellowed in cooking. In the Padang region of Indonesia, this sambal is made from a blend of chilis, many of which cannot be easily sourced on this side of the globe. We've crafted our recipe to be close to the original while using more available ingredients.

> Water as necessary to simmer the tomatillos and chilis
>
> 12 ounces (340 g) fresh tomatillos (about 6 small), husked, rinsed of any sticky residue, and halved through the stem end
>
> 12 ounces (340 g) fresh green serrano chilis (about 8), stemmed
>
> 12 ounces (340 g) fresh green jalapeño chilis (about 4), stemmed
>
> ½ cup (120 ml) neutral-flavored oil, such as canola or vegetable oil
>
> 6 small shallots (about ¾ ounce or 22 g *each*), peeled and minced
>
> 12 medium garlic cloves, peeled and minced
>
> 2 tablespoons (25 g) granulated white sugar
>
> 1½ teaspoons kosher salt

Bottom to top: Tomato-Lemongass Sambal (page 217) on ground beef in a Boston lettuce cup and Green Sambal (page 218) on ground beef in a radicchio cup

1. Bring a large saucepan of water to a boil over high heat. Add the tomatillos and both chilis. Boil just until tender, about 3 minutes. Drain in a colander set in the sink.

2. Put the softened tomatillos and chilis in a food processor. Cover and process until a smooth puree forms.

3. Set a large skillet over medium-high heat for a minute or two. Add the oil, then the shallots and garlic. Fry, stirring often, until the garlic is golden and everything's a bit crisp around the edges, about 2 minutes.

4. Pour the tomatillo puree into the skillet; stir in the sugar and salt. Reduce the heat to low. Cook, stirring more and more frequently to prevent scorching, until thickened and paste-like, in fact almost dry, about 20 minutes.

5. Turn off the heat and take the skillet off the burner. Transfer to five *clean* ½ pint (236 ml) jars or other containers, leaving about ½ inch (1 cm) headspace in each. Cover or seal. Cool at room temperature for no more than 30 minutes, then refrigerate or freeze.

Next

We love this sambal on steamed, roasted, or air-fried green vegetables, including broccoli, asparagus, and Brussels sprouts.

Peanut-Tamarind Sambal

MAKES: about 2 cups (480 ml)
FRIDGE: up to 3 weeks
FREEZER: up to 1 year

Here's a more unusual chili sauce, our version of sambal pecel (pronounced *PUH-chell*). It's actually a kaleidoscope of fiery chilis, peanuts, and galangal. That last is a cousin to ginger: It's less spiky, has more of a citrus flavor, and is found in almost all Asian supermarkets. If you can't find

galangal, substitute about 2 teaspoons finely grated fresh ginger and 1 teaspoon finely grated grapefruit zest. This sauce should be fairly dry, less wet than our Fiery Red Sambal (page 217). It's more for sprinkling than drizzling.

> 6 tablespoons (80 ml) neutral-flavored oil, such as canola or vegetable oil
>
> 4 medium *fresh* red chilis, preferably red Fresno chilis, stemmed
>
> 5 *fresh* red bird's eye chilis, stemmed
>
> 5 medium garlic cloves, peeled
>
> One 1 inch (2.5 cm) piece of fresh galangal, peeled and roughly chopped
>
> 1¾ cups (250 g) unsalted roasted shelled peanuts
>
> ½ cup (108 g) packed light brown sugar
>
> 4 fresh or dried makrut lime leaves, the center spines removed
>
> 2 teaspoons (10 g) tamarind paste
>
> 2 teaspoons kosher salt

1. Set a small skillet over medium-high heat for a minute or two. Add the oil and heat until shimmering and waggly. Or use the chopstick test (see page 192). Add both kinds of chilis, the garlic, and galangal. Fry, stirring often, until the chilis begin to blister and soften, about 2 minutes. Turn off the heat and set the skillet off the burner. Cool for 5 minutes.

2. Pour and scrape the contents of the skillet into a food processor. Add the peanuts, brown sugar, makrut lime leaves, tamarind paste, and salt. Cover and process to form a coarse paste, stopping the machine at least once to scrape down the inside of the canister.

3. Transfer to two *clean* ½ pint (236 ml) jars or other containers, leaving about ½ inch (1 cm) headspace in each. Cover or seal. Cool at room temperature for no more than 30 minutes, then refrigerate or freeze.

Next

This sambal is great as a dip for raw vegetables, particularly cucumbers and celery. It's also a solid addition to canned broths to squeeze in some spicy flavors.

Sour-Funky Sambal

MAKES: about 2 cups (480 ml)
FRIDGE: up to 3 weeks
FREEZER: up to 1 year

Our last, funky-hot, red sambal is perhaps our most unusual. It's our version of sambal plecing, an Indonesian chili sauce originally from Lombok Island. It's traditionally served on top of blanched, leafy greens, like Asian water spinach. It's also terrific as a final condiment on wok-tossed cabbage leaves, spinach, or green beans.

⅓ cup (80 ml) neutral-flavored oil, such as canola or vegetable oil

2 teaspoons (11 g) shrimp paste, preferably an oily bottling

8 ounces (225 g) red Fresno chilis (about 8 medium), stemmed, halved lengthwise, and seeded

2 long thin bird's eye chilis, stemmed

2 medium shallots (about 1 ounce or 30 g *each*), peeled and roughly chopped

1 pound (450 g) globe tomatoes (about 2 medium), roughly chopped

2 tablespoons (30 ml) lime juice

1 teaspoon (5 g) dark brown sugar

1 teaspoon kosher salt

1. Set a medium skillet over medium-high heat for a minute or two. Pour in the oil, then dollop in the shrimp paste without breaking it up. Fry undisturbed until fragrant, about 1 minute. Use a slotted spoon to transfer the mound or patty of paste to a food processor.

2. Add both kinds of chilis and the shallots to the skillet. Cook, stirring often, until the chilis blister and soften a bit, about 2 minutes. Use a slotted spoon to transfer these to the food processor.

3. Add the tomatoes to the skillet. Cook, stirring often, just until they begin to soften, about 2 minutes. Turn off the heat and set the skillet off the burner. Use that slotted spoon to transfer the tomatoes to the food processor. Cool the oil for 5 minutes, then pour it into the food processor too.

4. Add the lime juice, brown sugar, and salt. Cover and pulse several times, until the mixture is like a chunky salsa, uncovering the machine to scrape down the inside of the canister at least once.

5. Transfer to two *clean* ½ pint (236 ml) jars or other containers, leaving about ½ inch (1 cm) headspace in each. Cover or seal. Cool at room temperature for no more than 30 minutes, then refrigerate or freeze.

Tip
Less is more when it comes to processing this sauce. You want a chunky consistency for the best garnish on those leafy greens.

Lemon-Ginger Mazavaroo

MAKES: about 2 cups (480 ml)
FRIDGE: up to 3 weeks
FREEZER: up to 1 year

Here's our version of a classic Mauritian chili sauce, made from super hot chilis, tamed (if slightly) by lemon juice. It can be green or red, depending on the chilis used. This version is red, simply because red bird's eye chilis are easier to track down on this side of the globe. You can also substitute green bird's eye chilis (sometimes called Thai hots) for a slightly brighter flavor. Think of this chili sauce as a lemony version of Tabasco sauce…and use it accordingly.

14 ounces (400 g) *fresh* red bird's eye chilis, stemmed and seeded (if desired)

½ cup (120 ml) neutral-flavored oil, such as canola or vegetable oil

6 medium garlic cloves, peeled and halved lengthwise

1 tablespoon (6 g) finely grated lemon zest

6 tablespoons (75 ml) lemon juice

1 tablespoon (15 g) minced peeled fresh ginger

2 teaspoons kosher salt

Fermented Chili
Sauce (page 223)
with fried chicken
wings

1. Combine all the ingredients in a food processor (for a slightly chunkier sauce) or a blender (for a smoother sauce, particularly if you use a turbo blender). Cover and process or blend to create a slushy paste, stopping the machine to scrape down the inside of the canister as necessary.

2. Transfer to two *clean* ½ pint (236 ml) jars or other containers, leaving about ½ inch (1 cm) headspace in each. Cover or seal, then refrigerate or freeze.

Tip

These chilis are *hot*. Wear culinary kitchen gloves to prevent a chemical burn. Strip off the gloves, then (even so) pour some oil into your hands and wash them well with soap and water.

Peri Peri Sauce

MAKES: about 2 cups (480 ml)
FRIDGE: up to 3 weeks
FREEZER: up to 1 year

Peri peri sauce (or piri piri sauce) is an African staple, usually made with super hot peri peri chilis, although red bird's eye chilis will do in a pinch. We actually prefer to tame the sauce (a bit!) by cutting down on the sheer bulk of the chilis and substituting a couple of jarred roasted red bell peppers for a softer finish, more in keeping with even *our* high-heat tolerance. We also add plenty of aromatics and spices, so our homemade version is far better than any from a bottle. We love our sauce as a garnish with sour cream on any bean soup.

- ¼ cup (60 ml) red wine vinegar
- 2 tablespoons (30 ml) olive oil
- 2 tablespoons (30 ml) lemon juice
- 2 jarred whole roasted red bell peppers, seeded and torn to smaller bits
- 8 fresh peri peri chilis or red bird's eye chilis, stemmed and seeded (if desired)
- ¼ cup (8 g) *packed* cilantro leaves

- 1 small shallot (about ¾ ounce or 22 g), peeled and chopped
- 4 medium garlic cloves, peeled and halved lengthwise
- 2 teaspoons kosher salt
- ½ teaspoon ground black pepper
- Water as necessary to blend a smooth sauce

1. Add the vinegar, oil, lemon juice, roasted peppers, chilis, cilantro, shallot, garlic, salt, and pepper (in that order!) to a blender. Cover and blend, adding water in 1 tablespoon (15 ml) increments as necessary, until a smooth, thick sauce forms.

2. Transfer to two *clean* ½ pint (236 ml) jars or other containers, leaving about ½ inch (1 cm) headspace in each. Cover or seal, then refrigerate or freeze.

Next

We also use peri peri sauce as a grill marinade, usually combined with other oils and aromatic liquids, like sesame oil and ginger juice or olive oil and dry vermouth.

Fermented Chili Sauce

MAKES: about 2 cups (480 ml)
FRIDGE: up to 2 weeks after fermentation
FREEZER: up to 1 year

Here's our version of a Middle Eastern chili sauce, shatta, made with fermented red chilis. For safety reasons (that is, since we're not processing these jars in a canner), we advocate fermenting the chilis in the fridge, rather than on the counter. It takes a little longer but the results are less likely to go bad. The sauce is sour, chunky, a bit funky, and even a smidge fizzy at its best.

- 1 pound 3 ounces (540 g) *fresh* red jalapeño chilis and/or red Fresno chilis, stemmed and thinly sliced
- 1½ tablespoons (18 g) kosher salt
- 1 tablespoon (12.5 g) granulated white sugar
- ½ cup (120 ml) apple cider vinegar
- 1 teaspoon (6 g) finely grated lemon zest
- 2 tablespoons (30 ml) lemon juice, preferably freshly squeezed
- Olive oil as necessary to cover the sauce

1. Mix the chilis, salt, and sugar in a large bowl until the chilis are well and evenly coated. Pour and scrape the contents of the bowl into a large nonreactive container, preferably a 1 quart (1 liter) glass jar. Cover tightly and refrigerate until a little funky, even fizzy, but with a bright, clean aroma (nothing rotten), from 6–9 days.

2. Drain the chilis in a colander set in the sink. Shake the colander a few times to get rid of excess moisture.

3. Put the chilis in a blender. Add the vinegar, lemon zest, and lemon juice. Cover and blend until looser than a paste, still grainy, definitely not slushy.

4. Transfer to two *clean* ½ pint (236 ml) jars or other containers, leaving about ½ inch (1 cm) headspace in each. Slowly pour olive oil to float over the top and cover the sauce below (of each jar or whatever you've used). Cover or seal, then refrigerate or freeze.

Next

Quite hot, this sauce is terrific as a dip for pita or a topper on just about any Middle Eastern spread or salad, baba ghanoush to labneh, hummus to tabbouleh.

Easy Red Chili Paste

MAKES: about 2 cups (480 ml)
FRIDGE: up to 1 month
FREEZER: up to 1 year

Although this is the first of our chili pastes, it rides the line between a paste and a sauce—that is, between a cooking ingredient (a paste) and a condiment (a sauce). You can use it as the base for fried rice, a garnish with a burger, and even a dip for salty potato chips when thinned with a little more oil. The paste is made from red Fresno chilis, among our favorites. As you'll see, we suggest removing about half the seeds to keep the sauce from being too unhinged. Feel free to push it into the wilds.

- 1 pound (450 g) *fresh* red Fresno chilis (about 20 medium)
- 2 small shallots (about ¾ ounce or 22 g *each*), peeled and chopped
- 2 medium garlic cloves, peeled and chopped
- ¼ cup (60 ml) olive oil
- 1 teaspoon kosher salt
- ½ teaspoon ground cumin

1. Stem the chilis, then halve each lengthwise. Remove the seeds and membranes from about half of the chilis. (Wear culinary kitchen gloves to protect you and your loved ones! Or afterwards, coat your hands with oil, then wash them well with soap and water.)

2. Place the chilis, shallots, and garlic in a food processor. Cover and process until finely chopped, about like a relish.

3. Set a medium skillet over medium heat for a minute or two, then pour in the oil. Add *every speck* of the chili mixture from the food processor along with the salt and cumin. Cook, stirring more and more frequently to prevent scorching, until the sauce is thickened enough that you can see the bottom of the skillet when you drag a wooden spoon through it, about 10 minutes.

4. Turn off the heat and set the skillet off the burner. Cool for 1–2 minutes. Transfer to two *clean* ½ pint (236 ml) jars or other containers, leaving about ½ inch (1 cm) headspace in each. Cover or seal. Cool at room temperature for no more than 30 minutes, then refrigerate or freeze.

More

Double the garlic and/or sweeten the sauce by adding up to 2 teaspoons (9 g) granulated white sugar with the cumin.

Calabrian Chili Paste

MAKES: 2 cups (480 ml)
FRIDGE: up to 1 month
FREEZER: up to 1 year

Jarred Calabrian chilis put this traditional, straightforward chili paste within easy reach. We call for soft, luxurious chilis packed in oil; but we'll be the first to admit that the oil in the jars is often not the best quality. So we drain the chilis, then use a better-quality olive oil in the sauce. We also use a blender, rather than a food processor, for a creamier paste. All in all, this one is a no-cook wonder that you can dollop on pizza or focaccia…or enjoy alongside chunks of Parmigiano-Reggiano with thin slices of toasted bread. Although you can stir a little into dairy-free tomato sauces for pasta, this paste is probably more useful as a condiment.

> One 10 ounce (285 g) jar of red Calabrian chilis (or peppers) packed in oil
>
> ½ cup (120 ml) olive oil, preferably extra virgin olive oil
>
> 1 tablespoon (15 ml) white balsamic vinegar
>
> 4 medium garlic cloves, peeled and halved lengthwise
>
> Kosher salt as necessary for your taste

1. Drain and stem the chilis and put in a blender. Add (in this order) the olive oil, vinegar, and garlic. Cover and blend until quite smooth, stopping the machine occasionally to scrape down the inside of the canister.

2. Taste for salt. If needed (the jarred chilis can be very salty), add a little and blend until incorporated. Transfer to two *clean* ½ pint (236 ml) jars or other containers, leaving about ½ inch (1 cm) headspace in each. Cover or seal, then refrigerate or freeze.

More

Make the paste more sour by substituting (and maybe even doubling) white wine vinegar for the white balsamic vinegar.

Garlicky Chili Paste

MAKES: about 2 cups (480 ml)
FRIDGE: up to 3 weeks
FREEZER: up to 1 year

If you love garlic, you've come to the right paste! We spread garlic and other aromatics out across a skillet in order to give them more room to react with the scalding scallion oil. The technique results in something like a cross between a traditional chili paste and a chili crisp. It will be quite oily. It will even separate in storage with a layer of oil on top. Bring it back to room temperature and stir the oil into the paste before using. This vinegar-free paste is probably best as an addition to soups, stews, and pasta sauces, rather than a condiment.

> ½ pound (225 g) *fresh* red Fresno chilis (about 10 medium), stemmed, seeded, and minced
>
> 1 small red onion, peeled and *minced*
>
> 30 medium garlic cloves, peeled and *minced*
>
> ¼ cup (60 g) minced peeled fresh ginger
>
> 1 tablespoon (12 g) kosher salt
>
> 1 cup (240 ml) neutral-flavored oil, such as canola or vegetable oil
>
> 8 medium scallions, trimmed of straggly roots and thin green tops, then halved lengthwise

1. Spread the chilis, onion, garlic, ginger, and salt in an even layer across a 10 inch (25 cm) skillet, preferably cast iron or stainless steel.

2. Pour the oil into a medium saucepan and add the scallions. Set the pan over medium heat and cook, stirring once in a while, until the scallions are sizzling and beginning to brown, about 4 minutes.

3. Use tongs or a slotted spoon to remove *and discard* the (hot!) scallions. Pour the sizzling oil over the ingredients in the skillet. When the sizzling stops, stir well to combine evenly.

4. Transfer to two *clean* ½ pint (236 ml) jars or other containers, leaving about ½ inch (1 cm) headspace in each. Cover or seal. Cool at room temperature for no more than 30 minutes, then refrigerate or freeze.

Next

Simply stirring a little of this chili paste into jarred marinara sauce will make a much more complex sauce for cooked pasta.

Aji Amarillo Paste

MAKES: about 2 cups (480 ml)
FRIDGE: up to 1 month
FREEZER: up to 1 year

This yellow chili paste is often used in Peruvian (and now other South American) cooking. It's usually made from *fresh* aji amarillo (that is, a varietal of yellow chilis) but these can be hard to find in supermarkets outside of Latin and South America. Unfortunately, the jarred versions have lost some of their slightly sour yet floral flavor; so we find the best substitutes are dried amarillo chilis, which means we have to compromise on the color. The dried chilis will never yield a bright yellow paste but they offer a flavor closer to the original.

5 ounces (140 g) dried aji amarillo (amarillo chilis—about 16), stemmed

Boiling water as necessary to soak the chilis

4 medium garlic cloves, peeled and halved lengthwise

½ cup (120 ml) olive oil

2 tablespoons (30 ml) lime juice, preferably freshly squeezed

½ teaspoon kosher salt

1. Put the stemmed chilis in a large bowl and submerge them in boiling water. Set a heat-safe, nonreactive small plate on top of the chilis to weight them down in the water. Soak at room temperature until soft—that is, for quite a while, about 45 minutes.

2. Uncover and drain the chilis in a colander set in the sink. Use kitchen shears to open each one. Discard the seeds and any off-white membranes.

3. Put the chilis in a food processor and add the garlic, olive oil, lime juice, and salt. Cover and process to make a fairly smooth puree, stopping the machine at least once to uncover and scrape down the inside of the canister.

4. Transfer to two *clean* ½ pint (236 ml) jars or other containers, leaving about ½ inch (1 cm) headspace in each. Cover or seal, then refrigerate or freeze.

Next

Make an easy dipping sauce for carrot sticks, celery stalks, or even tortilla chips by putting all the following in a food processor: a spoonful of aji amarillo paste, some minced shallot and garlic, a hefty mound of mayonnaise, some crumbled feta, a little ketchup or tomato puree, and a squeeze of lime juice. Cover and process until smooth.

Garlicky Chili Paste (page 225) in
a skillet, ready to be bottled

Left to right: Aji Amarillo Paste (page 226), Aji Panca Paste (page 229), and Red Curry Paste (page 230)

Aji Panca Paste

MAKES: about 2 cups (480 ml)
FRIDGE: up to 1 month
FREEZER: up to 1 year

Panca chilis are a sweeter, low-heat chili from South America with an almost berry-like flavor. Although we sometimes tame some of the heat of super hot peppers, we like as much heat as possible with these almost elegant chilis. So we like to keep the seeds, even though they result in a grainier paste. (You have the option of removing all or some of the seeds if you want to smooth out the paste.) The flavors are deep and rich, like reduced red wine with chilis and a lemon wedge on the side…if that makes any sense. It makes a great base with other aromatics for a pot of chili.

> 5⅔ ounces (160 g) dried aji panca (or panca chili — about 14), stemmed
>
> Boiling water as necessary to soak the chilis
>
> ¼ cup (60 ml) olive oil
>
> 1 tablespoon (15 ml) lemon juice
>
> 1 teaspoon kosher salt
>
> Additional water as necessary to create a smooth puree

1. Put the stemmed chilis in a large bowl, submerge them in boiling water, and set a heat-safe, nonreactive small plate on top of the chilis to weight them down. Soak at room temperature until soft—that is, for quite a while, about 45 minutes.

2. Drain the chilis in a colander set in the sink. Use kitchen shears to halve each one, retaining the seeds if desired.

3. Put the chilis (and seeds if using) in a food processor and add the olive oil, lemon juice, and salt. Cover and process to make a fairly smooth puree, adding water in 1 tablespoon (15 ml) increments as necessary and stopping the machine

at least once to uncover and scrape down the inside of the canister.

4. Transfer to two *clean* ½ pint (236 ml) jars or other containers, leaving about ½ inch (1 cm) headspace in each. Cover or seal, then refrigerate or freeze.

Next
For a chicken or pork marinade, whisk 2 parts aji panca paste with 1 part red wine vinegar, 1 part soy sauce, and 1 part pisco (a sugarcane rum) *by volume*. Also, whisk in some minced garlic and a sprinkling of ground cumin.

Smoky Macadamia Nut Chili Paste

MAKES: about 3 cups (720 ml)
FRIDGE: up to 1 month
FREEZER: up to 1 year

Although you might expect to find dried chipotles or even canned chipotles in adobo sauce in a smoky chili paste like this one, we use dried morita chilis because they add a pleasant sweetness alongside the oil-rich nuts. This chili paste is not as hot as some others, so it makes a mellow base for stir-fries or larbs. And it's great stirred into pizza sauce to add a pop to your next homemade pie. Or whisk a little of this paste into warmed tomato puree to dollop onto the next four-cheese pizza you pick up on the way home.

> 2¼ ounces (64 g) dried morita chilis (about 12), stemmed, halved, and seeded
>
> Boiling water as necessary to soak the chilis
>
> ½ cup plus 2 tablespoons (150 ml) neutral-flavored oil, such as canola or vegetable oil
>
> 1 large yellow or white onion, peeled and sliced into 2 inch (5 cm) rounds
>
> 5 medium garlic cloves, peeled and halved lengthwise
>
> ½ cup (75 g) unsalted shelled macadamia nuts
>
> 2 teaspoons (9 g) granulated white sugar
>
> 1 teaspoon kosher salt
>
> Additional water as necessary to create a smooth puree

1. Put the chilis in a heat-safe bowl and pour the boiling water over them to submerge. Set a heat-safe, nonreactive small plate on the chilis to weight them down. Soak at room temperature for 20 minutes.

2. Meanwhile, set a large skillet over medium heat for a minute or two. Add 2 tablespoons (30 ml) oil, then the onion slices and garlic. Cook undisturbed until the onion slices have charred a bit, about 6 minutes. Flip them and the garlic pieces over and repeat this process on the other side. Scrape and pour the contents of the skillet into a food processor. Cool for a few minutes.

3. Uncover the chilis, drain them in a colander set in the sink, and add them to the food processor along with the nuts, sugar, and salt. Cover and process until smooth, adding water by 1 tablespoon (15 ml) increments to create a smooth paste, stopping the machine at least once to scrape down the inside of the canister.

4. Clean and dry the large skillet. Set it over medium-high heat for a minute or two. Pour in the remaining ½ cup (120 ml) oil, then scrape every speck of the chili paste from the canister into the skillet. Cook, stirring more and more often to prevent scorching, until the oil has been absorbed and the mixture is bubbling, a little reduced, and quite fragrant, about 2 minutes.

5. Turn off the heat and set the skillet off the burner to cool at room temperature for a couple of minutes. Transfer to three *clean* ½ pint (236 ml) jars or other containers, leaving about ½ inch (1 cm) headspace in each. Cover or seal. Cool at room temperature for no more than 30 minutes, then refrigerate or freeze.

More

For much more heat, add up to 1 tablespoon (5 g) red pepper flakes to the food processor with the nuts.

Red Curry Paste

MAKES: about 2 cups (480 ml)
FRIDGE: up to 1 month
FREEZER: up to 1 year

This red chili paste is familiar from Southeast Asian cooking, particularly Thai braises with coconut milk. The paste needs to be *smooth*. But even with a turbo blender or a high-powered food processor in a home kitchen, it's hard to get some aromatics like lemongrass, ginger, and garlic to blend so there aren't any grainy bits. To aid the texture, we call for lemongrass, ginger, and garlic *pastes*, sold in tubes near the fresh herbs in most supermarkets (as we do in many of the subsequent recipes). With these purchased pastes, we can then create a fiery, silky base for many braises, stews, soups, and even stir-fries. Use this paste for any Asian or Asian-inspired recipe that calls for red curry paste.

- 1¾ ounces (50 g) dried guajillo chilis (about 10), stemmed, halved lengthwise, and seeded
- 10 árbol chilis, stemmed (do not seed for lots of heat)
- Boiling water as necessary to soak the chilis
- 2 tablespoons (32 g) shrimp paste
- 2 tablespoons (30 g) garlic paste
- 2 tablespoons (30 g) ginger paste
- 2 tablespoons (30 g) lemongrass paste
- 1 tablespoon (6 g) finely grated lime zest
- 1 tablespoon (8 g) ground coriander
- 1 tablespoon (8 g) ground cumin
- 1 tablespoon (12 g) kosher salt
- 2 teaspoons onion powder
- 1½ teaspoons ground *white* pepper
- Additional water as necessary to create a smooth puree

1. Put both chilis in a heat-safe bowl. Pour in enough boiling water to submerge them. Set a heat-safe, nonreactive small plate on top of the chilis to weight them down. Soak at room temperature for 20 minutes.

2. Uncover and drain the chilis in a colander set in the sink. Transfer to a food processor and add the shrimp paste, garlic paste, ginger paste, lemongrass paste, lime zest, coriander, cumin, salt, onion powder, and white pepper. Cover and process until smooth, adding water by 1 tablespoon (15 ml) increments through the feed tube and stopping the machine at least once to scrape down the inside of the canister, until a thick, smooth paste forms.

3. Transfer to two *clean* ½ pint (236 ml) jars or other containers, leaving about ½ inch (1 cm) headspace in each. Cover or seal, then refrigerate or freeze.

Next
For a stir-fry (as a general rule), fry about 2 tablespoons of this chili paste in oil before you crumble in ground meat or cooked rice.

Yellow Curry Paste

MAKES: about 2 cups (480 ml)
FRIDGE: up to 1 month
FREEZER: up to 1 year

We nixed the traditional shrimp paste or fermented fish paste in our version of yellow curry paste because we wanted a cleaner flavor without any added funkiness, mostly to let the caramelized notes of roasted garlic open up among the flavors. We'll admit that the flavors dull a bit in freezing: There's just no way around that problem with this complex blend of aromatics. Still, to be able to pull a jar of your homemade yellow curry paste out of the freezer and make absolutely incredible fried rice or a dumpling dipping sauce is worth the small-ish compromise in flavor. And there's no doubt that even frozen and thawed, it still tastes far more complex and aromatic, not to mention spicier, than any canned or bottled version on the market.

5 large heads of garlic

8 tablespoons (120 ml) neutral-flavored oil, such as canola or vegetable oil

10 árbol chilis, stemmed (and seeded if you want to knock down the heat)

Boiling water as necessary to soak the chilis

4 large shallots (about 1¾ ounces or 50 g *each*), peeled and *thickly* sliced

3 tablespoons (45 g) ginger paste

3 tablespoons (45 g) lemongrass paste

¼ cup (8 g) packed fresh cilantro leaves

3 tablespoons (24 g) yellow curry powder

1 tablespoon (8 g) ground dried turmeric

2 teaspoons ground coriander

2 teaspoons kosher salt

1. Position the rack in the center of the oven. Heat the oven to 375°F (190°C), no fan or convection.

2. Slice the top quarter off each head of garlic to expose the cloves inside. Rub them all with a total of 2 tablespoons (30 ml) oil. Seal in an aluminum foil packet, set on a lipped baking sheet, and roast until the cloves are soft and golden, about 45 minutes. Transfer to a cooling rack, open the packet, and cool at room temperature for about 20 minutes.

3. Meanwhile, put the chilis in a heat-safe bowl and pour in boiling water to submerge them. Set a heat-safe, nonreactive small plate on top of them to weight them down. Soak at room temperature for 20 minutes.

4. Set a medium skillet over medium heat for a minute or two. Add the remaining 6 tablespoons (90 ml) oil, then the shallots. Cook, stirring often, until softened, about 3 minutes. Scrape the contents of the skillet into a food processor and cool for 5 minutes.

5. Squeeze the mushy garlic pulp out of the heads and into the food processor. Uncover and drain the chilis in a colander set in the sink and add them, too. Add the ginger paste, lemongrass paste, cilantro, curry powder, turmeric, coriander, and salt. Cover and process until a smooth paste forms, stopping the machine at least once to scrape down the inside of the canister.

6. Transfer to two *clean* ½ pint (236 ml) jars or other containers, leaving about ½ inch (1 cm) of headspace in each. Cover or seal. Cool at room temperature for no more than 30 minutes, then refrigerate or freeze.

Next

For a poaching sauce for fish, shrimp, mussels, or clams, whisk a few tablespoons of the paste into 2 cups canned coconut milk along with a pinch of brown sugar and a squeeze of lime juice.

Green Curry Paste

MAKES: about 2 cups (480 ml)
FRIDGE: up to 3 weeks
FREEZER: up to 1 year

Here's a basil-laced chili paste that has a fresh, bright flavor, thanks to both Thai basil and fresh chilis. If you can't find Thai basil, substitute sweet or Italian basil leaves, but reduce the amount by half. For a wild lunch, smear small amounts of the paste on a slice of bread before building and browning a grilled cheese as you normally would.

- 4¼ ounces (120 g) *fresh* green serrano chilis (about 12), stemmed, halved lengthwise, and seeded
- 4¼ ounces (120 g) *fresh* medium green jalapeño chilis (about 6), stemmed, halved lengthwise, and seeded
- 6 tablespoons (14 g) packed Thai basil leaves (no stems)
- ¼ cup (60 g) ginger paste
- ¼ cup (60 g) garlic paste
- 3 tablespoons (45 g) lemongrass paste
- 2 tablespoons (15 g) ground coriander
- 1 tablespoon (16 g) shrimp paste
- 1 tablespoon (6 g) finely grated lime zest
- 1 tablespoon (8 g) ground cumin
- 1 tablespoon (12 g) kosher salt
- Water as necessary to create a smooth paste

1. Put both chilis, the basil, ginger paste, garlic paste, lemongrass paste, coriander, shrimp paste, lime zest, cumin, and salt in a food processor.

Cover and process until a smooth paste forms, adding water in 1 tablespoon (15 ml) increments as necessary and stopping the machine at least once to scrape down the inside of the canister.

2. Transfer to two *clean* ½ pint (236 ml) jars or other containers, leaving about ½ inch (1 cm) headspace in each. Cover or seal, then refrigerate or freeze.

Next

This paste makes an excellent stock for simmering thick fish fillets. Use the paste in a 1-to-6 ratio *by volume* with chicken or vegetable broth to make a simmering sauce, then slide the fillets in to simmer at a low bubble for a few minutes, just until cooked through.

Black Mole

MAKES: about 4 cups (960 ml)
FRIDGE: up to 1 month
FREEZER: up to 1 year

Black mole (aka mole negro) is an art form from Oaxaca. Since making the paste is an involved process, we feel it's worth the effort to make extra for the freezer (and for gifts). The best mole is made from a blend of dried chilis, often with guajillos in the mix. However, we've subbed those out for moritas to give the paste a smokier flavor. For a more traditional sauce, swap out those moritas for guajillos.

- 2 ounces (58 g) dried mulato chilis (about 6), stemmed, seeded, and broken into pieces
- 1 ounce (30 g) dried morita chilis (about 6), stemmed, seeded, and broken into pieces
- 1 ounce (30 g) dried pasilla chilis (about 4), stemmed, seeded, and broken into pieces
- 4 dried Calimyrna or Adriatic (aka Turkish) figs, stemmed
- Boiling water as necessary to soak the chilis
- ¼ pound (115 g) plum tomatoes (about 2 medium), quartered
- 1 ripe plantain, peeled and cut into 1 inch (2.5 cm) rounds
- 1 cup (240 ml) vegetable broth

¼ cup (40 g) pepitas (small shelled pumpkin seeds)

3 medium garlic cloves, peeled and halved lengthwise

2 tablespoons (18 g) white sesame seeds

1 ounce (28 g) unsweetened chocolate, chopped

1 tablespoon (21 g) honey

1 teaspoon ground cinnamon

1 teaspoon kosher salt

½ teaspoon ground allspice

½ teaspoon ground cloves

½ teaspoon ground black pepper

Additional water as necessary to create a smooth paste

3 tablespoons (45 ml) neutral-flavored oil, such as canola or vegetable oil

1. Put all the chili pieces and the dried figs in a heat-safe bowl. Pour in boiling water until submerged. Set a heat-safe, nonreactive small plate on top of the items to weight them down. Soak at room temperature for 20 minutes.

2. Meanwhile, position an oven rack 6 inches (15 cm) from the broiler; heat the broiler. Place the tomatoes cut sides up and the plantains on a lipped baking sheet. Broil until well browned in spots, turning once, about 2 minutes.

3. Scrape the contents of the baking sheet into a food processor. Uncover and drain the chilis and figs. Add them as well. Also add the broth, pepitas, garlic, sesame seeds, chocolate, honey, cinnamon, salt, allspice, cloves, and black pepper. Cover and process, adding water by 1 tablespoon (15 ml) increments and occasionally scraping down the inside of the canister, until a smooth paste forms.

4. Set a very large skillet over medium heat for a minute or two. Pour in the oil, then add every speck of the mole from the canister. Watch out for splatters. Stir until the oil incorporates and the mole comes to a bubble, about 2 minutes.

5. Turn off the heat and remove the skillet from the burner. Cool for 1–2 minutes. Transfer to four *clean* ½ pint (236 ml) jars or other containers, leaving about ½ inch (1 cm) headspace in each.

Cover or seal. Cool at room temperature for no more than 1 hour, then refrigerate or freeze.

Next
Whisk this mole with broth until it's the consistency of marinara sauce, then bring to a simmer in a skillet. Add cut-up boneless skinless chicken breasts or thighs and simmer until tender.

Shortcut Black Mole

MAKES: about 3 cups (720 ml)
FRIDGE: up to 1 month
FREEZER: up to 1 year

Although we need the traditional dried mulato chilis to make this easier version of the classic black mole, we don't have to soak them first. Instead, they cook in this simplified sauce with canned chipotles in adobo sauce. Our secret is the almond butter, which adds a depth of flavor close to what we might get from a larger range of aromatics.

2 tablespoons (30 ml) neutral-flavored oil, such as canola or vegetable oil

1 small white or yellow onion, peeled and chopped

2 medium garlic cloves, peeled and thinly sliced

1 canned chipotle in adobo sauce, stemmed and chopped (keep the seeds for heat)

3 cups (720 ml) vegetable broth

¼ cup (38 g) raisins

1.3 ounces (37 g) dried mulato chilis (about 4), stemmed, seeded, and torn into tiny pieces

2 tablespoons (11 g) unsweetened cocoa powder

1 tablespoon (9 g) yellow cornmeal

1 teaspoon dried oregano

1 teaspoon ground cumin

1 teaspoon kosher salt

½ teaspoon ground cinnamon

¼ cup (68 g) almond butter

1. Set a medium saucepan over medium heat for a minute or two, then swirl in the oil. Add the onion and garlic and cook, stirring often, until browned

Top to bottom:
Red Mole (page 235),
Green Mole (page 236),
and Black Mole (page 232)

at the edges, about 5 minutes. Add the chipotle and cook, stirring often, until fragrant, about 1 minute.

2. Stir in the broth, raisins, dried chilis, cocoa powder, cornmeal, oregano, cumin, salt, and cinnamon. Continue cooking, stirring more and more frequently to prevent scorching, until the liquid has been reduced to two-thirds of its original volume, about 8 minutes.

3. Turn off the heat and set the pan off the burner for 5 minutes. Pour and scrape every drop from the pan into a food processor and add the almond butter. Cover and process until a thick puree, stopping and uncovering the machine at least once to scrape down the inside of the canister.

4. Transfer to three *clean* ½ pint (236 ml) jars or other containers, leaving about ½ inch (1 cm) headspace in each. Cover or seal, then refrigerate or freeze.

Next

To make a simmering sauce, mix this shortcut mole negro with chicken or vegetable broth in a ratio of 1 part mole to 4 parts broth *by volume*. Bring to a simmer, stirring constantly to dissolve, before adding boneless center-cut pork loin chops or even beef meatballs. Simmer slowly, adding more broth as necessary.

Red Mole

MAKES: about 4 cups (960 ml)
FRIDGE: up to 1 month
FREEZER: up to 1 year

This red chili paste (aka mole rojo) includes tomatoes for a lush finish. It's also simpler in its flavors than Black Mole (page 232). It's a terrific simmering sauce for shellfish, chicken, or pork. For a simmering sauce, mix 1 part mole with 4 parts broth (*by volume*); or go for a combo of broth and beer or even broth and wine. From there, you can add it to softened vegetables like onions, garlic, and carrots, before adding shrimp

(in or out of the shell), boneless chicken thighs, or even diced pork shoulder meat.

> **2.1 ounces (60 g) dried guajillo chilis (about 12),** stemmed, seeded, and torn into tiny pieces
>
> **¾ ounce (24 g) dried New Mexican red chilis (about 4),** stemmed, seeded, and torn into tiny pieces
>
> **¼ cup (38 g) raisins**
>
> **Boiling water as necessary to soak the chilis and raisins**
>
> **1 pound (450 g) plum tomatoes (about 4 *large*),** quartered
>
> **½ cup (120 ml) vegetable broth**
>
> **¼ cup (38 g) roasted unsalted shelled peanuts**
>
> **1 tablespoon (6 g) masa harina (ground masa for tamales)**
>
> **2 teaspoons dried oregano**
>
> **1 teaspoon kosher salt**
>
> **½ teaspoon dried thyme**
>
> **½ teaspoon ground cinnamon**
>
> **½ teaspoon ground cloves**
>
> **½ teaspoon ground black pepper**
>
> **¼ teaspoon ground star anise**
>
> **Additional water as necessary to create a smooth paste**
>
> **3 tablespoons (45 ml) neutral-flavored oil, such as canola or vegetable oil**

1. Put both chilis and the raisins in a heat-safe bowl. Add enough boiling water to submerge everything. Set a heat-safe, nonreactive small plate on the ingredients to weight them down. Soak at room temperature for 20 minutes.

2. Meanwhile, position a rack 6 inches (15 cm) from the broiler; heat the broiler. Place the tomatoes cut sides up on a lipped baking sheet and broil until browned in spots, turning once, about 2 minutes.

3. Scrape the contents of the baking sheet into a food processor. Uncover and drain the chilis and raisins and add them as well. Add the broth, peanuts, masa, oregano, salt, thyme, cinnamon, cloves, black pepper, and star anise. Cover and process, adding water by 1 tablespoon (15 ml) increments and occasionally scraping down the inside of the canister, until a smooth paste forms.

4. Set a very large skillet over medium heat for a minute or two. Pour in the oil, then add every speck of the mole from the canister. Watch out for splatters. Stir until the oil incorporates and the mole comes to a bubble, about 2 minutes.

5. Turn off the heat and remove the skillet from the burner. Cool for 1–2 minutes. Transfer to four *clean* ½ pint (236 ml) jars or other containers, leaving about ½ inch (1 cm) headspace in each. Cover or seal. Cool at room temperature for no more than 30 minutes, then refrigerate or freeze.

Next
Even burritos or tamales benefit from mole rojo. Make the simmering sauce we suggest in the headnote, bring it to a simmer, and pour it over those burritos or tamales.

Shortcut Red Mole

MAKES: about 3 cups (720 ml)
FRIDGE: up to 1 month
FREEZER: up to 1 year

If you want to skip working with dried chilis, our easy version of this Oaxacan red paste may fit the bill. We bring on toasted, smoky flavors with both canned chipotles in adobo sauce as well as smoked paprika. Note, however, that we call for *pure* ancho chili powder, not the more common North American blend.

- 2 tablespoons (30 ml) neutral-flavored oil, such as canola or vegetable oil
- 2 small yellow or white onions, peeled and chopped
- *At least* 4 medium garlic cloves, peeled and thinly sliced
- 3 canned chipotles in adobo sauce, stemmed and chopped
- 1 tablespoon (15 ml) adobo sauce from the can
- 2 cups (480 g) tomato puree
- 1 cup (240 ml) vegetable broth
- 3 tablespoons (24 g) *pure* ancho chili powder
- 1 tablespoon (8 g) mild smoked paprika
- 2 teaspoons ground cumin
- 1 teaspoon kosher salt
- ⅛ teaspoon ground cloves
- ¼ cup (65 g) tahini

1. Set a medium saucepan over medium heat for a minute or two, then swirl in the oil. Add the onion and garlic; cook, stirring often, until browned at the edges, about 5 minutes. Add the chipotles and cook, stirring often, until fragrant, about 1 minute.

2. Stir in the adobo sauce, tomato puree, broth, ancho chili powder, smoked paprika, cumin, salt, and ground cloves. Continue cooking, stirring more and more frequently to prevent scorching, until the liquid has been reduced to half of its original volume, about 10 minutes.

3. Turn off the heat and set the pan off the burner for 5 minutes. Pour and scrape every drop from the pan into a food processor. Add the tahini. Cover and process until a thick puree forms.

4. Transfer to three *clean* ½ pint (236 ml) jars or other containers, leaving about ½ inch (1 cm) headspace in each. Cover or seal, then refrigerate or freeze.

Next
This mole works really well with duck or chicken leg quarters, and even turkey thighs, simmered slowly with root vegetables and broth in a covered pot in the oven. Or make a barbecue mopping sauce by whisking about 1 cup mole with hefty splashes of apple cider vinegar and beer.

Green Mole

MAKES: about 4 cups (960 ml)
FRIDGE: up to 1 month
FREEZER: up to 1 year

This is our lightest mole: a little sour from the tomatillos, fiery from the fresh jalapeños, and loaded with cilantro. Also known as mole verde, it's the best mole for fish of almost any sort. To make a simmering sauce, mix 1 part mole with 5 parts broth (and/or wine) *by volume*. Bring the combined sauce to a simmer, then cook uncovered for a bit to reduce and concentrate the flavors before adding fish fillets or even chunks of cod or halibut. Because the sauce is so flavorful, frozen fish fillets work great!

- 1 pound (450 g) fresh small tomatillos, husked, rinsed to remove any sticky residue, and halved through the stem ends
- 1 cup (160 g) pepitas (small shelled pumpkin seeds)
- 4 tablespoons (60 ml) neutral-flavored oil, such as canola or vegetable oil
- 1 small yellow or white onion, peeled, halved, and sliced into thin half-moons
- 4 medium garlic cloves, peeled and thinly sliced
- 1½ cups (55 g) *packed* fresh cilantro leaves
- 1 cup (240 ml) vegetable broth
- 3 medium *fresh* green jalapeño chilis, stemmed, halved lengthwise, and seeded
- 2 teaspoons dried oregano
- 1 teaspoon kosher salt
- Water as necessary to create a smooth paste

1. Position an oven rack 4 inches (10 cm) from the broiler; heat the broiler. Put the tomatillos cut side up on a lipped baking sheet. Broil undisturbed until charred in spots, about 2 minutes. Scrape the contents of the baking sheet into a food processor.

2. Set a small skillet over medium-low heat for a minute or two. Add the pepitas and toast, stirring often, until they brown lightly and begin to pop, about 2 minutes. Pour these into the food processor as well.

3. Return the skillet to medium heat and swirl in 2 tablespoons (30 ml) oil. Add the onion and garlic and cook, stirring occasionally, until browned at the edges, about 4 minutes. Pour and scrape the contents of the skillet into the food processor.

4. Add the cilantro, broth, jalapeños, oregano, and salt to the food processor. Cover and process, adding water in 1 tablespoon (15 ml) increments and stopping the machine at least once to scrape down the inside of the canister, until a smooth paste forms.

5. Set a very large skillet over medium heat for a minute or two. Pour in the remaining

2 tablespoons (30 ml) oil, then add every speck of the mole from the canister. Watch out for splatters. Stir until the oil incorporates and the mole comes to a bubble, about 2 minutes.

6. Turn off the heat and remove the skillet from the burner. Cool for 1–2 minutes. Transfer to four *clean* ½ pint (236 ml) jars or other containers, leaving about ½ inch (1 cm) headspace in each. Cover or seal. Cool at room temperature for no more than 30 minutes, then refrigerate or freeze.

More

For a spicier mole verde, substitute 1 green habanero for 1 of the jalapeños. Or go all out and substitute lard for the oil!

Go-to Harissa

MAKES: about 2 cups (480 ml)
FRIDGE: up to 1 month
FREEZER: up to 1 year

This North African chili paste—or sauce, depending on how loose you make it—is actually a bit sweeter than it is fiery, thanks to the less assertive dried chilis in the mix. Although often served as a dip or condiment with various Middle Eastern dishes, we love it with mayonnaise on a burger or as a dip for French fries, particularly when mixed 50/50 with unseasoned rice vinegar.

- 2⅔ ounces (75 g) dried guajillo chilis (about 15), stemmed, split lengthwise, and seeded
- 1¾ ounces (50 g) dried ancho chilis (about 5), stemmed, split lengthwise, and seeded
- Boiling water as necessary to soak the chilis
- ½ cup (120 ml) olive oil
- 4 medium garlic cloves, peeled and halved lengthwise
- 1½ teaspoons ground coriander
- 1½ teaspoons ground cumin
- 1 teaspoon *ground* caraway seeds
- 1 teaspoon kosher salt
- Additional water as necessary to create a thick paste

1. Put both chilis in a heat-safe bowl and pour in enough boiling water to submerge them. Set a heat-safe, nonreactive small plate on the chilis to weight them down. Soak at room temperature for 20 minutes.

2. Uncover and drain the chilis in a colander set in the sink. Shake the colander a couple of times to get rid of excess moisture.

3. Transfer the chilis to a food processor. Add the olive oil, garlic, coriander, cumin, caraway seeds, and salt. Cover and process, adding water in 1 tablespoon (15 ml) increments as necessary and stopping the machine at least once to uncover it and scrape down the inside of the canister, until a thick, mushy paste forms.

4. Transfer to two *clean* ½ pint (236 ml) jars or other containers, leaving about ½ inch (1 cm) headspace in each. Cover or seal, then refrigerate or freeze.

More

For a hotter harissa, substitute some árbol chilis for a few of the other dried chilis, keeping the overall weight of the chilis constant. Or simply add up to ½ teaspoon ground cayenne with the other spices to the food processor.

Rose Harissa

MAKES: about 2 cups (480 ml)
FRIDGE: up to 1 month
FREEZER: up to 1 year

This complex harissa is a coarse paste, stocked with not only chilis but plenty of spices (including dried roses) *and* laced with tomatoes for a sweeter, sophisticated finish. All in all, this is a versatile chili paste that would be welcome with onions and other aromatics as the base of a dairy-free braise.

> 3 ounces (85 g) dried New Mexican red chilis (about 14), stemmed, seeded, and cut into small pieces
> 7 dried árbol chilis, stemmed and seeded
> 5 dry-packed sun-dried tomatoes

> Boiling water as necessary to soak the chilis and sun-dried tomatoes
> 1 tablespoon (6 g) cumin seeds
> 2 teaspoons coriander seeds
> 1 teaspoon caraway seeds
> 4 medium garlic cloves, peeled and halved lengthwise
> ¼ cup (60 ml) olive oil
> 2 tablespoons (30 ml) lemon juice
> 2 tablespoons (2 g) dried culinary rosebuds (see recipe headnote, page 100)
> 1 tablespoon (15 g) tomato paste
> 1 tablespoon (15 ml) white wine vinegar
> 2 teaspoons (10 g) pomegranate molasses
> 1½ teaspoons mild smoked paprika
> 1 teaspoon (5 ml) rose water
> 1 teaspoon kosher salt
> Additional water as necessary to create a smooth paste

1. Place both chilis and the sun-dried tomatoes in a heat-safe bowl. Pour in enough boiling water to submerge them. Set a heat-safe, nonreactive small plate on top of the items to weight them down. Soak at room temperature for 20 minutes.

2. Meanwhile, set a small skillet over medium-low heat for a minute or two. Add the cumin, coriander, and caraway seeds; toast until fragrant, stirring often, about 1 minute. Pour the seeds into a blender.

3. Uncover and drain the chilis and sun-dried tomatoes in a colander set in the sink. Shake the colander a few times to get rid of excess moisture.

4. Transfer the chilis and sun-dried tomatoes to the blender. Add the garlic, olive oil, lemon juice, rosebuds, tomato paste, vinegar, pomegranate molasses, smoked paprika, rose water, and salt. Cover and blend, adding water in 1 tablespoon (15 ml) increments through the hole in the lid and stopping the machine at least once to uncover and scrape down the inside of the canister, until a fairly smooth, thick paste forms.

5. Transfer to two *clean* ½ pint (236 ml) jars or other containers, leaving about ½ inch (1 cm)

Rose Harissa (page 238)
with roasted potatoes

headspace in each. Cover or seal, then refrigerate or freeze.

Next

Spoon this harissa on eggs (particularly deviled eggs!). Serve it with crackers and creamy dips. Toss it with cut-up potatoes before roasting or air-frying. Or whir it into hummus.

Smoky-Sweet Harissa

MAKES: about 2 cups (480 ml)
FRIDGE: up to 1 month
FREEZER: up to 1 year

We love this simple if whimsical harissa, a sort of cross-cultural chili paste. It's a blend of canned chipotles in adobo sauce (for a smoky flavor), fresh chilis (for a brighter bite), and a jarred roasted red pepper (for a sweet finish).

- ⅔ ounce (18 g) dried New Mexican red chilis (about 3), stemmed, seeded, and torn into small bits
- Boiling water as necessary to soak the chilis
- 1 jarred roasted red bell pepper, seeded and torn up
- ½ cup (120 ml) olive oil
- 3 canned chipotles in adobo sauce, stemmed and seeded
- 1 tablespoon (15 ml) adobo sauce from the can
- 1 teaspoon ground coriander
- 1 teaspoon ground cumin
- 1 teaspoon kosher salt
- 1 teaspoon ground black pepper

1. Place the chilis in a heat-safe bowl and pour in enough boiling water to submerge them. Set a heat-safe, nonreactive small plate on the chilis to weight them down. Soak at room temperature for 20 minutes.

2. Uncover and drain the chilis in a colander set in the sink. Shake the colander a few times to get rid of excess moisture.

3. Transfer the chilis to a blender. Add the roasted red pepper, olive oil, canned chipotles, adobo sauce, ground coriander, ground cumin, salt, and pepper. Cover and blend, stopping the machine once to open it and scrape down the inside of the canister, until a mushy paste forms.

4. Transfer to two *clean* ½ pint (236 ml) jars or other containers, leaving about ½ inch (1 cm) headspace in each. Cover or seal, then refrigerate or freeze.

More

Roast a medium red bell pepper yourself: Use tongs to place it over a gas burner turned to high and turn repeatedly until blackened. Seal in a bag and set aside at room temperature for 30 minutes. Peel off the blackened bits, then stem and seed the pepper for this recipe.

Shortcut Gochujang

MAKES: about 2 cups (480 ml)
FRIDGE: up to 1 month
FREEZER: up to 1 year

The Korean chili paste gochujang has become a favored ingredient not only in Korean cuisine but across Asian and even North American cooking. It's a salty, spicy mix, the base of many stews, stir-fries, and braises. As here, it's made with gochugaru (ground red chili flakes). But it's traditionally a fermented paste, a vibe we get with red miso paste, a decidedly funky, fermented ingredient. Gochujang also usually includes glutinous rice, sometimes malted barley, and lots of aromatics. We found we can adjust the number of ingredients to create something that's close to the original but far easier to prepare. It's a fine house gift whenever you're invited for the weekend.

1⅓ cups (320 ml) water

⅔ cup (133 g) granulated white sugar

⅓ cup (104 g) light corn syrup

1 cup (120 g) gochugaru

6 tablespoons (90 g) *red* miso paste

2½ tablespoons (38 ml) toasted sesame oil

1 tablespoon (15 ml) *unseasoned* rice vinegar

½ teaspoon kosher salt

1. Stir the water, sugar, and corn syrup in a small saucepan set over medium-high heat until the sugar dissolves. Bring to a boil, stirring occasionally. Boil for 4 minutes. Turn off the heat and remove the pan from the burner.

2. Stir in the gochugaru and red miso paste until smooth. Add the sesame oil, vinegar, and salt. Stir until a thick paste forms, about 2 minutes. (It will thicken more as it cools.)

3. Transfer to two *clean* ½ pint (236 ml) jars or other containers, leaving about ½ inch (1 cm) headspace in each. Cover or seal, then refrigerate or freeze.

Next

This version of gochujang is an excellent marinade for meats headed for the grill. Either smear it directly over the cuts or thin it out with equal parts rice vinegar and honey for a more complex marinade.

4

Pickles, Preserved Vegetables, and Syrupy Fruits

We can't imagine a summer weekend meal without a vat of pickles. We also find it hard to picture an autumn evening without fruits in syrup ready for ice cream. And most weekdays all year long, we can hardly figure out how to eat lunch without oil-cured tomatoes or artichoke hearts on hummus.

Yes, there are lots of pickles, preserved vegetables, and syrupy fruit contrivances at the supermarket. But they don't taste like homemade! They're lackluster: less herbal, delectable, or tempting. And all around mushier, to boot. When we make our own classic dills, when we soak apples in honey syrup, or when we preserve garlic cloves in oil, we're left with some of the best things our kitchen can produce.

In this chapter, we range wider than in any other: from sparky Horseradish Pickles (page 251) to surprisingly delicate Gingered Watermelon Rinds (page 278); from super easy Pickled Red Onions (page 258) to classic Prunes in Armagnac (page 290); from old-school Harvard Beets (page 276) to newfangled Dried Pears in Fennel-Orange Syrup (page 294). All in all, it's a big pantry of fine condiments, add-ons, garnishes, and even sides.

Vinegar-brining and sugar-preserving vegetables and fruits are arts, although both based in science. There's the exacting ratio for the salt in the brine or the sugar in the syrup. If the brine is too salty or the syrup too sweet, either will overwhelm every other flavor. Worse yet, if a brine is not salty enough, it won't permit osmosis, blocking the salt and other flavors from getting inside the cucumbers or carrots. And if there's not the proper amount of salt or sugar in a pickled or preserved condiment, it can quickly go bad and rot. Don't be tempted to shortchange our amounts in the service of some notion of better nutrition. And don't ever use a sugar substitute in place of white or brown sugar.

In fact, this whole chapter is about exacting ratios. If we add too many aromatics, we'll mask what we've preserved. If we add too few, there's little point to our work. As we said, it's an art. Okay, maybe not quite the art that traditional fermentation is (we'll get to that in the next chapter!), but a lot of know-how has gone into centuries of saving back the harvest for the leaner days ahead. We hope we can add our hard-won ratios to that know-how and bring you the best small-batch successes for your fridge.

Yes, your *fridge*. Most of what you'll make in this chapter doesn't freeze well. Pickled things end up soggy after freezing, since the salt has already broken down some of the cellular structure before the thaw does its inevitable damage. Some sugar-preserved fruits thaw into almost tasteless nonsense because the sugary stickiness has infiltrated every speck of the fruit that had held microscopic ice crystals in the freezer. So without a freezer in the offing for much of this chapter, you'll have to enjoy these sour and sweet wonders in the weeks after they're made. Or give some away and make lots of new friends.

Let's finesse a couple of the common ingredients in this chapter, then talk about some specific techniques as well as a way to up your bartending with the leavings in some canning jars.

Mixed pickling spice

You'll find this blend in the spice aisle of almost every supermarket. There are wide variations among the bottlings. Most include allspice, crushed bay leaves, cardamom, cloves, and black peppercorns. Some add cinnamon, coriander, dried lemon peel, red pepper flakes, and/or mace.

▲ When you make your own pickling spice, you can tailor it to your taste!

A few even have preservatives, like sulfiting agents. Read the labels and pick the one that matches your taste.

Or make your own. Here's our favorite: Combine 2 tablespoons (12 g) yellow mustard seeds, 2 tablespoons (12 g) allspice berries, 1 tablespoon (6 g) coriander seeds, 2 *green* cardamom pods, 8 whole cloves, 2 small cinnamon sticks, and a strip of dried orange or lemon peel in a ziplock bag and seal shut. Set the bag on a cutting board, hold the seal closed, and crush the spices with the bottom of a heavy saucepan or rolling pin (taking care not to tear the bag and minding your fingers at the bag's seal). Alternatively, *coarsely* grind the spices in a spice grinder. Pour the crushed spices into a small bowl and add up to 1 teaspoon red pepper flakes and/or ¼ teaspoon grated nutmeg. Also, crumble a few dried bay leaves into micro bits and add these to the bowl. Stir well, then store in a sealed jar in a cool, dark pantry for up to 1 year.

Salt

We've already discussed our preference for kosher salt in the introduction (page 20), but the matter bears even more explanation here.

Weigh the salt, if at all possible. There are varying grinds of kosher salt. The best results in this chapter will be achieved with the best precision.

As you might suspect, we never call for pink curing salt, which is often used to preserve meat. We also don't call for pickling or canning salt, although you *can* substitute it for kosher salt. However, pickling or canning salt has a finer grain than kosher salt. If you want to use pickling salt, use about *two-thirds* the recipe's stated amount *by volume*. And since pickling or canning salt is expensive, it's frankly more cost-effective to buy a box of kosher salt and have it on hand for all our recipes.

But *no table salt*. In most cases, it includes anti-caking agents to let it pour freely. Those can fall out of suspension after the salt has dissolved, sometimes hours later, sometimes days later. They'll cloud the brine.

Does that matter? We think so. Nobody wants pickled murk. But it can also obscure dire problems. As vegetables and fruits degrade, they begin to cloud brines and syrups, offering a clue as to when they've gone beyond their prime. If the muck is present from the get-go, how can you tell if it's time to chuck the jar?

Jars

Many of these pickling recipes call for a large glass canning jar. We often advocate for a 1 or 2 quart (1 or 1.9 liter) jar. For one thing, the vegetables can be tightly packed in the jar to make sure everything is submerged in the brine or syrup. For another, most jars (rather than, say, crocks) are easier to store in the fridge.

The jars must be *scrupulously* cleaned. Yes, you can use the dishwasher trick, as we suggest in the introduction (see page 19). But not everyone's hot water heater is set as high as it needs to be to

▲ Bigger jars more easily hold pickles and their brine.

sterilize the jars. Not everyone has a powerful dishwasher. *And* we're working here with refrigerator pickling and a few times with a more exacting (if shortcut) countertop fermentation process. Either technique can result in bad bugs or their toxic residue if you haven't properly sanitized the containers. We strongly recommend that you boil the jar(s) and lid(s) in a large pot of water for about 5 minutes.

If you use another container or a crock, it should have no reactive glazes or dyes. Plus, the vegetables or fruit *must be fully covered* in the brine or syrup. If you pour in either and find it comes only halfway or even a third of the way up the vegetables, you must add more brine in the same *water-vinegar-salt ratio by volume* or more syrup in the same *water-sugar ratio by volume* (and heated or not, as the recipe indicates) until the vegetables or fruit are covered.

Pickling v. refrigerator fermentation

Many of these vinegar-based recipes undergo a *refrigerator* pickling process. Vegetables or fruits are put in a brine, then chilled for a day, two days, a week, or maybe more, depending on how

quickly osmosis happens at lower temperatures. There's not much to do here but be patient. We always date the lids with an indelible marker to know when the pickling process started.

A few of these pickles undergo outright fermentation, a process beyond pickling, either in the refrigerator or with a shortcut, countertop, just-a-few-hours method in line with our overall faster techniques and smaller batches. But even though we use these slightly more complicated processes in this chapter, we avoid traditional fermentation because we're not canning the results and have zero chance to kill off any bad bugs that may develop. We're also not checking pH values. And we're making small batches that seem to preclude the more involved folderol of traditional fermentation techniques.

Even though we're not pulling out our pH strips, we still must be exacting about the required acid. Use *only* what we call for, usually distilled white vinegar (for more information, see page 21 of the introduction). Don't substitute rice vinegar, white wine vinegar, or white balsamic vinegar (all of which have a higher pH) for distilled white vinegar (which is more acidic and thus more preserving).

Unfortunately, refrigerator fermentation is not an exact science. There are many factors at play: how long the brine takes to chill evenly, the temperature of the vegetables before they go into the jar, and even the specific density of those vegetables and other aromatics. Refrigerator fermentation generally takes 5 to 7 days. Be patient but check often for the results that match your taste.

Safety first

Follow your nose: Pleasantly sour is as pleasantly sour smells. But in like manner, rotten is as rotten smells. Do not consume any pickle that has a musty, stinky, or acrid aroma. Discard any pickles with a brine that has turned so murky that you can't see your hand on the other side of the container.

▲ Use a thin fork to keep your fingers out of delicate brines and syrups.

▲ Many sweet-and-sour mixtures become ready-made shrubs for refreshing cocktails or mocktails.

To get the longest life out of refrigerator pickles, use firm, ripe vegetables without any brown or mushy spots.

Never stick even your clean fingers in a jar. Instead, use a clean fork to remove pickles. Rather than serving up a whole jar for, say, a picnic or a patio party, take out as many pickles as you want, then reseal the jar and put it back in the fridge. Don't return any removed pickles to the pickling jar. Instead, cover these in a separate little dish and refrigerate them to enjoy within a day or two.

Make shrubs!

In this chapter, we've got a lot of fruit packed in sweet-and-sour syrups. After you've enjoyed the fruit, don't discard the syrup! You've got a ready-made, vinegary shrub for a patio drink on a summer evening. Strain a tablespoon or two of the syrup into a 12 ounce (180 ml) glass, then add ice and top with sparkling water. Or go all out and shake a drizzle of the shrub with vodka, gin, or rum over ice in a cocktail shaker. Strain over fresh ice, then top with club soda, ginger beer, or tonic.

Ready, set...

Get ready for the *sweet* and the *sour*, the vinegar and the sugar. These pickled, cured, and preserved vegetables and fruits will last you from morning to night, from brunch with pickled kumquats on smoked salmon to dessert with sweet kumquats in a brandy syrup spooned over raspberry sorbet. You may have thought you got into cold canning over the prospect of small batches of jellies, chutneys, or even relishes, but you'll become a lifetime cold canner with the recipes in this chapter.

COLD CANNING

Classic Dill Pickles

MAKES: 7–9 pickles
FRIDGE: up to 3 weeks after steeping
FREEZER: no

Who doesn't love to crunch into a dill pickle along with a turkey sandwich on rye? And who doesn't love to sneak a dill pickle as an afternoon snack? A lot of traditional canning recipes ask you to steep the cucumbers in an unseasoned brine *before* you steam- or pressure-preserve them in their pickling brine to keep them crunchy through the canning process. Since we're doing the whole job in the fridge, our work is *so much easier*: basically, just cucumbers, a brine, and crunchy results. Use only the seeds of the spices, not ground versions, for a clear, beautiful brine.

- 4 cups (960 ml) water
- ¼ cup (60 ml) distilled white vinegar
- ¼ cup (48 g) kosher salt
- 2 tablespoons (20 g) mustard seeds
- 2 tablespoons (12 g) dried juniper berries
- 1 tablespoon (6 g) coriander seeds
- 8 whole cloves
- 2 dried bay leaves
- Additional water for rinsing the cucumbers
- 1¾ pounds (800 g, or 7 to 9) medium Kirby or pickling cucumbers, each fairly thin and about 5 inches (13 cm) long
- 4 large bushy fresh dill sprigs

1. Bring the water, vinegar, salt, mustard seeds, juniper berries, coriander seeds, cloves, and bay leaves to a boil in a medium saucepan set over high heat, stirring occasionally. Turn off the heat, cover the pan, and set it off the burner. Steep at room temperature for 2 hours, until cool to the touch.

2. Rinse the cucumbers with water, gently scrubbing them with a new sponge or a wad of paper towels (without nicking the skins). Stuff the cucumbers and dill sprigs into one *clean* 2 quart (1.9 liter) jar or other container. Make sure the dill is distributed among the cucumbers.

3. Pour the vinegar mixture through a fine-mesh strainer into the jar, leaving about ½ inch (1 cm) headspace. Make sure no cucumber sticks out of the brine. Cover or seal, then refrigerate to steep for at least 5 days before enjoying.

More
For heat, add either 2–4 dried árbol chilis or 1 teaspoon red pepper flakes to the vinegar mixture before boiling.

Half Sour Pickles

MAKES: 7–9 pickles
FRIDGE: up to 3 weeks after steeping
FREEZER: no

If you know deli lingo, you know that half sour pickles are crunchy, bright-green pickles, not the duller green of more familiar long-soured pickles. Half sours have a distinct snap and much gentler flavor. This recipe is our first refrigerator ferment: There's no vinegar; but we're using a shortcut method, not standard fermentation, giving the jar a little bump toward true fermentation at room temperature before squirreling it away in the fridge. This way, we don't push the limits of what cold canning can accomplish with pickles. In any event, sterilize the jar and don't be tempted to make substitutions. And use only *distilled* water for best results (since the chlorine in tap water or chemicals in well water can halt fermentation).

- 1 medium garlic clove, peeled and thinly sliced
- 1 teaspoon coriander seeds
- 1 teaspoon yellow mustard seeds
- 1 teaspoon black peppercorns
- 2 dried bay leaves
- 1¾ pounds (800 g, or 7 to 9) medium Kirby or pickling cucumbers, each fairly thin and about 5 inches (13 cm) long
- Distilled water for rinsing the cucumbers
- 2 fresh thyme sprigs
- 4 cups (960 ml) *distilled* water
- ¼ cup (48 g) kosher salt

1. Put the garlic, coriander, mustard seeds, black peppercorns, and bay leaves in one *clean* 2 quart (1.9 liter) jar or other container.

2. Rinse the cucumbers with *distilled* water, gently scrubbing them with a new sponge or a wad of paper towels (without nicking the skins). Stuff the cucumbers and thyme sprigs into the jar.

3. Whisk the 4 cups (960 ml) *distilled* water and salt in a bowl until the salt dissolves. Pour this brine over the cucumbers and aromatics, leaving about ½ inch (1 cm) headspace. If the brine does not cover everything, make more in that same ratio *by volume* to fill the container. (Make sure no cucumber sticks out of the brine.) Cover or seal; set aside *at room temperature* for 12–16 hours.

4. Refrigerate to steep until the cucumbers are crisp and starting to get sour, 5–6 days, before enjoying. (The longer the pickles sit in the brine, the saltier and more sour they'll get.)

More
For a completely nontraditional take, swap out the thyme sprigs for other leafy herbs: tarragon, rosemary, dill, parsley, cilantro, or parsley.

Garlic Sour Pickles

MAKES: 7–9 pickles
FRIDGE: up to 3 weeks after steeping
FREEZER: no

Somewhat translucent and intensely flavored, garlic sour pickles are the prize in most delis: terrific with corned beef or pastrami sandwiches, even better with chopped liver. But they're too powerful for some. Bruce grew up in a house divided: those who liked half sour pickles (see page 247) and the hardier lot who liked these. There's lots of garlic here; the cloves may turn bluish-green during pickling. Although safe if submerged in the brine, it's best to toss them out when you're done with the pickles. For the clearest brine, use dill and mustard *seeds*.

1¾ pounds (800 g, or 7 to 9) medium Kirby or pickling cucumbers, each fairly thin and about 5 inches (13 cm) long
Distilled water for rinsing the cucumbers
10 medium garlic cloves, peeled
2 dried bay leaves
2 teaspoons dill seeds
2 teaspoons yellow mustard seeds
4 cups (960 ml) *distilled* water
¼ cup (48 g) kosher salt

1. Rinse the cucumbers with *distilled* water, gently scrubbing them with a new sponge or a wad of paper towels (without nicking the skins). Stuff the cucumbers, garlic, and bay leaves in one *clean* 2 quart (1.9 liter) jar or other container. Add the dill and mustard seeds; gently shake the jar to distribute the seeds.

2. Whisk the 4 cups (960 ml) *distilled* water and salt in a bowl until the salt dissolves. Pour this brine over the cucumbers and aromatics, leaving about ½ inch (1 cm) headspace. If the brine does not cover everything, make more in that same ratio *by volume* to fill the container. Cover or seal. Refrigerate to steep for 2 weeks before enjoying.

Next
Dice these pickles into a fine relish to add as a layer in grilled cheese sandwiches.

Fiery Pickles

MAKES: 7–9 pickles
FRIDGE: up to 3 weeks after steeping
FREEZER: no

Cucumbers take to heat like few other vegetables: a sweet, watery undertow among fiery (and in this case, numbing) spices. As with our half sours (page 247), these undergo a quick shortcut countertop ferment before they go in the fridge, so they develop a more complex sour flavor than vinegar alone would afford.

Left to right: Half Sour Pickles (page 247) and Garlic Sour Pickles (page 248)

- 4 cups (960 ml) *distilled* water
- ¼ cup (48 g) kosher salt
- 2 tablespoons (10 g) Szechuan peppercorns
- 1 tablespoon (5 g) red pepper flakes
- 1 tablespoon (12.5 g) granulated white sugar
- 1¾ pounds (800 g, or 7 to 9) medium Kirby or pickling cucumbers, each fairly thin and about 5 inches (13 cm) long
- Additional *distilled* water for rinsing the cucumbers

1. Bring the 4 cups (960 ml) *distilled* water, salt, peppercorns, red pepper flakes, and sugar to a boil in a medium saucepan set over high heat, stirring occasionally. Turn off the heat, cover the pan, and set it off the burner. Steep at room temperature for 2 hours, until cool to the touch.

2. Rinse the cucumbers with distilled water, gently scrubbing them with a new sponge or a wad of paper towels (without nicking the skins). Stuff the cucumbers into one *clean* 2 quart (1.9 liter) jar or other container.

3. Pour the brine (spices and all) into the jar, leaving about ½ inch (1 cm) headspace. If the brine does not cover everything, make more in that same ratio *by volume* to fill the container. (Make sure no cucumber sticks out of the brine.) Cover or seal; set aside *at room temperature* for 12–16 hours. Then refrigerate to steep for 1 week before enjoying.

More

Spice the pickles by adding *2 green* cardamom pods, 1 star anise pod, and/or 1 tablespoon coriander seeds to the salt mixture before bringing it to a boil.

Green Tea Pickles

MAKES: about 25 pickle chunks
FRIDGE: up to 3 weeks after steeping
FREEZER: no

Green tea lends an herbaceous flavor to cucumber pickles, a musky but vibrant base to the otherwise sour brine. We find that the flavors are best balanced with hot chilis to bring a little brightness to the mix. We like these cucumbers cut into chunks because the flavor is so intense that there's really no way to finish a whole pickle with a sandwich. Put out a chunked bunch with toothpicks and cold beers some evening on the patio.

- 4 cups (960 ml) *distilled* water
- ¼ cup (48 g) kosher salt
- 4 green tea bags (see MORE below)
- 1¾ pounds (800 g, or 7 to 9) medium Kirby or pickling cucumbers, each fairly thin and about 5 inches (13 cm) long, cut into 2 inch (5 cm) chunks
- Additional *distilled* water for rinsing the cucumbers
- 2 *fresh* red serrano chilis, stemmed and halved lengthwise (keep those seeds!)

1. Bring the 4 cups (960 ml) *distilled* water and salt to a boil in a medium saucepan set over high heat, stirring occasionally. Turn off the heat and add the tea bags. Cover the pan, set it aside, and steep at room temperature for 2 hours, until cool to the touch.

2. Rinse the cucumbers with *distilled* water, gently scrubbing them with a new sponge or a wad of paper towels (without nicking the skins). Stuff the cucumbers and halved chilis into one *clean* 2 quart (1.9 liter) jar or other container. Make sure the chilis are distributed among the cucumbers.

3. Remove the tea bags. Pour the tea brine into the jar, leaving about ½ inch (1 cm) headspace. Cover or seal, then refrigerate to steep for 4 days before enjoying.

More

Vary this recipe based on the green tea: Sencha will offer a softer flavor, in some cross-sensory ways like the last light of a summer evening; matcha, much more vegetal flavors with soft, musky notes; and either gunpowder or hojicha will bring on darker, more roasted notes.

Horseradish Pickles

MAKES: 14–18 half pickle slices
FRIDGE: up to 3 weeks after steeping
FREEZER: no

We split the cucumbers lengthwise for this recipe so more of that sparky horseradish flavor gets into each slice. But there's a compromise: Halving them means they're not as crunchy after they're pickled, since they do get softer. Still, the flavor's hard to beat: sweet and vinegary with a nose-spanking bash. Just as a technique note: Once we add vinegar to the brine, we no longer need to worry about distilled water because we've upped the sour game without resorting to even low-grade, refrigerator fermentation.

- 3 cups (720 ml) water
- 1 cup (240 ml) apple cider vinegar
- ½ cup (100 g) granulated white sugar
- ¼ cup (48 g) kosher salt
- 2 tablespoons (30 g) jarred prepared white horseradish
- 1 tablespoon (15 g) mixed pickling spice
- 2 medium garlic cloves, peeled and smashed
- 1¾ pounds (800 g, or 7 to 9) medium Kirby or pickling cucumbers, each fairly thin and about 5 inches (13 cm) long
- Additional water for rinsing the cucumbers

1. Bring the water, vinegar, sugar, salt, horseradish, pickling spice, and garlic to a boil in a medium saucepan set over high heat, stirring occasionally. Turn off the heat, cover the pan, and set it off the burner. Steep at room temperature for 2 hours, or until cool to the touch.

2. Rinse the cucumbers with tap water, gently scrubbing them with a new sponge or a wad of paper towels (without nicking the skins). Halve each cucumber lengthwise. Stuff them into one *clean* 2 quart (1.9 liter) jar or other container.

3. Pour the vinegar mixture into the jar, leaving about ½ inch (1 cm) headspace. Cover or seal, then refrigerate to steep for 3 days before enjoying.

Next
Finely chop one or two horseradish pickles and add to chicken, tuna, or salmon salad.

Mustard Pickles

MAKES: 16 pickle spears
FRIDGE: up to 3 weeks after steeping
FREEZER: no

Because the flavor of dried mustard is so strong and earthy, particularly as it seeps into the cucumber *quarters*, we don't need to let these garlicky pickles undergo a long refrigerator fermentation to get the characteristic funkiness that's decidedly best with deli sandwiches. But since the ground mustard clouds the brine, don't push the storage time of this pickle.

- 1½ cups (360 ml) distilled white vinegar
- 2 tablespoons (42 g) honey
- 1½ tablespoons (25 g) ground dried mustard
- 1½ teaspoons mixed pickling spice
- 1½ teaspoons kosher salt
- 1 pound 2 ounces (500 g, or 4 to 5) medium Kirby or pickling cucumbers, each fairly thin and about 5 inches (13 cm) long
- Water for rinsing the cucumbers

1. Bring the vinegar, honey, ground mustard, pickling spice, and salt to a boil in a medium saucepan set over high heat, stirring occasionally. Turn off the heat, cover the pan, and set it off the burner. Steep at room temperature for 2 hours, or until cool to the touch.

2. Rinse the cucumbers with tap water, gently scrubbing them with a new sponge or a wad of paper towels (without nicking the skins). Quarter each cucumber *lengthwise*. Stand these spears up in one *clean* 1 quart (1 liter) jar or other container.

3. Pour the vinegar mixture into the jar, leaving about ½ inch (1 cm) headspace in each. Make sure no cucumber spear sticks out of the brine. Cover or seal, then refrigerate to steep for 2 days before enjoying.

More

Cut one of these spears into tiny bits and stuff one or two bits into a pitted date. Halve thinly sliced US-style bacon (or streaky bacon) widthwise, *then* lengthwise, and wrap a slice around the date; repeat for as many dates as you'd like. Air-fry at 350°F (175°C) for about 15 minutes or bake at 375°F (190°C) until warm and aromatic, about 25 minutes.

Zucchini Pickles

MAKES: about 4 cups (960 ml)
FRIDGE: up to 3 weeks after steeping
FREEZER: no

Sort of like more traditional cucumber pickles but softer and more luxurious, zucchini rounds easily become great refrigerator pickles. These have a sweet-and-sour finish, the better to pair with their pronounced vegetal flavors. However, zucchini are, by nature, watery. Salt them first to get rid of excess moisture so that the rounds retain some crunch after the pickling process.

> 1½ pounds (680 g) medium zucchini, sliced into rounds between ¼ and ½ inch thick (about 1 cm thick)
>
> 1 small yellow or white onion, peeled and sliced into ¼-inch-thick (0.5-cm-thick) rounds, the rounds then separated into rings
>
> 2 tablespoons (24 g) kosher salt
>
> 1 cup (240 ml) apple cider vinegar
>
> ¾ cup (175 g) granulated white sugar
>
> ½ teaspoon yellow mustard seeds
>
> ¼ teaspoon ground dried turmeric

1. Mix the zucchini rounds and onion rings in a large bowl. Sprinkle the salt over the top and toss repeatedly and well until all of the vegetables are evenly salted. Set aside at room temperature for 2 hours.

2. Dump the vegetables into a large colander set in the sink and let them drain for a few minutes. Shake the colander to remove excess moisture, then blot handfuls of the vegetables dry with paper towels before setting them aside.

3. Put the vinegar, sugar, mustard seeds, and turmeric in a very large saucepan. Set it over medium-high heat and stir until the sugar dissolves. Bring to a boil.

4. Add the zucchini and onions, bring back to a simmer, and reduce the heat to medium-low. Simmer, stirring occasionally, just until the vegetables are tender, about 8 minutes.

5. Turn off the heat and remove the pan from the burner. Cool for a few minutes, then ladle the contents of the pan into four *clean* ½ pint (236 ml) jars or one *clean* 1 quart (1 liter) jar or other container, leaving about ½ inch (1 cm) headspace in each. Cover or seal, then refrigerate to steep for 1 week before enjoying.

More

The ground dried turmeric clouds the brine. Keep it clearer by omitting the ground turmeric and using a 1 inch (2.5 cm) piece of fresh turmeric instead: Peel it and slice into paper-thin rounds, then add to the saucepan with the zucchini and onions.

Bread and Butter Pickles

MAKES: about 4 cups (960 ml)
FRIDGE: up to 3 weeks after steeping
FREEZER: no

Summer wouldn't be summer without a jar of these sweet but savory pickles in the fridge. They can make an appearance with burgers, hot dogs, grilled anything, or even purchased hummus. Be exacting when you cut the cucumbers. You want even slices. To be a perfectionist, use a mandoline, even a hand-held one. But wear a cut-proof glove to protect your fingers.

Bread and Butter Pickles
(page 252)

1 pound (450 g) medium Kirby or pickling cucumbers, sliced into ½ inch (1 cm) rounds (about 4 cups sliced)

1 tablespoon (12 g) kosher salt

Water to rinse the cucumbers

1 small yellow or white onion, peeled and very thinly sliced

¾ cup (180 ml) distilled white vinegar

¾ cup (150 g) granulated white sugar

¼ cup (60 ml) apple cider vinegar

3 tablespoons (39 g) dark brown sugar

3 tablespoons (30 g) brown mustard seeds

1 teaspoon yellow mustard seeds

¼ teaspoon celery seeds

⅛ teaspoon ground cloves

⅛ teaspoon ground dried turmeric

1. Toss the cucumber slices and salt in a large bowl until well coated. Cover and refrigerate for 1½ hours.

2. Pour the cucumbers into a large colander set in the sink and shake the colander to drain. Rinse the cucumbers with cool water and shake again to drain as well as you can.

3. Wipe out the bowl and pour the cucumber slices back into it. Add the onion and mix until well combined. Pack these vegetables into four *clean*, *heat-safe*, ½ pint (236 ml) jars or one *clean*, *heat-safe*, 1 quart (1 liter) jar or other container.

4. Bring the distilled vinegar, white sugar, cider vinegar, brown sugar, both types of mustard seeds, the celery seeds, ground cloves, and turmeric to a boil in a large saucepan set over high heat, stirring constantly until the sugar dissolves.

5. Pour the hot vinegar mixture over the vegetables in the jars, leaving about ½ inch (1 cm) headspace in each. Cool the jar(s) at room temperature for no more than 1 hour. Cover or seal, then refrigerate to steep for 2 days before enjoying.

More

If you want to see a video on how to make these pickles, check out the one on our YouTube channel, Cooking With Bruce & Mark.

Sweet Gherkins

MAKES: 16–18 gherkins
FRIDGE: up to 3 weeks after steeping
FREEZER: no

What kid doesn't love a sweet gherkin? It represents about the best thing anyone can do to a vegetable! But for us adults, the problem can be its texture, not its flavor. A hot sugar solution poured over the gherkins will render them unpleasantly soft. Make sure you give the sugar mixture time to cool somewhat. However, it should still be slightly warm so that it can better infuse the little pickles.

1½ cups (300 g) granulated white sugar

1 cup (240 ml) apple cider vinegar

1 tablespoon (12 g) kosher salt

One 2 inch (5 cm) cinnamon stick

¼ teaspoon celery seeds

¼ teaspoon fennel seeds

⅛ teaspoon ground dried turmeric

⅛ teaspoon vanilla extract

13 ounces (380 g) small gherkins, preferably cornichons, no more than 2 inches (5 cm) each (between 16 and 18)

1. Bring the sugar, vinegar, salt, cinnamon stick, celery seeds, fennel seeds, turmeric, and vanilla to a boil in a medium saucepan set over high heat, stirring constantly until the sugar dissolves. Turn off the heat, remove the pan from the burner, and cool for 1 hour, until just warm to the touch.

2. Pack the gherkins into two *clean* ½ pint (236 ml) jars or one *clean* 1 quart (1 liter) jar or other container, leaving about ½ inch (1 cm) headspace in each. Pour the brine over them. Cover or seal, then refrigerate to steep for 3 days before enjoying.

More

For slightly more savory gherkins, add up to 1 teaspoon yellow mustard seeds and 1 teaspoon coriander seeds with the other spices before you bring them to a boil.

Cornichons

MAKES: 16–18 cornichons
FRIDGE: up to 3 weeks after steeping
FREEZER: no

Proper cornichons should be *sour*, as well as small. (Measure the proper amount *by weight*, not by number.) To go all out, try to find raw *cornichons* at large supermarkets. They're a specific variety of little gherkins. Failing those, you can indeed use more standard gherkins, so long as they are small, as you'll see in the ingredient list. Once pickled, cornichons are absolutely essential on a cheese board. They're also terrific with just about any appetizer spread. And they're great with baked salmon salad and whitefish salad.

> 2 cups (480 ml) distilled white vinegar
>
> 2 tablespoons (24 g) kosher salt
>
> ½ teaspoon allspice berries
>
> ½ teaspoon juniper berries
>
> ½ teaspoon black peppercorns
>
> 13 ounces (380 g) small gherkins, preferably cornichons, no more than 2 inches (5 cm) each (between 16 and 18)

1. Bring the vinegar, salt, allspice berries, juniper berries, and peppercorns to a boil in a medium skillet set over high heat, stirring until the salt dissolves. Turn off the heat and set the pan off the burner for about 1 hour, until just warm to the touch.

2. Pack the gherkins into four *clean* ½ pint (236 ml) jars, two *clean* 1 pint (472 ml) jars, or one *clean* 1 quart (1 liter) jar or other container, leaving about ½ inch (1 cm) headspace. Pour the barely warm brine over them. Cover or seal, then refrigerate to steep for 3 days before enjoying.

Next
Cornichons are essential for tartar sauce. Chop them and mix with mayonnaise, a little lemon juice, a little granulated white sugar, and (if desired) some chopped fresh parsley leaves and/or minced red onion.

Pickled Jalapeño Rings

MAKES: about 4 cups (960 ml)
FRIDGE: up to 3 weeks after steeping
FREEZER: no

Well, not *just* jalapeños. Our version of the Tex-Mex restaurant staple is a mix of the chilis plus carrots and onions, a customer favorite with chips, nachos, and tacos. We make batches of this pickle all summer as the chilis come in from our garden, spicier and spicier as the weather heats up and the plants fire up the capsaicin. To make sure the chilis stay crisp, time the cooking from the moment they (and the vegetables) go into the pan, not from the time the liquid returns to a simmer.

> 1½ cups (360 ml) water
>
> 1 teaspoon kosher salt
>
> ½ teaspoon cumin seeds
>
> 4 ounces (115 g) baby carrots (that is, small snacking carrots), cut into ¼-inch-thick (0.5-cm-thick) rounds
>
> 4½ ounces (128 g) peeled fresh pearl onions or thawed frozen pearl onions (about 1 cup for either)
>
> 12 large fresh jalapeño chilis, stemmed and cut into ½-inch-thick (1-cm-thick) rounds
>
> 1½ cups (360 ml) distilled white vinegar

1. Stir the water, salt, and cumin seeds in a large saucepan until the salt dissolves. Set the pan over medium-high heat and bring to a simmer, stirring once or twice.

2. Add the carrots. Stir well and cook for 3 minutes from the moment the carrots go in the pan.

3. Add the pearl onions. Stir well and cook, stirring occasionally, for 1 minute from the moment the onions go in the pan.

4. Add the jalapeño rings. Cook, stirring occasionally, for 2 minutes from the moment the chilis go in the pan.

5. Turn off the heat and remove the pan from the burner. Stir in the vinegar. Cool at room temperature for 1 hour.

6. Ladle the contents of the pan into four *clean* ½ pint (236 ml) jars, two *clean* 1 pint (472 ml) jars, or one clean 1 quart (1 liter) jar or other container, leaving about ½ inch (1 cm) headspace. Cover or seal, then refrigerate to steep for 2 days before enjoying.

Tip
Jalapeño chilis have gotten milder and milder, thanks to morphing varietals that fit North American and European palates. You can find the old-school hot ones at farmers' markets. Or grow your own! They're super easy in pots on the patio. And as we've said, most get hotter as the season wears on.

Cowboy Candy

MAKES: about 4 cups (960 ml)
FRIDGE: up to 1 month
FREEZER: no

IYKYK. If not, just wait! Candied jalapeño rings are irresistible all summer long on hot dogs, grilled cheese sandwiches, and burgers, as well as alongside cheese and crackers or just about any dip you bring outside to the patio to better enjoy the evening light. (Try them with French onion dip and thick-cut ruffled potato chips!) Although you can eat these candied jalapeños the moment they're cool, they get better as they sit in the spicy syrup.

- 3 cups (600 g) granulated white sugar
- 2 cups (480 ml) distilled white vinegar
- 1 teaspoon kosher salt
- 1 pound 7 ounces (650 g) fresh jalapeño chilis, stemmed and cut into ¼-inch-thick (0.5-cm-thick) rounds

1. Combine the sugar, vinegar, and salt in a large saucepan. Set over medium-high heat and stir until the sugar dissolves. Raise the heat to high and bring to a boil. Boil undisturbed for 1 minute.

2. Stir in the jalapeños. Cook, stirring occasionally, for 5 minutes from the time the liquid comes back to a boil. The chilis should morph from bright green to a dull, dark, olive green.

3. Turn off the heat and remove the pan from the burner. Use a slotted spoon to transfer the jalapeños to four *clean* ½ pint (236 ml) jars, two *clean* 1 pint (472 ml) jars, or one *clean* 1 quart (1 liter) jar. Pour the syrup from the pan into the jars to cover the jalapeños and come within ½ inch (1 cm) of the top of the jar. (There may be excess syrup, depending on the jars or containers you've used. See the MORE section below.) Cover or seal. Cool at room temperature for no more than 1 hour, then refrigerate.

More
Strain the excess chili syrup to get rid of any solids, then store in a sealed container in the fridge for up to 1 month. Add a splash to margaritas or other cocktails in place of sugar or other sweeteners.

Pickled Cubanelles

MAKES: about 20 cubanelle strips
FRIDGE: up to 1 month after steeping
FREEZER: no

Why buy tasteless, limp, pickled cubanelles when you can pick out the best peppers to start with, add some aromatics, and keep the cubanelles crunchier and less wan? There's quite a range of heat among cubanelles. The ones in the supermarket are probably milder than the ones from a farmers' market. Even so, there are super hot ones everywhere. Take care if you've got kids eating these crunchy, sweet-sour pickles. (And if you *do* have kids eating them, kudos to you.)

Cowboy Candy (page 256) on a bagel with cream cheese and smoked salmon

14 ounces (400 g) medium cubanelle peppers (about 5)

2¼ cups (540 ml) distilled white vinegar

2 tablespoons (30 ml) balsamic vinegar

1 tablespoon (12.5 g) granulated white sugar

1 tablespoon (6 g) fennel seeds

1 tablespoon (12 g) kosher salt

1 teaspoon dried oregano

1. Stem the peppers, then slice each lengthwise into 4 strips. Pack them into one *clean, heat-safe,* 1 quart (1 liter) jar or other container.

2. Bring both vinegars, the sugar, fennel seeds, salt, and oregano to a boil in a medium saucepan set over medium-high heat, stirring at first to dissolve the sugar. Pour the hot vinegar syrup over the cubanelles, leaving about ½ inch (1 cm) headspace.

3. Cool at room temperature for 1 hour. Cover or seal, then refrigerate to steep for 2 days before enjoying.

Next

The brine from a spent jar of these pickles makes an excellent brine for chicken before you grill or fry it. Strain the brine, measure it, then mix with the same amount of water (*by volume*) in a large bowl. Add the chicken pieces, cover, and refrigerate, stirring occasionally, for no more than 2 hours.

Pickled Red Onions

MAKES: about 4 cups (960 ml)
FRIDGE: up to 1 month after steeping
FREEZER: no

These are a staple for tacos. Also, salads. Also, sandwiches. Also, hummus. Or dips of almost any sort. There are lots of methods touted for making pickled red onions: cook the onions in the vinegar; pour cold vinegar over them; make a vinegar brine and cool it before pouring it over the onions. As you can see, we don't advocate putting hot liquid

on the onions because we want to preserve as much crunch as possible. But then the onions need a bit of time to marinate. We also add a little sugar because it makes the onions more delectable *and* preserves their color.

2 teaspoons black peppercorns

2 medium red onions, peeled, trimmed, halved through the root ends, and sliced into paper-thin half-moons

1 cup (240 ml) white wine vinegar

1 cup (240 ml) water

¼ cup (50 g) granulated white sugar

2 tablespoons (24 g) kosher salt

1. Divide the peppercorns between four *clean* ½ pint (236 ml) or two *clean* 1 pint (472 ml) jars or other containers. Pack the sliced onions into the jars.

2. Whisk the vinegar, water, sugar, and salt in a bowl or measuring vessel until the sugar and salt dissolve. Pour this mixture evenly over the onions, leaving about ½ inch (1 cm) headspace in each jar. Cover or seal, then refrigerate to steep for 2 days before enjoying.

More

Divide 1 teaspoon cumin seeds, 1 teaspoon coriander seeds, and/or 6 whole cloves between the jars.

Cocktail Onions

MAKES: about 4 cups (960 ml)
FRIDGE: up to 1 month after steeping
FREEZER: no

You can't make a gimlet without a cocktail onion. And why use a pale, processed version from a jar when you can make cocktail onions that retain their spicy vibrancy and have a bit more herbal flavor? Use only *fresh* pearl onions. Yes, it's a pain to peel them. But the frozen ones just get too mushy.

Water to blanch the pearl onions

2½ pounds (1.1 kg) fresh pearl onions (do not use frozen)

A big bowl of ice water to cool down the pearl onions

4 cups (1 quart or 960 ml) water

½ cup (96 g) plus 1 teaspoon kosher salt

1½ cups (360 ml) apple cider vinegar

½ teaspoon celery seeds

½ teaspoon dill seeds

½ teaspoon yellow mustard seeds

1. Bring a large saucepan of water to a boil over high heat. Add the pearl onions and blanch for 1 minute from the moment they go in the water. Drain the onions in a colander set in the sink, then transfer to a large bowl of ice water. Cool for 10 minutes.

2. Pick up an onion, cut off the root end, and gently squeeze the softer, inner onion out of its wet, papery skin. Repeat with the remaining onions. Discard the skins.

3. Whisk 4 cups (960 ml) water and ½ cup (65 g) salt in a large bowl until the salt dissolves. Add the onions. Refrigerate for 24 hours.

4. Bring the vinegar, celery seeds, dill seeds, mustard seeds, and remaining 1 teaspoon salt to a boil in a large saucepan set over medium-high heat. Drain the onions and add them to the pan. Bring the liquid back to a boil, then turn off the heat and remove the pan from the burner. Cool at room temperature for no more than 1 hour.

5. Pack the onions and their brine into four *clean* ½ pint (236 ml) jars, two *clean* 1 pint (472 ml) jars, or one *clean* 1 quart (1 liter) jar, leaving about ½ inch (1 cm) headspace in each. Cover or seal, then refrigerate to steep for 2 days before enjoying.

More

Add heat by adding up to 4 dried árbol chilis with the various seeds.

Pickled Ginger

MAKES: about 4 cups (960 ml)
FRIDGE: up to 1 month after steeping
FREEZER: no

What sort of ginger should you use for gari or pickled ginger, familiar from sushi counters? If it were easy to find, we'd call for only young, baby ginger because of its mild flavor and high sugar count, preferably with almost no skin, just a translucent outer coating. But we have to go with what's available in North American and European markets. So look for juicy ginger roots that look like palms with lots of knobs (or fingers). The skin should be supple and fragrant, certainly not a husk (with fibrous ginger inevitably underneath). We forgo the now-customary food coloring. The ginger can stand on its own.

1½ pounds (680 g) fresh ginger, preferably the knobs off larger sections, peeled

Water to blanch and cool down the ginger

2 cups (240 ml) *unseasoned* rice vinegar

½ cup (100 g) granulated white sugar

1 tablespoon (12 g) kosher salt

1. Thinly slice the ginger into coins and strips. We use a mandoline (with cut-safe gloves!) but you can use a sharp, thin knife if you've got lots of patience.

2. Bring a medium saucepan of water to a boil over high heat. Add the ginger and cook for exactly 40 seconds from the second the ginger hits the water. Drain *immediately* in a colander set in the sink, then repeatedly rinse with cold water to stop the cooking, shaking the colander to rearrange the ginger pieces and get rid of as much water as possible.

3. Clean and dry your hands or put on culinary kitchen gloves. Pick up the ginger by handfuls and gently but firmly squeeze them dry over the sink before packing into four *clean*, *heat-safe*, ½ pint

Cocktail Onions (page 258)

(236 ml) jars or two *clean, heat-safe,* 1 pint (472 ml) jars or other containers.

4. Bring the vinegar, sugar, and salt to a boil in a small saucepan set over high heat, stirring often at first to dissolve the sugar. Divide the hot syrup between the jars, leaving about ½ inch (1 cm) headspace in each. Cover or seal. Cool at room temperature for no more than 1 hour, then refrigerate to steep for 2 days before enjoying.

Next
Beyond sushi and maki, pile pickled ginger on a smear of mayonnaise (particularly Kewpie mayonnaise) with your next tuna or salmon burger.

Pickled Turmeric

MAKES: about 4 cups (960 ml)
FRIDGE: up to 1 month after steeping
FREEZER: no

Here's our version of a Gujarati specialty: haldi ka achar (sometimes just called achar or achaar). Essentially, it's lemon-pickled fresh turmeric, a vibrant bite of sour-herbal flavor that's guaranteed to perk up curries, stews, and braises when used as a garnish. Although we prefer turmeric's straightforward, earthy-musky flavor, check the MORE section to use the more traditional spice blend for the brine.

> 1⅓ pounds (605 g) fresh turmeric, peeled and julienned (about 4 cups)
>
> 2 teaspoons kosher salt
>
> 1½ cups (360 ml) lemon juice, preferably freshly squeezed
>
> A neutral-flavored oil, such as canola or vegetable oil, as necessary to cover the vegetable

1. Toss the turmeric matchsticks and salt in a large bowl until the bits are well salted. Pack the strips into four *clean* ½ pint (236 ml) jars or two *clean* 1 pint (472 ml) jars or other containers, making sure none stick up to impede sealing the jars.

2. Divide the lemon juice evenly between the jars. Add enough vegetable oil to cover the turmeric strips, leaving about ½ inch (1 cm) headspace in each jar.

3. Cover or seal tightly, then refrigerate, shaking the jars about every 2 days but making sure the turmeric is always submerged in the lemon juice. Steep for 1 week before enjoying.

More
If you want to add more of the traditional spice blend, stem, split, and thinly slice up to 2 red bird's eye chilis and add them to the jars before the lemon juice. And add 2 teaspoons yellow mustards seeds, crushed, and 1 teaspoon fenugreek seeds to each jar. The lemon juice will get murkier from the crushed seeds.

Pickled Green Tomatoes

MAKES: about 28 tomato quarters
FRIDGE: up to 1 month after pickling
FREEZER: no

Pickled green tomatoes are briny, sour, and crunchy. They're great with just about any deli sandwich, just about anything off the grill, or even on their own as a mid-afternoon appetite quencher. They're made with unripe tomatoes, not tomato varietals that ripen green. Unripe, the tomatoes are a bit astringent and quite hard. Both problems are solved by the boiling brine poured over the quarters.

> 1 pound 1 ounce (480 g) *small,* unripe green tomatoes (about 7), quartered
>
> 1 cup (240 ml) distilled white vinegar
>
> 1 cup (240 ml) water
>
> 2 medium garlic cloves, peeled and smashed
>
> 2 tablespoons (24 g) kosher salt
>
> 1 tablespoon (12.5 g) granulated white sugar
>
> 1 teaspoon dried dill
>
> ½ teaspoon ground dried turmeric

1. Pack (but don't crush) the green tomato quarters in four *clean, heat-safe,* ½ pint (236 ml) jars; two *clean, heat-safe,* 1 pint (472 ml) jars; or one *clean, heat-safe,* 1 quart (1 liter) jar or other container.

2. Stir the vinegar, water, garlic, salt, sugar, dill, and turmeric in a medium saucepan set over medium-high heat until the sugar dissolves. Bring to a full boil, stirring occasionally.

3. Pour the hot brine over the tomato quarters, leaving about ½ inch (1 cm) headspace in the jar(s). Cover or seal. Cool at room temperature for no more than 1 hour, then refrigerate to steep for 3 days before enjoying.

More
Add up to 1 teaspoon yellow mustard seeds, ½ teaspoon ground dried ginger, and/or ½ teaspoon ground black pepper with the other spices in the brine.

Giardiniera

MAKES: about 4 cups (960 ml)
FRIDGE: up to 1 month after steeping
FREEZER: no

To get the perfect, luxurious texture, this Italian blend of pickled vegetables is traditionally *cooked* as the vegetables and brine are steamed or boiled inside a canner. Since we're not using that old-school method, we must *simmer* the vegetables in the brine before we bottle them. It's a bit of work; but the results are flavorful, briny, sour, and crunchy, a perfect condiment with hard aged cheeses and sliced salami.

- 1⅓ cups (320 ml) white wine vinegar
- 1⅓ cups (320 ml) distilled white vinegar
- 1⅓ cups (320 ml) water
- 4 teaspoons (17 g) granulated white sugar
- 4 teaspoons (16 g) kosher salt
- ½ teaspoon black peppercorns
- ½ teaspoon red pepper flakes
- 4 whole cloves
- 2 dried bay leaves
- ½ pound (225 g) *small* cauliflower florets (about 2 cups)
- 6 ounces (170 g) baby carrots (or small snacking carrots), each cut *lengthwise* into thirds
- 3 ounces (85 g) fresh pearl onions, peeled; or thawed frozen pearl onions (about ¾ cup of either)
- 1 medium red or yellow bell pepper, stemmed, cored, and cut into ½-inch-wide (1-cm-wide) strips
- 1 large celery stalk, trimmed, halved lengthwise, and cut into 2 inch (5 cm) pieces
- 2 tablespoons (30 ml) olive oil

1. Stir both vinegars, the water, sugar, salt, peppercorns, red pepper flakes, cloves, and bay leaves in a very large saucepan until the sugar dissolves. Set it over medium-high heat and bring to a boil, stirring occasionally.

2. Add the cauliflower, carrots, onions, bell pepper, and celery. Cook, stirring occasionally, for 10 minutes from when the vegetables hit the liquid.

3. Turn off the heat and remove the pan from the burner. Divide the oil between four *clean* ½ pint (236 ml) jars, two *clean* 1 pint (472 ml) jars, or one *clean* 1 quart (1 liter) jar or other container. Add the vegetables, aromatic spices, and as much brine as you can, leaving about ½ inch (1 cm) headspace in the jar(s). Cool at room temperature for no more than 1 hour. Cover or seal, then refrigerate to steep for 2 days before enjoying.

Next
Giardiniera is terrific in omelets and frittatas. Drain some of the vegetables, then add them to the eggs about as you would any other ingredient.

Dilly Beans

MAKES: about 4 cups (960 ml)
FRIDGE: up to 1 month after steeping
FREEZER: no

Although pickled green beans are usually made with fatter, more traditional green beans, we can use more tender and flavorful French green beans (aka haricots verts) in refrigerator pickling because we're not worried about turning them mushy from the canning process. We end up with thinner beans, almost tidbits, arranged in pretty layers or standing up straight in the jars. The results are more pleasing to the eye *and* more delicious for the palate.

> 2 pounds (900 g) thin green beans, preferably haricots verts
>
> Water to blanch the green beans and a big bowl of ice water to cool them down
>
> 2 medium garlic cloves, peeled and thinly sliced
>
> 1 teaspoon yellow mustard seeds
>
> 1 teaspoon red pepper flakes
>
> 4 fresh dill sprigs
>
> 1 cup (240 ml) water
>
> 2 cups (480 ml) distilled white vinegar
>
> 2 tablespoons (24 g) kosher salt

1. Tip and tail the green beans, then trim them to fit in the container(s) you've chosen (see step 3), either standing up or lying on their sides.

2. Bring a large saucepan of water to a boil over high heat. Add the beans and blanch for 1 minute from the time they hit the water. Drain in a colander set in the sink, then dump the beans into a large bowl of ice water.

3. Divide the garlic, yellow mustard seeds, red pepper flakes, and dill sprigs among four *clean*, *heat-safe*, ½ pint (236 ml) jars; two *clean*, *heat-safe*, 1 pint (472 ml) jars; or one *clean*, *heat-safe*, 1 quart (1 liter) jar or other container(s). Drain the beans and put them in the jars, too, either standing up like soldiers or lying on their sides.

4. Bring 1 cup (240 ml) water, the vinegar, and salt to a boil in a medium saucepan set over high heat, stirring until the salt dissolves. Pour this very hot mixture over the beans, leaving about ½ inch (1 cm) headspace in the jar(s). Cover or seal. Cool at room temperature for no more than 1 hour, then refrigerate to steep for 3 days before enjoying.

Next
Drain and mince a few dilly beans to add to chicken or tuna salad.

Vinegary Cherry Tomatoes

MAKES: about 4 cups (960 ml)
FRIDGE: up to 3 weeks after steeping
FREEZER: no

Vinegar lovers, take heart! Here's a recipe that mutes the sweetness of tomatoes while maintaining their more fruit-like flavor notes. Maybe a pickle like this one isn't a big surprise. If you love salads, you already know tomatoes love vinegar. In that case, pickling cherry tomatoes makes them even more irresistible. The only trick is to use very small cherry tomatoes, not the larger ones commonly found still on the vine, nor even the oversized ones often at the supermarket's salad bar. Smaller tomatoes fit better in the jars. One note: The longer they sit, the more sour they get!

> 1 pound (450 g) *small* cherry tomatoes (about 2 pints)
>
> 2 medium garlic cloves, peeled
>
> 1 teaspoon black peppercorns
>
> 2 fresh thyme sprigs
>
> 1¼ cups (300 ml) white wine vinegar
>
> 1¼ cups (300 ml) water
>
> 2 tablespoons (25 g) granulated white sugar
>
> 1 tablespoon (12 g) kosher salt

1. Poke each tomato with a toothpick or bamboo skewer a few times to help the brine get in.

2. Pack the tomatoes, garlic, peppercorns, and thyme evenly into four *clean* ½ pint (236 ml) jars, two *clean* 1 pint (472 ml) jars, or one *clean* 1 quart (1 liter) jar or other container.

3. Bring the vinegar, water, sugar, and salt to a boil in a medium saucepan set over medium-high heat, stirring until the sugar dissolves. Once the mixture is at a full boil, turn off the heat and set the pan off the burner to cool at room temperature for 15 minutes.

4. Pour the warm brine into the jar(s), leaving about ½ inch (1 cm) headspace. Cover or seal. Refrigerate to steep for 2 days before enjoying.

Next
We love these tomatoes in grain salads, particularly ones with wheatberries, millet, or brown rice. Or even in lentil salads with lots of shredded carrots.

Pickled Asparagus

MAKES: about 32 asparagus pickles
FRIDGE: up to 2 weeks after steeping
FREEZER: no

The key to successful pickled asparagus is threefold: 1) pencil-thin asparagus spears that 2) are firm enough to stand up straight when held in your hand and 3) have leaf-like bracts that are quite tight at the top of the spears. You can shave thicker spears down with a vegetable peeler, but they'll inevitably get floppy and won't result in still-crunchy pickles. We keep the spices here fairly simple, although we love the little bit of warmth the cinnamon stick adds to the sour brine.

> 1¾ pounds (790 g) pencil-thin asparagus spears (about 32), trimmed of their woody ends
> 2 cups (480 ml) distilled white vinegar
> 2 cups (480 ml) water
> ½ cup (100 g) granulated white sugar
> 2 tablespoons (24 g) kosher salt
> 1 medium garlic clove, peeled and minced
> One 3 inch (7.5 cm) cinnamon stick
> 2 dried bay leaves

1. Stand the spears up in a *clean, heat-safe,* tall, 1 quart (1 liter) jar or other vessel. Trim the bottom of any spears that would keep you from sealing the jar, so that they're all about ½ inch (1 cm) from the top of the jar.

2. Bring the vinegar, water, sugar, salt, garlic, cinnamon stick, and bay leaves to a full boil in a medium saucepan set over medium-high heat, stirring constantly at first until the sugar dissolves. Pour this hot brine over the asparagus spears in the jar. They should all be submerged.

3. Cool at room temperature for no more than 1 hour. Cover or seal, then refrigerate to steep for 2 days before enjoying.

Tip
When we serve these as a snack before dinner we provide long-handled forks so everyone can nab a spear without handling the entire lot in the dish.

Pickled Celery

MAKES: about 4 cups (960 ml)
FRIDGE: up to 1 month after steeping
FREEZER: no

Celery stays crunchier during refrigerator pickling than its near flavor-kin, fennel. So it's a better choice to go along with potato pancakes, corned beef, tagines, or even grilled chops. Since celery offers vaguely anise notes, we feel it also benefits from a bigger range of flavors as a counter-balance: a little aromatic from dill, a little bright from lemon zest, and a more complicated mix of spices from the pickling blend. One warning: The brine *will* quickly turn cloudy. Keep the pickled celery cold in the fridge and use it within the time we recommend.

> 12 celery stalks, cut lengthwise into halves or even thirds, each piece then cut into ½ inch (1 cm) segments (about 4 cups)
> 6 fresh dill sprigs
> 2 tablespoons (12 g) finely grated lemon zest
> 2 teaspoons dehydrated onion flakes
> 1⅓ cups (320 ml) white wine vinegar
> ⅔ cup (160 ml) water
> 6 tablespoons (75 g) granulated white sugar
> 2 tablespoons (15 g) mixed pickling spice
> 2 tablespoons (24 g) kosher salt

Left to right: Vinegary Cherry Tomatoes (page 263) and Pickled Asparagus (page 264)

1. Divide the celery, dill, zest, and dehydrated onion among four *clean*, *heat-safe*, ½ pint (236 ml) jars or two *clean*, *heat-safe*, 1 pint (472 ml) jars. Or put it all in one *clean*, *heat-safe*, 1 quart (1 liter) jar or other container.

2. Bring the vinegar, water, sugar, pickling spice, and salt to a full boil in a medium saucepan set over medium-high heat, stirring at first until the sugar dissolves.

3. Pour this hot brine over the celery mixture in the jar(s), leaving about ½ inch (1 cm) headspace in each jar. Cool at room temperature for no more than 1 hour. Cover or seal, then refrigerate to steep for 2 days before enjoying.

More
We love a couple of these pickled celery bits in martinis!

Pickled Red Cabbage

MAKES: about 4 cups (960 ml)
FRIDGE: up to 1 month after steeping
FREEZER: no

Not sauerkraut, but *pickled* cabbage. The difference has to do with the missing funky sourness, made by the room-temperature fermentation that sauerkraut undergoes to create that flavor. That said, pickled red cabbage is *definitely* sour, little threads that are a wake-up call on a plate or in a sandwich. It's also incredibly staining. (Trust us.) Pickled red cabbage makes an easy side salad when mixed with other chopped vegetables and a little olive oil.

> 12 ounces (340 g) finely shredded cored red cabbage (about 6 cups)
> 2 teaspoons kosher salt
> 1 cup (240 ml) red wine vinegar
> 1 cup (240 ml) water
> 2 tablespoons (25 g) granulated white sugar
> ½ teaspoon ground black pepper

1. Toss the cabbage and salt in a large bowl until the cabbage is evenly salted. Set aside at room temperature for 2 hours.

2. Clean and dry your hands or put on culinary kitchen gloves (which will protect your hands from long-lasting stains). Pick up the cabbage by handfuls and squeeze them dry over the sink before putting them in a second bowl.

3. When all the cabbage has been squeezed, stir in the vinegar, water, sugar, and black pepper until well combined (the sugar must fully dissolve).

4. Pack this mixture into four *clean* ½ pint (236 ml) jars, two *clean* 1 pint (472 ml) jars, or one *clean* 1 quart (1 liter) jar or other container(s), leaving about ½ inch (1 cm) headspace in the jar(s). Cover or seal, then refrigerate to steep for 2 days before enjoying.

Tip
The easiest way to shred cabbage is to cut the head in half, core it, and shred it through the large holes of a box grater starting with a rounded side. Or you can just buy shredded red cabbage in bags in the produce section (although the packaged pieces will have dried out a bit and the pickle won't be as tender).

Pickled Radishes

MAKES: about 4 cups (960 ml)
FRIDGE: up to 1 month after steeping
FREEZER: no

These crunchy wonders are the perfect snack before dinner, especially if you have a little dish of ground black pepper or even Sweet Red Chili Sauce (page 349) nearby for dipping. There are dozens of types of radishes on the market. Use almost any you like, provided they have a uniform size and aren't bigger than golf balls (the slices have to fit in the jars!). We cool the brine a bit before pouring it onto the radish slices to 1) keep them a little crunchier and 2) preserve more of their peppery spike.

1 pound (450 g) radishes, cleaned, trimmed, and sliced into thin rounds

1½ cups (360 ml) water

1¼ cups (300 ml) *unseasoned* rice vinegar

1 cup (200 g) granulated white sugar

1 tablespoon (12 g) kosher salt

1. Divide the radishes among four *clean* ½ pint (236 ml) jars or two *clean* 1 pint (472 ml) jars. Or put them all in one *clean* 1 quart (1 liter) jar.

2. Bring the water, vinegar, sugar, and salt to a full boil in a medium saucepan set over medium-high heat, stirring at first until the sugar dissolves. Turn off the heat, remove the pan from the burner, and cool at room temperature for 10 minutes.

3. Pour this brine over the radishes, leaving about ½ inch (1 cm) headspace in the jar(s). Cool at room temperature for no more than 1 hour. Cover or seal, then refrigerate to steep for 2 days before enjoying.

Next
Pickled radishes are great with fried chicken, especially Korean fried chicken in a ginger sauce.

Gingery Pickled Broccoli

MAKES: about 4 cups (960 ml)
FRIDGE: up to 3 weeks after steeping
FREEZER: no

The flavor of these pickled florets rides the line between our refrigerator pickling and more standard, funky fermentation. The amount of natural sugar in the vegetable lets us push the pickle closer to the old-school method even in the fridge (about as we will do with kimchis in the next chapter). We've added lots of fresh ginger, then balanced its spark with plenty of spices. The results are probably better served with cocktails than as a condiment, although we've certainly eaten our share with Korean pancakes like yachaejeon and buchimgae.

1 pound (450 g) *small* broccoli florets, each about 1½ x 1 inch (4 x 2.5 cm); or larger florets stemmed and broken into smaller pieces

3 medium garlic cloves, peeled and minced

1 tablespoon (15 g) minced peeled fresh ginger

1½ teaspoons dill seeds

1 teaspoon coriander seeds

1 teaspoon brown mustard seeds

1¼ cups (320 ml) *unseasoned* rice vinegar

1¼ cups (320 ml) water

2 tablespoons (25 g) granulated white sugar

2 teaspoons kosher salt

1. Mix the broccoli, garlic, ginger, dill seeds, coriander seeds, and mustard seeds in a large bowl until the spices and aromatics are even throughout. Pack this spiced broccoli mixture into four *clean* ½ pint (236 ml), two *clean* 1 pint (472 ml) jars, or one *clean* 1 quart (1 liter) jar or other container.

2. Whisk the vinegar, water, sugar, and salt in a large bowl until the sugar dissolves. Pour over the broccoli mixture in the jars, leaving about ½ inch (1 cm) headspace in the jar(s). Cover or seal, then refrigerate to steep for 1 week before enjoying.

Next
Finely chop the pickled florets to add them to grain salads or as a final condiment (with chili crisp!) to simple vegetable stir-fries.

Fiery Sugar Snaps

MAKES: about 4 cups (960 ml)
FRIDGE: up to 3 weeks after steeping
FREEZER: no

Sugar snap peas are so flavorful that they readily take to spicy aromatics and a brine to become crunchy sweet-and-sour pickles. If you want to go all out, use your own Red Curry Paste (page 230). You *must* trim the peas of their leafy ends. You *can* also zip out the tough fibrous membranes along the inner curves if you don't like the chewy texture…or leave them be for a simpler prep.

1 pound (450 g) sugar snap peas, trimmed

1 cup (240 ml) *unseasoned* rice vinegar

1 cup (240 ml) water

2 medium garlic cloves, peeled and smashed

1 tablespoon (18 g) red curry paste (or use your own homemade, page 230)

1 tablespoon (12.5 g) granulated white sugar

2 teaspoons kosher salt

1. Pack the sugar snap peas like standing soldiers in four *clean* ½ pint (236 ml) jars or two *clean* 1 pint (472 ml) jars. Or pack them in layers of standing soldiers in a *clean* 1 quart (1 liter) jar or other vessel.

2. Bring the vinegar, water, garlic, curry paste, sugar, and salt to a full boil in a medium saucepan set over medium-high heat, stirring at first to dissolve the paste and the sugar. Turn off the heat, remove the pan from the burner, and cool to room temperature, about 2 hours.

3. Stir the brine again, then divide it between the jars or pour it into the single, larger jar, leaving about ½ inch (1 cm) headspace. Cover or seal, then refrigerate to steep for 1 week before enjoying.

More
Substitute yellow curry paste for a milder flavor or green curry paste for a wilder, funkier flavor.

Hot and Sour Pickled Okra

MAKES: about 4 cups (960 ml)
FRIDGE: up to 2 weeks after steeping
FREEZER: no

The best okra for pickles are the smallest, thinnest spears you can find. The fatter and larger the spear, the tougher it is. Fresh okra can be tough to track down outside of the US South, but you can usually find it in the produce section of East Indian markets. Because we don't cook the okra,

but instead soak it in a hot brine, it never develops any of its unattractive slime. These crisp pickles are the perfect accompaniment to sweet, frozen drinks on a summer evening.

Up to 2 fresh green serrano chilis, stemmed and thinly sliced

2 medium garlic cloves, peeled and thinly sliced

1 teaspoon caraway seeds

1 teaspoon black peppercorns

1 pound (450 g) *small thin* okra pods, stemmed

1½ cups (360 ml) white wine vinegar

1½ cups (360 ml) water

2 tablespoons (24 g) kosher salt

1 tablespoon (12.5 g) granulated white sugar

1. Divide the chili slices, garlic, caraway seeds, and peppercorns evenly between two *clean, heat-safe,* 1 pint (472 ml) jars or other containers. (The okra spears will generally not fit easily in ½ pint or 236 ml jars.)

2. Pack the okra into the jars by standing them up like soldiers. It helps to reverse their directions: some with tips down, some with tips up. Make sure none are so tall that you can't seal the jars.

3. Bring the vinegar, water, salt, and sugar to a full boil in a medium saucepan set over medium-high heat, stirring at first until the salt and sugar dissolve.

4. Pour the brine over the okra in the jars, leaving about ½ inch (1 cm) headspace in each. Cover or seal. Cool at room temperature for no more than 1 hour, then refrigerate to steep for 1 week before enjoying.

More
Omit the caraway seeds and peppercorns. Instead, add 2 teaspoons mixed pickling spice to the pan with the salt and sugar before boiling.

Spicy-Garlicky Cauliflower Pickles

MAKES: about 4 cups (960 ml)
FRIDGE: up to 1 month after steeping
FREEZER: no

We keep these pickled cauliflower florets from becoming too squishy by cooling the brine before we pour it into the jars. The florets need to soften a little, but not as much as in more traditional canning. We want to preserve as much crunch as we can! The brine will get murky after a bit because of the way cauliflower breaks down with salt. Use your nose to determine whether the pickles are still good. Be safe, not sorry.

- 2 pounds (900 g) *small* cauliflower florets (each about 1½ x 1 inch or 4 x 2.5 cm), any tough stems removed
- 2 fresh red jalapeño or Fresno chilis, stemmed and thinly sliced
- 8 medium garlic cloves, peeled and thinly sliced
- ½ teaspoon cumin seeds
- ½ teaspoon brown mustard seeds
- 1¼ cups (300 ml) distilled white vinegar
- 1¼ cups (300 ml) water
- 2 teaspoons (9 g) granulated white sugar
- 2 teaspoons kosher salt

1. Divide the florets, chilis, garlic, cumin seeds, and mustard seeds between four *clean* ½ pint (236 ml) jars, two *clean* 1 pint (472 ml) jars, or one *clean* 1 quart (1 liter) jar.

2. Bring the vinegar, water, sugar, and salt to a full boil in a medium saucepan set over medium-high heat, stirring at first until the sugar and salt dissolve. Turn off the heat and set the pan off the burner. Cool at room temperature for 15 minutes.

3. Fill the jar(s) with the still-warm brine, leaving about ½ inch (1 cm) headspace in each. Cover or seal. Cool at room temperature for no more than 1 hour, then refrigerate to steep for 3 days before enjoying.

Next
Skip the raita and serve these pickles next to rice and a curry of just about any sort. The pickles also make a great taco topping.

Pickled Tarragon Carrots

MAKES: about 4 cups (960 ml)
FRIDGE: up to 1 month after steeping
FREEZER: no

These small, crunchy, sweet-and-sour carrots are perfect treats, salty and garlicky, with that summery, herbal flavor of tarragon to balance the sweetness. When we call for *baby* carrots, we're not talking about immature carrots but rather those that have been cut down to fit a child's hand, sometimes called *snacking carrots*.

- Water to blanch and cool down the carrots
- 1 pound (450 g) baby (or snacking) carrots
- 4 fresh tarragon sprigs
- 4 medium garlic cloves, peeled and thinly sliced
- 1 teaspoon coriander seeds
- 1 teaspoon black peppercorns
- 1 dried bay leaf, broken in two even pieces
- 1¼ cups (300 ml) white wine vinegar
- 1¼ cups (300 ml) water
- ¼ cup (50 g) granulated white sugar
- 1 tablespoon (12 g) kosher salt

1. Bring a large saucepan of water to a boil over high heat. Add the carrots and cook for 3 minutes from the moment they hit the water, until just barely tender. They should be crunchy but not raw.

2. Drain in a colander set in the sink and rinse repeatedly with cold water to stop the cooking. Shake the colander repeatedly to get rid of excess water.

Front to back: Spicy-Garlicky Cauliflower Pickles (page 269) and Pickled Tarragon Carrots (page 269)

3. Pack the carrots, tarragon sprigs, garlic, coriander seeds, peppercorns, and bay leaf pieces into two *clean* 1 pint (472 ml) jars or one *clean* 1 quart (1 liter) jar or other container.

4. Bring the vinegar, 1¼ cups (300 ml) water, sugar, and salt to a full boil in that same pan set over medium-high heat, stirring at first to dissolve the sugar. Turn off the heat and set the pan off the burner. Cool at room temperature for 15 minutes.

5. Divide the brine among the jars or pour it into the larger jar, either way leaving about ½ inch (1 cm) headspace. Cover or seal. Cool at room temperature for no more than 1 hour, then refrigerate to steep for 3 days before enjoying.

More

For heat, stem and thinly slice 1 fresh red serrano chili and divide it among the jars with the carrots, herbs, and spices.

Pickled Eggplant

MAKES: about 4 cups (960 ml)
FRIDGE: up to 3 weeks after steeping
FREEZER: no

Don't fear raw eggplant, particularly after it's been salted to draw out excess moisture and then packed in olive oil. It becomes pure luxury: soft, fragrant, almost ambrosial in texture (but with lots of pucker). Pickled eggplant is great on a cheese or charcuterie board, so long as there are firm or even aged cheeses on the board. It's also great as a garnish with curries and tomato-based stews. And it's particularly appealing with salmon fillets off the grill, or wings out of the air fryer.

- 3 small eggplants (about 8 ounces or 225 g *each*)
- 1½ teaspoons kosher salt
- 1 cup (240 ml) red wine vinegar
- 4 medium garlic cloves, peeled and thinly sliced
- 1 teaspoon red pepper flakes
- 10 basil leaves
- Olive oil as necessary to cover the pickle

1. Peel the eggplants, then slice them into 1-inch-thick (2.5-cm-thick) rounds. Slice each of these rounds into ¼ inch (a little more than 0.5 cm) strips.

2. Toss the eggplant strips and salt in a large bowl until the strips are well and evenly salted. Set aside at room temperature for 4 hours.

3. Lay out lots of paper towels, then pour the eggplant strips onto them and gently press the strips between paper towels to remove as much moisture as you can without smashing the eggplant.

4. Put the strips back in their large bowl, then add the vinegar, garlic, and red pepper flakes. Toss well to combine. Divide this mixture along with the basil leaves between four *clean* ½ pint (236 ml) jars, two *clean* 1 pint (472 ml) jars, or one *clean* 1 quart (1 liter) jar or other container.

5. Pour enough olive oil into the jar(s) to cover the vegetables and aromatics, leaving about ½ inch (1 cm) headspace. It's important to create an anaerobic environment in the jars. In other words, every speck of eggplant must be submerged in the oil to prevent rot. Use a toothpick or a wooden skewer to get rid of any air pockets in the jar(s). Cover or seal, then refrigerate to steep for 2 days before enjoying.

Tip

Smaller eggplants have fewer seeds and are usually sweeter than larger ones.

Sweet-and-Sour Butternut Squash

MAKES: about 4 cups (960 ml)
FRIDGE: up to 3 weeks after steeping
FREEZER: no

Butternut squash is a great pickling vegetable because it's sweet and firm, so it retains some crunch while naturally balancing the vinegar and spices. Of course, you can make this recipe even easier by buying cubed butternut squash in the produce department. You'll need about 1¼ pounds (565 g) prepared squash…then you'll need to cut each piece into the smaller pieces required here.

- 1½ pounds (680 g) butternut squash (about 1 small), peeled, seeded, and cut into ½ inch (1 cm) cubes
- 1 tablespoon (12 g) kosher salt
- Water to rinse the squash
- 1¼ cups (300 ml) apple cider vinegar
- ½ cup (120 ml) water
- ½ cup (108 g) light brown sugar
- One 1 inch (2.5 cm) piece of fresh ginger, about the thickness of your thumb, peeled and sliced into thin rounds
- 2 medium garlic cloves, peeled and smashed
- 1 tablespoon (6 g) black peppercorns
- 6 whole cloves

1. Toss the butternut squash cubes and salt in a large bowl until the squash is well and evenly salted. Set aside at room temperature for 2 hours.

2. Pour the cubes into a colander set in the sink. Rinse well and repeatedly, shaking the colander to get rid of excess moisture. Pack the cubes into two *clean*, *heat-safe*, 1 pint (472 ml) jars or other containers.

3. Stir the vinegar, ½ cup (120 ml) water, brown sugar, ginger, garlic, peppercorns, and cloves in a medium saucepan set over medium-high heat until the brown sugar dissolves. Bring to a full boil, stirring occasionally. Reduce the heat to low and simmer for 10 minutes, stirring once or twice.

4. Pour the *hot* vinegar mixture through a strainer into the jars, leaving about ½ inch (1 cm) headspace in each. Cover or seal, then refrigerate to steep for 2 weeks before enjoying.

Next
These are the perfect pickles for banderillas, the appetizer skewers served with drinks in tapas bars. Skewer the cubes with Cornichons (page 255), Cocktail Onions (page 258), and Zucchini Pickles (page 252).

Pickled Jicama

MAKES: about 4 cups (960 ml)
FRIDGE: up to 1 month after steeping
FREEZER: no

Jicama is sturdier than you think. Raw, it's got a big crunch; a light, surprisingly watery texture; and a bright, almost cucumber flavor. It retains all those when pickled! The only trouble is peeling the thing. Unfortunately, prepared jicama, often available as cubes or sticks near the cut-up celery in the produce section, doesn't do well in this recipe. The cut vegetable has already lost a lot of its texture and flavor (because it's lost a lot of its moisture), so it's best to prep your own. For the easiest job peeling the behemoth, look for a jicama that has a smooth skin without many indentations or rough spots…and no mushy bits.

- 1 pound (450 g) jicama (about 1 medium)
- 1 tablespoon (12 g) kosher salt
- 1 cup (240 ml) *unseasoned* rice vinegar
- 1 cup (240 ml) water
- 3 tablespoons (38 g) granulated white sugar

1. Peel the jicama (a paring knife works better than a vegetable peeler) and slice it into ½-inch-thick (1-cm-thick) rounds. Slice each of these into matchsticks about 4 inches (10 cm) long. In fact, look at the jars or containers you'll use and cut the matchsticks to fit.

2. Mix the jicama sticks and salt in a large bowl until the vegetable is well salted. Set aside at room temperature for 2 hours.

3. Drain any liquid in the bowl, holding back the jicama with your clean hands as you tip the bowl over the sink. Lay paper towels on your work surface and pour the jicama pieces onto them. Blot them all dry with more paper towels.

4. Stand the jicama sticks up like soldiers in two *clean*, *heat-safe*, 1 pint (472 ml) jars or other containers.

5. Bring the vinegar, water, and sugar to a boil in a small saucepan set over high heat, stirring at first to dissolve the sugar. Pour the boiling solution over the jicama sticks, leaving about ½ inch (1 cm) headspace in each. Cover or seal. Cool at room temperature for no more than 1 hour, then refrigerate to steep for 2 days before enjoying.

Next
You need this pickled jicama for tacos!

Lime-Sesame Pickled Daikon

MAKES: about 4 cups (960 ml)
FRIDGE: up to 3 weeks after steeping
FREEZER: no

A daikon is a long, tubular, white root vegetable, as juicy as jicama but with a flavor more like a radish. It's somehow both refreshing and a little spicy. It morphs into tasty pickles with a little flavor boost, here not only with lime and sesame, but also orange zest and mirin (a sweetened rice wine). Look for fresh daikons that have no brown or mottled spots, an even color (more white than off-white), and a distinctly radish-like aroma. With this recipe, you've got the best garnish for a platter of grilled vegetables.

> 2 tablespoons (18 g) white sesame seeds
> 1½ pounds (680 g) daikon (about 1 medium)
> ½ cup (120 ml) *unseasoned* rice vinegar
> ¼ cup (60 ml) mirin
> ¼ cup (60 ml) lime juice, preferably freshly squeezed
> ¼ cup (60 ml) water
> 2 teaspoons (4 g) finely grated orange zest
> 2 teaspoons kosher salt

1. Toast the sesame seeds in a small skillet set over medium-low heat, stirring often, until lightly browned and fragrant, about 2 minutes. Pour the seeds into a large bowl and set aside at room temperature.

2. Use a vegetable peeler to peel the daikon. Then use that peeler to make long, thin strips from the vegetable (about 4 cups' worth). Pack these strips into four *clean* ½ pint (236 ml) jars, two *clean* 1 pint (472 ml) jars, or one *clean* 1 quart (1 liter) jar or other container.

3. Add the vinegar, mirin, lime juice, water, zest, and salt to the bowl with the sesame seeds. Whisk to combine. Pour this mixture over the daikon strips, leaving about ½ inch (1 cm) headspace in the jar(s). Use a spoon or a wooden skewer to push any strips into the marinade so they're all submerged.

4. Cover or seal, then shake the jars to mix up the spices among the strips. Again make sure the vegetable is covered in the brine. Refrigerate to steep for 2 days before enjoying.

More
Add up to 1 teaspoon red pepper flakes and/or 4 whole cloves to the pickling brine with the sesame seeds.

Pickled Daikon and Carrots

MAKES: about 4 cups (960 ml)
FRIDGE: up to 3 weeks after steeping
FREEZER: no

This pickle is ubiquitous at Vietnamese restaurants, tucked into bánh mì, garnishing fresh salads, and served with the fresh leafy herbs to be rolled up in rice paper wrappers with pork or shrimp. We also love this pickle on turkey sandwiches with lots of deli mustard. And we've been known to open a jar when we splurge on a hunk of pâté. We call for julienned vegetables: a tricky technique. You can often find julienned carrots in the produce section, sometimes sold as *matchstick carrots*. Julienned daikon is harder to track down. Peel and slice the root into ½-inch-thick (about 1-cm-thick) rounds, then slice these into matchsticks of the same width.

> One 10-ounce (285 g) bag of matchstick or julienned carrots
>
> 8 ounces (225 g) daikon (about half of 1 small), peeled and julienned (see headnote)
>
> 4 teaspoons (17 g) granulated white sugar
>
> 1 teaspoon kosher salt
>
> ¾ cup (180 ml) *unseasoned* rice vinegar
>
> Water as necessary to submerge the vegetables

1. Toss the carrots and daikon in a large bowl until well combined. Distribute the mixture among four *clean* ½ pint (236 ml) jars, two *clean* 1 pint (472 ml) jars, or one *clean* 1 quart (1 liter) jar or other container.

2. Divide the sugar and salt evenly between the jars or sprinkle them into the single one. Divide the vinegar evenly between the jars or pour it into the single jar. Fill the jars with enough water to submerge the vegetables but also leave about ½ inch (1 cm) headspace.

3. Cover or seal *tightly*, then shake the jars to mix well. Make sure the vegetables are still submerged. If not, open and rearrange. Refrigerate to steep for 2 days before enjoying.

Next
If you're not a fan of sauerkraut on hot dogs, try this condiment instead!

Sweet-and-Sour Pickled Beets

MAKES: about 4 cups (960 ml)
FRIDGE: up to 3 weeks after steeping
FREEZER: no

Beets take to pickling! The vinegar is a great balance to their sweet, earthy flavor. Although sweet-and-sour beets are often thickened with cornstarch, we prefer a more watery brine. Its texture doesn't interfere with the complex flavors and keeps the sturdy root vegetable pickle fresher and thus more appealing.

> Water to steam the beets
>
> 2 pounds (900 g) *small* red beets (none more than 2½ inches or 6.5 cm in diameter), trimmed, peeled, and cut into ¼-inch-thick (0.5-cm-thick) disks
>
> ½ cup (120 ml) red wine vinegar
>
> ¼ cup (85 g) honey
>
> ¼ cup (60 ml) water
>
> 1 teaspoon allspice berries
>
> 1 teaspoon yellow mustard seeds
>
> One 3 inch (7.5 cm) cinnamon stick, broken in half widthwise
>
> ½ teaspoon kosher salt
>
> ¼ teaspoon red pepper flakes

1. Pour about 1 inch (2.5 cm) water in a large saucepan, then fit it with a vegetable steamer. Bring the water to a boil over high heat. Add the beet slices to the steamer, cover, reduce the heat to low, and steam until crisp-tender, about 10 minutes. Cool for a few minutes, then transfer the beet slices to two *clean*, *heat-safe*, 1 pint (472 ml) jars or one *clean*, *heat-safe*, 1 quart (1 liter) jar or other container.

2. Bring the vinegar, honey, ¼ cup (60 ml) water, allspice, mustard seeds, cinnamon pieces, salt, and red pepper flakes to a simmer in a small saucepan set over medium-high heat, stirring often at first to dissolve the honey. Reduce the heat to low and simmer *slowly* for 3 minutes.

3. Pour the hot vinegar mixture over the beets, covering them until there's only ½ inch (1 cm) headspace in the jar(s). If you've used two jars, make sure each gets a piece of the cinnamon stick and a fairly even amount of spices. Cover or seal. Cool at room temperature for no more than 1 hour, then refrigerate to steep for 2 days before enjoying.

Next
These pickled beets are wonderful with baba ghanoush or a cold tomato-eggplant salad.

Horseradish-Pickled Beets

MAKES: about 4 cups (960 ml)
FRIDGE: up to 3 weeks after steeping
FREEZER: no

These are large beet chunks, pickled in a horseradish-laced brine for bold flavor (along with a little ground dried ginger to bring out more earthy tones). Given the size of the chunks, this pickle works best in one 1 quart (1 liter) jar. One note: The brine will be cloudy because of the ground ginger, so don't be tempted to press the shelf life of these beets.

> 2 pounds (900 g) medium red beets (6–8 beets), trimmed, peeled, and quartered
>
> Water to simmer the beets
>
> 1 tablespoon (15 g) jarred prepared white or red horseradish
>
> 1 teaspoon kosher salt
>
> ½ teaspoon ground dried ginger
>
> 1¼ cups (300 ml) distilled white vinegar
>
> ¼ cup (60 ml) water
>
> ¼ cup (50 g) granulated white sugar

1. Put the beet quarters in a large saucepan and add enough water to cover them by 1 inch (2.5 cm). Bring to a boil over medium-high heat. Cover, reduce the heat to low, and simmer until tender when poked with the point of a knife, about 12 minutes.

2. Drain the beets in a colander set in the sink and cool for a few minutes. Pack the quarters into one *clean*, *heat-safe*, 1 quart (1 liter) jar or other container. Spoon the horseradish into the jar, then add the salt and ground ginger. Set aside.

3. Bring the vinegar, ¼ cup (60 ml) water, and sugar to a boil in a small saucepan set over high heat, stirring often at first until the sugar dissolves. Pour this hot mixture over the beet quarters. Cover or seal. Cool at room temperature

for no more than 1 hour, then refrigerate to steep for 2 days before enjoying.

More

For a brighter flavor, omit the ground dried ginger and substitute up to 1 tablespoon (15 g) minced peeled fresh ginger.

Pickled Roasted Beets

MAKES: about 4 cups (960 ml)
FRIDGE: up to 3 weeks after pickling
FREEZER: no

If you think you're not into beets, this may be the recipe to jump-start your appreciation of the root vegetable. Roasting beets before pickling them gives them a slightly bittersweet and certainly more sophisticated flavor. It calms their characteristic earthiness a bit, too. As with some other beet recipes, this one works best with a 1 quart (1 liter) jar or other container, so that it can easily hold the larger beet quarters.

> 2 pounds (900 g) *small* red beets (about 10), trimmed and peeled
>
> 1 teaspoon kosher salt
>
> ¼ teaspoon celery seeds
>
> ¼ teaspoon red pepper flakes
>
> ¾ cup (180 ml) apple cider vinegar
>
> ¼ cup (60 ml) water
>
> ¼ cup (85 g) honey

1. Position the rack in the center of the oven; heat the oven to 400°F (200°C), no fan or convection. Wrap the beets in a tightly sealed aluminum foil packet, set it on a baking sheet, and roast until tender when pierced with a knife, about 45 minutes.

2. Set the packet on a wire rack and (carefully!) open it. Cool for a few minutes, then cut the beets into quarters. Put them in a medium bowl and toss with the salt, celery seeds, and red pepper flakes until well coated. Pack all of this into one *clean*, *heat-safe*, 1 quart (1 liter) jar or other container.

3. Bring the vinegar, water, and honey to a boil in a small saucepan set over high heat, stirring often at first to dissolve the honey. Pour this hot syrup over the beets. Cover or seal. Cool at room temperature for no more than 1 hour, then refrigerate for 1 day before enjoying.

More

Add one 3 inch (7.5 cm) cinnamon stick and/or 2 *green* cardamom pods to the jar with the seasoned beet quarters.

Harvard Beets

MAKES: about 4 cups (960 ml)
FRIDGE: up to 3 weeks after steeping
FREEZER: no

What's with calling beets in a more-sweet-than-sour syrup "Harvard beets"? One theory is that the beets were so named after Harvard picked crimson as its school color in the early twentieth century. Another is that this is actually an English pickle from the town of Harwood that got sweeter as it crossed the Atlantic and was slowly mispronounced to its current name. Whatever the reason, the syrup is usually thickened with cornstarch—but we prefer an old-school sugar syrup because the flavors are more complex and so more pleasing.

    2 pounds (900 g) medium red beets (no more than
        3½ inches or 9 cm in diameter, 6–8 beets)
    Water to simmer the beets
    1 teaspoon ground black pepper
    ½ teaspoon kosher salt
    1¼ cups (250 g) granulated white sugar
    ¾ cup (180 ml) water
    6 tablespoons (90 ml) apple cider vinegar
    6 tablespoons (90 ml) red wine vinegar

1. Trim and peel the beets, then slice them into ¼-inch-thick (0.5-cm-thick) rounds. Place in a large saucepan and fill it with enough water to cover the slices by 1 inch (2.5 cm). Set the pan over medium-high heat and bring to a boil, stirring occasionally. Reduce the heat to low and simmer until the slices are crisp-tender when pierced with a knife, about 15 minutes.

2. Drain the slices in a colander set in the sink. Cool for a few minutes. Layer them with the pepper and salt in one *clean*, *heat-safe* 1 quart (1 liter) jar or other container.

3. Bring the sugar, ¾ cup (180 ml) water, and both vinegars to a boil in a medium saucepan set over high heat, stirring often at first to dissolve the sugar. Boil undisturbed for 1 minute.

4. Pour this hot syrup over the beet slices. Cover or seal. Cool at room temperature for no more than 1 hour, then refrigerate to steep for 2 days before enjoying.

Next

Make beet hummus by putting a couple of Harvard beet slices with lots of drained, canned chickpeas, some tahini, a little lemon juice, salt, and pepper in a food processor; cover and process until smooth.

Preserved Lemons

MAKES: 6 preserved lemons
FRIDGE: up to 1 month after brining
FREEZER: no

Salty preserved lemons are a staple in tagines, Moroccan stews, and much North African cooking. In addition to salty, ours are spicy from dried chilis—an added bonus. They're terrific as an addition to grain salads, pilafs, chopped vegetable salads, and even tabbouleh, purchased or homemade. In general, you eat only the rind of the lemons, not the squishy, inner flesh. Because

Left to right:
Pickled Roasted
Beets (page 275)
and Harvard Beets
(page 276)

we preserve these in the fridge, we have to open the lemons to give the salt and sugar a chance to get inside from the get-go.

- 1½ cups (300 g) granulated white sugar
- 1½ cups (175 g) kosher salt
- 6 small lemons (*each* about 2⅛ inches or 5.5 cm long and about 2 ounces or 58 g), scrubbed clean (see TIP)
- 4 dried árbol chilis
- 4 dried bay leaves

1. Mix the sugar and salt in a medium bowl until well combined.

2. Stand a lemon on its end and use a sharp knife to cut an X from the top down about two-thirds of the way. Repeat with the remaining lemons. Gently pry them open, like petals of a flower. Stuff the center and gaps in these petals with some of the sugar-salt mixture.

3. Pack the stuffed lemons into one *clean* 1 quart (1 liter) jar or other container. Shove the chilis and bay leaves among the lemons. Pour the remainder of the sugar-salt mixture over the lemons. Cover or seal, then refrigerate to brine for 3 weeks. At that time, the lemons should be submerged in liquid and ready to use. From now on, keep the lemons in and under the brine; rearrange any that stick up. Rinse the lemons before using.

Tip

Lemons are often coated in a food-grade, waxy seal to preserve them on the market's shelf. Before making preserved lemons, remove this coating so the salt and sugar can penetrate the skins: Wash the lemons under cool water, using a new sponge to rub them all over, even the ends, without nicking any of the zest.

Gingered Watermelon Rinds

MAKES: about 4 cups (960 ml)
FRIDGE: up to 3 weeks after steeping
FREEZER: no

Pickled watermelon rind is a *sticky*-sweet treat from the US South, served at barbecues and almost every summertime family reunion. You might expect these rind bits to be sour, given that the first part of this chapter is all about pickling. But there's a long tradition of pickling in sugar syrups…and more to come in this chapter! The bits of watermelon rind are like glacéed fruit, if somewhat larger. We didn't put this recipe back with other fruits preserved in sugar syrups because pickled watermelon rind is most often eaten at a Southern meal where you'd find any cucumber pickle.

- 1 pound (450 g) watermelon rind, any green outer skin peeled off and any fleshy red or pink bits removed, then cut into 1½ inch (4 cm) cubes (about 4 cups)
- ¼ cup (48 g) kosher salt
- Water to rinse, simmer, and cool the rind
- 2 cups (400 g) granulated white sugar
- 1 cup (240 ml) apple cider vinegar
- 1 tablespoon (15 g) minced peeled fresh ginger

1. Toss the cubed rind and salt in a large bowl until the rind bits are well and evenly coated. Cover and refrigerate for 24 hours.

2. Drain the cubes in a colander set in the sink. Rinse repeatedly with cool water to get off some of the salt, shaking the colander to rearrange the cubes and to get rid of as much water as you can.

3. Pour the cubes into a large saucepan and add enough water to cover the cubes by 2 inches (5 cm). Set the pan over medium-high heat and bring to a simmer. Reduce the heat to low and simmer slowly for 10 minutes. Drain the cubes again in that colander and rinse them repeatedly with cool water to stop the cooking.

4. Stir the sugar, vinegar, and ginger in the same large saucepan set over medium-high heat until the sugar dissolves. Bring to a full boil, stirring occasionally. Add the rind cubes and bring back to a boil, stirring often. Reduce the heat to low and simmer until tender, about 12 minutes.

5. Turn off the heat and remove the pan from the burner. Set aside at room temperature until cool to the touch, about 2 hours.

6. Divide the rind and syrup between four *clean* ½ pint (236 ml) jars, two *clean* 1 pint (472 ml) jars, or one *clean* 1 quart (1 liter) jar or other container, leaving about ½ inch (1 cm) headspace in the jar(s). Cover or seal. Refrigerate to steep for 2 days before enjoying.

Tip
The best way to make this pickle might be to save back watermelon rinds as you eat the melon. Cut the rind into 6 x 8 inch (15 x 20 cm) strips and wrap in plastic. They'll last about a week, covered, in the fridge. After that, you can peel off the green exterior and any fleshy bits of interior remaining on the rinds.

Sweet-and-Sour Cherries

MAKES: about 4 cups (960 ml)
FRIDGE: up to 2 weeks after steeping
FREEZER: no

These sweet cherries are steeped in a vinegar-laced sugar syrup to create a great condiment with barbecued or smoked meats. They can also be cut up and sprinkled over chopped, vinegar-based salads. The cherries take a while to steep, about 2 weeks. After that, it's safe to keep them around for only a short while because they will start to degrade. We leave the pits in the cherries so we don't break the skin's seal and let too much of the vinegary syrup inside. We also leave the stems on so they're easier to handle on cheese or charcuterie boards.

> 3 cups (600 g) granulated white sugar
> 1½ cups (360 ml) *white* balsamic vinegar
> Two 2-inch-wide (5-cm-wide) strips of orange zest
> 2 star anise pods
> 1 teaspoon fennel seeds
> 1½ pounds (680 g) *sweet* cherries, such as bing (about 3 cups), not pitted or stemmed

1. Combine the sugar, vinegar, orange zest, star anise pods, and fennel seeds in a large saucepan. Set over medium-high heat and stir until the sugar dissolves. Bring to a boil, stirring occasionally. Boil undisturbed for 2 minutes.

2. Turn off the heat, remove the pan from the burner, and stir in the cherries. Set aside at room temperature until cool to the touch, about 2 hours.

3. Transfer the cherries to four *clean* ½ pint (236 ml) jars, two *clean* 1 pint (472 ml) jars, or one *clean* 1 quart (1 liter) jar or other container, leaving about ½ inch (1 cm) headspace in the jar(s). Cover or seal, then refrigerate to steep for 2 weeks before enjoying.

Next
These cherries make a great addition to a salad with a soft cheese like Camembert, lots of chopped endive, and toasted pecans. Just remember to stem and pit the pickled cherries before using.

Spiced Pickled Cherries

MAKES: about 4 cups (960 ml)
FRIDGE: up to 3 weeks after steeping
FREEZER: no

These spiced cherries are great with almost anything battered and fried: chicken, fish, even artichoke hearts. Air-fried, too! (And boy, have we written books on that subject!) The cherries are also terrific with pâté or chopped liver, as well as alongside any runny cheese like goat Brie.

- 2 cups (480 ml) *unseasoned* rice vinegar
- ¾ cup (180 ml) water
- ½ cup (100 g) granulated white sugar
- ¼ cup (48 g) kosher salt
- 1 teaspoon black peppercorns
- 6 whole cloves
- 2 dried bay leaves
- 1 pound (450 g) large sweet cherries, such as bing cherries, pitted and halved (about 2½ cups)

1. Bring the vinegar, water, sugar, salt, peppercorns, cloves, and bay leaves to a simmer in a medium saucepan set over high heat, stirring constantly at first to dissolve the salt and sugar. Boil undisturbed for 1 minute.

2. Turn off the heat and remove the pan from the burner. Set aside until cool to the touch, about 3 hours.

3. Meanwhile, pack the cherries into four *clean* ½ pint (236 ml) jars, two *clean* 1 pint (472 ml) jars, or one *clean* 1 quart (1 liter) jar or other container.

4. Pour the cooled vinegar mixture over the cherries, leaving about ½ inch (1 cm) headspace in the jar(s). There may be a little extra syrup, but make sure all the spices go into the jar(s). Cover or seal, then refrigerate to steep for 2 days before enjoying.

More

You can use an equivalent amount of thawed, frozen cherries for this recipe. But make sure you save any liquid in the package after thawing and add it to the sugar mixture before boiling.

Pickled Spiced Pears

MAKES: about 4 cups (960 ml)
FRIDGE: up to 3 weeks after steeping
FREEZER: no

Reinvent the martini with a piece of pickled pear instead of an olive. But before you can use these tasty pears in a cocktail, you'll need to cut the halves down to smaller bits because we keep the pears in halves for preserving. Overall, we find they're more versatile in larger chunks: sliced for a cheese board or sandwiches, chunked for a salad or pilaf, or left in halves for a barbecue side.

- 3 cups (600 ml) white wine vinegar
- 2¼ cups (450 g) granulated white sugar
- The zest in strips from 1 medium orange
- One 2 inch (5 cm) piece of fresh ginger, about the width of your pinky, peeled and thinly sliced
- 1 teaspoon black peppercorns
- 1 teaspoon allspice berries
- One 3 inch (7.5 cm) cinnamon stick
- 10 whole cloves
- 5 ounces (145 g) *small* semi-firm pears, such as Bosc (about 6), stemmed, peeled, halved, and cored

1. Put the vinegar, sugar, orange zest, ginger, peppercorns, allspice berries, cinnamon stick, and cloves in a very large saucepan. Set it over medium-high heat and stir until the sugar dissolves. Bring to a low simmer (not a boil), stirring occasionally.

2. Add the pear halves and bring back to a low simmer. Reduce the heat to very low and simmer very slowly until the pears are cooked through, occasionally rearranging the halves, between

Top to bottom: Pickled Spiced Pears (page 280) and Sweet-and-Sour Cherries (page 279)

15 and 25 minutes, depending on the varietal. They're done when they've begun to turn translucent and a knife easily pierces them.

3. Turn off the heat and remove the pan from the burner. Use a slotted spoon to transfer the pear halves to one *clean*, *heat-safe*, 1 quart (1 liter) jar or other container.

4. Return the pan to the burner and bring the remaining liquid to a boil over high heat, stirring occasionally. Boil until reduced by about one-third from its original volume and slightly thickened, about 5 minutes. Strain the syrup through a fine-mesh sieve into the jar or container with the pear halves. Cover or seal, then refrigerate to steep for 1 week before enjoying.

Next

The vinegary syrup left from these pears is an excellent marinade or even a barbecue mop. Thin it out with an equal amount of wine or beer *by volume* before using.

Pickled Spiced Plums

MAKES: about 4 cups (960 ml)
FRIDGE: up to 3 weeks after steeping
FREEZER: no

Because plums have a gorgeous, summery, sweet flavor, we keep the other spices in this syrupy pickling brine to a minimum. And because a plum's skin is relatively tough, we prick the fruit so that the brine can indeed permeate it. It's crucial to use small plums so they can fit in the jar and be covered with that brine. If you need more brine, you'll need to repeat step 2, making a half or full batch of cooked brine to cover the plums in the jar.

> 2 pounds (900 g) *small*, firm red or purple plums (do not use Italian prune plums)
> 2 cups (400 g) granulated white sugar
> 1⅓ cups (320 ml) red wine vinegar

> Two ¼-inch-thick (0.5-cm-thick) slices of peeled fresh ginger
> One 3 inch (7.5 cm) cinnamon stick, broken into a few small pieces
> 8 whole cloves
> ½ teaspoon kosher salt

1. Use a toothpick or a bamboo skewer to pierce each plum repeatedly. Figure on 12–15 pokes per plum.

2. Put the sugar, vinegar, ginger, cinnamon stick, cloves, and salt in a large saucepan. Set it over medium-high heat and bring to a boil, stirring frequently at first to dissolve the sugar. Boil for 1 minute.

3. Add the plums, bring back to a boil, and remove immediately from the heat. Set aside at room temperature until cool to the touch, about 3 hours.

4. Use a slotted spoon to transfer the plums to one *clean* 1 quart (1 liter) jar. Strain the brine over the plums. Press them down to make sure they're submerged. Cover or seal, then refrigerate to steep for 1 week before enjoying.

More

For a much deeper flavor, replace the red wine vinegar with ⅔ cup white wine vinegar plus ⅔ cup balsamic vinegar.

Pickled Grapes

MAKES: about 4 cups (960 ml)
FRIDGE: up to 3 weeks after steeping
FREEZER: no

Pickled grapes make the best snacks! They're boldly spiced and certainly less sweet than off-the-vine grapes, but not as assertive as more traditional pickles and so perhaps a gentler afternoon treat. Pickled grapes are also great to put out anytime someone drops over for a glass of iced tea in the summer or a cup of hot tea in the winter.

½ cup (120 ml) red wine vinegar

½ cup (168 g) honey

¼ cup (60 ml) balsamic vinegar

3 tablespoons (41 g) dark brown sugar

2 tablespoons (30 ml) water

2 tablespoons (32 g) pomegranate molasses

1 small shallot (about ¾ ounce or 22 g), peeled and minced

1 teaspoon kosher salt

6 *green* cardamom pods

Two 2-inch-long (5-cm-long) strips of lemon zest

1⅓ pounds (605 g) red seedless grapes, stemmed (about 4 cups)

1. Mix the red wine vinegar, honey, balsamic vinegar, brown sugar, water, pomegranate molasses, shallot, salt, cardamom pods, and lemon zest in a large saucepan. Set the pan over medium-high heat and stir until the brown sugar dissolves. Bring to a boil, stirring occasionally.

2. Add the grapes, bring back to a boil, and remove from the heat. Set aside at room temperature until cool to the touch, about 2 hours.

3. Use a slotted spoon to transfer the grapes into four *clean* ½ pint (236 ml) jars, two *clean* 1 pint (472 ml) jars, or one *clean* 1 quart (1 liter) jar or other container. Strain the syrup through a fine-mesh sieve over the grapes in the jar(s), leaving about ½ inch (1 cm) headspace. Cover or seal, then refrigerate to steep for 3 days before enjoying.

More

For a much more assertive flavor, substitute date vinegar for the red wine vinegar and date syrup for the honey.

Pickled Kumquats

MAKES: about 4 cups (960 ml)
FRIDGE: up to 3 weeks after steeping
FREEZER: no

For a sour pop in cocktails, on a cheese board, with sliced smoked meats, or even alongside grilled brats, you've got to have a jar of these pickled kumquats on hand. For the proper pickling, the kumquats should be sliced into quite thin rounds, no more than ¼ inch (0.5 cm) thick. You'll need a sharp knife for the task. We find the heavier the knife, the better—so skip the paring knife. Or use a mandoline along with a hand guard or a cut-safe glove.

2 pounds (900 g) kumquats, thinly sliced and *seeded*

1¾ cups (350 g) granulated white sugar

1 cup (240 ml) white wine vinegar

1 cup (240 ml) water

¼ cup (48 g) kosher salt

One 4 inch (10 cm) piece of fresh ginger, about the size of your thumb, peeled and thinly sliced

1. Pack the kumquat slices into four *clean, heat-safe* ½ pint (236 ml) jars, two *clean, heat-safe* 1 pint (472 ml) jars, or one *clean, heat-safe* 1 quart (1 liter) jar or other container.

2. Put the sugar, vinegar, water, salt, and ginger in a medium saucepan. Set it over medium-high heat and bring to a boil, stirring constantly at first to dissolve the sugar and salt. Boil undisturbed for 1 minute.

3. Turn off the heat and take the pan off the burner. Cool at room temperature for 10 minutes. Pour the syrupy brine over the kumquats, leaving about ½ inch (1 cm) headspace in the jar(s). Cover or seal, then refrigerate to steep for 2 days before enjoying.

Next

For the best burger, top the patty with these pickled kumquats and Pickled Jalapeño Rings (page 255) or even Jalapeño Relish (page 167).

Garlic Confit (page 285)

Garlic Confit

MAKES: about 3 cups (720 ml)
FRIDGE: up to 6 weeks
FREEZER: up to 1 year

Freshly peeled garlic is the best bet for preserved softened garlic in oil, creating a milder, more caramelized flavor. But peeling the heads and cloves is admittedly a pain. Perhaps in the spirit of our shortcut recipes, a purchased jar of peeled garlic cloves is the easiest way to go. Note that the results will not be as stellar; but by adding some aromatics, we can make up for the inadequacies caused by long storage. So go ahead: Buy the giant jar of peeled cloves at a big-box store. A jar of garlic confit and a crunchy baguette make the perfect start for an evening at home.

> 2 cups extra virgin olive oil, plus more as necessary
> About 80 peeled garlic cloves (from about 10 medium heads)
> 3 short fresh rosemary sprigs
> 3 fresh thyme sprigs
> 3 dried árbol chilis
> 3 dried bay leaves

1. Combine all the ingredients in a medium saucepan. Set it over low heat and bring to a low simmer. Simmer slowly, reducing the heat more as necessary and stirring occasionally, until the garlic is tender and golden but not deeply browned, about 30 minutes.

2. Use a slotted spoon to transfer the garlic cloves to three *clean* ½ pint (236 ml) jars or other containers. Strain the oil into the jars, leaving about ½ inch (1 cm) headspace in each. Use a long toothpick or a bamboo skewer to move the vegetables around and get rid of any air pockets. Make sure no clove is sticking up above the oil. Add extra oil, if necessary. Cool at room temperature for no more than 1 hour. Cover or seal, then refrigerate or freeze.

Next

Don't throw out the oil, even after you've used the garlic. It's an excellent start for skillet sautés and many stews or braises—an aromatic punch of flavors.

Roasted Tomatoes in Oil

MAKES: about 4 cups (960 ml)
FRIDGE: up to 3 weeks
FREEZER: up to 1 year

These are homemade sun-dried tomatoes—or oven-dried, as the case might be. They're a glory with pasta, appetizers, or salads. Look for small plum tomatoes, sized so they'll fit in the jars. Although we recommend using two 1 pint (472 ml) jars, you can indeed use ½ pint (236 ml) jars but you'll need to squish and maybe even juice the tomatoes to get several in each jar. You needn't use extra virgin olive oil for *roasting* the tomatoes, but its brighter, floral flavors are essential when filling the jars.

> 5 pounds (2.25 kg) *small* plum tomatoes, halved lengthwise
> 6 tablespoons (90 ml) olive oil
> 2 teaspoons kosher salt
> 1 teaspoon ground black pepper
> Extra virgin olive oil as necessary to cover the tomatoes

1. Position the rack in the center of the oven; heat the oven to 275°F (135°C), no fan or convection.

2. Place the tomatoes cut side up on a large lipped baking sheet. Drizzle with the 6 tablespoons (90 ml) oil, then sprinkle with the salt and pepper.

3. Roast, gently rearranging the tomatoes occasionally to compensate for hot spots and charred bits, until shriveled and even caramelized, about 3 hours. Transfer to a wire rack and cool at room temperature for 1 hour.

➡

4. Pack the tomatoes into two *clean* 1 pint (472 ml) jars or other containers. Fill the jars with *extra virgin* olive oil, leaving about ½ inch (1 cm) headspace in each jar. Use a long toothpick or a bamboo skewer to move the vegetables around and get rid of any air pockets. No tomato can stick out of the oil. Cover or seal, then refrigerate or freeze.

More

For a more sophisticated flavor, sprinkle the tomato halves with 1 teaspoon fennel pollen before roasting.

Seared Mushrooms in Oil

MAKES: about 4 cups (960 ml)
FRIDGE: up to 3 weeks after marinating
FREEZER: no

Mushrooms need a little more care when they're preserved in oil. They lose some of their earthy flavor both when heated and during storage. To compensate, we plunge them into boiling *vinegar* to give them a bump. And we season the olive oil with aromatics so it'll add even more flavor. Unfortunately, seared mushrooms don't survive the freezing process well. You'll just have more jars to give away.

> 2 pounds (900 g) Baby Bella or cremini mushrooms, cleaned and cut into ½-inch-thick (1-cm-thick) slices
>
> 2 tablespoons (24 g) kosher salt
>
> 2 cups (480 ml) white wine vinegar
>
> 1 cup (240 ml) extra virgin olive oil, plus more as necessary
>
> 1 dried árbol chili or other dried long thin red chili, stemmed
>
> ¼ teaspoon ground black pepper

1. Toss the mushroom slices with the salt in a large bowl until the slices are well coated. Set a plate over the mushrooms to weight them down, preferably a plate that fits just down in the bowl. Set aside at room temperature for 1½ hours.

2. Remove the plate and drain the mushrooms in a colander set in the sink, shaking it several times to get rid of excess moisture. Do not rinse. Lay paper towels across your work surface, then spread the mushrooms slices onto the paper towels in a single layer. Top with more paper towels and press gently to blot dry.

3. Bring the vinegar to a boil in a large saucepan set over high heat. Add the mushrooms, then bring the liquid back to a boil, stirring occasionally. Cook for 4 minutes, stirring often. Drain the mushrooms again in that colander, then repeat that paper towel–blotting process.

4. Set a large heavy pan, preferably cast iron, over medium-high heat until smoking. Add as many mushrooms slices as will fit in a single layer. Sear until browned at the edges, even charred a bit in places, about 1 minute. Turn the slices over and brown or char again. Transfer the mushrooms to a bowl and soldier on with more batches.

5. Cool the seared mushrooms for about 15 minutes, then pack them into four *clean* ½ pint (236 ml) jars or two *clean* 1 pint (472 ml) jars or other containers.

6. Heat the 1 cup (240 ml) oil, the chili, and black pepper in a small saucepan set over medium-low heat until warm but not simmering. Pour into the jars with the mushrooms, leaving about ½ inch (1 cm) headspace in each. Use a long toothpick or a bamboo skewer to move the vegetables around and get rid of any air pockets. The mushrooms must be covered in oil; add more olive oil as necessary. Cover or seal. Cool at room temperature for no more than 1 hour. Refrigerate to marinate for at least 2 days before enjoying.

Next

Don't throw that oil away when you've eaten the mushrooms. Strain it and use it for salad dressings—for example, with red wine vinegar in a 1-part-vinegar-to-3-part-oil ratio *by volume*.

Roasted Bell Peppers in Oil
(page 288) on toasted baguette
with soft goat cheese

Roasted Bell Peppers in Oil

MAKES: about 4 cups (960 ml)
FRIDGE: up to 3 weeks
FREEZER: up to 1 year

We find that a lot of bell peppers stored in oil are fairly tasteless. After sitting in a neutral oil or even a highly refined, less expensive olive oil, they need a squeeze of lemon juice or a splash of vinegar to bring back the fresher flavors that faded during storage. So we shortcut the process by steeping the peppers in a brine before packing them in oil. Choose bell peppers without any brown marks or mushy spots. The stems should be desiccated but not easily splintered.

> 3 pounds (1.4 kg) red and/or yellow bell peppers (about 13 medium)
>
> 1 cup (240 ml) white wine vinegar
>
> 1 cup (240 ml) water
>
> ¼ cup (50 g) granulated white sugar
>
> 1½ teaspoons kosher salt
>
> Extra virgin olive oil as necessary to cover the pepper strips

1. Char the peppers over an open flame, either using a grill or the burner of a gas stove. (Or set an oven rack about 6 inches or 15 cm from the broiler, heat the broiler, lay the peppers on a large lipped baking sheet, and broil, turning occasionally, until blackened all around.) Set the charred peppers in a large bowl and cover with plastic wrap or seal them in two large zip-closed plastic bags. Set aside at room temperature for 20 minutes.

2. Uncover or unwrap the peppers. Remove the stem and a little of the pepper around it from each, then scrape or peel off any blackened skin. Use a small spoon to scoop out and discard all the seeds and membranes in each. Cut the peppers into ½-inch-wide (1-cm-wide) strips and put them in a large bowl.

3. Bring the vinegar, water, sugar, and salt to a boil in a small saucepan set over high heat, stirring constantly at first to dissolve the sugar. Pour this boiling syrup over the pepper strips. Stir well and set aside at room temperature, stirring occasionally, until cool to the touch, about 3 hours.

4. Reserve 2 tablespoons of the soaking syrup. Drain the pepper strips and pack them into four *clean* ½ pint (236 ml) jars or two *clean* 1 pint (472 ml) jars or other containers. Add the reserved syrup, then fill the jars with more olive oil, leaving about ½ inch (1 cm) headspace in each. Use a long toothpick or a bamboo skewer to move the vegetables around and get rid of any air pockets. The pepper strips must be submerged in the oil. Cover or seal, then refrigerate or freeze.

More

Add up to 2 tablespoons (6 g) fresh rosemary leaves to the brine before boiling in step 3.

Marinated Artichokes

MAKES: about 4 cups (960 ml)
FRIDGE: up to 3 weeks after marinating
FREEZER: no

These artichoke hearts are superior to any you could buy: velvety, herbal, and surprisingly fresh in flavor. You may wonder why you didn't always make your own. One problem: Some small artichokes are not truly *baby* artichokes, but smaller mature ones from farther down a stem. In this case, the mature-but-still-small artichokes will have a hairy center, not exactly delectable after being marinated in oil. Search out the for-real immature artichokes. You can pry one open to make sure you have the true article.

1 pound (450 g) baby artichokes (about 5 inches or 13 cm in circumference, about 10 artichokes)

4 cups (960 ml) water

2 cups (480 ml) dry white wine, such as Chardonnay

½ cup (120 ml) white wine vinegar

6 medium garlic cloves, peeled

1 tablespoon (12 g) kosher salt

1 tablespoon (6 g) black peppercorns

6 fresh thyme sprigs

2 dried bay leaves

Olive oil as necessary to cover the artichokes

1. Peel the artichokes' stems with a vegetable peeler to remove any rough, fibrous outer bits. If the stems are woody, rather than soft, you'll simply need to remove them. Remove any of the hard, fibrous outer leaves (perhaps more than you think!) and cut the top quarter off each artichoke.

2. Bring the water, wine, vinegar, garlic, salt, peppercorns, thyme, and bay leaves to a boil in a very large saucepan set over high heat. Add the prepared artichokes. Bring back to a boil, reduce the heat to low, and cook, stirring occasionally, for 10 minutes.

3. Drain the artichokes and aromatics in a colander set in the sink. Reserve the garlic cloves; discard the remaining spices and aromatics. Pack the artichokes and garlic cloves into two *clean* 1 pint (472 ml) jars or other containers. Fill the jars with olive oil, leaving about ½ inch (1 cm) headspace in each. Use a long toothpick or a bamboo skewer to move the vegetables around and get rid of any air pockets. Cover or seal, then refrigerate to marinate for 3 days before enjoying.

Next

Make a simple supper with some cooked spaghetti and a jar of these artichoke hearts. Cut each in half, toss with warm spaghetti along with some chopped tomatoes, fresh basil leaves, and some of the oil from the jar. Garnish with lots of finely grated Parmigiano-Reggiano and ground black pepper.

Marinated Roasted Vegetables

MAKES: about 4 cups (960 ml)
FRIDGE: up to 3 weeks after marinating
FREEZER: up to 1 year

This old-school Italian vegetable preserve of eggplant, zucchini, and summer squash makes a tasty treat year-round, especially since you can freeze the jars and return them to room temperature without a lot of problems with the vegetables' texture. Whether you use two 1 pint (472 ml) jars or one 1 quart (1 liter) jar, make sure they have a wide mouth so it's relatively easy to get the vegetables inside. Also, make sure every bit of vegetable is submerged in the oil. If you store a jar in the fridge, let it fully solidify before turning it on its side so the vegetables remain stuck in the oil.

1 small eggplant (about 6½ ounces or 185 g), stemmed and cut into ¼-inch-thick (0.5-cm-thick) rounds

2 small zucchini (about 4 ounces or 115 g *each*), sliced into ¼-inch-thick (0.5-cm-thick) rounds

2 small yellow summer squash (about 4 ounces or 115 g *each*), sliced into ¼-inch-thick (0.5-cm-thick) rounds

Up to 2 fresh red bird's eye chilis, stemmed

2 teaspoons kosher salt

¼ cup (60 ml) olive oil

Two 3 inch (7.5 cm) fresh rosemary sprigs

Four fresh basil leaves

Extra virgin olive oil as necessary to cover the vegetables

1. Position the rack in the center of the oven; heat the oven to 350°F (175°C), no fan or convection.

2. Lay the vegetables and chilis in a single layer on a large lipped baking sheet. Avoid crowding! Work in batches, as necessary. Sprinkle the vegetables and chilis with the salt, then drizzle with ¼ cup (60 ml) oil (or divided amounts, if you're working in batches).

➡

3. Roast until softened and browning at the edges, about 35 minutes. Transfer the pan with the vegetables to a cooling rack and cool to room temperature, about 1 hour.

4. Pack the vegetables and chilis into two *clean* 1 pint (472 ml) jars or one *clean* 1 quart (1 liter) jar or other container. Tuck the rosemary sprigs and basil leaves among the vegetables. Pour olive oil into the jar(s) to cover the vegetables but leave about ½ inch (1 cm) headspace in the jar(s). Use a long toothpick or a bamboo skewer to move the vegetables around and get rid of any air pockets. Make sure the vegetables are fully covered in the oil. Cover or seal, then refrigerate to marinate for 3 days before enjoying.

Next
Either discard the chilis when serving or slice them into tiny rounds to go with the vegetables. To serve, pour the vegetables and oil out on a large plate or small platter, then offer toothpicks and lots of napkins on the side.

Spiced Peach Quarters

MAKES: about 4 cups (960 ml)
FRIDGE: up to 3 weeks after steeping
FREEZER: no

Time was, you couldn't have fried chicken in the US South without spiced peaches as a side dish. They were also in one compartment of every relish tray (next to the scallions soaking in salt water) at every 1960s dinner party across the country. These days, they're a bit of a throwback but still really tasty, particularly with heavier foods, like smoked ham or barbecued brisket.

- 1⅓ cups (320 ml) water
- 1 cup (200 g) granulated white sugar
- 2 tablespoons (30 ml) white wine vinegar
- One 3 inch (7.5 cm) cinnamon stick, broken in half widthwise
- 1 teaspoon allspice berries
- 1 teaspoon whole cloves
- ½ teaspoon kosher salt
- 2½ pounds (1.1 kg) ripe peaches (about 5 large), peeled, quartered, and pitted

1. Bring the water, sugar, vinegar, cinnamon stick, allspice berries, cloves, and salt to a simmer in a large saucepan set over high heat, stirring constantly at first to dissolve the sugar. Boil undisturbed for 1 minute.

2. Add the peach quarters and bring back to a boil. Reduce the heat to low and simmer slowly for 10 minutes.

3. Turn off the heat and set the pan off the burner. Use a slotted spoon to pack the peach quarters into two *clean* 1 pint (472 ml) jars or one *clean* 1 quart (1 liter) jar or other container.

4. Pour the remaining syrup over the peach quarters, leaving about ½ inch (1 cm) headspace in the jar(s). Make sure the spices are distributed evenly among the peaches in the jar(s). Cover or seal. Cool at room temperature for no more than 1 hour, then refrigerate to steep for 2 days before enjoying.

Next
The syrup that remains in the jar is great for cocktails if you need a slight vinegary twist and decidedly herbal-peach flavor. For example, use it instead of sugar in a blender to make a frozen margarita.

Prunes in Armagnac

MAKES: about 4 cups (960 ml)
FRIDGE: up to 3 weeks after steeping
FREEZER: up to 6 months

Armagnac, a brandy distilled in Gascony, France, has long been prized for its oaky, smooth, elegant finish…and has long been paired with prunes to be ladled over slices of vanilla cake or spooned up alongside fine chocolates. We feel that the assertive flavors of Armagnac are nicely balanced with a little black tea, which offers some bitter tannins and mellows the sweet flavors, all in a bid to bring the prunes forward. Look for plump prunes, not desiccated or hard.

- 2 teaspoons loose black tea, preferably Assam or black oolong
- 2 cups (480 ml) *boiling* water
- ½ cup (108 g) packed light brown sugar
- 1¼ pounds (565 g) pitted prunes
- 1 vanilla bean, halved lengthwise
- 1 cup (240 ml) Armagnac

1. Put the tea in a large heat-safe bowl. Add the boiling water and steep for 5 minutes. Strain through a fine-mesh sieve into a medium saucepan.

2. Add the brown sugar and set the pan over medium-high heat. Bring to a boil, stirring constantly at first to dissolve the brown sugar. Boil undisturbed for 2 minutes. Turn off the heat, remove the pan from the burner, and stir in the prunes. Set aside at room temperature, stirring occasionally, until cool to the touch, about 2 hours.

3. Use a slotted spoon or two forks to lift the prunes out of the syrup one by one. Pack them into four *clean* ½ pint (236 ml) jars, two *clean* 1 pint (472 ml) jars, or one *clean* 1 quart (1 liter) jar or other container. Nestle the vanilla bean halves among the prunes, slicing the bean into smaller segments as necessary.

4. Whisk the Armagnac into the remaining liquid in the pan. Pour this mixture into the jar(s), covering the prunes and leaving about ½ inch (1 cm) headspace in the jar(s). Make sure the prunes are submerged in the syrup. Cover or seal, then refrigerate to steep for at least 3 days before enjoying or freezing.

Next
The soaking syrup makes a fine cocktail: In a cocktail shaker, stir 1 part syrup with ice, 3 parts brandy, and ½ part Cointreau (*by volume*). Strain into chilled martini glasses.

Apples in Syrup

MAKES: about 1 quart (1 liter)
FRIDGE: up to 1 month
FREEZER: up to 1 year

Here's our version of a Greek treat that preserves whole apples in a sugary syrup. We confess we've put out bowls, spoons, a filled quart jar of these, and a container of Greek yogurt for our overnight guests and called it *breakfast*. The apple varietal traditionally used is hard to track down outside of the Aegean. We've used more common, *small* apples. You could also substitute large crab apples. In any event, the apples are sometimes spiced, although our base recipe is straightforward. Look for additional spices in the MORE section.

- 3 pounds (1.4 kg) very small, semi-tart, firm apples (no more than 4 ounces or 115 g each), such as small Cortlands or Empires
- 2½ cups (500 g) granulated white sugar
- ¾ cup (180 ml) water
- 2 tablespoons (30 ml) lemon juice
- ¼ teaspoon vanilla extract

1. Stem the apples, then peel them. Remove their cores, leaving them whole. The easiest way to do this is to dig into the apple from the former stem section with a melon baller, scooping down to remove the seeds and fibrous bits without breaking the apple. (If you break one or two, they're still usable, just not as aesthetically pleasing.)

2. Bring the sugar, water, lemon juice, and vanilla extract to a boil in a very large saucepan or a pot over high heat, stirring often at first to dissolve the sugar.

➡

3. Add the apples and reduce the heat to low. Cover and cook, basting and turning often, for 30 minutes.

4. Uncover and continue cooking, *gently* basting and turning even more frequently, until the apples are tender and slightly translucent and the syrup is a very pale honey color, 5–10 minutes.

5. Turn off the heat and set the pan off the burner. Cool for 1–2 minutes, then use a slotted spoon to transfer the apples to one *clean, heat-safe, wide-mouth* 1 quart (1 liter) jar or other container. Pour in the syrup, leaving about ½ inch (1 cm) headspace in the jar. Cover or seal. Cool at room temperature for no more than 1 hour, then refrigerate or freeze (upright to make sure the apples are submerged).

More
Add one 3 inch (7.5 cm) cinnamon stick, 4 whole cloves, 4 allspice berries, and/or 2 *green* cardamom pods with the vanilla extract.

Cherries in Almond Syrup

MAKES: about 4 cups (960 ml)
FRIDGE: up to 1 month
FREEZER: up to 1 year

When you've got a jar or two of these cherries on hand, you've got a ready dessert—just dish out some vanilla ice cream. Or forget about dessert and start your weekend morning with French toast or waffles, plenty of butter, and some of these cherries with their syrup.

> 1 cup (240 ml) water
> 1 cup (200 g) granulated white sugar
> 1 pound (450 g) sweet cherries, such as bing cherries, stemmed, halved, and pitted
> ½ cup (120 ml) amaretto (an almond liqueur) or sweetened almond syrup for coffee drinks

1. Combine the water and sugar in a medium saucepan set over high heat. Stir constantly to dissolve the sugar. Bring to a boil, stirring occasionally.

2. Add the cherries and bring back to a boil. Reduce the heat to low and simmer slowly, stirring occasionally, for 3 minutes. Use a slotted spoon to transfer the cherries to four *clean* ½ pint (236 ml) jars or two *clean* 1 pint (472 ml) jars or other containers.

3. Raise the heat to high under the syrup in the pan and bring it to a boil. Boil, stirring occasionally, until reduced to about two-thirds of its original volume, about 3 minutes. Stir in the amaretto or almond syrup.

4. Set the syrup aside for about 30 minutes to cool. Pour it into the jars, leaving about ½ inch (1 cm) headspace in each. Make sure the cherries are covered in the syrup. Cover or seal, then refrigerate or freeze.

More
To make SPICED CHERRIES IN ALMOND SYRUP, add one 3 inch (7.5 cm) cinnamon stick, one 2 inch (5 cm) knob of fresh peeled ginger, and/or 1 star anise pod to the pan with the cherries.

Pear Quarters in Spiced Syrup

MAKES: about 4 cups (960 ml)
FRIDGE: up to 1 month
FREEZER: up to 1 year

Here's the perfect match to thinly sliced prosciutto or salami, as well as room-temperature cheese of just about any sort. The perfume-rich pears soak up the lemony ginger syrup to become somehow more irresistible. Even for breakfast! These pear quarters are wonderful with unsweetened yogurt; make sure you stir some of the syrup into the yogurt.

4 cups (960 ml) water

1 cup (200 g) granulated white sugar

Half of a small lemon, thinly sliced and seeded

One 1 inch (2.5 cm) piece of fresh peeled ginger (about as wide as your thumb), thinly sliced

6 whole cloves

2 pounds (900 g) firm pears, preferably Bosc (about 4, at 8 ounces or 225 g *each*), stemmed, peeled, quartered, and cored

½ cup (165 g) honey

1. Bring the water and sugar to a boil in a large saucepan set over high heat, stirring constantly at first to dissolve the sugar.

2. Add the lemon slices, ginger, and cloves. Then submerge the pear quarters into the syrup. Reduce the heat to very low and simmer *slowly*, gently rearranging the quarters once in a while to make sure they've all been in the syrup, until a paring knife can easily go into a quarter and they've turned somewhat translucent, 15–25 minutes (depending on the pears' firmness and the varietal).

3. Turn off the heat and set the pan off the burner. Use a slotted spoon to transfer the pear quarters to two *clean, heat-safe, wide-mouth*, 1 pint (472 ml) jars or one *clean, heat-safe, wide-mouth*, 1 quart (1 liter) jar.

4. Return the saucepan to high heat and bring the syrup to a boil. Boil, stirring occasionally, until reduced to about half its original volume, about 7 minutes. Stir in the honey until dissolved.

5. *Strain* the hot syrup through a sieve over the pear quarters in the jar(s), leaving about ½ inch (1 cm) headspace. Make sure the pears are submerged in the syrup. Cover or seal. Cool at room temperature for no more than 1 hour, then refrigerate or freeze.

More

Try a PEAR COSMO: Fill a cocktail shaker with ice, then add 4 parts vodka, 1 part pear syrup from one of these jars, and 1 part cranberry juice (*by volume*). Add a squeeze of lime juice, cover, and shake well. Strain into chilled martini glasses.

Dried Pears in Fennel-Orange Syrup

MAKES: about 4 cups (960 ml)
FRIDGE: up to 1 month
FREEZER: up to 1 year

Since there's vinegar in this syrup and since we're using dried pears with their firmer texture, this condiment straddles the border between dinner and dessert. The pear halves are terrific with roasts, particularly pork or lamb. But they're also welcome with pound cake or sugar cookies. Look for dried pears *without* many brown spots but *with* some give or wiggle.

1 pound (450 g) dried pear halves

Water to simmer the dried pears

1¾ cups (420 ml) apple cider vinegar

2 tablespoons (30 g) minced peeled fresh ginger

2 teaspoons fennel seeds

One 3 inch (7.5 cm) cinnamon stick

2 long strips of orange zest

2 cups (400 g) granulated white sugar

1. Place the pear halves in a large saucepan, then add water to cover by a depth of 1 inch (2.5 cm). Bring to a boil over medium-high heat, stirring occasionally. Reduce the heat to low and simmer *slowly* just until the pear halves are tender, 8–10 minutes. Drain in a colander set in the sink.

2. Combine the vinegar, ginger, fennel seeds, cinnamon stick, and orange zest in that same pan and bring to a boil over high heat, stirring once in a while. Turn off the heat and remove the pan from the burner. Cover and set aside at room temperature until cool to the touch, about 2 hours.

3. Strain the vinegar mixture into a medium saucepan. Discard the aromatics. Add the sugar and place the pan over high heat. Bring to a boil, stirring constantly at first to dissolve the sugar.

➡

Dried Pears in Fennel-Orange Syrup (page 294) with whipped cream on pound cake

Boil, stirring occasionally, until syrupy and slightly thickened, about 5 minutes.

4. Turn off the heat and set the pan off the burner. Stir in the pear halves. Set aside at room temperature until cool to the touch, about 2 hours.

5. Transfer the pears and syrup to two *clean* 1 pint (472 ml) jars or one *clean* 1 quart (1 liter) jar, leaving about ½ inch (1 cm) headspace. Cover or seal, then refrigerate or freeze (upright so the pears stay in the syrup).

Next

For a more sophisticated finish, add 2 tablespoons (30 ml) Campari or Aperol to the syrup with the pears in step 4.

Figs in Honey Syrup

MAKES: about 3 cups (720 ml)
FRIDGE: up to 1 month
FREEZER: up to 1 year

Preserving figs in a sugary syrup is a centuries-long tradition, a way to save that precious, perishable fruit for months. However, ripe figs are incredibly fragile. So for the best results with this recipe, don't look for the perfect figs for snacking. Instead, choose firmer figs, ripe but not yet…um, voluptuous. Adriatic, Calimyrna, *or* Black Mission figs will work in this recipe.

> 1¼ cups (250 g) granulated white sugar
> 1 cup (240 ml) white wine vinegar
> ¾ cup (180 ml) water
> 3 tablespoons (63 g) honey
> 1 pound (450 g) fresh ripe but firm figs, stemmed and halved through the former stem ends

1. Bring the sugar, vinegar, water, and honey to a boil in a large saucepan set over medium-high heat, stirring constantly at first to dissolve the sugar and honey. Boil for 1 minute.

2. Remove the pan from the heat and let the bubbling stop. Gently add the fig halves, stirring or folding quite gently to get them in the syrup without breaking them apart. All the fig halves should be submerged.

3. Set the pan over low heat and bring to a low simmer, stirring *very gently* once in a while. Lower the heat as much as you can and simmer very slowly for 10 minutes, stirring as gently as possible one or two times.

4. Turn off the heat and set the pan off the burner. Cool at room temperature until barely warm, about 1 hour.

5. Use a slotted spoon to transfer the fig halves to three *clean* ½ pint (236 ml) jars or other containers. Pour the syrup over the figs, leaving about ½ inch (1 cm) headspace in each jar. Make sure the figs are covered in the syrup. Cover or seal, then refrigerate or freeze.

More

Introduce some herbal notes by adding up to 1 tablespoon stemmed thyme leaves with the honey. Or use a floral-based honey, such as star thistle or blueberry blossom.

Pineapple in Black Pepper Syrup

MAKES: about 4 cups (960 ml)
FRIDGE: up to 1 month after steeping
FREEZER: up to 1 year

Black pepper gives pineapple chunks in syrup a decidedly urbane twist, a nice treat with cheese (particularly hard, aged cheeses) or grilled sausages. The black pepper should be *coarsely* ground so that the syrup remains relatively clear. If possible, grind your own—or look for coarsely ground black pepper in the spice aisle.

3 cups (720 ml) water

1½ cups (300 g) granulated white sugar

3 pounds (1.4 kg) fresh pineapple (about 1 large), trimmed, peeled, cored, and *finely* chopped (about 5 cups)

2 teaspoons coarsely ground black pepper

½ teaspoon vanilla extract

1. Put the water and ½ cup (100 g) sugar in a medium saucepan. Set it over high heat and stir until the sugar dissolves. Bring to a full boil.

2. Add the pineapple chunks, then reduce the heat to very low. Simmer *slowly*, gently stirring once in a while, until the pineapple is tender when poked with a fork but not soft, about 10 minutes.

3. Use a slotted spoon to transfer the pineapple chunks to four *clean*, *heat-safe*, ½ pint (236 ml) jars or two *clean*, *heat-safe*, 1 pint (472 ml) jars or other containers.

4. Return the pan to high heat and stir in the remaining 1 cup (200 g) sugar until dissolved. Bring to a boil. Boil, stirring occasionally, until reduced to about half the syrup's original volume, about 7 minutes. Stir in the pepper and vanilla. Boil for 1 more minute.

5. Pour the hot syrup over the pineapple chunks in the jars, leaving about ½ inch (1 cm) headspace in each. Cover or seal. Cool at room temperature for no more than 1 hour, then refrigerate or freeze.

More

Vary the pepper by using coarsely ground Aleppo pepper or even sour green peppercorns.

Oranges in Brandy Syrup

MAKES: 6 preserved oranges
FRIDGE: up to 1 month after steeping
FREEZER: no

Preserved oranges are an Old World treat, originating back in a time before global shipping lanes, when oranges were short-seasoned and precious. We've added brandy to the syrup to give these oranges a boozy finish, best as a dessert with a dollop of crème fraîche (so long as you've also got crunchy cookies nearby).

6 small navel oranges (about 3½ ounces or 100 g *each*), gently scrubbed clean

2 cups (400 g) granulated white sugar

1 cup (240 ml) water

1 cup (240 ml) brandy

1. Use a vegetable peeler or a sharp paring knife to remove the zest from two of the oranges in long strips. Set the zest strips aside.

2. Use a paring knife to peel those two oranges, then peel the remaining four oranges as well, as if you were going to make orange supremes from all of them (see pages 31–32). But do not make supremes. Instead, leave the oranges whole but get as much of the white pith off as you can.

3. Bring the sugar and water to a boil in a large saucepan set over high heat, stirring constantly at first to dissolve the sugar. Add the oranges, reduce the heat to low, and simmer for 2 minutes, turning the oranges gently once or twice.

4. Use a slotted spoon to divide the oranges between two *clean*, *heat-safe* 1 pint (472 ml) jars or put in one *clean*, *heat-safe* 1 quart (1 liter) jar or container.

5. Return the syrup in the pan to a simmer over medium-high heat. Add the reserved zest and boil for 3 minutes. Turn off the heat and set the pan off the burner. Cool at room temperature for 1 hour.

Oranges in Brandy
Syrup (page 297)

6. Remove and discard the zest strips. Stir in the brandy. Divide this syrup between the two jars or pour it into one jar, leaving about ½ inch (1 cm) headspace. Make sure the oranges are submerged. Cover or seal, then refrigerate to steep for 2 weeks before enjoying.

More

Make the syrup even more elegant by swapping out the plain brandy for cognac, Armagnac, or even Calvados.

Kumquats in Cognac Syrup

MAKES: about 25 preserved kumquats
FRIDGE: up to 1 month after steeping
FREEZER: no

Preserving sour kumquats in a sugary cognac syrup may be one of the finest things we've done over the years. Both the fruit and the syrup are worth preserving, the first for light desserts with coffee cake or cookies; the second, for cocktails, including wild, new takes on Manhattans and Old Fashioneds.

Water to blanch the kumquats
1 pound (450 g) kumquats (about 25), gently scrubbed clean
1½ cups (360 ml) water
¾ cup (150 g) granulated white sugar
2 cups (480 ml) cognac, plus more if needed

1. Bring a medium saucepan with lots of water to a boil over high heat. Add the kumquats and blanch for 1 minute. Drain in a colander set in the sink. Cool for 10 minutes, then pierce each kumquat a few times with a toothpick or bamboo skewer.

2. Bring 1½ cups (360 ml) water and the sugar to a boil in the same medium saucepan, stirring constantly at first to dissolve the sugar. Add the pierced kumquats, reduce the heat to low, and *simmer* for 5 minutes. (Do not boil!)

3. Use a slotted spoon to transfer the kumquats to two *clean, heat-safe, wide-mouth*, 1 pint (472 ml) jars or other containers.

4. Bring the syrup in the pan back to a boil over high heat, stirring occasionally. Continue to boil, stirring occasionally, until the syrup is reduced to about half its volume, about 5 minutes.

5. Turn off the heat and remove the pan from the burner. Stir in the cognac. Divide the syrup between the two jars, leaving about ½ inch (1 cm) headspace in each. If you don't have enough liquid, top each jar with more cognac. Make sure all the kumquats are submerged. Cover or seal. Cool at room temperature for no more than 1 hour, then refrigerate for at least 2 weeks to steep before enjoying.

More

Serve the syrup from the jars as a cordial in front of a roaring fire some frosty night.

5

Kimchis and Sauerkrauts

If most of the chili-laced condiments in Chapter 3 and many of the pickles in the previous chapter are bright or fiery, get ready for all that's earthy, sometimes fiery, and often mildly sour. Get ready for lots of refrigerator ferments and our only true room-temperature ferments...although all in small batches, as per our promise of a quicker technique for smaller, safer batches. You don't need to make a 5-gallon drum of kimchi or sauerkraut. You can make 1 quart and have enough for several meals or maybe one big barbecue with friends.

Home-fermenting became a craze during the pandemic, but it seems to be suffering the sourdough tragedy: A way to fill extra time has become too complicated in a once-again busy world. Fortunately, small batches of kimchis and sauerkrauts don't require quite the effort, although they do require patience: not time working, but time waiting.

Almost all of our *kimchis* as well as our recipe for a Salvadoran-style curtido are fermented in the fridge, perhaps a new way for some of us to think about an age-old process. True, refrigerator fermentation doesn't happen as quickly as room-temperature fermentation. But once it begins, it continues apace, mostly because of the natural sugar content of some of the vegetables (or in one case, from an added rice porridge).

Sauerkrauts are another matter. Although they're not all made with cabbage, almost all undergo classic, room-temperature fermentation. (There's one that employs a super shortcut process with vinegar as an aid to its final flavor.) As such, this process must be more exacting because it involves the chemical reactions that are necessary to bring on those prized flavors but that can also sadly lead to bad results. In all cases, a busted jar or a popped lid is a no-go *at any moment in the process*, even after the sauerkraut has been transferred to the refrigerator.

Let's start with a couple ingredient notes, then move on to the important points you need to keep you and yours safe *and* have a small batch of the best kimchi or sauerkraut around.

Gochugaru flakes

This vibrantly red, dried, Korean chili seasoning is sometimes sold as flakes (or coarsely ground bits) and sometimes as a more finely ground powder. We call for only the flaked or coarsely ground variety for our kimchis. You can use either interchangeably, but not the powdery stuff: It makes too much of a murky mess in the final product.

One flavor note: Gochugaru is much hotter than standard North American chili powder, but a tad milder than *old-school* red pepper flakes, and much milder than ground dried cayenne.

Distilled water

Tap water is chlorinated. Well water may have inadvertent minerals, some even beneficial for your health. Although you can use tap water (or well water, if you live in the country as we do) to wash the vegetables, use distilled water for the final fermentation in the jars. Neither tap or well water is good for the process on two counts: Some chemicals, like chlorine, can impede fermentation. Others, particularly in well water, may cloud the brine, turning a condiment unpleasantly murky.

By weight, please

Because refrigerator and room-temperature fermentation is an exacting science, we strongly recommend that you measure the ingredients *by weight*. To that end, you need a kitchen scale. And while we're at it, make sure it's a digital scale so it can measure down to very small amounts. In this chapter, to get the ratios right and keep you safe, we often call for even kosher salt *by weight*, not by volume. Don't be tempted to guess what a tablespoon or two of kosher salt can weigh. Fermentation is a gorgeously satisfying process, a mad-scientist project that results in tasty fare. But like all science projects, it comes with risks. Given all that, break out the scale.

Salting and seasoning kimchi

For proper results in our refrigerator ferments, make sure every leaf of cabbage for kimchi is well coated in the spice mixture or the rice porridge. To do so, it's best to work with your hands, not a wooden spoon or a silicone spatula. And since we want to keep contamination at bay, we strongly recommend wearing a pair of culinary kitchen gloves. Yes, generations of kimchi makers have used their bare hands. We're just not as sure of personal hygiene. If you must forgo the gloves, first wash your hands well with warm soapy water, even under your fingernails, scrubbing them with a sponge to get off as much dirt as possible before thoroughly rinsing them.

Fermenting kimchi in the fridge

All but one of our kimchis are fermented in the refrigerator. However, they're ready immediately (or almost immediately) after they're made. They'll be fresh and bright, but they won't have the sour funkiness many of us prize from fermentation.

As a general rule, it takes about 10 days for kimchi to begin to ferment and get a little funky in the fridge. The longer you leave it after that, the funkier it'll get.

In traditional Korean cuisine, most of our kimchis would *not* be eaten fresh. Even so, we love those salty, spicy flavors in fresh kimchi, almost like a sophisticated cabbage salad. However, for the true flavor, be patient. Keep tasting (with a clean fork!). Good umami things come to those who wait.

Massaging the brine for sauerkraut

If you're not familiar with making sauerkraut, you may be surprised at one of the stranger techniques: salting vegetables to draw out the natural moisture, then massaging them to extract as much of that natural brine from the vegetables as you can for the fermenting process.

▲ Wear culinary kitchen gloves to evenly distribute the spice paste for kimchi.

▲ Gently rub, massage, and squeeze salted cabbage to create some brine in the bowl.

COLD CANNING

Again, we strongly recommend wearing culinary kitchen gloves. And never reuse those gloves. Yes, you can scrupulously clean and dry your hands, as we stated just above for kimchi. But remember: You're trying to avoid contaminants. Culinary kitchen gloves are your best bet.

To massage the cabbage and/or other ingredients like carrots or turnips for sauerkraut, don't press hard on or smoosh the salted vegetables. Skip any techniques you might know for deep-tissue massage and instead gently massage the vegetables against the inside of the bowl, as you might give someone in *mild* pain an easy back rub. The point here is to extract the leached moisture and to soften the vegetables *a bit*. You'll know you've got it right when you end up with a puddle of brine yet still distinct shreds of vegetable in the bowl.

Tamping the salted vegetables into the jar

Once you've got the salting and seasoning process underway, you'll need to pack the vegetables into a jar. You've got to work at this a bit for two reasons.

One, you want as compact a mixture as possible to get rid of any extraneous air pockets or bubbles in the jar. Even in the fridge, fermentation *must* remain an anaerobic process (that is, without free-floating oxygen) to keep rot at bay.

And two, you're pressing down to extract even more natural brine, more than you created during the massaging process, so that the vegetables are submerged and (as you know now) out of the oxygen-rich air.

To get the job done, we use a fermentation tamping dowel. It must be scrupulously cleaned after each use. You can also use the cleaned end of a handle-less rolling pin. Or a cleaned, small, silicone spatula. The point is to get the shreds under the brine.

▲ For the best fermentation technique, we recommend a tamping dowel to get the vegetables below the level of the brine.

Jars

Most of these recipes make 1 quart (about 1 liter). We *always* boil our jars for kimchi and sauerkraut. Yes, you can use the dishwasher trick, as we discussed in the main introduction to this book (page 19). But for the recipes in this chapter, more than for those in any other chapter, the jars should be *sterilized*. We also boil the lids and sealing bands or rings in that big pot of water.

Fermentation weights and lids

Although you can use standard canning lids— either the one-piece, screw-on lid, or the two-piece set of a lid and a sealing band—please invest in a fermentation weight…and if you want to go all out, in a specialty lid designed to release excess gas during fermentation.

Here's the skinny: A fermentation *weight* is a glass disk that fits in a standard canning jar. It also has a button on one side. Sterilize it with the jar in boiling water, then set it flat side down on top of the vegetable mixture. Use the button to force it down further into the sauerkraut or kimchi, pressing firmly enough that some of the brine comes up and over the top of the weight.

▲ Use a fermentation weight to keep the vegetables under the brine.

As you'll see, we also advocate for a circle cut from a green cabbage leaf to be set on top of the vegetables in the brine but still underneath this weight. This circle cut-out in effect creates a double layer of protection for your hard work.

By contrast to a weight, a specialty fermentation *lid* is not necessary, although we often use one. It's a silicone ring, again with a button on one side. It, too, should be sterilized in boiling water. Set it on the lip of the jar (not on top of the vegetables), then secure it in place with the traditional sealing band or ring for canning jars. The fermentation lid has a small, one-way hole in that button that lets gasses escape as fermentation happens. In essence, it saves you from burping the jar every day. We find it invaluable not to have to ask Siri for a daily reminder to keep a jar of sauerkraut from cracking because of the built-up pressure from those gasses in a sealed jar. More on that, just below.

Burping the jars

If you *don't* use a fermentation *lid*, you'll need to release the excess gas (and the resulting pressure) in the jars. As fermentation proceeds, you'll notice some fizziness around the contents in the jar, a sure sign of success but also a signal to take action and release the pressure. Open the jar to burp it and perhaps tamp everything even farther under the brine. One warning: When you open the jar, some of the liquid inside may spray or sputter because the whole thing is indeed under pressure. Consider working in the sink to make cleanup easier. (Again, you needn't go through this rigamarole if you've used a specialty fermentation *lid* to seal the jar.)

And while we're at it, you might want to store kimchi and sauerkraut jars in a small baking pan in your fridge or on the counter to catch excess liquid that can even escape under pressure from a sealed lid. In fact, we often store room-temperature ferments in the sink of our back pantry so we can wash overflow or sputtered brine down the drain.

Safety first

Let's lay down three hard-and-fast commandments for home fermentation, even in small batches.

1. As our grandmothers would say: *If it's in the brine, it's fine; if it's in the air, beware.* In other words, every speck of vegetable matter must be submerged in the brine. True, for some *refrigerator* kimchis, you might not see a lot of brine until the second or third day. But once you do, press down all the vegetable matter so it's submerged. A fermentation weight (discussed above) is the best tool for keeping everything under the brine.

2. No matter what any social media influencer says, you *cannot* freeze any of these ferments. Doing so invites rot to the party. And rot may well entail a trip to the hospital. It's actually not the freezing that's the problem. It's the thawing. Vegetables break down in the thaw, losing their

cellular coherence, which then allows other organic matter, trapped in those shreds, to leach into the brine. Voilà, gastric disaster, if not worse.

3. Use clean utensils *every* time you dip into kimchi or sauerkraut. To serve either, pull out as much as you'd like with a clean fork, then put that fork in the dishwasher and get a clean serving piece. Never put an open jar on the table and let everyone dig in. And while we're at it, no double-dipping on your part in the kitchen! Do not sample the condiment and then stick that same fork back in the jar.

Ready, set...

Now that we're covered the basics, you're ready to make small batches of some of the finest condiments in this book. In many of these recipes, we're not reinventing the wheel. Our Go-to Sauerkraut (page 317) is about as traditional as you can get! But we are cutting down on the yields so that 1) the craft itself is more easily within reach, and 2) you're ready for an outdoor deck party or a terrific weekday condiment with just about any lunch, all without hauling around a giant vat or jug of soured vegetables, some of which inevitably gets tossed out. Faster and more economical: That's the core ethic of cold canning.

Go-to Kimchi

MAKES: about 2 quarts (a little less than 2 liters)
FRIDGE: up to 6 weeks
FREEZER: no

This kimchi is our most versatile: It can be enjoyed almost immediately as a vibrant, mildly spicy condiment—a variation on fresh, unfermented kimchi; or it can be fermented in the fridge for at least a week to gain a sour edge. The most important thing is to make sure the napa cabbage is free of blemishes or darkened bits…and certainly without any squishy spots. Be particular at the supermarket when choosing the cabbage: It should have green leaves that verge to white, fairly tight to the head, with the stem end remnant still white or just barely off-white.

> One 3 pound (1.36 kg) head of napa cabbage
>
> 2 quarts (8 cups or 1.9 liters) *distilled* water, plus additional to rinse the cabbage
>
> ¾ cup (145 g) kosher salt
>
> 3 tablespoons (45 ml) fish sauce
>
> 3 tablespoons (50 g) coarsely ground gochugaru or gochugaru flakes (see page 301)
>
> 2 tablespoons (30 ml) toasted sesame oil
>
> 2 tablespoons (30 ml) *unseasoned* rice vinegar
>
> 1 teaspoon (5 ml) ginger juice
>
> 2 medium garlic cloves, peeled and minced
>
> 5 ounces (140 g) carrots (about 2 large), peeled and shredded through the large holes of a box grater
>
> 8 medium scallions, trimmed and cut widthwise into 1 inch (2.5 cm) segments (green parts, too)

1. Remove and discard any blemished outer leaves from the cabbage. Cut off the root end by about 1 inch (2.5 cm). Cut the cabbage into quarters *lengthwise*. Then cut each of these quarters *widthwise* into 2 inch (5 cm) segments.

2. Whisk the *distilled* water and salt in a large bowl until the salt dissolves. Add the cabbage sections and press down to submerge. Set a *clean* plate on top of the cabbage to keep it submerged. Set aside at room temperature for 2 hours.

3. Scoop out and save 1 cup (240 ml) of the salt brine. Drain the cabbage with the remaining brine in a colander set in the sink. Rinse well with additional *distilled* water, gently turning the segments to make sure they're all rinsed. *Gently* squeeze each one over the sink to dry it out without squishing it.

4. Rinse and clean the large bowl. Combine the fish sauce, gochugaru, oil, vinegar, ginger juice, and garlic until uniform. Add the cabbage sections, the carrots, and scallions. Clean and dry your hands or wear culinary kitchen gloves. Mix well to combine.

5. Pack this mixture tightly into one *clean* 2 quart (1.9 liter) glass jar or other nonreactive container, leaving 1 inch (2.5 cm) headspace in the jar. Press down gently but firmly to remove all the air pockets. As much of the brine as possible should come above the leaves. Ideally, they should all be submerged. Use a fermentation weight to hold everything down, if desired. Cover or seal, then store in the refrigerator for at least 24 hours or up to 6 weeks, unsealing and burping twice during the first week, then less frequently. As soon as there's enough brine, push the vegetable matter down under it. Use a clean fork to take out some of the kimchi each time, making sure the remainder stays under the brine.

Next

The best burger is a medium-rare patty on a toasted whole-wheat bun with (Kewpie!) mayonnaise and this kimchi.

Go-to Kimchi (page 306)

Summer Kimchi

MAKES: about 1 quart (about 1 liter)
FRIDGE: up to 2 weeks
FREEZER: no

Sometimes called raw (or shang) kimchi, this kimchi isn't fermented, even with our fridge technique. As such, it won't last as long as some other kimchis; but the flavor is light, even refreshing, a great treat in the summer heat when cabbages are fresh and you want a bump of flavors to go along with almost anything off the grill.

> One 1½ pound (680 g) head of napa cabbage
> 3 tablespoons (36 g) kosher salt
> 3 tablespoons (45 ml) *unseasoned* rice vinegar
> 2½ tablespoons (55 g) sambal oelek (or your own homemade Fiery Red Sambal, page 217)
> 1 tablespoon white sesame seeds, toasted
> 2 teaspoons (10 ml) toasted sesame oil
> 6 medium garlic cloves, peeled and minced

1. Cut the root end off the cabbage by about 1 inch (2.5 cm). Cut the cabbage in half *lengthwise*, then cut each half into 2 inch (5 cm) sections *widthwise*.

2. Put these sections in a large bowl and add the salt. Toss well to coat, massaging the salt *gently* into the cabbage with clean, dry hands or while wearing culinary kitchen gloves. Set aside at room temperature for 2 hours.

3. Dump the cabbage and any liquid in the bowl into a colander set in the sink. Rinse the cabbage pieces, rearranging them so they're all rinsed. *Gently* squeeze each section of cabbage dry over the sink.

4. Clean and dry the bowl. Whisk the vinegar, sambal oelek, sesame seeds, sesame oil, and garlic in it until well combined. Clean and dry your hands or wear new culinary kitchen gloves. Add the cabbage sections and mix well by hand to combine.

5. Pack this mixture tightly into one *clean* 1 quart (1 liter) glass jar or other nonreactive container, leaving 1 inch (2.5 cm) headspace in the jar. Press down gently but firmly to remove all the air pockets and release as much liquid as possible. It may not cover the cabbage, but more will leach out over the next several days. Cover or seal, then store in the refrigerator for at least 24 hours or up to 2 weeks, pressing down the cabbage once there's enough liquid to keep it submerged.

Next

Make a KIMCHI PANCAKE! Whisk ½ cup (60 g) all-purpose or plain flour and ½ cup (120 ml) water in a bowl. Drain and chop 1 cup (about 6 ounces or 170 g) of this kimchi, then stir it into the batter. Heat a medium nonstick skillet over medium heat and swirl in a little vegetable oil. Spread the batter in the skillet into a flat, compact pancake. Cook for about 5 minutes, until golden brown, then flip and continue cooking until golden on the other side, adding a little more oil if desired. Slip out onto a cutting board, cool for a few minutes, then slice into squares or pie wedges.

Napa Cabbage Kimchi

MAKES: about 2 quarts (a little less than 2 liters)
FRIDGE: up to 6 weeks
FREEZER: no

This is our most traditional kimchi, our version of baechu kimchi, made with a glutinous rice paste. Although usually fermented at room temperature, we can get a fine, earthy edge in the fridge if we're patient…about 1 week should do it until the mixture starts to take on that prized, funky-sour flavor. For this kimchi, the liquid will not appear in the jar until a few days in the fridge. After that, use a fermentation tamping dowel or the clean, flat end of a handle-less rolling pin to mash the vegetables down below the level of the liquid…or set a fermenting weight over the kimchi in the jar.

One 3 pound (1.36 kg) head of napa cabbage

2 quarts (8 cups or 1.9 liters) plus 1½ cups (360 ml) *distilled* water, plus additional to rinse the cabbage

¾ cup (145 g) kosher salt

3 tablespoons (24 g) glutinous rice flour

2 tablespoons (25 g) granulated white sugar

1 cup (270 g) coarsely ground gochugaru or gochugaru flakes (see page 301)

½ cup (120 ml) fish sauce

8 medium garlic cloves, peeled and minced

One 2 inch (5 cm) piece of fresh ginger (about the width of your thumb), peeled and finely chopped

8 ounces (225 g) daikon (about 1 small), peeled and shredded through the large holes of a box grater

2½ ounces (70 g) carrot (about 1 large), peeled and shredded through the large holes of a box grater

16 medium scallions, trimmed and cut widthwise into 2 inch (5 cm) segments (the green parts, too)

1. Cut the root end off the cabbage by about 1 inch (2.5 cm). Cut the cabbage in half *lengthwise*, then cut each half *widthwise* into 2 inch (5 cm) sections.

2. Whisk the 2 quarts (1.9 liters) *distilled* water and the salt in a large bowl until the salt dissolves. Add the cabbage sections and press down to submerge. Set a clean plate on top of the cabbage to keep it under the brine. Set aside at room temperature for 2 hours.

3. Drain the cabbage in a colander set in the sink. Rinse well with additional *distilled* water, gently turning the pieces to make sure they're all rinsed. Clean and dry your hands or put on culinary kitchen gloves. *Gently* squeeze each segment over the sink to dry it without squishing it. Clean and dry the bowl; return the cabbage to it.

4. Whisk the remaining 1½ cups (360 ml) *distilled* water, the rice flour, and sugar in a small saucepan set over medium heat until smooth. Bring to a simmer, whisking constantly to prevent scorching or forming lumps. Continue cooking, whisking constantly, until the mixture thickens to a paste, 2–3 minutes. Turn off the burner and remove the pan from the heat. Stir in the gochugaru, fish sauce, garlic, and ginger until well combined.

Scrape this mixture into a small bowl and cool at room temperature for 10 minutes.

5. Add the daikon, carrot, and scallions to the cabbage pieces. Pour and scrape the rice porridge into the bowl. Clean and dry your hands or put on new culinary kitchen gloves. *Gently* mix well by hand to combine. Take your time, maybe 2–3 minutes.

6. Pack this mixture tightly into one *clean* 2 quart (1.9 liter) glass jar or other nonreactive container, leaving 1–2 inches (2.5–5 cm) headspace in the jar but pressing down with a fermentation tamping dowel or other device to get rid of the air pockets. There may not be enough brine released to cover the vegetables. Cover or seal, then store in the refrigerator for at least 24 hours, or up to 6 weeks. The liquid will begin to appear in 2 or 3 days. At this point, press all the vegetable matter below the liquid. Add a fermentation weight, if desired. After about 2 weeks, you'll need to unseal and burp the jar every few days. Use a clean fork to remove some of the kimchi each time, making sure that the remainder stays under the brine.

Next

To make KIMCHI DIP, drain and chop about 1 cup (about 6 ounces or 170 g) of this kimchi. Put it in a food processor with 8 ounces (225 g) softened cream cheese, 8 ounces (225 g) sour cream, and a splash of soy sauce. Cover and process until creamy-smooth.

White Kimchi

MAKES: about 2 quarts (a little less than 2 liters)
FRIDGE: up to 6 weeks
FREEZER: no

A kimchi without heat? Yep, our version of baek (or white) kimchi is a light, bright ferment, although it can be enjoyed almost immediately for an even fresher flavor. There's no additional brine; the necessary liquid will come from the pureed pear and onion (plus more and more as the salt works its magic).

> One 3 pound (1.36 kg) head of napa cabbage
>
> 12 ounces (340 g) daikon (about 1 medium), peeled and shredded through the large holes of a box grater
>
> ⅓ cup (65 g) kosher salt
>
> *Distilled* water for rinsing the vegetables
>
> 1 medium Shinseiki (or Asian) pear (about 6 ounces or 170 g), stemmed, peeled, cored, and quartered
>
> 1 small yellow or white onion, peeled and quartered
>
> 6 medium garlic cloves, peeled
>
> One 2 inch (5 cm) piece of fresh ginger (about the width of your thumb), peeled and chopped
>
> 2 tablespoons (25 g) granulated white sugar
>
> ½ cup (120 ml) fish sauce
>
> 3 medium scallions, trimmed and cut widthwise into 2 inch (5 cm) sections (green parts, too)

1. Cut the root end off the cabbage by about 1 inch (2.5 cm) Cut the cabbage in half *lengthwise*, then cut each half *widthwise* into 2 inch (5 cm) sections.

2. Clean and dry your hands or put on culinary kitchen gloves. Toss the cabbage sections, shredded daikon, and salt in a large bowl until the vegetables are well and evenly salted. Set a clean plate on top of the vegetables to hold them down and set aside at room temperature for 2 hours.

3. Drain the contents of the bowl in a colander set in the sink. Rinse the cabbage and daikon well with *distilled* water, rearranging the pieces and bits a few times. *Gently* squeeze the cabbage sections

and daikon shreds dry over the sink. Clean and dry the bowl.

4. Put the pear, onion, garlic, ginger, and sugar in a food processor. Cover and process until finely chopped, almost a puree, stopping the machine at least once to scrape down the inside of the canister. Pour and scrape this mixture into the clean bowl; stir in the fish sauce until well combined.

5. Add the cabbage sections, daikon, and scallions. Clean and dry your hands or put on new culinary kitchen gloves. *Gently* mix well by hand to combine. Take your time, maybe 2–3 minutes.

6. Pack this mixture tightly into one *clean* 2 quart (1.9 liter) glass jar or other nonreactive container, leaving 1–2 inches (2.5–5 cm) headspace in the jar. Press down gently but firmly to remove all the air pockets and until the brine comes above the leaves. Use a fermentation weight, if desired. Cover or seal, then store in the refrigerator for at least 24 hours or up to 6 weeks, unsealing and burping the jar twice during the first week, then less frequently. Use a clean fork to take out some of the kimchi each time, making sure that the remainder stays under the brine.

Next
To make a wild version of KIMCHI UDON, boil and drain some udon noodles. Mix them with some of this kimchi (drained or not, depending on how soupy you want the dish), as well as a little melted butter, a splash of toasted sesame oil, about the same amount of soy sauce, and a healthy pinch of sugar. Toss well and dig in.

Radish Kimchi

MAKES: about 2 quarts (a little less than 2 liters)
FRIDGE: up to 1 month
FREEZER: no

This is our version of kkakdugi, a traditional kimchi made from cubed daikon. It won't ferment as readily as cabbage-based kimchi, but it will start to get sour after a week or so in the fridge. It also won't keep as long as some other kimchis in this chapter. It's so light and delicious, it works as a great appetizer with toothpicks to pick up the cubes. (Have lots of cold beer on hand!)

- 4 pounds (1.8 kg) daikons (about 6 medium or 4 large)
- 2 tablespoons (25 g) granulated white sugar
- 2 tablespoons (24 g) kosher salt
- ¾ cup (200 g) coarsely ground gochugaru or gochugaru flakes (see page 301)
- ¼ cup (60 ml) fish sauce
- 4 medium scallions, trimmed and thinly sliced
- 6 medium garlic cloves, peeled and minced
- 1 tablespoon (15 ml) ginger juice
- *Distilled* water to make up the required volume of brine

1. Peel the daikons, then cut each into ¾–1 inch (2–2.5 cm) cubes. Transfer to a large bowl and add the sugar and salt. Clean and dry your hands or put on culinary kitchen gloves. Mix until the cubes are well and evenly coated. Set aside at room temperature for 2 hours.

2. Drain the daikon *and reserve* any brine in a separate bowl. In the large bowl, combine the drained daikon, gochugaru, fish sauce, scallions, garlic, and ginger juice, plus about ¼ cup (60 ml) of the reserved brine. If you don't have enough brine, add *distilled* water to make the necessary amount. Clean and dry your hands or put on new culinary kitchen gloves. Mix by hand until well combined.

3. Pack tightly into one *clean* 2 quart (1.9 liter) glass jar or other nonreactive container, leaving 1–2 inches (2.5–5 cm) headspace in the jar. Press down gently but firmly to remove all the air pockets. The brine must come above the cubes. Use a fermentation weight, if desired. Cover or seal, then store in the refrigerator for at least 24 hours or up to 1 month, unsealing and burping the jar twice during the first week, then less frequently. Use a clean fork to take out some of the daikon cubes each time, making sure that the remainder stay under the brine.

Next
We love these cubes alongside scrambled eggs for a quick, tasty lunch.

Savoy Cabbage Kimchi

MAKES: about 2 quarts (a little less than 2 liters)
FRIDGE: up to 6 weeks
FREEZER: no

Savoy cabbage looks more like the standard, round, green cabbage that appears in North American and European supermarkets, except the leaves are crinkled (even frilly), less waxy, and less elastic. This kimchi is vegan, since we omit the fish sauce that appears in other recipes in a bid for a fresher flavor. The technique is admittedly more labor-intensive because you must massage a spice paste onto the savoy leaves. They're delicate, particularly at their ends, so work gently to avoid a mush.

- One tight large head of savoy cabbage (about 2 pounds 6 ounces or 1.1 kg)
- 2 tablespoons (24 g) kosher salt
- 1 small yellow or white onion, peeled and quartered
- ½ cup (150 g) canned crushed pineapple in juice
- Up to ½ cup (135 g) coarsely ground gochugaru or gochugaru flakes (see page 301)
- One 3 inch (7.5 cm) piece of fresh ginger (about the width of your thumb), peeled and finely chopped
- 6 medium garlic cloves, peeled
- 2 tablespoons (30 ml) soy sauce
- 2 tablespoons (25 g) granulated white sugar
- *Distilled* water for rinsing the cabbage leaves

Top to bottom:
Savoy Cabbage
Kimchi (page 311),
Radish Kimchi
(page 311), and
Cucumber Kimchi
(page 314)

1. Remove and discard (or compost) the outer leaves from the cabbage. Quarter the head, then cut out the tough core from each quarter. Clean and dry your hands or put on culinary kitchen gloves. *Gently* massage the salt among, inside, and on the leaves of the quarters. Set the quarters in a large bowl, set a clean stainless-steel saucepan or a heavy plate with a nonreactive glaze on top of them to weight them down, and set aside at room temperature for 2 hours.

2. Put the onion, pineapple, gochugaru, ginger, garlic, soy sauce, and sugar in a food processor. Cover and process to create a paste, stopping the machine at least once to scrape down the inside of the canister.

3. Remove the saucepan or plate from the cabbage. Press down on the quarters in the bowl to extract some of the liquid. Turn the quarters this way and that to get as much liquid out as you can, removing them one by one from the bowl. Reserve this salty liquid. Separate the leaves from the quarters, put them in a large colander, and rinse with *distilled* water, rearranging the leaves repeatedly to make sure they're all well rinsed. Spread paper towels across your work surface, spread the leaves out on it, and blot them dry with more paper towels.

4. Clean and rinse the large bowl. Return the leaves to it. Scrape all of the onion paste over the leaves. Clean and dry your hands or put on new culinary kitchen gloves. Mix well, massaging gently and making sure *all* the leaves are coated in the paste.

5. Pack tightly into one *clean* 2 quart (1.9 liter) glass jar or other nonreactive container. Add as much as the reserved salty liquid as will fit in the jar yet leave a 1 inch (1 cm) headspace. Press down gently but firmly to remove all the air pockets and until the brine comes above the leaves. They must be covered. Use a fermentation weight, if desired. Cover or seal, then store in the refrigerator for at least 24 hours or up to 2 weeks, unsealing and burping the jar twice during the first week, then less frequently. Use a clean fork to

take out some of the kimchi each time, making sure that the remainder stays under the brine.

Next

Make PEANUT BUTTER–KIMCHI NOODLES. Boil and drain soba or Asian wheat noodles. Whisk some of this kimchi with unsweetened, natural-style peanut butter in a bowl, then add the warm noodles and toss well to coat.

Baby Bok Choy Kimchi

MAKES: about 1 quart (about 1 liter)
FRIDGE: up to 6 weeks
FREEZER: no

We use only *baby* bok choy for this kimchi because 1) the little heads are more tender than the larger ones, 2) they have a more herbaceous flavor without any bitterness, and 3) they can stay whole while fermenting, making this a great condiment on a plate: a compact head of sour kimchi. Unfortunately, baby bok choy can be sandy. Be scrupulous when cleaning it in step 1.

> 2 quarts (8 cups or 1.9 liters) *distilled* water, plus more to clean the bok choy
> ½ cup (95 g) kosher salt
> 1 pound 5 ounces (600 g) baby bok choy (6–7 heads)
> ¼ cup (68 g) coarsely ground gochugaru or gochugaru flakes
> 2 tablespoons (30 g) purchased lemongrass paste
> 2 tablespoons (30 g) minced peeled fresh ginger
> One 4 inch (10 cm) piece of daikon, peeled and shredded through the large holes of a box grater
> 3 medium garlic cloves, peeled and minced

1. Whisk the 2 quarts (8 cups or 1.9 liters) *distilled* water and salt in a large bowl until the salt dissolves.

2. Gently spread the leaves of the bok choy heads and rinse out every speck of sand and dirt with *distilled* water, taking care to keep the heads whole. Add the cleaned bok choy to the brine and set a plate over it to keep it submerged. Set aside at room temperature for 4 hours.

3. Scoop out and reserve 1 cup (240 ml) of the brine. Drain the bok choy and remaining brine in a colander set in the sink.

4. Stir the gochugaru, lemongrass paste, ginger, daikon, and garlic in a small bowl to form a chunky paste. Clean and dry your hands or put on culinary kitchen gloves. In a large bowl, smear and spread this paste by hand between and among the leaves of the bok choy, including the outside of the heads.

5. Pack the boy choy tightly into one *clean* 1 quart (1 liter) glass jar or other nonreactive container. Press down to extract some liquid, then add some of the reserved brine to make sure every speck of boy choy is covered. Press down gently again to remove any air pockets. Use a fermentation weight, if desired. Cover or seal, then store in the refrigerator for at least 24 hours or up to 6 weeks, unsealing and burping the jar twice during the first week, then less frequently. Use a clean fork to take out some of the kimchi each time, making sure that the remainder stays under the brine.

Next

To make KIMCHI-SHRIMP SALAD, chop one or two of the kimchi bok choy heads. Add them to a bowl with cooked and drained soba noodles, some unseasoned rice vinegar, a little soy sauce, and toasted sesame oil. Add a little grated fresh ginger and cooked shelled cocktail shrimp. Toss well and serve.

Cucumber Kimchi

MAKES: about 1 quart (about 1 liter)
FRIDGE: up to 10 days after steeping
FREEZER: no

This kimchi is more of a pickle than a standard kimchi, a sort of culinary and even cultural intersection that preserves a lot of the summery flavors of Kirby (or pickling) cucumbers. Make sure you gently scrub the cucumbers with a new sponge under running cool water to remove any grime. This pickle doesn't last long because of the problems of rot. However, it doesn't stick around for even a week in our house, what with sandwiches, burgers, and hot dogs in the offing.

> 2 pounds (900 g) Kirby or pickling cucumbers, cleaned, halved lengthwise, and sliced widthwise into ¼-inch-thick (0.5-cm-thick) rounds
>
> 1 tablespoon (12 g) kosher salt
>
> *Distilled* water for rinsing the cucumber
>
> ½ small yellow or white onion, peeled and thinly sliced
>
> 3 medium garlic cloves, peeled and minced
>
> ¼ cup (60 ml) *toasted* sesame oil
>
> 2 tablespoons (35 g) coarsely ground gochugaru or gochugaru flakes (see page 301)
>
> 1 tablespoon (15 g) minced peeled fresh ginger
>
> 1 teaspoon (5 ml) fish sauce
>
> 1 teaspoon (2 g) finely grated lime zest

1. Toss the cucumber slices and salt in a large bowl until the slices are evenly and well salted. Set aside at room temperature for 20 minutes.

2. Drain the cucumber slices in a colander set in the sink and rinse them well with *distilled* water, repeatedly rearranging them to get them all rinsed. Clean and dry your hands or put on culinary kitchen gloves. Gently squeeze the cucumber slices dry by the handful over the sink.

3. Clean and dry the bowl. Return the cucumber slices to it. Add the onion, garlic, oil, gochugaru, ginger, fish sauce, and lime zest. Stir until well combined.

4. Pack the mixture into one *clean* 1 quart (1 liter) glass jar or other nonreactive container. Cover or seal, then refrigerate to steep for at least 1 day before enjoying.

Next
This kimchi is a great addition to a rice bowl: Put cooked but still warm brown rice in a bowl and top with sliced grilled flank or skirt steak, some of this kimchi, a little toasted sesame oil, some chili sauce (preferably Tomato-Lemongrass Sambal, page 217), and thinly sliced scallions.

Carrot Kimchi

MAKES: about 1 quart (about 1 liter)
FRIDGE: up to 3 weeks after fermenting
FREEZER: no

This last kimchi begins to cross the line into a sauerkraut because it's fermented at room temperature, not in the fridge. Carrots take a little patience to get them to ferment and the fridge slows the process down too much for us to start the mix in the chill. The resulting flavor is something like a cross between kimchi and sauerkraut because of the spicy notes from the gochugaru and the sweet-funky notes from the fermented carrots.

- 1½ pounds (680 g) carrots, peeled and shredded through the large holes of a box grater
- 8 ounces (225 g) daikon (about 1 medium), peeled and shredded through the large holes of a box grater
- 2 tablespoons (24 g) kosher salt
- 2 medium scallions, trimmed and thinly sliced
- 2 medium garlic cloves, peeled and thinly sliced
- 1 tablespoon (15 g) minced peeled fresh ginger
- 2 teaspoons (10 ml) fish sauce
- 1 teaspoon (6 g) coarsely ground gochugaru or gochugaru flakes (see page 301)
- 1 leaf of green cabbage

1. Mix the carrots, daikon, and salt in a large bowl until the vegetables are well and evenly salted. Set aside at room temperature for 1 hour.

2. Clean and dry your hands or put on culinary kitchen gloves. *Gently but firmly* massage the vegetables until the carrots give off a puddle of orange liquid, 3–4 minutes. Stir in the scallions, garlic, ginger, fish sauce, and gochugaru until well combined.

3. Tightly pack this mixture into one *clean* 1 quart (1 liter) glass jar or other nonreactive container, leaving about 1 inch (2.5 cm) headspace in the jar. Press down to compact to get rid of all the air pockets and to let the liquid come up over the top of the vegetables so that they're submerged.

4. Take the cabbage leaf and cut a round from it that will fit on top of the vegetables in the jar. Set this cabbage circle in the jar and press down until it seals the jar and is covered by the liquid. Set a fermentation weight on top.

5. Cover or seal, either with a traditional canning lid and sealing band or with a fermentation lid and sealing band (see page 304). Set aside at room temperature for 1 week to ferment, uncovering the jar to burp it once a day if you haven't used a fermentation lid.

6. Transfer to the fridge and store, sealed, for up to 3 weeks. Use a clean fork to take out some of the kimchi each time, making sure that the remainder stays under the brine.

More
For a bigger bump of flavor, double the garlic and/or ginger. Also, add a star anise pod to the jar with the vegetables.

Front to back: Go-to Sauerkraut (page 317), Red Cabbage Sauerkraut (page 318), and Jalapeño Sauerkraut (page 326) on hot dogs

Go-to Sauerkraut

MAKES: about 1 quart (about 1 liter)
FRIDGE: up to 3 weeks after fermenting
FREEZER: no

Here's our most straightforward sauerkraut: cabbage and salt. It's a small batch, just 1 quart (about 1 liter), enough for a few meals or an outdoor picnic. It's just a matter of patience before you have the best sauerkraut around: light, not terribly sour, vegetal, and great for your health and your meal all at once. Because this sauerkraut is fermented at room temperature, you *must* be very exacting about the weights. You're doing chemistry! Although we can say that 16 grams of kosher salt is about 1 tablespoon plus 1 teaspoon, it's important to go beyond that approximation and work with weights alone. Buy a digital kitchen scale, if only for your own safety.

> One 2¼ pound (1 kg) tight head of green (or white) cabbage
>
> 0.56 ounce (16 g) kosher salt, plus more as necessary
>
> *Distilled* water to make more brine

1. Remove any loose or bruised outer leaves from the cabbage. Cut the cabbage into quarters through its stem, then stem and core each quarter. Take off one firm outer leaf from one quarter and set it aside. Slice the quarters *crosswise* into ¼ inch (0.5 cm) shreds. Weigh out *exactly* 28.2 ounces (800 g) of the shreds. Save the rest for another use.

2. Toss the shreds with the salt in a large bowl until the cabbage is well and evenly salted. Set aside at room temperature for 3 hours.

3. Clean and dry your hands or put on culinary kitchen gloves. Gently but consistently squeeze and massage the cabbage in the bowl until softened and compacted with a good-size puddle of brine sitting in the bowl, 4–5 minutes.

4. Pack the salted cabbage (but not the brine) into one *clean* 1 quart (1 liter) glass jar. Press down firmly, either with a fermentation dowel or the clean, flat end of a handle-less rolling pin, until there are no air pockets left and 1–2 inches (2.5–5 cm) headspace in the jar.

5. Pour the brine from the bowl on top. If it settles down into the jar and leaves some cabbage exposed to the air, make more brine in a ½-teaspoon-kosher-salt-to-½-cup-*distilled*-water (2-g-to-120-ml) ratio and pour it into the jar. There should be about ½ inch (1 cm) headspace in the jar above the brine's level.

6. Take the reserved cabbage leaf and cut out a round to fit in the jar and cover the cabbage. Set it down into the brine on top of the shreds. Set a fermentation weight on top of the cabbage leaf, pressing down until some of the brine comes over the sides of the weight. Cover or seal, either with a standard lid and sealing band or with a fermentation lid and sealing band (see page 304).

7. Set aside at room temperature for 1 week to ferment, until sour and a bit funky. If you haven't used a fermentation lid, unseal the jar and burp it every day to get rid of the built-up gasses. If at any time you find the sauerkraut is sour enough for your liking, stop the process by moving the jar to the fridge. Once fermented, store in the fridge for up to 3 weeks, making sure any remaining cabbage stays under the brine when you remove some to enjoy.

Next

What's a hot dog off the grill without sauerkraut? And Coarse-Grained Mustard (page 363). On a toasted whole-wheat bun, of course.

Shortcut Vinegary Red Sauerkraut

MAKES: about 1 quart (about 1 liter)
FRIDGE: up to 3 weeks
FREEZER: no

If you don't want to go to the trouble of fermenting sauerkraut, this recipe will help you take a step toward that wilder path leading to more authentic versions. This sauerkraut is somewhat like a vinegary salad…in fact, it's got added vinegar to get the process moving. The flavors are close to but decidedly more acidic than traditional sauerkraut. You can enjoy it right away or you can let it mellow in the fridge for a week or so, just until it develops a bit of that basic, earthy tonality familiar from a more standard sauerkraut.

> One 2 pound (900 g) tight head of red cabbage (you'll use about half of it)
> 0.59 ounce (17 g) kosher salt
> 1¼ cups (300 ml) distilled white vinegar
> ⅔ cup (160 ml) water
> 1 tablespoon (6 g) black peppercorns
> 1 teaspoon caraway seeds
> 1 teaspoon yellow mustard seeds
> 1 teaspoon granulated white sugar
> 8 allspice berries
> Additional water for rinsing the leaves

1. Cut the cabbage half in two through its core. Remove the core from each section. Slice one half and a bit of the other *crosswise* into ¼ inch (0.5 cm) shreds. Weigh out exactly 16.5 ounces (470 g). If not enough, shred more of the head to compensate. Save the remainder for another use.

2. Toss the shreds and salt in a large bowl until the cabbage is well and evenly salted. Set aside at room temperature for 3 hours.

3. Meanwhile, bring the vinegar, water, peppercorns, caraway seeds, mustard seeds, sugar, and allspice berries to a boil in a small saucepan set over medium-high heat, stirring occasionally. Turn off the heat, remove the pan from the burner, and cool at room temperature until barely warm, about 1 hour. Pour the mixture into a large bowl.

4. Dump the cabbage shreds into a colander set in the sink. Rinse them well under cool water, rearranging them as you go. Clean and dry your hands or put on culinary kitchen gloves. Squeeze the shreds dry by the handful over the sink, dropping them into the bowl with the vinegar mixture. Stir well when they're all in the bowl.

5. Pack the cabbage and brine into one *clean* 1 quart (1 liter) glass jar. Press down firmly, either with a fermentation dowel or the clean, flat end of a handle-less rolling pin, until there are no air pockets left and 1 inch (2.5 cm) headspace in the jar. Make sure every speck of cabbage is submerged. Use a fermentation weight, if desired. Cover or seal, then refrigerate.

More
Add more spices to the brine: one 2 inch (5 cm) cinnamon stick, 3 or 4 whole cloves, and/or 1 teaspoon coriander seeds.

Red Cabbage Sauerkraut

MAKES: about 1 quart (about 1 liter)
FRIDGE: up to 3 weeks after fermenting
FREEZER: no

Although this traditional sauerkraut uses slightly sweeter red cabbage, the fermentation works a little miracle, turning the red (or really, purple) cabbage a gorgeous shade of pink. The flavors are a little more complex than our Go-to Sauerkraut (page 317) because the sweetness of the red cabbage lends itself to a wider range of added spices.

One 2¼ pound (1 kg) tight head of red cabbage

0.56 ounce (16 g) kosher salt, plus more as necessary

1 teaspoon caraway seeds

1 teaspoon yellow mustard seeds

2 dried bay leaves

Distilled water to make more brine

1. Remove any loose or bruised outer leaves from the red cabbage. Cut the cabbage into quarters through its stem, then stem and core each quarter. Take off one firm outer leaf from one quarter and set it aside. Slice the quarters *crosswise* into ¼ inch (0.5 cm) shreds. Weigh out *exactly* 28.2 ounces (800 g) of the shreds. Save the rest for another use.

2. Toss the shreds, salt, caraway seeds, and mustard seeds in a large bowl until the cabbage is well and evenly salted. Set aside at room temperature for 2 hours.

3. Clean and dry your hands or put on culinary kitchen gloves. Gently but consistently squeeze and massage the cabbage in the bowl until softened and compacted with a good-size puddle of brine sitting in the bowl, 4–5 minutes.

4. Pack the salted cabbage and spices (but not the brine) into one *clean* 1 quart (1 liter) glass jar, sticking the bay leaves into the mixture as you pack it in. Press down firmly, either with a fermentation dowel or the clean, flat end of a handle-less rolling pin, until there are no air pockets left and 1–2 inches (2.5–5 cm) headspace in the jar.

5. Pour the brine from the bowl on top. If it settles down into the jar and leaves some cabbage at the top exposed to the air, make more brine in a ½-teaspoon-kosher-salt-to-½-cup-*distilled*-water (2-g-to-120-ml) ratio and pour it into the jar. There should be about ½ inch (1 cm) headspace in the jar above the level of the brine.

6. Take the reserved cabbage leaf and cut out a round to fit in the jar and cover the cabbage mixture. Set it down into the brine on top of the shreds. Set a fermentation weight on top of the cabbage leaf, pressing down until some of the liquid comes over the sides of the weight. Cover or seal, either with a standard lid and sealing band or with a fermentation lid and sealing band (see page 304).

7. Set aside at room temperature for 1 week to ferment, until sour and a bit funky. If you haven't used a fermentation lid, unseal the jar and burp it every day to get rid of the built-up gasses. If at any time you find the sauerkraut is sour enough for your liking, stop the process by moving the jar to the fridge. Once fermented, store in the fridge for up to 3 weeks, making sure any remaining cabbage stays under the brine when you remove some to enjoy.

Next

We love this sauerkraut on avocado toast: First a slice of whole-wheat toast, then a smear of mayonnaise, then this drained sauerkraut, then the peeled, seeded avocado half smashed on top.

Caraway-Cranberry Sauerkraut

MAKES: about 1 quart (about 1 liter)
FRIDGE: up to 3 weeks after fermenting
FREEZER: no

This is our version of Lithuanian sauerkraut, made with cabbage, carrots, and cranberries. It's sweeter than some of our other sauerkrauts and so perhaps a better place to start home fermentation if you're wary because you were forced to eat horrid, canned sauerkraut as a kid. This one's light and fizzy, given all the natural sugars, especially after it's been in the fridge for a while. It's a great side dish on its own but even better in a turkey club.

One 2¼ pound (1 kg) tight head of green (or white) cabbage

2 ounces (60 g) carrot (about 1 medium), peeled and shredded through the large holes of a box grater

0.56 ounce (16 g) kosher salt, plus more as necessary

1 teaspoon caraway seeds

6 fresh whole cranberries

Distilled water to make more brine

1. Remove any loose or bruised outer leaves from the red cabbage. Cut the cabbage into quarters through its stem, then stem and core each quarter. Take off one firm outer leaf from one quarter and set it aside. Slice the quarters *crosswise* into ¼ inch (0.5 cm) shreds. Weigh out *exactly* 26.5 ounces (750 g) of the shreds. Save the rest for another use.

2. Toss the cabbage shreds, carrot, and salt in a large bowl until the vegetables are well and evenly salted. Set aside at room temperature for 3 hours.

3. Clean and dry your hands or put on culinary kitchen gloves. Gently but consistently squeeze and massage the cabbage mixture in the bowl until softened and compacted with a good-size puddle of brine sitting in the bowl, 4–5 minutes. Stir in the caraway seeds and cranberries.

4. Pack the cabbage mixture (but not the brine) into one *clean* 1 quart (1 liter) glass jar. Press down firmly, either with a fermentation dowel or the clean, flat end of a handle-less rolling pin, until there are no air pockets left and 1–2 inches (2.5–5 cm) headspace in the jar.

5. Pour the brine from the bowl on top. If it settles down into the jar and leaves some vegetable matter at the top exposed to the air, make more brine in a ½-teaspoon-kosher-salt-to-½-cup-*distilled*-water (2-g-to-120-ml) ratio and pour it into the jar. There should be about ½ inch (1 cm) headspace in the jar above the level of the brine.

6. Take the reserved cabbage leaf and cut out a round to fit in the jar and cover the cabbage mixture. Set it down into the brine on top of the shreds. Set a fermentation weight on top of the cabbage leaf, pressing down until some of the

liquid comes up over the sides of the weight. Cover or seal, either with a standard lid and ring or with a fermentation lid and ring.

7. Set aside at room temperature for 1 week to ferment, until sour and a bit funky. If you haven't used a fermentation lid, unseal the jar and burp it every day to get rid of the built-up gasses. If at any time you find the sauerkraut is sour enough for your liking, stop the process by moving the jar to the fridge. Once fermented, store in the fridge for up to 3 weeks, making sure any remaining vegetable stays under the brine when you remove some to enjoy.

More
Fire it up with up to 1 teaspoon red pepper flakes added with the caraway and cranberry.

Apple Sauerkraut

MAKES: about 1 quart (about 1 liter)
FRIDGE: up to 3 weeks after fermenting
FREEZER: no

Apple and onion add a lot of sweetness to this ferment, making a sauerkraut that offers a nice contrast to spicy sausages off the grill or a grilled flank steak with a chili marinade. Be extra exacting with this one because of the higher sugar content. If the ferment starts to smell acrid, it's been contaminated in some way and should be tossed out. Otherwise, you've got a delightful sauerkraut that even helps with your diet plan—a forkful in the afternoon curbs snack cravings.

One 2¼ pound (1 kg) tight head of red cabbage

10 ounces (285 g) sweet apple, preferably a Honeycrisp apple (about 1 large), stemmed, peeled, cored, and shredded through the large holes of a box grater

1 medium red onion, peeled, halved, and sliced into very thin half-moons

0.56 ounce (16 g) kosher salt, plus more as necessary

1 teaspoon caraway seeds

Distilled water to make more brine

1. Remove any loose or bruised outer leaves from the red cabbage. Cut the cabbage into quarters through its stem, then stem and core each quarter. Take off one firm outer leaf from one quarter and set it aside. Slice the quarters *crosswise* into ¼ inch (0.5 cm) shreds. Weigh out *exactly* 21.2 ounces (600 g) of the shreds. Save the rest for another use.

2. Toss the cabbage shreds, apple, onion, salt, and caraway seeds in a large bowl until everything is well and evenly salted. Set aside at room temperature for 2 hours.

3. Clean and dry your hands or put on culinary kitchen gloves. Gently but consistently squeeze and massage the cabbage mixture in the bowl until softened and compacted with a good-size puddle of brine sitting in the bowl, 4–5 minutes.

4. Pack the cabbage mixture (but not the brine) into one *clean* 1 quart (1 liter) glass jar. Press down firmly, either with a fermentation dowel or the clean flat end of a handle-less rolling pin, until there are no air pockets left and 1–2 inches (2.5–5 cm) headspace in the jar.

5. Pour the brine from the bowl on top. If it settles down into the jar and leaves some cabbage mixture at the top exposed to the air, make more brine in a ½-teaspoon-kosher-salt-to-½-cup-*distilled*-water (2-g-to-120-ml) ratio and pour it into the jar. There should be about ½ inch (1 cm) headspace in the jar above the level of the brine.

6. Take the reserved cabbage leaf and cut out a round to fit in the jar and cover the cabbage mixture. Set it down into the brine on top of the shreds. Set a fermentation weight on top of the cabbage leaf, pressing down until the brine comes up over the sides of the weight. Cover or seal, either with a standard lid and sealing band or with a fermentation lid and sealing band (see page 304).

7. Set aside at room temperature for 1 week to ferment, until sour and a bit funky. If you haven't used a fermentation lid, unseal the jar and burp it every day to get rid of the built-up gasses. If at any time you find the sauerkraut is sour enough for your liking, stop the process by moving the jar to the fridge. Once fermented, store in the fridge for up to 3 weeks, making sure any remaining shreds stay under the brine when you remove some to enjoy.

Tip
For heat, tuck a couple of stemmed dried árbol chilis into the brine.

Pineapple Sauerkraut

MAKES: about 1 quart (about 1 liter)
FRIDGE: up to 3 weeks after fermenting
FREEZER: no

Here, sauerkraut gets even sweeter, and a little tropical…if that makes any sense. We wanted to make one sauerkraut that had a bit more sweetness to it, but excess sugar is not really the friend of room-temperature fermentation. Or perhaps *too much* of a friend, allowing bad bugs to proliferate. The best alternative for a sweeter sauerkraut is fresh pineapple: lots of sweetness, plus some protective enzymes. This admittedly whimsical sauerkraut is the perfect topper for strongly flavored meats and root vegetables: venison, buffalo, and goat, of course, but also steamed rutabaga or turnips (with lots of butter). Although we often recommend using kitchen culinary gloves, we *strongly* do so here because we're trying to keep contaminants to a minimum. For the same reason, buy a fresh, whole pineapple, rather than a precut one.

Clockwise from bottom: Pineapple Sauerkraut (page 321), Celery Root Sauerkraut (page 323), Fennel Sauerkraut (page 325), and Beet Sauerkraut (page 324)

One 1½ pound (680 g) tight head of green (or white) cabbage

One 2 pound (900 g) small pineapple

0.7 ounce (20 g) kosher salt, plus more as necessary

Distilled water to make more brine

1. Remove any loose or bruised outer leaves from the cabbage. Cut the cabbage into quarters through its stem, then stem and core each quarter. Take off one firm outer leaf from one quarter and set it aside. Slice the quarters *crosswise* into ¼ inch (0.5 cm) shreds. Weigh out *exactly* 17.6 ounces (500 g) of the shreds. Save the rest for another use.

2. Peel, quarter, and core the pineapple. Weigh out 10.5 ounces (300 g) and finely chop this amount. Save the rest for another use.

3. Toss the cabbage shreds, pineapple, and salt in a large bowl until everything is well and evenly salted. Set aside at room temperature for 1 hour.

4. Put on culinary kitchen gloves. *Very* gently squeeze and massage the cabbage mixture in the bowl until softened and compacted with a good-size puddle of brine sitting in the bowl, 4–5 minutes. The pineapple will give off a lot of liquid, but it shouldn't be crushed to bits during this process.

5. Pack the cabbage mixture (but not the brine) into one *clean* 1 quart (1 liter) glass jar. Press down firmly, either with a fermentation dowel or the clean, flat end of a handle-less rolling pin, until there are no air pockets left and 1–2 inches (2.5–5 cm) headspace in the jar. Pour the brine from the bowl on top, leaving about ½ inch (1 cm) headspace in the jar. If there's not enough brine, make more in a ½-teaspoon-kosher-salt-to-½-cup-*distilled*-water (2-g-to-120-ml) ratio.

6. Take the reserved cabbage leaf and cut out a round to fit in the jar and cover the cabbage mixture. Set it down into the brine on top of the shreds. Set a fermentation weight on top of the cabbage leaf, pressing down until some of the liquid comes up over the sides of the weight. Cover or seal, either with a standard lid and sealing band

or with a fermentation lid and sealing band (see page 304).

7. Set aside at room temperature for 1 week to ferment, until sour and a bit funky. If you haven't used a fermentation lid, unseal the jar and burp it every day to get rid of the built-up gasses. If at any time you find the sauerkraut is sour enough for your liking, stop the process by moving the jar to the fridge. Once fermented, store in the fridge for up to 3 weeks, making sure any shreds stay under the brine when you remove some to enjoy.

More

Add up to 1 teaspoon coriander seeds and/or 1 teaspoon brown mustard seeds with the salt.

Celery Root Sauerkraut

MAKES: about 1 quart (about 1 liter)
FRIDGE: up to 3 weeks after fermenting
FREEZER: no

Celery root (aka celeriac) gives sauerkraut a more savory, vegetal flavor, not really like celery, more like the earthiness of a root vegetable combined with mild, anise notes. You're going to lose a lot of the celery root when you trim it because you have to get rid of *every* bit of brown and *every* hint of squishiness. Shredding a celery root with a box grater is tough work. Wear a cut-proof kitchen glove to be extra safe.

One 1½ pound (680 g) tight head of green (or white) cabbage

One 1½ pound (680 g) celery root (or celeriac)

0.56 ounce (16 g) kosher salt, plus more as necessary

1 teaspoon celery seeds

Distilled water to make more brine

1. Remove any loose or bruised outer leaves from the cabbage. Cut the cabbage into quarters through its stem, then stem and core each quarter.

Take off one firm outer leaf from one quarter and set it aside. Slice the quarters crosswise into ¼ inch (0.5 cm) shreds. Weigh out *exactly* 14.1 ounces (400 g) of the shreds. Save the rest for another use.

2. Cut off the brown skin, any hairy bits, and all the waggly roots from the celery root. Trim off every speck of brown and any squishy bits so you're left with a creamy white core. (The trimmings are great for compost!) Shred the core through the large holes of a box grater. Weigh out *exactly* 14.1 ounces (400 g) of the shreds. Save the rest for another use.

3. Toss the cabbage, celery root, salt, and celery seeds in a large bowl until everything is well and evenly salted. Set aside at room temperature for 3 hours.

4. Clean and dry your hands or put on culinary kitchen gloves. Gently but consistently squeeze and massage the cabbage mixture in the bowl until softened and compacted with a good-size puddle of brine sitting in the bowl, 4–5 minutes.

5. Pack the cabbage mixture (but not the brine) into one *clean* 1 quart (1 liter) glass jar. Press down firmly, either with a fermentation dowel or the clean, flat end of a handle-less rolling pin, until there are no air pockets left and 1–2 inches (2.5–5 cm) headspace in the jar.

6. Pour the brine from the bowl on top. If it settles down into the jar and leaves some vegetable matter at the top exposed to the air, make more brine in a ½-teaspoon-kosher-salt-to-½-cup-*distilled*-water (2-g-to-120-ml) ratio and pour it into the jar. There should be about ½ inch (1 cm) headspace in the jar above the level of the brine.

7. Take the reserved cabbage leaf and cut out a round to fit in the jar and cover the cabbage mixture. Set it into the brine on top of the shreds. Set a fermentation weight on top of the cabbage leaf, pressing down until some of the liquid comes over the sides. Cover or seal, either with a standard lid and sealing band or with a fermentation lid and sealing band (see page 304).

8. Set aside at room temperature for 1 week to ferment, until sour and a bit funky. If you haven't used a fermentation lid, unseal the jar and burp it every day to get rid of the built-up gasses. If at any time you find the sauerkraut is sour enough for your liking, stop the process by moving the jar to the fridge. Once fermented, store in the fridge for up to 3 weeks, making sure any remaining vegetable stays under the brine.

More
Add more flavor depth by mixing 1–2 teaspoons coriander seeds into the cabbage blend before it goes into the jar.

Beet Sauerkraut

MAKES: about 1 quart (about 1 liter)
FRIDGE: up to 3 weeks after fermenting
FREEZER: no

Beets add an earthy sweetness to sauerkraut, not as powerful as pineapple or apple, but just pleasing enough to take the edge off the sour, base flavors of the fermented cabbage. Beets themselves won't produce as much water as cabbage when salted, so we need to add a little extra to the mix to make sure we create the proper brine for fermentation.

> One 1¾ pound (800 g) tight head of green (or white) cabbage
> 8 ounces (225 g) purple beet (about 1 large)
> ½ cup (120 ml) *distilled* water
> 0.56 ounce (16 g) kosher salt, plus more as necessary
> 1 teaspoon celery seeds
> More *distilled* water to make more brine

1. Remove any loose or bruised outer leaves from the cabbage. Cut the cabbage into quarters through its stem, then stem and core each quarter. Take off one firm outer leaf from one quarter and set it aside. Slice the quarters *crosswise* into ¼ inch (0.5 cm) shreds. Weigh out *exactly* 21.6 ounces (600 g) of the shreds. Save the rest for another use.

2. Trim and peel the beet. Grate it through the large holes of a box grater. (A cut-proof kitchen glove saves your knuckles.) Weigh out *exactly* 7 ounces (200 g). Save the rest for another use.

3. Toss the cabbage, beet, ½ cup (120 ml) *distilled* water, salt, and celery seeds in a large bowl until everything is well and evenly salted. Set aside at room temperature for 2 hours.

4. Put on culinary kitchen gloves to prevent staining. Gently but consistently squeeze and massage the cabbage mixture in the bowl until softened and compacted, 4–5 minutes.

5. Pack the cabbage mixture (but not the brine) into one *clean* 1 quart (1 liter) glass jar. Press down firmly, either with a wooden tamping press designed for such or the flat end of a cleaned rolling pin until there are no air pockets left and 1–2 inches (2.5–5 cm) headspace in the jar.

6. Now pour the brine from the bowl on top. If it settles down into the jar and leaves some vegetable matter at the top exposed to the air, make more brine in a ½-teaspoon-kosher-salt-to-½-cup-*distilled*-water ratio (2-g-to-120-ml) and pour it into the jar. There should be about ½ inch (1 cm) headspace in the jar above the level of the brine.

7. Take the reserved cabbage leaf and cut out a round to fit in the jar and cover the cabbage mixture. Set it down into the brine on top of the shreds. Set a fermentation weight on top of the cabbage leaf. Cover or seal, either with a standard lid and sealing band or with a fermentation lid and sealing band (see page 304).

8. Set aside at room temperature for 1 week to ferment, until sour and a bit funky. If you haven't used a fermentation lid, unseal the jar and burp it every day to get rid of the built-up gasses. If at any time you find the sauerkraut is sour enough for your liking, stop the process by moving the jar to the fridge. Once fermented, store in the fridge for up to 3 weeks, making sure any remaining vegetable stays under the brine when you remove some to enjoy.

More

For a more elegant presentation, julienne the trimmed and peeled beet, cutting it into very thin matchsticks. Use the same weight (8 ounces) as specified in the recipe.

Fennel Sauerkraut

MAKES: about 1 quart (about 1 liter)
FRIDGE: up to 3 weeks after fermenting
FREEZER: no

Fennel makes a gorgeously refined sauerkraut: hints of anise flavor throughout the earthier, sour notes. It's a great addition to most sandwiches… and the brine itself can be a healthy drink, particularly when mixed with plain seltzer, a refreshing if bold sip. Fennel is often speckled with brown bruises, *all of which* must be removed. We often buy a little extra fennel, just to make sure we have enough. We easily use up any excess in stews and salads.

> One 1½ pound (680 g) tight head of green (or white) cabbage
>
> 1 pound (450 g) fennel bulbs (about 2 medium)
>
> 0.56 ounce (16 g) kosher salt, plus more as necessary
>
> 1 teaspoon fennel seeds
>
> *Distilled* water to make more brine

1. Remove the outer leaves and browned bits from the cabbage. Cut the remaining cabbage into quarters through its stem end. Core each section. Take off one firm outer leaf from one quarter and set it aside. Slice the remaining pieces *crosswise* into ¼ inch (0.5 cm) shreds. Weigh out *exactly* 17.5 ounces (500 g). Save the remainder for salads and slaws.

2. Trim the fennel of its stalks and fronds, removing about the top 2 inches (5 cm) from each head. Also, trim off the woody bottoms. Then cut off and discard any brown marks. Grate the remaining fennel through the large holes of a box grater. Weigh out *exactly* 10.5 ounces (300 g). Save the remainder for salads.

3. Toss the cabbage shreds, fennel, and salt in a large bowl until the vegetables are well and evenly salted. Set aside at room temperature for 3 hours.

4. Clean and dry your hands or put on culinary kitchen gloves. Gently but consistently squeeze and massage the vegetables, until softened and compacted with a good-size puddle of brine sitting in the bowl, 4–5 minutes. Stir in the fennel seeds.

5. Pack the vegetables (but not the brine) into one *clean* 1 quart (1 liter) glass jar. Press down firmly, either with a fermentation dowel or the clean, flat end of a handle-less rolling pin, until there are no air pockets left and 1–2 inches (2.5–5 cm) headspace in the jar.

6. Pour the brine from the bowl on top. If it settles down into the jar and leaves some vegetables exposed to the air, make more brine in a ½-teaspoon-kosher-salt-to-½-cup-*distilled*-water (2-g-to-120-ml) ratio and pour it into the jar. There should be about ½ inch (1 cm) headspace above the level of the brine.

7. Take the cabbage leaf and cut out a round to fit in the jar and cover the cabbage mixture. Set it down into the brine on top of the shreds. Set a fermentation weight on top of the cabbage leaf, pressing down until the liquid comes up over the sides of the weight. Cover or seal, either with a standard lid and sealing band or with a fermentation lid and sealing band (see page 304).

8. Set aside at room temperature for 1 week to ferment, until sour and a bit funky. If you haven't used a fermentation lid, unseal the jar and burp it every day to get rid of the built-up gasses. If at any time you find the sauerkraut is sour enough for your liking, stop the process by moving the jar to the fridge. Once fermented, store in the fridge for up to 3 weeks, making sure any remaining vegetables stay under the brine when you remove some to enjoy.

Next

The brine can be the base of a cold soup. Add it to the blender with cucumbers, carrots, and a little shallot. Then add a little plain cashew cream or cashew yogurt (the brine will curdle sour cream or dairy yogurt).

Jalapeño Sauerkraut

MAKES: about 1 quart (about 1 liter)
FRIDGE: up to 3 weeks after fermenting
FREEZER: no

We love the fiery, citrus-like burst that fresh jalapeños bring to sauerkraut. It tames the funky undertones and turns the condiment into a rather astoundingly bright concoction, terrific as a vinegary topper for tacos. Rather than adjusting the total number of jalapeños to control the heat, seed one, two, or all of them.

> One 2¼ pound (1 kg) tight head of green (or white) cabbage
>
> 0.56 ounce (16 g) kosher salt, plus more as necessary
>
> 4 ounces (112 g) fresh jalapeño chilis (about 4 large), stemmed, seeded (if desired), and thinly sliced
>
> *Distilled* water to make more brine

1. Remove any loose or bruised outer leaves from the cabbage. Cut the cabbage into quarters through its stem, then stem and core each quarter. Take off one firm outer leaf from one quarter and set it aside. Slice the quarters *crosswise* into ¼ inch (0.5 cm) shreds. Weigh out *exactly* 26.5 ounces (750 g) of the shreds. Save the rest for another use.

2. Toss the shreds and salt in a large bowl until the cabbage is well and evenly salted. Set aside at room temperature for 3 hours.

3. Clean and dry your hands or put on culinary kitchen gloves. Gently but consistently squeeze and massage the cabbage in the bowl until softened and compacted with a good-size puddle of brine sitting in the bowl, 4–5 minutes. Add the jalapeño slices and toss well.

4. Pack the vegetable mixture (but not the brine) into one *clean* 1 quart (1 liter) glass jar. Press down firmly, either with a fermentation dowel or the clean, flat end of a handle-less rolling pin, until there are no air pockets left and 1–2 inches (2.5–5 cm) headspace in the jar.

5. Pour the brine from the bowl on top. If it settles down into the jar and leaves some cabbage at the top exposed to the air, make more brine in a ½-teaspoon-kosher-salt-to-½-cup-*distilled*-water (2-g-to-120-ml) ratio and pour it into the jar. There should be about ½ inch (1 cm) headspace in the jar above the level of the brine.

6. Take the reserved cabbage leaf and cut out a round to fit in the jar and cover the cabbage mixture. Set it down into the brine on top of the shreds. Set a fermentation weight on top of the cabbage leaf, pressing down until some of the liquid comes up over the sides of the weight. Cover or seal, either with a standard lid and sealing band or with a fermentation lid and sealing band (see page 304).

7. Set aside at room temperature for 1 week to ferment, until sour and a bit funky. If you haven't used a fermentation lid, unseal the jar and burp it every day to get rid of the built-up gasses. If at any time you find the sauerkraut is sour enough for your liking, stop the process by moving the jar to the fridge. Once fermented, store in the fridge for up to 3 weeks, making sure any remaining vegetable stays under the brine when you remove some to enjoy.

Next
This sauerkraut is terrific when mixed with a hot chili sauce for an over-the-top condiment. Mix it with a splash of sriracha or a bit more of your own homemade Thick Red Chili Sauce (page 349).

Turmeric-Onion Sauerkraut

MAKES: about 1 quart (about 1 liter)
FRIDGE: up to 3 weeks after fermenting
FREEZER: no

Turmeric lends a strong, savory note to sauerkraut…and onions, a decided sweetness, especially if you use a sweet onion like a Vidalia. It's a bold topping for whitefish salad on a crunchy cracker. Because turmeric is so staining, we *strongly* recommend culinary kitchen gloves when you prepare this sauerkraut.

> One 1½ pound (680 g) tight head of green (or white) cabbage
>
> 1 pound (450 g) medium sweet onions, preferably Vidalia (about 2 medium)
>
> 0.56 ounce (16 g) kosher salt, plus more as necessary
>
> ½ teaspoon ground dried turmeric
>
> *Distilled* water to make more brine

1. Remove any loose or bruised outer leaves from the cabbage. Cut the cabbage into quarters through its stem, then stem and core each quarter. Take off one firm outer leaf from one quarter and set it aside. Slice the quarters *crosswise* into ¼ inch (0.5 cm) shreds. Weigh out *exactly* 15 ounces (425 g) of the shreds. Save the rest for another use.

2. Peel and quarter the onions. Slice them into very thin shreds. Weigh out *exactly* 13 ounces (370 g). Save the rest for another use (like the already-prepped onion base for a skillet sauté).

3. Toss the cabbage, onion, salt, and turmeric in a large bowl until the cabbage is well and evenly salted. Set aside at room temperature for 2 hours.

4. Put on culinary kitchen gloves. Gently but consistently squeeze and massage the vegetable mixture in the bowl until softened and compacted with a good-size puddle of brine sitting in the bowl, 4–5 minutes.

5. Pack the vegetable mixture (but not the brine) into one *clean* 1 quart (1 liter) glass jar. Press down firmly, either with a fermentation dowel or the clean, flat end of a handle-less rolling pin, until there are no air pockets left and 1–2 inches (2.5–5 cm) headspace in the jar.

6. Pour the brine from the bowl on top. If it settles down into the jar and leaves some cabbage at the top exposed to the air, make more brine in a ½-teaspoon-kosher-salt-to-½-cup-*distilled*-water (2-g-to-120-ml) ratio and pour it into the jar. There should be about ½ inch (1 cm) headspace in the jar above the level of the brine.

7. Take the reserved cabbage leaf and cut out a round to fit in the jar and cover the cabbage mixture. Set it down into the brine on top of the shreds. Set a fermentation weight on top of the cabbage leaf, pressing down until some of the liquid comes up over the sides of the weight. Cover or seal, either with a standard lid and sealing band or with a fermentation lid and sealing band (see page 304).

8. Set aside at room temperature for 1 week to ferment, until sour and a bit funky. If you haven't used a fermentation lid, unseal the jar and burp it every day to get rid of the built-up gasses. If at any time you find the sauerkraut is sour enough for your liking, stop the process by moving the jar to the fridge. Once fermented, store in the fridge for up to 3 weeks, making sure any remaining vegetable stays under the brine when you remove some to enjoy.

More

Add up to 1 teaspoon black peppercorns to the vegetable mixture after you've massaged it but before you pack it into the jar.

Gin Sauerkraut

MAKES: about 1 quart (about 1 liter)
FRIDGE: up to 3 weeks after fermenting
FREEZER: no

This sauerkraut is not made with gin itself, but crafted with the botanicals that make gin so tasty. All those dried spices, including some whole berries and seeds, will never soften during fermentation, so make sure you avoid them when you serve the condiment.

> One 2¼ pound (1 kg) tight head of green (or white) cabbage
>
> Long wide strips of zest from 1 small lemon
>
> 1 tablespoon (15 ml) lemon juice
>
> 1 tablespoon (8 g) juniper berries, lightly crushed
>
> 1 tablespoon (15 g) grated peeled fresh ginger
>
> 0.56 ounce (16 g) kosher salt, plus more as necessary
>
> 2 teaspoons coriander seeds, lightly crushed
>
> 1 teaspoon decorticated (husked and removed from the pods) cardamom seeds
>
> 1 star anise pod, broken into its individual chambers
>
> ⅛ teaspoon grated nutmeg
>
> *Distilled* water to make more brine

1. Remove any loose or bruised outer leaves from the cabbage. Cut the cabbage into quarters through its stem, then stem and core each quarter. Take off one firm outer leaf from one quarter and set it aside. Slice the quarters *crosswise* into ¼ inch (0.5 cm) shreds. Weigh out *exactly* 28.2 ounces (800 g) of the shreds. Save the rest for another use.

2. Toss the cabbage, lemon zest, lemon juice, juniper berries, ginger, salt, coriander seeds, cardamom seeds, star anise, and nutmeg in a large bowl until the cabbage is well and evenly salted. Set aside at room temperature for 3 hours.

3. Clean and dry your hands or put on culinary kitchen gloves. Gently but consistently squeeze and massage the cabbage mixture in the bowl until softened and compacted with a good-size puddle of brine sitting in the bowl, 4–5 minutes.

4. Pack the cabbage mixture (but not the brine) into one *clean* 1 quart (1 liter) glass jar. Press down firmly, either with a fermentation dowel or the clean, flat end of a handle-less rolling pin, until there are no air pockets left and 1–2 inches (2.5–5 cm) headspace in the jar.

5. Pour the brine from the bowl on top. If it settles down into the jar and leaves some cabbage at the top exposed to the air, make more brine in a ½-teaspoon-kosher-salt-to-½-cup-*distilled*-water (2-g-to-120-ml) ratio and pour it into the jar. There should be about ½ inch (1 cm) headspace in the jar above the level of the brine.

6. Take the reserved cabbage leaf and cut out a round to fit in the jar and cover the cabbage mixture. Set it down into the brine on top of the shreds. Set a fermentation weight on top of the cabbage leaf, pressing down until some of the liquid comes up over the sides of the weight. Cover or seal, either with a standard lid and sealing band or with a fermentation lid and sealing band (see page 304).

7. Set aside at room temperature for 1 week to ferment, until sour and a bit funky. If you haven't used a fermentation lid, unseal the jar and burp it every day to get rid of the built-up gasses. If at any time you find the sauerkraut is sour enough for your liking, stop the process by moving the jar to the fridge. Once fermented, store in the fridge for up to 3 weeks, making sure any remaining vegetable stays under the brine when you remove some to enjoy.

Tip
Crush the various dried spices on a cutting board by pressing down with a large saucepan.

Pistachio-Duqqa Sauerkraut

MAKES: about 1 quart (about 1 liter)
FRIDGE: up to 3 weeks after fermenting
FREEZER: no

Duqqa (or sometimes *dukkah*) is a Middle Eastern spice blend. We combine some of its flavors (along with pistachios!) into this surprising, flavorful sauerkraut. The spice blend gives the ferment a warming twist. Rather than shredding the cabbage by hand, we use a box grater or a food processor to produce much smaller bits of cabbage. We find the relish-like texture works better with the complex spice blend. One note: The pistachios must be fresh. If they have the slightest acrid odor, you may end up with a burst sauerkraut jar. Taste one to know they're good to go.

> One 2¼ pound (1 kg) tight head of green (or white) cabbage
> 0.56 ounce (16 g) kosher salt, plus more as necessary
> ¼ cup (28 g) finely chopped *unsalted* roasted shelled pistachios
> 2 tablespoons (18 g) white sesame seeds
> ½ teaspoon fennel seeds
> ½ teaspoon coriander seeds
> ½ teaspoon cumin seeds
> *Distilled* water to make more brine

1. Remove and discard any loose outer leaves from the cabbage. Take off one outer leaf and set it aside. Quarter and core the cabbage. Grate the quarters through the large holes of a box grater or quarter them and run through the shredding blade of a food processor.

2. Toss the cabbage with the salt in a large bowl until the shreds are evenly and well coated. Add the pistachios and the sesame, fennel, coriander, and cumin seeds.

3. Don't hesitate. Clean and dry your hands or put on culinary kitchen gloves. Gently but consistently squeeze and massage the cabbage mixture in the bowl until softened and compacted with a good-size puddle of brine sitting in the bowl, 4–5 minutes.

4. Pack the cabbage and spice mixture (but not the brine) into one *clean* 1 quart (1 liter) glass jar. Press down firmly, either with a fermentation dowel or the clean, flat end of a handle-less rolling pin, until there are no air pockets left and 1–2 inches (2.5–5 cm) headspace in the jar.

5. Pour the brine from the bowl on top. If it settles down into the jar and leaves some cabbage at the top exposed to the air, make more brine in a ½-teaspoon-kosher-salt-to-½-cup-*distilled*-water (2-g-to-120-ml) ratio and pour it into the jar. There should be about ½ inch (1 cm) headspace in the jar above the level of the brine.

6. Take the reserved cabbage leaf and cut out a round to fit in the jar and cover the cabbage mixture. Set it down into the brine on top of the shreds. Set a fermentation weight on top of the cabbage leaf, pressing down until some of the liquid comes up over the sides of the weight. Cover or seal, either with a standard lid and sealing band or with a fermentation lid and sealing band (see page 304).

7. Set aside at room temperature for 1 week to ferment, until sour and a bit funky. If you haven't used a fermentation lid, unseal the jar and burp it every day to get rid of the built-up gasses. If at any time you find the sauerkraut is sour enough for your liking, stop the process by moving the jar to the fridge. Once fermented, store in the fridge for up to 3 weeks, making sure any remaining vegetable stays under the brine when you remove some to enjoy.

More
For a deeper flavor, substitute toasted sesame seeds for the white ones.

Carrot Sauerkraut

MAKES: about 1 quart (about 1 liter)
FRIDGE: up to 3 weeks after fermenting
FREEZER: no

We've got a few ferments that don't involve cabbage…and we call them *sauerkraut* for convenience, because they take on the earthy-funky flavors of the more traditional condiment, even when lacking the quintessential vegetable. Carrots retain a great deal of their natural sweetness in this ferment. In fact, they'll be sweeter if you use small-ish carrots: not immature carrots, and not the so-called *baby carrots* (which are cut down to snacking size)—but just not the thick, giant roots often bagged at the supermarket. The smaller carrots will morph into a remarkable condiment that adds a kick to hot dogs or brats off the grill.

> 2¼ pounds (1 kg) carrots, peeled
>
> 2 tablespoons (30 g) minced peeled fresh ginger
>
> 0.56 ounce (16 g) kosher salt, plus more as necessary
>
> 1 green cabbage leaf
>
> *Distilled* water to make more brine

1. Grate the carrots through the large holes of a box grater. Weigh out *exactly* 28.2 ounces (1¾ pounds or 800 g) of the shreds. Save the rest for another use.

2. Mix the carrots, ginger, and salt in a large bowl until the carrots are evenly and well coated. Set aside at room temperature for 1 hour.

3. Clean and dry your hands or put on culinary kitchen gloves. Gently but consistently squeeze and massage the carrot mixture in the bowl until softened and compacted with a good-size puddle of orange brine in the bowl, 3–4 minutes.

4. Pack the carrot mixture (but not the brine) into one *clean* 1 quart (1 liter) glass jar. Press down firmly, either with a fermentation dowel or the clean, flat end of a handle-less rolling pin, until there are no air pockets left and 1–2 inches (2.5–5 cm) headspace in the jar.

Bottom to top: Carrot Sauerkraut (page 330) and Turmeric-Onion Sauerkraut (page 327)

5. Pour the brine in the bowl on top. If it settles down into the jar and leaves some carrot at the top exposed to the air, make more brine in a ½-teaspoon-kosher-salt-to-½-cup-*distilled*-water (2-g-to-120-ml) ratio and pour it into the jar. There should be about ½ inch (1 cm) headspace in the jar above the level of the brine.

6. Take the cabbage leaf and cut out a round to fit in the jar and cover the carrot mixture. Set it down into the brine on top of the shreds. Set a fermentation weight on top of the cabbage leaf, pressing down until some of the liquid comes up over the sides of the weight. Cover or seal, either with a standard lid and sealing band or with a fermentation lid and sealing band (see page 304).

7. Set aside at room temperature for 1 week to ferment, until sour and a bit funky. If you haven't used a fermentation lid, unseal the jar and burp it every day to get rid of the built-up gasses. If at any time you find the condiment is sour enough for your liking, stop the process by moving the jar to the fridge. Once fermented, store in the fridge for up to 3 weeks, making sure any carrot or ginger stays under the brine when you remove some to enjoy.

Next
Drain the fermented carrots, squeeze them a bit dry over the sink, and add them to latkes or potato pancakes.

Rutabaga Sauerkraut

MAKES: about 1 quart (about 1 liter)
FRIDGE: up to 3 weeks after fermenting
FREEZER: no

Fermenting rutabaga without cabbage gives you a funky, mustardy condiment, a wild concoction for your next backyard barbecue or the perfect condiment to put on corned beef or pastrami sandwiches. You should try a Reuben sandwich with this stuff! Because rutabagas don't put off much water, we have to add more to create a proper brine.

> 2 pounds (900 g) rutabaga
> 0.7 ounce (20 g) kosher salt, plus more as necessary
> ¼ cup (60 ml) *distilled* water, plus more to make more brine
> 1 green cabbage leaf

1. Peel the rutabaga(s) and slice off any brown or discolored bits, then shred the vegetable through the large holes of a box grater. Weigh out *exactly* 28.2 ounces (800 g) of the shreds. Save the rest for another use.

2. Toss the rutabaga and salt in a large bowl until everything is well and evenly salted. Set aside at room temperature for 3 hours.

3. Clean and dry your hands or put on culinary kitchen gloves. Gently but consistently squeeze and massage the rutabaga in the bowl, adding ¼ cup (60 ml) *distilled* water as you go, until the vegetable is softened and compacted with a good-size puddle of brine sitting in the bowl, 4–5 minutes.

4. Pack the rutabaga (but not the brine) into one *clean* 1 quart (1 liter) glass jar. Press down firmly, either with a fermentation dowel or the clean, flat end of a handle-less rolling pin, until there are no air pockets left and 1–2 inches (2.5–5 cm) headspace in the jar.

5. Pour the brine from the bowl on top. If it settles down into the jar and leaves some rutabaga at the top exposed to the air, make more brine in a ½-teaspoon-kosher-salt-to-½-cup-*distilled*-water (2-g-to-120-ml) ratio and pour it into the jar. There should be about ½ inch (1 cm) headspace in the jar above the level of the brine.

6. Take the cabbage leaf and cut out a round to fit in the jar and cover the rutabaga. Set it down into the brine on top of the shreds. Set a fermentation weight on top of the cabbage leaf, pressing down until some of the liquid comes up over the sides of the weight. Cover or seal, either with a standard lid and sealing band or with a fermentation lid and sealing band.

7. Set aside at room temperature for 1 week to ferment, until sour and a bit funky. If you haven't used a fermentation lid, unseal the jar and burp it every day to get rid of the built-up gasses. If at any time you find the condiment is sour enough for your liking, stop the process by moving the jar to the fridge. Once fermented, store in the fridge for up to 3 weeks, making sure any remaining rutabaga stays under the brine when you remove some to enjoy.

Tip
The smaller the rutabaga, the less dry and mealy inside. For the best results, use two 1 pound (450 g) rutabagas.

Turnip Sauerkraut

MAKES: about 1 quart (about 1 liter)
FRIDGE: up to 3 weeks after fermenting
FREEZER: no

This is our version of sauerruben, a German condiment that's a cousin to sauerkraut, made by fermenting turnips rather than cabbage. The results are earthy, much bolder and less sweet than a standard cabbage ferment. We add some black pepper because we think its subtle spike (tamed after fermentation) balances the funkier notes in the turnips. By the way, when we call for *white turnips*, we mean those with a pale purple tint at the top near the leaves.

> 2 pounds (900 g) white turnips (5–6 medium), trimmed of leaves and roots, then peeled, any brown spots discarded
>
> 0.7 ounce (20 g) kosher salt, plus more as necessary
>
> 1 tablespoon (6 g) coarsely ground black pepper
>
> 1 green cabbage leaf
>
> *Distilled* water to make more brine

1. Use a vegetable peeler to make long, wide, ribbon-like strips (like wide ride noodles) from the turnips.

2. Toss these in a large bowl with the salt and pepper. Immediately, clean and dry your hands or put on culinary kitchen gloves. Gently but consistently squeeze and massage the turnip mixture, until the shreds have softened and compacted, with a good-size puddle of brine sitting in the bowl, 4–5 minutes.

3. Pack the turnip (but not the brine) into one *clean* 1 quart (1 liter) glass jar. Press down firmly, either with a fermentation dowel or the clean, flat end of a handle-less rolling pin, until there are no air pockets left and 1–2 inches (2.5–5 cm) headspace in the jar.

4. Pour the brine from the bowl on top. If it settles down into the jar and leaves some turnip at the top exposed to the air, make more brine in a ½-teaspoon-kosher-salt-to-½-cup-*distilled*-water (2-g-to-120-ml) ratio and pour it into the jar. There should be about ½ inch (1 cm) headspace in the jar above the level of the brine.

5. Take the cabbage leaf and cut out a round to fit in the jar and cover the turnip mixture. Set it down into the brine on top of the shreds. Set a fermentation weight on top of the cabbage leaf, pressing down until some of the liquid comes up over the sides of the weight. Cover or seal, either with a standard lid and sealing band or with a fermentation lid and sealing band.

6. Set aside at room temperature for 1 week to ferment, until sour and a bit funky. If you haven't used a fermentation lid, unseal the jar and burp it every day to get rid of the built-up gasses. If at any time you find the sauerkraut is sour enough for your liking, stop the process by moving the jar to the fridge. Once fermented, store in the fridge for up to 3 weeks, making sure any remaining turnip stays under the brine when you remove some to enjoy.

Next
We love to add the drained sauerkraut to ham and cheese sandwiches, then crisp them in a skillet with some melted butter.

Curtido (page 335)

Curtido

MAKES: about 1 quart (about 1 liter)
FRIDGE: up to 10 days after fermenting
FREEZER: no

This is closer to a slaw than traditional sauerkraut. It has Salvadoran origins and can be eaten fresh before fermentation starts or fermented a bit longer in the fridge (as we do with most of our kimchis). It's certainly less finicky than traditional sauerkraut. But it will never have those decidedly funky flavors. Still, it's a great way to make a small batch of a simple vegetable ferment with minimal effort (and no fiery heat, as in kimchi). Because of the lower salt content *and* the higher amounts of sugar in the carrots and onion, our recipe's results don't last very long, even in the fridge. Eat up!

- One 1 pound (450 g) bag of shredded green cabbage (not slaw mix)
- 6 cups (1340 ml) *boiling distilled* water, plus more *distilled* water for rinsing
- 1 large carrot, peeled and shredded through the large holes of a box grater
- 1 small red onion, peeled, halved, and sliced into very thin half-moons
- 2 teaspoons kosher salt
- 1 teaspoon dried oregano
- ½ cup (120 ml) apple cider vinegar

1. Place the cabbage shreds in a large colander set in the sink. *Slowly* pour the boiling *distilled* water over them, stirring them at least once so they all get blanched. Rinse with *distilled* water, stirring repeatedly, until cool. Shake the colander to get rid of excess moisture.

2. Clean and dry your hands or put on culinary kitchen gloves. Squeeze the cabbage shreds dry by small handfuls and transfer to a large bowl. Stir in the carrot, onion, salt, and oregano until uniform. Set aside at room temperature for 10 minutes.

3. Stir in the vinegar and toss well. Pack the mixture (brine and all) into one *clean* 1 quart (1 liter) glass jar. Pack it down tightly, either with a fermentation tamping dowel or the flat end of a clean, handle-less rolling pin, until there are no air pockets left and the liquid covers every speck of vegetable matter by about 1 inch (about 2.5 cm).

4. Set a fermentation weight on top of the mixture, pressing down so the liquid comes up to cover part of the weight. Cover or seal the jar, then refrigerate for 3 days before enjoying. The longer the mixture sits in the fridge, the bolder the flavors will become. But the moment it starts to have an acrid or rotten odor, it has gone beyond its prime and should be tossed.

Next
The drained slaw is an excellent topping for tacos or tostados, particularly grilled or fried fish tacos.

6

Savory Sauces, Spreads, and Dips

You may have never considered making ketchup, barbecue sauce, or mustard, much less Worcestershire sauce! If you *have*, you're already our people. If you haven't, join the tribe! It's high time you upped your game with better condiments for burgers, dogs, and brats, as well as almost anything off the grill. Not to mention sandwiches, wraps, and sliders. And of course, French fries and onion rings.

These bottles and jars put in an appearance at picnics and barbecues, at outdoor summer events and alongside winter braises, with soups and salads. Many can even be used on their own as dips for cut-up vegetables.

We call these *savory* sauces to make a distinction between them and the sweeter dessert sauces up next. But no doubt about it: There's sugar or some sort of sweetener in many of these recipes. Sugar and its kin (like honey or maple syrup) bring forward sour, bitter, herbal, and even floral notes, sometimes lost in the dense mix of ingredients that make up a barbecue sauce. What's more, many tasty things you'll enjoy with these condiments—fried shrimp, deli turkey, or shoestring fries, to name a few—are salty and pair well with a bit of sweetness.

Why make your own sauce? It'll be tastier. More layered in its flavors. More forward on the palate. With a more complex blend of spices. So just more pleasing all around. Better food means a happier life. Even if you're ordering in, open a homemade condiment for whatever is about to show up at the door.

Jars and containers

Throughout this chapter, we've stuck to our guns (or jars?) by mostly calling for our standard ½ pint (236 ml) glass containers. We've done so for the sake of convenience, assuming you, like us, now have a stash of these jars on hand. As always, feel free to use 1 pint (472 ml) jars for some of these. Or a mix-and-match set of what you have on hand, provided you remember that too much headspace leads to oxidation, which leads to the trash.

▲ It's easy to get Gold Barbecue Sauce (page 358) into a decorative bottle with a narrow funnel.

That said, these sauces and condiments look lovely in decorative bottles and fancy jars. The pretty ones are also preferable if you intend to give a jar as a gift. If the sauce is still hot when it's transferred to the jar, make sure you're working with tempered glass or a heat-safe bottle. And make sure you leave headspace in the bottle or decorative jar if you're freezing the condiment because it will expand and can burst the lid. Finally, if you're using a decorative container, like a small crock, make sure it has no reactive glaze or dye, including a clear glaze that may indeed react unfavorably with acidic ingredients. Any container should be marked as *food-safe*, as well as heat- and freezer-safe.

Truth be told, decorative bottles or jars can be a pain to fill. The necks can be absurdly narrow or comically wide. The bottle itself may be unstable when you pour sauce into it. If you're intent on decorative bottles or crocks, invest in an array of culinary funnels so your house gifts will be gorgeous, not sticky.

Blending or processing sauces

We call for either a blender or a food processor in some of these recipes. Problem is, even the best blenders or food processors for home use never work with complete efficiency. So you have to stop the machine at least once to scrape down the inside of the canister and make sure you get a proper emulsion of the ingredients.

Yes, scraping down the inside can apply to even specialty blenders like a Nutribullet, where little mustard seeds can get stuck on the top of the canister and lost in the rush. Go the extra mile and open up or take off a canister to scrape down its insides. It's better than crunching on an unblended seed in a sandwich.

The longer you run the machine, the smoother the ketchup, barbecue sauce, or mustard. But smoother *within reason*. More powerful blenders like a Blendtec, Vitamix, or Nutribullet will produce smoother sauces. But oil-rich sauces can begin to turn mayonnaise-like in their consistency if you take them too far. It's a matter of taste, which then brings up the question…

How thick is thickened?

You'll see all sorts of visual cues in these recipes. For example, "reduce the sauce to one-third of its original volume." Or "reduce until moundable on a spoon." These demarcations indicate the final texture of the condiment. But we'll admit they're quirky, even idiosyncratic.

Sometimes, you just know. Steak sauce and duck sauce should be thinner than Dijon mustard.

Often, it's a matter of taste. We prefer a firmer, thicker ketchup; you might like a looser,

▲ Very thick Banana Ketchup (page 344) and looser Tomato Ketchup (page 340)

more pourable one. To that end, unless there's a special indicator of how thick a sauce should be, adjust our timings to suit your preference. Stop when a ketchup is a bit wetter, or blend until a mustard is creamier (particularly if the seeds have been soaked in advance).

There is one other problem when it comes to the final consistency: If there's sugar in the ingredients and the sauce has been cooked for a while, the sugar will liquefy on the stove and will remain liquid in a blender or food processor, then harden in the fridge, becoming much firmer than it appeared at the end of cooking or blending. When it comes to sauces with sugar in them, there's admittedly some finesse needed to get the results you prefer. That finesse is born out of experience. In other words, the more you make, the more you'll know.

Does freezing affect ketchups and the like?

Yes and no. As a general rule, the looser the sauce, the less it will be affected by freezing and thawing. Even so, we've frozen hundreds of jars of paste-like mustard over the years and seen few problems in the texture.

Although freezing may leave many of the flavors intact, it can dull chilis and some dried spices, particularly so-called *warming spices*, like ground allspice or grated nutmeg. The only real way to perk up those flavors after thawing is with acid. Consider serving thawed condiments with lemon juice, white balsamic vinegar, or even sriracha on the side to bring on more pizzazz.

In any event, there *must* be no sign of oxidation after the thaw—that is, no browning (or worse, blackening) along the top surface or at its edge against the side of the jar. And certainly no discoloration down inside the jar! If you see the signs of oxidation or rot, toss out the contents of the jar or bottle, then *thoroughly sanitize* the container. Most likely, there was a contaminant or a leak of some sort when you bottled the sauce.

Mustards in storage

Mustard seeds are *hydrophilic*, meaning that they capture more and more water as they sit, in the same way that oats or wheat berries do. So prepared, cooked, or even just blended mustard preparations can stiffen in storage, depending on how much residual moisture was in the seeds from the get-go. (The more they've dried out in storage, the more water they can then accommodate from their surroundings.) Mustard seeds stored in the freezer for long keeping may well be the worst of the bunch, losing lots of moisture in microscopic bits in the thawing process, even if you can't immediately tell from looking at them.

You might actually like the consistency of a drier mustard. Tastes do vary! We tend to like smoother, looser sweet mustards and drier, coarser spicy mustards. But in any event, we often find that we have to loosen up a mustard after a week or two in the fridge or after long storage in the freezer. To do so, put the mustard in a food processor, add about 2 tablespoons (30 ml) water, cover, and process, dribbling in more water through the feed tube to get the desired consistency. You can also swap out water for vegetable oil, but we find it changes the consistency too much—enough in some cases that the mustard takes on the texture of mayonnaise. We definitely don't want that! But again, tastes vary.

Ready, set…

We'll admit we're hitting the competent stride of the committed cold canner with these recipes. But hey, making ketchup, barbecue sauce, or mustard is not in the least difficult. Some of these are even no-cook recipes. And you'll end up with bigger, better flavors on your plate with little effort. Plus, it's deeply satisfying when you open the fridge and see…um, the *sauces* of your labors.

Tomato Ketchup

MAKES: about 3 cups (720 ml)
FRIDGE: up to 1 month
FREEZER: up to 1 year

We know we're risking it all with our own version of ketchup, particularly for North Americans, who have distinct preferences about what ketchup looks and tastes like. But we're proud of our spiced concoction that uses corn syrup for body and more vinegar than standard bottlings, mostly because we prefer a sour flavor amid the sweetness from the tomato paste and the dried spice notes.

> 12 ounces (340 g) tomato *paste* (do not use tomato puree)
>
> 1 cup (312 g) light corn syrup
>
> 1 cup (240 ml) distilled white vinegar
>
> ½ cup (120 ml) water
>
> 2 tablespoons (25 g) granulated white sugar
>
> 2 teaspoons kosher salt
>
> ½ teaspoon ground allspice
>
> ½ teaspoon ground cloves
>
> ½ teaspoon onion powder
>
> ¼ teaspoon garlic powder

1. Combine all the ingredients in a large saucepan. Set over medium-low heat and whisk until smooth.

2. Raise the heat to medium and bring to a simmer, whisking very often. Reduce the heat to low and simmer *slowly*, whisking occasionally, until reduced by between one-fourth and one-third of its original volume. The final reduction depends on how thick you like ketchup. But keep in mind that it thickens as it cools. When it's ready in the pan, it should have plopping bubbles like magma in a volcanic core.

3. Turn off the heat and remove the pan from the burner. Cool for 5 minutes, then transfer to three *clean* ½ pint (236 ml) jars or other containers, leaving at least ½ inch (1 cm) headspace in each. Cover or seal. Cool at room temperature for no more than 1 hour, then refrigerate or freeze.

Tip

The quality of the ketchup is directly affected by the quality of the tomato paste. Search out Italian brands, which usually offer more tomato flavor (although are also priced accordingly).

Curried Ketchup

MAKES: about 2 cups (480 ml)
FRIDGE: up to 1 month
FREEZER: up to 1 year

You can't have curry wurst without curried ketchup! But even if you're not into the intricacies of German comfort food, you might want to try our version of curried ketchup. It's not terribly sweet (or sour, for that matter), but more vegetal and full-bodied than many bottlings. Much will depend on the curry powder you use. The standard yellow variety can be wan. Look for better yellow curry powder blends, particularly blends with fenugreek and cardamom in the mix, in Indian markets and online spice outlets.

> 2 tablespoons (30 ml) olive oil
>
> 1 small yellow or white onion, peeled and *minced*
>
> 2 medium garlic cloves, peeled and *minced*
>
> 3 tablespoons (18 g) yellow curry powder
>
> 1 tablespoon (6 g) mild paprika
>
> ½ teaspoon ground dried mustard
>
> ¼ teaspoon ground cloves
>
> 2 cups (255 g) canned tomato *puree* (do not use tomato paste)
>
> 2 tablespoons (42 g) honey
>
> 1 tablespoon (15 ml) apple cider vinegar
>
> 1 tablespoon (15 ml) Worcestershire sauce (or use your own homemade, page 372)
>
> 1 teaspoon kosher salt

1. Set a medium saucepan over medium heat for a minute or two. Swirl in the oil, then add the onion. Cook, stirring often, just until softened, about 4 minutes.

2. Stir in the garlic, curry powder, paprika, dried mustard, and cloves. Cook, stirring constantly,

With sausage and fries, two containers of Tomato Ketchup (page 340) and one container of Curried Ketchup (page 340)

until aromatic, for about 15 seconds. Stir in the tomato puree, honey, vinegar, Worcestershire sauce, and salt. Bring to a simmer, stirring constantly. Simmer, still stirring constantly, until just slightly thickened like spaghetti sauce, about 3 minutes.

3. Turn off the heat and remove the pan from the burner. Cool to room temperature, about 2 hours.

4. Pour and scrape the contents of the pan into a blender. Cover and blend until smooth, stopping the machine at least once to scrape down the inside of the canister. Transfer to two *clean* ½ pint (236 ml) jars or other containers, leaving at least ½ inch (1 cm) headspace in each. Cover or seal, then refrigerate or freeze.

Next

If you want the whole (German!) megillah, slice bratwurst or knackwurst into 3 inch (7.5 cm) sections, then grill or fry them. Serve with toothpicks and lots of the curried ketchup.

Five-Spice Ketchup

MAKES: about 4 cups (960 ml)
FRIDGE: up to 1 month
FREEZER: up to 1 year

Here's a ketchup made from *fresh* tomatoes. As such, it requires more time on the stove; but the payoff is worth it, given the terrific blend of sweet and sour this ketchup brings to French fries or hamburgers. The sauce is flavored with warming spices as well as a fresh chili. As to five-spice powder, you can find it in the spice aisle of almost all supermarkets…or you can make your own (see the MORE section).

- 4 pounds (1.8 kg) plum tomatoes (about 30 medium), cut into eighths
- 1 large red onion, peeled and chopped
- 1 fresh Anaheim chili, stemmed, cored, seeded, and chopped
- 2 medium garlic cloves, peeled and smashed
- 1½ teaspoons five-spice powder

- ½ teaspoon ground *white* pepper
- 1 cup (240 ml) *unseasoned* rice vinegar
- ¾ cup (162 g) packed dark brown sugar
- 2 tablespoons (30 ml) soy sauce

1. Place the tomatoes, onion, chili, and garlic in a very large saucepan. Set over low heat, cover, and cook, stirring often, until the mixture gets soupy, about 10 minutes.

2. Uncover and stir in the five-spice powder and white pepper. Continue cooking, stirring more frequently, until the tomatoes have broken down and mixture has reduced to about two-thirds of its original volume, about 50 minutes. Turn off the heat and remove the pan from the burner. Cool at room temperature for 10 minutes.

3. Set a food mill over a clean large saucepan. (For an alternative to a food mill, see page 16.) In batches, grind the tomato mixture through the mill into the pan below. Discard (or compost) the tomato skins and other solids in the mill. Stir the vinegar, brown sugar, and soy sauce into the milled tomato sauce until smooth.

4. Set the pan with the tomato sauce over medium heat and bring to a simmer, stirring often. Reduce the heat to low and simmer slowly, stirring more and more frequently, then almost constantly, until thickened enough that you can run a wooden spoon across the bottom of the pan and the line you make will hold its shape for a second or two, about 1 hour.

5. Turn off the heat and remove the pan from the burner. Cool at room temperature for no more than 30 minutes. Transfer to four *clean* ½ pint (236 ml) jars or other containers, leaving at least ½ inch (1 cm) headspace in each. Cover or seal, then refrigerate or freeze.

More

Although traditional five-spice powder is made with a blend of specialty spices, make a close approximation with more common spices: Blend 1 part ground cloves, 1 part ground star anise, 3 parts ground cinnamon, 3 parts ground dried ginger, and 3 parts ground black pepper. Bottle and store in a cool cupboard for up to 1 year. For more authenticity, substitute ground Szechuan peppercorns for the black pepper.

Plum Ketchup

MAKES: about 3 cups (720 ml)
FRIDGE: up to 1 month
FREEZER: up to 1 year
May be traditionally canned (see page 436)

Plums make a great substitute for tomatoes in ketchup. They're sweeter, of course. But they also have herbaceous and floral notes, making this ketchup a great dip with warm pita or a topper for spicy sausages. Make sure the plums are ripe, a bit soft, and heavy to the hand with juice.

- 2½ pounds (1.1 kg) ripe red plums of any varietal, halved, pitted, and chopped
- 1 small yellow or white onion, peeled and diced
- 2 medium garlic cloves, peeled and minced
- 1 cup (240 ml) white wine vinegar
- ¾ cup (162 g) packed light brown sugar
- 1 tablespoon (15 g) tomato paste
- 1½ teaspoons kosher salt
- ½ teaspoon ground cloves
- ¼ teaspoon grated nutmeg
- ¼ teaspoon ground dried cayenne

1. Combine all the ingredients in a large saucepan set over medium-high heat. Stir constantly to dissolve the brown sugar. Bring to a boil, stirring often.

2. Reduce the heat to low and simmer slowly, stirring more and more frequently to break up the plums against the inside of the pan, until thickened and applesauce-like, 15–20 minutes.

3. Turn off the burner and remove the pan from the heat. Cool at room temperature for 1 hour. Pour and scrape the contents of the pan into a blender, cover, and blend until smooth—or use an immersion blender right in the saucepan.

4. Transfer the sauce to three *clean* ½ pint (236 ml) jars or other containers, leaving at least ½ inch (1 cm) headspace in each. Cover or seal, then refrigerate or freeze.

Next
Use this ketchup in cocktail sauce with some malt vinegar, a little prepared white horseradish, as much sriracha as you want, and a splash of lemon juice.

Blueberry-Jalapeño Ketchup

MAKES: about 2 cups (480 ml)
FRIDGE: up to 1 month
FREEZER: up to 1 year

Blueberries turn ketchup into a wonder: a little sweeter, sure, but also a little earthier, with lots of summery notes. The final consistency is a matter of preference. We prefer this sauce a bit chunky, although that texture is not in keeping with standard, smooth ketchup. For a smoother sauce, you can use an immersion blender right in the pan; or transfer the sauce to a blender, cover, and whirl into a smoother puree.

- 4 cups (540 g) fresh blueberries or thawed frozen blueberries (with any juice)
- 1 small red onion, peeled and *minced*
- 1 medium fresh green jalapeño chili, stemmed, seeded, and *minced*
- ¾ cup (162 g) packed light brown sugar
- ¼ cup (60 ml) red wine vinegar
- 2 tablespoons (30 g) minced peeled fresh ginger
- ½ teaspoon kosher salt
- ¼ teaspoon ground cumin

1. Combine all the ingredients in a medium saucepan. Set it over medium-high heat and use a potato masher or the back of a wooden spoon to mash the berries into pulp. Bring the mixture to a boil, stirring almost constantly.

2. Reduce the heat to low and simmer *slowly*, stirring more and more frequently until almost constantly, until thickened and the consistency of a thick barbecue sauce, about 20 minutes.

3. Turn off the heat and remove the pan from the burner. Cool at room temperature for no more than 30 minutes. Transfer to two *clean* ½ pint (236 ml) jars or other containers, leaving at least ½ inch (1 cm) headspace in each. Cover or seal, then refrigerate or freeze.

Next
For a great dip with salty potato chips, blend some of the ketchup with lots of sour cream, a little Worcestershire Sauce (see page 372), and dehydrated minced onion.

Banana Ketchup

MAKES: about 2 cups (480 ml)
FRIDGE: up to 1 month
FREEZER: up to 1 year

Here's our version of a Filipino fruit ketchup (or sauce)—a giant blend of flavors. The original is naturally brown (as here), although often dyed red in commercial bottlings to match Western-style ketchup. Use this sauce on hamburgers, with grilled pork, on chicken skewers, or alongside plantain tostones.

> 2 tablespoons (30 ml) neutral-flavored oil, such as canola or vegetable oil
>
> 1 small yellow or white onion, peeled and finely chopped
>
> 1 fresh *red* jalapeño chili, stemmed and minced (seeded, if desired)
>
> 3 medium garlic cloves, peeled and minced
>
> 1 tablespoon (15 g) minced peeled fresh ginger
>
> ½ teaspoon ground dried turmeric
>
> ¼ teaspoon ground allspice
>
> 4 large *ripe* bananas, peeled and mashed
>
> ⅔ cup (160 ml) apple cider vinegar
>
> 2 tablespoons (42 g) honey
>
> 2 tablespoons (30 ml) gold or light rum

> 1 tablespoon (15 g) tomato paste
>
> 1 tablespoon (15 ml) soy sauce
>
> ½ teaspoon kosher salt

1. Set a medium saucepan over medium heat for a minute or two. Swirl in the oil, then add the onion. Cook, stirring occasionally, until softened, about 4 minutes. Add the jalapeño, garlic, ginger, turmeric, and allspice. Stir until fragrant, about 30 seconds.

2. Stir in the bananas, vinegar, honey, rum, tomato paste, soy sauce, and salt. Bring to a simmer, stirring quite often. Reduce the heat to low and simmer slowly, stirring more and more frequently, then almost constantly, until so thick that the sauce is moundable on a spoon.

3. Turn off the heat and remove the pan from the burner. Cool at room temperature for 15 minutes. Pour and scrape every drop from the pan into a blender. Cover and blend until smooth, stopping the machine at least once to scrape down the inside of the canister.

4. Transfer to two *clean* ½ pint (236 ml) jars or other containers, leaving at least ½ inch (1 cm) headspace in each. Cover or seal. Cool at room temperature for no more than 30 minutes, then refrigerate or freeze.

Next
To make Filipino spaghetti, cook and drain spaghetti. In a large saucepan, cook cut-up hot dogs in a little oil until lightly browned. Remove the hot dogs. Add chopped onion, bell pepper, and minced garlic. Cook a few minutes, then crumble in ground beef and stir until browned. Add 1 part tomato sauce, 1 part Banana Ketchup, and 1 part beef broth all *by volume*, plus a little tomato paste and a sprinkling of sugar. Cook and stir until slightly thickened, then add the spaghetti and hot dogs. Toss to coat. Grate Velveeta over the top.

Center: Banana Ketchup (page 344), then clockwise from bottom left: Mushroom Ketchup (page 346), Kecap Manis (page 346), Steak Sauce (page 347), and Hoisin Sauce (page 348)

Mushroom Ketchup

MAKES: about 2 cups (480 ml)
FRIDGE: up to 1 month
FREEZER: up to 1 year

This one's an old-school condiment, dating back centuries and used then as we might use steak sauce now. It's sweet-sour but umami-rich, a little earthy-funky from the mushrooms, not quite as thick as a ketchup and decidedly brown. As an alternative to steak sauce, warm the ketchup and use it as a dip, as you would use beef broth for a French dip sandwich.

- 1 pound (450 g) white or brown button mushrooms, cleaned
- 1 tablespoon (12 g) kosher salt
- 1½ cups (360 ml) water
- 1 cup (240 ml) malt vinegar
- 2 medium shallots (about 1 ounce or 30 g *each*), peeled and very thinly sliced
- 3 medium garlic cloves, peeled and very thinly sliced
- 3 tablespoons (40 g) dark brown sugar
- 1 teaspoon dried thyme
- 1 teaspoon ground black pepper
- ½ teaspoon ground allspice
- ½ teaspoon ground cloves
- 1 tablespoon (15 ml) Worcestershire sauce (or use your own homemade, page 372)
- 1 tablespoon (7 g) cornstarch

1. Put the mushrooms in a food processor, cover, and pulse repeatedly to finely chop them, stopping the machine once or twice to rearrange any large chunks. Pour and scrape every speck of the mushrooms into a medium saucepan. Add the salt and toss well. Cover and set aside at room temperature for at least overnight or up to 24 hours to leach moisture from the mushrooms.

2. Uncover and add the water, vinegar, shallots, garlic, brown sugar, thyme, black pepper, allspice, and cloves. Set the pan over medium-high heat and stir until the brown sugar dissolves. Bring to a boil, stirring often.

3. Reduce the heat to low and simmer slowly, stirring often, until reduced to about half its original volume, about 15 minutes. Turn off the heat, remove the pan from the burner, and cool at room temperature for 1 hour.

4. Set up a jelly bag over a bowl (for alternatives to a jelly bag, see page 17). Pour the mushroom mixture into the bag and drain, squeezing occasionally to get out as much liquid as you can. This process can take an hour or two.

5. Discard the solids and pour the strained liquid into a clean medium saucepan. Set it over medium-high heat and bring to a simmer. Meanwhile, whisk the Worcestershire sauce and cornstarch in a small bowl to create a smooth slurry. When the mushroom liquid is bubbling, add the cornstarch mixture and whisk until thickened and translucent, only a few seconds.

6. Turn off the heat and remove the pan from the burner. Cool at room temperature for no more than 30 minutes. Transfer to two *clean* ½ pint (236 ml) jars or other containers, leaving about ½ inch (1 cm) headspace in each. Cover or seal, then refrigerate or freeze.

More

For a more authentic flavor, substitute demerara sugar *by weight* for the dark brown sugar.

Kecap Manis

MAKES: about 2 cups (480 ml)
FRIDGE: up to 1 month
FREEZER: up to 1 year

Kecap manis (*kay-CHAP mahn-EES*) is an Indonesian-Dutch condiment, originally perhaps a sweetened soy sauce mixture, but now made with more aromatics, making it the drizzle you didn't even know you needed for fried rice, stir-fries, and scrambled eggs. Or the dip to perk up some rotisserie chicken pieces after you've crisped them in an air fryer. Our version calls for a little extra time at the stove so that we can skip various thickeners, including the xanthan gum found in modern preparations. We love the salty-aromatic goodness of this sauce along with malt vinegar on onion rings.

- 1⅓ cups plus 1 tablespoon (300 g) packed dark brown sugar
- 1⅓ cups (320 ml) soy sauce
- 6 medium garlic cloves, peeled and smashed
- One 2 inch (5 cm) piece of fresh ginger (about the width of your thumb), peeled and sliced into thin rounds
- 3 star anise pods
- 1 tablespoon (8 g) ground black pepper

1. Mix all the ingredients in a small saucepan set over low heat, stirring until the brown sugar dissolves. Keeping the heat on low, bring the mixture to the barest bubble at the edges, stirring often. Keep it at this very low bubble, lowering the heat as much as necessary and stirring often, until about as thick as maple syrup, about 20 minutes. The point here is to create a slow reduction from a barely active simmer.

2. Turn off the heat and remove the pan from the burner. Cool at room temperature for no more than 30 minutes. Transfer to two *clean* ½ pint (236 ml) jars or other containers, leaving about ½ inch (1 cm) headspace in each. Cover or seal, then refrigerate or freeze.

More
For a much more authentic flavor, omit the brown sugar and grate 10½ ounces (300 g) palm sugar (preferably) or jaggery through the *small* holes of a box grater or a Microplane and into the pan. It'll take about 5 minutes of stirring for the palm sugar to dissolve.

Steak Sauce

MAKES: about 3 cups (720 ml)
FRIDGE: up to 1 month
FREEZER: up to 1 year

We modeled this sauce on the classic A.1., which means we've put raisins and oranges in the mix, as the original does. However, we think ours has a better balance of sweet *and sour* since we've upped the vinegar a bit and added tamarind concentrate. Or to put it another way, this version is not sticky sweet, a better contrast to the natural sweetness of a strip steak off the grill.

- ½ cup (76 g) raisins
- 6 plump pitted Medjool dates
- 1 cup (240 ml) *boiling* water
- 2 tablespoons (30 ml) neutral-flavored oil, such as canola or vegetable oil
- 2 small shallots (about ¾ ounce or 22 g *each*), peeled and thinly sliced
- 1 medium garlic clove, peeled and thinly sliced
- 1 fresh red bird's eye chili, stemmed, seeded, and minced
- 1 cup (200 g) granulated white sugar
- 2 tablespoons (42 g) molasses or black treacle
- 1 cup (240 ml) orange juice, preferably freshly squeezed
- 1 cup (240 ml) red wine vinegar
- ¼ cup (60 g) tomato paste
- 2 tablespoons (32 g) tamarind *concentrate* (do not use tamarind paste)
- 2 tablespoons (30 ml) soy sauce
- 1 tinned anchovy fillet, chopped
- 2 tablespoons (12 g) finely grated orange zest
- 1 teaspoon kosher salt
- 1 teaspoon ground black pepper
- ½ teaspoon dried thyme
- ¼ teaspoon ground cloves

1. Put the raisins and dates in a small bowl and cover them with the boiling water. Set aside while you continue with the recipe.

➡

2. Set a medium saucepan over medium heat for a minute or two. Swirl in the oil, then add the shallots, garlic, and chili. Cook, stirring often, until lightly browned, about 5 minutes.

3. Stir in the sugar and molasses. Melt the sugar and let the mixture come to a bubble. Cook, stirring almost constantly to prevent scorching, for 3 minutes.

4. Stir in the orange juice and vinegar. The sugar will clump but keep stirring until it melts. Add the dried fruits and their soaking water, the tomato paste, tamarind concentrate, soy sauce, anchovy fillet, orange zest, salt, pepper, thyme, and cloves. Bring to a simmer, stirring almost constantly. Continue simmering, stirring quite often, until the mixture is reduced to about two-thirds of its original volume, about 10 minutes. Turn off the heat, remove the pan from the burner, and cool at room temperature for 30 minutes.

5. Pour the sauce into a blender, cover, and blend until smooth, stopping the machine at least once to scrape down the inside of the canister. Transfer to three *clean* ½ pint (236 ml) jars or other containers, leaving about ½ inch (1 cm) headspace in each. Cover or seal, then refrigerate or freeze.

More
If you want a completely smooth steak sauce, pour the contents of the blender through a fine-mesh sieve to get rid of any small bits before bottling.

Hoisin Sauce

MAKES: about 2 cups (480 ml)
FRIDGE: up to 1 month
FREEZER: up to 1 year

The word *hoisin* comes from the word for seafood in Cantonese, but the sauce doesn't contain any seafood. Instead, it's a thick, sweet, vegetable condiment, made with a fermented bean paste. It sometimes includes sweet potatoes, but they pose a problem in fridge storage and so require a more traditional canning method. Our version is close to authentic recipes, but we've adapted some ingredients to keep the recipe more in line with North American and European supermarkets and to cut down on the long cooking for our speedier cold-canning ethic. Doenjang gives the sauce a pleasant funkiness; tahini, a thick texture without long cooking.

> ⅔ cup (320 g) doenjang (see TIP)
> ⅔ cup (160 ml) water
> ½ cup (108 g) packed dark brown sugar
> 2 tablespoons (32 g) tahini
> 2 tablespoons (30 ml) *unseasoned* rice vinegar
> 2 medium garlic cloves, peeled and minced
> 2 teaspoons rice flour
> 1 teaspoon five-spice powder (or use your own homemade: see the MORE section with the Five-Spice Ketchup recipe on page 342)
> 1 tablespoon (15 ml) *dark* soy sauce (see TIP)

1. Stir the doenjang, water, brown sugar, tahini, vinegar, garlic, rice flour, and five-spice powder in a medium saucepan set over medium heat until the doenjang and brown sugar dissolve. Bring to a simmer, stirring occasionally.

2. Reduce the heat to low and simmer slowly, stirring more and more often, until thickened, about 2 minutes. Turn off the heat and remove the pan from the burner. Cool for 15 minutes.

3. Pour and scrape the contents of the pan into a blender and add the dark soy sauce. Cover or blend until smooth, scraping down the inside of the canister at least once.

4. Transfer to two *clean* ½ pint (236 ml) jars or other containers, leaving about ½ inch (1 cm) headspace in each. Cover or seal, then refrigerate or freeze.

Tip
Doenjang (or "thick sauce") is a fermented soybean paste, common in Korean cooking. It's used as a soup base, a marinade, or a condiment. Dark soy sauce is a specialty soy sauce: darker, richer, and less salty than more familiar bottlings. Substitute standard soy sauce only in a pinch.

Thick Red Chili Sauce

MAKES: about 2 cups (480 ml)
FRIDGE: up to 1 month
FREEZER: up to 1 year

Store-bought red chili sauce, like the familiar Heinz bottle, is a pale imitation of its origins. It's become an overly sweet, barely spicy tomato sauce, sort of like tomato ketchup but with a tiny bit more heft. Our take on this classic sauce returns it to its roots: a fiery but sweet-and-sour mix of spices in a tomato base. Hot paprika will result in a slightly less burning sauce; cayenne, much more incendiary.

- 12 ounces (340 g) tomato *paste* (do not use tomato puree)
- 1 cup (240 ml) water
- ½ cup (108 g) *packed* light brown sugar
- ¼ cup (84 g) honey
- 6 tablespoons (90 ml) red wine vinegar
- 2 teaspoons (10 ml) Worcestershire sauce (or use your own homemade, page 372)
- 2 teaspoons hot paprika or ground dried cayenne
- 2 teaspoons kosher salt
- 1 teaspoon garlic powder
- 1 teaspoon ground black pepper
- ½ teaspoon ground allspice
- ¼ teaspoon ground cinnamon
- ¼ teaspoon ground cloves

1. Combine all the ingredients in a medium saucepan set over medium-high heat, stirring until the brown sugar and honey dissolve. Bring to a simmer, stirring almost constantly.

2. Reduce the heat to low and simmer slowly, stirring more and more frequently, then almost constantly, until thickened and ketchup-like, about 10 minutes.

3. Turn off the heat and remove the pan from the burner. Cool at room temperature for no more than 30 minutes. Transfer to two *clean* ½ pint (236 ml) jars or other containers, leaving at least ½ inch (1 cm) headspace in each. Cover or seal, then refrigerate or freeze.

Next

The best cocktail sauce is made with this sauce plus a generous scoop of prepared white horseradish, a little Worcestershire sauce, about the same amount of lemon juice, and a healthy dose of stemmed and minced fresh dill.

Sweet Red Chili Sauce

MAKES: about 3 cups (720 ml)
FRIDGE: up to 1 month
FREEZER: up to 1 year

We love translucent red chili sauce, but we can't stand the sugary, tasteless versions in many bottlings of what's sometimes called "Thai sweet chili sauce." We want the sauce to bring some heat to the game! So we've crafted the familiar dipping sauce into something with plenty of fire and lots of dark, rich notes in a deceptively translucent mix. We can't imagine egg rolls without it. Or summer rolls. Or turkey sandwiches. Or fried chicken wings.

- ¾ cup (180 ml) plus 1 tablespoon (15 ml) water
- ¾ cup (180 ml) *unseasoned* rice vinegar
- ¾ cup (150 g) granulated white sugar
- 2 tablespoons (30 ml) dry vermouth or *unsweetened* apple juice
- 2 tablespoons (30 ml) soy sauce
- 6 medium garlic cloves, peeled and *minced*
- 2 tablespoons (30 g) minced peeled fresh ginger
- 5 tablespoons (75 g) sambal oelek (or use your own homemade Fiery Red Sambal, page 217)
- 1 tablespoon (5 g) red pepper flakes
- 1 tablespoon (7 g) cornstarch
- 1–2 drops red food coloring, optional

Left to right, with egg rolls: Sweet Red Chili Sauce (page 349) and Thick Red Chili Sauce (page 349)

1. Combine ¾ cup (180 ml) water, the vinegar, sugar, vermouth, soy sauce, garlic, and ginger in a medium saucepan. Stir over medium-high heat until the sugar dissolves. Bring to a boil, stirring frequently. Boil for 1 minute. Stir in the sambal and red pepper flakes. Boil for 2 minutes, stirring occasionally.

2. Whisk the cornstarch with the remaining 1 tablespoon (15 ml) water in a small bowl to make a smooth slurry. Pour and scrape this slurry into the boiling sauce. Continue cooking, stirring constantly, until thickened, just a few seconds.

3. Turn off the heat and remove the pan from the burner. Stir in the food coloring, if desired. Cool at room temperature for no more than 30 minutes. Transfer to three *clean* ½ pint (236 ml) jars or other containers, leaving at least ½ inch (1 cm) headspace in each. Cover or seal, then refrigerate or freeze.

More
Thin out this sauce with wine or beer to make a mop for pork or beef on the grill.

Classic Barbecue Sauce

MAKES: about 2 cups (480 ml)
FRIDGE: up to 1 month
FREEZER: up to 1 year
May be traditionally canned (see page 436)

We call this ketchup-based barbecue sauce *classic*, not because it's our favorite, but because it is closest to most North American bottlings—with two key differences. One, we add smoked paprika for a woody base, reminiscent of a barbecue pit. And two, we use distilled white vinegar, rather than the more common apple cider vinegar, because the plainer, brighter vinegar lets the spices show through more readily.

1½ cups (412 g) tomato ketchup (or use your own homemade Tomato Ketchup, page 340)
½ cup (120 ml) distilled white vinegar
½ cup (120 ml) water
¼ cup (54 g) packed light brown sugar
¼ cup (60 ml) soy sauce
2 tablespoons (32 g) prepared yellow mustard (or use your own homemade Prepared Yellow Mustard, page 361)
1 tablespoon (6 g) mild smoked paprika
1 teaspoon ground cumin
1 teaspoon onion powder

1. Whisk all the ingredients in a medium saucepan set over medium heat until the brown sugar dissolves. Bring to a simmer, whisking often.

2. Reduce the heat to low and simmer slowly, whisking more and more often, until reduced to about two-thirds of its original volume yet still pourable, like a bottled barbecue sauce, about 10 minutes.

3. Turn off the heat and remove the pan from the burner. Cool at room temperature for no more than 30 minutes. Transfer to two *clean* ½ pint (236 ml) jars or other containers, leaving about ½ inch (1 cm) headspace in each. Cover or seal, then refrigerate or freeze.

More
For a gluten-free barbecue sauce, substitute tamari sauce for the soy sauce and make sure the ketchup and mustard are both gluten-free.

Vinegary Barbecue Sauce

MAKES: about 2 cups (480 ml)
FRIDGE: up to 1 month
FREEZER: up to 1 year
May be traditionally canned (see page 436)

Here's our favorite among our barbecue sauces. It's a sour but sophisticated pop, best with smoked meat as well as anything charred on the grill.

Because the sugar content is relatively low, this sauce is also a great barbecue mop. Slather it onto chicken, turkey, pork, or beef during the last few minutes of cooking for a big burst of flavors.

- 1 cup (240 ml) *unsweetened* apple juice
- ½ cup (120 ml) distilled white vinegar
- ½ cup (120 ml) apple cider vinegar
- ¼ cup (60 ml) water
- 2 tablespoons (25 g) granulated white sugar
- 1 tablespoon (16 g) prepared yellow mustard (or use your own homemade Prepared Yellow Mustard, page 361)
- 2 teaspoons (14 g) molasses or black treacle
- 2 teaspoons (10 g) tamarind paste
- 1 teaspoon ground black pepper
- ½ teaspoon red pepper flakes
- ½ teaspoon kosher salt

1. Whisk all the ingredients in a medium saucepan set over medium heat until the sugar dissolves. Bring to a simmer, whisking often.

2. Reduce the heat to low and simmer slowly, whisking more and more often, until slightly thickened, like thick salad dressing (that is, not a big reduction), about 5 minutes.

3. Turn off the heat and remove the pan from the burner. Cool at room temperature for no more than 30 minutes. Transfer to two *clean* ½ pint (236 ml) jars or other containers, leaving about ½ inch (1 cm) headspace in each. Cover or seal, then refrigerate or freeze.

More

For a more complex flavor, substitute malt vinegar for the apple cider vinegar.

Brown Sugar Barbecue Sauce

MAKES: about 2 cups (480 ml)
FRIDGE: up to 1 month
FREEZER: up to 1 year

Of all our barbecue sauces, this one seems made for pork: loin, chops, ribs, roasts, ham, sausages, you name it. It's quite thick from all the sugar and the somewhat longer reduction. There's a lot of body to stand up to the intricate blend of spices. With its mounding consistency and layered flavors, we feel this sauce is best as a dip for whatever comes *off* the grill, rather than as a grill mop for protein before it goes over the fire.

- One 15 ounce (425 g) can of tomato *sauce*
- 6 ounces (170 g) tomato *paste*
- ⅔ cup (160 g) packed dark brown sugar
- 3 tablespoons (45 ml) apple cider vinegar
- 1½ tablespoons (32 g) molasses or black treacle
- 1 tablespoon (15 ml) Worcestershire sauce (or use your own homemade, page 372)
- 2 teaspoons (10 ml) bottled liquid smoke
- 2 teaspoons ground dried mustard
- 2 teaspoons mild paprika
- 1 teaspoon onion powder
- 1 teaspoon kosher salt
- ½ teaspoon celery seeds
- ½ teaspoon garlic powder
- ¼ teaspoon ground cloves
- ¼ teaspoon ground dried cayenne

1. Whisk all the ingredients in a medium saucepan set over medium heat until the brown sugar dissolves. Bring to a simmer, whisking often.

2. Reduce the heat to low and simmer slowly, whisking more and more frequently, then almost constantly, until quite thickened, even *moundable*, about 18 minutes.

3. Turn off the heat and remove the pan from the burner. Cool at room temperature for no more than 30 minutes. Transfer to two *clean* ½ pint

(236 ml) jars or other containers, leaving about ½ inch (1 cm) headspace in each. Cover or seal, then refrigerate or freeze.

Next

There's not a lot of heat in this sauce…and we prefer to skip red pepper flakes because they dull over time. Instead, mix this sauce with a squirt of sriracha just before using to spice it up.

Five-Alarm Barbecue Sauce

MAKES: about 2 cups (480 ml)
FRIDGE: up to 1 month
FREEZER: up to 1 year

Fiery barbecue sauces are all the rage. We love the burn, but we also want to taste the spices and aromatics laced throughout. To get that balance, we use plenty of chilis but we also use a can of cola for its slightly caramelized flavors that allow the fruit notes from the chilis and even the cinnamon to stand out. This one cooks for longer than some of the previous barbecue sauce recipes. Control its final consistency by removing it a little early for a wetter sauce or letting it cook down for sauce that can mound on a spoon. The former is better as a barbecue mop; the latter, as a dip or spread.

- 2 teaspoons (10 ml) olive oil
- 1 small yellow or white onion, peeled and *minced*
- 2 medium garlic cloves, peeled and *minced*
- 1 ounce (28 g) dried New Mexican red chilis (4–5 small), stemmed, seeded, and torn into small pieces
- 1 ounce (28 g) dried ancho chilis (about 2 medium), stemmed, seeded, and torn into small pieces
- 2 large *fresh* green jalapeño chilis, stemmed, seeded (if desired), and *minced*
- 12 ounces (180 ml) cola (do not use diet cola)
- ¾ cup (180 ml) water
- ½ cup (85 g) thick sweet tomato-based chili sauce, such as Heinz (or use your own homemade Thick Red Chili Sauce, page 349)

- 2 tablespoons (30 ml) red wine vinegar
- ½ teaspoon ground cinnamon
- ½ teaspoon kosher salt

1. Set a large saucepan over medium heat for a minute or two. Swirl in the oil, then add the onion and garlic. Cook, stirring often, just until beginning to soften. Do not brown the garlic.

2. Add the New Mexican reds, anchos, and jalapeños. Cook, stirring often, until aromatic, about 20 seconds. Stir in the cola, water, chili sauce, vinegar, cinnamon, and salt until well combined.

3. Bring the sauce to a simmer, stirring occasionally. Cover, reduce the heat to low, and cook for 15 minutes, stirring once in a while. Uncover and continue simmering, stirring more and more often, until viscous, like a thin syrup, about 20 minutes.

4. Turn off the heat and remove the pan from the burner. Cool at room temperature for 30 minutes. Pour and scrape the sauce into a blender or a food processor. Cover and blend or process until smooth, stopping the machine at least once to scrape down the inside of the canister.

5. Transfer to two *clean* ½ pint (236 ml) jars or other containers, leaving about ½ inch (1 cm) headspace in each. Cover or seal, then refrigerate or freeze.

Next

For a great dipping sauce for chips or quesadillas, mix 1 part five-alarm sauce with 3 parts ranch dressing (*by volume*). Add a little onion power and ground black pepper for more flavor.

Five-Alarm Barbecue Sauce
(page 353)

Raspberry-Chipotle Barbecue Sauce

MAKES: about 4 cups (960 ml)
FRIDGE: up to 1 month
FREEZER: up to 1 year

You'll be tempted to head out to the grill with this sweet-spicy-smoky sauce, but we find it's also a great spread for turkey sandwiches (particularly a turkey club with mayo) or in vegetable wraps. Control the smoky heat by adjusting the amount of canned chipotles (and by seeding them, if desired). When we originally wrote a version of this recipe for *Cooking Light* magazine, it almost broke the algorithm with the number of downloads!

- 2 cups (510 g) canned tomato puree
- 1 cup (120 g) fresh raspberries or thawed frozen raspberries
- 1 cup (270 g) *seedless* raspberry jam
- ½ cup (108 g) packed dark brown sugar
- 6 tablespoons (90 ml) apple cider vinegar
- ⅓ cup (112 g) honey
- *Up to* 4 canned chipotles in adobo sauce, stemmed, seeded (if desired), and *minced*
- 1 small shallot (about ¾ ounce or 22 g), peeled and *minced*
- 2 medium garlic cloves, peeled and minced
- 2 tablespoons (30 g) Worcestershire sauce (or use your own homemade, page 372)
- 2 tablespoons (43 g) molasses or black treacle
- 1 teaspoon ground cloves
- 1 teaspoon kosher salt
- ½ teaspoon ground allspice
- ½ teaspoon mild smoked paprika
- ½ teaspoon ground black pepper

1. Combine all the ingredients in a large saucepan. Set the pan over medium heat and stir constantly until the jam and brown sugar dissolve, smashing the raspberries against the side of the pan to get as much pulp and juice from them as you can. Bring to a simmer, stirring occasionally.

2. Reduce the heat to very low and simmer *slowly*, stirring more and more often, until reduced to about 4 cups (960 ml), thick enough that you can make a line with a wooden spoon in the bottom of the pan that holds its shape for a few seconds, about 1 hour. You'll need to stir almost constantly during the last 10 or 15 minutes.

3. Turn off the heat and remove the pan from the burner. Cool at room temperature for 15 minutes, then transfer to four *clean* ½ pint (236 ml) jars or other containers, leaving about ½ inch (1 cm) headspace in each. Cover or seal. Cool at room temperature for no more than 1 hour, then refrigerate or freeze.

Next
This sauce is too thick to be a barbecue slather for long cooking on the grill. Instead, smear it on chicken or pork during the last minute or two over the grill's heat, just to reduce it without charring it.

Peanut Butter–Ginger Barbecue Sauce

MAKES: about 3 cups (720 ml)
FRIDGE: up to 1 month
FREEZER: up to 1 year

This sauce is a wild mix of flavors: not just peanut butter and ginger, but sesame, soy, and honey, too. Bruce first developed a version for that barbecue sauce article in *Cooking Light*, a wild creation to finish off the magazine's long run. Although *Cooking Light* is unfortunately out of print, one of our former editors occasionally writes us to say she still pulls out an old copy and whips up a batch. Now we've preserved the recipe here! It's a sweet, smooth sauce...and not cooked, so it lacks the deeper, caramelized notes from some of our other barbecue sauces. Of our lot of barbecue sauces, this one is great on its own as a dip for egg rolls, dumplings, or vegetable pancakes.

1 cup (240 ml) soy sauce

¾ cup (200 g) smooth peanut butter

½ cup (120 ml) *unseasoned* rice vinegar

6 tablespoons (125 g) honey

6 tablespoons (80 g) packed light brown sugar

¼ cup (60 ml) *toasted* sesame oil

3 tablespoons (45 g) minced peeled fresh ginger

2 medium garlic cloves, peeled and minced

2 teaspoons ground black pepper

1 teaspoon onion powder

1. Whisk all the ingredients in a large bowl until smooth. It will take some work to get the peanut butter and honey dissolved. A large bowl is best because you'll inevitably slosh some of the sauce onto the counter. Or work in the sink to easily clean up the splashes.

2. Transfer to three *clean* ½ pint (236 ml) jars or other containers, leaving about ½ inch (1 cm) headspace in each. Cover or seal, then refrigerate or freeze.

Next
This peanut-based sauce is terrific with cooked and drained noodles, particularly udon or thick spaghetti, or even soba noodles. Mix the sauce with a little water to thin it out, add hot drained noodles, and toss with lots of thinly sliced bell peppers, cucumbers, and carrots.

Peachy Barbecue Sauce

MAKES: about 3 cups (720 ml)
FRIDGE: up to 1 month
FREEZER: up to 1 year
May be traditionally canned (see page 436)

Fruit-based barbecue sauces are a grilling favorite because the natural sugars in the fruit caramelize into deeper, richer flavors. However, the sauces can get cloyingly sweet. So we opt for all-fruit preserves or spreads as a way to cut down on the added sugar. The results are more complex than you might think, given the recipe's name. We love this sauce as a dip for bratwurst or even hot dogs, so long as there's also some sauerkraut (like Red Cabbage Sauerkraut, page 318) or kimchi (like Napa Cabbage Kimchi, page 308) on the side.

20 ounces (567 g) *all-fruit* peach preserves or spread (about 2 cups)

2 cups (480 ml) vegetable broth

¾ cup (180 ml) dark rum, such as Myers's; or unsweetened apple cider

½ cup (85 g) thick sweet tomato-based chili sauce, such as Heinz (or use your own homemade Thick Red Chili Sauce, page 349)

¼ cup (60 ml) apple cider vinegar

2 small shallots (about ¾ ounce or 22 g each), peeled and *minced*

2 tablespoons (30 ml) soy sauce

1½ tablespoons (24 g) Dijon mustard (or use your own homemade Dijon Mustard, page 361)

1 tablespoon (15 g) minced peeled fresh ginger

2 teaspoons ground black pepper

¼ teaspoon ground cloves

1. Whisk all the ingredients in a medium saucepan set over medium heat until the all-fruit preserves dissolve. Bring to a simmer, whisking often.

2. Reduce the heat to low and simmer slowly, whisking more and more frequently, then almost constantly, until a little thickened, like a thin porridge, about 15 minutes. (The sauce will set up more as it cools.)

3. Turn off the heat and remove the pan from the burner. Cool at room temperature for no more than 30 minutes. Transfer to three *clean* ½ pint (236 ml) jars or other containers, leaving about ½ inch (1 cm) headspace in each. Cover or seal, then refrigerate or freeze.

Next
For a creamy dip, mix the sauce with a little mayonnaise, some sriracha, a splash of lemon juice, and a dash of garlic powder.

Roasted Garlic–Maple Barbecue Sauce

MAKES: about 2 cups (480 ml)
FRIDGE: up to 1 month
FREEZER: up to 1 year

This barbecue sauce has the strongest flavor among our lot, partly because of the large amount of roasted garlic, but also because of the big blend of spices and even the more delicate notes from maple syrup. If you want a stronger maple flavor, use a darker maple syrup, more suited to baking than pancakes. The sauce is great with lamb or game.

- 1 large garlic head
- 1 tablespoon (15 ml) olive oil
- 12 ounces (340 g) tomato *paste*
- ¾ cup (160 g) maple syrup
- ⅓ cup (80 ml) *unseasoned* rice vinegar
- One 4½ ounce (128 g) can of chopped mild green chilis
- 1 small yellow or white onion, peeled and *minced*
- 1 medium garlic clove, peeled and minced
- 2 tablespoons (30 ml) Worcestershire sauce (or use your own homemade, page 372)
- ½ teaspoon ground allspice
- ½ teaspoon ground coriander
- ¼ teaspoon vanilla extract
- ½ teaspoon ground cloves

1. Position a rack in the oven's center; heat the oven to 400°F (200°C), no fan or convection.

2. Slice about ½ inch (1 cm) off the top of the garlic head, exposing the cloves inside. Set the head, cut side up, on a small piece of aluminum foil. Drizzle the head with the oil, then seal the foil tightly closed over the top. Roast until the cloves are soft and sweet, about 40 minutes. Transfer to a wire rack, carefully open the packet, and cool for 15 minutes.

3. Squeeze the mushy pulp out of their husks into a large saucepan set over medium heat. Add the remaining ingredients, stirring constantly at first to dissolve the syrup and tomato paste. Bring to a simmer, stirring occasionally. Reduce the heat to low and simmer slowly, stirring more and more often, until thickened like hot (not refrigerated!) split-pea soup, about 15 minutes.

4. Turn off the heat and remove the pan from the burner. Cool at room temperature for 10 minutes. Set a fine-mesh strainer over a bowl and strain the sauce through the strainer, catching the liquid below. Use the back of a wooden spoon to press the solids against the mesh to extract more of their liquid, but without pressing so hard that the pulp starts to come through. Discard the solids.

5. Transfer the sauce to two *clean* ½ pint (236 ml) jars or other containers, leaving about ½ inch (1 cm) headspace in each. Cover or seal, then refrigerate or freeze.

Next

This sauce is terrific on a loaded baked potato with butter, shredded cheese, Pickled Jalapeño Rings (page 255), and sour cream.

Pineapple-Sesame Barbecue Sauce

MAKES: about 2 cups (480 ml)
FRIDGE: up to 1 month
FREEZER: up to 1 year

This pineapple-based barbecue sauce is our version of huli huli sauce, a staple in Hawaiian grilling: a sweet, gingery concoction that works both as a marinade and a mop, mostly for chicken, but also for pork or even (utterly unconventionally) lamb. The sauce should be chunky, not smooth, a nice contrast as a dip if you've got a sliced leg of lamb off the grill. If you want to get even more authentic, substitute bottled black bean–garlic sauce for the hoisin sauce.

1 cup (275 g) tomato ketchup (or use your own homemade Tomato Ketchup, page 340)

1 cup (215 g) packed light brown sugar

⅔ cup (160 ml) soy sauce

⅔ cup (160 g) crushed pineapple in juice

¼ cup (60 ml) toasted sesame oil

¼ cup (60 g) sriracha

2 tablespoons (30 g) minced peeled fresh ginger

2 tablespoons (30 ml) *unseasoned* rice vinegar

2 tablespoons (32 g) hoisin sauce (or use your own homemade Hoisin Sauce, page 348)

2 medium garlic cloves, peeled and minced

1. Combine all the ingredients in a medium saucepan set over medium heat, stirring constantly until the brown sugar dissolves. Bring to a simmer, stirring occasionally.

2. Reduce the heat to low and simmer slowly, stirring more and more often, until reduced to about two-thirds of its original volume, with a consistency sort of like Thousand Island dressing (although not the same color), about 10 minutes.

3. Turn off the heat and remove the pan from the burner. Cool at room temperature for no more than 30 minutes. Transfer to two *clean* ½ pint (236 ml) jars or other containers, leaving about ½ inch (1 cm) headspace in each. Cover or seal, then refrigerate or freeze.

Next

To make HULI-HULI CHICKEN, coat up to 4 bone-in skin-on chicken thighs with 1 cup of this sauce, cover, and marinate overnight in the fridge. Prepare the grill for high, direct-heat cooking. Grill the thighs directly over the heat, turning a couple of times, until cooked through, about 15 minutes. Baste repeatedly with more of the sauce during the last 2 or 3 minutes on the grill.

Gold Barbecue Sauce

MAKES: about 3 cups (720 ml)
FRIDGE: up to 1 month
FREEZER: up to 1 year

A barbecue sauce without tomatoes of some sort? Even ketchup? You bet! Mustard gives this sauce a spiky, vibrant flavor. Our version of Carolina Gold is best as a dip with smoked brisket or ribs.

2¼ cups (570 g) prepared yellow mustard (or use your own homemade Prepared Yellow Mustard, page 361)

½ cup (108 g) packed light brown sugar

¼ cup (85 g) honey

2 tablespoons (30 ml) Worcestershire sauce (or use your own homemade, page 372)

2 tablespoons (30 ml) apple cider vinegar

2 tablespoons (30 ml) soy sauce

1 teaspoon ground black pepper

Up to ½ teaspoon ground cayenne, optional

1. Combine all the ingredients in a medium saucepan set over medium heat, stirring constantly until the brown sugar and honey dissolve. Bring to a simmer, stirring occasionally.

2. Reduce the heat to low and simmer slowly, stirring more and more often, until thickened about like gravy, about 10 minutes.

3. Turn off the heat and remove the pan from the burner. Cool at room temperature for 10 minutes. Transfer to three *clean* ½ pint (236 ml) jars or other containers, leaving about ½ inch (1 cm) headspace in each. Cover or seal. Cool at room temperature for no more than 30 minutes, then refrigerate or freeze.

Next

We love to thin this sauce in this ratio: 2 parts olive oil, 1 part white wine vinegar, and 1 part gold barbecue sauce *by volume*. Grill some romaine lettuce halves or halved endive spears, then serve with this sauce drizzled over the charred greens.

Clockwise from bottom: Gold Barbecue Sauce (page 358), Peanut Butter–Ginger Barbecue Sauce (page 355), and Roasted Garlic–Maple Barbecue Sauce (page 357)

Alabama White Sauce

MAKES: about 3 cups (720 ml)
FRIDGE: up to 2 weeks
FREEZER: no

Yankees sometimes think that Alabama white sauce is nothing more than mayonnaise with vinegar and black pepper. It actually should be a much more complicated, layered sauce, occasionally with horseradish, sometimes with lemon juice, and often with plenty of aromatics. We've opted for them all! White sauce is usually served with smoked brisket or pork shoulder, but it's equally good with a corned beef sandwich or even as a dip for ribs off the grill. Because of the emulsified eggs, this sauce cannot be frozen.

- 2 large eggs
- ½ cup (120 ml) apple cider vinegar
- 2 tablespoons (32 g) prepared yellow mustard (or use your own homemade Prepared Yellow Mustard, page 361)
- 2 tablespoons (25 g) granulated white sugar
- 1½ tablespoons (23 g) prepared white horseradish
- 2 teaspoons (10 ml) lemon juice
- 2 teaspoons ground black pepper
- 1 teaspoon (5 ml) Worcestershire sauce (or use your own homemade, page 372)
- 1 teaspoon (5 ml) hot red pepper sauce, such as Tabasco sauce
- 1 teaspoon garlic powder
- 1 teaspoon onion powder
- 1 teaspoon kosher salt
- 2 cups (480 ml) neutral-flavored oil, such as canola or vegetable oil

1. Combine the eggs, vinegar, prepared mustard, sugar, horseradish, lemon juice, black pepper, Worcestershire sauce, hot sauce, garlic powder, onion powder, and salt in a blender.

2. Cover, then remove the lid's center knob. Begin blending, pouring in the oil in a thin stream to create a thick, white, mayonnaise-like sauce.

3. Transfer to three *clean* ½ pint (236 ml) jars or other containers, leaving about ½ inch (1 cm) headspace in each. Cover or seal, then refrigerate.

Next

This barbecue sauce is not for mopping or grilling. It's for dipping *after* grilling or smoking. Or it's for burgers off the grill (with lots of kimchi, particularly Go-to Kimchi on page 306).

Char Siu Sauce

MAKES: about 3 cups (720 ml)
FRIDGE: up to 1 month
FREEZER: up to 1 year

If you stop at the front counter of many Chinese markets, you'll likely see red-stained char siu or barbecued pork hanging from hooks or laid out on the chopping block. The meat itself is a go-to ingredient for stir-fries, although we also love to use it in wraps with lots of fresh vegetables and Pickled Daikon and Carrots (page 273). This recipe is our simplified version of the classic sauce for that meat preparation, although we *can't* omit one key ingredient: red fermented tofu. You'll probably find it at Asian supermarkets and from online suppliers. It adds both the characteristic color and the slightly sweet-funky flavor.

- 12 ounces (340 g) red fermented tofu, drained
- 1 cup (320 g) hoisin sauce (or use your own homemade, page 348)
- 1 cup (240 ml) soy sauce
- 1 cup (215 g) packed dark brown sugar
- ½ cup (120 ml) unsweetened Chinese rice wine, preferably Shaoxing; or dry sherry
- ½ cup (170 g) honey
- 2 teaspoons five-spice powder (or use your own homemade, see the MORE section with the Five-Spice Ketchup recipe on page 342)
- 2–3 drops red food coloring, optional

1. Combine all the ingredients in a blender. Cover and blend until smooth, stopping the machine at least once to scrape down the inside of the canister.

2. Pour and scrape the contents of the blender into a medium saucepan. Set it over medium heat and bring to a simmer, stirring quite often. Cook, stirring almost constantly, until thickened a bit, about 5 minutes. The final sauce should be a bit wet but not *moundable*.

3. Turn off the heat and remove the pan from the burner. Cool at room temperature for 15 minutes. Transfer the sauce to three *clean* ½ pint (236 ml) jars or other containers, leaving about ½ inch (1 cm) headspace in each. Cover or seal, then refrigerate or freeze.

Next

To make char siu (Cantonese-style barbecued pork) with this sauce: Slice a boneless pork butt or shoulder into strips about 2 inches (5 cm) thick. Coat these well with the sauce, then cover and refrigerate overnight. Position a rack in the top third of the oven and heat it to 475°F (250°C), no fan or convection. Place a metal rack in a lipped baking sheet, then lay the pork on top. Roast for 10 minutes, then reduce the heat to 375°F (190°C) and continue roasting for 15 minutes. Turn the pork and roast for another 15 minutes. Thin out some of the char siu sauce with a little hot water, baste the pork, and roast for about 5 minutes. Turn, baste, and continue roasting for about 5 minutes or until an instant-read meat thermometer registers 150°F (65°C). Cool for at least 10 minutes before slicing and serving.

Prepared Yellow Mustard

MAKES: about 2 cups (480 ml)
FRIDGE: up to 1 month
FREEZER: up to 1 year

This mustard is our version of the US standard, the store-bought mustard served on hot dogs and brats across the country. This mustard is *prepared*—that is, in the sense of fully cooked. In fact, it's the *only* fully cooked mustard among our offerings. It's not terribly spicy. But we don't add any sugar—we prefer some spike! If you want a sweeter finish, add Sweet Pickle Relish (page 163) or English Piccalilli (page 173) to your sandwiches.

> 1 cup (240 ml) water
> 1 cup (96 g) ground dried mustard
> ¾ cup (180 ml) distilled white vinegar
> 2 teaspoons all-purpose flour
> 1½ teaspoons kosher salt
> ½ teaspoon ground dried turmeric
> ¼ teaspoon garlic powder
> ⅛ teaspoon mild paprika

1. Combine all the ingredients in a small saucepan set over medium heat, whisking until smooth. Bring to a boil, whisking often.

2. Reduce the heat to low and simmer, whisking all the while, until a bit thickened, somewhat like pancake batter, about 5 minutes.

3. Turn off the heat and remove the pan from the burner. Cool at room temperature for no more than 15 minutes. Transfer to two *clean* ½ pint (236 ml) jars or other containers, leaving about ½ inch (1 cm) headspace in each. Cover or seal, then refrigerate or freeze.

Next

To make a dip for pretzels, mix the mustard with mayonnaise and sour cream in equal parts *by volume*. Stir in a little granulated sugar, even less dehydrated onion, and prepared white horseradish to taste.

Dijon Mustard

MAKES: about 2 cups (480 ml)
FRIDGE: up to 1 month after ripening
FREEZER: up to 1 year after ripening

Right up front, we have to admit that this Dijon mustard is coarse in its texture. Part of the problem is that home-kitchen equipment, even super-powered turbo blenders, will never get a

Right to left, with soft pretzels:
Coarse-Grained Mustard
(page 363) and Dijon Mustard
(page 361)

mustard as smooth as commercial blenders. But honestly? We prefer the brighter pop and bigger texture of coarsely ground mustard seeds. If you've never had a homemade full-bodied mustard, go easy at first taste. This one's got the nose-bopping flavor of Pommery mustard. That said, any mustard calms down in storage, especially if frozen.

- ½ cup (120 ml) white wine vinegar
- 1 small shallot (about ¾ ounce or 22 g), peeled and thinly sliced
- 2 medium garlic cloves, peeled and crushed
- 2 tablespoons (12 g) coriander seeds
- 1 teaspoon caraway seeds
- 1 teaspoon allspice berries
- 1 cup (240 ml) dry white wine, such as Chardonnay; or *unsweetened* apple juice
- ¾ cup (72 g) yellow mustard seeds
- 6 tablespoons (36 g) brown mustard seeds
- 3 tablespoons (38 g) granulated white sugar
- 2 teaspoons kosher salt
- Water to create a paste

1. Combine the vinegar, shallot, garlic, coriander seeds, caraway seeds, and allspice berries in a small saucepan set over medium heat. Bring to a simmer, stirring occasionally. Turn off the heat and remove the pan from the burner. Cover and set aside at room temperature until cool to the touch, about 1 hour.

2. Strain the vinegar mixture through a fine-mesh strainer into a blender. Discard the solids in the strainer. Add the wine, both mustard seeds, the sugar, and salt to the strained vinegar. Cover and blend until a coarse paste forms, or even longer for a somewhat smoother texture (it'll never be super creamy). Stop the machine at least once to scrape down the inside of the canister and add water in 1 tablespoon (15 ml) increments to make sure the paste is moving over the blades.

3. Uncover and transfer to two *clean* ½ pint (236 ml) jars or other containers, leaving about ½ inch (1 cm) headspace in each. Cover or seal, then refrigerate for 1 week to ripen. Then enjoy or freeze.

Next

If you want to go nuts with a ham and cheese sandwich, spread a little of this mustard inside the sandwich, then spread the outside of both pieces of bread with mayonnaise. Fry in a nonstick skillet set over medium heat until toasty and brown, turning once, about 2 minutes per side.

Coarse-Grained Mustard

MAKES: about 2 cups (480 ml)
FRIDGE: up to 1 month after ripening
FREEZER: up to 1 year after ripening

Watch carefully as this mustard blends. If you're using a Nutribullet or a turbo blender, you'll need to stop the machine repeatedly to make sure you're *not* making a puree. Also, the more water you add, the smoother the mustard can become…but be careful: Too much water and it'll quickly turn soupy.

- ¾ cup (180 ml) moderately sweet white wine, such as a Riesling; or *unsweetened* apple juice
- ⅔ cup (64 g) yellow mustard seeds
- ⅔ cup (64 g) brown mustard seeds
- ¼ cup (60 ml) malt vinegar
- 2 tablespoons (30 ml) Worcestershire sauce (or use your own homemade, page 372)
- 1 medium garlic clove, peeled and crushed
- 2 teaspoons kosher salt
- ½ teaspoon ground allspice
- ½ teaspoon ground caraway seeds
- ⅛ teaspoon grated nutmeg
- ⅛ teaspoon ground cloves
- Water to create a coarse paste

1. Combine the wine, both mustard seeds, the vinegar, Worcestershire sauce, garlic, salt, allspice, caraway seeds, nutmeg, and cloves in a blender. Cover and blend, adding water in 1 tablespoon (15 ml) increments as necessary to create a spreadable mixture. It should be a bit saucy, yet thicker than prepared mustard, so more substantial.

Add just enough liquid so the seeds blend evenly and fully without turning into a wet puree. Turn off the machine at least once and scrape down the inside of the canister.

2. Uncover and transfer the mustard to two *clean* ½ pint (236 ml) jars or other containers, leaving about ½ inch (1 cm) headspace in each. Cover or seal, then refrigerate for 1 week to ripen. Then enjoy or freeze.

Tip

Ground caraway can be hard to find—and expensive to boot. Grind whole caraway seeds by putting about 1 teaspoon on a cutting board, then rocking the bottom edge of a heavy saucepan back and forth across them until powdery. (Watch for escapees!) Or you can use a mortar with a pestle.

Honey Mustard

MAKES: about 2 cups (480 ml)
FRIDGE: up to 1 month after ripening
FREEZER: up to 1 year after ripening

We prefer the texture of a *smooth* honey mustard. Given the limitations of home equipment, our preferences mean we must move from mustard seeds to ground dried mustard for this recipe. Problem is, the flavor of that powder is often muted, from both the grinding process and long storage. To compensate, we add a little wasabi powder to give the mustard the bop-in-the-kisser power we love. You can omit the wasabi powder, but the mustard will be much (much!) tamer.

- 6 tablespoons (125 g) honey
- ¼ cup (60 ml) neutral-flavored oil, such as canola or vegetable oil
- ¼ cup (60 ml) apple cider vinegar
- ¼ cup (54 g) packed light brown sugar
- 1¼ cups (120 g) ground dried mustard
- 2 teaspoons kosher salt
- 1 teaspoon wasabi powder, optional

1. Combine the honey, oil, vinegar, and brown sugar in a small saucepan set over low heat. Stir until the brown sugar and honey dissolve. Warm thoroughly, stirring often. *Do not* let the mixture come to a simmer.

2. Turn off the heat and remove the pan from the burner. Whisk in the ground mustard, salt, and wasabi powder, if using, to form a smooth paste. Cool at room temperature for 15 minutes.

3. Transfer to two *clean* ½ pint (236 ml) jars or other containers, leaving about ½ inch (1 cm) headspace in each. Cover or seal, then refrigerate for 2 weeks to ripen. Then enjoy or freeze.

Next

To make HONEY MUSTARD DIP for pretzels or vegetables, mix 1 part honey mustard with 2 parts mayonnaise (*by volume*). Add a squeeze of lemon juice for brightness or maybe a dash of sriracha.

Brown Mustard

MAKES: about 2 cups (480 ml)
FRIDGE: up to 1 month after ripening
FREEZER: up to 1 year after ripening

Here's our powerhouse of a mustard, best with fully loaded deli sandwiches, although it's admittedly a go-to in our house for hot dogs and even chicken clubs. It's quite spicy, thanks to all those brown mustard seeds…and a little coarse in texture. Remember that mustard seeds can go rancid quickly: Store extra in the freezer.

- 1½ cups (144 g) brown mustard seeds
- ⅔ cup (160 ml) water, plus more as necessary to create a thick paste
- ½ cup (120 ml) white wine vinegar
- ¼ cup (54 g) packed dark brown sugar
- ¼ cup (60 ml) olive oil
- 2 teaspoons kosher salt
- 1 teaspoon ground coriander
- ½ teaspoon ground allspice

1. Combine the mustard seeds, ⅔ cup (160 ml) water, the vinegar, brown sugar, oil, salt, coriander, and allspice in a blender. Cover and blend, adding water in 1 tablespoon (15 ml) increments as necessary to create a spreadable mixture, a bit saucy, but thicker and more substantial. Add just enough liquid that the seeds blend evenly and fully without turning into a wet puree. Turn off the machine at least once to scrape down the inside of the canister.

2. Uncover and transfer the mustard to two *clean* ½ pint (236 ml) jars or other containers, leaving about ½ inch (1 cm) headspace in each. Cover or seal, then refrigerate for 1 week to ripen. Then enjoy or freeze.

Next

For a mustard barbecue mop, whisk 3 parts brown mustard with 1 part brown sugar and 1 part apple cider vinegar (*by volume*). Whisk in a splash of olive oil, a pinch of garlic powder, and a pinch of ground dried cayenne. Use the mop only for the last 10 minutes or so of grilling to prevent scorching.

Wheat Beer Mustard

MAKES: about 4 cups (960 ml)
FRIDGE: up to 1 month
FREEZER: up to 1 year

Wheat beer (or Hefeweizen) adds a sweet complexity to this otherwise assertive mustard that includes the surprising spark of lemon zest for a little more brightness. The mustard is great in wraps of all sorts, particularly those stocked with lots of fresh or roasted vegetables—along with a smear of soft goat cheese to balance the flavors.

> One 12 ounce (360 ml) bottle of wheat beer (do not use a flavored wheat beer)
> 1 cup (240 ml) white balsamic vinegar
> 1 cup (96 g) yellow mustard seeds
> ½ cup (48 g) brown mustard seeds
> 1 tablespoon (12 g) kosher salt

> 1 teaspoon (6 g) finely grated lemon zest
> 1 teaspoon ground cinnamon
> ½ teaspoon ground allspice
> ½ teaspoon ground cloves
> ½ teaspoon ground black pepper

1. Combine all the ingredients in a large bowl. Cover and set aside at room temperature for 48 hours.

2. Pour and scrape the contents of the bowl into a food processor (work in batches, as necessary). Cover and process to a grainy paste, stopping the machine at least *twice* to scrape down the inside of the canister, about 4 minutes.

3. Transfer the mustard to four *clean* ½ pint (236 ml) jars or other containers, leaving about ½ inch (1 cm) headspace in each. Cover or seal, then refrigerate or freeze.

More

This mustard is the best dip for pretzel rods!

Fiery Brown Mustard

MAKES: about 2 cups (480 ml)
FRIDGE: up to 1 month after ripening
FREEZER: up to 1 year after ripening

This mustard is about as spicy as you can imagine, with fewer sweet notes and a big punch of heat, thanks to the cayenne. When that spice is combined with the nose-spank from both brown and yellow mustard seeds, the results are nothing if not eye-opening, if not eye-watering. Given the nature of this wild concoction, we don't add many dried spices because we want that heat to come through unobstructed. However, if you'd like to add more flavor depth, see the MORE section.

One 12 ounce (360 ml) bottle of dark beer, preferably a brown ale or an unflavored stout

½ cup (48 g) yellow mustard seeds

¼ cup (24 g) brown mustard seeds

3 tablespoons (37 g) dark brown sugar

2 tablespoons (42 g) honey

2 teaspoons kosher salt

Up to 1 teaspoon ground dried cayenne

½ teaspoon ground allspice

Water to create a thick spread

1. Pour the beer into a small bowl and add both kinds of mustard seeds. Stir, cover, and set aside at room temperature for 2 hours.

2. Uncover and scrape every speck of the beer mixture into a blender. Add the brown sugar, honey, salt, cayenne, and allspice. Cover and blend to create a fairly smooth spread, adding water in 1 tablespoon (15 ml) increments as necessary to get a *moundable* but not dry consistency. Stop the blender at least once to scrape down the inside of the canister.

3. Transfer the mustard to two *clean* ½ pint (236 ml) jars or other containers, leaving about ½ inch (1 cm) headspace in each. Cover or seal, then refrigerate for 1 week to ripen. Then enjoy or freeze.

More

For more flavor, add ½ teaspoon ground cinnamon, ¼ teaspoon grated nutmeg, and/or ¼ teaspoon ground cardamom to the blender.

Maple Mustard

MAKES: about 2 cups (480 ml)
FRIDGE: up to 1 month after ripening
FREEZER: up to 1 year after ripening

The success of this fairly sweet and delicate mustard depends on the quality of the maple syrup. For the best, search out online suppliers who will ship from Vermont, northern New England, or eastern Canada. If possible, use *baking* or dark maple syrup, sometimes called *grade A*

dark color in the US and *grade B very dark* in Canada. We nixed the mustard seeds in this recipe in favor of ground dried mustard to keep the overall flavors more muted in a bid to bring forward the autumnal feel of the maple syrup. To help with the cost of so much ground dried mustard, look for larger packagings from online spice purveyors.

1¼ cups (96 g) ground dried mustard

¾ cup (180 ml) water

¼ cup (80 g) dark maple syrup

¼ cup (60 ml) apple cider vinegar

2 teaspoons kosher salt

1 teaspoon ground black pepper

1. Combine all the ingredients in a medium bowl. Stir until the mixture forms a smooth paste.

2. Transfer to two *clean* ½ pint (236 ml) jars or other containers, leaving about ½ inch (1 cm) headspace in each. Cover or seal, then refrigerate for 2 weeks to ripen. Then enjoy or freeze.

More

For a much darker, richer flavor with bitter notes and a decidedly umami finish, substitute pure birch syrup for the maple syrup. Look online for suppliers in Alaska or western Canada.

Molasses Mustard

MAKES: about 2 cups (480 ml)
FRIDGE: up to 1 month after ripening
FREEZER: up to 1 year after ripening

Molasses (or treacle) adds slightly bitter if sweet tannic notes to this mustard, a more refined condiment all around, certainly more so than Honey Mustard (page 364). By soaking the mustard seeds, we soften them and end up with a somewhat smoother mustard, too. That said, the final consistency is largely dependent on the type of blender you use. A turbo blender will result in a smoother mustard with soaked seeds. You can get a fairly smooth mustard from a standard blender but you have to stop the machine repeatedly to rearrange the contents and you may have to add a little more water than usual to keep things blending.

1 cup (120 ml) *warm* water
1 cup (96 g) brown mustard seeds
¼ cup (85 g) molasses or black treacle
¼ cup (24 g) ground dried mustard
1½ tablespoons (23 ml) apple cider vinegar
1 tablespoon (8 g) ground dried ginger
1 tablespoon (12 g) kosher salt
Additional water to create a thick spread

1. Combine the warm water and mustard seeds in a blender canister. Cover and set aside at room temperature for 2 hours.

2. Add the molasses, ground mustard, vinegar, ground ginger, and salt. Cover and blend until a thick, saucy spread forms, adding more water in 1 tablespoon (15 ml) increments as necessary and stopping the machine at least once to scrape down the inside of the canister.

3. Uncover and transfer the mustard to two *clean* ½ pint (236 ml) jars or other containers, leaving about ½ inch (1 cm) headspace in each. Cover or seal, then refrigerate for 1 week to ripen. Then enjoy or freeze.

Next
This mustard makes a great salad dressing. Whisk a small dollop of it with lots of olive oil and some white wine vinegar. Add a little ground black pepper and mild paprika, then taste and season for salt.

Garlic Mustard

MAKES: about 2 cups (480 ml)
FRIDGE: up to 1 month after ripening
FREEZER: up to 1 year after ripening

Raw garlic is too powerful a flavor, even for a spicy mustard. And roasting garlic cloves brings on perhaps unwanted caramelized notes, which can be a bit overpowering on a sandwich or in a wrap

to many tastes. To solve the problems, we boil the garlic cloves in their husks to tame and soften them. Although we usually call for medium garlic cloves in our recipes, this one calls for *large* cloves. Even when we've tamed the cloves, we still want as much garlic flavor as possible!

1 cup (96 g) yellow mustard seeds
½ cup (120 ml) water
16 *large* garlic cloves (do not peel)
½ cup (120 ml) olive oil
½ cup (120 ml) white wine vinegar
1 tablespoon (12 g) kosher salt
Up to 5 shots of red hot sauce, such as Tabasco or Cholula
Additional water to create a thick spread

1. Put the mustard seeds and ½ cup (120 ml) water in a blender canister. Cover and set aside at room temperature for 2 hours.

2. Meanwhile, put the garlic cloves in a small saucepan and fill the pan with water to submerge them. Set the pan over high heat and bring to a boil, stirring once or twice. Reduce the heat to medium-low and simmer until the garlic has softened, about 12 minutes. Turn off the heat, remove the pan from the burner, and cool to room temperature, about 1 hour.

3. Drain the cloves in a colander set in the sink, then squeeze the soft pulp from the husks into the blender. Discard the husks. Add the oil, vinegar, salt, and hot sauce. Cover and blend until a thick, saucy spread forms, adding more water in 1 tablespoon (15 ml) increments as necessary and stopping the machine at least once to scrape down the inside of the canister.

4. Uncover and transfer the mustard to two *clean* ½ pint (236 ml) jars or other containers, leaving about ½ inch (1 cm) headspace in each. Cover or seal, then refrigerate for 1 week to ripen. Then enjoy or freeze.

More
For a more elegant finish, substitute white balsamic vinegar for the white wine vinegar.

Center: Fiery Brown Mustard (page 365), then clockwise from bottom: Szechuan-Inspired Red Mustard (page 369), Garlic Mustard (page 367), and Molasses Mustard (page 366)

Super Hot Yellow Mustard

MAKES: about 2 cups (480 ml)
FRIDGE: up to 1 month
FREEZER: up to 1 year

If you grew up going to American-Chinese restaurants, as we did, you know this mustard as the forbidden sauce on the table, the condiment your mother warned you about. She needn't have worried. It's a wonderful addition to a well-stocked fridge, great on egg rolls and fried noodles, but also terrific with fried chicken or shrimp.

- 1½ cups (144 g) *hot* ground yellow mustard powder, preferably S&B hot mustard
- 2 tablespoons (25 g) granulated white sugar
- 1½ tablespoons (18 g) kosher salt
- 1 tablespoon (6 g) ground *white* pepper
- ¾ cup (180 ml) very hot tap water
- ½ cup (120 ml) *unseasoned* rice vinegar
- ¼ cup (60 ml) neutral-flavored oil, such as canola or vegetable oil

1. Whisk the ground mustard, sugar, salt, and pepper in a medium bowl until uniform. Whisk in the hot water, then whisk in the vinegar and oil to form a smooth paste.

2. Transfer to two *clean* ½ pint (236 ml) jars or other containers, leaving about ½ inch (1 cm) headspace in each. Cover or seal, then refrigerate or freeze.

Tip
Can you use standard ground dried mustard? Yes, but the condiment won't have that characteristic, obstreperous burst of flavor.

Szechuan-Inspired Red Mustard

MAKES: about 2 cups (480 ml)
FRIDGE: up to 1 month after ripening
FREEZER: up to 1 year after ripening

We'll admit up front that this mustard is our whimsical invention, crafted to capture the fiery flavor of ground er jing tiao chili (found in the chili powder) and pair it with the up-the-nose quality of good mustard. In other words, this mustard is not for the faint of…well, palate, if not heart.

- 1 cup (96 g) yellow mustard seeds
- ¼ cup (24 g) ground dried mustard
- ½ cup (120 ml) water
- ½ cup (120 ml) *unseasoned* rice vinegar
- 6 tablespoons (90 ml) rice wine, preferably Shaoxing; or dry vermouth
- 2 tablespoons (12 g) coarsely ground red Szechuan chili powder (see page 190)
- 2 teaspoons kosher salt
- Additional water to create a smooth puree

1. Combine all the ingredients in a blender canister. Cover and blend until a coarse but not dry spread forms, stopping the machine at least once to scrape down the inside of the canister and adding water in 1 tablespoon (15 ml) increments to get a smooth but not wet consistency.

2. Transfer to two *clean* ½ pint (236 ml) jars or other containers, leaving about ½ inch (1 cm) headspace in each. Cover or seal, then refrigerate for 1 week to ripen. Then enjoy or freeze.

More
For deeper flavors, add up to 2 teaspoons five-spice powder (or use your own homemade, see the MORE section of the Five-Spice Ketchup recipe on page 342), 1 teaspoon ground coriander, and/or ½ teaspoon ground cinnamon to the blender.

Spicy Peanut Sauce

MAKES: about 2 cups (480 ml)
FRIDGE: up to 1 month
FREEZER: up to 1 year

Break out the satay! Or egg rolls! Or spring rolls! Or sliced cucumbers! We can't imagine not having a jar of this spicy sauce in our fridge. You can tame the heat a bit by using fewer chilis than we suggest, but we love that fiery pop against the complicated blend of ingredients, less sweet than commercial bottlings, less like peanut butter in sauce form, more textural from the ground peanuts, and more layered from all the spices.

- 8 dried árbol chilis, stemmed, the seeds shaken out and discarded
- *Boiling* water to soak the chilis
- 1½ cups (90 g) *unsalted* roasted peanuts
- 1 medium shallot (about 1 ounce or 30 g), peeled and roughly chopped
- 3 medium garlic cloves, peeled and halved
- 1 lemongrass stalk, trimmed of tough bottoms, fibrous tops, and all outer leaves, the remainder minced
- 2½ tablespoons (32 g) granulated white sugar
- 1 tablespoon (15 g) minced peeled fresh ginger
- 1 tablespoon (15 g) tamarind paste
- 1 tablespoon (16 g) hoisin sauce (or use your own homemade, page 348)
- 1 teaspoon ground coriander
- ½ teaspoon kosher salt
- ¼ cup (60 ml) neutral-flavored oil, such as canola or vegetable oil
- 1 cup (240 ml) water

1. Put the árbol chilis in a medium bowl and cover with boiling water. Set a heat-safe plate on top of them to weight them down. Soak at room temperature for 10 minutes.

2. Meanwhile, put the peanuts in a food processor, cover, and pulse until finely ground, about like very coarse sand. Set aside.

3. Uncover the bowl and drain the chilis in a colander set in the sink. Transfer to a blender and add the shallot, garlic, lemongrass, sugar, ginger, tamarind paste, hoisin sauce, coriander, and salt. Cover and blend until a thick puree forms, stopping the machine at least once to scrape down the inside of the container.

4. Set a medium saucepan over medium heat for a minute or two. Add the oil, then scrape all of the chili paste from the blender into the pan. Cook, stirring often, until fragrant, about 2 minutes.

5. Add the ground peanuts and stir to coat. Pour in the 1 cup (240 ml) water and bring to a simmer, stirring often. Simmer, stirring almost constantly, until slightly thickened, somewhat like thick pancake batter, about 3 minutes.

6. Turn off the heat and remove the pan from the burner. Cool at room temperature for no more than 30 minutes. Transfer to two *clean* ½ pint (236 ml) jars or other containers, leaving about ½ inch (1 cm) headspace in each. Cover or seal, then refrigerate or freeze.

More

For a more authentic flavor, substitute kecap manis for the hoisin sauce—and use your own homemade Kecap Manis (page 346).

Duck Sauce

MAKES: about 3 cups (720 ml)
FRIDGE: up to 1 month
FREEZER: up to 1 year

There's no duck in duck sauce! Instead, it's an apricot-based, sweet-and-sour (or actually, *more-sweet*-than-sour) sauce that's always served at American Chinese restaurants. It's made for egg rolls and steamed ribs…as well as roast duck (or chicken). We also find it rather refreshing when mixed with sriracha as a dip for cucumbers and carrots on the deck in the evening.

Top to bottom: Duck Sauce (page 370) and Spicy Peanut Sauce (page 370) with crunchy Chinese noodles

10 ounces (285 g) *fresh* ripe peaches (about 2 medium), peeled, pitted, and finely chopped

8 ounces (225 g) *dried* apricots, finely chopped

1½ cups (360 ml) unsweetened apple juice

⅔ cup (160 ml) *unseasoned* rice vinegar

¼ cup (54 g) packed light brown sugar

1 tablespoon (12.5 g) granulated white sugar

1 tablespoon (15 ml) soy sauce

2 teaspoons (10 g) minced peeled fresh ginger

½ teaspoon kosher salt

¼ teaspoon ground dried mustard

¼ teaspoon red pepper flakes

1. Combine all the ingredients in a medium saucepan set over medium heat, stirring constantly until the brown sugar dissolves. Bring to a simmer, stirring occasionally.

2. Reduce the heat to very low and simmer *slowly*, stirring more and more frequently to prevent scorching, until the fruit is soft and the mixture is beginning to thicken, about 10 minutes.

3. Turn off the heat and remove the pan from the burner. Cool at room temperature for 20 minutes.

4. Use an immersion blender in the pan to create a chunky puree. Alternatively, transfer about *half* of the sauce to a blender, cover, and blend until smooth; then stir this puree back into the remainder in the pan.

5. Transfer to three *clean* ½ pint (236 ml) jars or other containers, leaving about ½ inch (1 cm) headspace in each. Cover or seal, then refrigerate or freeze.

Next

To make a sweet-and-sour salad dressing, whisk 3 parts neutral-flavored oil (like canola or vegetable oil) with 1 part white wine vinegar (*by volume*). Whisk in a little of this duck sauce, as well as a pinch of garlic powder and onion powder.

Worcestershire Sauce

MAKES: about 4 cups (960 ml)
FRIDGE: up to 2 months after ripening
FREEZER: up to 1 year after ripening

If you're questioning who would make homemade Worcestershire sauce, you've never made it. And we know lots of people who have! Of the tens of thousands of recipes we've published and posted over twenty-five years, this recipe has won the most followers and the most praise online. It's an aromatic burst of flavor, the best thing you can have in your fridge for marinades, cocktail sauce, and even Bloody Marys.

1⅓ cups (320 ml) malt vinegar

1⅓ cups (320 ml) distilled white vinegar

⅔ cup (226 g) molasses or black treacle

⅔ cup (160 ml) soy sauce

⅓ cup (80 g) tamarind *concentrate* (do not use tamarind paste)

⅓ cup (33 g) yellow mustard seeds

¼ cup (48 g) kosher salt

1 large yellow or white onion, peeled and roughly chopped

4 medium garlic cloves, peeled and smashed

One 2 ounce (55 g) tin of anchovy fillets, drained and roughly chopped

10 dried árbol chilis, stemmed and seeded

One 1 inch (2.5 cm) piece of fresh ginger (about the width of your thumb), peeled and thinly sliced

8 *green* cardamom pods, cracked open (plus their seeds)

One 2 inch (5 cm) cinnamon stick

1 tablespoon whole cloves

1 tablespoon coriander seeds

1 tablespoon black peppercorns

1 teaspoon ground dried turmeric

1 star anise pod

⅔ cup (133 g) granulated white sugar

1. Combine everything *except the sugar* in a large pot. Bring to a boil over medium-high heat, stirring often. Reduce the heat to low and simmer for 10 minutes, stirring often.

2. Meanwhile, put the sugar in a small nonstick skillet and melt it over low heat until golden caramel, about 7 minutes.

3. Pour the melted sugar into the pot. Be careful! Everything will roil. Continue stirring as the sugar clumps, then melts again. Turn off the heat and remove the pot from the burner. Cool at room temperature for 2 hours. Pour into a large glass jar, cover, and refrigerate to ripen for at least 3 weeks or up to 5 weeks.

4. Strain the mixture through a fine-mesh sieve into a bowl. Drip for about 1 hour. Discard the solids. Transfer the sauce to four *clean* ½ pint (236 ml) jars or other containers, leaving about ½ inch (1 cm) headspace in each. Cover or seal, then refrigerate or freeze.

Next

The best marinade for steaks is simply this sauce. Rub a little on them, then cover and refrigerate for 2–3 hours before grilling, roasting, or pan-frying.

7

Sweet Sauces and Dips

Desserts just got better. Rather than hot fudge thickened with hydrogenated shortening, purchased strawberry sauce made with allegedly *natural* flavors, or applesauce with too much sugar, we've got a range of delightful, sweet sauces: from simple to complex, from syrupy to sticky, from pear sauce (with yogurt for breakfast!) to cajeta (a famed goat milk caramel).

Most of these sweet sauces are pretty easy, just a matter of getting them to the right consistency or set. After that, they're ready for ice cream. Or pound cake. Or quick bread. Or cookies. Most are best spooned onto whatever treat you've got on a plate, although a few, like Cranberry Applesauce (page 378), can be dished up on their own. Even more, a few of the sauces, like Pineapple Sauce (page 392) and Blackberry Sauce (page 393), can be mixed with (more) white wine vinegar and (less) canola oil to create a (very) sweet barbecue mop.

You'll probably want to give these results away as house gifts, simply because it's nice to spread the bounty around. So you'll want to put them in decorative jars. We recommend glass all around because you can skip any problems with reactive glazes; but also consider using wide-mouthed jars because getting a thicky, sticky dessert sauce out of the narrow opening in a jar is like Sisyphus pushing caramel sauce uphill. Everybody knows the pain of trying to get some ice cream sauce out of a jar that's so narrow it can only accommodate an iced tea spoon. And who wants to drive to their grandmother's house to borrow an iced tea spoon just to have some toffee sauce?

Before we turn to our selection of small-batch sweet sauces, let's talk through a few of the common ingredients in this chapter and one of the more finicky points in our shortcut technique.

Chocolate

In a few of these recipes, we call for chocolate, perhaps to make proper hot fudge or chocolate sauce. Pay attention to the *type* of chocolate: unsweetened, in some cases; but other types as well, usually determined by the percentage of cocoa solids in the mix.

The best chocolate, even for cooking, is graded by its cocoa solid content: for example, about 70 percent cocoa solids make up what we would call *bittersweet* chocolate; about 50 percent, *semisweet* chocolate. We recommend a certain percent of cocoa solids in the chocolate, so the overall balance of flavors won't be quite so sweet—even in some of the dessert sauces.

To chop chocolate, you can use a sharp knife on a cutting board, rocking it through the bars or chunks. However, you'll inevitably create chocolate dust, some of which may even melt and stick to the cutting board because of the blade's friction. A better tool is a chocolate fork, designed to break chocolate into larger bits, which then melt evenly but slowly without a lot of waste on the cutting board.

▲ A chocolate fork is the best tool for chopping chocolate.

You can also find chocolate shavers on the market. We don't recommend them. They yield pretty curls for cakes and such, but those curls are too thin for proper melting. They scorch easily over the heat, which then renders the chocolate bitter.

Heavy or whipping cream

As far as US or Canadian cooks are concerned, whipping cream has a fat content between 30 and 36 percent; heavy cream, a fat content greater than 36 percent. Since we're not beating either into whipped cream in our recipes, both will work, depending on your preferences (and budget).

Things are a tad different in the UK, EU, Australia, and New Zealand. Single cream has a fat content of around 20 percent, give or take a little. You can use it in these recipes, although they won't be as rich or satisfying. Whipping cream has a higher fat content, somewhere near 35 percent, and is ideal here. In no case should you use double cream with a fat content of around 48 percent; it's too rich for these recipes.

How thick should the sauce be?

Most of these sauces are reduced in some way, although few reduce as much as many of the savory sauces in the previous chapter and none as far as the chutneys way back in the second chapter. Look, instead, for a decided thickening while maintaining lots of essential moisture. Remember: A dessert sauce will continue to set as it cools because of the melted sugar in the mix.

To be honest, the final consistency is a matter of taste. You can take a sauce further than we suggest for a thicker, stickier sauce, one that might have to be loosened in the microwave before it can be spooned onto ice cream. Our preference (and timings) are mostly for looser sauces, more pourable or spoonable than spreadable.

Ready, set...

We'll admit that some of these sauces are not traditionally found in canning and preserving books, although Mark's grandmother certainly squirreled away more than her share of both applesauce and butterscotch sauce during the autumn. Even so, both in the spirit of and in our appeal for a well-stocked fridge or freezer, we wanted to include some of our favorite dessert sauces as well as our go-to autumn treats like Pear-Ginger Sauce (page 381) among our small-batch, quick-cook recipes. These days, life needs a little something sweet, right? If we can make that happen with as few steps as possible, it's worth the effort!

Butterscotch Sauce
(page 385), reduced
less at back for a
thinner pour and
more at front for a
thicker consistency

Applesauce

MAKES: about 3 cups (720 ml)
FRIDGE: up to 2 weeks
FREEZER: up to 6 months

If you're going to the trouble to make applesauce, you might as well do it right: You need a food mill for the *smoothest* consistency, although alternative methods will yield acceptable results. Believe it or not, there's actually a time-saving bonus to making a small batch of applesauce with a food mill: You don't have to peel or core the apples, always one of our least-favorite kitchen tasks. All those bits of peel, core, and seeds get left behind in the mill. If you compost, there's organic matter right at hand. And if you use our preferred apple for applesauce (McIntosh!), the applesauce will have a beautiful, pale, pink hue.

- 1¾ pounds (795 g) tart juicy apples, preferably McIntosh (5–7 large)
- 2 cups (480 ml) water
- 1 tablespoon (21 g) honey
- ¼ teaspoon kosher salt
- ⅛ teaspoon ground cinnamon

1. Cut the apples up into chunks (peels, cores, and all) and put in a medium saucepan. Add the water, honey, salt, and cinnamon. Set the pot over medium-high heat and bring to a boil, stirring occasionally to dissolve the honey. Reduce the heat to low, cover, and simmer for 5 minutes.

2. Uncover and continue cooking, stirring often, until the apples are quite soft, about 15 minutes. Turn off the heat, remove the pan from the burner, and cool at room temperature for 20 minutes.

3. Set up a food mill over a large bowl (for an alternative to a food mill, see page 16). Pour some of the apple mixture into the food mill and grind it through, letting the pulpy solids fall into the bowl below and leaving the seeds, cores, skins, and other bits behind. Repeat this process until you've ground all the apples and their liquid.

4. Discard the solids in the food mill. Transfer the applesauce to three *clean* ½ pint (236 ml) jars or other containers, leaving about ½ inch (1 cm) headspace in each. Cover or seal, then refrigerate or freeze.

More

Add other spices with the cinnamon: ⅛ teaspoon ground allspice, grated nutmeg, ground mace, and/or ground dried ginger. Or omit the cinnamon and add 2 teaspoons (10 g) minced peeled fresh ginger to the saucepan.

Cranberry Applesauce

MAKES: about 4 cups (960 ml)
FRIDGE: up to 2 weeks
FREEZER: up to 6 months

Although we love the almost creamy texture of plain applesauce put through a food mill, we also like to make a small batch of cranberry-laced applesauce and keep it chunkier, the better to let little sparks of cranberry show through the sweet sauce. This applesauce is admittedly less work and may be a great way to convince you to try the more elaborate version with a food mill. Again, our preferred apple will yield a pink-toned sauce. Other apples, like Gala or Honeycrisp, will yield a paler, almost white sauce, even with the cranberries in the mix.

- 2 pounds (900 g) tart juicy apples, preferably McIntosh (6–8 large)
- 1 cup (115 g) fresh cranberries or thawed frozen cranberries
- ¾ cup (180 ml) water
- ¼ cup (50 g) granulated white sugar
- 2 tablespoons (25 g) light brown sugar
- 1 tablespoon (15 ml) lemon juice
- ¼ teaspoon kosher salt

1. Stem, peel, and halve the apples. Core them and cut into small chunks.

Front to back: Pear Sauce (page 380)
and Applesauce (page 378)

2. Combine the apples, cranberries, water, white sugar, brown sugar, lemon juice, and salt in a medium saucepan. Set over medium-high heat and bring to a boil, stirring occasionally to dissolve the honey. Reduce the heat to low, cover, and simmer for 5 minutes.

3. Uncover and continue cooking, stirring often, until the apples are quite soft, about 15 minutes. Turn off the heat, remove the pan from the burner, and cool at room temperature for no more than 20 minutes.

4. Use a potato masher or the back of a wooden spoon to smash the apples and cranberries into a chunky sauce. Transfer to four *clean* ½ pint (236 ml) jars or two *clean* 1 pint (472 ml) jars or other containers, leaving about ½ inch (1 cm) headspace in each. Cover or seal, then refrigerate or freeze.

Next
We love to serve cranberry applesauce for dessert with a big spoonful of plain Greek yogurt and a drizzle of honey, or even date syrup.

Sugar-Free Applesauce

MAKES: about 4 cups (960 ml)
FRIDGE: up to 2 weeks
FREEZER: up to 6 months

As we discussed in our sugar-free jam recipes, the absence of sugar causes a textural problem that has to be accommodated in some way. For a sugar-free applesauce, we use frozen unsweetened apple juice concentrate, which offers a ton of body since it's so reduced. We recommend using fairly sweet apples for this sauce…which means it will be paler than our other applesauces.

- 14 ounces (400 grams) sweet apples, such as Braeburn or Gala (4–6 large)
- ¼ cup (60 ml) thawed frozen *unsweetened* apple juice concentrate

- ½ cup (120 ml) water
- 2 tablespoons (30 ml) lemon juice

1. Stem, peel, and halve the apples. Core them and cut into small chunks.

2. Combine the apples, apple juice concentrate, water, and lemon juice in a medium saucepan. Set the pan over medium-high heat and bring to a boil, stirring constantly at first to dissolve the sugar, then occasionally as the mixture comes to a boil.

3. Reduce the heat to low, cover, and simmer slowly, stirring occasionally, until the apples are quite soft. Turn off the heat, remove the pan from the burner, and cool at room temperature for no more than 20 minutes.

4. Use a potato masher or the back of a wooden spoon to smash the apples into a chunky sauce. Transfer to four *clean* ½ pint (236 ml) jars or two *clean* 1 pint (472 ml) jars or other containers, leaving about ½ inch (1 cm) headspace in each. Cover or seal, then refrigerate or freeze.

More
Spice this applesauce by adding up to 1 teaspoon ground apple pie spice mixture to the pan with the lemon juice.

Pear Sauce

MAKES: about 3 cups (720 ml)
FRIDGE: up to 2 weeks
FREEZER: up to 6 months

Pears are pure luxury: super sweet, juicy, and fragrant. Unfortunately, the ones that show up in our supermarkets are about as luxurious as rocks on a mountain trail. Search out better pears at farm stands and farmers' markets. Look for soft, fragrant, heavy pears, such as Bartlett or Comice, that will produce the smoothest sauce. For the best aesthetics, use green or yellow pears, not brown. The color will be so pale that you won't believe how much flavor the sauce packs.

2½ pounds (1.1 kg) ripe fragrant semi-soft green or
   yellow pears (5–7 large)
2 cups (480 ml) water
½ cup (100 g) granulated white sugar
¼ teaspoon kosher salt

1. Cut the pears into chunks (peels, cores, and all) and put in a medium saucepan. Add the water, sugar, and salt. Set the pot over medium-high heat and bring to a boil, stirring constantly at first to dissolve the sugar, then occasionally. Reduce the heat to low, cover, and simmer for 20 minutes.

2. Uncover and continue cooking, stirring often, until the pears are quite soft, about 10 minutes. Turn off the heat, remove the pan from the burner, and cool at room temperature for 20 minutes.

3. Set up a food mill over a large bowl (for an alternative to a food mill, see page 16). Pour some of the pear mixture into the food mill and grind it through, letting the pulpy solids fall into the bowl below and leaving the seeds, cores, skins, and other bits behind. Repeat this process until you've ground all the pears and any juice through the mill. Discard the solids in the food mill.

4. Transfer the pear sauce to three *clean* ½ pint (236 ml) jars or other containers, leaving about ½ inch (1 cm) headspace in each. Cover or seal, then refrigerate or freeze.

Next
Sprinkle the servings with ground cinnamon or grated nutmeg.

Pear-Ginger Sauce

MAKES: about 4 cups (960 ml)
FRIDGE: up to 2 weeks
FREEZER: up to 6 months

Here's a pear sauce that's much like the consistency of applesauce but with a much bigger flavor profile. Although pears and ginger are a common pairing, we find that ginger often overwhelms the more delicate perfume from the pears. In fact, fresh ginger is just too assertive. Ground dried ginger is a little more subtle. But even so, maple syrup tames its muted if still spiky notes, yielding a much more mellow sauce, perfect as a snack on a rainy afternoon.

2¼ pounds (1 kg) ripe fragrant semi-soft green or
   yellow pears, such as Bartlett or Comice
   (4–6 large), stemmed, peeled, and cut into chunks
½ cup (160 g) maple syrup
½ cup (120 ml) water
2 teaspoons ground dried ginger
¼ teaspoon kosher salt

1. Put the pears, maple syrup, water, ground ginger, and salt in a medium saucepan. Set over medium-high heat and stir constantly until the syrup dissolves. Bring to a boil, stirring occasionally. Reduce the heat to low, cover, and simmer slowly, stirring occasionally, until the pears are tender enough to be mashed by a fork, about 20 minutes.

2. Uncover and stir to check to see if there's liquid in the pan. If so, raise the heat to medium-high and cook, stirring constantly, until it reduces to a syrup. If not, move ahead. Turn off the heat, remove the pan from the burner, and cool at room temperature for 15 minutes.

3. Pour and scrape the contents of the pan into a food processor. Cover and process until a smooth puree forms, stopping the machine at least once to scrape down the inside of the canister.

4. Transfer the pear sauce to four *clean* ½ pint (236 ml) jars or two *clean* 1 pint (472 jars) or other containers, leaving about ½ inch (1 cm) headspace in each. Cover or seal, then refrigerate or freeze.

More
For more complex flavors, swap out the maple syrup for date syrup or birch syrup.

Chocolate Sauce

MAKES: about 3 cups (720 ml)
FRIDGE: up to 3 weeks
FREEZER: up to 1 year

Here's a perfect example of why cold canning is a modern wonder: You'll make just enough of this classic, smooth, luscious dessert sauce to have on hand for a while, plus a little more for the freezer in the months ahead, and perhaps a jar for a friend. The sauce is smooth and rich…and perhaps even better heated. If you've used a glass jar, don't heat it in the microwave. The sauce's consistency can turn grainy. Rather, set the jar of sauce in a small saucepan with warm tap water for a few minutes, stirring occasionally.

> 1½ cups (300 g) granulated white sugar
>
> ¼ cup (21 g) unsweetened cocoa powder
>
> 1 cup (240 ml) heavy or whipping cream
>
> Water for the double boiler
>
> 8 tablespoons (1 stick, 4 ounces, or 115 g) unsalted butter, cut into small pieces
>
> 4 ounces (115 g) *unsweetened* chocolate, chopped
>
> 1 tablespoon (15 ml) vanilla extract
>
> ½ teaspoon kosher salt

1. Whisk the sugar, cocoa powder, and cream in a large bowl until pasty.

2. Set up a double boiler with about 1 inch (2.5 cm) of water in the bottom portion. (Either use a standard double boiler or set a metal or heat-safe bowl into a medium saucepan without it touching the water below.) Add the butter and chocolate to the top portion of the double boiler or the bowl. Bring the water to a simmer over medium heat, stirring the chocolate and butter repeatedly until smooth. Add the cocoa powder paste and whisk constantly until smooth and rich, about 5 minutes.

3. Turn off the heat, watch out for the steam, and remove the top portion of the double boiler or the bowl from the pan. Whisk in the vanilla and salt until smooth, then cool at room temperature for no more than 20 minutes.

4. Transfer to three *clean* ½ pint (236 ml) jars or other containers, leaving about ½ inch (1 cm) headspace in each. Cover or seal, then refrigerate or freeze.

More

Whisk in ½ teaspoon ground cinnamon with the vanilla.

Hot Fudge Sauce

MAKES: about 4 cups (960 ml)
FRIDGE: up to 3 weeks
FREEZER: up to 1 year

Dark and rich, this fudge sauce is best when warmed and drizzled on a sundae (which then must be topped with sweetened whipped cream and chopped nuts). The sauce will set up firm in the fridge, so it's never perfect when you open the jar…unless you like a little on a spoon with peanut butter for a snack! To loosen the sauce, set the jar in a small saucepan with hot tap water and stir the fudge sauce occasionally. One warning: The flavor and texture of the sauce degrade if you repeatedly loosen and chill it again. Best then to pack it into smaller jars.

> ⅔ cup (160 ml) heavy or whipping cream
>
> ⅔ cup (132 g) granulated white sugar
>
> ⅔ cup (104 g) light corn syrup
>
> Water for the double boiler
>
> 8 ounces (225 g) *bittersweet* chocolate (between 60 and 70% cocoa solids), chopped
>
> 4 ounces (115 g) *unsweetened* chocolate, chopped
>
> 6 tablespoons (¾ stick, 3 ounces, or 90 g) unsalted butter, cut into small pieces
>
> 2 teaspoons (10 ml) vanilla extract
>
> ¼ teaspoon kosher salt

1. Stir the cream, sugar, and corn syrup in a small saucepan set over low heat until the sugar dissolves. Reduce the heat further and keep warm, stirring occasionally. Do not simmer.

Left to right: Hot Fudge Sauce (page 382) on vanilla ice cream and White Chocolate Sauce (page 384) on chocolate ice cream

2. Set up a double boiler with about 1 inch (2.5 cm) of water in the bottom portion. (Either use a standard double boiler or set a metal or heat-safe bowl into a medium saucepan without it touching the water below.) Add both kinds of chocolate and the butter to the top portion of the double boiler or the bowl. Bring the water to a simmer over medium heat, stirring the chocolate and butter repeatedly until smooth.

3. *Whisk* the warmed cream mixture into the chocolate mixture in a slow, steady stream. Continue whisking constantly until the sauce is thick and shiny, about 10 minutes. Do not boil. Reduce the heat further if the mixture starts to simmer or remove the double boiler momentarily from the heat to cool things down, still whisking all the while.

4. Turn off the heat, watch out for the steam, and remove the top portion of the double boiler or the bowl from the pan. Whisk in the vanilla and salt until smooth. Cool at room temperature for no more than 20 minutes.

5. Transfer to four *clean* ½ pint (236 ml) jars or other containers, leaving about ½ inch (1 cm) headspace in each. Cover or seal, then refrigerate or freeze.

Next
Warm some of this hot fudge sauce and use it as a dip for pretzel rods or thick-cut ruffled potato chips.

White Chocolate Sauce

MAKES: about 3 cups (720 ml)
FRIDGE: up to 3 weeks
FREEZER: up to 1 year

For the best white chocolate sauce, look for white chocolate made with cocoa butter as the primary ingredient, rather than hydrogenated shortening. As a general rule, most white chocolate chips are not the best quality white chocolate; bars are a better bet. And one more thing: Most white chocolate has been deodorized to remove much of the assertive cocoa flavor. However, there are some artisanal brands that actually retain the natural chocolate flavor from the cocoa solids. We much prefer these so-called *non-deodorized* white chocolate bars for rich, creamy dessert sauces like this one.

> 1 cup (240 ml) heavy or whipping cream
> 2 tablespoons (30 g) unsalted butter
> 1 pound (450 g) white chocolate, chopped
> 1 tablespoon (15 ml) vanilla extract
> 2 tablespoons white (that is, clear) crème de cacao (or use your own homemade Cacao Liqueur, page 431), optional
> ¼ teaspoon kosher salt

1. Combine the cream and butter in a small saucepan set over low heat. Warm until the butter melts, stirring occasionally.

2. Place the chopped white chocolate in a large bowl. Pour the warmed cream mixture over the white chocolate. Stir until the white chocolate melts and the mixture is smooth. Stir in the vanilla and crème de cacao, if using, as well as the salt. Cool at room temperature for no more than 15 minutes.

3. Transfer to three *clean* ½ pint (236 ml) jars or other containers, leaving about ½ inch (1 cm) headspace in each. Cover or seal, then refrigerate or freeze.

More
For a more assertive cocktail flavor, better for spooning onto pound cakes or unfrosted carrot cakes than onto ice cream, substitute brandy for the crème de cacao.

Butterscotch Sauce

MAKES: about 2 cups (480 ml)
FRIDGE: up to 3 weeks
FREEZER: up to 1 year

Homemade butterscotch sauce has so much more of that prized sticky texture *and* so many more caramelized notes from the melted sugar than any commercial bottling ever could have. However, you can't use this sweet sauce straight out of the jar because it hardens in the fridge. You'll need to loosen it a bit, either by setting the jar in a pan of warm water or microwaving a serving or two in a small bowl on high in 5-second bursts, stirring after each.

- 1 cup (240 ml) heavy or whipping cream
- 8 tablespoons (1 stick, ¼ pound, or 115 g) unsalted butter, cut into small pieces
- 1½ cups (325 g) packed light brown sugar
- ½ teaspoon lemon juice, preferably freshly squeezed
- 1 tablespoon (15 ml) vanilla extract
- 1 tablespoon (15 ml) whiskey
- ½ teaspoon kosher salt

1. Pour the cream into a small saucepan and set it over very low heat. Warm it but do not let it simmer in any way, even in small bubbles around the inside rim of the pan. Keep warm as you continue with the recipe.

2. Melt the butter in a large saucepan set over medium heat. Add the brown sugar and lemon juice and stir well to melt the sugar. Bring the mixture to a boil, stirring often. Reduce the heat to low and simmer slowly, stirring quite often, until the mixture appears smooth, not at all grainy, about 3 minutes.

3. Pour in the warm cream in a steady, thin stream, stirring as much as you can. Be careful: The mixture will roil like magma. Continue stirring until the roiling stops and the mixture is merely boiling. Cook, stirring almost constantly, until very thick with magma-style bubbles, about 4 minutes.

4. Turn off the heat and remove the pan from the burner. Whisk in the vanilla, whiskey, and salt until well combined.

5. Transfer to two *clean*, *heat-safe*, ½ pint (236 ml) jars or other containers, leaving about ½ inch (1 cm) headspace in each. Cover or seal. Cool at room temperature for no more than 1 hour, then refrigerate or freeze.

Next
This sauce is great in a simplified trifle: Layer it with thin slices of pound cake or ladyfingers, fresh blackberries, and sweetened whipped cream in a large bowl. Since you'll need to warm the sauce to get it to drizzle when layering, let the sauce fall on the cake or berries, rather than the whipped cream.

Toffee Sauce

MAKES: about 2 cups (480 ml)
FRIDGE: up to 3 weeks
FREEZER: up to 1 year

Although we've mostly tried to steer clear of candy thermometers in these sweet sauce recipes, we need one for this sticky sauce because we're essentially making candy (or toffee, as the case might be), if still in sauce form. The sauce has a deep, rich flavor, with a few bitter notes from the caramelized sugar and the molasses or treacle.

- ½ cup (120 ml) heavy or whipping cream
- 12 tablespoons (1½ sticks, 6 ounces, or 170 g) unsalted butter, cut into small pieces
- 1 cup (215 g) packed dark brown sugar
- 2 tablespoons (43 g) molasses or black treacle
- ½ teaspoon ground cinnamon
- ¼ teaspoon kosher salt

1. Pour the cream into a small saucepan and set it over very low heat. Warm it but do not let it simmer in any way, even in small bubbles around the inside rim of the pan. Keep warm as you continue with the recipe.

2. Melt the butter in a large saucepan set over medium-low heat, stirring occasionally, but do not brown. Add the brown sugar, molasses or treacle, cinnamon, and salt. Cook, stirring constantly, until the mixture morphs from looking muddy to looking foamy and opaque, about 5 minutes.

3. Clip a candy thermometer to the inside of the pan. Pour in the warm cream in a thin, steady stream, stirring as much as you can. The mixture will roil like mad. Stir constantly as the sugar remelts. Continue cooking, stirring almost constantly, until the thermometer registers 235°F (113°C), about 5 minutes.

4. Turn off the heat and remove the pan from the burner. Cool at room temperature for no more than 30 minutes. Stir well, then transfer to two *clean* ½ pint (236 ml) jars or other containers, leaving about ½ inch (1 cm) headspace in each. Cover or seal, then refrigerate or freeze.

Next
This sticky sauce makes a great filling for sandwich cookies. Warm it so that it's a little loose, then spread it on the flat side of a sugar cookie or a chocolate wafer cookie (even purchased cookies). Top with a second cookie, flat side down.

Salted Caramel Sauce

MAKES: about 2 cups (480 ml)
FRIDGE: up to 3 weeks
FREEZER: up to 1 year

There's no call for a candy thermometer for this sauce because we're just melting sugar until it's golden brown. But here's the tricky part: Melted sugar continues to caramelize off the heat. It's so molten that it keeps on cooking. And the darker the caramel, the more bitter the flavors. Actually, that last is the good news. You can adjust the

flavor of this sauce based on your preference. Very dark and you're bold. Golden and you're a gentler soul. We knew it: Food is personality!

> 1 cup (240 ml) heavy or whipping cream
> 2 cups (400 g) granulated white sugar
> ½ cup (120 ml) water
> 4 tablespoons (½ stick, 2 ounces, or 58 g) unsalted butter, cut into small pieces
> 1½ teaspoons kosher salt

1. Pour the cream into a small saucepan and set it over very low heat. Warm it but do not let it simmer in any way, even in small bubbles around the inside rim of the pan. Keep warm as you continue with the recipe.

2. Mix the sugar and water in a large pan set over medium heat, stirring until the sugar dissolves. Continue cooking, stirring occasionally, until the mixture is golden, golden brown, brown, or even dark brown.

3. Whisk the warmed cream into the sugar syrup in a slow, steady stream, stirring as much as you can. The mixture will roil like magma. Keep stirring until the roiling stops, then until the sugar remelts in the sauce. Simmer, stirring almost constantly, for 2 minutes.

4. Add the butter and salt. Stir well until the butter melts and the sauce is smooth. Turn off the heat, remove the pan from the burner, and cool at room temperature for no more than 30 minutes. Stir well, then transfer to two *clean* ½ pint (236 ml) jars or other containers, leaving about ½ inch (1 cm) headspace in each. Cover or seal, then refrigerate or freeze.

Next
You'll need this dessert sauce for a SALTED CARAMEL MARTINI: Drizzle about 2 tablespoons (30 ml) of the sauce in the inside of a chilled martini glass. Then shake 4 tablespoons (2 ounces or 60 ml) Irish cream liqueur and 3 tablespoons (1½ ounces or 45 ml) vanilla-flavored vodka with lots of ice in a cocktail shaker until very cold. Strain into the martini glass.

Salted Caramel Sauce (page 386)

Coconut Caramel Sauce

MAKES: about 2 cups (480 ml)
FRIDGE: up to 1 month
FREEZER: up to 1 year

Although we've got plenty of caramel dessert sauces with cream, this one is a vegan alternative. But don't just think of it as a dairy-free dessert sauce. Consider it a decadent treat on its own: lots of coconut flavor, a little corn syrup for body, and an amber color for eye-catching appeal. It's perfect on chocolate oat-milk ice cream.

> 1 cup (245 g) full-fat coconut milk
> 2 cups (400 g) granulated white sugar
> ½ cup (156 g) light corn syrup
> ¼ cup (60 ml) water
> ¼ cup (57 g) coconut oil

1. Pour the coconut milk into a small saucepan and set it over very low heat. Warm it but do not let it simmer in any way, even in small bubbles around the inside rim of the pan. Keep warm as you continue with the recipe.

2. Stir the sugar, corn syrup, and water in a large saucepan set over medium heat until the sugar dissolves. Cook, stirring occasionally, until the mixture comes to a simmer and turns a dark amber, about 7 minutes.

3. *Whisk* in the coconut oil. The mixture will roil a bit but keep whisking until smooth. Whisk in the warmed coconut milk in a thin, steady stream, whisking as much as you can, despite the roiling and the steam. Keep whisking until it calms down to a simmer, the sugar has remelted, and the mixture is smooth.

4. Turn off the heat, remove the pan from the burner, and cool at room temperature for no more than 30 minutes. Stir well, then transfer to two *clean* ½ pint (236 ml) jars or other containers, leaving about ½ inch (1 cm) headspace in each. Cover or seal, then refrigerate or freeze.

Next
Stir some of this sauce into lots of salted, roasted peanuts, then spread on a silicone-lined baking sheet. Cool in the fridge for at least 1 hour to create a chewy, sticky, peanut caramel candy.

Praline Sauce

MAKES: about 3 cups (720 ml)
FRIDGE: up to 3 weeks
FREEZER: up to 1 year

If you're looking for a nut-filled dessert sauce, you've come to the right recipe: It's like candied Texas pralines in sauce form, or a weird, wild cross between Wet Walnuts (page 396) and Toffee Sauce (page 385).

> ½ cup (70 g) pecan pieces
> 2½ cups (540 g) packed light brown sugar
> 1½ cups (360 ml) full-fat evaporated milk
> 3 tablespoons (1½ ounces or 45 g) unsalted butter, cut into small pieces
> 1 teaspoon (5 ml) vanilla extract
> ¼ teaspoon kosher salt

1. Set a small skillet over low heat for a minute or two. Add the pecans and toast, stirring often, until lightly browned and aromatic, about 4 minutes. Pour the pecans into a bowl and cool for 20 minutes. Chop into small pieces on a cutting board by rocking a large knife through them.

2. Combine the brown sugar, evaporated milk, and butter in a medium saucepan set over medium-low heat, stirring until the brown sugar dissolves and the butter melts. Continue cooking, stirring almost constantly, until steadily simmering.

3. Reduce the heat to low and continue cooking, stirring almost constantly, until thickened, smooth, and syrupy, about 7 minutes. Turn off the heat, remove the pan from the burner, and stir in the toasted pecans, vanilla, and salt until uniform. Cool at room temperature for 15 minutes.

4. Stir well, then transfer to three *clean* ½ pint (236 ml) jars or other containers, leaving about ½ inch (1 cm) headspace in each. Cover or seal, then refrigerate or freeze.

Next
This sauce is a great topping for butter pecan ice cream. Or a decadent drizzle over a slice of pecan pie. Or a sweet smear on a slice of toasted quick bread. Or use a thin layer of sauce as the middle layer of a vanilla layer cake, covering the cake with caramel or chocolate frosting.

Peanut Butter Sauce

MAKES: about 3 cups (720 ml)
FRIDGE: up to 3 weeks
FREEZER: up to 1 year

Here's a culinary trick: By including melted marshmallows in a peanut butter dessert sauce, we can create a creamy, almost light sauce, not the sticky mess you might expect from so much peanut butter. This sauce *requires* standard creamy peanut butter, not natural-style. The sauce needs the added fat found in the more standard bottling.

- 1½ cups (360 ml) full-fat evaporated milk, plus more as necessary for a smooth sauce
- 1⅓ cups (415 g) light corn syrup
- 6 standard-sized marshmallows
- 1⅓ cups (375 g) *standard* smooth peanut butter
- 2 teaspoons (10 ml) vanilla extract
- ¼ teaspoon kosher salt

1. Combine the evaporated milk, corn syrup, and marshmallows in a medium saucepan set over medium heat. Cook, stirring often to dissolve the corn syrup, until the marshmallows melt. Bring to a simmer and cook, stirring almost constantly, for 1 minute.

2. Turn off the heat and remove the pan from the burner. *Whisk* in the peanut butter, vanilla, and salt until smooth. Cool at room temperature for 1 hour, whisking in more evaporated milk in 1 tablespoon (15 ml) increments if the mixture becomes too thick. The final sauce should be thick and sticky but pourable, like honey or molasses.

3. Stir well, then transfer to three *clean* ½ pint (236 ml) jars or other containers, leaving about ½ inch (1 cm) headspace in each. Cover or seal, then refrigerate or freeze.

More
Bump up the flavors by adding up to ½ teaspoon ground cinnamon, ¼ teaspoon ground mace, and/or ¼ teaspoon ground dried ginger with the vanilla.

Marshmallow Sauce

MAKES: about 3 cups (720 ml)
FRIDGE: up to 1 month
FREEZER: up to 1 year

Back in the day, Bruce was a confirmed maven of super-sweet, rich marshmallow sauce on Carvel vanilla ice cream. The sauce is indeed a rich, ooey-gooey indulgence. We make it strictly old-school: with unflavored gelatin and light corn syrup. If you're going to the trouble, you might as well do all the things for the most luxurious, softest dessert topping imaginable. One note: After 1 week in the fridge or after thawing from the freezer, the sauce may separate. Stir well to recombine.

- 1 cup (240 ml) water
- 1 teaspoon (3.25 g) unflavored gelatin
- 1½ cups (300 g) granulated white sugar
- 1 cup (315 g) light corn syrup
- ¼ teaspoon kosher salt
- 1 teaspoon (5 ml) vanilla extract

1. Place ½ cup (120 ml) water in the bowl of a stand mixer or a large bowl that will accommodate a hand mixer. Sprinkle the gelatin over the water. Set aside.

2. Combine the remaining ½ cup (120 ml) water, the sugar, corn syrup, and salt in a small saucepan set over medium-low heat. Stir until the sugar dissolves. Bring to a simmer, stirring occasionally. Clip a candy thermometer to the inside of the pan and continue cooking undisturbed until the temperature reaches 240°F (116°C).

3. With the stand mixer or a hand-held mixer running at low speed, pour the hot sugar syrup into the water and gelatin in a slow, steady stream. Continue beating at low speed for 2 minutes to cool.

4. Once the mixture has cooled a bit and started to get frothy, add the vanilla and raise the speed to high. Beat until thick, fluffy, and light, 10–12 minutes.

5. Transfer to three *clean* ½ pint (236 ml) jars or other containers, leaving about ½ inch (1 cm) headspace in each. Cover or seal, then refrigerate or freeze.

More

For a boozy marshmallow sauce, add 1 tablespoon (15 ml) whiskey, brandy, or bourbon with the corn syrup.

Strawberry Sauce

MAKES: about 2 cups (480 ml)
FRIDGE: up to 3 weeks
FREEZER: up to 1 year

We believe a strawberry dessert sauce should actually be *chunky* with bits of strawberry throughout. Otherwise, it becomes something like loose strawberry jam, which isn't the best contrast to a sundae's creamy ice cream. Having said that, it's a matter of preference *how* chunky the sauce is. Chop the berries finer for a smoother sauce, if that's your pleasure. And only use fragrant *fresh* strawberries. Frozen strawberries just don't have enough punch to make a great dessert topper.

> 1 cup (200 g) granulated white sugar
> ½ cup (120 ml) plus 2 teaspoons (10 ml) water
> 1 pound (450 g) strawberries, hulled and chopped (about 2 cups)
> 1 tablespoon (15 ml) lemon juice
> ¼ teaspoon vanilla extract
> ¼ teaspoon kosher salt
> 2 teaspoons (5 g) cornstarch or corn flour

1. Stir the sugar and ½ cup (120 ml) water in a medium saucepan set over medium heat until the sugar dissolves. Bring to a boil, stirring occasionally. Boil undisturbed for 1 minute.

2. Add the strawberries, lemon juice, vanilla, and salt. Bring back to a full boil. Reduce the heat to low and simmer slowly, stirring occasionally, until thickened quite a bit, reminiscent of pancake syrup, about 15 minutes. Use a flatware tablespoon to skim any foam from the sauce.

3. Whisk the cornstarch and the remaining 2 teaspoons (10 ml) water in a small bowl to form a smooth slurry. Stir the slurry into the sauce and cook, stirring constantly, until thickened, just a few seconds.

4. Turn off the heat, remove the pan from the burner, and cool at room temperature for 15 minutes. Transfer to two *clean* ½ pint (236 ml) jars or other containers, leaving about ½ inch (1 cm) headspace in each. Cover or seal, then refrigerate or freeze.

More

For BALSAMIC STRAWBERRY SAUCE, use balsamic vinegar in place of the water in the cornstarch slurry.

Front to back in a banana split: Strawberry
Sauce (page 390), Marshmallow Sauce
(page 389), and Pineapple Sauce (page 392)

Pineapple Sauce

MAKES: about 3 cups (720 ml)
FRIDGE: up to 3 weeks
FREEZER: up to 1 year

You can't have a banana split without pineapple sauce. Feel free to buy chopped, cored, fresh pineapple in the produce section to make this recipe simpler. Because pineapple sauce is super sweet, we bump up the lemon juice as a compensation to round out the flavors.

- 4 cups (680 g) roughly chopped cored peeled fresh pineapple
- ½ cup (100 g) granulated white sugar
- ½ cup (108 g) *packed* light brown sugar
- ¼ cup (60 ml) lemon juice
- ¼ teaspoon kosher salt

1. Put the pineapple chunks in a food processor and pulse until minced and juicy. Do not puree.

2. Pour and scrape the pineapple and juice into a medium saucepan. Stir in both sugars, the lemon juice, and salt. Set the pan over medium heat and stir constantly until the sugars dissolve. Bring to a simmer, stirring often.

3. Reduce the heat to low and simmer slowly, stirring almost constantly, until reduced to two-thirds of its original volume and the juice surrounding the pineapple has become syrupy, about 15 minutes. The bits of pineapple should be almost translucent.

4. Turn off the heat, remove the pan from the burner, and cool at room temperature for 15 minutes. Transfer to three *clean* ½ pint (236 ml) jars or other containers, leaving about ½ inch (1 cm) headspace in each. Cover or seal, then refrigerate or freeze.

Next
Use this sauce as an easy glaze over warm cakes or quick breads. Or try it over orange gelato or refreshing lemon sorbet.

Lemon Sauce

MAKES: about 4 cups (960 ml)
FRIDGE: up to 3 weeks
FREEZER: up to 1 year

This sauce is tart and bright, but not as thick as lemon curd. Rather, it's a thickened lemon sauce to go on pound cake or quick breads…or berry ice cream. Although the sauce requires a lot of lemon juice, freshly squeezed is best. You'll need about nine lemons to get 1⅓ cups juice.

- Water for the double boiler
- 2 cups (400 g) granulated white sugar
- 2 cups water (240 ml)
- 1⅓ cups (320 ml) lemon juice, preferably freshly squeezed
- 2 tablespoons (14 g) cornstarch or corn flour
- 2 teaspoons (10 ml) lemon extract
- ¼ teaspoon kosher salt
- 10 tablespoons (1 stick plus 2 tablespoons, 5 ounces, or 142 g) unsalted butter, cut into small pieces

1. Set up a double boiler with about 1 inch (2.5 cm) of water in the bottom portion. (Either use a standard double boiler or set a metal or heat-safe bowl into a medium saucepan without it touching the water beneath.) Add the sugar, water, lemon juice, cornstarch, lemon extract, and salt to the top portion of the double boiler or the bowl. Bring the water to a simmer over medium heat, *whisking* the lemon mixture constantly.

2. Add the butter and continue whisking almost constantly until the sauce is smooth, thickened, and translucent, about 15 minutes.

3. Turn off the heat, watch for steam, and remove the top half from the double boiler or the bowl from the pan. Cool at room temperature for 15 minutes. Transfer to four *clean* ½ pint (236 ml) jars or two *clean* 1 pint (472 ml) jars or other containers, leaving about ½ inch (1 cm) headspace in each. Cover or seal, then refrigerate or freeze.

Next

For LEMON-COCONUT SAUCE, substitute pulp-free, no-added-sugar coconut water for the water.

Blackberry Sauce

MAKES: about 2 cups (480 ml)
FRIDGE: up to 3 weeks
FREEZER: up to 1 year

By now you know that we prefer a chunky dessert sauce to a smooth one. It's all about texture for us. We feel that a sauce should bear some likeness to its origins (in this case, blackberries). If you like a smoother sauce, chop the blackberries before using, but not enough to juice them and lose essential moisture. Or just use thawed frozen blackberries (plus their thawed juice), which will more readily break down in the sauce.

- 2 cups (300 g) fresh blackberries (about 1 pint) or thawed frozen blackberries (with their juice)
- ¼ cup (50 g) granulated white sugar
- 2 tablespoons (30 ml) water
- ½ teaspoon (1 g) finely grated lemon zest
- 1 tablespoon (15 ml) lemon juice
- ¼ teaspoon kosher salt
- 2 teaspoons (5 g) cornstarch or corn flour

1. Put the blackberries, sugar, 1 tablespoon (15 ml) water, lemon zest, lemon juice, and salt in a medium saucepan. Set the pan over low heat and stir gently until the sugar melts and the blackberries begin to give off their juice. Don't crush the blackberries—let them remain as whole as possible.

2. Whisk the remaining 1 tablespoon (15 ml) water and the cornstarch in a small bowl to form a smooth slurry. Stir into the blackberry mixture, then cook, stirring gently, until thickened, just a few seconds.

3. Turn off the heat, remove the pan from the burner, and cool at room temperature for 15 minutes. Transfer to two *clean* ½ pint (236 ml)

jars or other containers, leaving about ½ inch (1 cm) headspace in each. Cover or seal, then refrigerate or freeze.

Next

Beyond ice cream, use this sauce on pancakes. Or better yet, drizzle onto a chunky or mousse pâté. Or simply drizzle it over sautéed duck or chicken livers. Wow!

Raspberry-Orange Sauce

MAKES: about 2 cups (480 ml)
FRIDGE: up to 3 weeks
FREEZER: up to 1 year

This sauce is like a classic raspberry coulis, a puree without any seeds, but with a bit of buzz from the Grand Marnier, which also adds a sophisticated bitterness to the otherwise sweet sauce. Omit the Grand Marnier for no buzz and a simpler flavor. Instead, substitute 1 tablespoon (17 g) thawed frozen orange juice concentrate plus 1 tablespoon (15 ml) water.

- ½ cup (100 g) granulated white sugar
- ½ cup (120 ml) water
- 4 cups (480 g) fresh raspberries or thawed frozen raspberries (with their juice)
- 1 tablespoon (6 g) finely grated orange zest
- ¼ teaspoon kosher salt
- 2 tablespoons (30 ml) Grand Marnier
- 1 tablespoon (7 g) cornstarch or corn flour

1. Combine the sugar and water in a medium saucepan set over medium heat, stirring until the sugar dissolves. Bring to a boil, stirring occasionally. Boil undisturbed for 1 minute.

2. Add the raspberries, orange zest, and salt. Cook, stirring often to smash up the berries, until the mixture is the consistency of loose jam, about 4 minutes. Use a flatware tablespoon to skim any foam from the mixture.

Raspberry-Orange
Sauce (page 393) on
cheesecake

3. Whisk the Grand Marnier and cornstarch in a small bowl to form a smooth slurry. Whisk into the raspberry mixture and cook, whisking constantly, until thickened, just a few seconds.

4. Turn off the heat, remove the pan from the burner, and cool at room temperature for 5 minutes. Strain the sauce through a fine-mesh sieve into a bowl, gently scraping the puree against the mesh to extract as much juice and pulp as possible, leaving only the seeds behind. Discard the seeds.

5. Transfer to two *clean* ½ pint (236 ml) jars or other containers, leaving about ½ inch (1 cm) headspace in each. Cover or seal, then refrigerate or freeze.

Next
For RASPBERRY BRANDY SAUCE, omit the orange zest and substitute brandy for the Grand Marnier.

Apple Dessert Sauce

MAKES: about 2 cups (480 ml)
FRIDGE: up to 3 weeks
FREEZER: up to 1 year

This sauce is by no means applesauce. It's a sweet, dense dessert sauce, sort of like the filling for apple pie morphed into an ice cream or pound cake topper. We also love the sauce layered into trifles or spread on slices of toasted zucchini or banana bread.

- 2 tablespoons (30 g) unsalted butter
- 1¼ pounds (565 g) tart firm apples, such as Granny Smith (about 4 large), stemmed, peeled, halved, cored, and cut into ½-inch-thick (1-cm-thick) slices
- 2 tablespoons (30 ml) apple brandy, plain brandy, or unsweetened apple juice
- ⅓ cup (67 g) granulated white sugar
- ¼ cup (54 g) *packed* light brown sugar
- ½ teaspoon ground cinnamon
- ¼ teaspoon kosher salt
- ⅛ teaspoon grated nutmeg
- 2 tablespoons (30 ml) lemon juice
- 1 teaspoon (5 ml) vanilla extract
- 1 teaspoon (3 g) cornstarch or corn flour

1. Melt the butter in a large saucepan set over medium heat. Add the apples and cook, stirring often, until softened, about 7 minutes.

2. Add the brandy (be careful of flames), then both sugars, the cinnamon, salt, and nutmeg. Stir until the sugars melt. Cook, stirring almost constantly, until the mixture begins to reduce and the sugars caramelize to a golden brown, about 4 minutes.

3. In a small bowl, whisk the lemon juice, vanilla, and cornstarch to make a smooth slurry. Stir the slurry into the simmering sauce and cook, stirring constantly, until thickened, just a few seconds.

4. Turn off the heat, remove the pan from the burner, and cool at room temperature for 15 minutes. Transfer to two *clean* ½ pint (236 ml) jars or other containers, leaving about ½ inch (1 cm) headspace in each. Cover or seal, then refrigerate or freeze.

More
Make APPLE-GINGER TOPPING SAUCE by omitting the vanilla and substituting ginger juice for the lemon juice.

Coffee Sauce

MAKES: about 2 cups (480 ml)
FRIDGE: up to 1 week
FREEZER: up to 1 year

Because of the cream, this sauce won't keep very long in the fridge. No worries: It wouldn't last anyway! It's splendidly decadent, even as a sweetener in your morning coffee with a few other flavors (except vanilla). We tested this sauce with instant espresso and the results were disappointing. If you don't have an espresso maker or a mocha maker at home, stop by a local coffeehouse and order 6 shots to go.

> ¾ cup (180 ml) espresso
> 1¼ cups (300 ml) heavy or whipping cream
> ½ cup (100 g) granulated white sugar
> 1 tablespoon (7 g) cornstarch or corn flour
> 1 tablespoon water
> ¼ teaspoon vanilla extract
> ¼ teaspoon kosher salt

1. Combine the espresso, cream, and sugar in a small saucepan set over low heat, stirring until the sugar dissolves. Warm just below a simmer, with only a bubble or two around the pan's inner rim.

2. Whisk the cornstarch and water in a small bowl to form a smooth slurry. Stir the slurry into the coffee mixture and cook, stirring constantly, until thickened, about 10 seconds. Stir in the vanilla and salt.

3. Turn off the heat and remove the pan from the burner. Cool at room temperature for 15 minutes. Transfer to two *clean* ½ pint (236 ml) jars or other containers, leaving about ½ inch (1 cm) headspace in each. Cover or seal, then refrigerate or freeze.

Next
To make MACCHIATO, brew 2–4 ounces (30–60 ml) espresso. Froth 12 ounces (180 ml) milk of any sort until steaming and foamy. Pour the espresso into the milk and add up to 1 tablespoon (15 ml) of this sauce. Drizzle with Caramel Syrup (page 426), if desired.

Wet Walnuts

MAKES: about 3 cups (720 ml)
FRIDGE: up to 6 weeks
FREEZER: up to 1 year

These sugary walnuts are a bygone favorite on sundaes and banana splits. They well deserve a comeback. There's no need for a candy thermometer because we're simply making a sticky syrup to hold the walnuts in place. As you probably know, nuts go rancid quickly at room temperature, sometimes within a month. Store extra in the freezer for up to 1 year.

> 1 cup (200 g) granulated white sugar
> 1 cup (240 ml) water
> ½ cup (156 g) light corn syrup
> ½ cup (150 g) honey
> 2 cups (225 g) walnut pieces, roughly chopped
> ¼ teaspoon kosher salt

1. Combine the sugar, water, corn syrup, and honey in a large saucepan set over medium heat. Stir until the sugar and honey dissolve and the mixture turns translucent. Bring to a boil, stirring occasionally. Boil undisturbed for 2 minutes.

2. Add the walnuts and salt and stir well to combine. Bring back to a boil and cook, stirring constantly, until sticky and candy-like, about 2 minutes. Be careful and don't let the sugar syrup darken too much. Remove the pan from the heat and continue stirring if it turns dark brown.

3. Turn off the heat and remove the pan from the burner. Cool at room temperature for 15 minutes. Transfer to three *clean* ½ pint (236 ml) jars or other containers, leaving about ½ inch (1 cm) headspace in each. Cover or seal, then refrigerate or freeze.

Next
Skip dessert and use the walnuts as a breakfast topper for oatmeal or unsweetened Greek yogurt.

Front to back: Wet Walnuts (page 396)
and Dulce de Leche (page 398)

Dulce de Leche

MAKES: about 2 cups (720 ml)
FRIDGE: up to 3 weeks
FREEZER: up to 1 year

This originally Latin American—but now global—golden, rich, caramel sauce is definitely a labor of love: It is one of the simpler recipes in this book in terms of its ingredients, but one of the most time-consuming to make. The results, however, prove worth the effort: a sticky, creamy, slightly tannic, decidedly elegant sauce that's great on ice cream, with cakes and quick breads, and even drizzled into fussy, cream-based cocktails.

> 8 cups (2 quarts or 1.92 liters) *whole* milk
> 1½ cups (500 g) granulated white sugar
> 1 teaspoon baking soda

1. Mix the milk, sugar, and baking soda in a large saucepan set over medium heat and stir until the sugar dissolves. Bring to a boil, stirring occasionally. Reduce the heat to *very* low and simmer *slowly*, stirring once in a while, for 1 hour.

2. Continue simmering, stirring more and more often, then constantly after about 20 minutes, until the mixture is caramel-colored and thickened into a sauce, about 1 more hour (about 2 hours *total*).

3. Turn off the heat, remove the pan from the burner, and cool at room temperature for 15 minutes. Transfer to two *clean* ½ pint (236 ml) jars or other containers, leaving about ½ inch (1 cm) headspace in each. Cover or seal, then refrigerate or freeze.

Next

Make shortcut ALFAJORES! Bake or buy fairly thick, buttery shortbread rounds and sandwich them with a smear of dulce de leche. (If you bake your own cookies, they must be cooled to room temperature on a wire rack before sandwiching.)

Easy Dulce de Leche

MAKES: about 2 cups (480 ml)
FRIDGE: up to 3 weeks
FREEZER: up to 1 year

If you don't want to spend more than an hour standing at the stove, this simplified dulce de leche is your best bet for a creamy, caramel sauce. Yes, it still takes a long time to make, but the effort involved is so much less. The streamlined version is made in a *bain-marie*—that is, a baking pan filled with water and set in the oven. The sauce still requires a bit of stirring and it's admittedly not quite as luxurious as the more standard, stirred-forever version, mostly because not as much air gets into it to lighten it. But that said, it's thicker and even a bit stickier, so it has its own charms.

> Two 14 ounce (400 g) cans of full-fat sweetened condensed milk
> Hot water as necessary for the cake pan

1. Position a rack in the center of the oven; heat the oven to 425°F (220°C), no fan or convection.

2. Pour the sweetened condensed milk into a 9 inch (23 cm) round cake pan. Set the pan in a large roasting pan. Add enough hot tap water to the roasting pan to come about halfway up the side of the cake pan. Slip the roasting pan into the oven (be careful that no water sloshes into the condensed milk) and bake for 1 hour.

3. Check the water level and add more hot tap water to the roasting pan, if necessary. Continue baking until caramel-colored and thickened, stirring once in a while and adding more hot water to the roasting pan as necessary, about 1 more hour.

4. Carefully remove the cake pan from the hot water and cool on a wire rack at room temperature for 20 minutes. Transfer the caramel mixture to two *clean* ½ pint (236 ml) jars or other containers, leaving about ½ inch (1 cm) headspace in each. Cover or seal, then refrigerate or freeze.

More

Stir up to ½ teaspoon ground cinnamon and/or ¼ teaspoon grated nutmeg into the condensed milk during the second hour of baking.

Cajeta

MAKES: about 2 cups (480 ml)
FRIDGE: up to 3 weeks
FREEZER: up to 1 year

Cajeta is a goat milk version of dulce de leche— and so a little more savory, a little more sophisticated, and utterly decadent all around. Goat milk is naturally low-fat, so we need to be more careful as the natural sugars caramelize (because they're not as protected). We also have to use a candy thermometer to make sure we get the right set. *And* we must stir almost constantly during that final hour of cooking. But a jar of cajeta is one of the most incredible gifts you can bring a friend.

8 cups (2 quarts or 1.92 liters) goat milk
2 cups (400 g) granulated white sugar
2 teaspoons baking soda

1. Combine the goat milk, sugar, and baking soda in a large saucepan. Set it over low heat and stir until the sugar dissolves. Bring to a simmer, then reduce the heat even further and cook, stirring occasionally, for 1 hour.

2. Attach a candy thermometer to the inside of the pan. Continue cooking, stirring almost constantly at first and then just constantly after about 20 minutes, until the temperature reaches 240°F (115°C) and the sauce is golden and thick, about 40 minutes, or even a bit more in total for this second step.

3. Turn off the heat, remove the pan from the burner, and cool at room temperature for 15 minutes. Transfer to two *clean* ½ pint (236 ml) jars or other containers, leaving about ½ inch (1 cm) headspace in each. Cover or seal, then refrigerate or freeze.

Next

Make easy CAJETA EMPANADAS: Cut one or two purchased, raw pie crusts into 4 inch (10 cm) rounds. Put a small spoonful of cajeta in the center of each. Fold into a half-moon, then crimp the rounded edges closed with the tines of a fork. Gently roll each filled empanada in sugar laced with ground cinnamon. Bake on a parchment-lined baking sheet in a 375°F (190°C) oven until lightly browned, about 12 minutes. Cool on a wire rack for at least 10 minutes before enjoying.

8

Infused Oils, Vinegars, Syrups, and Liqueurs

Our final chapter moves far beyond what would have been preserved in an old-school water bath or steam canner. But these recipes still hold tight to our new way to think about saving back the best of the seasons. Most of these oils, vinegars, syrups, and liqueurs can be stored in the fridge for quite some time, even months…and many in the freezer for more than a year (or actually, almost indefinitely, although that's well beyond USDA guidelines).

owever, they're not shelf stable. True, *commercially* produced basil oil or raspberry liqueur can often be kept in a cool, dark pantry for a very long while. But those have been refined in some way, with added flavors and colorings, all in a bid to keep them fresher longer.

By contrast, ours have small bits of herbs or fruit in the mix, even microscopic specks, all of which can rot over time, even when held in something like an alcohol-rich syrup. True, rot mostly happens in the presence of oxygen. Also true, many of these oils and liqueurs become almost anaerobic (or no-oxygen) environments in and of themselves. But we can't help little specks of this or that from floating to the surface and beginning the natural degradation of organic material. So to the fridge or freezer with all of these, as with everything in this book.

Even so, the results are astounding. The flavors, more layered than commercial bottlings. The colors, brighter or deeper. The spices or herbs, more present. The uses, manifold: from cocktails to salad dressings, marinades to richly flavored sauces, desserts to after-dinner shots. Some of the oils make excellent finishing drizzles on whatever you make. Some of the syrups can turn a supermarket cake or pie into something more worthy of a fine bakery. We can only hope that better food is the reason you're now wholeheartedly into cold canning.

Let's talk through a few common ingredients in this chapter, then turn to some specifics about the techniques.

Vinegar

In these recipes, we're not making vinegar from scratch. Yes, we love the complicated craft of it: fermenting a fruit mixture (essentially creating a fruit wine), then introducing bacteria to eat the ethanol (the boozy stuff in any alcohol) and turn it into acetic acid (aka vinegar). But we felt starting from scratch was outside the spirit of the quick and easy methods we're advocating. So we start our recipes with premade vinegar: white wine, distilled white, or some other sort.

That said, not all vinegars are created equal. You often get what you pay for. No, you don't have to splurge on an expensive bottle of white wine vinegar, best for drizzling on grilled vegetables. But you should consider something beyond the cut-rate store brand, if only to create a better balance among the flavors.

White balsamic vinegar

Several times in this chapter (and elsewhere in the book), we call for this specialty vinegar. Do not confuse white balsamic with standard, dark balsamic vinegar (and certainly not with syrupy, aged balsamic vinegar). White balsamic is made from grapes, preferably Trebbiano grapes, like more standard balsamics. However, the grape must is not cooked in the open but instead pressure-cooked so that it never has a chance to oxidize (aka turn brown). The resulting vinegar is aged in casks for only a short while, so it's gold-toned and quite beautiful in the light. It has a delicately sweet flavor, perhaps more readily recognizable as *grape* than standard balsamic. It's the perfect ingredient for infused vinegars when we want other flavors to show through.

Vodka and grain alcohol

Many of our infused liqueurs begin with a *high-proof* vodka, preferably around 100 proof (or about 50 percent distilled spirit by volume). You'll need to read the labels to see if you've got the higher proof we suggest. It will act as more of a preservative than standard vodka and it will actually bring more of the flavors from the berries, fruit, or coffee beans forward.

Can you use regular vodka? Yes, but the results will be less complex, somehow duller. If you insist on using a lower-proof vodka, you should store the results in the freezer. In no case should you ever use a flavored vodka.

We also call for grain alcohol—that is, a neutral-flavored spirit—usually with a very high proof, around 180 or 190 proof, almost completely ethanol. In these cases, we're looking not only for the punch from the booze but also for the protection that the larger quantity of ethanol provides. You should dole out homemade, grain-alcohol-based liqueurs in small portions because they're potent and unforgiving, if tasty and beautiful.

Freezing and thawing frozen oils

Most of the syrups, liqueurs, and even vinegars in this chapter will freeze and thaw with no problems. In fact, some of the syrups and liqueurs can be stored in the freezer but won't ever freeze solid.

By and large, the oils, vinegars, and liqueurs will retain a brighter color if stored in the freezer. And oils in particularly will preserve much of their layered flavors because their solidification creates an almost fully anaerobic environment.

That said, infused oils will harden. They may even do so in the fridge. Before you freeze an oil, make sure you've put it in a tempered glass container if you intend to thaw it with warm water (see below.) Also, make sure any bits of particulate ingredients or spices are submerged in the oil (that is, not exposed to the air). It's best to freeze oils standing up until they harden. Then

▲ Thaw cold or even frozen infused oils like Chive Oil (page 404) in a saucepan of warm water.

you can turn them on their sides to make room for other things in your freezer.

To thaw a frozen oil in a tempered glass jar, you can leave it at room temperature, perhaps for up to 48 hours. If you're in a hurry, fill a large skillet or saucepan with warm tap water, unseal and uncover the bottle of oil, and set it uncovered side up in the warm water. Let stand for perhaps 1 hour, changing the warm water at least once to make sure the oil is softening without cooling the water too much. Stir occasionally for even better results.

Decorative bottles

For these recipes, you're free to use the more standard, *clean* ½ pint (236 ml) or 1 pint (472 ml) canning jars we've been using all along. But these jars may not be pretty enough to be gifts or even perhaps for your own use. You may well want to search out decorative jars or bottles to hold what you make.

Make sure the glass is tempered, especially if you're pouring a hot vinegar or sugar syrup into it. And make sure the glass has no tint or dyes

▲ Infused vinegars, oils, and liqueurs deserve beautiful bottles.

▲ Thin, small funnels are made for bottles with narrow necks.

that could leach into what you make. If you want to store your work in pottery vessels, remember that both vinegars and liqueurs are particularly reactive and so shouldn't come into contact with suspect glazes. But then again, why would you want to put a beautiful liqueur in a bottle you can't see through?

Small funnel for glass jars

If you're going to use decorative glass bottles to hold what you make, you're going to need a tiny funnel because the necks of these bottles are often quite narrow. Even more standard bottles, like a clean liquor bottle, have fairly narrow openings. It's hard to pour straight down into the bottle from a bowl, even with a tapered ladle. The best tool is a narrow funnel. But beware: You'll need to pour slowly since the syrup, liqueur, or (particularly) the oil may be thick and so take its own sweet time getting through the funnel and into the bottle. Hey, you got this far! Be patient a little longer to fill the bottle.

Ready, set…

We might be a little beyond the notion of canning with these final recipes, but we're certainly still in the quick and easy spirit of our book: saving back fresh fruits, herbs, and vegetables to make gorgeous finishing oils and vinegars to have on hand for drizzles for salads or sides, or to keep stocked up with liqueurs you can sip by the fire. In New England, it's a great comfort to know that the pantry is well stocked as the fire crackles and the wintry night sets in.

Basil Oil

MAKES: about 2 cups (480 ml)
FRIDGE: up to 2 weeks
FREEZER: up to 1 year

There's nothing quite like basil oil: fresh, summery, a treat in salad dressings or simply drizzled on soft goat cheese for an elegant appetizer with super crunchy rye crackers. Because the basil never gets fully cooked in this recipe, you might want to choose organic basil... or even grow your own without pesticides or chemical fertilizers. And because the basil is still relatively fresh, the oil can't be stored in the fridge for long (but up to 1 year in the freezer).

> Water for blanching the basil
> 6 ounces (170 g) fresh basil (about 4 bunches), stems and all
> A big bowl of ice water
> 3 cups (720 ml) olive oil
> ½ teaspoon kosher salt

1. Bring a large saucepan of water to a boil over high heat. Add the basil and blanch for 15 seconds from the time the herb hits the water. Use a slotted spoon to immediately get the basil into the bowl of ice water. Or drain the pan in a colander set in the sink and scrape the basil into the ice water. Cool for a minute or two.

2. Drain well in a colander set in the sink, then spread paper towels on your work surface. Spread the basil on the paper towels and gently blot dry with more paper towels.

3. Chop the blotted basil, then transfer to a blender and add the oil and salt. Cover and blend until fairly smooth but not emulsified, stopping the machine at least once to scrape down the inside of the canister.

4. Strain the oil through a fine-mesh sieve or a colander lined with cheesecloth, either one set over a medium bowl. Use the back of a wooden spoon to press the basil solids against the mesh or cheesecloth to extract as much of the juice as possible. Discard the basil solids.

5. Transfer the oil to two *clean* ½ pint (236 ml) jars or one *clean* 1 pint (472 ml) jar, bottle, cruet, or decanter, leaving about ½ inch (1 cm) headspace in each. Cover or seal, then refrigerate or freeze.

More

Use this technique to make almost any leafy herb oil (dill, tarragon, parsley, or cilantro, for example). Substitute other leafy herbs *by weight* for the basil.

Chive Oil

MAKES: about 2 cups (480 ml)
FRIDGE: up to 2 weeks
FREEZER: up to 1 year

Although we prefer olive oil as the base for Basil Oil (left), we think it competes too much with the chives in this infused oil. So we resort to a neutral-flavored oil to get more chive essence into every drop. Given the amount of solids that remain in this oil, it will solidify in the fridge and will need to come back to room temperature before using. As a bonus, it will keep its bright green color even after freezing.

> Water for blanching the chives
> 4 ounces (115 g) fresh chives (about 4 small bunches)
> A big bowl of ice water
> 3 cups (720 ml) neutral-flavored oil, such as canola or vegetable oil
> ½ teaspoon kosher salt

1. Bring a large saucepan of water to a boil over high heat. Add the chives and blanch for 10 seconds from the time the chives hit the water. Use a slotted spoon to immediately get the chives into the bowl of ice water. Or drain the pan in a colander set in the sink and scrape the chives into the ice water. Cool for a minute or two.

2. Drain well, then spread paper towels on your work surface. Spread the chives on the paper

Chive Oil (page 404)
with steamed dumplings

towels and gently blot dry with a top layer of paper towels.

3. Transfer the chives to a blender and add the oil and salt. Cover and blend until fairly smooth but not emulsified, stopping the machine at least once to scrape down the inside of the canister.

4. Strain the oil through a fine-mesh sieve or a colander lined with cheesecloth, either set over a medium bowl. Use the back of a wooden spoon to press the chives against the mesh to extract as much of the juice as possible. Discard the solids.

5. Transfer the oil to two *clean* ½ pint (236 ml) jars or one *clean* 1 pint (472 ml) jar, bottle, cruet, or decanter, leaving about ½ inch (1 cm) headspace in each. Cover or seal, then refrigerate or freeze.

Next
Drizzle this oil over steamed or grilled fish. Or use it with equal parts *unseasoned* rice vinegar as a dip for dumplings or spring rolls.

Rosemary-Garlic Oil

MAKES: about 4 cups (960 ml)
FRIDGE: up to 2 months
FREEZER: up to 1 year

Here's a wallop of an infused oil, perhaps best in a barbecue mop or a marinade rather than straight on in a salad dressing. In fact, the garlic itself is still potent, even after soaking; but you can save it back in a sealed container in the fridge for up to a week to mince for sautés, braises, and stews. Note that the length of the skewers is smaller than those you usually find in the supermarket. Cut the standard skewers to the right size with scissors.

> 2 cups (480 ml) neutral-flavored oil, such as canola or vegetable oil
> 1½ cups (360 ml) olive oil, plus more if necessary
> 40 garlic cloves, peeled

> Four 4 inch (10 cm) bamboo skewers
> 6 rosemary sprigs

1. Pour both oils into a small saucepan and set over very low heat.

2. Skewer 6 to 8 garlic cloves along each of the 4 (shortened) skewers, stacking them fairly tight so you only see a line of garlic on each. Set the skewers in two *clean* 1-pint (472 ml) jars or other containers. Snip the top 4 inches (10 cm) off the rosemary sprigs and put 3 in each jar.

3. Smash the remaining garlic cloves with the side of a heavy knife or the bottom of a large saucepan. Scrape them into the warm oil; add the remaining bits of the rosemary sprigs, too. Continue heating the oil just until tiny bubbles form around the garlic cloves. Reduce the heat even further and barely simmer, just at this minimal level, for 10 minutes.

4. Turn off the heat and remove the pan from the burner. Cool at room temperature for no more than 1 hour. Strain the oil into the prepared jars, leaving about ½ inch (1 cm) headspace in each. The oil and rosemary *must* be submerged in the oil; add a little more olive oil if you need more to cover what's in the jars. Discard the solids in the pan. Cover or seal the jars, then refrigerate or freeze.

Tip
No piece of garlic or rosemary should ever stick up out of the oil, even in the fridge, to prevent rot. As you use this oil, remove the garlic cloves from the skewers as the level of the oil goes down. And just take out and discard the rosemary sprigs altogether.

Citrus Oil

MAKES: about 2 cups (480 ml)
FRIDGE: up to 2 months
FREEZER: up to 1 year

Use this intensely flavored oil as a dip for crunchy bread. Or as a drizzle over chopped salads. Or as a finishing touch for grilled fish fillets. Or as a garnish with steamed or roasted broccoli. There may be a waxy, protective coating on citrus. Gently scrub the lemons and oranges under cool, running water with a new sponge or a wad of paper towels without nicking the zest.

- 2 medium lemons
- 2 medium oranges
- 1 cup (240 ml) neutral-flavored oil, such as canola or vegetable oil
- 1 cup (240 ml) olive oil

1. Use a vegetable peeler to remove as much of the colorful zest (and none of the pith) in long strips from the lemons and oranges. Reserve the fruits for juicing or cooking.

2. Pour both oils into a small saucepan and add the zest. Set the pan over low heat and warm just until little bubbles appear around the edges of the zest. Turn off the heat, remove the pan from the burner, and cool to room temperature for 2 hours.

3. Strain the oil into two *clean* ½ pint (236 ml) jars or one *clean* 1 pint (472 ml) jar, bottle, cruet, or decanter, leaving about ½ inch (1 cm) headspace in each. Cover or seal, then refrigerate or freeze.

More

For a much more complex oil, use 1 lemon, 1 orange, 1 lime, and 1 small grapefruit.

Eighteen-Spice Chili Oil

MAKES: about 4 cups (960 ml)
FRIDGE: up to 3 months
FREEZER: up to 1 year

If you're going to the trouble of making our version of Chinese spiced chili oil, you might as well make enough to save back or pass around. So we've upped the yield a bit, in a bid to compensate for the effort. Our version is more aromatic than spicy. A huge blend of flavors, it makes an

excellent drizzle over most stir-fries, many braises, and even plain, steamed, purchased dumplings. You won't want take-out Chinese food without this oil on hand!

- 5 cups (1200 ml) neutral-flavored oil, such as canola or vegetable oil
- 3 cups (90 g) dried er jing tiao chilis, chopped or crushed (seeds and all)
- 4 medium scallions, trimmed and roughly chopped
- One 1 inch (2.5 cm) piece of fresh ginger, about the size of your thumb, peeled and thinly sliced
- 5 medium garlic cloves, peeled and smashed
- 3 tablespoons (18 g) dried *red* Szechuan peppercorns
- 2 tablespoons (12 g) cumin seeds
- 2 tablespoons (12 g) broken-up dried orange peel (look for it in the spice aisle)
- 1 tablespoon (12.5 g) granulated white sugar
- 1 tablespoon (6 g) fennel seeds
- 1 tablespoon (6 g) allspice berries
- 1 tablespoon (6 g) dried *green* Szechuan peppercorns
- 2 teaspoons whole cloves
- 1 whole nutmeg, cracked or smashed
- Two 3 inch (7.5 cm) cinnamon sticks
- 10 dried bay leaves
- 5 star anise pods
- 3 *black* cardamom pods, cracked open with a heavy saucepan or clean hammer
- 3 small pieces of dried sand ginger (see TIP)

1. Combine everything in a Dutch oven or small stockpot. Set over medium-low heat, stir well, and heat until tiny bubbles begin to form around the spices. The oil should be about 200°F (95°C).

2. Reduce the heat to maintain just this temperature, certainly no more. Warm for 1 hour, stirring often. Turn off the heat and take the pot off the burner. Cover and set aside at room temperature for 2 days.

3. Strain the oil into four *clean* ½ pint (236 ml) jars, or two *clean* 1 pint (472 ml) jars, or one *clean* 1 quart (1 liter) bottle, cruet, or decanter, leaving about 1 inch (2.5 cm) headspace in each. Cover or seal, then refrigerate or freeze.

Tip

Dried sand ginger, although obscure, is essential to this oil's flavor. It's one of four types of galangal, related to the more familiar ginger but with an earthier, less spiky flavor. When dried, it's sometimes packaged as *aromatic ginger* or *kencur*.

Eighteen-Spice Curry Oil

MAKES: about 4 cups (960 ml)
FRIDGE: up to 3 months
FREEZER: up to 1 year

Rather than using this highly flavored oil as the base of a dish (even a curry), consider it a finishing condiment that you can drizzle onto curries and Indian braises, of course, but also Asian noodle dishes, steamed vegetables, roasted shrimp, and grilled chicken breasts.

- 4½ cups (1020 ml) neutral-flavored oil, such as canola or vegetable oil
- 5 dried árbol chilis
- 1 tablespoon (6 g) ground dried turmeric
- 1 tablespoon (6 g) brown mustard seeds
- 1 tablespoon (6 g) cumin seeds
- 1 tablespoon (6 g) fennel seeds
- 1 tablespoon (6 g) fenugreek seeds
- 1 tablespoon (6 g) black peppercorns
- ½ teaspoon saffron threads
- 10 *green* cardamom pods
- 2 *black* cardamom pods, cracked open
- 10 whole cloves
- One 3 inch (7.5 cm) cinnamon stick
- 1 whole nutmeg, cracked open with a heavy saucepan or clean hammer
- 1 star anise pod
- 3 dried bay leaves
- 2 medium yellow or white onions, peeled and thinly sliced
- 4 medium garlic cloves, peeled and smashed
- One 4 inch (10 cm) piece of fresh ginger, about the size of your thumb, peeled and thinly sliced

1. Combine the oil, chilis, turmeric, mustard seeds, cumin seeds, fennel seeds, fenugreek seeds, peppercorns, saffron, green cardamom, black cardamom, cloves, cinnamon stick, nutmeg, star anise, and bay leaves in a Dutch oven or small stockpot. Set over low heat and heat until tiny bubbles begin to form around the spices. The oil should be about 200°F (95°C).

2. Add the onion, garlic, and ginger. Reduce the heat to maintain this temperature, certainly no more. Warm at the barest sizzle for 1 hour, stirring often. Turn off the heat and take the pot off the burner. Cover and set aside at room temperature for at least 2 hours—or for up to 24 hours for *much* stronger flavor.

3. Strain the oil into four *clean* ½ pint (236 ml) jars, or two *clean* 1 pint (472 ml) jar, or one *clean* 1 quart (1 liter) bottle, cruet, or decanter, leaving about 1 inch (2.5 cm) headspace in each. Cover or seal, then refrigerate or freeze.

Next

This oil can be used as part of a marinade. In general, we replace half the amount of oil called for in a marinade with the same amount of this curry oil, mostly so as not to overpower any other flavors.

Raspberry Vinegar

MAKES: about 3 cups (720 ml)
FRIDGE: up to 3 months after infusing
FREEZER: up to 1 year after infusing

Many commercial raspberry vinegars are doped with so-called *natural flavors* because raspberries are so delicate (and so costly) that the manufacturers try to cut a few corners. But we can get the flavor in a small batch by using real raspberries…but not too many of them to break the bank. Unfortunately, frozen raspberries are a bit dull for this vinegar: Only fresh will do. You'll end up with a tart, fruit-forward vinegar for drizzling over fish fillets or roasted carrots.

Front to back: Eighteen-Spice Curry Oil (page 408)
and Eighteen-Spice Chili Oil (page 407)

3 cups (360 g) fresh raspberries
2 cups (480 ml) white wine vinegar
½ cup (100 g) granulated white sugar

1. Place the raspberries in a *clean, heat-safe* medium bowl, 1 quart (1 liter) glass jar, or a nonreactive plastic container of about the same size.

2. Mix the vinegar and sugar in a medium saucepan set over medium-high heat, stirring constantly until the sugar dissolves. Warm, stirring occasionally, just until the mixture begins to simmer, only a few bubbles.

3. Pour the hot vinegar mixture over the berries. Set aside at room temperature to cool for about 2 hours. Cover and refrigerate to infuse for 4 days, shaking gently each day.

4. Set up a jelly bag over a pot or a bowl (for alternatives to a jelly bag, see page 17). Pour the raspberry vinegar through the bag or strainer. Press the solids gently to extract more juice without extracting cloudy, pulpy bits. Transfer to three *clean* ½ pint (236 ml) glass jars or other nonreactive containers, leaving about ½ inch (1 cm) headspace in each. Cover or seal, then refrigerate or freeze.

Next

To make RASPBERRY VINAIGRETTE, whisk 1 part raspberry vinegar with 3 parts olive oil *by volume*. Whisk in a pinch of garlic powder, dried thyme, and/or smoked paprika, if desired. Salt and pepper to your taste.

Plum Vinegar

MAKES: about 3 cups (720 ml)
FRIDGE: up to 2 months
FREEZER: up to 1 year

This sweet-sour vinegar is thicker than some of our others. We modeled it on crema di aceto prugna, an Italian specialty that is drizzled over cake or chocolate ice cream for a sophisticated dessert. The vinegar is less like an ingredient for the likes of salad dressings or marinades and more like a condiment. Think syrupy balsamic vinegar.

1½ cups (360 ml) white balsamic vinegar
½ cup (100 g) granulated white sugar
¼ teaspoon ground cinnamon
⅛ teaspoon ground cloves
1 pound (450 g) Italian prune plums (or ripe red plums, if you must), stemmed, quartered, and pitted

1. Combine the vinegar and sugar in a medium saucepan set over medium-high heat, stirring until the sugar dissolves. Add the cinnamon and cloves. Bring to a boil, stirring occasionally. Reduce the heat to very low and simmer *slowly*, stirring occasionally, for 5 minutes.

2. Add the plum quarters and continue simmering slowly, stirring occasionally, for 10 minutes. Lightly mash the plums against the insides of the pan as you stir the mixture.

3. Turn off the heat and remove the pan from the burner. Set aside at room temperature for 4 hours.

4. Set up a jelly bag over a pot or a bowl (for alternatives to a jelly bag, see page 17). Pour the plum vinegar through the bag or strainer. Press the solids gently to extract more juice without extracting cloudy, pulpy bits. Transfer to three *clean* ½ pint (236 ml) glass jars or nonreactive containers, leaving about ½ inch (1 cm) headspace in each. Cover or seal, then refrigerate or freeze.

Next

This vinegar is an excellent choice for dipping bread as a nibble before dinner. Or serve it with a chunk of aged Parmigiano-Reggiano and crunchy crackers. Or drizzle it on chopped raw vegetables, roasted root vegetables, or even grilled romaine lettuce halves.

Cranberry Vinegar

MAKES: about 2 cups (480 ml)
FRIDGE: up to 3 months
FREEZER: up to 1 year

Tart, brightly colored, and aromatic, this vinegar is a great choice for salads and marinades. You can use frozen cranberries, but you must let them come to room temperature before adding to the vinegar mixture. Otherwise, they'll chill it down, causing it to heat up more slowly and resulting in a cloudy vinegar.

> 1½ cups (360 ml) apple cider vinegar
> ¼ cup (50 g) granulated white sugar
> 12 ounces (340 g) fresh cranberries or thawed frozen cranberries

1. Mix the vinegar and sugar in a medium saucepan set over medium-high heat, stirring constantly until the sugar dissolves.

2. Add the cranberries and reduce the heat to low. Cook, stirring constantly, until the cranberries pop, about 5 minutes. Do not let the mixture come to a boil. Stirring constantly will help, but if it starts to boil, reduce the heat even further.

3. Turn off the heat, remove the pan from the burner, and cool at room temperature for 2 hours.

4. Set up a jelly bag over a pot or a bowl (for alternatives to a jelly bag, see page 17). Pour the cranberry vinegar through the bag or strainer. Gently press the cranberries to extract more juice without extracting cloudy, pulpy bits. Transfer to two *clean* ½ pint (236 ml) glass jars or nonreactive containers, leaving about ½ inch (1 cm) headspace in each. Cover or seal, then refrigerate or freeze.

Next
This vinegar is great in marinades for poultry. Add a splash with the oil and other aromatics, plus some kosher salt to make sure osmosis happens. But be careful: Too much vinegar can tighten muscle fibers. Use no more than 1 or 2 tablespoons for a bigger depth of flavor. Marinate in the refrigerator for no more than 4 hours.

Sour Cherry Vinegar

MAKES: about 2 cups (480 ml)
FRIDGE: up to 3 months after infusing
FREEZER: up to 1 year after infusing

This vinegar's flavor is surprisingly subtle, much more so than our Raspberry Vinegar (page 408), if still bright and fruity. What's more, sour cherries take more time than raspberries to infuse the vinegar. Although sour cherries can be hard to track down, feel free to use thawed frozen pitted sour cherries—but do not use canned sour cherries.

> 1 pound (450 g) sour cherries, stemmed and pitted
> 1¼ cups (300 ml) distilled white vinegar
> ½ cup (100 g) granulated white sugar

1. Place the cherries in a *clean, heat-safe* medium bowl, 1 quart (1 liter) glass jar, or a nonreactive plastic container of about the same size.

2. Mix the vinegar and sugar in a medium saucepan set over medium-high heat, stirring constantly until the sugar dissolves. Warm, stirring occasionally, just until the mixture begins to simmer, only a few bubbles.

3. Pour the hot vinegar mixture over the cherries. Cool at room temperature for 2 hours. Cover and refrigerate to infuse for 1 week, shaking gently each day.

4. Set up a jelly bag over a pot or a bowl (for alternatives to a jelly bag, see page 17). Pour the cherry vinegar through the bag or strainer. Press the solids gently to extract more juice without extracting cloudy, pulpy bits.

5. Transfer to two *clean* ½ pint (236 ml) glass jars or nonreactive containers, leaving about ½ inch (1 cm) headspace in each. Cover or seal, then refrigerate or freeze.

Clockwise from bottom: Cranberry Vinegar (page 411),
Sour Cherry Vinegar (page 411), Raspberry Vinegar
(page 406), and Plum Vinegar (page 410)

Next

To make SOUR CHERRY VINAIGRETTE, whisk 1 part sour cherry vinegar with 2 parts olive oil *by volume*. Whisk in a little minced shallot and about 1 teaspoon Dijon mustard, plus salt and pepper to taste.

Fig Vinegar

MAKES: about 2 cups (480 ml)
FRIDGE: up to 3 months after infusing
FREEZER: up to 1 year after infusing

Homemade fig vinegar often doesn't store well, either in the fridge or the freezer, because ripe figs are so soft they leave lots of (unseen!) residue in the vinegar, which oxidizes or eventually goes off. We solve that recurrent problem by using firmer dried figs. Use Calimyrna or white Adriatic figs so that the vinegar stays opalescent.

> 8 dried Calimyrna or white Adriatic (aka Turkish) figs
> 1 tablespoon (6 g) black peppercorns
> 2 cups (480 ml) white balsamic vinegar

1. Stem and finely chop 6 of the dried figs. Put these bits into one *clean, heat-safe* 1 quart (1 liter) glass jar or other nonreactive container. Add the peppercorns, too.

2. Warm the vinegar in a small saucepan over medium heat just until it's steaming, not simmering. Pour the vinegar over the chopped figs and peppercorns. Cool at room temperature for 2 hours. Cover and refrigerate to infuse for 1 week, shaking gently *every day*.

3. Set up a jelly bag over a pot or a bowl (for alternatives to a jelly bag, see page 17). Pour the fig vinegar through the bag or strainer. Press the solids *gently* to extract more juice without extracting cloudy, pulpy bits.

4. Stem the remaining 2 dried figs. Put them in either two *clean* ½ pint (236 ml) glass jars or 1 clean 1 pint (472 ml) glass jar or other nonreactive container. Pour the vinegar into the

jar(s), leaving about ½ inch (1 cm) headspace in each. Cover or seal, then refrigerate or freeze.

Next

This vinegar isn't thickened the way many commercial fig vinegars are. To make it more of a condiment or dipping sauce, whisk 2 teaspoons cornstarch or corn flour and 2 teaspoons water to form a slurry. Bring about 1 cup (240 ml) of the vinegar to the barest simmer in a small saucepan. Whisk in the slurry and cook until thickened, just a few seconds. Cool for at least 30 minutes before using.

Lemon-Sage Vinegar

MAKES: about 2 cups (480 ml)
FRIDGE: up to 3 months after infusing
FREEZER: up to 1 year after infusing

This infused vinegar is not sweet, although it does have the barest amount of added sugar, just to bring the lemon and herbal flavors to the foreground. Given its acidity, it's probably not a great dip for bread or vegetables on its own. Instead, consider it a perfect pairing with good olive oil to dress whatever fresh, green produce the summer brings.

> 2 cups (480 ml) white wine vinegar
> 2 medium garlic cloves, peeled and thinly sliced
> Long strips of zest from 2 medium lemons
> 6 fresh sage sprigs
> 1 teaspoon (3 g) granulated white sugar

1. Combine the vinegar, garlic, zest, and 5 of the sage sprigs in a small saucepan set over medium heat. Bring the mixture to the barest simmer, just a bubble or two, stirring often.

2. Turn off the heat, cover the pan, and remove from the burner. Set aside at room temperature to infuse for 24 hours.

3. Put the remaining sage sprig and the sugar in one *clean* 1 pint (472 ml) glass jar or nonreactive container. Strain the vinegar mixture through a fine-mesh sieve into the jar, leaving about ½ inch (1 cm) headspace. Cover or seal, then refrigerate or freeze.

Next
For fried or air-fried fish fillets or shrimp, marinate the seafood in this vinegar mixed with minced garlic and a couple of bay leaves. The fillets or shrimp should not sit in the vinegar at room temperature for more than 1 hour.

Lavender-Thyme Vinegar

MAKES: about 2 cups (480 ml)
FRIDGE: up to 3 months after infusing
FREEZER: up to 1 year after infusing

This vinegar has both a mild floral flavor with even a few herbal notes, and a gorgeous, pale violet color, thanks to both the lavender buds and the way the acid brings back their springtime color. It is also a fantastic gift, especially when presented in a decorative glass jar wrapped in a purple ribbon.

> 4 fresh thyme sprigs, the tender top parts only, each only about 4 inches (10 ml) long
> 1 teaspoon dried culinary lavender buds (see TIP on page 49)
> 2 cups (480 ml) white wine vinegar

1. Put the thyme and lavender buds in one *clean*, *heat-safe* 1 pint (472 ml) glass jar or other nonreactive container.

2. Warm the vinegar in a small saucepan set over medium heat just until steaming, not simmering.

3. Pour the vinegar over the thyme and lavender, leaving about ½ inch (1 cm) headspace in the jar. Cool at room temperature for no more than 1 hour. Cover and refrigerate to infuse for 4 days. Then enjoy or freeze.

More
Add some heat with 1 stemmed dried árbol chili. Or add a little brightness with a strip of lemon zest.

Tarragon Vinegar

MAKES: about 2 cups (480 ml)
FRIDGE: up to 3 months after infusing
FREEZER: up to 1 year after infusing

This vinegar replicates a classic ingredient in French cooking: slightly herbal, very sour, pale green, and quite refreshing when whisked into vinaigrettes or marinades. Although we call for a bunch of tarragon, use only the tender leaves if the stems seem at all woody. And make sure there are no squishy or brown spots.

> One 1 ounce (28 g) bunch of tarragon, trimmed to about 4 inches (10 cm) long, only the tender, upper leaves and stems
> 1¾ cups (420 ml) white wine vinegar

1. Put the tarragon in one *clean*, *heat-safe* 1 pint (472 ml) glass jar or other nonreactive container.

2. Warm the vinegar in a small saucepan set over medium heat just until steaming, not simmering.

3. Pour the vinegar over the tarragon, leaving about ½ inch (1 cm) headspace in the jar. Cool at room temperature for no more than 1 hour. Cover and refrigerate to infuse for 4 days. Then enjoy or freeze.

Next
Make that French classic, TARRAGON VINAIGRETTE: In a small bowl whisk together 3 parts olive oil and 1 part tarragon vinegar *by volume*. Whisk in a little minced shallot, Dijon mustard, and a drizzle of honey. Season with salt and pepper to taste.

Front to back:
Tarragon Vinegar
(page 414) and
Lavender-Thyme
Vinegar (page 414)

Fresh Chili Vinegar

MAKES: about 2 cups (480 ml)
FRIDGE: up to 2 months after infusing
FREEZER: up to 1 year after infusing

Blanching serrano chilis helps tame their heat. It also brings out some of the sweet, fruity notes of their natural sugars. And it intensifies the chilis' color…and so, by extension, the vinegar's. Don't get rid of the chilis' seeds. They bring desired heat to this bold vinegar.

> **Water as necessary for blanching the chilis**
> **3 fresh green serrano chilis, stemmed and split lengthwise**
> **A big bowl of ice water**
> **2 cups (480 ml) distilled white vinegar**

1. Bring a small saucepan of water to a boil over high heat. Add the chili halves and blanch for 20 seconds from the moment they hit the water.

2. Drain the chilis in a colander set in the sink and get them immediately into the bowl of ice water—or simply transfer them to the ice water with a slotted spoon. Chill for just 1 minute, then get those chili halves into two *clean, heat-safe* ½ pint (236 ml) glass jars or nonreactive containers or into one *clean, heat-safe* 1 pint (472 ml) glass jar or other container.

3. Warm the vinegar in that small saucepan set over medium heat, just until steaming, not simmering. Pour the warm vinegar over the chilis, leaving about ½ inch (1 cm) headspace in the jar(s). Cover or seal; refrigerate to infuse for 4 days. Then enjoy or freeze.

Next
For an Asian-inspired marinade, whisk the vinegar with equal parts soy sauce and toasted sesame oil *by volume*. Also, whisk in some minced garlic, scallion, and ginger. Because this marinade is pretty acidic, let seafood sit in it for no more than 1 hour in the fridge, and let cuts of meat sit in it for no more than 2 hours.

Dried Chili Vinegar

MAKES: about 2 cups (480 ml)
FRIDGE: up to 3 months after infusing
FREEZER: up to 1 year after infusing

Maybe the best part of making this fiery, earthy vinegar is the chilis you'll have left over when you've used up the vinegar itself. The now-pickled, rehydrated chilis can be minced to become a big flavor powerhouse in stir-fries or dairy-free braises. Or better yet, drizzle this on Chinese takeout, everything from wonton soup to chow fun…and it is particularly good when drizzled on anything in garlic or black bean sauce.

> **4–6 *dried* er jing tiao chilis, stemmed**
> **2 cups (480 ml) *unseasoned* rice vinegar**

1. Put the chilis in one *clean, heat-safe* 1 pint (472 ml) glass jar or other nonreactive container, breaking them as necessary to help them fit.

2. Warm the vinegar in a small saucepan set over medium heat just until steaming, not simmering.

3. Pour the vinegar over the chilis, leaving about ½ inch (1 cm) headspace in the jar. Cool at room temperature for no more than 1 hour. Cover and refrigerate to infuse for 4 days. Then enjoy or freeze.

More
For more assertive flavors, break a 3 inch (7.5 cm) cinnamon stick in half and place it in the jar with the chilis, along with 1 star anise pod and up to ½ teaspoon Szechuan peppercorns. Reduce the amount of the vinegar to 1¾ cups (420 ml).

Grenadine

MAKES: about 4 cups (960 ml)
FRIDGE: up to 3 months
FREEZER: up to 1 year

Grenadine is a red, pomegranate-based syrup that's used as a mixer in cocktails or a sweetener in lots of frozen drinks. Essentially, it's a simple sugar syrup made with pomegranate juice instead of water. We feel it's best to cook it a bit to condense the flavors, making them even more sour-sweet than many standard bottlings.

> 4 cups (960 ml) *unsweetened* pomegranate juice
>
> 4 cups (800 g) granulated white sugar
>
> Long strips of zest from 1 medium orange *and* 1 medium lemon
>
> ¼ cup (60 ml) lemon juice, preferably freshly squeezed

1. Combine all the ingredients in a large saucepan set over medium heat, stirring constantly until the sugar dissolves. Bring to a simmer, stirring occasionally.

2. Reduce the heat to very low and simmer slowly, stirring occasionally, until reduced to about two-thirds of its original volume, somewhat like warmed maple syrup, about 20 minutes.

3. Turn off the heat, remove the pan from the burner, and set aside at room temperature until cool to the touch, about 2 hours.

4. Transfer to four *clean* ½ pint (236 ml) jars, two *clean* 1 pint (472 ml) jars, or one *clean* 1 quart (1 liter) bottle or nonreactive container, leaving about ½ inch (1 cm) headspace in each. Cover or seal, then refrigerate or freeze.

Next

To make a TEQUILA SUNRISE, mix 4 ounces (½ cup or 120 ml) orange juice and 2 ounces (¼ cup or 60 ml) white or silver tequila with lots of ice in a highball glass. Add ½ ounce (1 tablespoon or 15 ml) grenadine. Wait a second: The grenadine will sink to the bottom, creating a layered look. Garnish with an orange wedge.

Tonic Syrup

MAKES: about 3 cups (720 ml)
FRIDGE: up to 3 months
FREEZER: up to 1 year

Tonic syrup is a complex blend of old-school spices and aromatics. Perhaps the most important ingredient is cinchona bark, the only easy source of quinine. There's actually a big range of cinchona varietals, producing barks of varying pungencies. Our favorite is red cinchona bark, with a slightly more tannic flavor. You'll find it in health-food stores and from dozens of online specialty shops. One warning: Red cinchona bark yields a pale red tonic syrup, perhaps not to everyone's liking, but gorgeous in a summery gin and tonic.

> 4 cups (960 ml) water
>
> 3 cups (600 g) granulated white sugar
>
> Long strips of zest and seeded juice of 2 medium lemons
>
> Long strips of zest and seeded juice of 2 medium oranges
>
> 1½ tablespoons (12 g) crumbled cinchona bark, preferably red cinchona bark
>
> 2 teaspoons citric acid
>
> 2 teaspoons coriander seeds
>
> 2 teaspoons juniper berries
>
> 1 large lemongrass stalk, trimmed of its woody root end and desiccated leaves, particularly on top, the inner parts thinly sliced
>
> 8 *green* cardamom pods, crushed

1. Combine all the ingredients in a large saucepan set over medium heat, stirring until the sugar dissolves. Bring to a boil, stirring often.

2. Reduce the heat to very low and simmer *slowly*, stirring occasionally, until reduced to about half of its original volume, somewhat like thin pancake syrup, about 35 minutes. Turn off the heat, remove the pan from the burner, and set aside at room temperature until cool to the touch, about 2 hours.

3. Strain the syrup into three *clean* ½ pint (236 ml) jars or nonreactive containers, leaving about ½ inch (1 cm) headspace in each. Discard the solids. Cover or seal, then refrigerate or freeze.

Next

To make a refreshing LIME-TONIC MOCKTAIL, combine 3 parts club soda or plain seltzer and 1 part tonic syrup *by volume* with lots of ice in a cocktail shaker or even a pitcher. Add a little lime juice to taste (up to half the amount of tonic syrup you used), as well as a few dashes of bitters. Stir well and strain over fresh ice.

Demerara Syrup

MAKES: about 4 cups (960 ml)
FRIDGE: up to 3 months
FREEZER: up to 1 year

Demerara sugar is a raw sugar, made strictly from sugarcane. Since it's not refined, it has a tan to golden-brown color and fairly large crystals. It's sometimes used as sanding (or decorative) sugar crystals on cakes and cupcakes. It makes a rich syrup, with molasses and vanilla undertones among the sweet. We played with ratios for years to try to tame the sheer sugary flavor of the syrup and let those other notes through. We've finally landed here, a compromise that's not as sweet as many a simple syrup. Use in any cocktail in place of simple syrup (although this syrup will darken the color of the quaff a bit).

> 4 cups (770 g) demerara sugar
> 2 cups (480 ml) water

1. Combine the sugar and water in a medium saucepan set over medium heat, stirring until the sugar dissolves. (It'll take a while because of the size of the crystals.) Bring to a boil, stirring often. Boil undisturbed for 30 seconds.

2. Turn off the heat, remove the pan from the burner, and set aside at room temperature until cool to the touch, about 2 hours.

3. Transfer to four *clean* ½ pint (236 ml) jars, two *clean* 1 pint (472 ml) jars, or one *clean* 1 quart

(1 liter) bottle or nonreactive container, leaving about ½ inch (1 cm) headspace in each. Cover or seal, then refrigerate or freeze.

Next

Did you know the classic OLD-FASHIONED was once made only with demerara syrup? Mix 2 ounces (¼ cup or 60 ml) bourbon, ½ ounce (1 tablespoon or 15 ml) demerara syrup, and a few dashes of bitters in a rocks glass. Add a few ice cubes and stir for 30 seconds. Garnish with a strip of orange zest (or an orange twist).

Coconut Syrup

MAKES: about 2 cups (480 ml)
FRIDGE: up to 3 months
FREEZER: up to 1 year

Coconut water is refreshing and light. But it's also watery. Yes, we've used it for jellies and other condiments in this book, but a thick coconut *syrup* needs a bigger flavor bump to be successful. So we combine coconut water with coconut sugar, which is made from the sap of coconut palms and has a deep, rich flavor, somewhat reminiscent of molasses. Because of the color of coconut sugar, this syrup will be pale or golden brown.

> 2 cups (310 g) coconut sugar
> 1 cup (240 ml) plain coconut water without any pulp
> ½ teaspoon vanilla extract

1. Combine all the ingredients in a small saucepan set over medium heat, stirring constantly until the coconut sugar dissolves. Bring to a boil, stirring occasionally.

2. Immediately turn off the heat, remove the pan from the burner, and use a tablespoon to skim any impurities from the surface. Set aside at room temperature until cool to the touch, about 2 hours.

3. Transfer to two *clean* ½ pint (236 ml) glass jars or other nonreactive containers, leaving about ½ inch (1 cm) headspace. Cover or seal, then refrigerate or freeze.

Clockwise from bottom: Tequila Sunrise with Grenadine (page 417), Lemon Soda with Lemon Syrup (page 420), and Mai Tai with Almond Syrup (page 420)

Next

To make COCONUT MARGARITA, pour equal amounts of tequila, Cointreau, and lime juice over ice in a cocktail shaker. Add a healthy splash of coconut syrup, then cover and shake until cold. Strain over fresh ice into a highball glass.

Lemon Syrup

MAKES: about 2 cups (480 ml)
FRIDGE: up to 3 months
FREEZER: up to 1 year

To make great lemon syrup, you need only sugar and lemons. The trick is the timing. If you cook the sugar long enough, it will thicken the lemon juice. Make sure that the mixture doesn't boil but simmers *slowly*. Otherwise, the sugar will caramelize and the syrup will be brown.

> 1¾ cups (350 g) granulated white sugar
> Long strips of zest from 3 medium lemons
> 1¾ cups (420 ml) lemon juice, preferably freshly squeezed

1. Combine all the ingredients in a medium saucepan set over medium heat, stirring constantly until the sugar dissolves. Bring to the barest simmer, stirring occasionally.

2. Reduce the heat to *very low* and simmer *slowly*, stirring occasionally, for 10 minutes. Turn off the heat, remove the pan from the burner, and set aside at room temperature until cool to the touch, about 2 hours.

3. Strain the syrup into two *clean* ½ pint (236 ml) glass jars or nonreactive containers, leaving about ½ inch (1 cm) headspace. Cover or seal, then refrigerate or freeze.

More

To make LEMON-GINGER SYRUP, add one 1 inch (2.5 cm) piece of fresh ginger (about the width of your thumb), peeled and thinly sliced.

Almond Syrup

MAKES: about 3 cups (720 ml)
FRIDGE: up to 2 months after infusing
FREEZER: up to 1 year after infusing

Here's our version of orgeat, an almond syrup, with a key change from commercial bottlings. We make ours with unskinned almonds for more flavor in every drop but (unfortunately) a darker color. It may even separate into dark and light layers when stored in the fridge. No worries: Just shake it up. You'll end up with tons of almond flavor for bartending, baking, or drizzling.

> 2 cups (285 g) whole unskinned almonds
> 3 cups (720 ml) water
> 2 cups (400 g) granulated white sugar
> 1 teaspoon orange flower water
> ¼ teaspoon almond extract

1. Position the rack in the center of the oven; heat the oven to 350°F (175°C), no fan or convection.

2. Spread the almonds on a large lipped baking sheet. Roast, stirring occasionally, until fragrant and lightly browned, about 10 minutes.

3. Pour the warm almonds into a food processor, cover, and process until *coarsely* chopped but with no big chunks, stopping the machine at least once to rearrange the almonds inside.

4. Pour the water into a big bowl. Add every speck of almonds from the food processor. Cover and refrigerate to infuse for 2 days.

5. Set up a jelly bag over a medium saucepan (for alternatives, see page 17). Pour the almond water into the bag. Let it drip for about 1 hour, squeezing the bag occasionally to extract as much liquid as possible.

6. Discard the almond solids. Set the pan over medium heat, add the sugar, and stir constantly until dissolved. Bring to a boil, stirring often.

7. Turn off the heat, remove the pan from the burner, and use a tablespoon to skim any impurities. Cool at room temperature for no more than 1 hour. Stir in the orange flower water and almond extract.

8. Transfer to three *clean* ½ pint (236 ml) jars or nonreactive containers, leaving about ½ inch (1 cm) headspace in each. Cover or seal, then refrigerate or freeze.

Next

To make a MAI TAI, pour all of the following over ice in a cocktail shaker: 1½ ounces (3 tablespoons or 45 ml) white rum, ½ ounce (1 tablespoon or 15 ml) almond syrup, ¼ ounce (1½ teaspoons or 8 ml) triple sec (or use your own homemade, page 434), and about 1 teaspoon lime juice (or a little more if you prefer a more sour drink). Cover and shake. Strain over fresh ice into a highball glass. Garnish with a maraschino cherry.

Coffee Syrup

MAKES: about 3 cups (720 ml)
FRIDGE: up to 2 months
FREEZER: up to 1 year

No matter how hard you work nor how precise you are, coffee syrup is really only as good as the coffee that goes into it. It's best to use espresso or very strong coffee, preferably from a French press—but strained to make sure you don't end up with any grinds in the translucent syrup. Once you have your own coffee syrup, you're on your way to your favorite coffeehouse drinks at home!

> 3½ cups (700 g) granulated white sugar
> 2½ cups (600 ml) strong coffee

1. Combine the sugar and coffee in a large saucepan set over medium heat, stirring constantly until the sugar dissolves. Bring to a boil, stirring often.

2. Turn off the heat, remove the pan from the burner, and set aside at room temperature until cool to the touch, about 2 hours.

3. Transfer to three *clean* ½ pint (236 ml) jars or nonreactive containers, leaving about ½ inch (1 cm) headspace in each. Cover or seal, then refrigerate or freeze.

Next

To make ALMOND ICED COFFEE, pour brewed coffee into a tall glass over ice. Add a little of this syrup as well as a little Almond Syrup (page 420). Stir well and topped with sweetened whipped cream.

Chai Syrup

MAKES: about 3 cups (720 ml)
FRIDGE: up to 2 months
FREEZER: up to 1 year

Well, not truly chai syrup. Instead, this is the spiced syrup used to make chai. It's fairly easy to pull off and you'll have a flavorful syrup for your next cup of strong black tea with milk.

> 2½ cups (600 ml) water
> 2 cups (400 g) granulated white sugar
> 1 cup (215 g) *packed* light brown sugar
> 1 teaspoon decorticated (husked and removed from the pods) cardamom seeds
> 1 teaspoon whole cloves
> 1 teaspoon allspice berries
> One 3 inch (7.5 cm) cinnamon stick, broken in half widthwise
> One 1 inch (2.5 cm) piece of fresh ginger (about the width of your thumb), peeled and thinly sliced into rounds

1. Combine all the ingredients in a large saucepan set over medium heat, stirring constantly until both sugars dissolve. Bring to a boil, stirring often.

2. Turn off the heat, remove the pan from the burner, and set aside at room temperature until cool to the touch, about 2 hours.

3. Strain the mixture through a fine-mesh strainer or a colander lined with cheesecloth into a medium bowl. Ladle into three *clean* ½ pint (236 ml) jars or nonreactive containers, leaving about ½ inch (1 cm) headspace in each. Discard the solids in the strainer. Cover or seal the syrup, then refrigerate or freeze.

Next

To make a HOLIDAY CHAI COCKTAIL, mix equal parts *by volume* of vodka, a coffee-flavored liqueur (or your own homemade, page 433), and canned coconut milk in a cocktail shaker. Stir until well combined, then add ice, a little of this chai syrup (maybe 1 tablespoon, ½ ounce, or 15 ml), and a tiny drizzle of molasses. Cover and shake, then strain into a chilled martini glass.

Lavender Syrup

MAKES: about 2 cups (480 ml)
FRIDGE: up to 2 months
FREEZER: up to 1 year

This syrup is potent! Use it in small measures in cocktails or frosting recipes. It has a pale lavender color that gets clearer and more intense once the lemon juice changes the pH. That said, you can also add a smidgen of violet food color…but be careful: Even a drop can turn the syrup a neon purple.

- 2 cups (480 ml) water
- 2 cups (400 g) granulated white sugar
- 3 tablespoons (24 g) dried culinary lavender buds (see TIP on page 49)
- 1 teaspoon (5 ml) lemon juice, preferably freshly squeezed
- No more than 1 drop of violet food color, optional

1. Combine the water, sugar, and lavender buds in a medium saucepan set over medium heat, stirring constantly until the sugar dissolves. Bring to a boil, stirring occasionally. Boil undisturbed for 1 minute.

2. Turn off the heat, remove the pan from the burner, and set aside at room temperature until cool to the touch, about 2 hours.

3. Strain the syrup through a fine-mesh strainer or a colander lined with cheesecloth into a medium bowl. Discard the solids. Stir in the lemon juice and food coloring, if desired.

4. Transfer to two *clean* ½ pint (236 ml) glass jars or other nonreactive containers, leaving about ½ inch (1 cm) headspace. Cover or seal, then refrigerate or freeze.

Next

Add a splash of lavender syrup to lemonade or limeade, or drizzle over chocolate or chocolate nut ice cream for a burst of floral flavor.

Rose Syrup

MAKES: about 2 cups (480 ml)
FRIDGE: up to 2 months
FREEZER: up to 1 year

Rose syrup packs a powerful flavor. It's amazing when drizzled into a very herbal gin over ice. It's also great when drizzled over tagines or Moroccan dishes, just the barest amount, to offer its herbal notes without adding too much sweetness.

- 2 cups (480 ml) water
- 2 cups (400 g) granulated white sugar
- ¼ cup (32 g) dried culinary rosebuds (see recipe headnote, page 100)
- 1 tablespoon (15 ml) rose water
- 1 teaspoon (5 ml) lemon juice, preferably freshly squeezed
- Pink food coloring, optional

1. Combine the water, sugar, and rosebuds in a medium saucepan set over medium heat, stirring constantly until the sugar dissolves. Bring to a boil, stirring occasionally. Boil undisturbed for 1 minute.

2. Turn off the heat, remove the pan from the burner, and set aside at room temperature until cool to the touch, about 2 hours.

3. Strain the syrup through a fine-mesh strainer or a colander lined with cheesecloth into a medium bowl. Discard the solids. Stir the rose water, lemon juice, and food coloring, if desired, into the syrup.

4. Transfer to two *clean* ½ pint (236 ml) glass jars or other nonreactive containers, leaving about ½ inch (1 cm) headspace. Cover or seal, then refrigerate or freeze.

More

For SPICED ROSE SYRUP, add *2 green* cardamom pods, a few allspice berries, 1 star anise pod, and/or 1 small 2 inch (5 cm) cinnamon stick with the dried rosebuds.

Elderberry Syrup

MAKES: about 3 cups (720 ml)
FRIDGE: up to 3 months
FREEZER: up to 1 year

Elderberry syrup is not only great in cocktails, it's been a folk remedy for colds for generations. Just mix a little with lemon juice and hot water. Or use the syrup to sweeten iced tea for a summertime quaff. You can most readily find dried elderberries in health-food stores and from online suppliers.

> 1 cup (250 g) *dried* elderberries
> 4 cups (960 ml) water
> One 1 inch (2½ inch) piece of fresh ginger (about the width of your thumb), peeled and thinly sliced
> One 2 inch (5 cm) cinnamon stick
> 10–12 whole cloves
> 1½ cups (300 g) granulated white sugar

1. Combine the elderberries, 2½ cups (600 ml) water, the ginger, cinnamon stick, and cloves in a medium saucepan set over medium heat. Bring to a boil, stirring occasionally.

2. Reduce the heat to low and simmer, stirring occasionally, until reduced to about half of its original volume, about 15 minutes.

3. Turn off the heat, remove the pan from the burner, and pour the elderberry mixture into a fine-mesh strainer or a cheesecloth-lined colander set over a bowl. Set aside to drip for 1 hour.

4. Meanwhile, combine the sugar and remaining 1½ cups (360 ml) water in a small saucepan set over medium heat, stirring until the sugar dissolves. Bring to a boil, stirring occasionally. Boil undisturbed for 1 minute. Turn off the heat, remove the pan from the burner, and cool for 15 minutes.

5. Discard the solids in the strainer or cheesecloth. Stir the sugar syrup into the elderberry infusion. Transfer to three *clean* ½ pint (236 ml) glass jars or other nonreactive containers, leaving about ½ inch (1 cm) headspace. Cover or seal, then refrigerate or freeze.

More

If you have leftover dried elderberries, you can brew them in hot water (as you would tea) to make a floral, hot infusion to soothe a sore throat.

Strawberry Syrup

MAKES: about 2 cups (480 ml)
FRIDGE: up to 3 months
FREEZER: up to 1 year

Get your pancakes ready! This syrup is loaded with strawberry flavor, a great treat for a weekend morning's breakfast. Beyond that, consider it a drizzle for vanilla cakes…or even painted with a pastry brush onto each layer of a layer cake before you add the frosting.

> 2 cups (400 g) granulated white sugar
> 1 cup (240 ml) water
> 2 pounds (900 g) fresh strawberries, hulled and chopped (about 4 cups chopped)
> ¼ teaspoon vanilla extract
> ¼ teaspoon kosher salt

Clockwise from bottom: Rose Syrup (page 422), Strawberry Syrup (page 423), Tonic Syrup (page 417), Caramel Syrup (page 426), and Lavender Syrup (page 422)

1. Combine the sugar and water in a medium saucepan set over medium heat, stirring constantly until the sugar dissolves. Bring to a boil, stirring occasionally.

2. Add the strawberries, vanilla, and salt. Bring back to a full boil, stirring often. Reduce the heat to low and simmer, stirring often, until the liquid is thick and the strawberries are super soft, almost mushy, about 12 minutes.

3. Turn off the heat, remove the pan from the burner, and use a tablespoon to skim any impurities from the surface. Cool at room temperature for 20 minutes.

4. Set up a jelly bag over a pot or a bowl (for alternatives to a jelly bag, see page 17). Pour in the strawberry syrup and let drip for 1 hour, occasionally pressing against the solids to extract as much liquid as you can.

5. Transfer to two *clean* ½ pint (236 ml) glass jars or other containers, leaving about ½ inch (1 cm) headspace in each. Cover or seal, then refrigerate or freeze.

More
Add up to 1 teaspoon black peppercorns or 1 small piece of dried orange peel with the vanilla.

Chocolate Syrup

MAKES: about 3 cups (720 ml)
FRIDGE: up to 3 months
FREEZER: up to 1 year

Not Chocolate *Sauce*. That's on page 382. Instead, this is a chocolate *syrup*, made for cocktails and drinks of all sorts. In fact, it's a great addition to coffee drinks, particularly those that are iced. It has a dark brown color thanks to the cocoa powder, rather than the more familiar clear bottlings made with natural and/or artificial flavors.

1½ cups (360 ml) water
1½ cups (300 g) granulated white sugar
½ cup (160 ml) light corn syrup
1 cup (85 g) unsweetened cocoa powder
1 tablespoon (15 ml) vanilla extract
¼ teaspoon kosher salt

1. Combine the water, sugar, and corn syrup in a medium saucepan set over medium heat, stirring until the sugar and corn syrup dissolve. Bring to a boil, stirring occasionally. Boil for 5 minutes, stirring often.

2. Reduce the heat to low and stir until the mixture is simmering, not boiling. *Whisk* in the cocoa powder until smooth. Bring back to a boil, whisking constantly. Boil, still whisking constantly, for 1 minute.

3. Turn off the heat, remove the pan from the burner, and stir in the vanilla and salt. Set aside at room temperature until cool to the touch, about 2 hours.

4. Transfer to three *clean* ½ pint (236 ml) jars or other containers, leaving about ½ inch (1 cm) headspace in each. Cover or seal, then refrigerate or freeze.

Next
To make that deli favorite, an EGG CREAM, put 3 tablespoons (45 ml) chocolate syrup in an iced tea glass. Stirring all the while, add ½ cup (120 ml) milk (of any sort) until the syrup is dissolved and the mixture is well blended. Add cold plain seltzer or club soda, stirring gently just until the fizzy water reaches the top of the glass. Immediately remove the spoon to preserve the foamy head.

Caramel Syrup

MAKES: about 2 cups (480 ml)
FRIDGE: up to 3 months
FREEZER: up to 1 year

Here's the perfect sweet syrup for cocktails, mocktails, and iced coffee drinks. It's also great as an iced tea sweetener, for a sophisticated twist. And it's a great dessert drizzle over cakes and pies, particularly nut pies. Just be cautious when you add the water to the melted sugar. It will sputter super heated sugar. Work with a long-handled spoon and stand back.

> 2 cups (400 g) granulated white sugar
> 1¾ cups (420 ml) room temperature water (do not use cool water!)

1. Mix the sugar and 1 cup (240 ml) water in a large saucepan set over medium heat, stirring constantly until the sugar dissolves. Raise the heat to medium-high and bring to a boil, stirring once or twice. Continue boiling, stirring occasionally, until the sugar caramelizes and the syrup turns golden, brown, or even dark brown, depending on how assertive a flavor you want the caramel to have. Do not let the mixture blacken. We prefer it the color of maple syrup.

2. Reduce the heat to medium. Drizzle in the remaining ¾ cup (180 ml) water. Be very careful: The sugar syrup will sputter and roil. Stir as much as possible. Once all the water is in, the sugar will have clumped. Continue cooking, stirring almost constantly, until the sugar dissolves again.

3. Turn off the heat, remove the pan from the burner, and set aside at room temperature until cool to the touch, about 3 hours.

4. Transfer to two *clean* ½ pint (236 ml) jars or other containers, leaving about ½ inch (1 cm) headspace in each. Cover or seal, then refrigerate or freeze.

Tip

Many caramel syrups add vanilla extract or flavoring as a shortcut. We prefer to control the bitterness and depth of the flavor by caramelizing the sugar properly: golden brown for a mild flavor or darker brown for a bolder, even tannic flavor.

Root Beer Syrup

MAKES: about 3 cups (720 ml)
FRIDGE: up to 3 months
FREEZER: up to 1 year

One holiday, we made a huge batch of this syrup, put it into small decorative bottles, and gave it away at every party we attended. Everybody was shocked to have homemade root beer syrup! Once you have it in hand, it's easy to turn it into root beer. Just stir as much as you like into club soda or plain seltzer in a glass with lots of ice. As to sourcing some of the more esoteric ingredients here, there are plenty of herbalist shops online with vast arrays of these goods.

> 6 cups (720 ml) water
> 3½ ounces (100 g) cut or chopped dried sarsaparilla root
> 1½ ounces (42 g) cut or chopped dried cherry bark
> 1 ounce (28 g) cut or chopped dried burdock root
> 6 small pieces (about 9 g) dried acacia bark
> 2 small pieces (about 4 g) dried licorice root
> One 2½ inch (6 cm) piece of fresh ginger (about the width of your thumb), peeled and roughly chopped
> 3 *green* cardamom pods, crushed
> 10 coriander seeds
> 6 whole cloves
> 6 allspice berries
> 1 star anise pod
> ¼ cup (85 g) molasses or black treacle
> 6 drops wintergreen extract
> About 2½ cups (500 g) granulated white sugar, or as necessary for the proper volume

1. Combine the water, sarsaparilla, cherry bark, burdock, acacia, licorice, ginger, cardamom pods, coriander seeds, cloves, allspice berries, and star anise pod in a very large saucepan set over medium-high heat. Bring to a boil, stirring occasionally. Reduce the heat to low and simmer *slowly*, stirring often, for 10 minutes.

2. Stir in the molasses or treacle until smooth. Continue simmering *slowly*, stirring often, for 5 minutes.

3. Stir in the wintergreen extract. Turn off the heat, remove the pan from the burner, and set aside at room temperature until cool to the touch, about 2 hours.

4. Strain the herbal mixture through a fine-mesh strainer or a cheesecloth-lined colander into a medium bowl set below. Measure the volume of the liquid. Stir in as much granulated sugar as liquid *by volume*.

5. Set the pan over medium-high heat and bring to a simmer, stirring constantly at first to dissolve the sugar. Bring to a boil, stirring occasionally. Boil undisturbed for 1 minute.

6. Turn off the heat, remove the pan from the burner, and again set aside at room temperature until cool to the touch, about 2 hours. Transfer to three *clean* ½ pint (236 ml) jars or other containers, leaving about ½ inch (1 cm) headspace in each. Cover or seal, then refrigerate or freeze.

Tip

Nobody needs a vat of root beer syrup. You might want to store it in much smaller containers. To get it into small glass bottles, you'll need a tiny funnel.

Cranberry Liqueur

MAKES: about 4 cups (960 ml)
FRIDGE: up to 3 months after infusing
FREEZER: at least 2 years after infusing

This liqueur is more of a traditional, boozy syrup because we steep cranberries in vodka, then add a sugar syrup made with cranberry juice concentrate for a big bump of flavor. It's a lovely sip (perhaps over ice) after a holiday meal.

> 12 ounces (340 g) fresh cranberries or thawed frozen cranberries (about 3 cups for either)
>
> 3 cups (720 ml) *100-proof* vodka (do not use flavored vodka)
>
> 1½ cups (300 g) granulated white sugar
>
> 1½ cups (360 ml) water
>
> ¼ cup (60 ml) *thawed* cranberry juice concentrate

1. Put the cranberries in a food processor, cover, and pulse until fairly finely chopped. Stop the machine at least once to rearrange cranberry chunks so they can be chopped.

2. Pour the chopped cranberries into a large nonreactive bowl and stir in the vodka. Cover and refrigerate to infuse for 3 weeks, stirring every few days.

3. Combine the sugar, water, and cranberry juice concentrate in a medium saucepan set over medium heat, stirring constantly until the sugar dissolves. Bring to a boil, stirring occasionally. Turn off the heat, remove the pan from the burner, and cool at room temperature for 2 hours.

4. Set up a jelly bag over a pot or a bowl (for alternatives to a jelly bag, see page 17). Strain the cranberry mixture through the jelly bag, letting it drip for about 1 hour. *Don't* squeeze the bag to keep that the flavored liqueur as clear as possible.

5. Stir the sugar syrup into the strained cranberry vodka. Transfer to one *clean* 1 quart (1 liter) glass bottle or nonreactive container. Cover or seal, then refrigerate or freeze.

➡

More

For SPICED CRANBERRY LIQUEUR, add one 3 inch (7.5 cm) cinnamon stick, 4 or 5 cloves, 1 or 2 *green* cardamom pods, and/or 1 star anise pod to the cranberry and vodka mixture before it steeps.

Raspberry Liqueur

MAKES: about 4 cups (960 ml)
FRIDGE: up to 3 months after infusing
FREEZER: at least 2 years after infusing

Here's our version of framboise, aka raspberry liqueur. Ours is actually somewhere between raspberry-flavored vodka and the more traditional, syrupy liqueur. As a side note, our version has a higher proof than most commercial bottlings, since it's made with vodka from the start. It's a great addition to cocktails, as well as a sweet shot on its own after dinner. But keep in mind that even just a shot is powerful.

> 5 cups (600 g) fresh raspberries or thawed frozen raspberries (plus all juice)
> 3½ cups (840 ml) *100-proof* vodka (do not use flavored vodka)
> 1 cup (200 g) granulated white sugar

1. Mash the raspberries with a potato masher or the back of a wooden spoon in a large nonreactive bowl to extract their juice and pulp.

2. Add the vodka and sugar and stir until the sugar dissolves. Cover and refrigerate for 2 weeks to infuse, stirring every 3 or 4 days.

3. Strain the raspberry mixture into one *clean* 1 quart (1 liter) glass bottle or nonreactive container. Cover or seal, then refrigerate or freeze.

Next
To make a RASPBERRY COSMOPOLITAN, pour 1½ ounces (3 tablespoons or 45 ml) raspberry liqueur, 1 ounce (2 tablespoons or 30 ml) cranberry juice, ½ ounce (1 tablespoon or 15 ml) Cointreau, and ½ ounce (1 tablespoon or 15 ml) lime juice into a cocktail shaker filled with ice. Cover and shake until cold, then strain into a martini glass.

Strawberry Liqueur

MAKES: about 4 cups (960 ml)
FRIDGE: up to 3 months after infusing
FREEZER: at least 2 years after infusing

To make the best strawberry liqueur, you need the freshest strawberries. Don't use frozen because they'll have lost some of their flavor in the thaw. Fresh strawberries should have that characteristic fragrance, particularly at their stems, almost irresistible. Only these will bring both the right color and flavor to this liqueur.

> 1½ pounds (680 g) very ripe sweet fresh strawberries, hulled and thinly sliced
> 2 cups (480 ml) neutral-flavored grain alcohol
> 1½ cups (300 g) granulated white sugar
> ¾ cup (180 ml) water

1. Stir the strawberries and alcohol in a large nonreactive bowl. Cover and refrigerate to infuse for 4 weeks, stirring every few days and making sure the strawberries are always submerged.

2. Combine the sugar and water in a medium saucepan set over medium heat, stirring constantly until the sugar dissolves. Bring to a boil, stirring occasionally. Turn off the heat, remove the pan from the burner, and cool at room temperature for 2 hours.

3. Set up a jelly bag over a pot or a bowl (for alternatives to a jelly bag, see page 17). Strain the strawberry mixture through the jelly bag, letting it drip for about 1 hour. *Don't* squeeze the bag to keep the flavored liqueur as clear as possible.

4. Stir the sugar syrup into the strained strawberry alcohol. Transfer to one *clean* 1 quart (1 liter) glass bottle or nonreactive container. Cover or seal, then refrigerate or freeze.

Raspberry Liqueur (page 428)

Next

To make a STRAWBERRY DAIQUIRI, muddle one hulled ripe strawberry in a cocktail shaker with 1 ounce (2 tablespoons or 30 ml) strawberry liqueur. Stir in 1 ounce (2 tablespoons or 30 ml) white rum and 1 ounce (2 tablespoons or 30 ml) lime juice. Add ice, cover, and shake until cold. Strain into a martini glass.

Blueberry Liqueur

MAKES: about 4 cups (960 ml)
FRIDGE: up to 3 months after infusing
FREEZER: at least 2 years after infusing

To make great blueberry liqueur, you need tiny low-bush blueberries, common to Maine and eastern Canada. Only these have enough blueberry flavor to stand up to the alcohol and sugar syrup. Unless you live in these areas, you'll probably only find the tiny blueberries in the freezer section of your supermarket. When you thaw them, use all the juice they produce as well as the berries.

> 10 ounces (340 g) fresh wild low-bush blueberries or thawed frozen wild low-bush blueberries (about 2 cups for either)
>
> 2 cups neutral-flavored grain alcohol
>
> 1½ cups (300 g) granulated white sugar
>
> 1½ cups (360 ml) water

1. Gently crush the blueberries in a large nonreactive bowl with a potato masher or your clean hands. Wear culinary gloves to prevent staining. Stir in the alcohol. Cover and refrigerate for 3 weeks to infuse, stirring every few days.

2. Combine the sugar and water in a medium saucepan set over medium heat, stirring constantly until the sugar dissolves. Bring to a boil, stirring occasionally. Turn off the heat, remove the pan from the burner, and cool at room temperature for 2 hours.

3. Set up a jelly bag over a pot or a bowl (for alternatives to a jelly bag, see page 17). Strain the blueberry mixture through the jelly bag, letting it drip for about 1 hour. *Don't* squeeze the bag to keep the flavored liqueur as clear as possible.

4. Stir the sugar syrup into the blueberry alcohol. Transfer to one *clean* 1 quart (1 liter) glass bottle or nonreactive container. Cover or seal, then refrigerate or freeze.

Next

To make a BLUEBERRY RUM FIZZ, muddle a few fresh blueberries with a pinch of granulated white sugar in a cocktail shaker. Stir in 2 ounces (¼ cup or 60 ml) white or silver rum, 1 ounce (2 tablespoons or 30 ml) lime juice, and 1 ounce (2 tablespoons or 30 ml) blueberry liqueur. Add ice, cover, and shake until cold. Strain into a martini glass and top with club soda for fizz.

Black Currant Liqueur

MAKES: about 4 cups (960 ml)
FRIDGE: up to 3 months after infusing
FREEZER: at least 2 years after infusing

We make black currant liqueur (crème de cassis) every summer because we grow a bumper crop of black currants at our house. Over the years, we've added red currants to the liqueur. Although untraditional, they add more sour flavor and improve the color, making the liqueur less inky and more vibrant. But trust us: There are no worries about the liqueur's flavor. Red currants can never overpower black currants.

> 2 heaping cups (350 g) stemmed black currants
>
> 1 heaping cup (300 g) stemmed red currants
>
> 3 cups plus 2 tablespoons (750 ml) neutral-flavored grain alcohol
>
> 2 cups (400 g) granulated white sugar
>
> 1 cup (240 ml) water

1. Gently crush the black and red currants in a large nonreactive bowl with a potato masher or your clean hands. Wear culinary gloves to prevent staining. Stir in the alcohol. Cover and refrigerate for 2 weeks to infuse, stirring every few days.

2. Combine the sugar and water in a medium saucepan set over medium heat, stirring constantly until the sugar dissolves. Bring to a boil, stirring occasionally. Turn off the heat, remove the pan from the burner, and cool at room temperature for 2 hours.

3. Set up a jelly bag over a pot or a bowl (for alternatives to a jelly bag, see page 17). Strain the currant mixture through the jelly bag, letting it drip for about 1 hour. *Don't* squeeze the bag to keep the flavored liqueur as clear as possible.

4. Stir the sugar syrup into the currant alcohol. Transfer to one *clean* 1 quart (1 liter) glass bottle or nonreactive container. Cover or seal, then refrigerate or freeze.

Next

A chilled shot or two of this liqueur in front of the fireplace with a bowl of toasted, salted nuts may be the best dessert after dinner with friends. Or add a small drizzle to a glass of white wine for a kir.

Cacao Liqueur

MAKES: about 4 cups (960 ml)
FRIDGE: up to 4 months
FREEZER: at least 2 years

This liqueur is not just sweet. It also has the bitter, somewhat tannic edge that crème de cacao used to have but has lost over the years. To get those deeper, more elegant flavors, we start with cacao nibs and steer clear of any chocolate syrup. Given its bolder flavor profile, this liqueur is probably not the best for sipping, but better in cocktails: up, over ice, or frozen.

9 ounces (255 g) cacao nibs (about 2 cups)
2½ cups (600 ml) aged rum (do not use dark rum)
Boiling water to fill the bowl
2 cups (400 g) granulated white sugar
1 cup (240 ml) water

1. Position a rack in the oven's center; heat the oven to 300°F (150°C), no fan or convection.

2. Spread the cacao nibs on a large lipped baking sheet. Toast, stirring occasionally, until warmed and quite fragrant, about 5 minutes. Set the baking sheet on a wire rack and cool for 10 minutes.

3. Divide the nibs between two *clean, heat-safe* 1 pint (472 ml) jars or other containers. Divide the rum evenly between them (1¼ cups or 300 ml in each). Cover or seal tightly. Set the jars in a large *heat-safe* bowl. They can be askew or tipped diagonally away from each other. Pour in the boiling water to fill *the bowl*, then leave at room temperature for 12 hours or overnight.

4. Remove the jars from the water bath and set them aside, still sealed, at room temperature for 24 hours.

5. Combine the sugar and 1 cup (240 ml) water in a medium saucepan set over medium heat, stirring constantly until the sugar dissolves. Bring to a boil, stirring occasionally. Turn off the heat, remove the pan from the burner, and cool at room temperature for 2 hours.

6. Set up a jelly bag over a pot or a bowl (for alternatives to a jelly bag, see page 17). Strain the cacao mixture through the jelly bag, letting it drip for about 1 hour. *Don't* squeeze the bag to keep the flavored liqueur as clear as possible.

7. Stir the sugar syrup into the cacao alcohol. Transfer to one *clean* 1 quart (1 liter) glass bottle or nonreactive container. Cover or seal, then refrigerate or freeze.

Front to back:
Black Currant Liqueur
(page 430) in a kir and
Triple Sec (page 434)
in a sidecar

Next

To make a CHOCOLATE MARTINI, pour 2 ounces (¼ cup or 60 ml) Irish cream liqueur, 1 ounce (2 tablespoons or 30 ml) vodka, and 1 ounce (2 tablespoons or 30 ml) cacao liqueur into a cocktail shaker. Add ice, cover, and shake until cold. Drizzle chocolate syrup (even your own homemade, page 425) around the inside of a martini glass, then strain this drink into the glass.

Coffee Liqueur

MAKES: about 4 cups (960 ml)
FRIDGE: up to 3 months after infusing
FREEZER: at least 2 years after infusing

This is a no-cook liqueur, so not as syrupy as some of our other offerings, but big on flavor, since the notes from coffee beans get more present in the silky texture of the sugar syrup. Use strongly flavored beans, preferably a dark roast for espresso.

> 4 cups (960 ml) aged rum (do not use dark rum)
> 2 cups (430 g) *packed* light brown sugar
> 6 ounces (170 g) dark-roasted coffee beans (about 2 cups), coarsely ground
> 1 teaspoon (5 ml) vanilla extract

1. Whisk the rum, sugar, coffee, and vanilla in a large bowl until the brown sugar dissolves. Cover and set aside at room temperature to infuse for 2 days.

2. Set up a jelly bag over a pot or a bowl (for alternatives to a jelly bag, see page 17). Strain the coffee mixture through the jelly bag, letting it drip for about 1 hour. *Don't* squeeze the bag to keep the flavored liqueur as clear as possible.

3. Transfer the liqueur to one *clean* 1 quart (1 liter) glass bottle or nonreactive container. Cover or seal, then refrigerate or freeze.

Next

Add a shot of this liqueur to your favorite coffee drink for a boozy alternative. Or simply mix 2 parts liqueur and 1 part heavy cream *by volume* for a decadent shot.

Hazelnut Liqueur

MAKES: about 4 cups (960 ml)
FRIDGE: up to 3 months after infusing
FREEZER: at least 2 years after infusing

Frangelico, eat your heart out! It's easy to make homemade hazelnut liqueur…and it's so much more complexly flavored, thanks to the toasted hazelnuts. We add a few coffee beans, brandy, and orange zest, just to deepen the overall profile, with more bass note than sharp acid pitch. The results are layered and very satisfying.

> 4 cups (500 g) raw whole hazelnuts
> 2 cups (480 ml) vodka (do not use flavored vodka)
> 2 cups (480 ml) brandy (do not use flavored brandy)
> 20 dark-roasted coffee beans
> 2 cups (400 g) granulated white sugar
> 1 cup (240 ml) water
> Long wide strips of zest from 1 medium orange,
> 1 teaspoon (5 ml) vanilla extract

1. Position a rack in the oven's center; heat the oven to 325°F (160°C), no fan or convection.

2. Spread the hazelnuts on a large lipped baking sheet. Toast, stirring often, until lightly browned and fragrant, about 10 minutes. Transfer the baking sheet to a wire rack and cool for 15 minutes.

3. Pour the still-warm hazelnuts into a clean large kitchen towel. Gather it together and rub the hazelnuts against the towel, taking off as much of their skins as you can. Pick out the hazelnuts and put them in a food processor. Cover and process until coarsely ground, stopping the machine at least once to rearrange the pieces.

4. Pour the ground hazelnuts into a large bowl and stir in the vodka, brandy, and coffee beans. Cover and set aside at room temperature to infuse for 1 week, stirring every day.

5. Combine the sugar, water, orange zest, and vanilla in a medium saucepan set over medium heat, stirring constantly until the sugar dissolves. Bring to a boil, stirring occasionally. Turn off the heat, remove the pan from the burner, and cool at room temperature for 2 hours.

6. Set up a jelly bag over a pot or a bowl (for alternatives to a jelly bag, see page 17). Strain the hazelnut mixture through the jelly bag, letting it drip for about 1 hour. Don't squeeze the bag to keep the flavored liqueur as clear as possible.

7. Pick the orange zest strips out of the cooled sugar syrup and discard. Stir the syrup into the hazelnut alcohol. Transfer to one *clean* 1 quart (1 liter) glass bottle or nonreactive container. Cover or seal, then refrigerate or freeze.

Next
To make an imaginative hazelnut cocktail, dissolve 1 tablespoon (21 g) honey in 1 tablespoon (15 ml) hot water until smooth. Pour into a cocktail shaker and add 1½ ounces (3 tablespoons or 45 ml) hazelnut liqueur, 1 ounce (2 tablespoons or 30 ml) gin, and ½ ounce (1 tablespoon or 15 ml) lemon juice. Add ice cubes, cover, and shake until cold. Strain into a chilled martini glass. Garnish with a small fresh rosemary sprig, if desired.

Triple Sec

MAKES: about 4 cups (960 ml)
FRIDGE: up to 6 months after infusing
FREEZER: at least 2 years after infusing

Sure, there are plenty of triple secs on the market. They're mostly pale imitations of what a fine orange liqueur should be. That said, commercial triple sec is clear because of colorless flavor additives. Ours has a gorgeous, pale orange, almost pink tint, more in keeping with the fruit that made the liqueur. If you've got your own homemade triple sec, your margaritas will never know what hit them! Plus, there's no going back. Look for dried *bitter* orange peel from online suppliers. We've come to the last recipe and by now, you're committed to the sheer joy of cold canning.

> 3¼ cups (780 ml) *100-proof* vodka (do not use flavored vodka)
> Long wide strips of zest from 3 large navel oranges
> 2½ tablespoons (12 g) *dried bitter* orange peel
> 1¾ cups (350 g) granulated white sugar
> 1 cup (240 ml) water

1. Stir the vodka, orange zest, and bitter orange peel in a large bowl. Cover and set aside at room temperature to infuse for 2 weeks, stirring about every few days but making sure the zest and peel stay submerged.

2. Combine the sugar and water in a medium saucepan set over medium heat, stirring constantly until the sugar dissolves. Bring to a boil, stirring occasionally. Turn off the heat, remove the pan from the burner, and cool at room temperature for 2 hours.

3. Set up a jelly bag over a pot or a bowl (for alternatives to a jelly bag, see page 17). Strain the orange mixture through the jelly bag, letting it drip for about 1 hour. Don't squeeze the bag to keep the triple sec as clear as possible.

4. Stir the sugar syrup into the orange alcohol. Transfer to one *clean* 1 quart (1 liter) glass bottle or nonreactive container. Cover or seal, then refrigerate or freeze.

Next
The best MARGARITA starts with equal parts white or silver tequila, triple sec, and lime juice *by volume* in a cocktail shaker. Add a pinch of granulated white or bar sugar to taste and lots of ice. Cover and shake until cold. Strain over fresh ice into a highball glass. Or make a SIDECAR by mixing 2 parts brandy, 1 part lemon juice, and 1 part triple sec in a cocktail shaker with ice; cover and shake. Strain in an up glass with a sugared rim.

How to Can Some of These Recipes the Traditional Way

Although we designed our recipes to make small batches that can be stored in the refrigerator or freezer, you may choose to can some of these in the traditional way to preserve cold-storage space in your kitchen or to make enough for holiday gifts for all your friends and family.

Before we get into the specifics, we must begin this discussion with three warnings.

- First, the texture and flavor of traditionally canned condiments will be different because of the second cooking inside the water-bath canner. We experimented with Peach Preserves (page 59): one jar for the fridge and one jar (using the same ingredient ratios) with traditional canning. No doubt: The one for the fridge had a brighter, peachier flavor with slightly sour undertones and a distinct perfume. It was also more brilliantly colored. The canned jar had notes of caramelized sugar, which indeed competed with the peach flavors. It did not have any sour undertones and had a darker, golden-brown color when held to the light.

- Second, can or process only the recipes so labeled with the heading in the storage guidelines. Our pickles and relishes, some jams, all chili crisps, all salsas, and most others *were not* developed with a proper pH for shelf-stable results.

- Third, we do not recommend *pressure* canning for any of these recipes. The ratios were not developed with the *lower* sugar amounts some pressure-canned condiments require. Pressure canning is so intense that all of our results would be distinctly compromised, even damaged.

Okay, on to traditional canning. Use only water-bath canning (or "boiling-water canning," to use the USDA's term). Here are the steps:

1. You must submerge and heat all jars, lids, sealing rings, funnels, and ladles in a large pot of *simmering* water (195°F or 90°C) for at least 5 minutes. Then you should leave the jars, lids, and sealing rings (but not the funnels and ladles) in the simmering water until you're ready to fill the jars. A jar lifter is the only way to protect your fingers from hot glass and metal. Look for jar lifters online or at specialty kitchen shops. One note: You must not *boil* the lids. Only simmering water will do. Boiling can compromise the adhesive ring (or the gasket) on the underside of the lid. (By the way, the USDA does not recommend using single-piece canning lids for shelf-stable products.)

2. Fill a water-bath canner with enough water to cover the jars you're using by about 2 inches (5 cm). Bring the water to a boil over high heat. A water-bath canner will come with its own instructions; each may be slightly different. However, all will have a low rack to keep the jars off the bottom of the pot. Yours should be tall enough to submerge the filled bottles by the stated amount of water.

3. Once your jam or jelly is ready to bottle according to the recipe, ladle it into the hot jars right away, filling the hot jars to the stated amount of headspace.

4. Wipe the rims with a damp, new paper towel. Set a lid, adhesive (or gasket) side down, on each jar, then screw on the sealing rings—in most cases, only until you feel resistance, not until tight. Air must be able to escape during canning. But check the guidelines for each lid manufacturer to make sure they concur with this tightening finesse. (Some have other markers for the right seal.)

5. Use a jar lifter to lower the filled and sealed jars into the *boiling* water and cover the canner. Wait until the water comes back to a vigorous boil. Now process (or boil) the jars for 10 minutes.

6. Turn off the heat and allow the jars to sit in the hot water for 5 minutes.

7. Remove the jars with a jar lifter and set them on a rack or a heat-resistant counter. As the jars cool, the lids will get sucked down for a tight seal. You may hear small pops to indicate the action. Once cool, you can tighten the sealing ring, or you can remove it to better see the seal around the lid as the jar sits on the shelf. (But don't pack a jar in your luggage without a tightened sealing ring!)

8. Label the date and perhaps the contents on the jars. Store the jars in a dark, cool pantry. Do not store them near furnaces, heating pipes, or under the sink. If any lid becomes unstuck, popped up, or bent during storage, throw out the jar and its contents. The lid must always have a concave center. There must be no discoloration or mold in the jar. The jars can remain at room temperature for perhaps 6 months but no more than 9 months. (Because we haven't been persnickety about the pH of these cold-canning recipes, err on the conservative side.)

One final note: Canning times change at higher altitudes. For every 1,000 feet (300 meters) above sea level, add one additional minute for the jars in the boiling water. For example, at 5,000 feet above sea level (or about 1,500 meters), add 5 additional minutes in the water bath.

Acknowledgments

THANK YOU

Mike Szczerban. It's hard to imagine that moment (eight years and eight books ago!) when we were sitting at the James Beard Awards at Chelsea Piers, spotted you across the banquet hall, and said to our agent, "We want to hitch our wagon to his."

Susan Ginsburg. Forty-one agented books from the two of us? And three ghostwritten bestsellers? Plus about five billion book proposals? And we're still on such good terms? Is that possible? With you, definitely, yes.

Eric Medsker. We're so glad we got obsessed with your photographer's eye on that first job, fifteen years ago, when you were an assistant (and a kid). And now this, the fourteenth book you've shot for us. Because you're that good (and that great to work with).

Catherine Bradshaw. We don't envy the fact that you get to face writerly anxiety head-on. We so appreciate your patience and kindness.

Pat Jalbert-Levine. Nobody could ask for a more efficient or capable production editor. It's a thankless job...until now.

The company we keep at Voracious and Little, Brown: Sally Kim, Morgan James, Juliana Horbachevsky, Katherine Akey, Kirin Diemont, Nyamekye Waliyaya, and Laura Palese, and editorial freelancers Deri Reed, Deborah Jacobs, Jayne Yaffe Kemp, and Elizabeth Parson. No book is an island, entire of itself. We are so fortunate to be a part of your main (to stretch Donne as far as we can).

Index

Note: Page references in *italics* indicate photographs; "var." indicates a recipe variation.

A

Aji Amarillo Paste, 226, *228*
Aji Panca Paste, *228*, 229
Alfajores, Shortcut, 396
Almond Raspberry Preserves
    (var.), 50
almond syrup
  Almond Iced Coffee, 421
  Almond Syrup, 420–21
  Apple-Amaretto Jelly, 72–74, *73*
  Cherries in Almond Syrup, 293
anchovies
  Black Olive Tapenade, *180*, 181
  Puttanesca Tapenade, 184
  Worcestershire Sauce, 372–73
apples. *See also* applesauce
  Apple-Amaretto Jelly, 72–74, *73*
  Apple-Caramel Jam, *73,* 75–76
  Apple-Cardamom Jam, 74–75
  Apple Chutney, 150–51, *152*
  Apple Dessert Sauce, 395
  Apple Jelly, 71
  Apple Pie Chutney, 151
  Apple Pie Conserve, *131,* 132
  Apple Sauerkraut, 320–21
  Apples in Syrup, 291–93, *292*
  Brandied Apple Preserves, 77
  Candy Apple Jelly, 71–72
  Mint Jelly, 141
  Nearly Sugar-Free Apple Chutney,
    153
  Oven-Roasted Apple Butter, 78
  Spiced Apple Preserves, 76
  Sugar-Free Apple Jam, 74
  Tarragon Jelly, 142
applesauce
  Applesauce, 378, *379*
  Cranberry Applesauce, 378–80
  Easy Apple Butter, 77–78
  Sugar-Free Applesauce, 380
apricots
  Apricot–Garam Masala Chutney,
    159
  Apricot-Gochujang Jam,
    64–65

  Apricot Preserves, *63,* 64
  Duck Sauce, 370–72, *371*
Armagnac, Prunes in, 290–91
artichokes
  Artichoke-Lemon Tapenade, 187
  Marinated Artichokes, 288–89
Asparagus, Pickled, 264, *265*

B

bacon
  Bacon Jam, 118, *119*
  Shallot-Bacon Jam, 121–22
balsamic vinegar
  Balsamic Strawberry Sauce (var.),
    390
  Blackberry-Balsamic Jam, 48
Banana Ketchup, 344, *345*
barbecue sauce
  Brown Sugar Barbecue Sauce,
    352–53
  Classic Barbecue Sauce, 351
  Five-Alarm Barbecue Sauce, 353,
    354
  Gold Barbecue Sauce, 358, *359*
  Peachy Barbecue Sauce, 356
  Peanut Butter–Ginger Barbecue
    Sauce, 355–56, *359*
  Pineapple-Sesame Barbecue
    Sauce, 357–58
  Raspberry-Chipotle Barbecue
    Sauce, 355
  Roasted Garlic–Maple Barbecue
    Sauce, 357, *359*
  Vinegary Barbecue Sauce,
    351–52
basil
  Basil Oil, 404
  Tomato-Basil Jam, 128
beans
  Corn–Black Bean Salsa, *199,*
    200–201
  Dilly Beans, 262–63
beets
  Beet Relish, 172
  Beet Sauerkraut, *322,* 324–25

  Beet Tapenade, 184, *185*
  Harvard Beets, 276, *277*
  Horseradish-Pickled Beets, 275
  Pickled Roasted Beets, 275–76,
    277
  Sweet-and-Sour Pickled Beets,
    274
berries. *See also specific berries*
  Four-Berry Holiday Jam,
    57–59, *58*
  Three-Berry Jam, 57
blackberries
  Blackberry-Balsamic Jam, 48
  Blackberry–Chia Seed Jam,
    49–50
  Blackberry Conserve, 129–30, *131*
  Blackberry-Lavender Jam, 49
  Blackberry Preserves, *46,* 47
  Blackberry Sauce, 393
  Sugar-Free Blackberry Jam,
    47–48
  Three-Berry Jam, 57
Black Currant Jelly, 87, *88*
Black Currant Liqueur, 430–31, *432*
Black Currant–Port Jam, 89
black treacle, 21
blender, 116
blueberries
  The Best Blueberry Preserves,
    42–44, *43*
  Blueberry–Chia Seed Jam, 45–47
  Blueberry-Jalapeño Ketchup,
    343–44
  Blueberry Liqueur, 430
  Blueberry-Onion Jam, *119,* 120
  Blueberry-Orange Jam, 44–45
  Four-Berry Holiday Jam,
    57–59, *58*
  Sugar-Free Blueberry Jam, 44
  Three-Berry Jam, 57
boiling-water canning, 436–37
Bok Choy, Baby, Kimchi, 313–14
bourbon
  Old Fashioned, 418
  Onion-Bourbon Jam, 118–20, *119*

Boysenberry Jam, 54–56
brandy
    Apple Dessert Sauce, 395
    Brandied Apple Preserves, 77
    Hazelnut Liqueur, 433–34
    Kumquats in Cognac Syrup,
        299
    Oranges in Brandy Syrup, 297–99,
        298
    Prunes in Armagnac, 290–91
    Raspberry Brandy Sauce (var.),
        395
    Sidecar, *432,* 434
Broccoli, Gingery Pickled, 267
Brown Mustard, 364–65
Brown Mustard, Fiery, 365–66,
    368
Butterscotch Sauce, *377,* 385

C
cabbage
    Apple Sauerkraut, 320–21
    Baby Bok Choy Kimchi, 313–14
    Beet Sauerkraut, *322,* 324–25
    Caraway-Cranberry Sauerkraut,
        319–20
    Celery Root Sauerkraut, *322,*
        323–24
    Chili Chow Chow, 177
    Curtido, *334,* 335
    Fennel Sauerkraut, *322,*
        325–26
    Gin Sauerkraut, 328–29
    Go-to Kimchi, 306, *307*
    Go-to Sauerkraut, *316,* 317
    Jalapeño Sauerkraut, *316,*
        326–27
    Napa Cabbage Kimchi,
        308–9
    Pickled Red Cabbage, 266
    Pineapple Sauerkraut, 321–23,
        322
    Pistachio-Duqqa Sauerkraut,
        329–30
    Red Cabbage Sauerkraut, *316,*
        318–19
    Savoy Cabbage Kimchi, 311–13,
        312
    Shortcut Vinegary Red
        Sauerkraut, 318
    Summer Kimchi, 308
    Sweet Chow Chow, 175
    Turmeric-Onion Sauerkraut,
        327–28, *331*
    White Kimchi, 310

Cacao Liqueur, 431–33
Cajeta, 399
Calabrian Chili Paste, 225
candy-making thermometer, 18
canning, traditional, 436–37
capers
    Black Olive Tapenade, *180,* 181
    Caper Tapenade, 183
    Puttanesca Tapenade, 184
Caponata, 178–79, *180*
caramel
    Cajeta, 399
    Caramel Syrup, *424,* 426
    Coconut Caramel Sauce, 388
    Dulce de Leche, *397,* 398
    Easy Dulce de Leche, 398–99
    Salted Caramel Sauce, 386, *387*
cardamom
    Apple-Cardamom Jam, 74–75
    Celery Root–Cardamom Jam,
        125–27, *126*
    Cranberry-Cardamom Chutney,
        157, 158–59
carrots
    Carrot-Ginger Relish, *165,* 168
    Carrot Jam, 122, *123*
    Carrot Kimchi, 315
    Carrot Marmalade, 112–13
    Carrot Sauerkraut, 330–32, *331*
    Giardiniera, 262
    Pickled Daikon and Carrots,
        273–74
    Pickled Tarragon Carrots, 269–71,
        270
    Spicy Carrot Jam, 122–24
    Super Sour Iranian-Style Pickle,
        179–81
Cashew-Coconut Chutney, Spicy,
    161, *162*
cauliflower
    English Piccalilli, 173, *176*
    Giardiniera, 262
    Spicy-Garlicky Cauliflower
        Pickles, 269, *270*
    Sticky Brown Cauliflower Pickle,
        174–75, *176*
    Super Sour Iranian-Style Pickle,
        179–81
Celery, Pickled, 264–66
Celery Root–Cardamom Jam,
    125–27, *126*
Celery Root Sauerkraut, *322,*
    323–24
Chai Jelly, 104
Chai Syrup, 421–22

char siu, preparing, 361
Char Siu Sauce, 360–61
cheesecloth, 17–18
cherries
    Cherries in Almond Syrup,
        293
    Cherry Pie Jam, 67–69, *68*
    Cherry-Pistachio Salsa Macha,
        205
    Peach–Sour Cherry Conserve,
        130–32, *131*
    Sour Cherry Preserves, 66
    Sour Cherry Vinegar, 411–13,
        412
    Spiced Black Cherry Jelly, 69
    Spiced Pickled Cherries, 280
    Sugar-Free Sweet Cherry
        Jam, 67
    Sweet-and-Sour Cherries, 279,
        281
    Sweet Cherry Preserves, 66–67
Chestnut Jam, 86
chia seeds
    Blackberry–Chia Seed Jam,
        49–50
    Blueberry–Chia Seed Jam,
        45–47
    Raspberry–Chia Seed Jam,
        54, *55*
Chicken, Huli-Huli, 358
chili crisp
    Almost Everything Chili Crisp,
        209
    Curried Chili Crisp, 215, *216*
    defined, 189
    Five-Spice Chili Crisp, 210–12
    Garlic-Scallion Chili Crisp, 212
    Gochugaru Chili Crisp, 213
    Shiitake–Szechuan Peppercorn
        Chili Crisp, *211,* 214
    Star Anise–Smoked Paprika Chili
        Crisp, 210, *211*
    Sumac-Cinnamon Chili Crisp,
        213–14
    Wasabi-Nori Chili Crisp, 215–17,
        216
chili-infused condiments
    about, 189–92
    and dairy, note about, 192
    list of recipes, 8–9
    storage and safety, 193
    types of, 189
chili paste
    defined, 189
    list of recipes, 8–9

chilis. *See also* chili-infused
condiments
Blueberry-Jalapeño Ketchup,
343–44
Chili Chow Chow, 177
Cowboy Candy, 256, *257*
dried, measuring and prepping,
190
Dried Chili Vinegar, 416
Eighteen-Spice Chili Oil, 407–8,
409
Five-Alarm Barbecue Sauce, 353,
354
Fresh Chili Vinegar, 416
Jalapeño Jam, 139–41, *140*
Jalapeño Relish, 167
Jalapeño Salsa, 198, *199*
Jalapeño Sauerkraut, *316,*
326–27
Pickled Jalapeño Rings, 255–56
Pineapple-Chili Chutney,
159–60
Raspberry-Chipotle Barbecue
Sauce, 355
Raspberry-Chipotle Jam,
53–54
Red Pepper Jam, *123,* 124
Rhubarb-Chipotle Chutney,
154–55
Strawberry-Jalapeño Jam, 37
Tamarind-Chili Jam, 128–29
Tomato-Ancho Jam, *126,* 127
chili sauce
defined, 189
list of recipes, 8–9
Chive Oil, 404–6, *405*
chocolate
Black Mole, 232–33, *234*
Chocolate Sauce, 382
Chocolate Syrup, 425
chopping, 375
cocoa solid content, 375
Hot Fudge Sauce, 382–84, *383*
Shortcut Black Mole, 233–35
White Chocolate Sauce, *383,*
384
chopstick test for hot oil, 192
chow chow
Chili Chow Chow, 177
Sweet Chow Chow, 175
Watermelon Rind Chow Chow,
177–78
chutney
defined, 115
list of recipes, 7–8

cilantro
Green Mole, *234,* 236–37
Mint Chutney, 160, *162*
Parsley–Pumpkin Seed Chutney,
160–61
Salsa Verde, *195,* 196
cinchona bark
Tonic Syrup, 417–18, *424*
cinnamon
Chai Syrup, 421–22
Spiced Cherries in Almond Syrup
(var.), 293
Spiced Rose Syrup (var.), 423
Sumac-Cinnamon Chili Crisp,
213–14
Citrus Oil, 406–7
Clementine-Ginger Marmalade,
109–10
Coarse-Grained Mustard, *362,*
363–64
coconut
Coconut Caramel Sauce, 388
Coconut-Lime-Ginger Jam (var.),
100
Coconut-Pecan Salsa Macha,
208–9
Coconut Syrup, 418–20
Holiday Chai Cocktail, 422
Lemon-Coconut Sauce (var.), 393
Pineapple-Coconut Jelly, 93–94
Spicy Coconut-Cashew Chutney,
161, *162*
Spicy Pineapple-Coconut
Conserve, 132–33
coffee
Coffee Jelly, 103–4
Coffee Liqueur, 433
Coffee Sauce, 396
Coffee Syrup, 421
Hazelnut Liqueur, 433–34
Holiday Chai Cocktail, 422
Cognac Syrup, Kumquats in, 299
Cointreau
Coconut Margarita, 420
Raspberry Cosmopolitan, 428
colanders, 17–18
cold canning
benefits of, 13–14
common ingredients, 20–22
freezing the recipes, 26
heat-processing the recipes,
25–26
how it works, 14–15
safety of, 14
shelf life of products, 25

storing preserves, 14–15
technical questions, 22–26
thawing the recipes, 26
tools for, 15–19
conserves
defined, 115
list of recipes, 7–8
corn
Corn–Black Bean Salsa, *199,*
200–201
Spicy Corn Relish, *165,* 166–67
Sweet Corn Relish, 166
Cornichons, 255
cover or seal, defined, 24–25
cranberries
Caraway-Cranberry Sauerkraut,
319–20
Chunky Cranberry Sauce, 144
Cranberry Applesauce, 378–80
Cranberry-Cardamom Chutney,
157, 158–59
Cranberry Liqueur, 427–28
Cranberry Vinegar, 411, *412*
Cranberry-Walnut Salsa Macha,
205–6, *207*
Cranberry Walnut Sauce, *143,* 146
Four-Berry Holiday Jam,
57–59, *58*
Smooth Cranberry Sauce, 142–44,
143
Spiced Cranberry Sauce, 145
Spicy Cranberry Conserve,
135–37
Sugar-Free Cranberry Sauce,
144–45
cranberry juice
Pear Cosmo, 294
Raspberry Cosmopolitan, 428
cream, heavy or whipping, 376
cucumbers. *See also* gherkins
Bread and Butter Pickles, 252–54,
253
Classic Dill Pickles, 247
Cucumber Kimchi, *312,* 314–15
Dill Pickle Relish, 164–66, *165*
Fiery Pickles, 248–50
Garlic Sour Pickles, 248, *249*
Green Tea Pickles, 250
Half Sour Pickles, 247–48, *249*
Horseradish Pickles, 251
Mustard Pickles, 251–52
Sweet Pickle Relish, 163–64, *165*
Cumin-Pineapple Salsa, *199,* 200
Curried Chili Crisp, 215, *216*
Curried Ketchup, 340–42, *341*

Curry Oil, Eighteen-Spice, 408, *409*
curry paste
    Green Curry Paste, 232
    Red Curry Paste, *228*, 230–31
    Yellow Curry Paste, 231–32
Curtido, *334, 335*

D

daikon
    Lime-Sesame Pickled Daikon, 273
    Pickled Daikon and Carrots, 273–74
    Radish Kimchi, 311, *312*
    White Kimchi, 310
Dal-Shallot Chutney, 163
Demerara Syrup, 418
Dijon Mustard, 361–63, *362*
dill
    Classic Dill Pickles, 247
    Dill Pickle Relish, 164–66, *165*
    Dilly Beans, 262–63
dips
    Honey Mustard Dip, 364
    Kimchi Dip, 309
    savory, list of recipes, 10
    sweet, list of recipes, 11
distilled white vinegar, 21
doenjang
    Hoisin Sauce, *345*, 348
drinks
    Almond Iced Coffee, 421
    Blueberry Rum Fizz, 430
    Chocolate Martini, 433
    Coconut Margarita, 420
    Egg Cream, 425
    Holiday Chai Cocktail, 422
    Lime-Tonic Mocktail, 418
    Macchiato, 396
    Mai Tai, *419*, 421
    Margarita, 434
    Old Fashioned, 418
    Pear Cosmo, 294
    Raspberry Cosmopolitan, 428
    Salted Caramel Martini, 386
    Sidecar, *432*, 434
    Strawberry Daiquiri, 430
    Tequila Sunrise, 417, *419*
Duck Sauce, 370–72, *371*
Dulce de Leche, *397*, 398
Dulce de Leche, Easy, 398–99
Duqqa-Pistachio Sauerkraut, 329–30

E

Egg Cream, 425
eggplant
    Caponata, 178–79, *180*
    Marinated Roasted Vegetables, 289–90
    Pickled Eggplant, 271
    Super Sour Iranian-Style Pickle, 179–81
Elderberry Jam, 56
Elderberry Syrup, 423
Empanadas, Cajeta, 399

F

fennel
    Dried Pears in Fennel-Orange Syrup, 294–96, *295*
    Fennel Relish, *170*, 171
    Fennel Sauerkraut, *322*, 325–26
Fermented Chili Sauce, *222*, 223–24
ferments
    fermenting process, 301–4
    list of recipes, 10
    refrigerator fermentation, 245, 301
    safety considerations, 304–5
    traditional fermentation, 245, 301
figs
    Dried Fig–Lemon Jam, 84–86, *85*
    Fig-Ginger Jam, 84
    Fig Jam, 83
    Fig-Olive Tapenade, 182–83
    Figs in Honey Syrup, 296
    Fig-Tamarind Chutney, 156–58, *157*
    Fig Vinegar, 413
fine-mesh strainer, 17
Five-Spice Chili Crisp, 210–12
Five-Spice Ketchup, 342–43
food mill, 16
food processor, 116
freezer condiments, 26
fruits. *See also specific fruits*
    syrups from, uses for, 246
    syrupy, list of recipes, 9
funnels, for glass jars, 403

G

Garam Masala–Apricot Chutney, 159
garlic
    Garlic Confit, *284*, 285
    Garlicky Chili Paste, 225–26, *227*
    Garlicky Sun-Dried Tomato Tapenade, 186
    Garlic Mustard, 367, *368*
    Garlic-Scallion Chili Crisp, 212
    Garlic Sour Pickles, 248, *249*
    Roasted Garlic–Maple Barbecue Sauce, 357, *359*
    Rosemary-Garlic Oil, 406
    Spicy-Garlicky Cauliflower Pickles, 269, *270*
    Yellow Curry Paste, 231–32
gherkins
    Cornichons, 255
    Sweet Gherkins, 254
Giardiniera, 262
ginger
    Apple-Ginger Topping Sauce (var.), 395
    Carrot-Ginger Relish, *165*, 168
    Chai Syrup, 421–22
    Clementine-Ginger Marmalade, 109–10
    Fig-Ginger Jam, 84
    Gingered Watermelon Rinds, 278–79
    Ginger Jam, 137
    Gingery Pickled Broccoli, 267
    Gochugaru Chili Crisp, 213
    Grape-Ginger Jelly, 41
    Lemon-Ginger Mazavaroo, 221–23
    Lemon-Ginger Syrup (var.), 420
    Lime-Ginger Jelly, 99–100
    Peach-Ginger Jam, 61–62
    Peanut Butter–Ginger Barbecue Sauce, 355–56, *359*
    Pear-Ginger Sauce, 381
    Pickled Ginger, 259–61
    Rhubarb-Ginger Jam, 70–71
gochugaru
    Gochugaru Chili Crisp, 213
    Shortcut Gochujang, 240–41
gochujang
    Apricot-Gochujang Jam, 64–65
    Shortcut Gochujang, 240–41
Gooseberry Jelly (var.), 87
grain alcohol
    Black Currant Liqueur, 430–31, *432*
    Blueberry Liqueur, 430
    for infused liqueurs, 402
    Strawberry Liqueur, 428–30
grapefruit
    Grapefruit Marmalade, *106*, 110
    Three-Citrus Marmalade, 111–12
grapes
    Concord Grape Jam, 38, *39*
    Concord Grape Jelly, 37–38

Grape-Ginger Jelly, 41
Green Grape Jam, 40
Pickled Grapes, 282–83
Red Grape Jam, *39,* 40–41
Spiced Grape Jelly, 42
Green Tea Pickles, 250
Grenadine, 417
Guava Jam, 99

H

harissa
Go-to Harissa, 237–38
Rose Harissa, 238–40, *239*
Smoky-Sweet Harissa, 240
Hazelnut Liqueur, 433–34
herbs, 22. *See also specific herbs*
hibiscus
Hibiscus Jelly, *101,* 102
Spiced Hibiscus Jelly, 102–3
hoisin sauce
Char Siu Sauce, 360–61
Hoisin Sauce, *345,* 348
Honey Mustard, 364
horseradish
Alabama White Sauce, 360
Horseradish-Pickled Beets, 275
Horseradish Pickles, 251
Pineapple-Horseradish Jam, 125,
126
Hot Fudge Sauce, 382–84, *383*

I

ingredients, 20–22
instant-read meat
thermometer, 18
Irish cream liqueur
Chocolate Martini, 433
Salted Caramel Martini, 386

J

jam (savory)
defined, 115
list of recipes, 7
jam (sweet)
defined, 29
list of recipes, 6–7
preparing, notes on, 29–31
jars
burping, 304
cleaning, 19
covering or sealing, 24–25
decorative, 337, 402–3
for pickling recipes, 244–45
sterilizing, 303
types of, 19

jellies
defined, 29
list of recipes, 6–7
preparing, notes on, 29–31
jelly bag, 16–17
Jicama, Pickled, 272–73
juniper berries
Gin Sauerkraut, 328–29
Tonic Syrup, 417–18, *424*

K

Kecap Manis, *345,* 346–47
ketchup
Banana Ketchup, 344, *345*
Blueberry-Jalapeño Ketchup,
343–44
Curried Ketchup, 340–42, *341*
Five-Spice Ketchup, 342–43
Mushroom Ketchup, *345,* 346
Plum Ketchup, 343
Tomato Ketchup, 340, *341*
kimchi
fermentation process, 301, 302
ingredient notes, 301
list of recipes, 10
salting and seasoning, 302
kitchen gloves, 18
kitchen scale, 301–2
Kiwi Jam, 94–96, *95*
kosher salt, 20, 301–2
kumquats
Kumquats in Cognac Syrup, 299
Pickled Kumquats, 283

L

lavender
Blackberry-Lavender Jam, 49
Lavender Syrup, 422, *424*
Lavender-Thyme Vinegar,
414, *415*
Lemongrass-Tomato Sambal,
217–18, *219*
lemons
Artichoke-Lemon Tapenade, 187
Citrus Oil, 406–7
Dried Fig–Lemon Jam,
84–86, *85*
Lemon-Ginger Mazavaroo,
221–23
Lemon Marmalade, *106,* 110–11
Lemon-Sage Vinegar, 413–14
Lemon Sauce, 392
Lemon–Summer Squash Relish,
169–71
Lemon Syrup, 420

Preserved Lemons, 276–78
Three-Citrus Marmalade, 111–12
White Currant–Lemon Jelly, *88,*
90–91
limes
Coconut Margarita, 420
Lime-Ginger Jelly, 99–100
Lime-Sesame Pickled
Daikon, 273
Lime-Tonic Mocktail, 418
liqueurs
about, 401–3
freezing and thawing, 402
list of recipes, 11
Lychee Jelly, 98

M

Macadamia Nut Chili Paste, Smoky,
229–30
Mai Tai, *419,* 421
mangoes
Classic Mango Chutney, 146–47,
148
Major Grey's Chutney, 147, *148*
Mango Jam, *95,* 97
Peach-Mango Jam, 62–64, *63*
Peach-Mango Salsa, *199,* 201
Shredded Mango Relish, *170,*
172–73
Sugar-Free Mango Chutney,
147–49
maple syrup
Maple Mustard, 366
Maple-Rhubarb Conserve, 134
Maple-Sesame Salsa Macha,
206–8
Roasted Garlic–Maple Barbecue
Sauce, 357, *359*
Marionberry Jam (var.), 47
marmalades
defined, 29
list of recipes, 7
preparing, notes on, 29–32
Marshmallow Sauce, 389–90, *391*
metric measurements, 23
Mint Chutney, 160, *162*
Mint Jelly, 141
miso
Shortcut Gochujang, 240–41
molasses, 21
Molasses Mustard, 366–67, *368*
Red Onion–Molasses Chutney,
150
Root Beer Syrup, 426–27
Worcestershire Sauce, 372–73

mole
  Black Mole, 232–33, *234*
  Green Mole, *234,* 236–37
  Red Mole, *234,* 235–36
  Shortcut Black Mole, 233–35
  Shortcut Red Mole, 236
mushrooms
  Mushroom Ketchup, *345,* 346
  Seared Mushrooms in Oil, 286
  Shiitake–Szechuan Peppercorn
    Chili Crisp, *211,* 214
mustard
  final consistency, 339
  list of recipes, 10
  Mustard Pickles, 251–52
mustard seeds, types of, 117

N
noodles
  Filipino spaghetti, preparing,
    344
  Kimchi-Shrimp Salad, 314
  Kimchi Udon, 310
  Peanut Butter–Kimchi Noodles,
    313
Nori-Wasabi Chili Crisp, 215–17, *216*
nuts. *See also* peanuts; pecans;
    walnuts
  Cherry-Pistachio Salsa Macha,
    205
  Chestnut Jam, 86
  Hazelnut Liqueur, 433–34
  Pineapple–Pine Nut Salsa Macha,
    202–4
  Pistachio-Duqqa Sauerkraut,
    329–30
  Smoky Macadamia Nut Chili
    Paste, 229–30
  Spicy Coconut-Cashew Chutney,
    161, *162*

O
oils
  for chili-infused condiments,
    191–92
  hot, chopstick test for, 192
  smoke points, 191–92
  types and temperatures,
    191–92
oils, infused
  about, 401–3
  Basil Oil, 404
  Citrus Oil, 406–7
  Eighteen-Spice Chili Oil, 407–8,
    409

Eighteen-Spice Curry Oil, 408,
    409
  freezing and thawing, 402
  Rosemary-Garlic Oil, 406
Okra, Hot and Sour Pickled,
    268
Olallieberry Jam (var.), 47
olive oil, 22
olives
  Anchovy-Free Tapenade,
    181–82
  Artichoke-Lemon Tapenade,
    187
  Beet Tapenade, 184, *185*
  Black Olive Tapenade, *180,* 181
  Caper Tapenade, 183
  Caponata, 178–79, *180*
  Fig-Olive Tapenade, 182–83
  Garlicky Sun-Dried Tomato
    Tapenade, 186
  Green Olive Tapenade, 182
  Puttanesca Tapenade, 184
  Spiced Tapenade, *185,* 186–87
onions
  Blueberry-Onion Jam, *119,* 120
  Cocktail Onions, 258–59, *260*
  Easy Onion Chutney, 149–50
  Onion-Bourbon Jam,
    118–20, *119*
  Pickled Red Onions, 258
  Red Onion–Molasses Chutney,
    150
  Turmeric-Onion Sauerkraut,
    327–28, *331*
oranges
  Blood Orange Marmalade, *106,*
    108–9
  Blueberry-Orange Jam, 44–45
  Citrus Oil, 406–7
  Dried Pears in Fennel-Orange
    Syrup, 294–96, *295*
  Fig-Tamarind Chutney, 156–58,
    157
  Oranges in Brandy Syrup, 297–99,
    298
  Raspberry-Orange Sauce,
    393–95, *394*
  Sour Orange Marmalade, 105–7,
    106
  Sugar-Free Orange Marmalade,
    106, 107–8
  Sweet Orange Marmalade,
    105
  Tequila Sunrise, 417, *419*
  Triple Sec, 434

P
Pancake, Kimchi, 308
Parsley–Pumpkin Seed Chutney,
    160–61
peaches
  Duck Sauce, 370–72, *371*
  Peach-Ginger Jam, 61–62
  Peach-Mango Jam, 62–64, *63*
  Peach-Mango Salsa, *199,* 201
  Peach Margarita Jam, 61
  Peach Melba Jam, 60–61, *68*
  Peach Preserves, 59
  Peach–Sour Cherry Conserve,
    130–32, *131*
  Peachy Barbecue Sauce, 356
  Spiced Peach Quarters, 290
  Sugar-Free Peach Jam, 60
Peanut Butter–Ginger Barbecue
    Sauce, 355–56, *359*
Peanut Butter–Kimchi Noodles,
    313
Peanut Butter Sauce, 389
peanuts
  Peanut-Tamarind Sambal,
    220
  Red Mole, *234,* 235–36
  Spicy Peanut Sauce, 370, *371*
pears
  Brown Sugar–Pear Preserves,
    80–81
  Dried Pears in Fennel-Orange
    Syrup, 294–96, *295*
  Pear Butter, 81
  Pear-Ginger Sauce, 381
  Pear Preserves, *79,* 80
  Pear Quarters in Spiced Syrup,
    293–94
  Pear Sauce, *379,* 380–81
  Pickled Spiced Pears, 280–82,
    281
  Sweet-and-Sour Pear Conserve,
    133–34
pecans
  Coconut-Pecan Salsa Macha,
    208–9
  Praline Sauce, 388–89
  Smoky Pecan–Cacao Nib Salsa
    Macha, 204–5
pectin, 21–22
peppers. *See also* chilis
  Peri Peri Sauce, 223
  Pickled Cubanelles, 256–58
  Red Pepper Jam, *123,* 124
  Roasted Bell Peppers in Oil, *287,*
    288

Smoky-Sweet Harissa, 240
Sweet Chow Chow, 175
Peri Peri Sauce, 223
Persimmon Jam, 97–98
piccalilli
    English Piccalilli, 173, *176*
    Southern Piccalilli, 174
pickle relish
    Dill Pickle Relish, 164–66, *165*
    Sweet Pickle Relish, 163–64, *165*
pickles and pickled foods
    about, 243–45
    list of recipes, 9
    mixed pickling spices for,
        243–44
    safety considerations, 245–46
pineapple
    Pineapple-Chili Chutney,
        159–60
    Pineapple-Coconut Jelly, 93–94
    Pineapple-Cumin Salsa, *199,*
        200
    Pineapple-Horseradish Jam, 125,
        126
    Pineapple in Black Pepper Syrup,
        296–97
    Pineapple Jam, 91–93, *92*
    Pineapple Jelly, 91, *92*
    Pineapple–Pine Nut Salsa Macha,
        202–4
    Pineapple Sauce, *391,* 392
    Pineapple Sauerkraut, 321–23,
        322
    Pineapple-Sesame Barbecue
        Sauce, 357–58
    Spicy Pineapple-Coconut
        Conserve, 132–33
Pine Nut–Pineapple Salsa Macha,
    202–4
pistachios
    Cherry-Pistachio Salsa Macha,
        205
    Pistachio-Duqqa Sauerkraut,
        329–30
plate test, 24
plums
    Pickled Spiced Plums, 282
    Plum Ketchup, 343
    Plum Preserves, *63,* 65–66
    Plum Vinegar, 410, *412*
    Spiced Plum Chutney, *152,*
        153–54
pomegranate
    Grenadine, 417
    Pomegranate Jelly, 94, *95*

pork char siu, preparing, 361
Port–Black Currant Jam, 89
Praline Sauce, 388–89
preserves
    defined, 29
    list of recipes, 6
    preparing, notes on, 29–31
Prunes in Armagnac, 290–91
Pumpkin Butter, 81–83, *82*
pumpkin seeds
    Black Mole, 232–33, *234*
    Cherry-Pistachio Salsa Macha,
        205
    Go-to Salsa Macha, 202, *203*
    Green Mole, *234,* 236–37
    Parsley–Pumpkin Seed Chutney,
        160–61

Q

Quince Jelly, 96–97

R

radishes. *See also* daikon
    Pickled Radishes, 266–67
raisins
    Apple Chutney, 150–51, *152*
    Apple Pie Chutney, 151
    Caponata, 178–79, *180*
    Fig-Tamarind Chutney, 156–58,
        157
    Lemon–Summer Squash Relish,
        169–71
    Major Grey's Chutney, 147, *148*
    Maple-Rhubarb Conserve, 134
    Red Mole, *234,* 235–36
    Rhubarb-Raisin Chutney, 154
    Shortcut Black Mole, 233–35
    Steak Sauce, *345,* 347–48
    Sweet-and-Sour Pear Conserve,
        133–34
raspberries
    Four-Berry Holiday Jam,
        57–59, *58*
    Peach Melba Jam, 60–61, *68*
    Raspberry–Chia Seed Jam,
        54, *55*
    Raspberry-Chipotle Barbecue
        Sauce, 355
    Raspberry-Chipotle Jam,
        53–54
    Raspberry Jam, 50–52
    Raspberry Jelly, *51,* 52
    Raspberry Liqueur, 428, *429*
    Raspberry-Orange Sauce,
        393–95, *394*

Raspberry Preserves, 50, *51*
Raspberry Vinegar, 408–10, *412*
Sugar-Free Raspberry Jam, 53
Three-Berry Jam, 57
recipes
    doubling, note about, 24
    yields from, 24, 117
Red Currant Jelly, *88* 89–90
red pepper flakes
    Gochugaru Chili Crisp, 213
    Star Anise–Smoked Paprika Chili
        Crisp, 210, *211*
    Wasabi-Nori Chili Crisp, 215–17,
        216
red Szechuan chili powder
    about, 190–91
    Almost Everything Chili Crisp,
        209
    Shiitake–Szechuan Peppercorn
        Chili Crisp, *211,* 214
    Szechuan-Inspired Red Mustard,
        368, 369
relishes
    defined, 115
    list of recipes, 8
rhubarb
    Maple-Rhubarb Conserve, 134
    Rhubarb-Chipotle Chutney,
        154–55
    Rhubarb-Ginger Jam, 70–71
    Rhubarb Jam, 70
    Rhubarb-Raisin Chutney, 154
    Strawberry-Rhubarb Jam, 36
Root Beer Syrup, 426–27
rosebuds, dried culinary, about,
    100
Rose Harissa, 238–40, *239*
Rose Jelly, 100, *101*
Rosemary-Garlic Oil, 406
Rosemary–Red Wine Jelly,
    138–39
Rose Syrup, 422–23, *424*
rum
    Blueberry Rum Fizz, 430
    Cacao Liqueur, 431–33
    Coffee Liqueur, 433
    Mai Tai, *419,* 421
    Peachy Barbecue Sauce, 356
    Pineapple-Rum Jam (var.), 93
    Strawberry Daiquiri, 430
Rutabaga Sauerkraut, 332–33

S

Sage-Lemon Vinegar, 413–14
Salad, Kimchi-Shrimp, 314

salsa macha
  Cherry-Pistachio Salsa Macha, 205
  Coconut-Pecan Salsa Macha, 208–9
  Cranberry-Walnut Salsa Macha, 205–6, *207*
  defined, 189
  Go-to Salsa Macha, 202, *203*
  Maple-Sesame Salsa Macha, 206–8
  Pineapple–Pine Nut Salsa Macha, 202–4
  Smoky Pecan–Cacao Nib Salsa Macha, 204–5
salsas
  defined, 189
  fresh, note about, 193
  list of recipes, 8
salt, 20, 244, 301–2
sambal
  Fiery Red Sambal, 217
  Green Sambal, 218–20, *219*
  Peanut-Tamarind Sambal, 220
  Sour-Funky Sambal, 221
  Sweet Red Chili Sauce, 349–51, *350*
  Tomato-Lemongrass Sambal, 217–18, *219*
sarsaparilla root
  Root Beer Syrup, 426–27
saucepans, 16, 116
sauces (savory)
  freezing and thawing, 339
  list of recipes, 10
  preparing, 337–38
  storing, 339
sauces (sweet)
  common ingredients, 375–76
  decorative jars for, 375
  final consistency, 376
  list of recipes, 11
  serving ideas, 375
sauerkraut
  fermentation process, 301
  ingredient notes, 301
  list of recipes, 10
  massaging brine for, 302–3
scale, digital, 301–2
scallions
  Garlic-Scallion Chili Crisp, 212
  Gochugaru Chili Crisp, 213

Sesame-Pineapple Barbecue Sauce, 357–58
sesame seeds
  Lime-Sesame Pickled Daikon, 273
  Maple-Sesame Salsa Macha, 206–8
  Pistachio-Duqqa Sauerkraut, 329–30
shallots
  Easy Red Chili Paste, 224–25
  Shallot-Bacon Jam, 121–22
  Shallot-Dal Chutney, 163
  Shallot Jam, 120–21
Shrimp-Kimchi Salad, 314
shrubs, preparing, 246
silicone bags, 19
soy sauce
  Char Siu Sauce, 360–61
  Kecap Manis, *345,* 346–47
  Peanut Butter–Ginger Barbecue Sauce, 355–56, *359*
  Worcestershire Sauce, 372–73
spices, 22
  Eighteen-Spice Chili Oil, 407–8, *409*
  Eighteen-Spice Curry Oil, 408, *409*
  Root Beer Syrup, 426–27
  Tonic Syrup, 417–18, *424*
spreads, savory, list of recipes, 10
squash. *See also* zucchini
  Lemon–Summer Squash Relish, 169–71
  Marinated Roasted Vegetables, 289–90
  Pumpkin Butter, 81–83, *82*
  Sweet-and-Sour Butternut Squash, 271–72
Star Anise–Smoked Paprika Chili Crisp, 210, *211*
Steak Sauce, *345,* 347–48
storage containers, 19
strainers, 17–18
strawberries
  Four-Berry Holiday Jam, 57–59, *58*
  Strawberry-Jalapeño Jam, 37
  Strawberry Jam, *33,* 34
  Strawberry Jewels, 34–35
  Strawberry Liqueur, 428–30
  Strawberry Preserves, 32–34, *33*
  Strawberry-Rhubarb Jam, 36
  Strawberry Sauce, 390, *391*

  Strawberry Syrup, 423–25, *424*
  Sugar-Free Strawberry Preserves, 35–36
sugar, 20
Sugar Snaps, Fiery, 267–68
sugar substitutes, 20
Sumac-Cinnamon Chili Crisp, 213–14
syrups
  about, 401–3
  freezing and thawing, 402
  list of recipes, 11
Szechuan peppercorns
  Fiery Pickles, 248–50
  Shiitake–Szechuan Peppercorn Chili Crisp, *211,* 214

T

tamarind
  Fig-Tamarind Chutney, 156–58, *157*
  Peanut-Tamarind Sambal, 220
  Steak Sauce, *345,* 347–48
  Tamarind-Chili Jam, 128–29
  Worcestershire Sauce, 372–73
tamping dowel, 303
tapenade
  Anchovy-Free Tapenade, 181–82
  Artichoke-Lemon Tapenade, 187
  Beet Tapenade, 184, *185*
  Black Olive Tapenade, *180,* 181
  Caper Tapenade, 183
  defined, 115
  Fig-Olive Tapenade, 182–83
  Garlicky Sun-Dried Tomato Tapenade, 186
  Green Olive Tapenade, 182
  Puttanesca Tapenade, 184
  Spiced Tapenade, *185,* 186–87
tarragon
  Pickled Tarragon Carrots, 269–71, *270*
  Tarragon Jelly, 142
  Tarragon Vinegar, 414, *415*
tea
  Chai Jelly, 104
tequila
  Coconut Margarita, 420
  Green Tequila Salsa, 197–98
  Margarita, 434
  Tequila Sunrise, 417, *419*
thermometers, 18
thyme
  Lavender-Thyme Vinegar, 414, *415*
  Peach-Thyme Jam (var.), 59

Toffee Sauce, 385–86
tofu
    Char Siu Sauce, 360–61
tomatillos
    Green Mole, *234, 236–37*
    Green Sambal, 218–20, *219*
    Green Tequila Salsa, 197–98
    Salsa Verde, *195,* 196
    Smooth Green Salsa, 196–97
tomatoes
    Brown Sugar Barbecue Sauce,
        352–53
    Caponata, 178–79, *180*
    Charred Salsa, 194, *195*
    Classic Barbecue Sauce, 351
    Curried Ketchup, 340–42, *341*
    Five-Spice Ketchup, 342–43
    Garlicky Sun-Dried Tomato
        Tapenade, 186
    Green Tomato Chutney, 156
    Hot Tomato Chutney, 155–56
    Pickled Green Tomatoes, 261–62
    Pineapple-Sesame Barbecue
        Sauce, 357–58
    Puttanesca Tapenade, 184
    Raspberry-Chipotle Barbecue
        Sauce, 355
    Red Mole, *234,* 235–36
    Roasted Garlic–Maple Barbecue
        Sauce, 357, *359*
    Roasted Tomatoes in Oil, 285–86
    Rose Harissa, 238–40, *239*
    Salsa Fresca, 193, *195*
    Shallot-Dal Chutney, 163
    Shortcut Red Mole, 236
    Simmered Salsa, 194–96
    Sour-Funky Sambal, 221
    Southern Piccalilli, 174
    Spicy Tomato Conserve, 134–35,
        136
    Tamarind-Chili Jam, 128–29
    Thick Red Chili Sauce, 349, *350*
    Tomato-Ancho Jam, *126,* 127
    Tomato-Basil Jam, 128
    Tomato Ketchup, 340, *341*
    Tomato-Lemongrass Sambal,
        217–18, *219*
    Vinegary Cherry Tomatoes,
        263–64, *265*

Tonic Syrup, 417–18, *424*
traditional canning, 436–37
triple sec
    Mai Tai, *419,* 421
    Triple Sec, 434
turmeric
    Pickled Turmeric, 261
    Turmeric-Onion Sauerkraut,
        327–28, *331*
Turnip Sauerkraut, 333

V
vegetable peeler, 15
vegetables. *See also specific
        vegetables*
    Marinated Roasted Vegetables,
        289–90
    preserved, list of recipes, 9
    salted, tamping down, 303
    squeezing out excess moisture,
        116
vinaigrettes
    Raspberry Vinaigrette, 410
    Sour Cherry Vinaigrette, 413
    Tarragon Vinaigrette, 414
vinegar, 21, 401. *See also
        vinaigrettes*
    Vinegary Barbecue Sauce, 351–52
vinegars, infused
    about, 401–3
    freezing and thawing, 402
    list of recipes, 11
vodka
    Chocolate Martini, 433
    Cranberry Liqueur, 427–28
    Hazelnut Liqueur, 433–34
    Holiday Chai Cocktail, 422
    for infused liqueurs, 402
    Pear Cosmo, 294
    Raspberry Liqueur, 428, *429*
    Salted Caramel Martini, 386
    Triple Sec, 434
volume measurements, 23

W
walnuts
    Apple Pie Conserve, *131,* 132
    Cranberry-Walnut Salsa Macha,
        205–6, *207*

Cranberry Walnut Sauce, *143,*
    146
Fig-Olive Tapenade, 182–83
Maple-Rhubarb Conserve, 134
Spicy Tomato Conserve, 134–35,
    136
Wet Walnuts, 396, *397*
Wasabi-Nori Chili Crisp, 215–17,
    216
water, distilled, 301
water-bath canning, 436–37
watermelon
    Gingered Watermelon Rinds,
        278–79
    Watermelon Rind Chow Chow,
        177–78
Wheat Beer Mustard, 365
whiskey
    Butterscotch Sauce, *377,* 385
    Old Fashioned, 418
white balsamic vinegar, 401
White Chocolate Sauce, *383,* 384
White Currant–Lemon Jelly, *88,*
    90–91
White Sauce, Alabama, 360
wine
    Black Currant–Port Jam, 89
    Quince-Wine Jelly (var.), 97
    Red Wine Jelly, 138
    Rosemary–Red Wine Jelly,
        138–39
    White Wine Jelly, 137–38
wooden spoons, 15
wooden spoon test, 116–17
Worcestershire Sauce, 372–73

Y
yellow mustard
    Prepared Yellow Mustard, 361
    Super Hot Yellow Mustard, 369

Z
zip-closed plastic bags, 19
zucchini
    Marinated Roasted Vegetables,
        289–90
    Sweet-and-Sour Zucchini Relish,
        168–69, *170*
    Zucchini Pickles, 252

About the Authors

Photograph by Eric Medsker

BRUCE WEINSTEIN and **MARK SCARBROUGH** are the authors of the bestselling *Instant Pot Bible* series of cookbooks, among more than thirty-five others. They are the owners of MediaEats, a culinary production company, were nominees for 2011 and 2015 James Beard Awards, won a 2015 IACP Award, and were the longest-serving columnists on WeightWatchers.com, as well as regular contributors to the *Washington Post*, *Eating Well*, *Fine Cooking*, and *Cooking Light*. They host a weekly podcast and can be found on most social media platforms, all under the name "Cooking with Bruce & Mark."

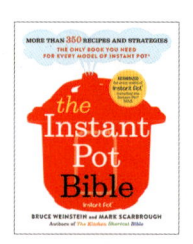

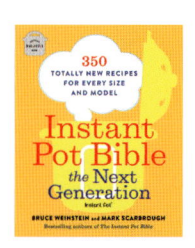
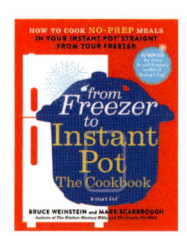
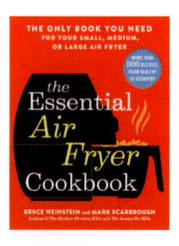
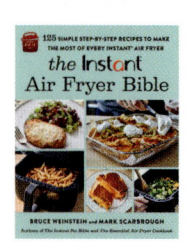
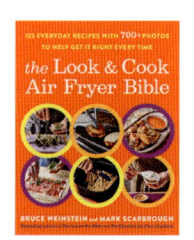
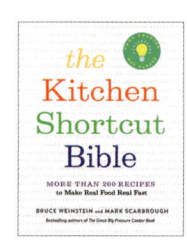